بداية المجتهد ونهاية المقتصد

THE DISTINGUISHED JURIST'S PRIMER

A Translation of Bidayat Al Mujtahid Wa Nihayat Al Muqtasid

VOLUME I

IBN RUSHD

Muhammad Bin Ahmad bin Muhammad Bin Rushd Al Hafeedh

Translated By

Imran Ahsan Khan Nyazee

Qadeem PRESS

AF721982

Qadeem Press Edition

Translation of the Qur'ān It should be perfectly clear that the Qur'ān is only authentic in its original language, Arabic. Since perfect translation of the Qur'ān is impossible, we have used the translation of the meaning of the Qur'ān throughout the book, as the result is only a crude meaning of the Arabic text.

Qur'ānic verses appear in speech marks proceeded by a reference to the Surah and verse number. Sayings (Hadith) of Prophet Muhammad (saw) appear in inverted commas along with reference to the Hadith Book and its Reporter.

CONTENTS OF VOLUME I

(IN BRIEF)

CONTENTS OF VOLUME I

In the Name of God, the Beneficent, the Merciful

FOREWORD

The interrelationship and interaction of human cultures and civilizations has made the contributions of each the common heritage of men in all ages and all places. Early Muslim scholars were able to communicate with their western counterparts through contacts made during the Crusades; at Muslim universities and centers of learning in Muslim Spain (al-Andalus, or, Andalusia) and Sicily to which many European students went for education; and at the universities and centers of learning in Europe itself (such as Salerno, Padua, Montpelier, Paris, and Oxford), where Islamic works were taught in Latin translations. Among the Muslim scholars well-known in the centers of learning throughout the world were al-Rāzī (Rhazes), Ibn Sīnā (Avicenna), Ibn Rushd (Averroes), al-Khwārizmī, and Ibn Khaldūn. Muslim scholars such as these and others produced original works in many fields. Many of them possessed encyclopedic knowledge and distinguished themselves in many disparate fields of knowledge.

In view of this, the Center for Muslim Contribution to Civilization was established in order to acquaint non-Muslims with the contributions Islam has given to human civilization as a whole. The Great Books of Islamic Civilization Project attempts to cover the first 800 years of Islam, or what may be called Islam's Classical Period. This project aims at making available in English a wide selection of works representative of Islamic civilization in all its diversity. It is made up of translations of original Arabic works that were produced in the formative centuries of Islam, and is meant to serve the needs of a potentially large readership. Not only the specialist and scholar, but the non-specialist with an interest in Islam and its cultural heritage will be able to benefit from the series. Together, the works should serve as a rich source for the study of the early periods of Islamic thought.

In selecting the books for the series, the Center took into account all major areas of Islamic intellectual pursuit that could be represented. Thus the series includes works not only on better-known subjects such as law, theology, jurisprudence, history and politics, but also on subjects such as literature, medicine, astronomy, optics and geography. The specific criteria, used to select individual books, were these: that a book should give a faithful and comprehensive account of its field; and that it should be an authoritative source. The reader thus has at his disposal virtually a whole library of informative and enlightening works.

Each book in the series has been translated by a qualified scholar and reviewed by another expert. While the style of one translation will naturally differ from another, the translators have endeavored, to the extent it was possible, to make the works accessible to the common reader. As a rule, the use of footnotes has been kept to a minimum, though a more extensive use of them was necessitated in some cases.

This series is presented in the hope that it will contribute to a greater understanding in the West of the cultural and intellectual heritage of Islam and will therefore provide an important means toward greater understanding of today's world.

May God Help Us!

Mohammad Ibn Hamad Al Thani
President of the Board of Trustees

ABOUT THIS SERIES

This series of Arabic works, made available in English translation, represents an outstanding selection of important Islamic studies in a variety of fields of knowledge. The works selected for inclusion in this series meet specific criteria. They are recognized by Muslim scholars as being early and important in their fields, as works whose importance is broadly recognized by international scholars, and as having had a genuinely significant impact on the development of human culture.

Readers will therefore see that this series includes a variety of works in the purely Islamic sciences, such as Qur'an, hadith, theology, prophetic traditions (sunna), and jurisprudence (fiqh). Also represented will be books by Muslim scientists on medicine, astronomy, geography, physics, chemistry, horticulture, and other fields.

The work, of translating these texts has been entrusted to a group of professors in the Islamic and Western worlds who are recognized authorities in their fields. It has been deemed appropriate, in order to ensure accuracy and fluency, that two persons, one with Arabic as his mother tongue and another with English as his mother tongue, should participate together in the translation and revision of each text.

This series is distinguished from other similar intercultural projects by its distinctive objectives and methodology. These works will fill a genuine gap in the library of human thought. They will prove extremely useful to all those with an interest in Islamic culture, its interaction with Western thought, and its impact on culture throughout the world. They will, it is hoped, fulfill an important rôle in enhancing world understanding at a time when there is such evident and urgent need for the development of peaceful coexistence.

This series is published by the Centre for Muslim Contribution to Civilization, which serves as a research centre under the patronage of H.H. Sheikh Khalifa bin Hamad al-Thani, Amir of Qatar. It is directed by a Board of Trustees chaired by H.E. Sheikh Mohammed bin Hamad al-Thani, the former Minister of Education of Qatar. The Board is comprised of a group of prominent scholars. These include H.E. Sheikh Gad al-Haq ali Taftazani, deputy Rector of Cairo Uinversity, and Dr Yusuf al-Qaradawi, Director of the Sira and Sunna Research Centre. At its inception the Centre was directed by the late Dr Mohammed Ibrahim Qazem, former Rector of Qatar University, who established its initial objectives.

The Centre is currently directed by Dr Kamal Nagi, the Foreign Cultural Relations Advisor of the Ministry of Education of Qatar. He is assisted by a Board compromising a number of academicians of Qatar University, in addition to a consultative committee chaired by Dr Ezz el-Din Ibrahim, former Rector of the University of the United Arab Emirates. A further committee acting on behalf of the Centre has been the prominent university professors who act under the chairmanship of Dr Raji Rammuny, Professor of Arabic at the University of Michigan. This committee is charged with making known, in Europe and in America, the books selected for translation, and in selecting and enlisting properly qualified university professors, orientalists and students of Islamic studies to undertake the work of translation and revision, as well as overseeing the publication process.

INTRODUCTION

Bidāyat al-Mujtahid is considered to be a book on *khilāf*, a discipline that records and analyzes the differences among Muslim jurists. It is sometimes treated as a book on comparative Islamic law that records the views of different schools and compares them, which is in fact the same thing as *khilāf*. Yet, this is not its declared purpose. Ibn Rushd states in this book, on various occasions and in different ways, that his purpose in writing this book, over which he spent more than twenty years, is the imparting of skills that make a student of law a competent jurist (*mujtahid*), someone who can independently derive the law from its sources. In an important passage, within the Book of *Ṣarf* (Exchange), he uses a simple analogy to point out the purpose of the book and also what the term jurist has come to mean in his own times and what it should mean.

> As our purpose is to record the issues that are expressly covered by the law or are very close to those expressly covered, we thought it desirable to record in this book seven well-known issues, which are like principles, or models, for the guidance of the (would-be) *mujtahid* in whatever he may encounter of the issues of this book. We have designed the book in such a way that with the help of its methodology he may attain the status of *ijtihād*, if he has acquired what is sufficient for him of *ʿilm al nahw* (grammar), language, and the methodology of *uṣūl al-fiqh*—and out of these it is sufficient to know what is proportionate to the requirements of this book or even less. It is by learning the relevant issues, and being equipped with these tools, that he deserves to be called a jurist (*faqīh*), not by merely learning too many details of *fiqh*, even if he has memorized the maximum that is possible for a human being. We find the (so called) jurists of our times believing that the one who has memorized the most opinions has the greatest legal acumen. Their view is like the view of one who thought that a cobbler is he who possesses a large number of shoes and not one who has the ability to make them. It is obvious that the person who has a large number of shoes will (some day) be visited by one whose feet the shoes do not fit. He will then go back to the cobbler who will make shoes that are suitable for his feet. This is the position of most of the *faqīh*s of these times.[1]

[1] See the third paragraph in the Book of *Ṣarf*.

He adds on another occasion:

> It is, however, a strength of this book that through it a person can attain, as we have said, the status of *ijtihād* as he proceeds, along with a knowledge of the Arabic language and of *uṣūl al-fiqh* that is sufficient for this purpose. It is for this reason that we thought that the most suitable title for this book would be if we name it: *Bidāyat al-Mujtahid wa Kifāyat al-Muqtaṣid.*[2]

To achieve this purpose, he rises above school bias and treats all the great jurists equally. He analyzes their methodology and is at times critical even of his own school. This makes his book unique in Islamic legal literature, and a powerful tool for legal instruction. Anyone who has the determination to read through and understand this powerful, yet difficult, book will not only understand the nature of Islamic law, but also develop skills that will help him derive the law independently. In short, he will be on his way to becoming a jurist.

The Author

Abū al-Walīd Muḥammad ibn Aḥmad ibn Rushd (d. 595/1198),[3] famous in the Medieval West under the name of Averöes, belonged to an important Spanish family. His grandfather (d. 520/1126),[4] who had the same name and with reference to whom Ibn Rushd is known as the grandson (*al-ḥafīd*), was a well-known Mālikī jurist, a *qāḍī*, and the *imām* of the Great Mosque of Cordova. His father too was a *qāḍī*. Ibn Rushd himself is better known as a philosopher or even as a physician, although he had been a *qāḍī* most of his life. He was born at Cordova in the year 520 of the Hijrah, the same year that his grandfather died. In his youth he received an excellent education in *fiqh*, *ḥadīth*, *kalām*, and medicine. Some of the well-known teachers mentioned by

[2] See the last paragraph in the Book of *Kitāba*.

[3] For a detailed description of the life and works of the Author see the excellent article "Ibn Rushd" in the *Encyclopaedia of Islam*; see also George F. Hourani, *Averroes on the Harmony of Religion and Philosophy* (London, 1961) 1–43. For his work as a jurist see R. Brunschvig, "Averroès Juriste", in *Études d'Orientalisme Dédiées a la Mémoire de Lévi-Provençal*, tome i (Paris, 1962) 35–68. Also published in *Études d'Islamologie: Droit Musulman* 2 (1976) 167–200. This article presents a reasonable overview of *Bidāyat al-Mujtahid*.

[4] He wrote a number of well-known works on Mālikī law. See Abū al-Walīd Muḥammad ibn Aḥmad ibn Rushd (1058/1126), *Fatāwá Ibn Rushd*, 3 vols. (Bayrūt: Dār al-Gharb al-Islāmī, 1987); *Al-Bayān wa-al-Taḥsīl wa-al-Sharḥ wa-al-Tawjīḥ wa-al Taʿlīl fī Masāʾil al-Mustakhraja*, 20 vols. (Bayrūt: Dār al-Gharb al-Islāmī, 1984–1987); and *al-Muqaddimāt al-Mumahhidāt li-Bayān mā Iqtaḍathū Rusūm al Mudawwana min al-Aḥkām al-Sharʿīyāt wa-al-Taḥṣīlāt al-Muḥkamāt li-Ummahāt Masāʾilihā al-Mushkilāt*, 3 vols. (Bayrūt: Dār al-Gharb al-Islāmī, 1988); see also *Jāmiʿ min al-Muqaddimāt* (ʿAmmān: Dār al-Furqān, 1985).

his biographers[5] are Muḥammad ibn Rizq, Ibn Bashkuwāl, Abū Jaʿfar Hārūn al-Tajallī, and Abū Marwān ibn Jurrayūl. These were the days when the Almoravid dynasty founded by Yūsuf ibn Tashfīn was replaced by the Almohad dynasty in North Africa (in 541) and the Andalusian provinces were conquered in the next few years. In 565 Hijrah, Ibn Rushd was a *qāḍī* at Seville. This he mentions himself in one of his works. In 567 he was a *qāḍī* at Cordova. In 578, at Marrākush, he succeeded Ibn Ṭufayl as the chief physician to Abū Yaʿqūb Yūsuf (558–80). Later he became the chief *qāḍī* of Cordova. He continued to enjoy the favour of the authorities even during the reign of Yaʿqūb al-Manṣūr (580–95). It was towards the end of his reign, when animosity was reflected towards philosophers due to political reasons, that Ibn Rushd was criticised by some jurists. This criticism, however, appears to be based on envy and not on doctrinal grounds. He died at Marrākush on 9 Safar 595, 11th December 1298. His body was taken to Cordova for burial.

Ibn Rushd's works on philosophy are well known. Some of these works are available in Latin translations and not in Arabic. Translations of his works on philosophy are available today in English and other languages.[6] In medicine he wrote the book *al-Kulliyāt fī al-Ṭibb.*[7] He is also said to have been interested in Astronomy. A reflection of this can be seen in the section on the sighting of the moon for Ramaḍān in this book. In the area of law, he mentions having written a book on *uṣūl al-fiqh*,[8] and expresses the desire to write a comprehensive and analytical book on the issues dealt with by Mālikī law. He says:

> We hope, God willing, after being free of this book, to compile a book for Mālik's school that assimilates the principles of his school and the well-known issues that work as principles for further derivation. This is what Ibn al-Qāsim did in *al-Mudawwana*. He reconciled that in which he did not have his opinion with what he possessed of the issues of Mālik in the same category and that resembled principles insofar as people (jurists) adopted them for purposes of practice and *taqlīd* in rendering *aḥkām* and verdicts.[9]

[5] Notable among these are Muḥammad ibn ʿAbd Allāh ibn Abbār (1199 1260), *al-Takmila li Kitāb al-Ṣila*, 2 vols. (Cairo: Maktab Nashr al-Thaqāfa al-Islāmīya, 1955–56) and ʿAbd al-Walīd al-Marrākushī (b. 1185), *al-Muʿjib fī Talkhīs Akhbār al-Maghrib* (1978).

[6] See, e.g., George F. Hourani, *Averroes on the Harmony of Religion and Philosophy* (London, 1961). This is the translation of *Kitāb Faṣl al-Maqāl*. See also Simon Van den Bergh, *Averroes' Tahafut al-Tahafut* (*The Incoherence of the Incoherence*) 2 vols. (London, 1954.

[7] See also Ibn Rushd, *Rasāʾil ibn Rushd al-Tibbīya* (Cairo, 1987).

[8] See the first issue under section 2.2.1.2 in the Book of Prayer.

[9] See the last paragraph in the Book of *Kitāba*. He adds on another occasion: "If Allāh were to grant me a long life, I will compile a book about the cases in the school of Mālik ibn Anas, arranging them in an organized manner, as that is the school followed in this peninsula, the peninsula of Andalus, so that the reader may attain the status of a *mujtahid* within Mālik's school. The enumeration of all the narrations, I think, is a task in which life terminates before it (the task) can come to an end". See section 56.7, the Book of *Qadhf*.

It appears that he never found time for the latter book. His book on *uṣūl al-fiqh* is not available in print, and it is not clear whether it is available in manuscript form either. It took him twenty years to compile *Bidāyat al-Mujtahid*. He says at the end of the Book of *Ḥajj* (which was the last portion he compiled):

> It was finalized on Wednesday, the ninth of Jumādī al-Ūlā, which is in the year five hundred and eighty-four. It is a part of *Kitāb al-Mujtahid*, which I have been compiling for more than twenty years or close to it. All praise is for Allāh, the Lord of the Worlds.[10]

The Significance and Method of *Bidāyat al-Mujtahid*

Is *Bidāyat al-Mujtahid* a manual of law like all other manuals, which record the opinions of jurists within their own school? Is it a book on *khilāf* that gives the different opinions of the jurists and records the reasons for their disagreement? Finally, is it a book of law that can be relied upon for opinions expressed by jurists? It serves all these purposes and is used as such by scholars all over the Muslim world, but it is intended by the Author, as has been explained above, to serve a much higher purpose. The true significance and method of this treatise on the law cannot be appreciated unless the nature of Islamic law itself is understood. A brief explanation, therefore, follows.

An exact parallel for Islamic law does not exist in modern legal systems; however, some aspects of its nature may be understood by looking at English common law. Islamic law is an unwritten law, that is, it does not exist in a codified form. English common law is also an unwritten law and it is based on principles that are contained in ancient decisions. The principles of Islamic law are stated, expressly or impliedly, in the Qurʾān and the *sunna* (decisions and practices) of the Prophet Muḥammad (God's peace and blessings be upon him). The principles of the common law may be modified and amended by the judges while deciding new cases arising before them, but some of the principles of Islamic law are relatively fixed and immutable.

It is difficult for the layman, however learned he may otherwise be, to determine on the basis of the principles of the common law what the ruling is on a case. It requires a judge skilled in the art of legal reasoning to decide a case. Likewise, deriving a ruling based on the principles of Islamic law is no easy matter for a layman, whether he is a scholar of *tafsīr* (interpretation of the

[10] See the last paragraph in the Book of *Ḥajj*.

Qur'ān) or of the science of *ḥadīth* (traditions). It requires a jurist (*mujtahid*), who has acquired special skills through rigorous training, to derive such a ruling. The reason is that though the principles of Islamic law are stated in the texts of the Qur'ān and the *sunna* they are not obvious through a direct reading of these texts. It is not possible to read one verse of the Qur'ān or one tradition and say that this is what it means, therefore, this is the law. In some cases, it may not be clear what the law is, even when it is stated explicitly in the texts. Take the case mentioned in the following verse of the Qur'ān:

> And those who accuse chaste women but bring not four witnesses, scourge them (with) eighty stripes and never (afterward) accept their testimony, and they indeed are the *fāsiqūn* (evil-doers), *except those who afterward repent and make amends*, (For such) lo! Allāh is Forgiving Merciful.[11]

There are three penalties mentioned in this text for a person who falsely accuses an honourable woman of having committed unlawful sexual intercourse: eighty stripes, non-acceptance of testimony in other cases, and the public imputation of *fisq*. The question here relates to the impact of the exception mentioned in the words "except those who afterward repent". If a person were found guilty of this offence and he repents promising not to do it again, would it be possible to waive all three penalties for him and let him go? In other words, does the exception apply to all three penalties, to two, or to just one of them?

It is possible here to assign a number of reasons for choosing one of the penalties and relinquishing the others. If such reasoning, however, is based on human reason and expediency alone it would not be acceptable. As the law derived finally would be declared a *ḥukm* (injunction) of Allāh, it is a matter of grave responsibility, and the person has to be careful in arriving at a final ruling. His own reasoning, however plausible it might be, has little value and is considered mere guesswork. He must, therefore, adduce further evidence from within the Qur'ān and the *sunna* in support of his opinion. When he does so, he has a reliable basis for showing the true intention of the Lawgiver. How can the layman, in this case, be sure about the true intention of the Lawgiver? This is clearly the task for the jurist, who will first declare the principles of interpretation that he is using, so that others who follow similar or different principles may be able to evaluate his opinion. He will then undertake a search for one or more principles of law that operate in this case,[12] and determine how the general principles as a whole interact to yield the final view.

[11] Qur'ān 24 : 4.

[12] It should be obvious that the principles of law are not the same thing as the principles of interpretation.

Take another case where three separate verses apparently indicate three different penalties for the same offence:

> As for those of your women who are guilty of *fāhisha* (lewdness), call to witness four of you against them. And if they testify (to the truth of the allegation) then confine them to the houses until death take them or until Allāh appoint for them a way.[13]
> And as for the two of you who are guilty of it (*fāhisha*), punish them both. And if they repent and improve, let them be. Lo! Allāh is Relenting, Merciful.[14]
> The *zānī* and the *zāniyya*[15] scourge ye each one of them with a hundred stripes. And let not pity for the twain withhold you from obedience to Allāh, if ye believe in Allāh and the Last Day. And let a party of the believers witness their punishment.[16]

Is the term *fāhisha* in the first two verses applied to mean the offence of *zinā* mentioned in the third verse, or does it mean something else? In either case the evidence has to be provided from the Qur'ān and *sunna*, and mere literal meanings of the term will have very little force, as grave penalties are being assigned to these acts. If it is assumed, on the basis of some evidence, that the offence is the same in all three verses, are all three penalties to be awarded? Is this possible? Is that the intention of the Lawgiver? The situation becomes highly complex when the *sunna* introduces two more penalties of exile for the unmarried person and stoning to death for the married. Can some of these laws be said to have superseded the others, that is, can one text in the Qur'ān and *sunna* be said to abrogate another text? If we make the assumption that one text can abrogate another, it amounts to choosing a principle of interpretation. Once we choose such a principle, we have to abide by it and apply it to other cases too where it may be applicable. We cannot turn around in another case and say that one text cannot abrogate the other, as in doing so we would be following our own fancy and not a consistent system. This is the crux of the matter. A *mujtahid* must define and declare all his principles of interpretation before he can attempt to interpret the law. Further, the system of interpretation he devises must be internally consistent, that is, one principle should not attempt to contradict or demolish the effect of another principle, as this would ultimately lead to an inconsistency in the derived law.

[13] Qur'ān 4 : 15.

[14] Qur'ān 4 : 16.

[15] The terms *zānī* and *zāniyya* are applied to mean a male and a female, whether married or unmarried, who indulge in unlawful sexual intercourse. It is incorrect to use the terms adulterer and adultress here, as many translators of the Qur'ān tend to do, insofar as the term adultery applies to unlawful sexual intercourse by married persons. The terms used here apply to all persons, whether married or unmarried.

[16] Qur'ān 24 : 3.

The schools of Islamic law, that is, those within the *Sunnī* schools are not sects; their disagreement is not based on theological issues. They represent groups of jurists who uphold different theories of interpretation of the law. Each school has its own set of principles for interpreting the texts. What is common among the four *Sunnī* schools is that they all agree on four sources of Islamic law. They disagree on other principles of interpretation. This is not to be seen as some kind disunity among the Muslims; it is a characteristic found in all legal systems. Take the case of the English common law again. The English common law as practised in England is different to some extent from that applicable in the United States of America, and these systems may differ somewhat from what is practised in Australia and New Zealand, yet they are all based on the English common law and have grown from it. Further, there may be several theories of interpretation within each system. The differences between the views of legal philosophers like Lon Fuller, H.L.A. Hart, and Ronald Dworkin, as well as many others, does not mean that they are talking about different legal systems, yet they are all proposing a different analysis of the methodology of the judge for the same law. It is the same in Islamic law. Each school is advocating a method of interpretation, which not only indicates the maturity of the law, but a richness and variety that helps accommodate a multiplicity of cultures within its fold.[17]

The schools of law did not appear all at once. In the first century of Islam, the law started growing to meet the needs of an expanding empire. The leaders in the law, to whom the people looked up for guidance, were the Companions of the Prophet (God's peace and blessings be upon him). The Companions, as is obvious, did not adopt a common methodology of interpretation. Some of the learned Companions settled in areas that became centres of learning. Within each centre of learning, a more or less common methodology of interpretation started evolving. This led, by the beginning of the second century, to at least two major organized systems of interpretation. The first system was devised by Imām Mālik, who lived in Medina, and the second by Imām Abū Ḥanīfa in Iraq. Both jurists had predecessors whose practices and methods they followed. These leaders in the law were considered the founders of schools because the comprehensive and internally consistent systems of interpretation followed by their respective schools are said to have been devised by these Imāms. In other words, the methodology through which the law had to be developed and derived from its sources was laid down by these jurists. Jurists within these schools derived the law independently, but they did not frame new theories of interpretation. They followed the rules chosen by

[17] The views of some Muslim scholars who see the jurists as having caused disunity among the Muslims is naive at best. Such views arise from a lack of understanding of the nature of this law.

their Imāms. By the end of the second century a new theory of interpretation was proposed by Imām al-Shāfiʿī. This was followed by the theory proposed by Imām Aḥmad ibn Ḥanbal. Another theory proposed by Dāwūd al-Ẓāhirī did not survive in the form of an established school.

Can one theory be said to be better than the other? This cannot be decided by the layman, not because he has no right to do so, but because he does not have the ability to prefer one to the other. The layman is known as the *muqallid*, or one who follows the opinion of another, that is, the layman who follows the opinion of an Imām or the preferred opinion of his school. This he does on the basis of faith that he has in the decisions of one school. It is the same thing as following the opinion of a physician in whom one has developed faith or that of a lawyer whose advice one values. The process is known as *taqlīd* in Islamic law. This process has been criticised by many modern scholars, and is deemed to have been the cause of stagnation and decadence. This criticism in unjustified as *taqlīd* is rampant in every area of human life today as it has been in the past, and the causes of stagnation and decadence lie elsewhere. A distinction needs to be made between the principle of *taqlīd* and the inability of jurists in a certain age to independently derive the law. It also needs to be distinguished from the social pressure that the conservative element may exert on a jurist who is competent to undertake *ijtihād*. Ibn Rushd narrates a story about his grandfather, who was forced to take back his opinion that clashed with the established doctrine of the school. The case relates to the time when the right of retaliation is to be exercised, if there are minors among the heirs of the victim.

> On the basis of this opinion, if the victim has heirs who include majors as well as minors, it is necessary to postpone retaliation till the minors grow up to exercise their option, especially when the minors exclude the adults (in inheritance), like children along with brothers.
>
> The *Qāḍī* (Ibn Rushd) says: This case came up in Cordoba, during the time of my grandfather (God bless him) and the jurists of his time issued the verdict according to the well-known narration (from Mālik), which requires that they should not wait for the minors (to grow up), but he, may Allāh have mercy on him, issued the verdict of waiting on the basis of analogy. His contemporaries declared this as abominable, due to the intensity of their *taqlīd*, so much so that he was compelled to issue a verdict in which he supported this school, and this (decision) can be found with people.[18]

It is also said that Jalāl al-Dīn Suyūṭī claimed the status of a *mujtahid* for himself. He was confronted by the jurists, who challenged him to a debate so that they could ascertain whether he was really a *mujtahid*. He declined on the

[18] See section 56.1.2. under the Book of *Qiṣāṣ*.

grounds that a *mujtahid* cannot engage in such an encounter with a *muqallid*, because the opponent must also be a *mujtahid* and there should be a third *mujtahid* to judge between them. Such jurists he maintained did not exist in his times.[19]

Taqlīd, as distinguished from blind conservatism, is the foundation of all relationships based on trust, like those between a patient and his doctor, a client and his lawyer, and a business and its accountant. It is a legal method for ensuring that judges who are not fully qualified *mujtahids* may be able to decide cases in the light of precedents laid down by independent jurists. It is similar to the case of a subordinate court following the precedent established by a higher court. On the other hand, a Muslim is at liberty to follow one school and then move to another if he is not satisfied, just as he can visit one doctor and then move to another. The system of *taqlīd* implies that as long as the layman does not get the training for becoming a doctor he cannot practise medicine, for example. In the case of medicine, such a person may be termed a quack and may even be punished today, but in the case of Islamic law he is assuming a much graver responsibility: he is claiming that the opinion he is expressing is the law intended by Allāh.

Does this mean that no new theory of interpretation can be proposed today? Certainly not. The Muslim jurists have never placed this restriction. They have never said that jurists should not exercise *ijtihād*. In fact, they maintain that if a person has the necessary ability, it is binding upon him to follow his own opinion. The only requirement is that whoever desires to interpret the law may either use one of the existing systems of interpretation, without mixing it with another to preserve internal consistency, or he should come up with a new theory of interpretation, in which case it would be binding upon him to use his own system. The only requirement is that he must declare his principles of interpretation so that other jurists should be able to judge his competence. In fact, there have been cases in Islamic legal history where new theories have been proposed, although they have been considered extensions of the existing theories rather than as completely indepedent methods. One such theory was proposed by the famous Imām al-Ghazālī, which was refined from the work of his teacher al-Juwaynī. This is the theory based on the purposes of the law, and it comes very close to the methods used in modern law. The full potential of his theory is yet to be utilized by the Muslims. Imām al-Ghazālī died in 505 Hijrah, and Ibn Rushd was born in the year 520.

Did Ibn Rushd lay a claim to the status of a *mujtahid*? He did not do so openly, but if he is claiming to impart skills to would-be *mujtahids* through his

[19] See the introduction to Jalāl al-Dīn Abū Bakr al-Suyūṭī *al-Ashbāh wa al Naẓā'ir* (Beirut, 1987) 15–16.

work, he is definitely implying that. His competence, his general tone in this book, and the way he prefers opinions expressed by other jurists bears ample testimony to the fact that he considered himself to be a full *mujtahid*. He even expresses new opinions, on several occasions, after declaring that no one had expressed them before him.

Ibn Rushd does not propose a new theory of interpretation in *Bidāyat al-Mujtahid*, although if his book on *uṣūl al-fiqh* is discovered we may find that this may very well be the case. He is fully aware of the developments before him, including the work of al-Ghazālī on the law. He begins the book with a brief statement on the principles of interpretation. He avoids technicalities and presents the principles in a few pages in a manner that only he is accomplished to do. He tries to find a common ground between the different principles of interpretation that are preferred by the leading schools. A thorough grasp of these details is essential for anyone who wishes to understand his book. The system of literal interpretation that he describes uses the terminology adopted by the majority of the schools as compared to the Ḥanafites. He describes how the law is conveyed to us in the form of reports about words, acts, and approvals. The way in which words are used, for example, and the way in which they relate to the acts of the subject determines what the derived law will be. He determines what is to be given preference when words and acts appear to convey different meanings. He does not consider consensus of opinion (*ijmāʿ*) to be an independent source of law, unless it is based directly on a text from the Qurʾān or the *sunna*.

The most important aspect of his method is the way he treats analogy (*qiyās*) and also general principles (*uṣūl*) arising from the texts. He divides analogy into two types: *qiyās al-ʿilla* and *qiyās al-shabah*. This is not to be confused with the division of analogy into *qiyās al-maʿnā* and *qiyās al-shabah* adopted by al-Shāfiʿī in his book *al-Risāla*. Ibn Rushd's method of *qiyās al-shabah* is a much wider form of extension as compared to the restricted form proposed by al-Shāfiʿī. Whenever the phrases like "held it to be similar to" or "considered it to be similar to" appear in his book, the underlying rule is that of *qiyās al-shabah*. The method of *qiyās al-shabah* is usually applied by Ibn Rushd to explain the extensions to the law made by the Mālikī jurists. This method may have much in common with analogy used in the modern law today.

The way Ibn Rushd can identify general principles related to an issue is simply remarkable. General principles play a greater role in the system of interpretation used by the Ḥanafites as well as the Malikīs, as compared to the Shafiʿite system in which the emphasis and preference is always given to the text of a sound tradition. These general principles are not based on the jurist's own reasoning or experience, but are based on the texts of the Qurʾān and *sunna*. What is significant is the way Ibn Rushd brings out these principles and explains their operation. This type of exposition is rare in Islamic legal literature, yet it may be essential for the modern lawyer.

When the details of Ibn Rushd's method are considered as a whole, and are related to each other, they begin to reveal a slightly different picture, and this may be termed a somewhat modified, if not a new theory of interpretation.

The arrangement of chapters, or of books as they are called, in the main book follows that in many other manuals of the law, especially Mālik's *al-Muwaṭṭaʾ*. This facilitates the tracing of issues in books that lack an index or a detailed table of contents. The only section that Ibn Rushd appears to have left out intentionally is the topic of *waqf.* It is the treatment of the topic in which Ibn Rushd's method differs from the rest. He begins each topic by stating the main proposition and then classifies it into its detailed components assigning them to detailed sub-chapters accordingly. Each sub-chapter is divided into detailed issues. The criterion for selecting these issues is described by Ibn Rushd on numerous occasions. He says that these issues are either expressly stated in the texts or are closely related to those that are. In this sense, they serve as the fundamental principles governing a topic. In other words, he discusses only those issues that need to be understood by the student of law, the would-be jurist, and the rest he can derive on his own.

> The purpose is the recording of the well-known issues over which disputes arose between the jurists of the regions together with the issues expressly stated by the *sharʿ*. This is so, and we have stated this more than once, because our intention in this book is to establish the issues expressly stated by the texts, agreed upon or disputed, and to mention those issues about which the texts are silent, but in which disagreement of the jurists of the regions has become well-known.[20]

Thus, all the detailed issues that may be found in other manuals are not covered by this book.

A distinct pattern can be seen in the statement and discussion of the detailed issues. Ibn Rushd first states the issue and then the opinions of the jurists. He does not give much importance to the author of the opinion; it is the opinion itself that is important. Thus, the opinion may be expressed by a Companion, an individual jurist, or by the leader of a school of law. He makes it a point, though, not to miss the opinions, if known, of the three well-known jurists: Mālik, Abū Hanīfa, and al-Shāfiʿī. If there are a large number of opinions on an issue, he classifies them into different groups and refers to them later as the first group, the second group, and so on. Once the opinions have been described he begins by giving the reasons for the formulation of an opinion. A pattern can be seen here too, and it is not too often that Ibn Rushd deviates

[20] See the last sections of the Book of *Kitāba*.

from this pattern. The first basis for an opinion are the texts of the Qurʾān and the *sunna*, that is, if the opinion is directly based on them. This is followed by a description of the methods of interpretation and preference (*tarjīḥ*) used by a jurist. If the jurist relied on analogy in addition to the texts, the basis for such analogy is described and analysed. The special methods of interpretation used by certain schools or jurists are given separate treatment. Thus, Imām Mālik may have used *maṣlaḥah mursala* or *istiḥsān*, or Abū Ḥanīfa may have used his method of preferring general principles. These are explained in detail by the Author. Commenting upon the use of *maṣlaḥa*, for example, he says:

> The rejection of the permissibility of marriage on account of (with the intention of) the inclusion of an additional heir is an analogy based upon *maṣlaḥa*, which is not permitted according to the majority of the *fuqahāʾ*. Taking interests into account in a genus that is remote from the genus that is desired for the establishment of the *ḥukm* according to (the principle of) *maṣlaḥa* led some jurists to the conclusion that upholding such an opinion amounts to legislating additional law, and the adoption of such an analogy dilutes the principle of submission to the *sharīʿa*, neither adding to it nor detracting from it. Yet reluctance to pay attention to *maṣlaḥa* might cause the people to be pushed, because of a lack of precedents in this genus, toward injustice. Such interests should be brought to the scholars of the *ḥikma* (philosophy) of the law, the learned who will not be accused of judging by it, especially nowadays when the qualified persons think that adoption of the letter of the law (apparent meaning) leads to injustice. The proper methodology of the learned scholar in this should be to examine the evidence in the circumstances of the case. If such evidence indicates that he (the *marīḍ*) intends betterment through the marriage, he should not prohibit the marriage, but if it indicates that he intends harm to his heirs, he should disallow it. This is the case in many things among skills and services where the professional is faced with opposing results in what he is trying to do upon the strength of his skill, for it is not possible to lay down fixed limits for the service. This (situation) is usually faced in the profession of medicine and also in various other professions.

Ibn Rushd always makes an attempt to accommodate traditions as far as possible even when they are conflicting with the general principles. If the general principle can be restricted to the extent of the impact of the tradition, he does not hesitate to do so. On many occasions, the criterion he uses for preferring an opinion is the final impact of the opinion on human affairs, that is, he focuses more on the result of the opinion rather than the opinion or the reasoning itself, as in the case cited above, though he tries to find the best reasoning in this case too. When Ibn Rushd is expressing his own opinion it is preceded by the phrase, "The Qāḍī said". This of course is the work of the scribe and not the Author's own language.

Ibn Rushd's method of presenting an issue and explaining its underlying reasoning is highly systematic; however, it must be mentioned that even in its translated form the book is not intended to be taken lightly. He expects the reader to be on his toes, remembering the rules of interpretation along with the evidences stated for an issue. On some occasions the reasoning is so complex that it can be understood only by sketching it out on paper. This means that if the reader is not careful, he will soon find himself facing a void. For the serious reader, however, this book is one of the most powerful tools of legal instruction. Working through the issues will be highly rewarding for him.

> It is likely that one who works through these issues and understands the principles of the causes that generated the disagreement of the jurists in them, will be able to derive what is required in each particular case, I mean, what is the answer for it in the opinion of each one of the *fuqahā'* of the regions, that is, in one particular issue itself, and will know when a jurist has opposed his own principle and when he has not. This is the case when an opinion has been related from him in that issue. If, however, a verdict has not been related from him or it has not reached the investigator of these principles, it is possible for him to come up with the answer in accordance with the principles of that jurist according to whose school he is rendering an opinion, and according to the truth to which his *ijtihād* leads him.[21]

At the end of the book Ibn Rushd makes an important statement in which he attempts to summarize the purpose of the *sharī'a*. In doing so he allows us a glimpse into his own personality.

> The *Qāḍī* (Ibn Rushd), may Allāh be pleased with him, said: It is necessary to know that the *aḥkām* of the *sharī'a* are divisible into two kinds. One of these kinds is adjudicated by the judges, and the majority of the *aḥkām* we have mentioned fall under this category. The second kind are those not adjudicated by the judges, and most of these are in the recommended (*mandūb*) category. This category of the *aḥkām* are like responding to the Muslim greeting (*salām*), blessing one who sneezes, and the like, which are mentioned by the jurists at the end of their books that are called *Jawāmi'*. We have also thought of mentioning the best known of this category, God willing.
>
> It is necessary, before this, to know that the legal *sunan* (practices) pertaining to conduct have as their purpose the virtues of the believer. Some of them refer to respect, to whom it is due, and to the expression of gratitude, to whom that is due. The *'ibādāt* are included in this category. These are the *sunan* relating to ethical values. Some of the *sunan* relate to the virtue call *'iffa* (chastity, abstinence from undignified habits), and are of two kinds: *sunan* laid down about food and beverages, and *sunan* laid down about marital affairs. Some *sunan* refer to the requirement of justice and abstention from tyranny. These are the categories of *sunan* that require the maintenance of a balance in financial dealings, and the maintenance of a balance in personal relations (physical contact). Related to this category are (the *aḥkām* of) *qiṣāṣ*, wars, and punishments, as the maintenance of

[21] See the section in the Book of *Kitāba* referred to above.

> justice is the aim of all of these. Among them are *sunan* laid down for individual integrity, and *sunan* laid down for all kinds of wealth and its valuation, through which is intended the attainment of the merit called generosity, and the avoidance of the meanness called *bukhl* (covetousness). *Zakāt* is included in this category from one aspect, and is included in the communal sharing of wealth from another; same is the case with charity (*ṣadaqāt*). There are *sunan* laid down for social life, which is the essential condition for human life, and the preservation of its benefits relating to conduct and knowledge, which are called statehood. It is for this reason that these *sunan* should be upheld by the leaders and the upholders of the *Dīn*. Among the important *sunan* for social life are those related to love and hate, and to cooperation for the maintenance of all these *sunan*, which is called *al-nahy ʿan al-munkar, waʾl-amr biʾl-maʿrūf* (prohibiting the blameworthy and requiring what is good), and which is love and hate, that is religious, which occurs either due to the evasion of these *sunan* or due to the evil intent of the believer in the *sharīʿa*. Most of what the jurists mention in the *Jawāmiʿ*, among their books, is that which deviates from the four categories that are the merit of chastity, the merit of justice, the merit of courage, and the merit of generosity, and all kinds of worship (*ʿibāda*) are like conditions for the fulfilment of these merits.[22]

THE TRANSLATION

This is the first time that an entire manual of Islamic law has been translated into English from the original Arabic. This means that the entire terminology of Islamic law has been rendered into English for the first time. The first manual that was rendered into English from a Persian translation was the *Hedaya*, which was translated in 1772 by Charles Hamilton on the order of Warren Hastings, the Governor-General of Bengal. This was not an exact translation of the original. It was more like a summary of al-Marghinānī's views, as they appeared in the Persian translation, expressed in Hamilton's language. The text in English does not conform with the statements of the Author in Arabic. Nevertheless, it was a commendable effort in those early days. Further, Hamilton's translation was meant to be used by the courts, and did not render into English the portions relating to the *ʿibādāt*. As the law in India was changed gradually, some more sections of the translation were deleted from the later editions. Some manuals, Mālikī and Shafiʿī, were translated into French, especially al-Nawawī's *Minhāj al-Ṭālibīn*, which was then translated into English from the French, but they suffered from various defects.[23]

The reason for the lack of translations of such legal texts is obvious. The type of language used by the jurists in their manuals is often so concise that it

[22] See the end of the Book of Judgments.

[23] See the comments made by Joseph Schacht, *Introduction to Islamic Law* (Oxford, 1964) 261–62.

defies rendition into another language. It is not the usual language that one finds in works relating to history or to literature. Most of the manuals were written to facilitate memorization by those aspiring to be judges. Each sentence carries within it an argument that has to be understood in the context of the issue and the underlying principles, many of which are not stated and their prior knowledge is assumed by the authors. It is for this reason that one finds the translations straying away from the original text and the arguments of the author. The task of translating such texts is further complicated by the lack of exact equivalents for the legal terminology employed by the jurists. Thus, there can be no simple formula for translating these texts, and the safest course appears to be to stay with the literal meaning, trying to preserve the intent of the author, even if this is at the expense of style. This was the method adopted for this translation.

Another feature of Islamic legal literature, as with any other technical subject, is that the authors assume a reasonable knowledge of the entire law, including the law realting to ritual, as well as a fair knowledge of legal theory (*uṣūl al-fiqh*). It is not merely a question of transmitting the text from one language into another. Such a knowledge may on some occasions be required of the reader of the translated text. An effort has been made to provide notes for the reader where the text is unduly complex; however, a full treatment of all difficult points is not possible, as that would turn into a full commentary and the sheer magnitude of the project makes that task difficult, at least for the present. A system of numbering the chapters and issues has been adopted to facilitate easy access. The translation of the Qurʾān by Marmaduke Pickthall has been followed generally; however, it has been necessary, several times, to change this to convey the exact meaning intended within the discussion of issues. Ibn Rushd has quoted about eighteen hundred traditions in this book in support of the arguments of the jurists, and on many occasions he refers to one of the *Saḥīḥ* compilations. It has not been possible to document all these traditions, as that would have expanded the project to at least twice its present size. The interested reader may refer to Aḥmad Ibn al-Ṣiddīq, *al-Hidāya fī Takhrīj Aḥādīth al-Bidāya*, 8 vols. (Beirut, 1407/1987).

There are at least three editions of *Bidāyat al-Mujtahid* in Arabic available in print. The only difference in these editions appears to be on how the publisher has divided them into volumes. The text has not been edited, though different manuscripts appear to have been used for compiling the published text. There are a number of typographical errors, and on one occasion a marginal note from one manuscript appears to have crept into the text. On another occasion some sentences have been copied out of order. Despite these errors the text appears to be in a sound and complete condition, and it can safely be assumed to be a complete copy of the Author's original text. The edition used for this translation was published at Beirut by Dār al-fikr, as two volumes in a single volume. There is no date on the book. The system of transliteration followed for this translation is that adopted by the Library of Congress, with slight modifications.

This translation was undertaken for the Center for Research on the Contribution to Muslim Civilization and was supported by a generous grant. It took over four years to complete.

Imran Ahsan Khan Nyazee
Ann Arbor, Michigan
1994

Dr Muhammad Abdul Rauf
Cairo
1994

PREFACE

Praise be to Allāh with all due praise, and prayers and blessings on His Prophet, Muhammad, his family and Companions.

My purpose in this treatise is to lay down in it for myself, by way of remembrance, the issues (*masāʾil*) of the *aḥkām*[1] that are agreed upon and those that are disputed, along with their evidences,[2] and to indicate those bases of the disputes that resemble general rules and principles, for the jurist may be presented with problems on which the law (*sharʿ*) is silent. The issues are mostly those that are expressly stated in the law, or are closely related to those that are so stated. They are the issues agreed upon by the Muslim jurists since the generation of the Companions (God be pleased with them) till such time that *taqlīd*[3] was rampant, or those over which a difference of opinion among them became widely known. Before recording these issues we will mention for you, as briefly as possible, the different channels through which the *aḥkām* of *sharīʿa* were received, the various categories[4] of such *aḥkām*, and the causes that necessitated controversy.

[1] The word *ḥukm* (pl. *aḥkām*) has been translated in various ways by different writers. Some of these meanings are: *sharīʿa* value, injunction, prescription, rule, and command, among others. None of these words, however, conveys the exact meaning of the term *ḥukm* as used in Islamic law, particularly the meaning implied by the *ḥukm waḍʿī* or the determining *ḥukm*. The term *sharīʿa*-value comes very close to capturing the whole meaning, but the term itself is too general and can be used for other meanings. It is, therefore, preferable to retain the term *ḥukm* and allow its meaning to unfold through the text. The term *ḥukm* is also used to mean "legal effects", particularly in contracts (*ʿuqūd*).

[2] The term *adilla* is the plural of *dalīl*, which literally means "guide", "proof", "evidence" and is used here as something that leads to another thing. Technically, the *dalīl* may be transmitted, that is, it may be a text, or it may be rational, like analogy (*qiyās*). The term "proof" is also used by some to denote *dalīl*. Also note the term *adilla tafṣīliyya* or "detailed proofs".

[3] *Taqlīd* means following the opinion of another without questioning the basis of such opinion or its *dalīl* (evidence). Technically it applies to a judicial method adopted by the jurists that ensured the application of the preferred opinion of a particular school in rendering judicial verdicts and in deciding cases. Perhaps, the author implies here that differences of opinion were encouraged during the time of the Companions but *taqlīd* put a stop to such an exchange of ideas and views.

[4] The categories of the *aḥkām* were fully developed by the classical jurists, but the origins can easily be traced back to the texts. The categories were also necessitated by the structure of Islamic law.

We say: The channels through which the *aḥkām* were received from the Prophet (God's peace and blessings be upon him) are three in genus: word, act, and approval. With respect to the *aḥkām* about which the Lawgiver is silent, the majority (*jumhūr*) say that the method of attaining them is analogy (*qiyās*). The Ẓāhirites[5] maintain that analogy in law (*sharʿ*) is illegal and that about which the Lawgiver is silent has no *ḥukm*. Reason, they say, supports this assertion as the incidents (occurring) among individuals are unlimited, while words, acts, and approvals are limited, and it is impossible to juxtapose the finite and the infinite.

The kinds of words through which the *aḥkām* are received, by means of transmitted evidences, are four in number; three are agreed upon while the fourth is disputed. The three that are agreed upon are the general word (*ʿāmm*) when applied to all its categories, the particular word (*khāṣṣ*) applied to its single category, the general word when its application is particular, and the particular word when its intended implication is general. Included in this is the use of the higher order meaning to denote the lower order meaning, and the employment of the lower order meaning to indicate the higher order meaning, as well as the indication of equivalent meanings.[6] The example of the first (of the four types of terms) is found in the words of the Exalted, "Forbidden unto you [for food] are carrion and blood and swine-flesh".[7] The Muslim jurists agreed that the word swine (*khinzīr*) includes all kinds of swine, unless it belongs to the category to which the name is not applied, except by way of equivocality (*ishtirāk*), like the term "swine of the sea (porpoise)".[8] The example of the general word implying the particular is found in the words of Allāh, "Take alms of their wealth, wherewith thou mayst purify them and mayst make them grow".[9] The Muslim jurists agreed

[5] The Ẓāhiriyya adopted a system of interpretation that emphasized the literal and the apparent meanings of the texts.

[6] This may sound confusing. The author is saying that the general word sometimes acts like itself and sometimes like the particular word. The same is true of the particular word; that is, it may act like itself or it may act like the general word. For instance, in the example of the verse of *zakāt* (see below), the term "wealth" is used as a general word without any restriction. The meaning it conveys is that *zakāt* is levied on all kinds of wealth; however, we know from other provisions of the *sharīʿa*, that *zakāt* is levied on certain kinds of wealth. The word "wealth" will, therefore, be read to mean certain kinds of wealth and not all kinds without restriction. In other words, the general word in this example is meant to convey a particular meaning. It is obvious that in this case the restricted implication of the word "wealth" is dictated by other provisions of the law. Take the other example of the use of the word "fie". This word has a particular implication, but we know that if merely saying "fie" is prohibited all other aggressive and rude behaviour must also be prohibited. The word "fie" is particular, but it has a general implication.

[7] Qurʾān 5 : 3.

[8] This is the name given to the porpoise, which in turn, according to the dictionary, is a name for a number of gregarious, toothed whales. *Porcus* in Latin is pig, while *piscis* is fish. The term used here in Arabic is *khinzīr al māʾ*.

[9] Qurʾān 9 : 103.

that *zakāt* is not obligatory on all kinds of wealth (*māl*).[10] The example of a particular word having a general intent is evident in the words of the Exalted: "Say not 'fie' unto them nor repulse them, but speak to them a gracious word".[11] This is the case of the indication of a higher order meaning through the lower as the prohibition includes beating, abuse, and whatever is more grievous.

The authority demanding the commission of an act uses either the form of a command or the form of a report implying a command. Similarly, the authority demanding omission of an act employs the form of a proscription (*nahy*), or the form of a report implying proscription. If words occur in these forms, is the demand for the commission of an act to be interpreted as an obligation (*wujūb*) or a recommendation (*nadb*)—as will be discussed under the definition of *wājib* and *mandūb*—or is interpretation to be abstained from till another evidence indicates either one of the two? There is a difference of opinion among the jurists in this, recorded in books on *uṣūl al-fiqh*.[12] Same is the case with the forms of proscription, whether they indicate disapproval (*karāha*) or prohibition (*taḥrīm*), or do not indicate either? In this too there is, recorded, a difference of opinion.

The entities to which the *ḥukm* is related[13] are indicated by it either through a word with a single meaning, and this is known in the discipline of *uṣūl al-fiqh* as *naṣṣ* (explicit)—there being no dispute about the obligation of acting in compliance with it—or through a word having more than one meaning and this is of two types. The word may indicate an equal disposition toward the different meanings and is known in *uṣūl al-fiqh* as *mujmal* (having equal probabilities) and there is no dispute that it does not obligate a *ḥukm*; or it may be inclined toward some of these meanings more than it is toward the others, and is known, with reference to such indicated meanings, as *ẓāhir* (manifest, apparent), and with reference to other (probable) meanings as *muḥtamal* (probable).[14] If such a word is used in an unqualified sense it is to be applied to its apparent meaning unless another evidence indicates its

[10] That is, it is applied to certain kinds of wealth; therefore, it is a case of a particular word applied to the specific.

[11] Qur'ān 17: 23.

[12] The term *uṣūl al-fiqh* has been called Islamic jurisprudence, legal theory, and methodology of Islamic jurisprudence, besides other things. It is best left untranslated. Technically it means "the knowledge of the principles that lead to the discovery or derivation of the *sharʿī aḥkām* from their detailed proofs in the sources of Islamic law".

[13] The *ḥukm* is always related to the act of the subject (*mukallaf*) and not to entities or things. It is the act of the subject related to things that is *ḥalāl* or *ḥarām* and not things in themselves. Thus the relationship of the *ḥukm* to entities is indirect.

[14] The division of words into *naṣṣ*, *mujmal*, *ẓāhir*, and *muḥtamal* is in conformity with the system of the Mutakallimūn. The division is slightly different in the system of the Ḥanafites, with some practical consequences.

application to its other probable meanings. Thus there occurs a difference of opinion among the jurists about the *aḥkām* of the Lawgiver. It, in fact, takes place mostly due to three meanings (reasons): the equivocality (*ishtirāk*) of the word applied to an entity with which the *ḥukm* is associated; the equivocality of the definite article "*al*" accompanying the genus of the entity, whether the whole is implied or a part; and the equivocality of the words used for commands and proscriptions. A fourth way, however, is to understand from the obligation of the *ḥukm* for a thing, the negation of things besides it, and from the negation of a thing the obligation of all things besides it. This is known as the (indirect) indication of the communication (*dalīl al-khiṭāb*).[15] It is a rule that is disputed, like the words of the Prophet (God's peace and blessings be upon him), "In the *sā'ima* out of cattle there is *zakāt*". Some have understood from this that there is no *zakāt* in cattle other than the *sā'ima* (pasturing animals).

Legitimate analogy (*qiyās*) is the assigning of the obligatory *ḥukm* for a thing to another thing, about which the law is silent, due to its resemblance to the thing for which the law has obligated the *ḥukm* or due to a common underlying cause (*ʿilla*)[16] between them. It is for this reason that legal analogy is of two types: *qiyās al-shabah* and *qiyās al-ʿilla*. The difference between legal analogy and the particular word implying a general meaning is that analogy can be undertaken only in the case of a particular word that implies just its single category.[17] The other similar cases are then joined with it, that is, those not covered by the text are joined to the one that is, due to a resemblance between them, not through an implication of the word. This is so because the extension of the *ḥukm* to an unstated yet implied category is not analogy, but an indication (connotation) of the word (*dalālat al-lafẓ*). These two kinds (of extensions of the *ḥukm* to the unstated entity) are very close as in both there is a joining of the explicit and the implicit cases and is often a cause of confusion for the jurists. Examples of analogy are the joining of one who drinks wine with the slanderer (*qādhif*) as regards the fixed punishment (*ḥadd*), and the joining of (the amount of) dower (*ṣadāq*) with the minimum scale (*niṣāb*) in the case of the cutting of the hand (of the thief). The joining, on the other hand, of things carrying usury (*ribā*) with food, things measured or eatables, is the case of a particular word implying the general. So ponder over this as it is a source of confusion.

[15] The term *khiṭāb*, literally address or communication, of the Lawgiver is distinguished by some from the text of the Qur'ān. The *khiṭāb* is eternal and the text is the evidence or *dalīl* of this *khiṭāb*, that is, it leads to the discovery of the meaning of the *khiṭāb*. The distinction indicates the meaning of the term *dalīl*.

[16] The term *ʿilla* too, like the term *ḥukm*, is sometimes translated as *sharīʿa*-value. See *supra* note 1.

[17] The distinction drawn by the author is crucial for understanding the nature of analogical reasoning (*qiyās*) in Islamic law.

It is possible for the Ẓāhirites to dispute the first genus (i.e. analogy), while they are not obliged to dispute the second (i.e., extension through implied meanings) for it is a case of authoritative transmission and he who rejects this rejects a style of communication (*khiṭāb*) employed by the Arabs.

The report of an act, according to many, is one of the channels through which the *aḥkām* are received. Some have said that reports of the Prophet's deeds (acts) do not yield *aḥkām*, as they do not have linguistic patterns. Those who accept that *aḥkām* can be received through acts differ about the kind of *ḥukm* indicated by them. Some say that they indicate obligation while others say that they indicate recommendation (*nadb*). The preferred opinion of the learned scholars is that if they occur as an explanation (*bayān*), of an obscure (*mujmal*) obligatory act, they indicate an obligation, and if they occur as an explanation of an obscure recommended act then they indicate recommendation. If they do not occur as an explanation for an obscure act, but belong to a recommended category, then they indicate recommendation. If they belong to the genus of permissible (*mubāḥ*) acts then they indicate permissibility. Approval (*iqrār*), on the other hand, indicates permissibility. These, then, are the kinds of channels through which the *aḥkām* are received.

Consensus (*ijmāʿ*) relies on one of these four channels, except that when it takes place on the basis of one of these channels, which is not definitive (*qatʿī*) the *ḥukm* is considered definitive due to predominant probability. *Ijmāʿ*, however, is not an independent source in itself unless reliance is placed on one of these (four) channels.[18] Had it been so it would have amounted to the establishment of additional law after (the time of) the Prophet (God's peace and blessings be upon him), as it would not have been based on one of the legally valid principles.

The functional terms denoting the *aḥkām* derived from these literal modes for the subjects (*mukallafūn*) are, as a whole, either a command for a thing or a proscription or a choice between the two. When the command is decisive and an omission (to do the act) invokes punishment the act is called obligatory (*wājib*). If there is reward (*thawāb*) for the act and punishment is absent it is called a recommended act (*mandūb*). Similarly, when the proscription is decisive and the commission of the act invokes punishment, the act is prohibited (*ḥarām*), and if there is an urging to abstain from the act without invoking punishment for commission it is called reprehensible (*makrūh*).[19] Where a choice has been given (between commission and omission) the act is permitted (*mubāḥ*). The kinds of *aḥkām* acquired through these channels are

[18] The evidence on which reliance is placed for purposes of *ijmāʿ* is called the *sanad* of *ijmāʿ*.

[19] The term "disapproved" will sometimes be used to indicate this category.

five: obligatory, recommended, prohibited, reprehensible or disapproved, and permissible.

The causes of conflict of opinion (*ikhtilāf*), by genus, are six.[20] First is the vacillation of the words between these four modes, that is between the general word meant as a particular word, or the particular word implying generality, or a general word implying generality, or a particular word intending a particular meaning, or there is present, or absent, an indirect indication of the communication. The second cause is the equivocality (*ishtirāk*) in words. This occurs sometimes in the individual word like the word "period" (*qurʾ*) that is applied both to purity (*ṭuhr*) and to menstruation (*ḥayḍ*); similarly, the word command (*amr*) whether it is to be given the (initial) meaning of obligation or of recommendation and the word proscription (*nahy*) whether it is to be given the meaning of prohibition or of disapproval. Sometimes it occurs in the compound word as in the words of Allāh: "Save those who afterward repent".[21] It is likely that this refers to the transgressing person (*fāsiq*) only and it is also probable that it refers to both the transgressor and the witness (*shāhid*). Thus, repentance can remove the consequences of transgression and it can also permit the testimony of the slanderer.[22] The third cause lies in the (different probabilities of the) grammatical structure. The fourth is the ability of the word to indicate its literal meaning, and an allegorical or metaphorical sense resulting from an implied omission or addition or from the reversal of the normal order of the sentence by advancing or deferring a word from its legitimate place, or it may be the vacillation of the word between its actual application and the figurative meaning. The fifth cause is the occasional use of the word in its absolute/unqualified (*muṭlaq*) meaning or in a qualified sense, like the unqualified use, on occasions, of the word slave (*raqabah;* literally neck) in manumission and then qualifying it with faith (*īmān*) at other times. The sixth cause is the conflict between two texts, in all kinds of words from which the law derives the *aḥkām*. Moreover, the conflict may exist between reported acts or approvals or between different kinds of analogy themselves, or the conflict may be between one of these four channels with another channel: that is, the conflict of a word with a reported act, approval, or analogy; the

[20] The accepted principle is that there is no conflict in the evidences of *sharīʿa*. The conflict exists in the mind of the jurist that he seeks to resolve through the science of *uṣūl al-fiqh*.

[21] Qurʾān 24: 5. The verse relates to those who falsely accuse chaste women: "And those who accuse honorable women but bring not four witnesses, scourge them (with) eighty stripes and never (afterward) accept their testimony. They indeed are the evildoers. Save those who afterward repent and make amends. (For such) lo! Allah is Forgiving, Merciful". Qurʾān 24 : 4, 5.

[22] The question here is whether repentance on the part of the slanderer (*qādhif*) will have the effect of waiving the restriction placed through the words, "and never (afterward) accept their testimony", (Qurʾān 24: 4) or it will only do away with the imputation, "they indeed are the evildoers". The exception, "save those who afterward repent", can be interpreted both ways.

conflict of a reported act with approval or analogy; and the conflict of approval with analogy.

The Qāḍī (Ibn Rushd) (God be pleased with him) said: After this brief discussion, we begin with our purpose, seeking the help of Allāh, and to do so we start with the Book of Purification (*Ṭahāra*) as is customary with them (the jurists).

I

THE BOOK OF (RITUAL) PURIFICATION (*ṬAHĀRA*)

The Muslim jurists agreed that *sharʿī* (legal) purity (*ṭahāra*) is of two types: purity from *ḥadath* (ritual impurity) and purity from *khabath* (physical impurity).[23] They also agreed that purity from *ḥadath* is of three kinds: ablution (*wuḍūʾ*), bathing (*ghusl*), and their substitute, ablution with clean earth (*tayammum*).[24] This is because of their inclusion in the verse of ablution,[25] which dealt with these issues. We shall begin, out of these, with a discussion of ablution. We say:

1.1. THE BOOK OF ABLUTION (*WUḌŪʾ*)

A comprehensive discussion of the principles of this (type of) worship (*ʿibāda*) is covered in five chapters. Chapter 1 relates to the evidence of its obligation—on whom it is obligatory and when; Chapter 2 is about the identification of its acts; Chapter 3 is about the identification of that with which it is performed, that is, water; Chapter 4 is about the identification of factors nullifying it; and Chapter 5 is about the identification of things with which it can be performed.

[23] Impurity (*najāsa*) is divided by the jurists into two kinds: actual (*ḥaqīqiya*) and technical or legal (*ḥukmiya*). The term *ḥadath* is applied to legal or technical impurity, while *khabath* to actual impurity. *Ḥadath* may be minor, which is removed through ablution, or it may be major (sexual defilement and menstruation) and is removed through bathing (*ghusl*). Similarly, actual *najāsa* may be heavy (*mughallaẓa*) or light (*mukhaffafa*).

[24] The term *wuḍūʾ* is also referred to as the minor (*sughrā*) ablution, while the term *ghusl* is referred to as the major (*kubrā*) ablution.

[25] Qurʾān 5 : 6.

1.1.1. **Chapter 1 The Evidence (*Dalīl*) of its Obligation**

The evidence of its obligation is in the Qur'ān, *sunna*,[26] and *ijmā*ʿ.[27] In the Qur'ān it is in the words of the Exalted: "O ye who believe, when ye rise up for prayer, wash your faces and your hands up to the elbows, and lightly rub your heads and (wash) your feet up to the ankles".[28] The Muslim jurists agreed that obedience to this communication is obligatory for each person on whom prayer is obligatory, when it is time for it(s) (performance). In the *sunna*, it is in the words of the Prophet (God's peace and blessings be upon him) "Allāh neither accepts prayers without purity nor charity out of purloined wealth [of spoils]", and in his saying, "Allāh does not accept prayers from one who has acquired *ḥadath* till he performs ablution". These two traditions are authentic according to the leading traditionists. Its evidence in *ijmā*ʿ is based on the absence of a transmission from any of the Muslims disputing its obligation. Had there been a dispute, it would necessarily have been transmitted because of the demands of practice.

Those on whom it is obligatory are the sane and pubescent.[29] This too is established through *sunna* and *ijmā*ʿ. In the *sunna*, it is found in the words of the Prophet (God's peace and blessings be upon him), "The pen [liability] has been lifted from [in the case of] three persons". He then mentioned the minor, till he attains puberty, and the insane person, till he recovers. There is no transmitted controversy about its proof in *ijmā*ʿ. The jurists (*fuqahā*') disagreed whether Islam is a requisite condition for its obligation. It is an issue that is of little benefit in *fiqh*, as it relates to the *ḥukm* of the hereafter.

Ablution becomes obligatory when it is time for prayer (*ṣalāh*) or when a person has intended an act for which ablution is a requisite condition, even if the act is not associated with a fixed time. About its obligation upon a person in a state of *ḥadath*, when it is time for prayer, there is no controversy because of the words of the Exalted, "O ye who believe, when ye rise up for prayer, wash your faces and your hands up to the elbows, and lightly rub your heads and (wash) your feet up to the ankles".[30] Thus, ablution is made obligatory at

[26] The term *sunna* applies to the practice of the Prophet (God's peace and blessings be upon him) as established through his words, acts, and tacit approval. The *sunna* is the source of Islamic law along with the Qur'ān. It is to be distinguished from the term *ḥadīth*, which is the bearer of the *sunna*. A *ḥadīth* may contain more than one *sunna*.

[27] The term "*ijmā*ʿ" refers to the consensus of Muslim jurists, in a determined period of time, on the scope and meaning of a principle or rule of Islamic law.

[28] Qur'ān 5 : 6.

[29] The term "pubescent" is being used here, for want of a better term, to mean a person who has attained puberty.

[30] Qur'ān 5 : 6.

the time of prayer, and one of the conditions (for the validity) of prayer is the commencement of the time of prayer. With respect to the evidence of its obligation at the time of intending an act, for which it is a condition, the discussion will be taken up under the description of the acts for which ablution is required, along with the (narration of the) differences among the jurists over this.

1.1.2. **Chapter 2 The Acts of Ablution**

The source for the identification of the acts of ablution is the description laid down in the words of the Exalted, "O ye who believe, when ye rise up for prayer, wash your faces and your hands up to the elbows, and lightly rub your heads and (wash) your feet up to the ankles",[31] and the method of performing ablution traced to the Prophet (God's peace and blessings be upon him) in the established narrations (*āthār*). To this are related twelve well-known issues that resemble fundamental principles. They are related to the identification of the requisite conditions, the elements, the description of the acts, their number, their specification, and the identification of the objects of the *aḥkām* of all these.

1.1.2.1. Issue 1: Whether intention (*niyya*) is a requisite condition

The jurists disagreed whether intention is a condition for the validity of ablution, although they had agreed on the stipulation of intention as a condition for worship (*ʿibādāt*), because of the words of the Exalted, "And they are ordered naught else than to serve Allāh, keeping religion pure for Him",[32] and because of the saying of the Prophet (God's peace and blessings be upon him), "The value of acts depends upon accompanying intentions", which is a well-known tradition. A group of jurists, including al-Shāfiʿī, Mālik, Ḥammād, Abū Thawr, and Dāwūd, was of the opinion that it (intention) is a condition. Another group said it is not a condition, and this was the opinion of Abū Ḥanīfa and al-Thāwrī. The reason for their disagreement is the vacillation of the term *wuḍūʾ* between being a pure ritual *ʿibāda*—I mean, not subject to rationalization and intended only for the pleasure of Allāh, like *ṣalāh* and similar forms of mere ritual worship—and between an *ʿibāda* that can also be rational, like washing of dirt. They did not differ about pure *ʿibāda* being in need of intention, and rational *ʿibāda* not being in need of it.

[31] Qurʾān 5 : 6.
[32] Qurʾān 98 : 5.

Ablution has a resemblance to both kinds of worship and a disagreement has, therefore, resulted. The reason is that it combines ritual worship and purification, and the aim of *fiqh* is to examine which one it resembles more strongly so that it may be linked to it.

1.1.2.2. Issue 2: *Aḥkām* of washing hands before touching utensils

The jurists differed about washing of hands before immersing a hand inside the water-utensil of ablution. Some have held that it is one of the practices (*sunan*) of ablution that is always recommended,[33] even when the hands are clean without a doubt. This is the better known opinion of Mālik and al-Shāfiʿī. It is also said that it is recommended in the case of a person doubting the purity of his hands. This too was an opinion narrated from Mālik. It is also said that washing of hands (before immersing them in the water inside a utensil) is obligatory on one waking up from sleep. This was Dāwūd's view and that of his disciples. Some have distinguished between nocturnal sleep and that of the day, and made it obligatory for nocturnal sleep, but not for that during the day. This is Aḥmad's opinion. Thus, four opinions are arrived at through this (discussion). First, that it is *sunna* in absolute terms (i.e. always undertaken). Second, that it is recommended for the person in doubt. Third, that it is obligatory on one awaking from sleep. Fourth, that it is obligatory on one waking up from nocturnal sleep and not that of the day.

The reason for their disagreement in this is their dispute over the meaning of Abū Hurayra's authentic tradition that the Prophet (God's peace and blessings be upon him) said, "When one of you wakes up from his sleep, let him wash his hand(s) before putting it into the water-can, for he does not know where his hand has spent the night". In some versions it is said, "let him wash it thrice". Those who did not see a contradiction between the additional requirement in this tradition and what is contained in the verse of ablution, interpreted the imperative word here in its apparent meaning of obligation (*wujūb*) and (thus) rendered the washing of hands from among the obligations of ablution. Those, among them, who considered the word "during the night" (*bayāt*) to imply nocturnal sleep, rendered it an obligation in the case of nocturnal sleep alone. Those who did not have a similar understanding of this, but understood from it sleep only, made it obligatory for all kinds of awakening from sleep, whether that of the day or night. Those who saw a conflict between the addition in this tradition and the verse of ablution—the apparent meaning in the verse of ablution being the enumeration of the

[33] The author is apparently using this term to mean *sunna muʾakkada* which depicts an act persistently performed by the Prophet (God's peace and blessings be upon him) as compared to *sunna ghayr muʾakkada* that applies to an act performed, by him, occasionally and for which the term recommendation (*mandūb*) has been used here.

obligations (*furūḍ*) of ablution—reconcile the two by shifting the apparent meaning, that is, obligation to mean recommendation (*nadb*). Those for whom this recommendation is emphatic (*muʾakkada*) due to the Prophet's persistent performance of this act, considered it a category of the *sunan*. Those for whom this recommendation was not emphatic, said it is from the category of *mandūb* (recommended) only. For them the washing of hands in this manner is required even when they are undoubtedly clean, I mean, those who considered it emphatic *sunna* and also those who said it is recommended. Those, among them, who did not comprehend from this tradition an obligatory underlying cause, so as to deem it a category of the particular word implying generality, recommended it only for one waking up from sleep. Those who deduced from it the cause of doubt deemed it to be of the category of the particular word implying generality and considered it to apply to every person in doubt, for it is close to the state of arising from sleep.

This tradition apparently is not intended for the *ḥukm* of (washing of) hands in ablution, but is intended for the *ḥukm* of the water with which ablution is to be performed, as purity is a stipulated condition for such water. The report about the Prophet (God's peace and blessings be upon him) washing his hands most of the time before handling the utensil is probably applicable to the *ḥukm* that washing hands in the beginning is one of the acts of ablution. It is also likely that it is related to the *ḥukm* for water, as it should not be polluted or become doubtful (as to purity), that is, if we say that doubt is an effective factor.

1.1.2.3. Issue 3: Elements: rinsing of mouth (*maḍmaḍa*) and snuffing water (*istinshāq*)

The jurists differed about rinsing of the mouth (*maḍmaḍa*) and snuffing (*istinshāq*). There are three opinions. First, that these practices are a *sunna* (emphatic recommendation) in ablution. This was the opinion of Mālik, al-Shāfiʿī, and Abū Ḥanīfa. Second, that they are obligatory (*farḍ*) in ablution. This was the view of Ibn Abī Laylā and some disciples of Abū Dāwūd. Third, that *istinshāq* is obligatory, while *maḍmaḍa* is recommended (*sunna*). This was the opinion of Abū Thawr, Abū ʿUbayda, and of a group of Ẓāhirites.

The reason for their disagreement, whether it is an obligation or a recommendation, is their dispute about the traditions reported on this issue, whether they amount to an addition over the verse of ablution, entailing a conflict. Those who considered that this addition, if deemed an obligation, conflicts with the verse—as the aim of the verse is to provide a foundation for this rule along with its explanation—shifted the implication of the traditions from the category of obligation to that of recommendation. Those who did not consider it as conflicting, assigned it its apparent meaning of obligation. Those for whom the authority of the Prophet's sayings and acts is equal (in strength), for purposes of assigning obligation, did not make a distinction between *maḍmaḍa* and *istinshāq*. Those for whom a saying is interpreted as an obligation and an act as recommendation distinguished between *maḍmaḍa* and *istinshāq*, as *maḍmaḍa* has been reported through the acts of the Prophet (God's peace and blessings be upon him) and not his command, while *istinshāq* is reported both from his commands and acts. The Prophet (God's peace and blessings be upon him) said, "When one of you performs *wuḍūʾ*, let him snuff up water into his nose and then let it out, while he who performs *istinjāʾ* (with stones) let him do it an odd number of times". It is narrated by Mālik in his *al-Muwaṭṭā* and by al-Bukhārī in his *Ṣaḥīḥ* from the tradition of Abū Hurayra.

1.1.2.4. Issue 4: Defining the area to be washed

The jurists agreed that washing of the whole face is one of the obligations of ablution, because of the words of the Exalted: "O ye who believe, when ye rise up for prayer, wash your faces". They differed about this on three points; namely, washing of the hairless part of the face between the beard and the ears, washing of the whole length of the beard, and the *takhlīl* of the beard (combing it with wet fingers).

The well-known opinion in Mālik's school is that the portion between the beard and the ears is not part of the face, though some Mālikites maintain that it is. Some jurists make a distinction between a person who is still beardless and a person with a beard. Thus, in the school (Mālik's) there are three opinions. Abū Ḥanīfa and al-Shāfiʿī said that it is a part of the face. With respect to the length of the beard, Mālik was of the opinion that it is obligatory that water flow on it, but it is not obligatory according to Abū Ḥanīfa and also al-Shāfiʿī in one of his two opinions. The reason for their disagreement over these two issues is the ambiguity of the term "face". With respect to the *takhlīl* of the beard, the opinion of Mālik was that it is not obligatory. Abū Ḥanīfa and al-Shāfiʿī had a similar view. Ibn ʿAbd al-Ḥakam, one of Mālik's disciples, made it obligatory.

The reason for their disagreement is the controversy about the authenticity of narrated traditions containing the command for *takhlīl* of the beard. The majority are of the view that they are not authentic and the narration in which the acts of the Prophet's ablution are reported do not contain anything about *takhlīl* of the beard.

1.1.2.5. Issue 5: Washing of hands and arms up to the elbows

The jurists agreed that the washing of the hands and the forearms are from among the obligations of ablution because of the words of the Exalted, "O ye who believe, when ye rise up for prayer, wash your faces". They disagreed about the inclusion of the elbows (in the forearms). The majority, Mālik, al-Shāfiʿī, and Abū Ḥanīfa, considered their inclusion as obligatory. Some of the Ẓāhirites, later Mālikites, and al-Ṭabarī were of the opinion that their inclusion in washing is not obligatory. The reason for their disagreement in this is the equivocality (*ishtirāk*) in the preposition *ilā* (to, up to) and the term *yadd* (hand), in the language of the Arabs. The preposition *ilā* sometimes denotes, in the usage of the Arabs, the limit (up to) and at other times gives the meaning of "with". The word *yadd* (hand), in the usage of the Arabs, is applied to three meanings: the hand; hand and forearms; hand, forearm, and upper arm. Those who rendered *ilā* as "with" or considered *yadd* as all three parts of the limb, deemed the inclusion of elbows for washing as obligatory. Those who understood from *ilā* the limit and from the term *yadd* whatever is lower than the elbows, and did not consider the limit as included in the defined category, did not include the elbows in washing. Muslim has reported in his *Ṣaḥīḥ* that Abū Hurayra used to first wash his right hand till the beginning of the upper arm, then the left in the same manner, followed by the washing of the right foot till the beginning of the calf and then the washing of the left in the same manner. He (Abū Hurayra) then said: "That is how I saw the Prophet of Allāh (God's peace and blessings be upon him) performing ablution". This is the proof given by those who made obligatory the inclusion of the elbows in washing.

When a word vacillates between two meanings it is necessary that it should not be assigned either meaning except through another evidence, even though in the case of *ilā* the meaning in the usage of the Arabs as being "limit" is more readily apparent than the meaning "with", and even though the term *yadd* is used more often to include whatever is below the forearm rather than what is above it. Thus, the opinion of those who did not include it is preferable from the aspect of the literal indication, and the opinion of those who did include it is clearer from the aspect of the narrated tradition, unless the tradition is interpreted only as a recommendation (*nadb*). The issue is probable either way, as is obvious. Some say that if "limit" is from the same genus as the term, it is included in it, but if it is not from the same genus it is not included.

1.1.2.6. Issue 6: Wiping (*masḥ*) of the head

The jurists agreed that wiping (*masḥ*) of the head is one of the obligations of ablution. They differed about the extent (of wiping) required. Mālik said that it is obligatory to wipe the whole of it (the head). Al-Shāfiʿī, some followers of Mālik, and Abū Ḥanīfa said that it is obligatory to wipe a part of it. Some followers of Mālik defined the minimum part to be a third, while others defined it as two-thirds. Abū Ḥanīfa, on the other hand, limited it to a fourth, and he also defined the part of the hand with which it is to be wiped as a fourth. He said, "Its wiping with less than three fingers is insufficient". Al-Shāfiʿī did not fix a limit for either.

The basis of this disagreement is due to the equivocality (*ishtirāk*) that is in (the particle) *bā*, in the usage of the Arabs. It is sometimes used as a mere addition for emphasis – as in the words of the Exalted, "*tanbut biʾdduhni*",[34] according to one who read "*tunbitu*" with a *ḍamma* for "*t*" and *kasra* for *bā* from the root *anbata*. At other times, the particle *bā* indicates the idea of a portion, as in the sentence "*akhadhtu bi thawbihi wa bi ʿaḍuḍih* (I held him [grabbed him] *bi* [by] his garment and his forearm)". There is no purpose in denying this, that is, the fact that *bā* may convey the idea of "a portion of". This is the opinion of the Kūfī school of grammar (*nahw*). Those who considered it superfluous have deemed obligatory the wiping of the entire head. Superfluous here means that it is added only for emphasis. Those who considered *bā* as indicating apportionment have deemed obligatory the wiping of only a part of the head. Those who preferred this meaning have argued on the basis of the tradition of al-Mughīra that "the Prophet (God's peace and blessings be upon him) performed ablution wiping his forehead and turban". It is reported by Muslim. If we accept that *bā* is superfluous, there still remains another probability, whether the obligation relates to the front part of names (like head) or to the back part.

1.1.2.7. Issue 7: Determination of the number

The jurists agreed that the obligation in ablution is to wash each washable limb once, one after the other, soaking these parts with water. Washing each (limb) twice or thrice is recommended (*mandūb*) for it is authentically reported that the Prophet (God's peace and blessings be upon him) performed ablution washing each (limb) once. On another occasion he washed twice, and on yet another occasion he was seen washing them thrice. The command, however, does not require washing each limb more than once, that is, the command laid down in the verse of *wuḍūʾ*.

They differed about the merit in repeating the wiping of the head. Al-Shāfiʿī was of the opinion that the person who washes his other limbs three times should preferably wipe his head thrice. The majority of the jurists saw no merit in repeating the *masḥ*. The reason for their disagreement (here) lies in their dispute over the acceptance of the addition contained in one tradition coming down through a single chain. The majority of the jurists do not use

[34] Qurʾān 23 : 20.

such a tradition. Most of the other traditions relating that he (the Prophet) washed thrice, including that related through Uthmān and others, state that he wiped only once. In some narrations from Uthmān, however, that describe the *wuḍū*ʾ of the Prophet (God's peace and blessings be upon him) it is stated that he (the Prophet) wiped his head thrice. Al-Shāfiʿī emphatically supported accepting this excess on the basis of the apparent generality of the narrations that the Prophet (God's peace and blessings be upon him) performed *wuḍū*ʾ repeating his acts twice and thrice. The generality, here, even though it arises from the word of a Companion is assigned to all the limbs in ablution. This addition, though, is not in the two *Ṣaḥīḥs*. If proved authentic it (the narration) must be followed, as that which fails to mention a thing cannot be a proof against that which does mention it. The majority of the jurists made obligatory the renewal of water for wiping on the analogy of the other limbs. It is narrated from Ibn Mājishūn that he said, "If the water is exhausted he may wipe with the moisture on his beard". This is the preference of Ibn Habīb, Mālik and al-Shāfiʿī.

It is recommended in the performance of *masḥ* that one begin with the forehead, passing the hands over the top up to the nape of the neck, and then bringing them (to the point) where he started. This is stated in the reliable tradition of ʿAbd Allāh Ibn Zayd al-Thābit. Some of the jurists preferred that one begin with the back of the head. This too is narrated from the description of the ablution of the Prophet from the tradition of al-Rubayyiʿ bint Muʿawwidh, except that it is not found in the *Ṣaḥīḥayn*.

1.1.2.8. Issue 8: Determination of the objects of wiping

The jurists disagreed about (the sufficiency of) *masḥ* over the turban (alone). This was permitted by Aḥmad Ibn Ḥanbal, Abū Thawr, al-Qāsim, Ibn Sallām and some others. It was prohibited by another group and by Mālik, al-Shāfiʿī, and Abū Ḥanīfa. Their disagreement arises from their dispute about the validity of acting upon the tradition related by al-Mughīra and others "that he [the Prophet] (God's peace and blessings be upon him) performed *masḥ* on his forehead and on his turban, and also upon the analogy of [the *masḥ* of] boots. It is for this reason that most of them stipulated that it be worn in a clean condition.[35] This tradition was rejected by some, either because it was deemed unauthentic by them or because the apparent meaning in the Qurʾān contradicted it, in their opinion, that is, the command in it about the *masḥ* of the head, or because it was not widely accepted in practice. This is according to those who require widespread practice for matters reported through

[35] That is, when the worshipper is in the ritual state of purity.

individual traditions, particularly in Medina, as is known about the school of Mālik, who stipulated widespread practice as a condition. The *ḥadīth* is reported by Muslim. Abū ʿUmar Ibn ʿAbd al-Barr said that it is a defective (*maʿlūl*) tradition. In some of its versions the wiping of the turban alone is mentioned, while that of the forehead is not. It is for this reason that some jurists did not stipulate with the wiping of the turban the wiping of the forehead as well, as the original requirement and its substitute cannot be combined together.

1.1.2.9. Issue 9: Wiping (*Masḥ*) of the ears

They (the jurists) disagreed about the wiping of the ears whether it is recommended (*sunna*) or an obligation (*farīḍa*), and whether the water is to be renewed. Some said it is obligatory and that water is to be renewed for (wiping) them. Those who expressed this opinion are a group from among Mālik's followers, as he considered the ears a part of the head. Abū Ḥanīfa and his followers considered their wiping as obligatory, and said that they are to be wiped along with the head with the same water. Al-Shāfiʿī considered their wiping as a *sunna* and stipulated the renewal of water for them. This opinion was held by another group of Mālik's followers and they maintained that it is Mālik's opinion, because it is narrated that he said "their *ḥukm* is the same as the *ḥukm* of *maḍmaḍa*". The disagreement—whether wiping of the ears is recommended or an obligation—stems from the controversy about the traditions transmitted on this issue, that is, the wiping of the ears by the Prophet (God's peace and blessings be upon him) whether it is an addition over what exists in the Qurʾān about the wiping of the head. Its *ḥukm* then is that it is a recommendation due to the conflict between it and the verse, if it is interpreted as an obligation. If, however, it is considered an explanation of an unelaborated word in the Qurʾān, its *ḥukm* becomes the *ḥukm* already existing for the head, that is, obligatory. Thus those who considered it obligatory deem it an explanation of the difficult (*mujmal*) word in the Qurʾān, while those who did not consider it obligatory deem it an addition, as in the case of *maḍmaḍa*. There are many traditions transmitted on this issue. Though they are not included in the two *Ṣaḥīḥs*, practice has become common according to these traditions.

With respect to the disagreement about the renewal of water for the ears, the cause is the vacillation of the term "ears", whether they are considered independent limbs for purposes of ablution or whether they form part of the head. One group gave a distinct opinion that they are to be washed with the face while another considered that the inside of the ears is to be wiped with the head and the outer parts to be washed with the face. The reason is their being equipoised between being part of the face or head. All this has no real significance in view of the common traditions about their *masḥ* and its widespread practice. Al-Shāfiʿī considers the repeated wiping of the ears as being recommended,[36] as he does in the case of wiping of the head.

1.1.2.10. Issue 10: Washing of the feet

The jurists agreed that the feet are limbs that are the object of ablution, but they differed about the method of purification required for them. A group of jurists, and these are the majority, said that their purity is attained by washing. Another group said that the obligation in their case is wiping. And yet another group said that their purity is achieved through either way; it depends upon the choice of the worshipper.

The reason for disagreement is based upon two well-known readings of the verse of *wuḍūʾ*, that is, the reading of those who read the word "feet" as the object of washing with a *naṣb* (accusative; final vowel *a*) in conjunction with limbs washed, and those who read it with a *khafḍ* (final vowel *i*) in conjunction with parts wiped. The reading with a *naṣb* clearly indicates washing, while reading it with a *khafḍ* evidently indicates wiping. Those who held that the obligation is specifically for one of these two types of purity, determined as washing or wiping, preferred one reading over the other, disposing of, by interpretation, the meaning of the other reading in favour of the reading that was preferable for them. Those who believed that the obvious implications of both readings were equal, and that one of these did not have a stronger indication than the other, rendered it as a *wājib mukhayyar* (obligation with a choice), like expiation for breaking an oath. This was the opinion of al-Ṭabarī and Dāwūd. The majority, however, have numerous ways of interpreting away the reading with a *khafḍ*, and the best of these is that the conjunction here relates to the pronounced form of the word, which is found in Arab usage.

The other party, and they are those who made wiping obligatory, interpreted the *naṣb* reading as being a conjunction related to the position of the immediately preceding word introduced by the genitive particle, which is like the direct object of the verb. The majority preferred this reading of theirs (in the accusative case) on the basis of reports established from the Prophet (God's peace and blessings be upon him) when he said about people who did not wash their feet, "Woe to the heels in the fire".[37] They said that this

[36] That is, he considers it to fall under the category known as *mandūb* (recommended). The phrase "al-Shāfiʿī recommended" is being used here as recommended by the Lawgiver not by al-Shāfiʿī. This may apply to the other categories of the *aḥkām*, and will be encountered frequently in what follows. The reader should note the distinction.

[37] The reference here is to ankles not properly washed in ablution.

indicates that washing of the feet is an obligation, as an obligation is that to which punishment is linked for non-observance. There is, however, no legal force in this; the warning was issued here about the people who chose to wash their feet but not their heels.[38] There is no doubt that those who made washing obligatory, made it so for the feet in their entirety, while those who made wiping obligatory, did so for the feet in their entirety, as did those who granted a choice in the two obligations. This may also be supported by what is related in a tradition, also recorded by Muslim, where it is said that "We began wiping our feet, when he [the Prophet] proclaimed, 'Woe to the heels in the fire'". This tradition, though it has been the practice to argue through it for the denial of wiping, is stronger in the indication of its permissibility rather than its prohibition, as the warning was issued for the neglect of completion and not for the type of *ṭahāra*; in fact, it is silent as to the type, which indicates their permissibility. The permissibility of wiping is also related from some of the Companions and the Tābiʿūn, but by way of implication.

Washing is more suitable for the feet than is wiping, just as wiping is more suitable for the head than is washing, as the dirt on the feet is usually not eliminated except by washing, while the dirt on the head is usually removed by wiping. Rational interests (*maṣāliḥ*) are probably not applicable as causes for obligatory acts of worship, and the law has, therefore, recognized both meanings in them: a meaning securing an interest and an *ʿibādī* (ritual) meaning requiring obedience. I mean by *maṣlaḥī* that which relates to the senses, and I mean by *ʿibādī* that which pertains to the purification of the self (*nafs*).

Likewise, those jurists, who permitted wiping, differed about whether ankles are to be included in wiping or washing. The disagreement stems from the equivocality of the preposition *ʿilā* (up to), that is, in the words of the Exalted, "up to the ankles". The discussion of the equivocality found in this word has preceded in the discussion of the words of the Exalted, "up to the elbows". The equivocality there was from two aspects, because of the word *yadd* and the word *ʿilā* while here it is due to the equivocality of the word *ʿilā* alone.

They disagreed about the connotation of the term *kaʿb*, because of the equivocality of the word *kaʿb* and the disagreement of language experts about its connotation. It is said that they are the two bones at the knot of the straps of the sandals, while it is also said that they are the two protruding bones on the sides of the (lower) calf. There is no dispute, as far as I know, about their inclusion in washing, according to those who maintain that they are the bones at the knot of the straps, for they are indeed parts of the foot. It is for this

[38] Since they started washing the fore-parts of the feet the heels had also to be washed.

reason that one group has said that if the defining limit is of the same category as the defined part, it is included in its ambit, that is, the thing introduced by the words "up to". If, however, it does not fall under the same category as the defined term, it is not covered by it, as in the words of the Exalted, "Then strictly observe the fast till [up to] nightfall".[39]

1.1.2.11. Issue 11: The sequence of the acts of ablution

They disagreed about the observance of a sequence in the acts of ablution as arranged in the verse. One group of jurists said that it (following the sequence) is a *sunna* (recommended). This is what is related by the later disciples of Mālik from the opinions in the school. It was also upheld by Abū Ḥanīfa, al-Thawrī, and Dāwūd. Another group of jurists said that it is an obligation, which was the opinion of Al-Shāfiʿī, Aḥmad, and Abū ʿUbayd. All this is about the sequence of the obligatory acts (of ablution) in relation to each other. As to the sequential ordering of the obligatory acts with recommended acts, it is regarded by Mālik as commendable (*mustaḥabb*), while Abū Ḥanīfa considered it to be a *sunna* (i.e. it should be acted upon as a *sunna*).

There are two reasons for their disagreement. First is the equivocality that arises from the conjunction *wāw* (and), as the conjunction is sometimes achieved through it in a sequential order, while at other times it is without such order. This is indicated through induction in the usage of the Arabs. On this point the grammarians are divided into two groups. The grammarians of Baṣra said that the *wāw* does not indicate an order or a sequence, it merely implies a connection of the words joined by it. The Kūfīs said that it does indicate an order as well as a sequence. Those who maintained that the *wāw* in the verse implies order, upheld the obligation of a sequence, while those who maintained that it does not imply a sequence, did not uphold its obligation. The second reason is based upon their difference related to the acts of the Prophet (God's peace and blessings be upon him), whether they are to be construed as an obligation or a recommendation. Those who interpreted them as obligatory, upheld the obligation of a sequence, as it is not related from him that he ever performed ablution without a definite sequence. Those who interpreted them to imply a recommendation said that sequential performance is a *sunna*. Those who made a distinction between acts prescribed as a *sunna* and as an obligation said that obligatory sequential ordering has to be in acts that are obligatory, but those who did not make such a distinction said that obligatory conditions may apply even to acts that are not obligatory.

[39] Qurʾān 2 : 187

1.1.2.12. Issue 12: The continuous performance of the acts

They disagreed about the (obligation of) continuous performance of the acts of ablution (without uncalled-for intervals between them). Mālik held that continuous performance is an obligation, when the acts are remembered along with the ability to perform them, relaxed only because of forgetfulness, or when they are remembered but there is a valid excuse, and the interval is not excessive. Al-Shāfiʿī and Abū Ḥanīfa said that continuous performance is not an obligation of ablution. The reason for disagreement is again the equivocality of the *wāw*, as the conjunction sometimes applies to adjacent things following each other, while at other times it applies to acts delayed with respect to others.

A group of jurists argued for the suspension of continuous performance on the basis of what is established from the Prophet (God's peace and blessings be upon him) that he occasionally performed ablution, and used to delay the washing of his feet till sometime later. The disagreement over this issue also arises from the interpretation of (following) these acts (of the Prophet) as an obligation or a recommendation.

Mālik made a distinction on the basis of intention and forgetfulness; the principle applying to the person who forgets is that he is excused, unless evidence to the contrary is established, because of the words of the Prophet (God's peace and blessings be upon him), "Liability for mistake and forgetfulness is removed from my *umma*". Similarly, a valid excuse, as is obvious from the dictates of the law, is effective in obtaining a concession.

A group of jurists said that invoking the name of Allāh at the beginning is an obligatory part of ablution. They argued for this on the basis of the words of the Prophet (God's peace and blessings be upon him), through a *marfūʿ* tradition: "There is no *wuḍūʾ* for the person who has not proclaimed the name of Allāh". This tradition has not been proved authentic according to the traditionists. Others have interpreted it as implying *niyya*, while some, as far as I know, have construed it as a recommendation.

These are the widely known principal issues in this topic (of ablution). They relate, as we have seen, either to the description of the acts of this ritual purification, or to the determination of their positions in relation to each other, or to the identification of the conditions and elements, and to all the rest that has been said.

1.1.2.13. Issue 13: Wiping over boots

One of the topics on this subject relates to *masḥ* over boots (*khuffayn*), as it is related to one of the acts of ablution (namely, washing of the feet). The discussion covering its principles relates to the study of seven issues: its permissibility; delineation of the object of *masḥ*; category of the object; its description, that is, the description of its object; its time; conditions; and factors nullifying it.

1.1.2.13.1. Sub-issue 1: Permissibility

There are three opinions about this. The widely known opinion, which was upheld by the majority of the jurists of the provinces, is that it is permitted absolutely. The second opinion permits it during a journey and not within settlements. The third opinion maintains its absolute prohibition, and is the most strict. All three opinions have been related from the first generation (of Islam) and also from Mālik.

The reason for their disagreement is the conflict thought to exist between the verse of ablution, commanding the washing of feet, with the traditions that permitted wiping, bearing in mind the fact that the verse itself was revealed later. This disagreement is to be found among the Companions in the first generation of Islam. Some of them maintained that the verse of ablution had abrogated these traditions, which is Ibn ʿAbbās's opinion. Those who upheld its permissibility argued on the basis of the report by Muslim that the tradition of Jarīr appealed to them, as it is related from him that he had seen the Prophet (God's peace and blessings be upon him) wiping his boots. It was said to him that this was prior to the revelation of *sūrat al-Māʾida*, but he said, "I converted to Islam after the revelation of *al-Māʾida*". The later jurists, who upheld its permissibility, said that there is no conflict between the verse and the traditions, as the command for washing feet is directed toward those who do not have boots, and the exemption has been granted to one wearing them. It is said that the interpretation of the verse based on the *khafḍ* version relates to wiping over boots. Those who made a distinction between travelling and being in a settlement, did so because most of the authentic traditions, conveying *masḥ* by the Prophet (God's peace and blessings be upon him) over his boots, relate to travel. Further, journey in itself depicts exemption and leniency. And, *masḥ* belongs to the category of leniency, as taking them off presents a hardship for the traveller.

1.1.2.13.2. Sub-issue 2: Defining the area to be wiped

The jurists of the regions disagreed about the delineation of the area (to be wiped). One group of jurists said that the obligation is for wiping the upper part of the boots, and that wiping the lower part, that is, the sole, is commendable. Mālik is one of those who upheld this, as is al-Shāfiʿī. Some of them deemed obligatory the wiping of the external and the internal parts of the boots, which is Ibn Nāfiʿ's opinion, from among the disciples of Mālik, while others deemed obligatory the wiping of the external part alone, and did not consider commendable the wiping of the inner part, which is the opinion of Abū Ḥanīfa, Dāwūd, Sufyān (al-Thawrī), and a group of jurists. Ashhab deviated from this and said that the obligation is for wiping the inner part or the external, whichever he (chooses) to wipe.[40]

The reason for their disagreement stems from the conflict of the traditions relevant to the subject, and the resemblance of wiping with washing. There exist two opposing traditions. The first is the tradition of al-Mughīra ibn Shuʿba, which says, "He (God's peace and blessings be upon him) wiped over his boots and inside them". The other is the tradition of ʿAlī, saying, "Had the *dīn* been structured upon opinions, the wiping of the lower part of the boots would have been better than wiping the upper part, but I have seen the Messenger of Allāh wiping the external part of his boots". Those who adopted an opinion based on the reconciliation of traditions interpreted the tradition of al-Mughīra to imply recommendation, and interpreted the tradition of ʿAlī to imply obligation. This is the preferable method. Those who adopted preference, either adopted ʿAlī's tradition or that of al-Mughīra. Those who gave predominance to al-Mughīra's tradition over ʿAlī's did so on the basis of analogy, that is, the analogy of *masḥ* upon washing, while those who gave predominance to ʿAlī's tradition did so because of its opposition to analogy or on the basis of a more reliable chain of transmission. Prominence in this issue goes to Mālik. I have no knowledge of the basis for those who permitted *masḥ* of the inner part alone, for they neither followed these traditions nor employed this analogy, that is, the analogy of wiping upon washing.

1.1.2.13.3. Sub-issue 3: Kinds of objects

About the kinds of objects that are to be wiped, the jurists upholding *masḥ* agreed upon wiping over boots, but they disagreed about socks (*jawrabayn*). One group of jurists permitted this, while another prohibited it. Among those who prohibited this are Mālik, Al-Shāfiʿī, and Abū Ḥanīfa. Those who permitted it include Abū Yūsuf and Muḥammad, the disciples of Abū Ḥanīfa, and Sufyān al-Thawrī.

The reason for their disagreement arises from their dispute over the authenticity of a tradition from the Prophet (God's peace and blessings be upon him) on this issue, which conveys that he wiped his socks as well as his sandals (*naʿlayn*). They also disputed as to whether analogy for other things can be constructed upon the wiping over boots, or whether it is a fixed ritual or non-rational interpretation upon which no analogy can be based nor can it be extended to other things. Those for whom the tradition did not prove authentic, or (information about) it did not reach them, and they did not employ analogy upon boots, restricted *masḥ* to the boots, while those who considered the tradition to be authentic, or upheld analogy upon boots,

[40] Note by the Editor of the original text: In the Fās manuscript it is stated: "While (wiping of) the external part is commendable".

permitted *masḥ* over socks. This tradition has not been recorded by the two Shaykhs, that is, al-Bukhārī and Muslim, but has been deemed authentic by al-Tirmidhī. Because of the vacillation of leather socks between boots and non-leather socks, there are two narrations from Mālik about wiping them: one prohibits it, while the other permits it.

1.1.2.13.4. Sub-issue 4: Description of boots

They agreed about wiping over boots that are in good condition, and disagreed about those that are torn. Mālik and his disciples said that one may wipe over them if the tear is minor. Abū Hanīfa limited the extent of the tear to the measure of three fingers. A group of jurists said that it is permitted to wipe over them as long as they can be described as boots, even when the tear is extensive. One such jurist from whom this is related is al-Thawrī. Al-Shāfiʿī, in one of his two opinions, held that the boot should not be torn from the front exposing the foot, even if the tear is small.

The reason for their disagreement derives from the question of whether the transference of the obligation, from washing (the feet) to wiping, is due to their being covered, that is, the feet being covered by the boots, or whether it is due to the hardship arising from taking off the boots and then wearing them after washing.[41] Those who said that it is due to covering did not allow wiping over torn boots, as the uncovering of the feet transfers the obligation from wiping to washing. Those who considered the underlying cause (*ʿilla*) to be hardship did not take into consideration the tear, when they could (still) be called boots. The distinction between a major and a minor tear[42] is based on *istiḥsān* and the removal of hardship. Al-Thawrī said that the boots of the Muhājirūn and the Anṣār were not devoid of tears, like the boots of other people, and had there been a prohibition in this regard it would have been laid down and related from them. I would say that this issue is one that is not expressed (in the texts), and had a *ḥukm* existed for it, along with the fact that tears in boots were common, the Prophet (God's peace and blessings be upon him) would have explained it. Allāh, the Exalted, has said, "We have revealed unto thee the Remembrance that thou mayst explain to mankind that which hath been revealed for them".[43]

1.1.2.13.5. Sub-issue 5: The time of wiping

The jurists also disagreed about (the extent of) its time. Mālik held that it is not limited by time, and one wearing boots may wipe over them, as long as he does not take them off or is not affected by a major impurity (*janāba*). Abū Ḥanīfa and al-Shāfiʿī held that it is limited by time.

[41] The word in the original is *nawʿ*. It should have been *nazʿ*—apparently a printing error.

[42] The word in the original is "boot"; obviously, it should be "tear".

[43] Qurʾān 16 : 44.

The reason for their disagreement is based upon the conflict of traditions about this. Three (relevant) traditions have been related. The first is a tradition of ʿAlī from the Prophet (God's peace and blessings be upon him) that he said, "The Prophet (God's peace and blessings be upon him) determined three days and accompanying nights for a traveller and a night and a day for the resident." It is recorded by Muslim. The second is the tradition of Ubayy ibn ʿUmāra that he said, "O Messenger of Allāh, do I wipe over my boots?" He said, "Yes". He said, "For a day?" He said, "Yes". He asked (again): "Two days?" He said, "Yes". He said, "And a third?" He said, "Yes, till you reach the seventh". He [the Prophet] then added, "Wipe for as long as you wish". This is recorded by Abū Dāwūd and al-Ṭaḥāwī. The third is the tradition of Ṣafwān ibn ʿAssāl, who said, "We were on a journey and were ordered not to take off our boots for three days and accompanying nights, except in the case of a major impurity, but not for urinating, sleep, or when answering the call of nature".

I would say that the tradition of ʿAlī is authentic, as it is recorded by Muslim. About the tradition of Ubayy ibn ʿUmāra, Abū ʿUmar ibn ʿAbd al-Barr has said that it is not established, and does not have a verified chain of narration, therefore, it cannot be used to oppose the tradition from ʿAlī. Though the tradition of Ṣafwān ibn ʿAssāl has not been recorded by al-Bukhārī or by Muslim, yet it has been considered sound by experts in traditions, like al-Tirmidhī and Abū Muḥammad ibn Ḥazm. Like ʿAlī's tradition, it conflicts in its apparent meaning with Ubayy's tradition. It is possible to reconcile the two by saying that the traditions of ʿAlī and Ṣafwān place a time limit in response to the question, while the tradition of Ubayy ibn ʿUmāra is explicit about the negation of such a limit, but the tradition of Ubayy has not been authenticated. It is, therefore, necessary to act according to the traditions of ʿAlī and Ṣafwān and that is better, although their implication conflicts with analogy: a time limit is not effective in annulling purity as factors that nullify it are impurities.

1.1.2.13.6. Sub-issue 6: Conditions for wiping over boots

The condition for the wiping over boots is that the feet, at the time of wearing the boot, should be clean through the purification of ablution. This is something agreed upon, except for a slight disagreement, which is attributed by Ibn al-Qāsim to Mālik, as reported by Ibn Lubāba in *al-Muntakhab*. The basis for the majority view rests on the traditions related by al-Mughīra and others, which state that when the Prophet (God's peace and blessings be upon him) wanted to take off his boots he said, "Let them be, for they (the feet) were clean when I put them on". Those deviating from the majority view interpreted this remark according to the literal meaning of cleanliness.

The jurists differed in this topic about the person who (while performing ablution) washes his feet, puts on his boots, and then completes the ablution, whether he is entitled to wipe over his boots (next time he performs ablution). Those who did not consider an ordered sequence to be obligatory (in ablution) and held that purity of each limb is valid before the purity of all the other limbs is completed, maintained that it is permissible. Those who held that a sequence is obligatory, and that purification of a limb is not valid before purification of all the limbs (preceding it), did not permit it. The first opinion was held by Abū Ḥanīfa, while the second was held by Mālik and al-Shāfiʿī, except that Mālik did not disallow this because of the sequence; he did so as the purity of this limb cannot be achieved except by washing the remaining limbs. (This is on account of) the words of the Prophet (God's peace and blessings be upon him), "I put them on when they were clean", meaning legal ceremonial purity. In some narrations from al-Mughīra the words are: "When you slip your feet into your boots, and they were then pure, wipe over them". On the basis of these rules the answer to the question about a person, who puts on one boot after washing his foot prior to washing the other, is provided by Mālik, who said that he is not to wipe over his boots for he wore them before the completion of (ritual) purification. This is also the opinion of al-Shāfiʿī, Aḥmad, and Isḥāq. Abū Ḥanīfa, al-Thawrī, al-Muzanī, al-Ṭabarī, and Dāwūd said that wiping is permitted. It was also the opinion of a group of Mālik's disciples, among whom are Muṭarrif and others. All of them agreed that if a person takes off one boot after washing the other foot and then puts it on, wiping is permitted to him.

Is it a condition for wiping over one boot that it should not be on a second boot (worn on top of the first soft boot)? There are two opinions about this from Mālik. The reason for disagreement is whether the obligation of wiping the inner boot is transferred to the outer boot, just as the obligation of washing the foot is transferred to the boot when it covers the foot? Those who held the second transference similar to the first allowed wiping of the outer boot, while those who did not hold it to be similar and found a distinction did not permit it.

1.1.2.13.7. Sub-issue 7: Factors nullifying this form of purification

They agreed that the factors nullifying this form of purification are the same factors nullifying ablution itself. They disagreed on whether taking off the boots nullifies this kind of purification. A group of jurists said that if a person takes off his boots and washes his feet, purification is maintained, but if he does not wash them and prays, his prayer is not counted, and he has to pray again after washing his feet. Those who maintained this include Mālik and his disciples, al-Shāfiʿī, and Abū Ḥanīfa. Mālik, however, maintained that if he delays this he has to renew ablution, conforming with the condition of continuous performance of the acts of ablution, which has preceded. Another group of jurists held that purity is maintained and he is not obliged to wash his feet, unless the person acquires some form of *ḥadath* (legal impurity) that nullifies his ablution. Among those who maintained this are Dāwūd and Ibn Abī Laylā. Al-Ḥasan ibn Ḥayy said that if he takes off his shoes, purity is annulled. Each of these three opinions was held by a group of the *Tābiʿūn*. This issue has not been explicitly mentioned (in the texts).

The reason for disagreement is whether wiping over boots is an independent act in itself or is a substitute for washing the feet once they are inside the boots. If we maintain that it is an independent act, purity must remain, even if he removes his boots, as in the case of a person whose feet are cut off after ablution. If we maintain that it is a substitute, it is possible to say that if he takes off his boots purification is annulled even if we stipulate immediate washing; and it is also possible to say that washing of the feet is enough to achieve purification, if we do not stipulate immediate washing. As to the stipulation of immediate washing at the time of removal of boots, it is weak, for it is something conjectural.

This is what we intended to establish in this chapter.

1.1.3. **Chapter 3 The Kinds of Water Used**

The basis for the obligation of purification with water are the words of the Exalted, "And (He) sends down water from the sky upon you, that thereby He might purify you",[44] and His words, ". . . and then ye find not water, then go to high clean soil and rub your faces and your hands (therewith)".[45]

The jurists agreed that all kinds of water are pure in themselves, purifying other things, except for the water of the sea, about which there was some disagreement in the first period. They (the dissenters) are defeated by the fact that sea-water is included within the unqualified use of the term "water" and also by the tradition recorded by Mālik, which is the saying of the Prophet, "Its water is pure, and its dead creatures are lawful". Although, this is a tradition whose authenticity is disputed, the law apparently supports it.

The jurists, similarly, agreed about things that alter the water and that are normally found in it (or that are not normally separated from it, like green moss), do not usurp its purification and the quality of purifying, except for slight disagreement recounted about stagnant water by Ibn Sīrīn, whose opinion here is also rejected on the ground that the absolute use of the term

[44] Qurʾān 8 : 11. Pickthall's translation altered.

[45] Qurʾān 4 : 43. Pickthall's translation altered.

"water" applies to stagnant water as well. They agreed about water that has been altered by impurity with respect to taste, colour, or smell, or with respect to more than one of these qualities, that it is not permitted for purposes of ablution or purification. They agreed that water in large quantities is not defiled by impurities that do not alter one of its (mentioned) qualities, and that it remains pure.

This is what they agreed upon in this topic, but they disagreed about six issues that are like rules and principles of the topic.

1.1.3.1. Issue 1: Water mixed with impurities without change in its attributes

They disagreed about water that contains impurities, but where none of its attributes is altered. One group of jurists said that it is pure irrespective of large or small quantities. This is one of the narrations from Mālik and is also upheld by the Ẓāhirites. Another group made a distinction between water in large and small quantities, saying that if there is little of it, it is impure and if there is much of it, it is not. They disagreed then about the demarcation separating small from large quantities (of water). Abū Ḥanīfa's opinion is that a large quantity of water is that in which a ripple caused by a person at one end does not reach the other side. According to al-Shāfiʿī the limit is the fill of two *qulla*s (containers), which weigh about five hundred *raṭl* (pounds). Some jurists did not impose any limit, though they held that impurities defile water in small quantities, even if its attributes are not changed. This is related from Mālik. It is also related that such water is not defiled, but that its use is undesirable. Thus, there are three opinions from Mālik about the use of small quantities of water in which small impure objects have been dropped. First, that it has thus been defiled, or it has been rendered unusable. Second, that it has not been defiled, so long as its attributes have not changed. Third, that its use is reprehensible.

The reason for disagreement here is based upon the conflict of the apparent meanings of traditions recounted on this matter. In the preceding tradition of Abū Hurayra—"When one of you wakes up from sleep"—the apparent meaning is that a small amount of impurity defiles a small amount of water. Similarly, in the tradition of Abū Hurayra established form the Prophet (God's peace and blessings be upon him) where he said, "No one should urinate in standing water and then use it for washing", from the apparent meaning of which it is understood that a small amount of impurity soils a small quantity of water. So also the proscription of washing in still water by the person who has acquired a major impurity. This is opposed to the implications of the tradition of Anas, which reports: "A bedouin went to the side of the mosque to relieve himself, and the people shouted at him. The Messenger of Allāh (God's peace and blessings be upon him) said, 'Leave him alone'. After the man had relieved himself the Messenger of Allāh (God's peace and blessings be upon him) ordered a pitcher of water to be poured over his urine". This tradition indicates through its apparent meaning that a minor impurity does not defile a small quantity of water, as it is obvious that this spot became clean with a pitcher of water. There is also the tradition of Abū Saʿīd al-Khudrī, recorded by Abū Dāwūd. He said, "I heard the Messenger of Allāh (God's peace and blessings be upon him) being asked whether the water of the well of Buḍāʿa could be used, and it was a well in which dog flesh, menstrual clothes, and dirt were cast. The Prophet (God's peace and blessings be upon him) said, "Nothing defiles water'".

The jurists attempted to reconcile all these traditions, but they differed in their methods of reconciliation and, therefore, their opinions differed. Those who decided to uphold the apparent meaning of the traditions of Anas about the bedouin and of Abū Saʿīd maintained that the two traditions of Abū Hurayra should not be subjected to rationalization;[46] and compliance with what they maintain is a mode of worship, and the fact that the water had become unusable does not mean that it had become impure. The Ẓāhirites exaggerated and went so far as to say that if a person were to pour urine into the water from a bowl, washing and ablution with it would not be considered reprehensible. Thus, those who held this opinion reconciled the traditions in this way. Those who considered the use of a small amount of water, which had some impurities dropped in it, as undesirable, also reconciled the traditions by construing the traditions of Abū Hurayra to imply mere undesirability, and interpreted the tradition of the bedouin (incident) and the tradition of Abū Saʿīd in their literal meaning, that is, validity (in the use of the water).

Al-Shāfiʿī and Abū Ḥanīfa reconciled the traditions of Abū Hurayra and Abū Saʿīd, applying the two traditions of Abū Hurayra to small quantities of water and the tradition of Abū Saʿīd to huge amounts. Al-Shāfiʿī maintained that the solution for this that reconciles all the traditions is related in the tradition of ʿAbd Allāh ibn ʿUmar from his father, recorded by Abū Dāwūd and al-Tirmidhī and declared as authentic by Abū Muḥammad ibn Ḥazm. ʿUmar said: "The Messenger of Allāh (God's peace and blessings be upon him) was asked about water and about the leftovers of beasts of prey and other animals. He [the Prophet] said, "If the water is more than two *qullahs* it does not retain impurity'". Abū Ḥanīfa maintained that the solution can be arrived at through analogy (reasoning). He connected the spreading of impurities in the water with the movement of water. If the quantity of water is so much that impurity cannot be conceived to move throughout it by a stir caused in the

[46] Perhaps, they can easily be rationalized on the basis of hygienic principles, but the interpretation here is literal, that is, unquestioned compliance.

water then the water is pure. Yet, the implication of the well-known tradition of the bedouin story appears to oppose those who hold these two opinions (i.e. the opinions of al-Shāfiʿī and Abū Ḥanīfa). For this reason the Shāfiʿites were constrained to distinguish between pouring water over impurities and dropping impurities in the water itself. They said that if it is poured over an impurity, as in the tradition about the bedouin, it does not remain impure, but if impurities are cast into the water, as in Abū Hurayra's tradition, it does. The majority of the jurists said that this is an arbitrary opinion. Yet, it does have a basis if pondered over carefully, because the jurists unanimously agree that a small amount of impurity does not affect a large amount of water, when the quantity of water is such that the impurity is not likely to spread through all its parts, and its essence would stand dissolved in such large amounts of water. In that case, it is not unlikely that if a small amount of impurity is dropped in a certain quantity of water it can get dissolved and spread throughout it, making it impure. If the same water were, instead, to be slowly poured over impurities, the essence of such impurity would gradually go and completely disappear before the disappearance of the water. In this way the last part of the water would have purified the defiled spot, as its ratio to what is left of the filth over which it is poured is the same as that of a large amount of water to a small amount of impurity. It is in this manner that certainty is attained about the disappearance of impurity, that is, by the falling of the last part of pure water on what remains of the essence of the impurity. For this reason they agreed that the amount of water with which ablution can be performed can purify a drop of urine falling on clothes or the body, but they disagreed when a drop falls into the same (little) amount of water.

The best view, in my opinion, is that of reconciliation, which interprets the traditions of Abū Hurayra, and those having the same implication, to mean abomination, and the traditions of Abū Saʿīd and Anas to imply permissibility. Such an interpretation retains the obvious meaning of the traditions, I mean, the traditions of Abū Hurayra, with their aim of indicating the effect of impurity on water. The definition of abomination, in my view, is what a person would naturally shy away from, and would consider to be filthy. Thus, whatever a person refrains from drinking, he must avoid using in attaining nearness to Allāh Almighty, and he should refrain from spilling over his outer body what he refrains from pouring within.

The argument of those who maintain that if the principle that a small amount of impurity defiles a small amount of water is upheld, water would never be able to purify anyone (or anything); the claim that the object outside the water that is intended to be purified would always make the water filthy, is an opinion that has no validity, though many later jurists have found it (this opinion) to be appealing. This is because of the explanation we have given about the ratio of the last part of water poured over the last part of impurity remaining at a spot as being the same as a large amount of water to a small quantity of impurity. We know certainly that large amounts of water dissolve the impurity and convert its essence to purity. The jurists, therefore, agreed that a small amount of impurity does not defile a large amount of water. If the person washing continuously pours water on the impure spot or on an impure limb, the water will necessarily remove the impurity because of its excess, whether the large amount of water is poured over impurity all at once or slowly in parts. These jurists, thus, argued on the basis of a unanimously agreed point for a matter that is disputed without realizing it. The two points are wide apart.

This is what seems appropriate to us in this issue based on the differences of the jurists in this, and through the preference of their opinions. If we were to follow this method in each issue, our opinion, we feel, would become lengthy and would tax time. As a precaution, we should stay with our original purpose, which we determined for ourselves, and if Allāh Almighty were to make things easy and we have ample life, this aim will be met too.

1.1.3.2. Issue 2: Water mixed with saffron and clean things

Water in which saffron or other things of which water is often free, are mixed, altering one of its attributes, is pure according to all the jurists, but loses its power to purify according to Mālik and al-Shāfiʿī. It purifies according to Abū Ḥanīfa as long as the change (in attributes) is not achieved through heating. The reason for disagreement stems from the understanding of the absolute term "water" as applied to such mixed water. Those who held that water so mixed is not covered by the unqualified term water, but is described by the things added, such as "the water of such and such thing", did not allow ablution with it, as ablution is to be performed with unadulterated water. Those who said that the term water still applies to water so mixed, allowed ablution with it. For the obvious inapplicability of the term to water heated with a non-polluted thing, they did not permit ablution with it; similarly, they did not permit it in the case of water extracted from vegetation, except for what is recorded in the book of Ibn Shaʿbān about the permissibility of using rose-water in the *jumuʿa* washing. The truth is that the verdict depends upon the quantities of the additives. With excessive mixing, the water may reach a state where the absolute term for water will not apply to it and will acquire a qualifying term, like the term bath water; or it may not reach such a state, especially when it is only the smell that has been altered. It is for this reason that some jurists did not take smell into account when prohibiting mixed water. The Prophet (God's peace and blessings be upon him) is reported to have said to Umm ʿAṭiyya, when she was about to bathe his (dead) daughter, "Bathe her with water and *sidr* (lotus), and in the last course of washing add some camphor". This is mixed water, but the mixture did not reach a state where it would negate the absolute term for water. Mālik, basing his judgment on the intensity of the mixture, made a distinction between weak and strong mixtures. He permitted weak mixtures, even when the attributes of the water were altered, but did not permit it in strong ones.

1.1.3.3. Issue 3: Water already used for purification

The jurists disagreed about water (already) used for purification and held three opinions. A group of jurists did not permit its use in purification under any circumstances, which is the opinion of al-Shāfiʿī and Abū Ḥanīfa. Another group considered it undesirable, but did not permit *tayammum* when it existed, which is the view of Mālik and his disciples. A group of jurists did not find any difference between this water and water in its absolute meaning, which was the opinion of Abū Thawr, Dāwūd, and his disciples. Abū Yūsuf deviated from all this and said that it is impure.

The reason for disagreement here also arises from the question of whether it is included in the unqualified term for water; some went as far as saying that the term bath-water is more appropriate for it than the term water. The Companions of the Prophet (God's peace and blessings be upon him) used to compete for the excess left over from the ablution of the Prophet, and it is obvious that some drops of the water used would fall into the utensil that contained the surplus.

On the whole, it is absolute water and does not end up with changed attributes through the dirt of the limbs that are washed with it, but if it is sullied, then its *ḥukm* is the same as that of water one of whose attributes has changed with something pure, though it is something repelling by nature; this is what was taken into account by those who considered it abominable. As for one who considered it filthy, there is no evidence to support him.

1.1.3.4. Issue 4: Water left over by Muslims and animals

The jurists agreed about the purity of the leftovers of Muslims and cattle, but they disagreed extensively about other categories. Some believed that the leftover of every animal is pure, while others made an exception in the case of swine alone. These two views are related from Mālik. Some jurists made an exception in the case of swine and dogs, which is al-Shāfiʿī's opinion. Some excluded the beasts of prey generally, which is Ibn al-Qāsim's opinion. Others maintained that leftovers of animals are subservient to the *ḥukm* of (their) flesh; if the flesh is prohibited the leftover is impure, if the flesh is abominable the leftover is abominable too, but if the flesh is permissible the leftover is pure. As to the leftover of an idolater, it is said that it is impure, while it is said that it is abominable only if he drinks ***khamr*** (wine), which is Ibn al-Qāsim's opinion. The same is the case for him of all animals that do not normally avoid filth, like filth-consuming wild hens, camels, and dogs.

Their disagreement is based on three points. First is the conflict of analogy with the obvious meaning of the Book. Second is its conflict with the literal meaning of the traditions. The third is the conflict of the traditions among themselves.

The point that death resulting without slaughter is legally the cause of impurity of the animal's carcass provides the basis for the analogy that life must be the basis for the purity of the body of the animal. If this is the case, then each living thing is pure, and whatever is pure its leftover must also be pure. The apparent meaning of the Book opposes this analogy in the case of swine and polytheists, as Allāh, the Exalted, has said about swine, "swine-flesh—for that verily is foul",[47] and that which is filthy in its essence is also impure. Thus, one group of jurists have excluded only swine from all living animals, while those who do not exclude it interpret the verse to imply derogation for it. As to the polytheists, the words of the Exalted are, "O ye who believe! The idolaters are unclean. So let them not come near the Inviolable Place of Worship".[48] Those who interpreted this too in its literal sense excluded the idolaters from the implication of the analogy, while those who considered this to be merely derogatory for them reimposed the requirement of analogy.

The traditions conflicted with the analogy about dogs, cats, and beasts of prey. The tradition about the dog is Abū Hurayra's, which is agreed upon for its authenticity, and it is the saying of the Prophet (God's peace and blessings be upon him), "If a dog licks a utensil belonging to one of you, he should purify it by washing it seven times". In some of its versions it says, "The first time with dust", and in others, "Cover it the eighth time with dust". With respect to the cat it is the tradition related by Qurra from Ibn Sīrīn from Abū Hurayra, who said, "The Messenger of Allāh (God's peace and blessings be upon him) said, 'The purification of a utensil, when a cat has licked it, is to wash it once or twice'". Qurra is a trustworthy narrator according to the traditionists. About the beasts of prey is the preceding tradition of Ibn ʿUmar from his father, who said, "that the Messenger of Allāh (God's peace and blessings be upon him) was asked about water and about the leftover of beasts of prey and other animals. He said, 'If the water is more than two *qullahs* it does not retain impurity'".

A conflicting tradition in this topic is the report from the Prophet (God's

[47] Qurʾān 6 : 146.
[48] Qurʾān 9 : 28.

peace and blessings be upon him) "that he was asked about the ponds between Mecca and Medina frequented by dogs and beasts of prey. He said, 'To them belongs what they carry in their bellies, and for you is what is left, a drink that is pure'". Similar to this is ʿUmar's tradition that was related by Mālik in his *al-Muwaṭṭaʾ*, which is the saying, "O owner of the pond, let's know not, for we follow up the beasts of prey and they follow us". Further, there is the tradition of Qatāda, also related by Mālik, "that Kabsha poured out water for his ablution and a cat came to drink from it. He tilted the utensil for it until it drank from it. He then said, 'The Messenger of Allāh (God's peace and blessings be upon him) said that it is not unclean. It is one of those (creatures) that move among you'". The jurists differed about the interpretation of these traditions and about their reconciliation with the stated analogy.

Mālik held the view that the leftover of a dog is to be spilled and the utensil is to be washed, as it is a ritual act of non-rational worship, for the water it has lapped up is not unclean. He did not require, according to the widely known opinion from him, the spilling of things other than water, which a dog had licked. The reason, as we have said, is the conflict with analogy according to him. He also believed that if it is to be understood from the tradition that a dog is unclean, it opposes the apparent meaning of the Book, that is, the words of the Exalted, "So eat of what they catch for you",[49] meaning thereby that if it had been unclean the prey would have become unclean by its touch. He supported this interpretation by the required number of washings, as number is not a condition in the washing of unclean things. He held that this washing is merely an act of worship. He did not rely on the remaining traditions as they were weak in his view.

Al-Shāfiʿī excluded the dog alone from all living animals maintaining that the literal meaning of the tradition implies the impurity of its leftover. He held, I think, that the uncleanliness lies in its saliva and not in the dog itself. Abū Ḥanīfa believed that the meaning of all these traditions laid down about the uncleanliness of the leftover of beasts of prey, cats, and dogs relates to the prohibition of their flesh (for eating). This pertains to the rule of a particular meaning intended generally. He said that the leftovers are dependent upon the (*ḥukm* of the) flesh of the animal.

Some jurists excluded from this a dog, cat, and beast of prey in conformity with the literal meaning of the related traditions, while some deemed the leftover of the dog and cat as pure, excluding only the beast of prey. (They declared clean) the leftover of the dog (considered unclean) because of the

[49] Qurʾān 5 : 4.

number of washings, as that is opposed by the obvious meaning of the Book, and also because of its conflict with Qatādah's tradition; if the underlying reason for the cleanliness of the cat is its moving around among people, then the dog does so too. With respect to the cat, (they declared it clean) by deciding to prefer Abū Qatāda's tradition over the tradition of Qurra from Ibn Sīrīn, and by preferring Ibn ʿUmar's tradition over that of ʿUmar and of others that convey the same meaning, because of its conflict with Abū Qatāda's tradition through the (indirect) indication of the text, that is, when the underlying reason for the cleanliness of the cat is its moving among people; it is to be understood from that that the leftovers of those (beasts) that do not move among people, namely the beasts of prey, is prohibited. Among those who held this opinion is Ibn al-Qāsim.

Abū Ḥanīfa upheld, as we have said, the uncleanliness of the leftover of a dog, and did not deem the number to be a condition for the purification of the utensil licked by the dog, as this is opposed, in his view, by analogy arising from the washing of unclean things, that is the point considered here is the removal of the filth alone. This conforms with his practice of rejecting individual narrations when they are opposed to the principles.

The Qāḍī (Ibn Rushd) said, "He thus used a part of the traditions and did not employ others; I mean, he used those that did not conflict with the principles, and did not use those that clashed with the principles. He supported this with the assertion that this was the opinion of Abū Hurayra, who had narrated the tradition. These, then, are the factors that moved the *fuqahā*ʾ to have such extensive disagreements on this issue and led them to dispute their implications. The issue is ratiocinative (*ijtihādiya*) and it is difficult to prefer some opinions over others. Perhaps, it is preferable to exclude from the purity of the leftovers those of the dog, swine, and the polytheist, because of the authenticity of the traditions about the dog, and also because it is better to adopt the obvious meaning of the Book, as against analogy, in maintaining the uncleanliness (of the leftovers) of swine and polytheists; similarly, the obvious meaning of the tradition. This is the opinion of the majority of the *fuqahā*ʾ, that is, maintaining the uncleanliness of the leftover of the dog. The directive of spilling of what has been licked by the dog is based on *ikhāla* (reasoned conviction: *mukhīl*) and is compatible (*munāsib*) with the law, because of the uncleanliness of the water that has been touched, I mean, that the usual implication of the law in requiring the spilling of a thing and of washing the utensil is usually on account of the uncleanliness of the thing. About the objection raised by them that had this been due to the uncleanliness of the thing the number of washings would not have been stipulated, it cannot be denied that the law may single out some form of pollution from others assigning it a different *ḥukm*, because of the intensity of the contamination".

The Qāḍī (Ibn Rushd) said: "My grandfather, may Allāh have mercy on him, ruled in the book *al-Muqaddimāt* that this tradition has a rational underlying cause, which is not related to uncleanliness, but is based on the likelihood that the dog licking the utensil is rabid, and the [viral] infection is to be feared. He said that it is for this reason that this number of seven has been laid down for its washing. This number has been used on many occasions in the law in relation to the treatment and medication for illnesses. What he expressed, may Allāh have mercy on him, is an outstanding view conforming with the method of the Mālikites. If we say that this water is not unclean, it is better to provide a rational underlying reason rather than saying that it is non-rational when water in itself is clean. Some people raised an objection to this, according to what has reached me, saying that a rabid dog does not go near water when it has hydrophobia. What they said is true when this canine illness has reached serious proportions, but it is not so when it is in its early stages. Their objection, therefore, has no foundation. Further, the tradition does not talk about water, and only the utensil has been mentioned. Perhaps, there is in its leftover some characteristic of a harmful nature, I mean, before rabies has reached more serious proportions. Such prescriptions in the law cannot be denied. Of a similar nature is the tradition about a fly falling on food, that it is to be immersed completely (and then thrown out). The underlying reason is that there is a disease in one of its wings, while in the other there is its antidote.

The opinion in Mālik's school that the reference in the tradition concerning the dog's licking relates only to a dog whose taking as a pet is forbidden, or that it is a street dog, is weak and remote from this cause, unless the claimant were to say that by this is meant a proscription of its restraining [as a pet]".

1.1.3.5. Issue 5: Leftovers from ritual purification

The jurists disagreed about the leftovers from purification expressing five opinions. One group held that the leftovers of purification are clean absolutely (and purifying). This is the opinion of Mālik, al-Shāfiʿī, and Abū Ḥanīfa. Another group said that it is not permitted for a man to purify himself with the leftover of a woman, but it is permitted for a woman to purify herself with the leftover of a man. A third group said that it is permitted for a man to purify himself with the leftover of a woman as long as she is not sexually defiled or menstruating. The fourth group maintained that it is not permitted for either one of them to undertake purification with the surplus water of the other, unless they started using it at the same time. Another group said that it is not permitted even if they commenced at the same time, which is Aḥmad ibn Ḥanbal's opinion.

The reason for disagreement is based upon the differences in the relevant traditions. There are four related traditions about this. First, the tradition that the Prophet (God's peace and blessings be upon him) used to wash away major ritual impurities along with his wives using the same utensil. Second, the tradition of Maymūna that he washed with the surplus left by his wife. Third, the tradition of al-Ḥakam al-Ghifārī that the Prophet (God's peace and blessings be upon him) prohibited the ablution by a man with the surplus left by a woman; this is recorded by Abū Dāwūd and al-Tirmidhī. Fourth is the tradition of ʿAbd Allāh ibn Sarjas, who said, "The Messenger of Allāh (God's peace and blessings be upon him) prohibited that a man may wash with the surplus left by a woman, or that a woman may wash with the surplus left by a man, unless they commence at the same time". The jurists adopted two kinds of methods for the interpretation of these traditions: a method of preference, and a method of reconciling some and preferring others.

Some jurists preferred the tradition about the Prophet's bathing along with his wives, drawing from the same vessel, over the rest of the traditions, for it was a tradition agreed upon by the compilers of the *ṣaḥīḥ* traditions, and because there was no distinction in their view between bathing at the same time or bathing with the surplus left by others. This is because bathing at the same time means that each is bathing with the surplus left by the other person, and further, because the tradition of Maymūna proved authentic along with this tradition, and was preferred over the tradition of al-Ghifārī. They, therefore, maintained the absolute purity of the leftovers of purification. Those who preferred the tradition of al-Ghifārī over the tradition of Maymūna, which is the opinion of Abū Muḥammad ibn Ḥazm, reconciled the tradition of al-Ghifārī with the tradition about the Prophet's bathing along with his wives, drawing from the same vessel. They also made a distinction between bathing together while drawing from the same vessel and bathing with a surplus left by the other. Thus, acting upon these two traditions alone, they permitted a man to undertake purification along with a woman drawing from the same vessel, and permitted her to purify herself with a surplus left by him; however, they did not permit him to do so with a surplus left over from her purification.

Those who used the method of reconciliation of all the traditions, except for the tradition of Maymūna, adopted the tradition of ʿAbd Allāh ibn Sarjas, for it is possible to accommodate the tradition of al-Ghifārī within it. So also the tradition of the Prophet bathing along with his wives, drawing from the same vessel. There is, however, an addition to it, which is that a woman also should not undertake purification with the surplus left over by a man. Further, it is opposed by Maymūna's tradition, which is recorded by Muslim. Yet some jurists have found a defect in it as some of its narrators used (doubting) statements like "I think" or "to the best of my knowledge, Abū al-Shaʿthāʾ related to me (such and such)". Those who did not permit either one of them to undertake purification with the leftover of the other nor allowed them to commence at the same time did so, perhaps, because the only tradition reaching them was that of al-Ḥakam al-Ghifārī. They, therefore, drew an analogy for a man from the case of the woman. I have no knowledge of the argument of those who prohibited only the left over of a woman who is sexually defiled or is menstruating, except that it is related from someone in the early generation, I believe from Ibn ʿUmar.

1.1.3.6. Issue 6: Ablution with the *nabīdh* (a beverage) of dates

Abū Ḥanīfa, in an opinion opposed by his disciples and all the jurists of the regions, permitted ablution with the *nabīdh* of dates during a journey on the basis of the tradition of Ibn ʿAbbās, which says: "Ibn Masʿūd went out with the Messenger of Allāh on the night of the *jinn* and the Messenger of Allāh asked him, 'Do you have any water?' He said, 'I have *nabīdh* in my container'. The Messenger of Allāh (God's peace and blessings be upon him) said, 'Pour out some'. He (the Prophet) performed ablution with it saying, 'It is a beverage and a purifying element'". He also quoted the tradition of Abū Rāfiʿ, the client of Ibn ʿUmar, derived from Ibn Maʿūd—which is almost the same—as follows: The Messenger of Allāh (God's peace and blessings be upon him) said, "It is good fruit and purifying water". They also claimed that this opinion is attributed to Companions like ʿAlī and Ibn ʿAbbās, and as there was no other Companion opposing them it amounted to a consensus. The traditionists, however, rejected this tradition because of the weak line of narrators (in its *isnād*). Furthermore, more reliable channels have related that Ibn Masʿūd was not with the Messenger of Allāh (God's peace and blessings be upon him) on the night of the *jinn*. The majority rejected this tradition on the basis of the words of the Exalted, "And ye find not water, then go to high clean soil and rub your faces and your hands (therewith)".[50] They said that He did not permit the use of anything beside water and clean soil. They also argued on the basis of the words of the Prophet (God's peace and blessings be upon him), "Clean soil constitutes the ablution of a Muslim, even if water is not to be found for ten seasons, and as soon as he finds water let him touch his face with it". They (the Ḥanafites) could have said that the term water is used in the absolute sense in the tradition (thus, including *nabīdh*), and it is an addition that does not constitute abrogation so that the Book should conflict with it, but then it is against their principle that an addition constitutes abrogation.

[50] Qurʾān 4 : 43.

1.1.4. Chapter 4 Factors Nullifying Ablution

The basis for this chapter are the words of the Exalted, "Or one of you cometh from the closet, or ye have touched women",[51] and the words of the Prophet (God's peace and blessings be upon him) that "Allāh does not accept prayers from one who is unclean, till he has performed ablution". In this chapter they agreed about the nullification of ablution due to urination, visit to the privy, passing wind, *madhy* (prostatic secretion prior to cohabitation), and *wady* (fluid preceding or following urination), on the basis of the authenticity of the traditions laid down in this, when such excreta and discharges occur in a state of health.

There are seven issues in this chapter, about which they disagreed, that are like the principles of this subject.

1.1.4.1. Issue 1: Unclean excretions from the body

The jurists of the regions disagreed about the invalidation of ablution resulting from unclean excretions from the body into three opinions. One group took into account excretions alone, whatever the outlet or the state in which it is excreted. This was the opinion of Abū Ḥanīfa, his disciples, al-Thawrī, Aḥmad, and a group among whom are Companions. They said that each unclean substance flowing from the body or excreted from it necessitates ablution, like blood, excessive nose-bleeding, drawing of blood, cupping, and vomiting, except for sputum in Abū Ḥanīfa's view. Abū Yūsuf, one of the disciples of Abū Ḥanīfa, said that ablution is necessary if it is a mouthful. None of them considered minor bleeding as significant, except for Mujāhid. Some other jurists took into account the passages through which the excretion occurs as factors affecting the nullification of ablution and limited these to the anus and the penis, saying that anything excreted from these two passages invalidates ablution, whatever its nature whether blood, or stone, or mucus, and whatever the condition of the body, whether in health or sickness. Those who held this opinion include al-Shāfiʿī, his disciples, and Muḥammad ibn ʿAbd al-Ḥakam from among the disciples of Mālik. Others took into account the passages and the type of excretions and also the manner of excretion. They said that normal excretions from these passages, like urine, faeces, *madhy*, *wady*, and wind, if passed in a state of health invalidate ablution. They did not take into account blood, bile, worms, nor the incontinence of urine. Those who upheld this opinion were Mālik and most of his disciples.

The reason for disagreement is that the unanimous conclusions of Muslim jurists over the invalidation of ablution due to whatever is excreted from the

[51] Qurʾān 4 : 43.

two passages, like faeces, urine, wind, and *madhy*, on the basis of the apparent meaning of the Book and also of the traditions, led to three possible interpretations. First, that the *ḥukm* be related only to the substance of these things, which are agreed upon, as in Mālik's opinion, may Allāh have mercy on him. The second likelihood is that the *ḥukm* be associated with these things insofar as they are pollutants excreted from the body, because ablution is purification and purification is (adversely) affected by pollution. The third possibility is that the *ḥukm* be related to them insofar as they are excrements from these two passages. According to the last two views the requirement of ablution, because of these forms of uncleanliness that are agreed upon, belongs to the category of a particular injunction intended to be general. Mālik and his disciples held that it is a particular category that is applied to its particular category. Al-Shāfiʿī and Abū Ḥanīfa agreed that the command belongs to the particular category intended to be general. Yet, they differed as to what is the generality intended here. Mālik preferred his opinion requiring that the principle is to maintain the particular within its sphere till an evidence indicates otherwise. Al-Shāfiʿī argued that what is intended is the passage and not what is excreted, because of their agreement over the obligation of ablution due to the passing of wind from (the passage) below, and that ablution is not an obligation when it is exhaled from above, although both are of the same category. The only difference between them is that of outlet. This indicates, it appears, that the *ḥukm* depends on the outlet, but this is weak, as the two kinds of winds are different with respect to characteristics and odour.

Abū Ḥanīfa argued that the factor of annulment is the unclean excrement (coming out through any outlet), because of the adverse effect of uncleanliness on ritual purity, and though this kind of purification is legal it resembles the actual physical purification, that is, freedom from filth. Further, (he argued) on the basis of the tradition of Thawbān "that the Messenger of Allāh (God's peace and blessings be upon him) vomited and then performed ablution"; and also on the basis of what is related from ʿUmar and Ibn ʿUmar (God be pleased with them) about the obligation of ablution due to a nosebleed. (Moreover, Abū Ḥanīfa argued) on the basis of what is related about the command of the Prophet (God's peace and blessings be upon him) for the continuously menstruating woman to perform ablution at the time of each prayer. The meaning of all these, according to Abū Ḥanīfa, is (that any) unclean excretion (from any passage annuls ablution). Al-Shāfiʿī and Abū Ḥanīfa agreed that factors nullifying ablution are effective even if they occur during sickness, because of the command of the Prophet (God's peace and blessings be upon him) requiring ablution before each prayer in the case of the continuously menstruating woman, which is an illness. As for Mālik, he was of the view that illness is effective in obtaining a concession on the analogy of the continuously menstruating woman, who was simply ordered to wash herself. The reason is that this tradition of Fāṭima bint Ḥubaysh is agreed upon for its authenticity, and there is a dispute only about the addition, that is, the order to perform ablution before each prayer. It has, however, been declared *ṣaḥīḥ* by Abū ʿUmar ibn ʿAbd al-Barr, on the analogy of one who bleeds incessantly as in the case of ʿUmar (God be pleased with him), who continued to perform his prayer while blood was flowing out of his wound.

1.1.4.2. Issue 2: Sleep

The jurists disagreed about sleep, expressing three opinions. One group of jurists held the view that it is a factor of annulment, and made ablution obligatory after it whether it was for a short or for a long duration. Another group held that it is not so, and they did not make ablution obligatory after it, unless the person was convinced, in accordance with the opinion of those who do not acknowledge doubt, that he had acquired *ḥadath*,[52] or when he was in a doubt that he had, in accordance with the opinion of those who consider doubt (as an effective factor). Some in the early generation used to depute a person to keep track of their state during sleep, that is, whether they had acquired *ḥadath*. Another group made a distinction between a light short sleep and a long deep sleep. They made ablution obligatory after a deep sleep, but not after light sleep. This is upheld by the *fuqahāʾ* of the regions, and by the majority.

As some (bodily) positions facilitate deep sleep as well as discharge of annulling elements more than other positions, the jurists differed about them. Mālik said that the person who sleeps reclining on his side or prostrate must perform ablution, whether the sleep was long or short, but one who sleeps in a sitting posture is under no obligation for ablution, unless such sleep becomes very long. His opinion about one (who sleeps while) bowing differed. He said once that his *ḥukm* is the same as that of the person standing, while he said another time that his *ḥukm* is that of the person prostrating. Al-Shāfiʿī said that whenever a person sleeps, whatever his posture, he is obliged to perform ablution, except for the person dozing off while sitting. Abū Ḥanīfa and his disciples said that there is no ablution for a person who sleeps, except for one sleeping on his side.

The basis for disagreement among them on this issue is the conflict of the relevant traditions. There are traditions whose apparent meaning implies that there is no ablution at all for a person who goes to sleep, like the tradition of Ibn ʿAbbās, "that the Messenger of Allāh (God's peace and blessings be upon

[52] The term *ḥadath* does not always involve pollution or filth or uncleanliness. For example, in the opinion of some jurists touching a woman or a human genital may be *ḥadath* in the sense of annulling ablution, though these acts do not constitute uncleanliness.

him) visited Maymūna and went to sleep at her place till they could hear him breathing. He then arose and prayed without performing ablution". There is the saying of the Prophet (God's peace and blessings be upon him) which is as follows: "If one of you dozes off during prayer, he should lie down till he is no longer sleepy (and then resume prayer). For it is possible that he intends to seek forgiveness of his Lord, but may err and slander himself". It is also related that the Companions of the Prophet (God's peace and blessings be upon him) used to doze off in the mosque till their heads would sink low. They prayed after this without performing ablution. All these are established traditions. There are also others whose obvious meaning indicates that sleep is a form of *ḥadath*. The clearest of these is the tradition of Ṣafwān ibn ʿAssāl in which he said, "We were on a journey with the Prophet (God's peace and blessings be upon him) when he ordered us not to take off our boots because of a visit to the privy, urination, or sleep, and that we should take them off only in case of sexual defilement". He thus held urination, visit to the privy, and sleep to be similar. It has been declared *ṣaḥīḥ* by al-Tirmidhī. Among these is also the preceding tradition of Abū Hurayra, which is the saying of the Prophet (God's peace and blessings be upon him), "When one of you wakes up from sleep, he should wash his hand before putting it into the water (utensil)". Its apparent meaning is that sleep necessitates ablution, whether it is short or long. Similarly, the apparent meaning of the verse of *wuḍūʾ*, according to those who derive such a meaning from the words of the Exalted, "O ye who believe! When ye rise up for prayer, wash your faces, and your hands up to the elbows, and lightly rub your heads and (wash) your feet up to the ankles",[53] that is, when you arise from sleep, in accordance with what is related from Zayd ibn Aslam and other early authorities.

As the apparent meanings of all these traditions were in conflict, the jurists decided the issue on the basis of one of two methods: the method of preference or the method of reconciliation. Those who applied the method of preference, either dropped the obligation of ablution after sleep completely on the basis of the apparent meaning of the traditions that drop it, or imposed it always after sleep, whether short or prolonged, on the basis of traditions that impose it, that is, in accordance with the prescribing tradition that was preferred by them or in accordance with the tradition that dropped it. Those who adopted the method of reconciliation interpreted the traditions prescribing ablution to apply to extended sleep, and interpreted the traditions waiving ablution to apply to a short sleep. This, as we have said, is the opinion of the majority, and reconciliation is better than preference, as far as it is possible, according to most experts on *uṣūl al-fiqh*.

[53] Qurʾān 5 : 6.

Al-Shāfiʿī interpreted the traditions so as to exempt, from among the positions of the person sleeping, the sitting posture alone, as this was established to be an authentic report about the Companions, that is, they used to sleep while sitting and then prayed without performing ablution. Abū Ḥanīfa made it obligatory only after sleep while reclining on the side, as this has been stated in a *marfūʿ* tradition, and in a saying of the Prophet (God's peace and blessings be upon him): "Ablution is obligatory on one who sleeps reclining on one side". The narration has been established from ʿUmar. Mālik said: Since sleeping can be a cause of annulment of ablution only on account of the fact that it makes easy the release of the cause of *ḥadath*. In forming his views, Mālik took into account three things: soundness, duration, and posture. He did not stipulate either duration or soundness for a posture that usually facilitates the occurrence of *ḥadath*, but he did do so for postures that normally do not do so (like standing or sitting).

1.1.4.3. Issue 3: Touching women

The jurists disagreed about the obligation of ablution for a person who touches a woman with his hand or with other sensuous limbs. One group held that one who touches a woman reaching out for her when there is no barrier or covering between the touching skins, is obliged to perform ablution. Similarly, one who kisses her, as a kiss, according to them, is a kind of touching, whether or not he derives pleasure from it. This opinion was upheld by al-Shāfiʿī and his disciples, except that he once made a distinction between the person touching and the person being touched, making ablution obligatory for the person touching to the exclusion of the person touched; another time he held that it was obligatory on both. A third time he made a distinction between women in the prohibited degree and a wife, making ablution obligatory in the case of (touching) the wife, but not in the case of women in the prohibited degree, while another time he held them to be similar. Others made ablution obligatory only when lustful pleasure is felt or it was intended. Upholders of this view go into details making a distinction in the case of the existence of a covering or otherwise, and in the case of particular limbs whose touching is harmful. In the case of kissing, they did not stipulate pleasure. This is the opinion of Mālik and the majority of his disciples. Some negated the obligation of ablution for the person touching women, which is the opinion of Abū Ḥanīfa. Each of these schools has predecessors from among Companions (holding these views), except the stipulation of pleasure, for I do not remember that any Companion stipulated this.

The reason for disagreement is the equivocality of the term "touching" in the usage of the Arabs. The Arabs apply it sometimes for touching that is by hand, and sometimes use it as an allusion to intercourse. A group of jurists, therefore, held that touching causing ablution according to the words of the Exalted, "or ye have touched women . . .",[54] means intercourse (which leads to major ablution, that is, bathing). Others maintained that the meaning here is that of touching by hand, and among them are those who considered it to be a general term intended for the particular, and, therefore, stipulated pleasure in it. There were those among them who deemed it a general term intended for the general, because of which they did not stipulate pleasure (for annulment). Those who stipulated pleasure were drawn to this by what restricts the generality of the verse, namely, the tradition that says that the Prophet (God's peace and blessings be upon him) used to touch ʿĀʾisha while prostrating, and perhaps she did too. The traditionists recorded the tradition of Ḥabīb ibn Abī Thābit from ʿUrwah from ʿĀʾisha: "He the Prophet (God's peace and blessings be upon him) used to kiss some of his wives and then go out to pray, but did not perform ablution. I said, 'Who could that be, but you, and she smiled'". Abū ʿUmar said that this tradition was deemed feeble by the scholars of Ḥijāz, but was considered *ṣaḥīḥ* by those of Kūfa. Yet, he held it to be authentic, saying that this tradition was also related through Maʿbad ibn Nubāta. Al-Shāfiʿī said that if the tradition of Maʿbad ibn Nubāta about kissing is established, I do not maintain the obligation of ablution for it, or for touching.

Those who made ablution obligatory upon touching by hand, argued that the term "touching" is used in its primary application to touching by hand and is applied metaphorically to intercourse, and if the word vacillates between the primary and metaphorical uses, it is better to confine it to the primary meaning, unless an evidence indicates the metaphorical meaning. The others could have said that when the use of a metaphorical term becomes frequent it is more expressive in its metaphorical sense than in its actual meaning, like the term *ghāʾiṭ*, which is more expressive in denoting a visit to the privy than it is in denoting depressed ground, which is its actual meaning. What I believe is that the word "touching", though it is equally expressive of both meanings, or almost equal, is more vivid, in my view, for denoting intercourse though it is a metaphor, as Allāh, the Glorious and Exalted, has used the terms *mubāshara*, "contact", and *mass*, "touching", for copulation and they denote the meaning of touching. It is on the basis of this interpretation of the verse that the argument is made for the permissibility of *tayammum* in the case of one with a major impurity, without requiring the assumption of advancing or delaying in the order of the words in the relevant texts, as will be coming up in what follows, and the conflict between the verse and the traditions is also removed on the basis of the other interpretation.

[54] Qurʾān 5 : 6.

The opinion of those who understood from the verse both meanings of touching (by hand or by way of intercourse) is weak, as the Arabs, when they use an equivocal term, intend thereby one of the meanings that can be indicated by the term and not all the meanings that may be indicated. This itself is obvious in their language.

1.1.4.4. Issue 4: Touching the penis

The jurists differed about it expressing three opinions. There are those who made ablution obligatory because of it, whatever the nature of the touch. This is the opinion of al-Shāfiʿī, his disciples, Aḥmad, and Dāwūd. Some of them did not make ablution obligatory at all in this case. These are Abū Ḥanīfa and his disciples. Both parties have predecessors among the Companions and the Tābiʿūn. A group of jurists made a distinction between touching it in a certain state and touching it in a different state. These jurists are further divided into sub-groups. Some made a distinction based on whether the person derives pleasure from it. Others made a distinction on the basis of whether he touches it with the inner part of the hand (palm) or with the outer part. They made ablution obligatory in the case of pleasure, but not in its absence; similarly, they (the other group) made it obligatory in the case of touching with the palm, but not in the case of touching with the outer part. These two considerations are related from the disciples of Mālik. It was as if the consideration of the inner part of the hand refers to the derivation of pleasure. Some jurists made a distinction on the basis of intention and forgetfulness, making ablution obligatory in the case of intention, but not in case of forgetfulness. This is related from Mālik, and is the opinion of Dāwūd and his disciples. Still others held that ablution following touching is recommended and not obligatory. Abū ʿUmar said that this is the settled view related from Mālik by his disciples from among the residents of *al-Maghrib*, but the narration varies.

The reason for disagreement is that there are two conflicting traditions in this. First is the tradition related from Busrah (daughter of Ṣafwān) that she heard the Messenger of Allāh (God's peace and blessings be upon him) saying, "When one of you touches his penis he should perform ablution". This is the best known tradition laid down about the obligation of ablution from touching the penis, is recorded by Mālik in his *al-Muwaṭṭaʾ*, and has been authenticated by Yaḥyā ibn Maʿīn and Aḥmad ibn Ḥanbal, but has been declared weak by the jurists of Kūfa. It is also related in the same meaning from Umm Ḥabība, and Aḥmad ibn Ḥanbal declared it to be authentic. A version similar in part is related through Abū Hurayra. Ibn al-Sakan held it to be authentic, though it has not been recorded by al-Bukhārī or Muslim. The second tradition, which opposes this, is related from Ṭalq ibn ʿAlī, who said,

"We came up to the Messenger of Allāh (God's peace and blessings be upon him) and there was a man with him, who appeared to be a bedouin. He said, 'O Messenger of Allāh! What do you say about a man who touches his penis after performing ablution?' He said, 'Is it not but a part of you?'" This has also been recorded by Abū Dāwūd and al-Tirmidhī, and has been declared authentic by many scholars among the Kūfīs and others.

The jurists chose to interpret these traditions in one of two ways: acceptance of one and rejection of the other by the method of preference or abrogation, or the method of reconciliation. Those who preferred the tradition of Busra or considered it to have abrogated the tradition of Ṭalq ibn ʿAlī upheld the obligation of ablution after touching of the penis, while those who preferred the tradition of Ṭalq ibn ʿAlī dropped the obligation of ablution resulting from the touch. Those who desired to reconcile the two traditions made ablution obligatory in one case, but not in the other, or they interpreted the tradition of Busra to indicate recommendation and the tradition of Ṭalq ibn ʿAlī to indicate the negation of obligation. The arguments adduced by each party for preferring the tradition of its choice are (too) many and their discussion is lengthy. They are available in their books, but the points of disagreement are those that we have indicated.

1.1.4.5. Issue 5: Eatables prepared on fire

The jurists in the first period disagreed about the obligation of ablution after eating what was cooked on fire, because of the conflict of the traditions related about it from the Messenger of Allāh (God's peace and blessings be upon him). The majority of the jurists of the regions after the first period agreed about dropping the obligation, for it was established for them that such was the practice of the four Caliphs, and also because of the tradition related from Jābir, who said, "One of the last commands of the Messenger of Allāh (God's peace and blessings be upon him) was to relinquish ablution after consuming what was cooked on fire". It is recorded by Abū Dāwūd. But a group of scholars from the traditionists, Aḥmad, Isḥāq, and a group besides them held that ablution is obligatory only after eating camel meat, because of an established tradition on this point from the Prophet (God's peace and blessings be upon him).

1.1.4.6. Issue 6: Laughter during prayer

Abū Ḥanīfa expressed a deviant opinion as he made ablution obligatory for one who laughs during prayer, because of a *mursal* tradition[55] of Abū al-ʿĀliyah,

[55] A *mursal* tradition is one in the *isnād* of which the Companion supposed to be its first narrator is not mentioned.

which states that a group of people laughed during prayer and the Prophet (God's peace and blessings be upon him) ordered them to repeat ablution and prayer. The majority rejected this tradition for its being a *mursal* and opposed to the principles, as it makes something a cause of invalidating ablution during prayer, but not when one is not praying. It is, however, a *mursal* that is sound.

1.1.4.7. *Issue 7: Ablution after carrying the dead*

One group of jurists deviated by making ablution obligatory because of carrying the dead. There is a tradition for it that is weak, "One who bathes the dead let him take a bath, and one who carries them let him perform ablution".

It is necessary to know that the majority of the jurists made ablution obligatory due to the loss of senses, whatever its cause, like fainting, insanity, or intoxication. All of them held it to be analogous to sleep, that is, they maintained that if sleep makes ablution obligatory in a state that normally leads to *ḥadath*, namely, sound sleep, it is appropriate that the loss of reason should cause this too.

These are the issues of this chapter that are agreed upon or are widely known to be disputed. We must now move to the fifth chapter.

1.1.5. **Chapter 5 Identification of Acts for which this form of Purification is Stipulated**

The basis of this chapter are the words of the Exalted, "O ye who believe! When ye rise up for prayer, wash your faces, and your hands up to the elbows, and lightly rub your heads and (wash) your feet up to the ankles",[56] and the words of the Prophet (God's peace and blessings be upon him), "Allāh does not accept prayer without purification nor charity from misappropriated proceeds".

The jurists, therefore, agreed that purification is one of the conditions of prayer, because of these evidences, though they differed on whether it is a condition of validity or a condition of obligation. They did not disagree that it is a condition for all forms of prayer, except the funeral prayer and prostration, that is, the prostration of recitation, for there is some deviant disagreement about that. The reason for this are the different possibilities in the meaning of the term "*ṣalāh*" (prayer). They differed as to whether the term applies to the funeral prayer and prostration on reciting certain Qur'ānic verses. Those who maintained that the term "*ṣalāh*" applies to the funeral prayer and to

[56] Qur'ān 5 : 6.

prostration (of recitation) itself, and these are the majority, stipulated this form of purification for it, while those who held that the term does not apply to them, as the funeral does not involve bowing or prostrations, and there is no standing or bowing in prostrations (of recitation) either, they did not stipulate this form of purification for it. There are four issues related to this chapter under this main issue.

1.1.5.1. Issue 1: Is this purification a condition for touching the muṣḥaf?

Mālik, Abū Ḥanīfa, and al-Shāfiʿī held that it is a condition for touching the *muṣḥaf* (copy of the Qurʾān), while the Ẓāhirites held that it is not. The reason for disagreement is whether the meaning of the words of the Exalted, "Which none toucheth save the purified",[57] refers to humans or angels, or whether this statement implies a prohibition or is just a report. Those who deemed the word "purified" to mean humans, and interpreted the statement as a prohibition, said that it is not permitted for anyone, but the purified to touch the *muṣḥaf*. Those who interpreted it as a report and interpreted the word "purified" as an allusion to angels said that there is no indication in the verse about the stipulation of purification as a condition for touching the *muṣḥaf*. And as there is no evidence in the Book or in the *sunna*, the matter is to be left to the original rule of non-liability, which is permissibility.

The majority argued for their opinion on the basis of the tradition of ʿAmr ibn Ḥazm "that the Prophet (God's peace and blessings be upon him) wrote: 'None but the purified touch the Qurʾān.'". The traditions of ʿAmr ibn Ḥazm are disputed among the scholars with respect to the obligation of acting upon them, as a writing error (*taṣḥīf*) occurred in them, though I have seen Ibn al-Mufawwaz declaring them as *sahīh* when reported by reliable narrators, for they are letters of the Prophet (God's peace and blessings be upon him). The same is said about the traditions of ʿAmr ibn Shuʿayb from his father from his grandfather, though the Ẓāhirites reject them. Mālik made an exemption in the case of minors touching the *muṣḥaf* when they are not purified, as they have not reached the age of liability.

1.1.5.2. Issue 2: Obligation of (minor) ablution for one involved in a major impurity

The jurists disagreed about the obligation of (performing the minor) ablution for a person who was sexually defiled, in certain cases. The first is when, having committed a major *ḥadath*, he wishes to continue sleeping. The majority upheld the recommendation of ablution, but not its obligation. The

[57] Qurʾān 56 : 79.

Ẓāhirites maintain that it is obligatory, because it is established from the Prophet (God's peace and blessings be upon him) through the tradition of ʿUmar that he asked the Messenger of Allāh (God's peace and blessings be upon him) what he had to do when he is involved in a major *ḥadath* (like intercourse or seminal discharge) during the night. The Messenger of Allāh (God's peace and blessings be upon him) said to him, "Perform ablution and wash your penis, and then go to sleep". This is also related from him through ʿĀʾisha. The majority chose to construe the command as a recommendation and to relegate the literal meaning due to its incompatibility with the obligation of purification when the intention is to go to sleep, that is, legal compatibility.

They (the majority) also argued for this on the basis of other traditions, the most authentic of which is the tradition of Ibn ʿAbbās that the Messenger of Allāh (God's peace and blessings be upon him) once returned from the privy and was brought food. It was said to him, "Should we not bring you (water for) purification?" He replied, "Am I going to pray that I should perform ablution?" In some versions, it was said to him, "Would you perform ablution?" He replied, "I have not resolved to pray as yet, so that I may perform ablution". Seeking support from this is weak, for it is one of the weakest kinds of implication of the text. They also argued on the basis of the tradition of ʿĀʾisha "that the Messenger of Allāh (God's peace and blessings be upon him) used to go to sleep after being involved in a major *ḥadath* without touching water". This, however, is a weak tradition.

Likewise, they disagreed about the obligation of ablution for the person with a major *ḥadath* when he wishes to eat or drink, or one who wishes to re-copulate. The majority decided to drop the obligation due to the lack of (legal) compatibility of purification with all these things, as purification has been prescribed in the law for solemn occasions (ritual) like prayers. In addition to this, there is a conflict of traditions on this issue. It is related from the Prophet (God's peace and blessings be upon him) "that he ordered that a person with *janāba*, wishing to repeat intercourse, should perform ablution". It is also related that he used to cohabit and then repeat it without performing ablution. Similarly, the prohibition of eating and drinking for a person with *janāba* is related from him, unless the person performed ablution. Its permissibility is also related from him.

1.1.5.3. Issue 3: Ablution for circumambulation (*ṭawāf*)

Mālik and al-Shāfiʿī stipulated ablution for circumambulation, while Abū Ḥanīfa held it to be unnecessary. The reason for disagreement is the vacillation of the *ḥukm* of circumambulation whether it should be associated with the *ḥukm* of prayers. On the one hand, there is the established report "that the Messenger of Allāh (God's peace and blessings be upon him) prohibited circumambulation to the menstruating woman, just as he prohibited her to pray". From this aspect *ṭawāf* resembles prayer. In some traditions circumambulation has been called prayer.

Abū Ḥanīfa's argument is that purification is not a condition for everything that is prohibited during menstruation, when it is to be performed after the cessation of menstruation. For example, fasting in the opinion of the majority (does not need ablution).

1.1.5.4. Issue 4: Reciting the *Qur'ān* and remembering *Allāh* without ablution

The majority maintained that it is permitted for a person who has not performed ablution to recite the Qur'ān and engage in the remembrance of Allāh. A group of jurist said that this is not permitted, unless he performs ablution.

The reason for disagreement are two established conflicting traditions. The first is the tradition of Abū Jahm, who said, "The Messenger of Allāh (God's peace and blessings be upon him) was coming from the side of *Bi'r Jamal* when he met a man who greeted him (with a *salām*). The Prophet did not return the greeting till he reached the side of the wall, where he rubbed his face and hands, and then returned the greeting". The second tradition is that of ʿAlī, "that nothing prevented the Messenger of Allāh (God's peace and blessings be upon him) from the recitation of the Qur'ān, except *janāba*".

The majority maintained that the second tradition had abrogated the first, while those who made ablution obligatory for the remembrance of Allāh preferred the first tradition.

1.2. THE BOOK OF BATHING (*GHUSL*) (THE MAJOR ABLUTION)

The basis for this kind of purification are the words of the Exalted, "And if ye are involved in a major *ḥadath*, purify yourself".[58] The discussion covering its rules—after having learned its obligation, on whom it is obligatory, and the identification of the thing to be used, which is unadulterated water—is undertaken in three chapters. The first chapter relates to the identification of the acts involved in this purification. The second relates to the factors invalidating it. The third chapter covers the *aḥkām* of the invalidation of this purification.

About the person on whom it is obligatory, it is incumbent upon each person who is under an obligation to pray, and there is no dispute about this.

[58] Qur'ān 5 : 6. Pickthall's translation changed.

Similarly, there is no dispute about its obligation, and its evidences are the same as those for ablution, which we have mentioned. Likewise, the *aḥkām* relating to the categories of water, whose discussion has preceded.

1.2.1. Chapter 1 Identification of the Acts of this Category of Purification

There are four issues related to this chapter.

1.2.1.1. Issue 1: Running the hand over the entire body

The jurists disagreed over whether running the hand over the entire body (i.e. massaging the skin while water is running over it) is a condition for this purification, as is the case in the purification of limbs while performing ablution, or whether it is sufficient to let water flow over the entire body without running the hand over the body. The majority of the jurists maintained that letting water flow over the body is enough. Mālik, most of his disciples, and al-Muzanī from among the disciples of al-Shāfiʿī held that if the person undertaking purification misses a single spot of his body over which he does not pass his hand, his purification remains incomplete.

The reason for disagreement is the equivocality of the term "*ghusl*", and the conflict of the apparent meanings of the traditions related about the description of bathing with the analogy of bathing based upon ablution. In the established traditions relevant to the subject of the Prophet's bath, and which are related through ʿĀʾisha and Maymūna, there is no mention of massaging the body; they only mention the flowing of water over it. In the tradition of ʿĀʾisha, she says, "When the Messenger of Allāh (God's peace and blessings be upon him) took a bath after sexual engagement, he would first wash his hands. He then poured water from his right hand over to the left hand with which he washed his genitals. Then he performed a minor ablution, like he did for his regular daily prayers. Thereafter, taking up water he would insert his fingers down to the roots of his hair and pour three handfuls of water over his head. Finally, he would let water flow over his entire body".

The description given in the tradition of Maymūna is similar to this, except that here he delayed washing his feet up to the end of the purification. In the tradition of Umm Salama too, when she asked the Prophet (God's peace and blessings be upon him) "whether she should undo her plaits while bathing after sexual engagement. The Prophet (God's peace and blessings be upon him) said, 'It is enough if you splash over your head three handfuls of water, then let water flow over yourself, and with that you are purified' ". This is the most persuasive tradition about dropping the requirement of massaging as compared to the other traditions, for it is not possible that a person describing her own purification would omit mentioning massage if it were included in his description for her of all the conditions of this ablution. Because of this, the jurists agreed that the descriptions provided in the traditions of ʿĀʾisha and Maymūna are complete descriptions, but what is laid down in the tradition of Umm Salama covers the obligatory essential elements (*arkān*), and minor ablution performed before the major ablution (bathing) is not a condition for it, except for an odd opinion attributed to al-Shāfiʿī, although his opinion exhibits some strength derived from the apparent meaning of the traditions The opinion of the majority exhibits analytical strength, for it is obvious that purification is a condition for the validity of ablution, and it is not ablution that is a condition for the validity of purification. This is a case of conflict between analogy and the apparent meaning of a tradition, and al-Shāfiʿī's method is to give predominance to the apparent meaning of a tradition over analogy.

A group of jurists adopted, as we have noted, the apparent meaning of the traditions and gave it predominance over analogy constructed upon ablution; therefore they did not make massaging obligatory. Others gave predominance to the analogy of this purification, built upon ablution, over the apparent meaning and made massaging of the body obligatory, as is the case in ablution. Those who preferred analogy made massaging obligatory, while those who preferred the apparent meaning over analogy did not consider massaging to be an obligation. I mean by analogy, the analogy of (this) purification based upon ablution.

There is weakness in the argument based on the application of the term "*ghusl*" to bathing, whether it is with massaging or without it, as the terms "purification" and "bathing" are applied, in the usage of the Arabs, equally to both meanings.

1.2.1.2. Issue 2: Intention as a prerequisite

They disagreed on whether intention is included in the conditions of this purification (*ghusl*), just like their disagreement in the case of the minor ablution. Mālik, al-Shāfiʿī, Aḥmad, Abū Thawr, Dāwūd, and his disciples held that intention is one of its conditions. Abū Ḥanīfa, his disciples, and al-Thawrī held that intention is not required, as in the case of minor ablution.

The reason for disagreement on the question of intention is the same as that in the case of the minor ablution, which has preceded.

1.2.1.3. Issue 3: Rinsing of the mouth and snuffing up water into the nostrils

They disagreed about *maḍmaḍa* and *istinshāq* in this category of purification too, like their disagreement in the case of the minor ablution, that is whether they are obligatory. A group of jurists held that these are not obligatory in bathing, while another group considered them obligatory. Those who maintained a negation of obligation include Mālik and al-Shāfiʿī, while those who made it obligatory include Abū Ḥanīfa and his disciples.

The reason for disagreement is the conflict of the apparent meaning of the tradition of Umm Salama with the traditions that were transmitted about the description of the Prophet's performance of minor ablution prior to his purification (bathing), because the traditions transmitted about the description of his minor ablution prior to his purification mention *maḍmaḍa* and *istinshāq*, while the tradition of Umm Salama mentions neither *maḍmaḍa* nor *istinshāq*. Those who considered the traditions of ʿĀʾisha and Maymūna as elaborations of the unexplained parts of the tradition of Umm Salama, and also as an explanation of the words of the Exalted, "And if ye are involved in a major *ḥadath*, purify yourselves",[59] made rinsing of the mouth and snuffing of water into the nostrils obligatory, while those who considered them as conflicting reconciled them so as to construe the implication of the traditions of ʿĀʾisha and Maymūna for a recommendation, and the implication of the tradition of Umm Salama as an obligation.

Because of this, they disagreed about the *ḥukm* of letting the hair loose, so as to let water reach its roots on the head (*takhlīl*), whether it is obligatory for this category of purification. Mālik deems it recommended, while others view it as obligatory. Those who made *takhlīl* obligatory supported their opinion with the report from the Prophet, "Under each hair is *janāba* (major *ḥadath*), so beautify the skin and let the hair get wet".

1.2.1.4. Issue 4: Continuous and sequential performance

They disagreed on whether a condition for this category of purification is continuous and sequential performance, as was their disagreement in the case of the minor ablution. The reason for disagreement is whether the acts of the Prophet are to be construed as obligatory or recommended. It has not been transmitted from the Prophet (God's peace and blessings be upon him) that he ever performed ablution, except in an ordered and sequential manner. A group of jurists held that sequence in this category of purification (*ghusl*) is more pertinent than it is in the minor ablution with respect to the head and the rest of the body, because of the words of the Prophet (God's peace and blessings be upon him) in the tradition of Umm Salama, "It is enough for you to splash over your head three handfuls of water, and then let water flow over your body". The conjunction particle "*thumma*" (then) implies sequence, without dispute, according to lexicologists.

[59] Qurʾān 5 : 6.

1.2.2. Chapter 2 Identification of the Factors Causing the Nullification of this Purification

The basis of this chapter are the words of the Exalted, "And if ye are involved in *janāba*, purify yourself",[60] and His words, "They question thee (O Muhammad) concerning menstruation. Say: It is a suffering, so let women alone at such times and approach them not till they are cleansed. And when they have purified themselves, then go in unto them as Allāh has enjoined upon you".[61]

The jurists agreed about the obligation of this major ablution (full washing) arising from two kinds of *ḥadath* (ritual pollution). First, is the flowing of *maniyy* (this is known as the major *ḥadath*) in sound health during sleep, or while awake, both in the case of a male and of a female, except for what is related from al-Nakhaᶜī, who did not require bathing for a woman after a wet dream. The majority agreed about the similarity of women to men with respect to wet dreams because of the established tradition of Umm Salama. She said, "O Messenger of Allāh! If a woman sees in her sleep what a man sees, does she have to take a bath?" He replied, "Yes, if she finds moisture". The second tradition, whose authenticity they also agreed about, relates to menstruation, and requires that bathing be performed, when it ceases. This is also based on the words of the Exalted, "They question thee (O Muhammad) concerning menstruation. Say: It is a suffering, so let women alone at such times and approach them not till they are cleansed. And when they have purified themselves, then go in unto them as Allāh has enjoined upon you".[62] Furthermore, it is based upon reports of the Prophet's instructions to ᶜĀʾisha and other women about bathing. They differed in this chapter about two issues that are like basic principles.

1.2.2.1. Issue 1: Obligation of purification after cohabitation

The Companions, may Allāh be pleased with them, disagreed about the obligation of purification following cohabitation. Some of them said that purification is obligatory after contact of the genitals, irrespective of the occurrence of ejaculation. This is upheld by the majority of the jurists of the provinces, Mālik, his disciples, al-Shāfiᶜī, his disciples, and a group of the Ẓāhirites. Another group of the Ẓāhirites maintained the obligation of purification in case of coition only.

The reason for their disagreement over this issue stems from the conflict of relevant traditions, for there are two established traditions whose authenticity

[60] Qurʾān 5 : 6.

[61] Qurʾān 2: 222. Pickthall's translation changed.

[62] Qurʾān 2: 222. Pickthall's translation changed.

is agreed upon by the traditionists. The Qāḍī (Ibn Rushd) said: "When I say established, I mean by it a tradition recorded by al-Bukhārī or Muslim, or one that is recorded by by both". One of these is the tradition of Abū Hurayra from the Prophet (God's peace and blessings be upon him), who said, "If he places himself between the four parts (thighs) of a woman, joining his genitals with hers, bathing becomes obligatory". The second tradition is from ʿUthmān, when it was said to him, "What do you think of the man who cohabits with his wife, but does not ejaculate?" He replied, "He is to perform (the minor) ablution like he does for prayers—I heard this from the Prophet (God's peace and blessings be upon him)".

The jurists were divided into two opinions about these traditions. The first is based upon abrogation, while the second follows what is agreed upon in case of conflict when neither preference nor reconciliation is possible. The majority maintained that Abū Hurayra's tradition abrogates that of ʿUthmān. Their argument is based upon what is related from Ubayy ibn Kaʿb, who said, "The Messenger of Allāh (God's peace and blessings be upon him) granted a concession in the early days of Islam, but later ordered bathing". It is recorded by Abū Dāwūd. Those who held that the conflict between these two traditions cannot be resolved through reconciliation or by preference maintained that recourse to what is agreed upon becomes necessary, which is the obligation of purification upon ejaculation. The majority preferred Abū Hurayra's tradition on the basis of analogy, saying that as consensus has occurred on the point that the contact of the genitals invokes the *ḥadd* penalty, it must also be the cause giving rise to bathing. They related that the analogy has been derived from the practice of the four Caliphs. The majority preferred it also on the basis of ʿĀʾisha's tradition and her reports from the Messenger of Allāh (God's peace and blessings be upon him), as recorded by Muslim.

1.2.2.2. Issue 2: Seminal discharge invoking purification

The jurists differed about the condition of seminal discharge that gives rise to the obligation of the major purification. Mālik took it into account when accompanied by (lustful) pleasure, while al-Shāfiʿī said that mere emission leads to the obligation of purification, irrespective of accompanying sensual pleasure. There are two reasons for their disagreement. The first is whether the term "*junub*" (being in a state of major ritual pollution) is also applicable to one who is involved in this way, though not in the normal manner. Those who held that it applies only to one who has become ritually polluted in the normal manner, did not require purification upon seminal discharge unaccompanied by pleasure. Those who held that it applies to seminal discharge whatever the manner, made purification obligatory because of it, even when unaccompanied by pleasure.

The second reason is the similarity of emission without pleasure with the blood of the irregularly bleeding woman. They disagreed whether the flow of such blood should give rise to the obligation of purification. We shall mention this in the chapter on menstruation, though it pertains to this topic too.

In Mālik's school there is a case discussed under this topic, which relates to a person who derives pleasure on provocation, but he ejaculates later after the pleasure has subsided (coitus interruptus). If he has bathed before this pleasureless ejaculation, it is said that he has to renew purification, while it is also said that he need not repeat it. The reason is that this type of ejaculation is accompanied by pleasure for part of the copulation, but not thereafter. Those who gave predominance to the state of pleasure said that purification is obligatory, while those who considered the absence of pleasure significant said that purification is not obligatory.

1.2.3. Chapter 3 *Aḥkām* of *Janāba* and Menstruation

1.2.3.1. *Section 1*: Janāba

The *aḥkām* about the form of major ritual pollution designated as *janāba* are covered in three issues.

1.2.3.1.1. Issue 1: Entry into the mosque in a state of *janāba*

The jurists disagreed about the entry of the *junub* into the mosque, expressing three opinions. One group of jurists prohibited this absolutely, which is the opinion of Mālik and his disciples. Another group, including al-Shāfiʿī, prohibited staying in the mosque and permitted one who is passing through it. The third group, including Dāwūd and his disciples, permitted this for all.

The reason for disagreement between al-Shāfiʿī and the Ẓāhirites is based on the vacillation of words of the Exalted, "O ye who believe! Draw not near unto prayer when ye are drunken, till ye know that which ye utter, nor when ye are [ritually] polluted, save when journeying upon the road, till ye have bathed",[63] between two interpretations. Is the use of words metaphorical, so that an implied word "place" is to be assumed inserted, that is, to read "Draw not near unto the place of prayer (the mosque)", and that the exemption for the traveller relates to the prohibition of staying in the place of prayer, or, whether no word is to be assumed implied and the verse is to be read as it is, where the traveller is in a state of *janāba* (sexual defilement), who lacks water (and can therefore perform *tayammum* and pray)? Those who held that a word

[63] Qurʾān 4 : 43.

is implied in the verse, permitted the *junub* to pass through the mosque, but those who did not take this to be the case did not have any evidence from the verse for prohibiting the *junub* from staying in the mosque. I do not know of any evidence for those who prohibited the *junub* to pass through the mosque, except the literal meaning of what is related from the Prophet (God's peace and blessings be upon him) that he said, "(Entry into) the mosque is not permitted to a *junub* nor to one menstruating." It is a tradition that is not established according to the traditionists. The disagreement of the jurists related to one menstruating, for purposes of this topic, is the same as that for the *junub*.

1.2.3.1.2. Issue 2: Touching the *muṣḥaf* in a state of ritual pollution

A group of jurists decided to permit this, but the majority prohibited it,[64] and they are those who prohibited touching it without ablution. The reason for their disagreement (over the case of the *junub*) is the same as that relating to the person who has not performed the minor ablution, that is, it is based on the words of the Exalted, "Which none toucheth save the purified".[65] We have already discussed the disagreement over the meaning of the verse. It is exactly the same disagreement as that relating to touching by the menstruating woman.

1.2.3.1.3. Issue 3: Recitation of the Qurʾān by the *junub*

The jurists differed about this, with the majority prohibiting it, and a group of jurists permitting it. The reason for their differences is the possibility of different interpretations of the tradition attributed to ʿAlī in which he states: "Nothing prevented the Prophet (God's peace and blessings be upon him) from the recitation of the Qurʾān, except *janāba*". One group of jurists said that the tradition does not give rise to a *ḥukm*, as it is only the impression of the narrator. Otherwise, how could one know that Qurʾān was not to be recited because of *janāba*, unless he informed him of this? The majority maintain that ʿAlī (God be pleased with him) would not say such a thing out of his own impression or conviction, and he said it after attaining sound knowledge.

A group of jurists considered the menstruating woman in the same position as the *junub*, while another group made a distinction between them, permitting the menstruating woman some recitation through *istiḥsān*, because of the length of the period of her menstruation. It is Mālik's opinion.

These, then, are the *aḥkām* of *janāba*.

[64] That is, they prohibited not only the *junub*, but also a person with a minor *ḥadath* from touching the *muṣḥaf*.

[65] Qurʾān 56 : 79.

1.2.3.2. *Section 2: The types of blood flowing from the uterus and related* aḥkām

The discussion of the principles related to the types of blood flowing from the uterus is covered in three subsections. The first is about the types of blood flowing from the uterus. The second is about the identification of indications of change from purity to menstruation, the signs denoting the transfer from menstruation to the period of purity or into extended menstruation, and of extended menstruation (unhealthy bleeding) into the period of purity. The third relates to the identification of the *aḥkām* of menses and extended menstruation, that is, acts prohibited and acts obligatory during it.

In each of these subsections, we shall mention issues that are like rules and principles for all that is covered in this chapter, in accordance with our aim of discussing issues agreed upon as well as those disputed.

1.2.3.2.1. *Sub-section 1: The types of blood flowing from the uterus*

The jurists agreed that the types of blood flowing from the uterus are three: menstrual blood, which flows (monthly) in a state of health; bleeding outside the regular monthly cycle of menstruation, which flows in a state of illness and is not menstrual blood according to the saying of the Prophet (God's peace and blessings be upon him), "It is blood from the (ailment of the) veins and not menstruation"; and (thirdly) postnatal bleeding, which occurs after childbirth.

1.2.3.2.2. *Sub-section 2: Indications of change from one to the other*

The identification of the indications distinguishing some of these types of blood from the others, and of the changing of the period of purity into menstruation and vice versa is based mostly on the knowledge of the usual dates of menstruation and those of purity. We will mention those that are like principles, and these are seven issues.

1.2.3.2.2.1. Issue 1: Maximum and minimum number of days for menstruation

The jurists disagreed about the maximum and minimum number of days of menstruation and the minimum number of days of the period of purity. It is related from Mālik that the maximum number of days for menstruation is fifteen, which is also al-Shāfiʿī's opinion. Abū Ḥanīfa said that the maximum number of days is ten. There is no minimum limit for the period of menstruation according to Mālik, who said that it could be a single flow of blood, though he does not take this minor discharge into account in calculating the periods in divorce. Al-Shāfiʿī said that the minimum period of menstruation is one day and a night. Abū Ḥanīfa said that the minimum is three days.

Narrations from Mālik differed about the minimum period of purity. It is related from him that it is ten days, it is related that it is eight days, and it is related that it is fifteen days, which was the inclination of his Baghdādī disciples. This is also the opinion of al-Shāfiʿī and Abū Ḥanīfa. Some jurists said that this period is seventeen days, which is the maximum according to consensus, as far as I think. There is no limit set for the maximum period of purity in their view. These are the views of the jurists regarding this subject. Those who have a minimum limit for menstruation regarded discharge for less than this minimum to be of the category of *istiḥāda* (unhealthy bleeding). Those who do not have a minimum fixed for menstruation, held that even a single flow must amount to menstruation. For those who have a maximum limit for menstruation, bleeding in excess of this limit is *istiḥāda*.

The summary of Mālik's views regarding this topic of menstruation, however, is that women are of two types: a starter and the experienced. A woman who has just started menstruating is to give up prayers upon seeing the first drop of blood till a period of fifteen days (if bleeding continues for so long). If it does not cease, she is from then on a *mustaḥāda* and is to start praying (after bathing). This was also al-Shāfiʿī's opinion. However, where Mālik said that she is to begin praying (only after fifteen days of bleeding) when she realizes that (further bleeding is not menstruation and) she is a *mustaḍāda*, al-Shāfiʿī required her (in addition to her fresh obligations) to pray *qaḍāʾ* for fourteen days that she has missed, except (she is not to repeat prayers for) the minimum period (which) for him is one day and one night. Another opinion from Mālik is that she is to count the number of days of someone her own age and then add three days. If bleeding has not ceased by then, she is deemed a *mustaḥāda*.

Mālik has two opinions about the woman who has been menstruating regularly but begins to suffer irregularity in bleeding. The first is that her menstruation is her usual period plus three days up to a total of fifteen days, which is the maximum period of menstruation. The second is to wait till the maximum period of menstruation, or she may try to distinguish (between the types of blood) if she is able to do that. Al-Shāfiʿī said that she acts in accordance with her usual period of menstruation.

All these opinions given by *fuqahāʾ* about the minimum period of menstruation, its maximum, and the minimum period for purity have no revelatory basis. The basis is experience and what each believed to be the usual occurrence. Each one of them said what he thought the common experience of women to be. It is difficult, however, to fix by experience limits for such things, because of the differences among women. The differences that arose about such things are those that we have mentioned.

They agreed generally that if bleeding extends beyond the maximum period of menstruation it is to be considered as *istiḥāda*, due to the words of the

Messenger of Allāh (God's peace and blessings be upon him) related by Fāṭima bint Hubaysh, who was told by the Prophet, "When menstruation commences, you should stop praying, and when the normal number of days for menstruation is over wash the blood away from you and pray".

The woman whose bleeding extends beyond the maximum period of menses will necessarily have gone beyond menstruation. Al-Shāfiʿī and Mālik, may Allāh have mercy on him, held, in one of two narrations from him (Mālik), about the woman accustomed to menstruation that she is to act according to her usual course, because of the tradition of Umm Salama recorded in *al-Muwaṭṭaʾ*: "A woman at the time of the Messenger of Allāh (God's peace and blessings be upon him) used to bleed copiously, so Umm Salama consulted the Messenger of Allāh (God's peace and blessings be upon him) concerning her. He said, 'She should take into account the number of days and nights for which she used to menstruate in a month prior to this affliction. She should give up praying for such a period each month. When this period is over she should take a bath, tie her private parts with a cloth, and pray'". They linked the *ḥukm* of the woman who is doubtful about menstruation with the *ḥukm* of a woman suffering from unhealthy bleeding (*istiḥāda*), who is in doubt about her normal menstruation. He (Mālik) also held the view about a woman who has started menstruating, upon reaching the age, that she should take into account the period of women her own age, for their periods are similar to hers. He, thus, deemed their *ḥukm* to be the same. As to the three additional days, to be sure, it is something unique to Mālik and his disciples, may Allāh have mercy on them. All other *fuqahāʾ*, except for al-Awzāʿī, opposed them in this, as it is not mentioned in the established traditions, though they relate a weak tradition for it.

1.2.3.2.2.2. Issue 2: The case of the woman whose menstruation ceases then begins again

Mālik and his disciples held that a woman whose bleeding is sporadic, bleeding for a day or two and becoming pure for the next day or two, is to add up the number of days for which she had a flow of blood, ignoring the days of purity. She is to bathe each day that she finds herself to be pure and pray, because even though she is not sure, it may be a period of purity. If the days of bleeding have added up to fifteen, she is a *mustaḥāda* from then on. This opinion was also upheld by al-Shāfiʿī. It is also related from Mālik that she is to add up her days of bleeding and measure them against her usual menstrual period. When these are equal she is to add another three days for the flow to cease, otherwise she is a *mustaḥāda*.

Considering the days in which there is no flow of blood as excluded from the count is incomprehensible, for they are either days of purity or of menstruation. If they are days of menstruation, it is necessary that they be added to the days of bleeding, but if they are the days of purity, then, there is no need to add up the (remaining) days of bleeding, since they are separated by the days of purity. What conforms with his (Mālik's) principles is that these are days of menses and not of purity, as the minimum period for purity is limited in his view, and it is more than a day or two. Think over this, and it will be evident, God willing.

The truth is that menstrual and postnatal blood flows and then ceases for a day or two, flowing again till the menstrual or postnatal period is over, just as it may flow for an hour or two in a day and then stop.

1.2.3.2.2.3. Issue 3: The minimum and maximum periods for postnatal bleeding

They disagreed about the maximum and minimum periods of postnatal bleeding. Mālik held that there is no minimum limit for it, which was also upheld by al-Shāfiʿī, Abū Ḥanīfa and a group of jurists maintained that it is limited. He said that it is fifteen days, while Abū Yūsuf, his disciple, said that it is eleven days. Al-Ḥasan al-Baṣrī fixed it at twenty days. As to the maximum period, Mālik once said that it is sixty days, retracting from it later and saying that women should be asked about it, but his disciples stood firm on the first opinion. This was also al-Shāfiʿī's opinion. The majority of the jurists from among the Companions maintained that it is forty days, which was upheld by Abū Ḥanīfa. It is said, however, that the periods of women in the same condition should be taken into account, and if she goes beyond that she is a *mustaḥāda*. Some jurists made a distinction between the birth of a male or female child, saying that for the male there are thirty days, for the female forty.

The reason for disagreement is the difficulty in relying upon experience, due to differences in women, and because there is no authoritative source that can be acted upon, as is the case in their disagreement about the days of menses and purity.

1.2.3.2.2.4. Issue 4: Blood seen by the pregnant woman

The jurists, both early and later, disagreed whether the blood seen by a pregnant woman is to be deemed as *ḥayḍ* or *istiḥāda*. Mālik, al-Shāfiʿī, in his more reliable opinion, and other jurists held that a pregnant woman can menstruate. Abū Ḥanīfa, Aḥmad, al-Thawrī, and others said that the pregnant woman does not menstruate, and the blood discharged from her is that of illness, unless she is having labour pains, in which case they agreed that it is to be deemed as postnatal bleeding and her *ḥukm* is the *ḥukm* of a menstruating woman with respect to the prohibition of prayers and other related *aḥkām*.

From Mālik and his disciples there are conflicting narrations about a menstruating pregnant woman with extended bleeding as to the shifting of the *ḥukm* of normal menstruation to that of *istiḥada*. One opinion is that her *ḥukm* is that of a menstruating woman, that is, she either bleeds for the maximum number of days for menstruation and then becomes a *mustaḥāda*, or she adds three days to her usual menstrual course, as long as the total does not exceed fifteen days. It is further said that she remains a normally menstruating woman for a period double that of the maximum for menstruation. It is also said that she doubles the maximum period of menstruation as a multiple of the month past in the gestation period; thus, in the second month she doubles the maximum number of days of menstruation twice, thrice in the third month, four times in the fourth, and so on as the months increase.

The reason for their disagreement on this issue stems from the difficulty of relying on experience and the obscurity of the subject. Sometimes the blood that a pregnant woman sees is the blood of menstruation, which is the case of an exceptionally strong woman and where the foetus is small, and it could be a double pregnancy as is related from Hippocrates and Galen, and the rest of the physicians. Sometimes the blood that she witnesses could be due to the weakness of the fetus, and its illness generally depends upon her frailty and illness, in which case it is the blood of a defect and illness, and usually it is the blood from a defect.

1.2.3.2.2.5. Issue 5: Mucus and pus (leucorrhoea)

The jurists disagreed about the yellow and brownish discharge (leucorrhoea) whether it amounts to menstruation. A group of jurists held that it is menstruation during the days of menstruation, which was the opinion of al-Shāfiʿī and Abū Ḥanīfa, and the same is related from Mālik. In *al-Mudawwana* it is related from him that the yellow and brown discharges are to be considered as menstruation during the menstrual days as well as in others, irrespective of the flow of blood with it. Dāwūd and Abū Yūsuf said that the yellow and brown discharges are not menstruation, unless accompanied by blood.

The reason for their disagreement is the conflict of the apparent meaning of the tradition of Umm ʿAṭiyya with that of ʿĀʾisha. It is related from Umm ʿAṭiyya that she said, "We did not attach significance to the yellow and brown discharge after bathing". It is related from ʿĀʾisha "that the women used to send her a folded scroll containing cotton on which there was the yellow and brown discharge from menstrual blood, asking her about prayers". She said, "Do not hasten things till you see that the white mucus [which denotes the end of menstruation and the beginning of purity] is white". Those who preferred ʿĀʾisha's tradition deemed the yellow and brown discharges as menstruation, whether it was found in the days of menstruation or otherwise, with blood or without it, because the *ḥukm* of a single thing cannot differ within itself (from its constituents). Those who desired to reconcile the two traditions said that the tradition of Umm ʿAṭiyya relates to the case after the cessation of bleeding, while ʿĀʾisha's tradition relates to the time immediately following it, or that the tradition of ʿĀʾisha relates to the period of menstruation, and that of Umm ʿAṭiyya relates to days free from menstruation.

A group of jurists followed the literal meaning of Umm ʿAṭīya's tradition and did not attach any significance to the yellow and brown discharges, either during days of menstruation or on other days, either immediately following the blood or after its cessation, because of the words of the Messenger of Allāh (God's peace and blessings be upon him), "The blood of menstruation is dark, and can be identified", and because the yellow and brown discharges are not blood. They are like all other discharges released by the womb, which is the opinion of Abū Muḥammad ibn Ḥazm.

1.2.3.2.2.6. Issue 6: Indications of purity

The jurists disagreed about the indications of purity. One group of jurists said that the indication of purity is when seeing the mucus becoming dry, which was the opinion of Ibn Ḥabīb from among the disciples of Mālik; this is so whether it is the practice of the woman to see the white mucus or reach purity by becoming dry. She becomes pure whichever one of these she sees. Another group of jurists made the distinction that if a woman is accustomed to seeing the white liquid, she does not become pure unless she actually sees it, but if she does not habitually get it, then her purity is attainedwhen she becomes dry. This is related in *al-Mudawwana* from Mālik. The reason for their disagreement is that some of them took into account the regular habit, while others considered the cessation of blood alone. It is also said that the one who is accustomed to reaching purity by becoming dry may reach purity by seeing the white matter, but the woman accustomed to seeing the white matter does not become pure by merely becoming dry. The opposite is also maintained, and all this is from Mālik's disciples.

1.2.3.2.2.7. Issue 7: When is the *mustaḥāda* considered to be menstruating normally

The jurists disagreed about a *mustaḥada*—if her bleeding continues indefinitely as to when she will be considered as menstruating normally, just as they disagreed about a woman with normal menstruation when her bleeding is extended, as to when she becomes a *mustaḥāda*, the discussion of which has preceded.

Mālik said that the *ḥukm* of the continuously bleeding woman is the same as the woman in purity, till the description of the blood changes to that of menstruation. This happens when the unhealthy bleeding continues beyond the minimum period of purity, and it is then that she is to be considered as menstruating normally, that is, when these two things come to pass together, the change in the blood and the passage of days in extended bleeding that can possibly be a period of purity, otherwise she is a *mustaḥāda*.

Abū Ḥanīfa said that she takes into account her normal days of menstruation, if she has experienced menstruation before, but if she has just begun menstruating, she passes the maximum period of menstruation, which is ten in his view. Al-Shāfiʿī said that she should try to distinguish between the distinctive signs, but if she has had menstrual experience earlier, she should follow that experience. If both factors are relevant to her, then there are two opinions from him. First, that she should follow the distinguishing signs, and second that she should follow her regular course.

The reason for their disagreement is that there are two conflicting traditions related to this. First is the tradition of ʿĀʾisha about Fāṭima bint Abī Ḥubaysh "that the Prophet (God's peace and blessings be upon him) ordered her, when she was having an extended bleeding, to give up praying for the number of days that she used to menstruate prior to this affliction, and then bathe and pray". The tradition of Umm Salama, which has preceded, and has been recorded by Mālik, has the same implication. The second tradition is recorded by Abū Dāwūd from the tradition of Fāṭima bint Abī Ḥubaysh that she had a sustained *istiḥāda* menstruation and the Messenger of Allāh (God's peace and blessings be upon him) said to her, "The blood of menstruation is dark, and can be identified. If it is like that then refrain from prayer, but if it is different then perform ablution and pray for it is blood from the veins". This tradition is declared authentic by Abū Muḥammad ibn Ḥazm.

Some jurists adopted the method of preference, while others adopted the method of reconciliation. Those who preferred Umm Salama's tradition, as well as others with the same implication, upheld the reckoning of days. Mālik, may Allāh be pleased with him, took into account the number of days alone in the case of a menstruating woman, when she was in doubt about the prolonged flow, but he did not take them into account for the woman who was in doubt about normal menstruation, that is, neither their number nor their dates within the month, as these were known. The text, however, pertains to a woman with an extended flow, who is in doubt about her normal menstruation. He (Mālik) applied the *ḥukm* to a sub-issue, but did not apply it to the main problem. This is strange, so think over it.

Those who preferred the tradition of Fāṭimah bint Abī Ḥubaysh took into account the colour (of blood). Some of them considered, along with the colour of blood, the passage of days that could be a period of purity during the extended bleeding. This is Mālik's opinion as related by ʿAbd al-Wahhāb. There were others who did not consider this. Those who reconciled the two traditions said that the first pertains to the woman who can identify the number of days in a month and their timing, while the second pertains to one who neither knows their number nor their timing, but recognizes the colour of blood. Some of these jurists held that even if she is not one of those who can distinguish (the blood) or the timing of the days, or one who knows their number, she is to abide by the tradition of Ḥamna bint Jaḥsh, which has been declared authentic by al-Tirmidhī. It states that the Messenger of Allāh (God's peace and blessings be upon him) said to her, "It is the gush of the devil. Observe menstruation for six or seven days, Allāh knows what (number) it is, then take a bath". The complete tradition will be coming up in the discussion of the *ḥukm* relating to the woman with extended bleeding in the period of purity.

These are the widely known issues in this chapter, and as a whole they come under four points. First, the identification of the change from purity to menses. Second, identification of the transfer from menses to purity. Third, identification of the transfer from normal to extended bleeding. Fourth, identification of the transfer from extended bleeding to normal menstruation, for which the traditions have been laid down. As to the other three cases, they are not expressly mentioned in the texts, that is, with respect to their determination. Same is the case with the transfer from postnatal bleeding to extended bleeding.

1.2.3.2.3. *Sub-section 3: The identification of the* aḥkām *of normal and extended bleeding*

The basis for this section are the words of the Exalted, "They question thee (O Muhammad) concerning menstruation. Say: It is an illness, so let women alone at such times and go not in unto them till they are cleansed. And when they have purified themselves, then go in unto them as Allāh has enjoined upon you",[66] and also the traditions pertaining to this, which we will be quoting.

The Muslim jurists agreed that menstruation prohibits four things. First, the act of the daily prayer and its obligation, that is, it is not obligatory for the menstruating woman to perform the prayer as *qaḍāʾ* (compensatory performance), unlike fasting (which has to be made up). Second, it prohibits the act of fasting, but not its delayed performance (*qaḍāʾ*). This is based on an established tradition from ʿĀʾisha, who said, "We were ordered to make up the days of fasting (which we missed on account of menstruation), but we were

[66] Qurʾān 2 : 222.

not ordered to perform compensatory prayers". A group of the Khārijites maintained that compensatory performance of prayer is obligatory. The third, in my reckoning, is circumambulation (*ṭawāf*) due to ʿĀʾisha's tradition when the Messenger of Allāh ordered her to do all that the pilgrims do except circumambulation of the House (as she was menstruating then). The fourth is coition due to the words of the Exalted, "So let women alone at such times and go not in unto them till they are cleansed".[67]

They differed about the *aḥkām* in a number of issues, and we shall mention those known most widely. These are five:

1.2.3.2.3.1. Issue 1: Cohabitation with the menstruating woman and what acts are permitted

The jurists disagreed about cohabitation with the menstruating woman and about the acts that are permissible. Mālik, al-Shāfiʿī, and Abū Ḥanīfa said that he can access the area above the waist (wrapper). Sufyān al-Thawrī and Dāwūd al-Ẓāhirī said that it is obligatory upon him to avoid only the outlet of blood.

The reason for their disagreement is the conflict of the apparent meaning of the traditions laid down on this issue with the likely interpretations of the verse of menstruation (*ḥayḍ*). It is stated in authentic traditions from ʿĀʾisha, Maymūna, and Umm Salama that the Prophet (God's peace and blessings be upon him), when one of them was menstruating, would order her to tie a waist-wrapper around her and then he would lie down with her. It is also related in the tradition of Thābit ibn Qays from the Prophet (God's peace and blessings be upon him) that he said, "Do everything with the menstruating woman, except coition". Abū Dāwūd has related from ʿĀʾisha that the Messenger of Allāh (God's peace and blessings be upon him) said to her, when she was menstruating, "Uncover your thighs." She said: "I did so, and he placed his cheek and his chest on my thighs. I leaned upon him till he was warm, for the cold had given him pains".

In the verse of menstruation, the words of the Exalted, "So let women alone at such times and go not in unto them till they are cleansed", vacillate between interpretation according to their general implication, except for what is restricted by an evidence, and between implying a general meaning intended for the particular, on the basis of the words of the Exalted, "Say: It is an illness", as the illness is confined to the outlet of blood. Those who interpreted the verse in its general meaning, that is, construing it in the general meaning till it is restricted by an evidence, exempted contact for what is above the waist-wrapper on the evidence from the *sunna*, for the restriction of the Book

[67] Qurʾān 2 : 222.

by the *sunna* is well-known to the experts of *uṣūl.* Those for whom the meaning was general intended for the particular, preferred this verse over the traditions prohibiting what is below the waist-wrapper, seeking support from traditions conflicting with the traditions prohibiting what is below the waist-wrapper.

There were some jurists who tried to reconcile these traditions with the meaning of the verse that is emphasized in the communication that it is an illness. They interpreted the traditions prohibiting what is below the waist-wrapper to imply mere undesirability, and interpreted the permitting traditions and the verse for permissibility. They preferred this interpretation of theirs on the basis of the *sunna* indicating that no part of the body of the menstruating woman is polluted, except for the outlet of blood. This is the tradition where "the Messenger of Allāh (God's peace and blessings be upon him) asked ʿAʾisha to fetch him a mat when she was menstruating. She said, 'I am menstruating.' He replied, 'Your menstruation is not in your hand'". Further, what is established about his resting his head on her thighs, when she was menstruating, and the saying of the Prophet (God's peace and blessings be upon him) "A believer is never unclean".

1.2.3.2.3.2. Issue 2: Intercourse in the period of purity before bathing

They disagreed about cohabiting with a woman (wife or slave girl) during the interval between the moment of cessation of blood and the time when she takes a bath. Mālik, al-Shāfiʿī, and the majority held that this is not permitted till she has a bath. Abū Ḥanīfa and his disciples held that this is permitted if she has been pure beyond the maximum period of menstruation, which according to him is ten days. Al-Awzāʿī held that if she has washed her private parts with water, cohabiting with her is permitted, that is, each menstruating woman becomes free from *ḥadath* once she purifies herself (after the cessation of bleeding). This was also Abū Muḥammad ibn Ḥazm's opinion.

The reason for their disagreement is based upon the possible interpretations of the words of the Exalted, "And when they have purified themselves, then go in unto them as Allāh has enjoined upon you",[68] whether the implication is purification by the termination of menstruation or purification with water. Further, if the purification is with water, does it imply purification of the entire body or purification of the private parts? "Purification" in the usage of the Arabs and in the technical legal meaning is an equivocal word used for these three meanings.

The majority preferred their view on the basis that the form of the verb "*tafaʿala*" is applied to the act of the subject (*mukallaf*), not to the act of

[68] Qurʾān 2 : 222.

others. Thus, the words of the Exalted, "*fa'idhā taṭahharna*" are clear in their meaning about washing with water as compared to the meaning of purity resulting from the termination of menstruation. It is obligatory to follow the apparent meaning, unless an evidence indicates the contrary. Abū Ḥanīfa preferred his view by maintaining that the word with the form *yafʿulna* in the words of the Exalted, "*ḥattā yaṭhurna*" is stronger in the meaning of purity that results from termination of menstruation, as compared to purification with water. The issue, as you see, is a matter of probability. It is necessary for those who understood one of these three meanings from the word derived from the root meaning "purity" in the words of the Exalted, "till they are cleansed", must infer the same meaning from the other derivation in the words of the Exalted, "And when they are purified, then go in unto them as Allāh has enjoined upon you". This is because it is not possible, or it is difficult (at the least), to accommodate within the same verse the two differing meanings, that is, cessation of blood from the word "*yaṭhurna*", and "full washing with water" from the word *taṭahharna*, as interpreted by the Mālikites, when arguing for Mālik. It is not customary with the Arabs to say, "Do not give so and so a *dirham* till he enters the house, and when he enters the mosque give him a *dirham*", but they say, "Do not give so and so a *dirham* till he enters the house, and when he enters the house give him a *dirham*", for the second sentence emphasizes the meaning contained in the first. Those who interpreted the words of the Exalted, "*till they are cleansed*", in the sense of termination of menses, and the words of the Exalted, "And when they have purified themselves", to mean purification with water are in the position of the person saying, "Do not give so and so a *dirham* till he enters the house, and when he enters the mosque give him a *dirham*". This meaning is not understood in the usage of the Arabs, unless there is an implied word and the assumed reading is, "And when they are cleansed [by cessation of blood] and have purified themselves [with full washing], then go in unto them as Allāh has enjoined upon you". This, however, is a far-fetched assumption, and no evidence is adduced by the person who claims it, unless he were to say that the obvious meaning of purification in the term "washing", is an evidence, but this is opposed by the greater and clearer probability of no implied assumption in the verse. This is because the implied assumption (of a word) is figurative, and interpreting the text in its actual connotation is better than construing it figuratively.

Consequently, it is the duty of the *mujtahid* here, when he reaches a point in his investigation like the one in this case, to weigh the two apparent probabilities, and the one he prefers in comparison with the other, he should accept. I mean by the two "apparent probabilities" that he is to compare the apparent meaning of the phrase "when they have purified themselves", indicating washing with water, against the obvious absence of an implied word in the verse, when preferring to interpret the word "*yathurna*" in its clear sense of cessation of blood. Whichever of the two clear probabilities is preferable in his view, he should act according to it. Thus, he should either not read an implied word into the verse and interpret the words, "when they have purified themselves", to mean purification (by termination of menses) or he should read the verse with an implied word and should interpret the words, "when they have purified themselves", to mean purification with water. On the other hand, he may measure the apparent meaning of the words, "when they have purified themselves", implying purification with water against the apparent meaning of the word "cleansed" implying purification (by termination of menses), then, whichever meaning appears appropriate to him should be assigned by interpretation to the other word too, and he should act upon it as if both words in the verse bear an identical meaning, that is, either in the sense of termination of the menses or of purification with water.

It is not in the nature of legal analysis to penetrate beyond this in such matters, so ponder over it, and here one is inclined to say: "Each *mujtahid* is right".

As to the consideration of the maximum period of menstruation by Abū Ḥanīfa in this issue, the argument is weak.

1.2.3.2.3.3. Issue 3: Cohabitation while the woman is menstruating

The jurist disagreed about the man who has intercourse with his wife when she is menstruating. Mālik, al-Shāfiʿī, and Abū Ḥanīfa said that he should seek Allāh's forgiveness and is not liable for anything. Aḥmad ibn Ḥanbal said that he should (in addition) give one or one-half *dīnār* as charity (atonement). A group of the traditionists said that if he has intercourse while she was bleeding, he would owe one *dīnār*, but if he cohabits with her after the bleeding has ceased he would owe one-half *dīnār*.

The reason for their disagreement over this is based on their dispute about the authenticity of the relevant traditions, or their weakness. It is related from Ibn ʿAbbās from the Prophet (God's peace and blessings be upon him) about the person who cohabits with his wife when she is menstruating that he should give one *dīnār* as charity. It is also related from him that he should give one-half *dīnār*. Another version of this tradition of Ibn ʿAbbās states that if he cohabits while she is bleeding he would be liable for one *dīnār*, but if he cohabits after the flow has ceased he is liable for one-half *dīnār*. In the same tradition it is related that he should give two-fifths of a *dīnār* as charity, which was al-Awzāʿī's opinion.

Those for whom these traditions were authentic acted according to them, while those for whom not a single one of these was authentic, and they are the majority, acted upon the principle of dropping the *ḥukm* till it is established through an evidence.

1.2.3.2.3.4. Issue 4: The woman with extended bleeding

The jurists disagreed about the woman with extended bleeding. A group of jurists made a single (full) purification (bathing) obligatory for her, which was to take place when she saw that her menstruation period was over in accordance with one of its indications, the discussion of which has preceded according to the opinions of these jurists. These jurists, who made a single purification obligatory for her, are divided into two groups. One group made it obligatory for her to perform (the minor) ablution for each prayer, while the other group recommended this, but did not make it obligatory. Those who made a single purification obligatory for her include Mālik, al-Shāfiʿī, Abū Ḥanīfa, their disciples, and the majority of the jurists of the regions with most of them making it obligatory for her to perform ablution for each prayer. Some of them did not make it obligatory, but recommended it, which is Mālik's opinion.

Another group, besides these groups, held that a woman with extended bleeding must purify (bathe) herself for each prayer, while a second group held that the obligation is to delay the noon prayer till the time of the middle prayer, and she should then purify herself and combine the prayers. Similarly she should delay the sunset prayer till the end of its time and the beginning of the time of *ʿishāʾ*, when she should purify herself a second time and combine the two prayers, and finally, she should purify herself a third time for the morning prayer. Thus, they made three purifications obligatory for her in one day and a night. One group of jurists held that she is obliged to purify herself only once for each period of one day and one night. Some of them did not fix a time for this, which is related from ʿAlī. Some maintained that she should purify herself from one period to the next.

Four opinions are thus arrived at in this issue. First that there is only one purification for her after the menstrual blood ceases to flow. Second, that she is to purify herself for each prayer. Third, that she is under an obligation to purify herself thrice in one day and night. Fourth, that she should purify herself once during one day and night.

The reason for their disagreement on this issue derives from the conflict of the apparent meaning of the traditions laid down in this regard. These are four widely known traditions, with one being agreed upon for its authenticity and three disputed. The tradition agreed upon for its authenticity is ʿĀʾisha's, who said, "Fāṭima daughter of Abū Ḥubaysh came to the Messenger of Allāh (God's peace and blessings be upon him) and said, 'O Messenger of Allāh! I am a woman who menstruates and is never pure. Should I abandon prayer?'

The Prophet (God's peace and blessings be upon him) said to her, 'No, for this is the blood of the veins and is not menstruation. When menstruation begins give up praying, but when it turns around, wash the blood from yourself and pray'". In some of the versions of this tradition the words, "And perform ablution for each prayer", are added. This addition is not recorded either by al-Bukhārī or by Muslim, but it is recorded by Abū Dāwūd and is authenticated by a group of traditionists.

The second tradition from ʿĀʾisha about Umm Ḥabība daughter of Jaḥsh, the wife of ʿAbd al-Raḥmān ibn ʿAwf, "that she menstruated continuously so the Messenger of Allah (God's peace and blessings be upon him) ordered her to wash for each prayer". This tradition is recorded as such by Isḥāq from al-Zuhrī, but the rest of the disciples of al-Zuhrī related "that she menstruated continuously and asked the Messenger of Allāh (God's peace and blessings be upon him) about it, so he said to her, 'It is the blood of the veins and not menstruation'". He then ordered her to wash and pray, and she used to wash for each prayer, for that was what she understood from him not that this is transmitted in the words of the Prophet (God's peace and blessings be upon him). This is the narration recorded by al-Bukhārī.

The third is the tradition of Asmāʾ bint ʿUmays, "She said, 'O Messenger of Allāh! Fāṭima bint Ḥubaysh has a prolonged menstruation'. The Messenger of Allāh (God's peace and blessings be upon him) said, 'Let her wash once for *ẓuhr* and *ʿaṣr*, once for *maghrib* and *ʿishāʾ*, and then let her wash for *fajr*, performing ablution for what is between these'". This is recorded by Abū Dāwūd.

The fourth tradition is that of Ḥamna bint Jaḥsh, which records: "The Messenger of Allāh (God's peace and blessings be upon him) gave her a choice between washing once for all the prayers, when she found that the blood of menstruation had ceased to flow, and between washing thrice in one day and night". This conforms with the tradition of Asmāʿ bint ʿUmays, except that in the latter case it apparently is an obligation, while in the former case it is an option.

As the apparent meanings of these traditions were in conflict, the jurists interpreted them differently formulating four opinions: an opinion based on abrogation, an opinion based on preference, an opinion based on reconciliation, and an opinion based on structure *bināʾ*. The difference between reconciliation and structure is that the person structuring them does not find a conflict in the traditions and combines them, but the person who reconciles them finds a conflict in the apparent meanings of the traditions; so think about this, the distinction is obvious.

Those who adopted the method of preference include those who preferred the tradition of Fāṭima bint Ḥubaysh, because of the existence of an agreement about its authenticity, and they acted on its obvious meaning, that is, to the effect that the Prophet (God's peace and blessings be upon him) did not order her to wash for each prayer, nor did he order her to combine the prayers after one purification or to do anything else required in the other opinions. This was adopted by Mālik, Abū Ḥanīfa, al-Shāfiʿī, and their disciples, and these jurists form the majority. Those who considered the addition stated in this tradition, that is, the order to perform ablution for each prayer, made this obligatory for her, but those who did not consider it as authentic did not deem it obligatory.

Those who adopted structured interpretation maintained that there is essentially no conflict between the traditions of Fāṭimah and Umm Ḥabība, one of whose narrators is Ibn Isḥāq. What is contained in the tradition of Umm Ḥabība is an addition over the content of Fāṭima's tradition. What is contained in the tradition of Fāṭima is a reply to a question whether that was the type of menstrual blood that prohibits prayer. The Prophet (God's peace and blessings be upon him) informed her that it is not menstrual blood that prevents the performance of prayers, but he did not inform her at all whether she was to purify herself for each prayer or at the time of the cessation of the menstrual flow. In Umm Ḥabība's tradition, he ordered her to do only one thing, which was purification for each prayer. The majority may nevertheless say that the delay of an explanation from the time of its need is questionable. If purification was necessary prior to each prayer, he would have informed her about it, and the contender cannot claim that there was no need as she was already aware of that. How could we assume that she was so knowledgeable when she was unaware even of the difference between extended bleeding and normal menstruation? The Prophet did not mention in his words "It is not menstruation" the obligation of purification after the cessation of menstrual blood, for it was known from his (God's peace and blessings be upon him) *sunna* that the termination of menstruation makes bathing obligatory. Therefore, he did not inform her about it as she was already aware of it. The case of purification before each prayer, however, is different unless the contender were to say that this addition had not been established before. This leads to the well-known issue, whether an addition amounts to abrogation. It is related in some versions of Fāṭima's tradition that the Prophet (God's peace and blessings be upon him) ordered her to take a bath. This, then, is the position of those who adopt interpretations based on preference and structure.

Jurists adopting the method of abrogation said that the tradition of Asmāʾ bint ʿUmays abrogated Umm Ḥabība's tradition. They argued for this on the basis of what is related by ʿĀʾisha "that Sahla bint Suhayl had extended bleeding and the Messenger of Allāh (God's peace and blessings be upon him) ordered her to bathe before each prayer. As this was strenuous for her, he ordered her to combine *ẓuhr* and *ʿaṣr* with a single bath, *maghrib* and *ʿishāʾ* with another, and that she should bathe a third time for the morning prayer".

Jurists adopting the method of reconciliation maintained that Fāṭima bint Ḥubaysh's tradition is to be interpreted as being addressed to a woman who can distinguish the days of normal menstruation from others, while Umm Ḥabība's tradition is interpreted as being addressed to a woman who cannot make such a distinction, and wastherefore ordered to bathe frequently for each time of prayer as a precaution. Because it is likely that each time she was about to pray she had reached the period of purification; and it was thus obligatory upon her to wash for each prayer. Asmāʾ bint ʿUmays's tradition, on the other hand, is to be interpreted as having been addressed to a woman who cannot distinguish between the days of normal menstruation and extended bleeding (due to the irregularity of the flow), as the flow ceases at times. When the flow ceases, this woman is under an obligation to bathe and to pray two prayers after the bath (*ẓuhr* and *ʿaṣr* together with one bath, *maghrib* and *ʿishāʾ* with another bath, and *ṣubḥ* with a third).[69]

Another group of jurists adopted the opinion based on an option between the traditions of Umm Ḥabība and Asmāʾ, arguing for this on the basis of Ḥamna bint Jaḥsh's tradition, which contains the words "that the Messenger of Allāh (God's peace and blessings be upon him) granted her an option". Among these jurists are some who said that the woman with an option is one who cannot distinguish the days of her menstrual flow, and there are others who said that she is the *mustaḥāda* irrespective of her being able to distinguish her menstrual cycle. This is the fifth opinion within the issue, but the option contained in Ḥamna bint Jaḥsh's tradition is between saying all the five daily prayers with one washing and purifying thrice in one day and a night. Jurists maintaining that she should bathe once each day made this obligatory for her, perhaps on the basis of doubt, and I am not aware of a tradition for this.

1.2.3.2.3.5. Issue 5: Cohabitation with a woman having extended bleeding

The jurists disagreed about cohabitation with a woman with extended bleeding, into three opinions. One group said that it is permitted to cohabit with her, and this is the opinion of the jurists of the provinces, and has been related from Ibn ʿAbbās, Saʿīd ibn al-Musayyab, and a group of the Tābiʿūn. Another group said that it is not permitted to cohabit with her, which is related from ʿĀʾisha, and is the opinion of al-Nakhʿī and al-Ḥakam. A third group said that her husband is not to cohabit with her, unless it becomes prolonged, which is Aḥmad ibn Ḥanbal's opinion.

[69] Statement in parentheses added to avoid possible misinterpretation.

The reason for disagreement stems from the dispute about whether permissibility of prayer in her case is an exemption resulting from the prescription of the obligation of prayer, or whether prayer has been permitted to her because her *ḥukm* is the same as that of a woman in a state of ritual purity? Those who maintained that this is an exemption did not permit the husband to cohabit with her, while those who maintained that her *ḥukm* is the same as that of a ritually pure person permitted it for her. On the whole, it is an issue that is not expressly stated in the texts. The distinction between a prolonged and a short period, on the other hand, is based upon *istiḥsān*.

1.3. THE BOOK OF *TAYAMMUM* (ABLUTION WITH CLEAN EARTH)

A comprehensive discussion of the principles of this subject is covered in seven chapters. The first chapter relates to the identification of the purification for which this purification forms a substitute. The second chapter is about the person to whom this form of purification is permitted. The third chapter is about the conditions for the permissibility of this purification. Chapter four is about the description of this purification. Chapter five relates to the thing with which this purification is performed. The sixth chapter is about factors nullifying it. Chapter seven is about acts for the validity and permissibility of which this purification is a condition.

1.3.1. **Chapter 1 Identification of Purification for which** ***Tayammum*** is a Substitute

The jurists agreed that this purification is a substitute for minor (*ṣughrā*) purification (i.e. *wuḍūʾ*), but they differed about major purification (*kubrā*). It is related from ʿUmar and Ibn Masʿūd that they did not view it as a substitute for major purification. ʿAlī and other Companions maintained that *tayammum* is a substitute for major purification, which was the view adopted by jurists generally.

The reason for their disagreement is the likelihood of different interpretations of the verse for *tayammum*, and that the traditions about *tayammum* for a person involved in *janāba* (the major *ḥadath*) did not prove to be authentic in their view. With respect to the different interpretations of the verse of *tayammum*, it is possible that the addressee in the words of the Exalted, "And ye find not water, then go to high clean soil and rub your faces and your hands (therewith)",[70] is just the person who has acquired a minor *ḥadath*, and it is also possible that it is addressed to both. Those for whom the term "touching", in the words of the Exalted, "Or ye have touched women", means copulation, the pronoun refers to both. Those for whom it means touching with the hand, it is more likely that the addressee is the person with a minor *ḥadath*. This is because the pronouns usually refer to the last mentioned thing. (The verse cannot have one possibility) unless a reading with a rearranged order in the verse is assumed, so that it is read as: "O ye who believe! When ye rise up for prayer, or one of you has come from the closet, or you have touched women, wash your faces, and your hands up to the elbows, and lightly rub your heads and [wash] your feet up to the ankles. And if ye are *junub* purify [bathe] yourself, and if ye are sick or on a journey, and ye find not water, then go to clean, high ground and rub your faces and your hands with some of it". Such an assumed reading is not allowed, except on the basis of an evidence, because an assumed reading is figurative, and it is better to read the text in its actual connotation instead of interpreting it figuratively. It may be said that there is a reason that necessitates the assumption of rearrangement; namely that its present order implies that illness and journey are causes of *ḥadath*. Yet this is not the case, if the conjunction "or" (*aw*), is considered here in the meaning of "and" which is found in the usage of the Arabs. This is one of the reasons that led to a disagreement over the issue.

Their disagreement over traditions relevant to this issue is obvious from what has been recorded by al-Bukhārī and Muslim "that a man came to ʿUmar, may Allāh be pleased with him, and said, 'I have been involved in *janāba* and cannot find water (to bathe).' He [ʿUmar] said, 'Do not pray.' ʿAmmār said, 'Do you not remember, O Amīr al-Muʾminīn [Commander of the believers], when you and I were tending the camels and became *junub*, but did not find water. As for you, you did not pray, but I rolled in the earth and prayed? The Prophet (God's peace and blessings be upon him) [on hearing our story] said, 'It would have been enough for you to stroke the earth with your hands, then to shake (the dust off) them, and then rub your face and hands'. ʿUmar said, 'Fear Allāh, O ʿAmmār.' He (ʿAmmār) said, 'If you like, I will not relate it'". In some versions it is stated that ʿUmar said to him, "Let it be at that". Muslim relates from Shaqīq that he said, "I was sitting with ʿAbd Allāh ibn Masʿūd and Abū Mūsā, when Abū Mūsā said, 'O Abū ʿAbd al-Raḥmān, what do you think about the person who becomes *junub* and does not find water for a month? How would he pray?' ʿAbd Allāh replied to Abū Mūsā saying, 'He is not to perform *tayammum* even if he does not find water for a month'. Abū Mūsā said, 'Then what about this verse in *ṣūrat al-Māʾida*,

[70] Qurʾān 5 : 5.

"And ye find not water, then go to high clean soil and rub your faces and your hands (therewith)?" ʿAbd Allāh said, 'If this concession were made for them, they would be ready to perform *tayammum* with earth when water appears cold to them'. Abū Mūsā said to ʿAbd Allāh, 'Did you not hear what ʿAmmār said to ʿUmar?'" He then proceeded to relate the preceding tradition. "ʿAbd Allāh replied, 'Did you not see that ʿUmar was not convinced by ʿAmmār's statement'".

The majority, however, maintained that this had been established by the traditions of ʿAmmār and ʿImrān ibn al-Ḥuṣayn, both recorded by al-Bukhārī, and that the forgetfulness of ʿUmar is not effective in the obligation to act upon the tradition of ʿAmmār. Further, they argued for the permissibility of *tayammum* for the *junub* and the menstruating woman on the basis of the general implication of the words of the Prophet (God's peace and blessings be upon him), "The earth has been deemed a mosque for me, and a means of purity". The tradition of ʿImrān ibn al-Ḥuṣayn states "that the Messenger of Allāh (God's peace and blessings be upon him) saw a person who had isolated himself and was not praying with the group. He said, 'Is it not good enough for you to pray with the group?' He said, 'O Messenger of Allāh (God's peace and blessings be upon him), I am *junub* and there is no water.' The Prophet (God's peace and blessings be upon him) said, 'You have the earth, that is good enough for you'".

They differed, because of the likelihood of such interpretations, about the person who does not have water whether he can cohabit with his wife? I mean, those who permit the *junub* to perform *tayammum*.[71]

1.3.2. Chapter 2 Persons Permitted to Undertake this Form of Purification

The jurists agreed unanimously that the persons permitted to undertake this purification are of two types: the sick and the traveller, when there is a lack of water. They disagreed about four other types: the sick person who can find water, but is afraid to use it; the resident who has no water; the healthy traveller who can find water, but fear prevents him from reaching it; and the person who is afraid to use water due to extreme cold.

[71] This is difficult to understand. *Ṭahāra* is not a requirement for copulation, unless the author means that in the absence of water intercourse will cause *janāba*, and the person will be unable to pray. This can, however, be true in the view of those who deny *tayammum* for the *junub*. Maybe, there is an omission in the text and it was meant to read: "I mean those who do *not* permit . . ."

About the *marīḍ* (sick person) who can find water, but is afraid to use it, the majority said that *tayammum* is permitted to him; similarly, in the case of the healthy person who fears death or severe illness because of the extreme coldness of water, and the person who is afraid to go out and reach the water, except that most of the jurists consider it obligatory for him to repeat prayers when he finds water. ʿAṭāʾ maintained that sick as well as the healthy persons who find water are not permitted to perform *tayammum*. Mālik and al-Shāfiʿī upheld the permissibility of *tayammum* for the healthy resident who lacks water. Abū Ḥanīfa said that *tayammum* is not permitted for the healthy resident, even if there is a lack of water.

The reason for their disagreement over these four issues are the fundamentals of this chapter. About the *marīḍ*, who is afraid to use water their disagreement centres on whether there is an implied additional word in the verse, that is in the words of the Exalted, "And if ye are sick or on a journey". Those who held that there is such an implied addition and the text means, "And if ye are sick, not able to use water", and that the pronoun "ye" in the words of the Exalted, "And ye find not water", refers to the traveller alone, (they) permitted *tayammum* for the sick person who is afraid to use water. Those who said that the pronoun in "And ye find not water", refers both to the *marīḍ* as well as the traveller, and that there is no implied addition in the verse, did not permit the *marīḍ* to perform *tayammum* if he can find water.

Their disagreement about the resident who lacks water relates to the dispute whether the pronoun in the words of the Exalted, "And ye find not water", refers to all kinds of persons in the state of *ḥadath*, that is, residents and travellers, or to travellers alone. Those who maintained that it refers to all types of persons in a state of *ḥadath*, permitted *tayammum* to residents, while those who maintained that it refers to the travellers alone, or to the sick and the travellers, did not permit *tayammum* to the resident who lacks water.

Their disagreement about the person who is afraid to go out and reach the water, was caused by their dispute over its analogy drawn from the person who cannot find water. Likewise, their disagreement over the case of the person who is afraid of using extremely cold water is caused by their differences over its analogy drawn from the case of the sick person who is afraid to use water.

Those who upheld the permissibility of *tayammum* for the *marīḍ*, supported their opinion on the basis of the tradition of Jābir about the wounded person, who bathed and died, and the Prophet (God's peace and blessings be upon him) permitted *masḥ* for such a person, saying: "They killed him, woe to them". In the same way they compared the healthy person, who is afraid to use water, to the case of the sick person on the basis of what is related about it from ʿAmr ibn al-ʿĀṣ, when he became *junub* on a cold night. He performed *tayammum* and recited the words of the Exalted, "Kill not yourself. Lo! Allāh is ever Merciful unto you".[72] He mentioned this to the Prophet (God's peace and blessings be upon him) who did not reprimand him.

1.3.3. Chapter 3 Conditions of Validity for this Form of Purification

The identification of the conditions of this type of purification relates to three issues, which are like principles. First, whether intention is a condition for this purification? Second, whether searching for water, when it is lacking, is a condition for the permissibility of this purification? Third, whether the advent of the time (of prayer) is a condition for the validity of *tayammum*.

1.3.3.1. Issue 1: Intention

The majority maintain that intention is a condition for *tayammum*, because it is a ritual non-rational worship. Zufar deviated saying that intention is not one of its conditions, and there is no need for intention. This is also related from al-Awzāʿī and al-Ḥasan ibn Ḥayy, but the claim is weak.

1.3.3.2. Issue 2: Seeking water

Mālik, may Allāh be pleased with him, stipulated the seeking of water (to ascertain non-availability prior to shifting to *tayammum*), as did al-Shāfiʿī. Abū Ḥanīfa did not lay down this condition. The reason for their disagreement over this is whether the person who does not find water without seeking it can be termed as one who lacks water, or whether the person lacking water is one who has sought it but could not find it? The truth is that the person convinced about a lack of water, either due to a prior (unsuccessful) search or without it, is one who lacks water. The person acting merely on his whim, however, cannot be one who lacks water. It is for this reason that the opinion in the school requiring repeated search in the same location is deemed weak, whereas the opinion stipulating initial search, when there is no convincing information about lack of water is deemed strong.

1.3.3.3. Issue 3: The advent of time (of prayer)

Some of the jurists stipulated this, which is the opinion of al-Shāfiʿī and Mālik, while others did not, which is the opinion of Abū Ḥanīfa, the Ẓāhirites, and Ibn Shaʿbān from among the disciples of Mālik.

The reason for their disagreement is whether the apparent meaning of the verse of ablution implies that *tayammum* and *wuḍūʾ* are not permitted, except

[72] Qurʾān 4 : 29.

when it is time for prayer, as in the words of the Exalted, "O ye who believe! When ye rise up for prayer . . ."[73] Thus, they made *wuḍū'* and *tayammum* obligatory at the time of rising up for prayer, which occurs when it is time for prayer. It follows from this that the *ḥukm* of *wuḍū'* and *tayammum* here is the same as the *ḥukm* for *ṣalāh*, that is just as time is a condition for the validity of prayer so, similarly, time is a condition for the validity of *wuḍū'* and *tayammum*. The *shar'* however has made an exemption in the case of ablution. Does *tayammum* then retain the original rule, or is this not an apparent implication of the verse and the words of the Exalted, "O ye who believe! When ye rise up for prayer . . ."[74] mean, "When ye resolve to undertake prayers?" Further, even if there is no assumption of an implied meaning in the verse, the only implication would be that the obligation of ablution and *tayammum* becomes due at the time of obligation of prayer, not that performance of *wuḍū'* and *tayammum* before the time of prayer is invalid, unless the rule is based upon the analogy of observing prayer before its time. In such a case, it would be preferable to say that the reason for disagreement in this is the analogy of *tayammum* upon prayer, but it is weak because its analogy upon *wuḍū'* would be better. This is a weak issue, so think over it, that is those who stipulate the advent of the time of prayer for its validity and render it a form of worship bound by time.

Limitations of time for the different kinds of worship are not imposed, except through a transmitted evidence. Imposition of a timing for *tayammum* would be justified if the finding of water were postponed till just before the advent of time, in which case this would not be a time-bound worship, but the issue would fall under the principle that the time arises when the lack of water is the moment of the beginning of the period of prayer. This is so as it is only at the beginning of the period of prayer that he can be sure of the availability or non-availability of water. It is for this reason that the school differed over the question: when should he perform *tayammum*? Is it to be at the beginning of the prescribed time (for prayer), in the middle, or at the end? Yet, there are certain situations in which it is known with certainty that he would not come across water, except at the time of prayer. Further, if water becomes available (after the performance of *tayammum*) he will only be obliged to terminate his *tayammum* (that is perform *wuḍū'*), not that it is invalid. The possibility of coming across water just before the beginning of the time of prayer and after its commencement is equal. Why, then, has the *ḥukm* of *tayammum* before the time of prayer been considered different from its *ḥukm* at its commencement, that is the undertaking of *tayammum* is prohibited before time, but it is not

[73] Qur'ān 5 : 6.
[74] Qur'ān 5 : 6.

prohibited at the advent of such time. Such views are not to be formulated, except on the basis of a transmitted evidence.

It follows from this logic that *tayammum* is to be delayed till close to the end of the time (for prayer), so think over it.

1.3.4. **Chapter 4 Descripton of this Form of Purification**

As to the description of this form of purification, it relates to three issues, which are the principles of this chapter.

1.3.4.1. Issue 1: The part of the hands to be rubbed

The jurists had four different opinions about the extent of the hands that Allāh has commanded people to rub in His words, "And ye find not water, then go to clean, high ground and rub your faces and your hands with some of it".[75] First, that the prescribed limit for this is the same as the limit in *wuḍūʾ* itself, which is up to the elbows. This is the widely known opinion in the school, and is upheld by the jurists of the provinces. Second, the obligation is to rub the palm of the hand only and this is maintained by the Ahl al-Ẓāhir and the traditionists. Third, that it is recommended up to the elbows, but the obligation is (to rub) the palms of the hands. This is related from Mālik. The fourth opinion is that the obligation extends up to the shoulder. This is a deviant opinion and has been related from al-Zuhrī and Muḥammad ibn Masalma.

The reason for their disagreement stems from the equivocality of the term "*yadd*" in the language of the Arabs. This is so as the term "*yadd*", in the language of the Arabs is used in three meanings: the hand only, which provides the primary use; the hand and the forearm; the hand, forearm, and upper arm. The second reason arises from the conflict of relevant traditions. The widely known tradition of ʿAmmār, in its various established channels, says, "It would have been enough for you to stroke with your hand, then shake it off them, and rub your face (with them) and your hands". In some versions it is stated that the Prophet (God's peace and blessings be upon him) said, "And that you rub your hands up to the elbows". It is also related from Ibn ʿUmar that the Prophet (God's peace and blessings be upon him) said, "*Tayammum* consists of two strokes: a stroke for the face, and another for the hands, up to the elbows". This is also related through Ibn ʿAbbās and other narrators.

The majority preferred these traditions over the tradition of ʿAmmār

[75] Qurʾān 5 : 6.

relying on the supporting analogy for it, that is the analogy of *tayammum* upon *wuḍūʾ*, the same factor which impelled them to prefer interpreting the term *yadd* in the sense which includes the palm and the forearm as against the hand alone, which is the apparent meaning. Those who claimed that it applies to both equally, and is not primarily applied to one of them as compared to the other, has erred, for "*yadd*", even if it is an equivocal term, primarily denotes hand, and is metaphorical for the part in excess of the hand. Every equivocal term is not obscure (*mujmal*). A term that is both obscure and equivocal is one that has been applied initially as an equivocal term. The jurists have held that it is not proper to argue on the basis of such a term. It is for this reason we say that the correct view is to believe that the obligation relates to the hands alone. This is so as the term *yadd* either applies primarily to hands as compared to all other limbs or its indication of the rest of the limbs, forearm and upper arm, is equal. It is necessary to decide on the basis of the established tradition when the meaning is more obvious. Giving predominance to analogy here over the tradition is incomprehensible. It is also incomprehensible to prefer on the basis of analogy traditions that have not been established. The *ḥukm* on the basis of the Book and the *sunna* is evident here, so ponder over it.

Those who held the limit to be up to the armpits maintained this as it is related in some versions of ʿAmmār's tradition that he said, "We used to perform *tayammum* along with the Messenger of Allāh (God's peace and blessings be upon him), and rubbed our faces and hands up to the shoulders". To construe those traditions as implying recommendation and the tradition of ʿAmmār as implying obligation is commendable as a method, for reconciliation is considered better than preference according to the experts of the juristic method, except that it is necessary to ascertain that the traditions are proved authentic.

1.3.4.2. Issue 2: Striking the earth

The jurists disagreed about the number of times the earth is to be struck for the purpose of *tayammum*. Some of them said it is once, while others said that it is twice. Those who said that it is twice include some who said that one stroke is for the face and one for the hands. These are the majority. When I say "majority", then the three (leading) jurists are counted among them, that is, Mālik, al-Shāfiʿī, and Abū Ḥanīfa. Some of them said that there are two strokes for each of them, that is two strokes for the hands and two strokes for the face.

The reason for their disagreement is that the verse gives no details about this, and the traditions are in conflict, while the analogy of *wuḍūʾ* for *tayammum* in all its instances is not agreed upon. What is stated by the established tradition of ʿAmmār about this is one stroke both for the face and the hands, but there are traditions in which it is required twice. The majority preferred these traditions on the basis of analogy of ablution for *tayammum*.

1.3.4.3. Issue 3: Earth reaching the limbs

Al-Shāfiʿī disagreed with Mālik, Abū Ḥanīfa, and others about the obligation of the earth reaching the limbs that are the object of *tayammum*. Abū Ḥanīfa did not consider this as obligatory, nor did Mālik, but al-Shāfiʿī upheld it as obligatory.

The reason for their disagreement is the equivocality found in the word "*min*" in the words of the Exalted, "And rub your faces and your hands with some of it (*minhu*)".[76] This is so as the word *min* is sometimes used to indicate a part, while at other times it is used to make a distinction between the categories. Those who held that it has been used here to indicate a part, made the transfer of the earth to the limbs of *tayammum* obligatory. Those who maintained that it indicates a distinction among categories said that transferring it is not obligatory. Al-Shāfiʿī preferred the interpretation implying a part on the basis of the analogy of ablution for *tayammum*, but this is opposed by the tradition of ʿAmmār that has preceded, for it contains the words, "then shake it off", and also the Prophet's performing *tayammum* at the wall.

The disagreement of the jurists about the obligation of a sequential order (of acts) in *tayammum*, as well as over the obligation of immediate performance (i.e. there should be no interval separating the rubbing of the face and the rubbing of the hands), is exactly the same as their disagreement about it in ablution, and the causes for disagreement there are the causes here; thus there is no point in reiterating them.

1.3.5. **Chapter 5 The Material Used for this Form of Purification**

This involves a single issue. They agreed about its validity with clean cultivable soil, but disagreed about its performance with what is besides soil from among the constituent parts found on land, like stones. Al-Shāfiʿī held that *tayammum* is not permitted except with pure earth. Mālik and his disciples held that *tayammum* is permitted, according to the widely known opinion, with whatever is found upon the surface of land with all its constituents, like pebbles, sand, and earth. Abū Ḥanīfa added to this saying (that it is permitted) with all kinds of solid matter produced by the earth, like lime, arsenic, gypsum, clay, and marble. Some of them, and these are the majority,

[76] Qurʾān 5 : 6.

stipulated that the soil must be on the surface of the earth. Aḥmad ibn Ḥanbal said that *tayammum* may be performed with dust from a garment or from wool.

The reason for their disagreement is based upon two factors. First, the equivocality of the term *ṣaʿīd* in the language of the Arabs, as it is sometimes applied to clean earth, and at other times to all the constituents on the surface of land, so much so that the interpretation of the derivatives of this term *ṣaʿīd* led Mālik and his disciples to permit it, in one of the narrations, with grass and snow; they said that these are also called *ṣaʿīd* in the primary use of the term, that is being upon the surface of the earth, but this argument is weak.

The second reason is the unqualified use of the term *arḍ* with respect to the permissibility of its use in some versions of the widely known tradition, and its restriction in others. It is the saying of the Prophet (God's peace and blessings be upon him), "The earth has been made a mosque for me, and a means of purity". In some versions the words, "The earth has been made a mosque for me, and a means of purity", have been recorded, while another version reads: "The earth has been made a mosque for me, and its soil a means of purity". Experts in juristic discourse have differed on whether the qualified term is to be construed as indeterminate or vice versa. The better known opinion in their view is that the indeterminate term is to be construed in terms of the qualified, but this is disputed. The opinion of Ibn Ḥazm is that the qualified term is to be construed in terms of the indeterminate, as the unqualified term has an additional meaning. Those who construed the unqualified term through the qualified term, and assigned the meaning of earth to clean surface material did not permit *tayammum* except with earth. Those who construed the qualified term through the unqualified term, and interpreted the term *ṣaʿīd* as all that is found on the surface of the earth, including its constituents, permitted *tayammum* with sand and pebbles.

That *tayammum* permits the use of all that is produced by the earth, however, is a weak claim since the term *ṣaʿīd* does not encompass all that is produced by the earth. The widest possible connotation of the term *saʿīd* points to all that is included in the soil, but not including lime and arsenic nor snow and grass. Allāh knows best.

The equivocality found in the word *ṭayyib* is also one of the causes of disagreement.

1.3.6. Chapter 6 Factors nullifying this form of purification

About the factors nullifying this form of purification, the jurists agreed that *tayammum* is invalidated by things that invalidate the original purification, which is ablution or bathing. They disagreed in this over two issues. First, does the intention of offering an obligatory prayer other than the obligatory *ṣalāh* that was intended with the *tayammum* invalidate it? Second, whether the existence of water invalidates it?

1.3.6.1. Issue 1: Intention to perform another obligatory prayer

Mālik maintained that the intention of a second prayer invalidates purification for the first prayer. The views of others are opposed to this. The basis for this disagreement revolves around two things. First, whether in the words of the Exalted, "O ye who believe! When ye rise up for prayer . . ", there is an implied text, that is, when ye arise from sleep, or when ye arise in an unclean state? Those who maintained that there is no implied text said that the apparent meaning of the verse indicates *wuḍūʾ* or *tayammum* for each prayer, but the *sunna* has restricted the meaning for *wuḍūʾ*, so *tayammum* retains the original rule. It cannot, however, be argued for Mālik on the basis of this (argument), because Mālik maintains that the verse contains an implied text, according to what he has related from Zayd ibn Aslam in his *al-Muwaṭṭaʾ*.

The second reason is based on the recurrence of the command with the advent of time for each prayer. This is what follows from Mālik's principles, that is, this argument may be adduced on his behalf, and the discussion of this issue has preceded. Those for whom the command does not recur, and they assumed an implied text in the verse, did not uphold that the intention to perform a second *ṣalāh* invalidates *tayammum*.

1.3.6.2. Issue 2: The existence of water

The majority held that the existence of water invalidates this purification. A group of jurists, however, maintained that its invalidation results only from the occurrence of a *ḥadath*. The basis of this disagreement is whether the existence of water removes the prevailing purification that was achieved with earth or whether it negates the initiation of purification with it (earth)? Those who maintained that it negates only the commencement of purification with earth (water being available) said that it is invalidated only by the occurrence of a *ḥadath*. Those who maintained that it (availability of water) invalidates the prevailing purity said that it is invalidated. The definition of the invalidating factor (water) is the eliminator of the prevailing purity.

The majority argued for their opinion on the basis of an established tradition, which is the saying of the Prophet (God's peace and blessings be upon him), "The earth has been made a mosque for me, and a means of purity, as long as water is not found". It is possible to understand from this that as soon as water is found this purification is terminated and removed, while it is also possible to understand it as implying that when water is found it is not valid to undertake this form of purification. The strongest support for the majority comes from the tradition of Abū Saʿīd al-Khudrī, which states that the Prophet (God's peace and blessings be upon him) said, "When you have found water let it touch your skin". The command here is interpreted by the majority to indicate immediate compliance, though it also leads to the preceding possibility, so think over it. Al-Shāfiʿī's acceptance, that the existence of water eliminates this purification, led him to say that *tayammum* does not, in fact, remove the *ḥadath*, that is, it does not generate purification removing the impurity, it merely has the effect of permitting prayer with the existence of the impurity. This is without foundation, as Allāh has called it purification. Some of the disciples of Mālik upheld this opinion saying that *tayammum* does not remove *ḥadath*, for had it done so, only a *ḥadath* would have invalidated it. The answer is that in the case of this purification the existence of water itself is a sort of *ḥadath* specific to it, according to the opinion that the existence of water eliminates it.

Those who upheld that the existence of water invalidates purification agreed that it does so before the commencement of prayer and after it, but they disagreed on whether it invalidates it during prayer. Mālik, al-Shāfiʿī, and Dāwūd held that the availability of water does not invalidate purification during prayer. Abū Ḥanīfa, Aḥmad, and others besides them maintained that it does invalidate it if water becomes available during prayer, and they are closer to preserving the original principle, for it is incompatible with the law to say that the availability of something does not invalidate purification during prayer, but invalidates it at other times. (Paradoxically) Abū Ḥanīfa's opinion had been denounced for a similar contradiction, that is, for holding that laughter during prayer invalidates *wuḍūʾ* (but not outside of prayer), though he was relying on a supporting tradition. Think over this issue, for the answer is evident. There is no evidence in what they (the critics of Abū Hanīfah) desired to use in support of their opinion; namely, the apparent meaning of the words of the Exalted, "And render not your actions vain",[77] as such a person is not annulling his prayer of his own volition; the prayer is annulled by the availability of water, as if he had acquired a *ḥadath* (such as passing wind).

1.3.4. Chapter 7 Acts for which this Form of Purification is a Condition

The majority agreed that acts whose validity or permissibility depends upon this form of purification are those for which ablution (*wuḍūʾ*) is a condition, like prayer, touching the *muṣḥaf*, and so on. They disagreed on whether more

[77] Qurʾān 47 : 33.

than one (obligatory) prayer is permissible with it (i.e. with one *tayammum*)? It is widely known in the Mālik's school that two mandatory prayers are never permitted with it. His opinion differed about two lapsed prayers. It is well-known that one *tayammum* is enough if one of the two prayers is mandatory and the other is supererogatory, if he prays the mandatory first, but if commences with the supererogatory, he cannot observe them with one *tayammum*. Abū Ḥanīfa held that it is permitted to observe two mandatory prayers with a single *tayammum*.

The basis for this disagreement is whether *tayammum* is required for each prayer, either due to the apparent meaning of the verse, or due to the obligation of the recurrence of the command, or due to both.

1.4. THE BOOK OF REMOVAL OF IMPURITIES (*NAJASĀT*)

The comprehensive discussion of the principles and rules of this form of purification is covered in six chapters. The first chapter is about the identification of the *ḥukm*, that is, whether it is obligatory or recommended from the aspect of being absolute, or is stipulated only as a condition for *ṣalāh*? The second chapter relates to the identification of the kinds of impurities. The third chapter is about the objects from which the removal of such impurities is obligatory. The fourth chapter is about the thing with which they are to be removed. The fifth chapter deals with the manner of their removal from each object. The sixth chapter relates to the etiquettes of the privy.

1.4.1. **Chapter 1 The *Ḥukm*** of this Form of Purification

The source of this chapter from the Book are the words of the Exalted, "Thy raiment purify",[78] and from the *sunna* the words of the Prophet (God's peace and blessings be upon him), "One who performs ablution should snuff up water and reject it, and one who uses stones [in purifying himself after excretion] should use the odd number [like three, five, etc.]". There is also the command of the Prophet (God's peace and blessings be upon him) for cleaning menstrual blood from clothes, and for pouring a pitcher of water over urine, as in the case of the bedouin. In addition, there is his saying about passing a grave in which two persons were buried that "they are being given some torment, but not for a major sin; one of them did not cleanse himself after urinating"

[78] Qur'ān 75 : 4.

The jurists agreed, because of the existence of these transmitted texts, that removal of impurities has been commanded by the law, but they differed over whether this was by way of obligation or recommendation, that is, as a *sunna*, as indicated earlier. One group of jurists said that the removal of impurities is obligatory, which was the opinion of Abū Ḥanīfa and al-Shāfiʿī. Another group of jurists said that it was *sunna muʾakkada* (emphatic), but is not an obligation (*farḍ*). One group said that it is an obligation when remembered, but is waived in the case of forgetfulness. Both opinions are related from Mālik and his disciples.

The reason for their disagreement over this issue stems from three factors. First, there is disagreement about the words of the Exalted, the Glorious, "Thy raiment purify"; whether these are to be taken literally or figuratively. The second reason is the conflict between the apparent meanings of the traditions with respect to this obligation. The third reason is their disagreement about the prescribed commands and proscriptions as related to a rational underlying cause; whether the underlying cause understood from these commands and proscriptions is a corroborative fact that moves the command from an obligation to a recommendation, and the proscription from a prohibition to disapproval, or whether it is not a corroborative fact, and that there is no difference here between rational and non-rational worship. Those who made such a distinction did so because most of the rational *aḥkām* in the law relate to ethical norms or to juristic interests, which are mostly recommended. Those who interpreted the words of the Exalted, "Thy raiment purify", to mean physical raiment said that purification from impurities is obligatory, while those who considered it as symbolic of purity of the *qalb* (heart) did not find any legal evidence in them.

Included in the conflicting traditions in this issue is the widely known tradition about two buried persons and the words of the Prophet (God's peace and blessings be upon him) that "they would be given some torment, but not for major sins; one of them did not cleanse himself after urinating". The apparent meaning of this tradition implies an obligation as torment relates only to an obligation. The tradition opposing this is that established from the Prophet (God's peace and blessings be upon him), that when he was assaulted while praying with the blood and viscera of a slaughtered camel placed upon him, he did not terminate his prayers. The apparent meaning of this is that had the removal of impurities (*najāsa*) been obligatory like the obligation of purification from ritual impurity (*ḥadath*), he would have terminated his prayers. Another related tradition is as follows: "While the Prophet (God's peace and blessings be upon him) was praying once in his sandals he cast them off; the people (praying with him) followed suit but he denied the need for this and said, 'I cast them off as Jibrīl informed me that there was filth on them'".

The apparent meaning is that had it been obligatory why would he have continued the prayer?

Those who adopted the method of preferring the apparent meaning of these traditions upheld obligation when the tradition requiring obligation was preferred, and upheld recommendation when the two traditions requiring a recommendation were preferred; I mean, that the two traditions imply that the removal of the sandals is in the category of an emphatic recommendation. Those who adopted the method of reconciliation include two groups. The first said that it is obligatory when remembering and when able to perform, and that the obligation is dropped in the case of forgetfulness and the incapacity to perform. The other group said that it is always an obligation, but is not a condition for the validity (proper performance) of prayer. This is the fourth opinion on the issue, and (the second part of it) is weak, because *najāsa* is to be removed during prayer.

In the same way, some of the jurists who distinguished between rational and non-rational forms of worship, that is, who deemed the non-rational as emphatic for purposes of obligation, made a distinction between a command prescribed for purification from legal impurity (*ḥadath*) and the command for actual impurity (*najāsa*), as it is known that the purpose of purification from *najāsa* is cleanliness, which is an ethical norm. Purification from *ḥadath*, on the other hand, is non-rational. They also sought support from the corroborating evidence of praying in sandals, as they did from the consensus about ignoring slight filth in some cases, when it is evident that one usually treads on filth with them.

1.4.2. **Chapter 2 The Kinds of Impurities**

The jurists agreed that the kinds of impurities are essentially four. First, carrion of warm-blooded animals not living in water. Second, flesh of swine, whatever the cause of its death. Third, blood of an animal that does not live in water, and is extracted from a living or dead animal when it flows out, that is, when it is excessive. Fourth, the urine and excrement of human beings. Most of the jurists agreed about the impurity of *khamr*, but there is disagreement about this among some of the traditionists. The jurists disagreed about things besides these. The principles of this chapter are covered in seven issues.

1.4.2.1. Issue 1: Carrion and dead sea animals

They disagreed about carrion that has no blood in it, and about dead sea animals. A group of jurists said that a carcass of a bloodless creature is clean; similarly, the dead sea creatures. This is Mālik's opinion and that of his disciples. A group of jurists maintained equivalence, with respect to impurity, between carrion of a warm-blooded and bloodless creatures, unless it was something over which there is agreement that it is not carrion like worms and what is produced in eatables, but they exempted dead marine animals from this, which is al-Shāfiʿī's opinion. Another group considered carrion and dead sea animals to be the same, exempting bloodless carrion, which is Abū Ḥanīfa's opinion.

The reason for their disagreement is based on their dispute over the meaning of the words of the Exalted, "Forbidden unto you are carrion . . ."[79] The reason, I think, is that they agreed that it belongs to a category of a general word intended for the particular, after which they differed as to which particular is meant here. Some of them exempt from this dead sea animals and carrion of bloodless creatures, some exempted dead sea animals only, while others made an exemption in the case of carrion of bloodless creatures alone. The reason for a disagreement over these exemptions is based upon their disagreement over the restricting evidence. The apparent argument of those who exempted bloodless carrion is based upon the established tradition from the Prophet (God's peace and blessings be upon him) relating to flies when they fall into food. They said that this indicates the cleanliness of flies, and there is no underlying reason for this except the fact that they are bloodless.

Al-Shāfiʿī's view is that this is particular to flies, because of the words of the Prophet (God's peace and blessings be upon him), "In one of its wings is disease and in the other its cure". Al-Shāfiʿī deemed weak the derivation from the tradition that the apparent meaning of the verse implies two separate prohibited impurities: carrion and blood. The first is acted upon by ritual slaughter for purification, because of which a slaughtered animal is permitted for consumption by agreement, while blood is not purified by slaughter and has a separate *ḥukm*. Thus, how is it possible to combine the two and maintain that blood is the cause of the prohibition of carrion? This is (a) strong (argument) as you can see, for if blood had been the cause of prohibition of carrion, the prohibition of eating (dead) animals would not have been lifted by slaughter. The prohibition of the blood still remaining in it and which has not been eliminated yet would have subsisted, and permissibility would only apply after the complete exhaustion of the blood from the animal; the cause having been removed, the effect would necessarily follow. If the cause is found, but the effect is absent, then, this is not the real cause. An example of this is the case of grape juice. If the prohibition is lifted from grape juice, it necessarily follows that intoxication be absent, that is if we believe intoxication to be the cause of prohibition.

[79] Qurʾān 5 : 3.

Those who exempted dead sea animals, adopted the established tradition of Jābir, which states "that they ate for several days of the whale that had been thrown out of the sea and that they derived their supplies from it. When they informed the Messenger of Allāh (God's peace and blessings be upon him) about this, he approved their act saying, 'Is something left of it?'" This is an evidence indicating that he did not permit this out of necessity arising from exhaustion or lack of food. They also argued on the basis of the words of the Prophet (God's peace and blessings be upon him), "Its water is pure and its dead creatures are permitted (for consumption)".

Abū Ḥanīfa, on the other hand, preferred the general meaning of the verse over this tradition, either because the verse is definitive and the tradition probable, or he held that this was an exemption for them, that is, the exemption in the tradition of Jābir, or because he held that the whale had died due to a cause, which was the turbulence of the sea that threw it out on the shore, as carrion is that which dies of its own without an external cause.

Another reason for their disagreement here is whether the pronoun in the words of the Exalted, "[The catch of the sea] and its food is permissible for you, a provision for you and for seafarers",[80] refers to the sea or to the fish itself. Those who associated it with the sea said that its food is that which is on the surface, while those who associated it with the catch said that what is permissible is only what is caught. In addition to this, the Kūfīs also relied on a tradition in which the prohibition of consuming fish floating on the surface is laid down, but which is weak according to the others.

1.4.2.2. Issue 2: Parts of dead animals

Just as the jurists differed about the (*ḥukm* of the) kinds of carrion they disagreed about (the *ḥukm* of) the parts of dead animals, which they had deemed as carrion by agreement. Thus, they concluded that flesh of the parts of *mayta* was also *mayta*, but they disagreed about bones and hair. Al-Shāfiʿī held that bones and hair were also *mayta*, while Abū Ḥanīfa held that they are not. Mālik made a distinction between hair and bones saying that bones are *mayta*, but not hair.

The reason for their disagreement relates to their dispute as to what activity in the limbs can be assigned the term "life". Those who maintained that the activity of growth and food intake depicts life said that when the activity of growth and food intake is absent from hair and bones they become *mayta*. Those who maintained that the term "life" is only applied to the senses, and as hair and bones do not possess the capacity to sense, they are not *mayta*. Those who distinguished between the two, assigned to bones the capacity to sense,

[80] Qurʾān 5 : 96. Pickthall's translation changed.

but not to hair. There is a disagreement about the capacity of the bones to sense, and the matter is disputed among the physicians. The evidence proving that food intake and growth are not that kind of life to the absence of which the term *mayta* can be applied is the agreement of all jurists that a part of an animal cut off when it is alive is *mayta*. This is based on a tradition, which is the saying of the Prophet (God's peace and blessings be upon him), "Whatever is cut off from an animal, when it is alive, is *mayta*". They agreed, however, that hair sheared from an animal is clean. Further, if the term *mayta* were to be applied to things whose growth and food intake has stopped, the uprooted vegetation would also be termed as *mayta*, as vegetation also shows growth and food intake. To this al-Shāfiʿī may reply that food intake, to the absence of which the term death is applied, is limited to beings endowed with the capacity to sense.

1.4.2.3. Issue 3: Skins of dead animals

They disagreed about the utilization of skins of dead animals. A group of jurists upheld the unconditional permissibility of the utilization of skins, whether tanned or not, while another group held the opposite view, that is, they are not to be utilized at all, even when tanned. A third group of jurists made a distinction between tanned an untanned skins, maintaining that tanning purifies them, which is al-Shāfiʿī's and Abū Ḥanīfa's opinion. There are two narrations from Mālik about this. The first is the same as that of al-Shāfiʿī, while the second is that tanning does not purify them, but they can be used if no moisture is involved. Those who maintained that tanning is a purifying factor, agreed that it purifies the skins of the animals that can be ritually slaughtered, that is, those permissible for consumption, but they disagreed about those to which ritual slaughter does not apply. Al-Shāfiʿī held that it purifies the skins of ritually slaughtered animals only, as slaughter is a substitute for the purpose of purification. Abū Ḥanīfa maintained the effectiveness of tanning in purifying the skins of all animals with the exception of swine. Dāwūd said that it purifies all, even the skins of swine.

The reason for their disagreement is the conflict of traditions on this issue. The absolute permissibility of its utilization is laid down in Maymūna's tradition, when the Prophet (God's peace and blessings be upon him) was passing by a carcass he said, "Would that you had made use of its skin". Its absolute prohibition is derived from the tradition of Ibn ʿAkīm, which states that "the Messenger of Allāh (God's peace and blessings be upon him) wrote that neither its hide nor its sinew are to be utilized". This was a year before his death. In some traditions the command conveys (the permissibility of) their utilization after tanning, but not before. The established tradition for this is that of Ibn ʿAbbās that the Prophet (God's peace and blessings be upon him) said, "When the hides are tanned they become purified".

The conflict of these traditions led the jurists to differ in their interpretation. One group adopted the method of reconciliation on the basis of the tradition of Ibn ʿAbbās, distinguishing between tanned and untanned skins. Another group adopted the method of abrogation, and relied on the tradition of Ibn ʿAkīm, because they date it as late as one year before the Prophet's death. A third group preferred Maymūna's tradition maintaining that it entails an addition over the tradition of Ibn ʿAbbās, as the prohibition of utilization prior to tanning cannot be derived from Ibn ʿAbbās's tradition, which speaks of purity, but utilization is different from purification. While each pure thing may be utilized, it is not necessary that each usable thing is pure.

1.4.2.4. Issue 4: Prohibition of blood

The jurists agreed that blood of land animals is unclean, but they differed about the blood of fish. Similarly, they disagreed about small quantities of blood of animals other than those of the sea.

A group of jurists said that the blood of fish is clean, and this is one of two opinions from Mālik and is also the opinion of al-Shāfiʿī. Another group of jurists said that it is unclean on the basis of the rule for blood. This is Mālik's opinion in *al-Mudawwana*. Similarly, a group of jurists said that small quantities of blood are overlooked, while others said that the *ḥukm* of large and small quantities is the same. The former view is held by the majority.

The reason for their disagreement over the blood of fish relates to their disagreement whether dead fish is *mayta*. Those who considered dead fish to be included in the general prohibition for *mayta*, deemed its blood to be the same, while those who exempted it from the general prohibition, exempted its blood on the same analogy. There exists a weak tradition related to this, and this is the saying of the Prophet (God's peace and blessings be upon him), "Two kinds of *mayta* and two kinds of blood have been permitted to us, locust and whale, and liver and spleen".

Their disagreement over large and small quantities of blood relates to the imposition of the qualified meaning over the absolute or the imposition of the absolute meaning over the qualified. The prohibition of blood has been laid down in absolute terms in the words of the Exalted, "Forbidden unto you are carrion and blood and swine-flesh",[81] while it is found in qualified terms in His words: "Say: I find not in that which is revealed to me aught prohibited to an eater that he eat thereof, except it be carrion, or blood poured forth, or

[81] Qurʾān 5 : 3.

swine-flesh—for that verily is foul".[82] Those who imposed the qualified meaning over the absolute meaning, and these are the majority, said that it is only blood that is "poured forth" that is prohibited and unclean. Those who decided according to the absolute meaning in preference to the qualified, said that blood "poured forth" is blood in large quantities, while that which is not "poured forth" is blood in small quantities, and both are prohibited. They also supported their view by saying that a thing which is unclean in essence cannot be clean in its constituent parts.

1.4.2.5. Issue 5: Pollution of urine

The jurists agreed about the uncleanliness of human urine and excrement, except for the urine of a male infant. They disagreed about what is besides this with respect to all animals. Al-Shāfiʿī and Abū Ḥanīfa held that urine and excrement of all animals are unclean, while a group of jurists upheld their absolute cleanliness, that is, offal of all animals from urine and excrement. A group of jurists said that the *ḥukm* of their urine and dung is dependent upon the *ḥukm* of their flesh. The animals whose flesh is prohibited, their urine and dung are prohibited and unclean, while the animals that are fit for consumption their urine and dung are clean, except for those animals that consume filth. The animals that are considered abominable (for food), their urine and dung are also abominable. This was Mālik's opinion, as well as that of Abū Ḥanīfa with respect to beasts of prey.

There are two reasons for their disagreement. The first is their dispute over the significance of the ordained permissibility of praying in the resting place of animals, the permission granted by the Prophet (God's peace and blessings be upon him) to the ʿUrniyīn to drink the urine and milk of camels, as well as the meaning of the prohibition of praying in the resting place of camels. The second reason is the analogy, for this purpose, of all other animals upon man. Those who constructed the analogy of all other animals upon man, maintaining that this belongs to the category of higher *qiyās*, did not consider the permissibility of praying in the resting places of animals as implying the cleanliness of their urine and dung, but deemed it to be a *ḥukm* resting upon a revelatory non-rational source. Those who interpreted the prohibition of praying in the resting places of camels to imply uncleanliness, and deemed the permissibility of drinking the urine of camels in the case of the ʿUrniyīn as medication, which is permitted on principle, said that all urine and dung is unclean. Those who interpreted the tradition permitting prayer in the resting places of animals as implying the cleanliness of their excrement and urine, as also in the case of the ʿUrniyīn, and deemed the prohibition of praying in the

[82] Qurʾān 6 : 146.

resting places of camels an act of worship and as conveying a meaning other than uncleanliness, the difference, according to them, between man and animals being that the excrement of man is repulsive by nature, while that of animals is not, deemed the excrement as being dependent upon (the permissibility) of the flesh of animals. Allāh knows best. Those who based the analogy of all other animals upon domesticated animals, deemed all excrement to be clean and not prohibited, except for the excrement of man.

The issue is subject to interpretation, and had it not been disallowed to issue an opinion that no one has expressed before among the widely known opinions, even when the issue is disputed, it would be said that the distinction be based upon those emitting an offensive smell and are considered filthy and those that do not emit such an odour and are not deemed filthy, especially those that have a pleasing smell, due to their agreement about the permissibility of ambergris, which according to most is the excrement of a marine animal, and about musk, which is a residue from the blood of an animal in which musk is formed, as is known.

1.4.2.6. Issue 6: Negligible filth

The jurists disagreed about small amounts of filth into three opinions. A group of jurists held that small and large quantities are the same. Among those who held this opinion is al-Shāfiʿī. Another group of jurists held that small amounts of filth are overlooked, and they fixed this to be an amount equal to the size of an impure (alloyed) *dirham*. Among those who held this opinion is Abū Ḥanīfa. Muḥammad ibn al-Ḥasan deviated from this saying that if the filth covers one-fourth or less of the dress, prayer is permitted in it. A third group of jurists held that small and large quantities of filth are the same, except in the case of blood as has been mentioned. This is Mālik's opinion. There are two narrations from him about menstrual blood, the one widely known being that it is similar to all other kinds of blood.

The reason for their disagreement is related to their dispute over the analogy of minor uncleanliness upon the exemption disregarding the remaining trace of filth in the case of cleaning with stones. Those who permitted such an analogy upheld the permissibility of minor uncleanliness, and for this reason they limited it to the size of a *dirham*, the size of which is the same as the size of the outlet. Those who held that these and other exemptions cannot serve as a basis for analogy, did not allow it.

The reason for the exemption granted by Mālik in the case of blood has already preceded, while the explanation of Abū Ḥanīfa's opinion is that filth is divided, according to him, into gross and light. In the case of gross filth, the amount of exemption is limited to the size of a *dirham*, while light filth is exempted up to the extent of a fourth of the dress. Light filth in his view is like the excrement of beasts of burden and those from which the streets are seldom free. This division by him into gross and light is excellent.

1.4.2.7. Issue 7: Semen

They disagreed about semen, whether it is unclean. A group, from among them, Mālik and Abū Ḥanīfa, held that it is unclean, while another group maintained that it is clean, which was the opinion of al-Shāfiʿī, Aḥmad, and Dāwūd.

There are two reasons for their disagreement. First is the variation in ʿĀʾisha's tradition. In some versions it says, "I used to wash off semen from the clothes of the Messenger of Allāh (God's peace and blessings be upon him), and he would go out to pray in them with water-marks on them." In others it says, "I used to scrape off semen from the clothes of the Messenger of Allāh (God's peace and blessings be upon him)", and that "he used to pray in them". The addition is recorded by Muslim. The second reason is the vacillation of semen between resemblance with the unclean excrements of the body and between resemblance with other clean secretions, like milk etc.

Those who reconciled all the traditions, interpreting washing to be for the purpose of cleanliness, and derived from scraping that does not purify an evidence of its purity, and made an analogy for semen upon other pure secretions, did not deem it unclean. Those who preferred the traditions of washing over those of scraping, and considered semen to be unclean, as it resembled, in their view, to unclean excrements more than clean secretions, maintained that it is unclean. So also those who believe that uncleanliness is removed by scraping. They said that scraping itself indicates its uncleanliness, as does washing. This is Abū Ḥanīfa's opinion. On this basis there is no proof with those who maintain their opinion (that semen is clean) on the words that "he used to pray in them", on the other hand, there is evidence in it for Abū Ḥanīfa that uncleanliness can be removed without water, which is contrary to the opinion of the Mālikites.

1.4.3. **Chapter 3 The Objects from which Impurities are to be Removed**

The objects from which impurities are to be removed are three, and there is no dispute about them. First is the body, then clothes, and finally the mosques and the places of prayer. The jurists agreed about these three objects as they are expressly mentioned in the Book and the *sunna*.

Clothes are mentioned in the words of the Exalted, "Thy raiment purify", according to those who interpreted this literally, and in the commands of the Prophet (God's peace and blessings be upon him) about washing away the blood of menstruation from clothes and about pouring water over the parts affected by the urine of the child who urinated in his lap. The mosques are covered by the command of the Prophet (God's peace and blessings be upon him) to pour a pitcher of water over the urine of the bedouin, who had urinated in a corner of the mosque. Similarly, it is established from the Prophet (God's peace and blessings be upon him) that "he ordered the washing of *madhy* from the affected parts of the body and the washing away of impurities from the two outlets".

The jurists differed aboutwhether the entire penis is to be washed because of *madhy* (prostatic secretion prior to cohabitation). This is based on the widely known tradition of ʿAlī from the Prophet (God's peace and blessings be upon him) when he was asked about prostatic fluid. He said, "He should wash his penis and perform ablution". The reason for the disagreement is whether the obligation relates to the entire affected object or to the actually affected parts of it. Those who maintained that it applies to the whole, that is, to the entire object to which the term is applied, said that the entire penis is to be washed, while those who maintained that it applies to the essential minimum part of the object said that only the affected part is to be washed on the analogy of urination.

1.4.4. **Chapter 4 The Means of Removal**

The Muslim jurists agreed that clean purifying water removes impurities from those three objects. They also agreed that stones can remove impurities from the two outlets. They disagreed about removal (of impurities) with what is besides these from among fluids and solid substances. A group of jurists held that anything clean can remove impurities whether it is a fluid or a solid, and whatever the affected object. This was upheld by Abū Ḥanīfa and his disciples. Another group of jurists said that impurities cannot be removed by things other than water, except for stones, which are agreed upon. This was upheld by Mālik and al-Shāfiʿī.

They also disagreed about the removal of impurities with bones and dung in the case of *istinjāʾ*. A group of jurists prohibited this, but permitted their use with other things that can clean, though Mālik exempted from these esteemed eatable things like bread. The same is said about things the use of which would be immoderate like gold and gems. One group restricted cleaning to stones only, which is the opinion of the Ẓāhirites, while another group permitted it with bones, but not dung, though this was considered abominable by them. Al-Ṭabarī deviated from all this and permitted in *istinjāʾ* wiping with all things clean and unclean.

The reason for their disagreement about the removal of impurities with things other than water and for objects other than the outlets is their dispute as to whether the purpose of removing impurities with water is only the destruction of the essence of the impurity, in which case other things destroying the essence would be deemed equivalent to water, or whether water has an additional attribute not found in other things. Those to whom no additional attribute was visible in water, upheld the validity of cleaning with all clean fluids and solids. This meaning was supported by the agreement over the removal of impurities from the outlets with things other than water. It is also supported by what is laid down in a tradition from Umm Salama who said to the Prophet (God's peace and blessings be upon him), "I am a woman having a long trailing dress and I walk over filthy spots". The Messenger of Allāh (God's peace and blessings be upon him) said to her (Umm Salama), "It (the impurity) is cleansed by what follows". In addition to this, there are traditions about similar cases recorded by Abū Dāwūd, like the words of the Prophet (God's peace and blessings be upon him), "If one of you walks over filth in his sandals, the dust is their purifier", as well as other similar reports.

Those who perceived an additional attribute in water, prohibited such cleaning except for the exempted case, which is that of the outlets (with stones). When the Ḥanafites demanded from the Shāfiʿites an explanation of such an additional attribute for water, the latter resorted to the argument that it is an act of worship, for they were not able to provide a rational reason for it. They even conceded that water does not do away with impurity in a rationally satisfying way, and the removal is assigned a legal recognition. There were extended discourses and polemics between them over the question of whether the removal of impurity with water is an act of worship or has a rational cause coming down as a precedent. The Shāfiʿites were constrained to establish a (special) legal virtue for water, which is not found in other things, in meeting the *aḥkām* of uncleanliness, though it is similar to other things in the (actual) removal of the substance (of pollutions).

The purpose (the Shāfiʿites added) is to meet the (requirements of the) *ḥukm* that singles out water as effective in the removal of the substance of impurities, as sometimes the impurity is already removed, but the *ḥukm* subsists. They thus relegated the purpose, although they had previously agreed with the Ḥanafites that purification from uncleanliness is not a legal purification, that is *sharʿī* and did not therefore require intention (*niyya*). If they had tried to distinguish themselves from them (the Ḥanafites) by saying that they did perceive in water a quality of dissolving impurity and contamination and of extracting them from clothes and bodies, a quality not found in other things—for which reason people rely on water for cleansing their bodies and clothes it would have been a better statement, while others are far from convincing. Perhaps it would be necessary to believe that the *sharʿ* (law) has relied on water for washing in each instance because of this inherent quality. If they had said so, they would have introduced into the prevailing *fiqh* something consistent with its meaning. The jurist resorts to saying that it (a certain thing) is an act of worship when his method imposes constraints upon him in arguing with the contender. Ponder over this, for it is evident from their treatment (of issues) on most occasions.

The reason for their disagreement about (the use of) animal droppings (in cleaning) is based on their dispute about the meaning of the proscription reported from the Prophet about it, that is, the prohibition by the Prophet (God's peace and blessings be upon him) that *istinjāʾ* is not to be performed with bones or dung. Those for whom the proscription indicated the invalidity of the thing itself did not permit it while those who did not view it as such, as uncleanliness has a rational meaning, interpreted this to mean abomination, but did not consider it as invalidating *istinjāʾ* itself. Those who made a distinction between bones and dung, did so because they considered dung as unclean.

1.4.5. **Chapter 5 The Description of the Act of Removal**

The jurists agreed about the manner with which impurities are removed, and it is of three types, washing, wiping, and sprinkling, because these have been mentioned in the law and established through the traditions. They agreed that washing applies to all kinds of impurities and for all locations of uncleanliness, and that wiping is permitted with stones for the outlets and with dry herbage for boots and sandals. They agreed, likewise, that the long trailing part of the female dress is purified by the dry herbage in accordance with the apparent meaning of the tradition of Umm Salama.

They disagreed on three points related to these things and which form the principles of this chapter. The first is about sprinkling, as to what kind of impurity that can be purified with it. The second is about wiping, as to what is its object and the kind of impurity it can remove, after agreeing about what we have mentioned. The third point is about the stipulation of number (of repetitions) for washing and wiping.

A group of jurists said that sprinkling is specific to the urine of a child, who has not weaned. Another group of jurists made a distinction in this about the urine of a male and that of a female, saying that the urine of the male is to be sprinkled over, while that of the female is to be washed. A third group said that washing is the prescribed purification for a thing the uncleanliness of which is confirmed, while sprinkling is for that which is doubted. This is the opinion of Mālik ibn Anas, may Allāh be pleased with him.

The reason for their disagreement stems from the conflict of the apparent meanings of the traditions related to the issue, that is, their disagreement over the meanings. This is so as there are two established traditions about sprinkling. First is the tradition of ʿĀʾisha "that children used to be brought to the Prophet (God's peace and blessings be upon him) and he used to pray for them and rub the top of their mouths with dates moistened in his own mouth as well as pet them. A child was brought to him and he urinated on him. He called for water and poured it over the affected spot but did not wash it." In some versions it says, "he sprinkled over it but did not wash it". This has been recorded by al-Bukhārī. The other is the widely known tradition of Anas in which he described the prayer of the Messenger of Allāh (God's peace and blessings be upon him) in his house saying, "I took hold of the mat that had become dark because of old age and sprinkled water over it". Some of the jurists acted in accordance with the implication of ʿĀʾisha's tradition saying that this is specific to the urine of the child, and they exempted it from other categories of urine. Others preferred the traditions about washing to this tradition. This is Mālik's opinion, who confined the use of sprinkling to what is in the tradition by Anas and which relates to a garment the impurity of which is doubted, according to the apparent meaning.

Those who distinguished between the urine of a male child from that of a female relied on what has been related by Abū Dāwūd from Abū al-Samḥ about the saying of the Prophet (God's peace and blessings be upon him), "The urine of the female (child) is to be washed, and that of the male is to be sprinkled over". Those who did not make this distinction relied upon the analogy of the female child over the male in whose case an established tradition is laid down.

A group of jurists permitted wiping of any smeared object, in accordance with Abū Ḥanīfa's opinion, if the substance of the impurity was so removed; similarly, in the use of rubbing on the basis of analogy drawn from the views of those who maintain that each thing that removes the impurity can purify. Another group of jurists did not permit this, except in the cases agreed upon, that is, the outlet, the trailing dress of a woman, and boots, which are to be wiped with dry herbage and not with an unclean or undried object. This is Mālik's opinion. These jurists did not extend wiping to objects other than those mentioned in the law, while another group extended it to other objects.

The reason for their disagreement over this is whether wiping has been laid down in those as an exemption or as a primary *ḥukm*. Those who said that it is an exemption did not extend it to other things, that this, they did not construct an analogy upon it, while those who said that it is a primary *ḥukm* among the *aḥkām* of impurities, like the *ḥukm* of washing, did extend it.

In their dispute about number (of repetitions), a group of jurists stipulated only the removal of impurity in washing and wiping, while another group stipulated number (of repetitions) in wiping with stones as well as in washing. Some of those who stipulated number in washing restricted it to those objects about which number has been specifically mentioned in the transmitted texts, while others extended this to the remaining impurities also. Jurists who did not stipulate number, neither for washing nor for wiping, are Mālik and Abū Ḥanīfa. Those who stipulated number in wiping with stones, that is, three stones and nothing less, include al-Shāfiʿī and the Ẓāhirites. Among those who stipulated number in washing, are some who restricted it to the object that has been mentioned in the texts, that is, washing a utensil seven times after it has been licked by a dog, are al-Shāfiʿī and those who adopted his opinion. Those who extended this stipulating washing of impurities seven times include, to the best of my knowledge, Aḥmad ibn Ḥanbal. Abū Ḥanīfa stipulates washing thrice in the case of impurities that cannot be perceived, that is, which are legal impurities.

The reason for their disagreement about this is the conflict of the interpreted meaning of this form of worship with the apparent implication of the tradition in which number has been laid down. Those for whom the meaning of the command conveyed the removal of the substance of the impurity itself, did not stipulate number at all. They deemed the stipulation of number in wiping with stones, laid down in the established tradition of Salmān that contains the command about not performing *istinjāʾ* with less than three stones, as a recommendation, so as to reconcile the interpreted meaning of the law with the implication of this tradition. They also deemed the number stipulated about washing of the utensil following licking by a dog as an act of worship not based upon impurity, as has preceded concerning Mālik's opinion. Those who decided according to the literal meaning of these traditions, exempting them from the interpreted principle of the law, restricted the prescribed number to stated objects. Those who preferred the literal meaning over the interpreted principle extended the condition of number to all the remaining impurities.

The evidence of Abū Ḥanīfa about washing thrice is the saying of the Prophet (God's peace and blessings be upon him), "When any of you wakes up from sleep let him wash his hand thrice before putting it into his utensil".

1.4.6. Chapter 6 The Etiquette of *Istinjāʾ*

The majority of the *aḥkām* of *istinjāʾ* and of visiting the privy are interpreted by the jurists as a recommendation (*nadb*). These are known through the *sunna*, and include seeking a remote place when answering the call of nature according to the opinion in the school—refraining from speech, the prohibition of performing *istinjā'* with the right hand, not touching the genitals with the right hand, and others besides these that have been laid down in the traditions.

They disagreed about one widely known issue and that is the facing of the *qibla* or turning the back to it while relieving oneself or urinating. The jurists have three opinions about it. First, that it is not permitted at all to face the *qibla* while relieving oneself, whether in the privy or at any other location. Second, that this is permitted absolutely. Third, that it is permitted within settlements and townships, but not in the desert or places other than settlements and towns.

The reason for their disagreement are two established but conflicting traditions. First is the tradition of Abū Ayyūb al-Anṣārī in which the Prophet (God's peace and blessings be upon him) is reported to have said, "When you visit the privy, do not face the *qibla* or turn your back toward it, but turn toward the east or the west".[83] The second tradition is related from ʿAbd Allāh ibn ʿUmar, who said, "I ascended the roof of my sister Ḥafṣa's house and saw the Messenger of Allāh (God's peace and blessings be upon him) on top of two bricks, answering the call of nature, with his face toward Syria and his back toward the *qibla*".

The jurists are divided over these two traditions into three opinions. The first opinion is based upon the method of reconciliation, the second on the method of preference, and the third is the method of resorting to the original permission when there is a conflict. I mean by original permission (*barā'a aṣlīya*), the absence of a *ḥukm*.

Those who adopted the method of reconciliation construed the tradition of Abū Ayyūb al-Anṣārī to relate to the desert (open spaces), when there is no cover, and construed the tradition of Ibn ʿUmar to relate to the existence of a cover. This is Mālik's opinion.

Those who adopted the method of preference, preferred the tradition of Abū Ayyūb, for in case of conflict of two traditions, one prescribing a law and the other conforming to the general principle, which in this case is the absence of a *ḥukm*, and it is not known which one precedes the other in time, it is necessary to adopt the tradition that lays down a law. The reason for being obliged to act according to one tradition that has been transmitted by reliable narrators and to relinquish the other, although it has also been reported by reliable narrators, and despite the possibility that one of them was later than the other or it was laid down before it, is that we are not permitted to relinquish a law that must be acted upon as an obligation in the face of a conjecture imposing an

[83] This is because Medina, where the Prophet lived is north of Mecca, the seat of the *qibla*.

abrogation for which we have no authority, unless it has been related that this tradition was later. The probabilities that are relied upon for the *aḥkām*, that is, those that impose the *aḥkām* or withdraw them, are limited by the law. Moreover, not every probability that may be agreed upon is accepted. Thus, they say that the liability to act is not imposed by probable conviction, but is imposed by a definitive rule, they mean by it the existence of a definitive rule that makes it obligatory to act according to a probability.

This method that we have described is the method of Abū Muḥammad ibn Ḥazm al-Andalusī. This is an excellent method based on the principles of juristic reasoning, and it relies on the rule that doubt cannot remove what has been established by an evidence from the law. Those who adopted the method of recourse to the underlying principle in case of conflict have erected it on the rule that doubt terminates the *ḥukm* and withdraws it, and it is as if there is no rule. This is the method of Dāwūd al-Ẓāhirī, but Abū Muḥammad ibn Ḥazm opposed him on this issue, even though he is one of his followers.

The Qāḍī (Ibn Rushd) said, "This is what we sought to establish in this book from the issues we thought take the course of principles, and these are what have been expressed more often in the law, that is, most of them relate to issues expressly stated in the law, either directly or inherently. When we remember anything of this nature, we verify it in this book. Most of what I have relied upon, with respect to attributing opinions to their authors, is from *Kitāb al-Istidhkār*,[84] and I permit (request) whosoever finds errors on my part to correct them. It is Allāh Who grants help and success."

[84] It has been found on certain occasions that opinions have incorrectly been attributed to the Ḥanafites and the Shāfiʿites or to the founders of these schools. This could be the case for other jurists too. Ascertaining whether each and every opinion has been correctly attributed to its author is beyond the scope of this translation.

II

THE BOOK OF PRAYER (*ṢALĀH*)

Prayer is divided initially, and as a whole, into two kinds: obligatory and recommended. The discussion covering the principles of this form of worship is confined to four categories, that is, four parts. Part One is about the identification of the obligation and matters related to it. Part Two is about the identification of its three conditions: the condition of obligation, condition of validity, and the condition of completion. Part Three covers the identification of its acts and words, and these are its essential elements (*arkān*). Part Four is about its delayed performance and the identification of forms of rectification following irregularity, for it is the delayed performance of an act that would not be deemed as lapsed had it been duly performed.

2.1. **Part 1: Identification of the Obligation**

In this part there are four issues that are taken to be the principles of this topic. The first issue is about the exposition of its obligation. The second issue is about the number of its (daily) obligations. The third issue is about the individual for whom it is obligatory. The fourth issue is about the consequential obligation because of intentional relinquishment.

2.1.1. Issue 1: The obligation

Its obligation is evident from the Book, the *sunna*, and consensus. The fact that it is so widely known makes its discussion unnecessary.

2.1.2. Issue 2: The number of obligatory daily prayers

There are two opinions about the number of daily obligations. First is the opinion of Mālik, al-Shāfiʿī, and the majority, which maintains that only five (daily) prayers are obligatory. The second is the opinion of Abū Ḥanīfa and his disciples which maintains that the *witr* prayer is also obligatory along with the five (daily) prayers. Their disagreement about whether the obligation established from the *sunna* is *wājib* or *farḍ* is of no consequence.[85]

The reason for their disagreement lies in conflicting traditions. The traditions that confine the obligation to five prayers are explicit, widely known and well-established. The most vivid of these is the tradition of *isrāʾ*, "When the obligation reached the number five, Mūṣā (Moses) said to him (Muḥammad), 'Turn back to your Lord, for your *umma* cannot bear this'. He said, 'So I did'. The Exalted said, 'They are five but they are fifty (in reward value), My decree is not altered'". Further, there is the widely known tradition of the bedouin, who asked the Prophet (God's peace and blessings be upon him) about it and the Prophet (God's peace and blessings be upon him) said, "Five prayers in a day and night". He asked (again), "Am I obliged for more besides these?" He replied, "No, unless you observe them voluntarily".

Among the traditions that convey the meaning of the obligation of *witr* is that of ʿAmr ibn Shuʿayb from his father and from his grandfather "that the Messenger of Allāh (God's peace and blessings be upon him) said, 'Allāh has added a prayer for you, and this is the *witr*, so keep it up'". They also include the tradition of Ḥāritha ibn Ḥudhāfa who said, "The Messenger of Allāh (God's peace and blessings be upon him) came out to us and said, 'Allāh has commanded you to observe a prayer, which is better for you than the red camels. This is the *witr*. He has determined that you observe it in the time between the night prayer (*ʿishāʾ*) and the morning prayer (*fajr*)'". In addition, there is the tradition of Burayda al-Aslamī "that the Messenger of Allāh (God's peace and blessings be upon him) said, 'The *witr* stands confirmed, and he who does not observe it is not one of us'".

Those who maintained that an addition (over the five daily prayers) amounts to an abrogation, and for whom these traditions (about *witr*) did not reach a level of authenticity sufficient to abrogate the widely known and established traditions (that confine the obligation to five), preferred them (the latter). Further, the limitation of five is established by the tradition of *isrāʾ* in the words of the Exalted, "My decree is not altered", which apparently imply that nothing is to be increased or decreased, though they convey a stronger probability of decrease. And what is revealed as an informative sentence (not a command) is not subject to abrogation. Those for whom the strength of the traditions, which imply an addition over five prayers, reached a level where it was obligatory to act according to them deemed it necessary to abide by the addition, especially those who held that an addition does not imply abrogation. This, however, is not Abū Ḥanīfa's opinion.

[85] The distinction between *farḍ* and *wājib* is maintained by the Ḥanafites.

2.1.3. Issue 3: The person for whom prayer is obligatory

The person for whom it is obligatory is every pubescent Muslim, and there is no dispute about this.

2.1.4. Issue 4: The obligation arising from intentional relinquishment

With respect to the obligation in the case of the person who relinquishes it intentionally, and when he is ordered to pray refuses to do so, but does not deny its obligation, a group of jurists said that he should be executed, while another group said that he is to be punished and confined. Among those who maintained that he is to be executed, some made his execution obligatory as a result of his disbelief (*kufr*). This is the opinion of Aḥmad, Isḥāq, and Ibn al-Mubārak. Others, who upheld his confinement and punishment till he resumes praying, determined it as a *ḥadd* penalty, which is the opinion of Mālik, al-Shāfiʿī, Abū Ḥanīfa, his disciples, and of the Ẓāhirites.

The reason for this disagreement stems from the conflict of traditions. It is established from the Prophet (God's peace and blessings be upon him) who said, "Shedding the blood of a Muslim does not become lawful, except in three cases: disbelief after faith, fornication after marriage, and killing a human being when it is not in retaliation for another life". It is also related from the Prophet (God's peace and blessings be upon him) in the tradition of Burayda that he said, "The distinguishing factor between them and us is prayer, so he who relinquishes it has committed disbelief". In the tradition of Jābir, the Prophet (God's peace and blessings be upon him) said, "It is the (basis for) distinction between obedience and disbelief", or he said, "Polytheism is nothing but the relinquishment of prayer". Those who understood from the term disbelief here to be actual rejection deemed this tradition to be a commentary on the words of the Prophet (God's peace and blessings be upon him) "disbelief after faith [occurring in the tradition quoted above]". Those who deemed it (the use of the term disbelief here) merely as censure and reproach said that it means that his acts are like those of the disbelievers and that he resembles the disbelievers. It is just like saying, "a fornicator does not commit fornication and remain a believer" or "a thief does not commit theft and remain a believer". Thus, they held that *ḥadd* penalty is not to be imposed in this case.

The opinion of those who said that he is to be executed by way of *ḥadd* (penalty) is weak. They have nothing to rely on, except for a weak *qiyās al-shabah*, if that is possible here, that is, the comparison of prayer, the foremost command, with murder, the foremost prohibition. The term "*kufr*" is literally applied to mean "denial", and it is known that the person relinquishing prayer is not denying, unless he relinquishes it with such a belief. We, therefore, have two choices. First, if we interpret the tradition in the sense of "disbelief", it is binding on us to construe that the Prophet (God's peace and blessings be upon him) meant a person who rejects it while disbelieving it, thus committing disbelief. Second, to assign to the term "*kufr*" a meaning other than its primary application, and this is possible in two ways. First, by assigning to the individual the *ḥukm* assigned to a disbeliever, that is, with respect to execution and the remaining *aḥkām* for the disbelievers, even when he is not denying belief. Second, by saying that all his acts are like those of the disbelievers by way of censure and deterrence, in view of the fact that a person who fails to perform the prayer resembles the disbelievers in his attitude, for the disbeliever does not pray. This is similar to the saying of the Prophet (God's peace and blessings be upon him), "The fornicator does not commit fornication and remain a believer".

The decision by interpretation that his *ḥukm* is the *ḥukm* of a disbeliever cannot be taken, except through an evidence, for it is a *ḥukm* that has not been established by the law in a way that a decision can be based upon it directly. As there is no evidence indicating actual disbelief, which amounts to denial in our view, it is necessary that it be construed in its allegorical sense and not in a manner that has not been established in the *sharᶜ*. In fact, its opposite has been established, which is that the shedding of his blood is not permissible as he does not fall under any of the three cases mentioned in the law. So ponder over this, for it is evident. Allāh knows best. This means that there are two choices for us. We may either imply the existence of an assumed word in the text, if we regard failure to pray tantamount to disbelief, in which case it conforms to its meaning in the law, or we may to interpret it in the metaphorical sense. The interpretation leading to the application of the *ḥukm* of a disbeliever in all its manifestations, while the person is a believer, is something that is inconsistent with the general principles, especially when the tradition establishes the cases in which execution is applied due to disbelief or as a *ḥadd*. For this reason, this opinion is similar to the doctrine of those who impute the sinners with *kufr* (disbelief).

2.2. Part 2: The Conditions of Prayer

This part contains eight chapters. The first chapter is about the identification of the timings. The second is about the call for prayer (*adhān*) and the call for commencement (*iqāma*). The third chapter relates to the identification of the direction in prayer (*qibla*). The fourth chapter relates to the covering of the private parts (*satr al-ᶜawra*) and the dress for prayer. The fifth chapter covers the stipulation of purification from impurities in prayer. The sixth chapter is about the identification of places where prayer can be undertaken and those where it cannot. The seventh chapter deals with the conditions of the validity of prayer. The eighth chapter is about intention (*niyya*), and the question of its stipulation in prayer.

2.2.1. Chapter 1 The Timings for Prayer

This chapter is first divided into two sections. The first relates to the identification of the timings for prayer. The second examines the timings during which prayer is forbidden.

2.2.1.1. *Section 1: The prescribed timings*

This section is also divided into two sub-divisions. The first relates to regular prayer timings within which a prayer has to be performed (extended[86] as well as preferred).[87] The second relates to timings for those facing a necessity.

2.2.1.1.1. *Division 1: The obligatory daily prayer timings*

The basis for this topic are the words of the Exalted, "Worship at fixed hours hath been enjoined on the believers".[88] The Muslim jurists agreed that the five (obligatory) prayers have five determined periods, performance of prayer during which is a condition for the validity of the prayer. (They also agreed) that each of these periods is divided into preferred and extended parts. They disagreed about the limits of such preferred and extended parts. There are five issues in this.

2.2.1.1.1.1. Issue 1

They agreed, except for a deviant disagreement attributed to Ibn ʿAbbās and a reported dispute over the time of performing Friday congregational prayer (*jumuʿa*), as will be mentioned, that the beginning of the timing for the midday (*ẓuhr*) prayer, before which praying not allowed, is the declining of the sun. They disagreed with respect to the *ẓuhr* period on two points, the end of its extended timing and the time that is preferable (for prayer).

Mālik, al-Shāfiʿī, Abū Thawr, and Dāwūd said that the end of its extended timing is when the shadow of a thing becomes equal to its length. Abū Ḥanīfa said, in one narration from him, that it is when the shadow of a thing becomes twice its length, which is the beginning of the period of the next prayer (*ʿaṣr*). According to another report from him, the last timing for the noon

[86] A period of time that is longer than the time needed to perform the prayer prescribed.

[87] A period in which performance of the prayer is considered to have greater merit.

[88] Qur'ān 4 : 103.

prayer is when the shadow of a thing is equal to its length, while the first timing for the *ʿaṣr* prayer is when the shadow is twice the length (of a thing), and the period between those when the shadow is the same as the length and when it is twice as much is not suitable for the noon prayer. This (latter opinion) was upheld by his two disciples, Abū Yūsuf and Muḥammad.

The reason for disagreement over this is the conflict of traditions. It is related about the prayer led by Jibrīl (Gabriel) "that he prayed *ẓuhr* with the Prophet (God's peace and blessings be upon him) on the first day when the sun declined, and on the second day when the shadow of each thing was equal to its length. He then said, 'The timing is what is between these'". It is related that the Prophet (God's peace and blessings be upon him) said, "Your stay on earth compared to that of nations who came before you is like the length of the time which is between the *ʿaṣr* prayer and sunset. The People of the Torah were given the Torah and they acted upon it till it was midday, and became unable (to continue) after that. It was then granted to them *qīrāṭ*[89] after *qīrāṭ*. The People of Injīl (New Testament) were then given the Injīl and they acted upon it till it was the time for *ʿaṣr*, being unable to do so after that. It was then granted to them in *qīrāṭ* at a time. We were given the Qurʾān and we acted upon it till it was sunset. It was then granted to us two *qīrāṭ*s at a time. The People of the Book said, 'O Lord, you have given these people two *qīrāṭ*s at a time, while you gave us one at a time, when our performance was for a greater period?' Allāh, the Exalted, replied, 'Have I done any injustice in compensating you?' They said, 'No'. He said, 'Then it is My benevolence, I grant to whom I will'".

Mālik and al-Shāfiʿī followed the tradition in which Jibrīl led the Prophet in prayer, while Abū Ḥanīfa followed the apparent meaning in the other tradition. The reason is that if the interval between the beginning of *ʿaṣr* and sunset is shorter than that from the beginning of *ẓuhr* up to the time of *ʿaṣr*, in accordance with the implication of this tradition, it is necessary that the beginning of the time for *ʿasr* be when the shadow is more than the height of a thing, and that this be the end of the time for *ẓuhr*. Abū Muḥammad ibn Ḥazm said, "It is not as they believe. I have examined the matter and found that the shadow is equal to the height when nine hours and a fraction of the day have passed". The Qāḍī (Ibn Rushd) said, "I am doubtful about the fraction, I believe he said a third".

The evidence of those who upheld the continuation of the timings, that is, continuation without a dividing break, is the saying of the Prophet (God's peace and blessings be upon him), "The time of a prayer does not end till the time of the next prayer begins". This is an established tradition.

[89] *Qīrāṭ* is a measure of small lengths.

Regarding the preferred, more meritorious part of the prayer period, Mālik said that for the individual (praying alone) it is the first part, but it is recommended that in congregational mosques the preferred timing be delayed slightly (to permit worshippers to join). Al-Shāfiʿī said that the first part of the prayer period is always preferred, except in case of extreme heat. The same view has also been related from Mālik. A group of jurists said that the first part is always preferred for the individual as well as the congregation in mild weather, heat as well as in cold.

Disagreement about this is due to the conflict of traditions. There are two established traditions about this. The first is the saying of the Prophet (God's peace and blessings be upon him), "When the heat is intense, delay the prayer till it is cool, for the intensity of heat is a breath of Hell". The second is the report "that the Prophet (God's peace and blessings be upon him) used to say the *ẓuhr* prayer at the time of the hottest hour". The tradition of Khabbāb, related by Muslim, contains the words, "They complained to him about the heat of the ***ramḍā'*** (scorching heat) and he did not heed their complaint". It is recorded by Muslim. Zuhayr, the narrator of the tradition, said that he asked his Shaykh, Abū Isḥāq, about it saying "Is it about *ẓuhr*?" He replied, "Yes". He said, "Is it about its prompt performance?" He said. "Yes".

A group of jurists preferred the tradition about delaying till it is cool as it is explicit and interpreted the other traditions according to this as these were not so explicit. Another group of jurists preferred the latter traditions, because of the general application of the words of the Prophet (God's peace and blessings be upon him) when he was asked the question, "What acts are the best?" He replied, "Prayer, at the first appointed time". The tradition is agreed upon by al-Bukhārī and Muslim. However, the addition in it, that is, "at the first appointed time", is disputed.

2.2.1.1.1.2. Issue 2

They disagreed about the *ʿaṣr* prayer on two points. The first is about the merging of its first timing with the end of the timing for the *ẓuhr* prayer. Second, about its own end. With respect to the merging of the timings, Mālik, al-Shāfiʿī, Dāwūd, and a group of jurists agreed that the beginning of the timing for *ʿaṣr* prayer is, in fact, the end of the period for *ẓuhr*, and this occurs when the shadow of a thing becomes equal to its height. Mālik, on the other hand, maintained that the last portion of the period for *ẓuhr* and the first portion of the period for *ʿaṣr*—a stretch of time sufficient for four (ordinary) *rakʿas*—is a common time for both prayers. According to al-Shāfiʿī, Abū Thawr, and Dāwūd the end of the period for *ẓuhr* is the point of time at which the timing for *ʿaṣr* begins, and is an indivisible moment. Abū Ḥanīfa, as we have said, maintained that the first timing for *ʿaṣr* is that when the shadow of a thing is twice its height, and the reason for his disagreement with them over this has preceded.

Mālik's disagreement with al-Shāfiʿī, and with those who adopted the same opinion as his on this issue, is based on the conflict of the tradition about Jibrīl with the tradition of ʿAbd Allāh ibn ʿUmar. In the prayer led by Jibrīl, it is stated that he prayed *ẓuhr* with the Prophet (God's peace and blessings be upon him) on the second day at the time at which he had prayed *ʿaṣr* on the first day. The tradition of ʿAbd Allāh ibn ʿUmar is that the Prophet (God's peace and blessings be upon him) said, "The timing of *ẓuhr* continues as long as the timing of *ʿaṣr* has not begun". This has been recorded by Muslim. Those who preferred the tradition about Jibrīl, deemed the timing as merged, while those who preferred the tradition of ʿAbd Allāh, did not consider the timings as merged. In the case of the tradition about Jibrīl, it is possible to interpret it in such a way that would agree with the tradition of ʿAbd Allāh, for it is likely that the narrator (of the tradition about Jibrīl) overemphasized the fact due to the proximity of the timings. The tradition about the *imāma* of Jibrīl has been declared *sahīh* by al-Tirmidhī, while Ibn ʿUmar's tradition has been recorded by Muslim.

In their disagreement about the last timing for *ʿaṣr*, there are two narrations from Mālik. The first maintains that the last timing is when the shadow of each thing is twice its height. This is also al-Shāfiʿī's opinion. The second narration maintains that the last timing continues as long as the sun has not turned yellow. This is also Aḥmad ibn Ḥanbal's opinion. The Ẓāhirites said that the timing ends just one *rakʿa*-time before sunset.

The reason for their disagreement is based on the existence of three traditions, the apparent meanings of which conflict. The first is the tradition of ʿAbd Allāh ibn ʿUmar, recorded by Muslim, which states, "When you pray *ʿaṣr*, there is time for it till the sun turns yellow". Some of the versions say, "The time for *ʿaṣr* prevails till the sun turns yellow". The second is the tradition of Ibn ʿAbbās about the *imāma* of Jibrīl, which states that "he prayed *ʿaṣr* with him on the second day when the shadow of each thing was twice its height". The third is the widely known tradition of Abū Hurayra, "Anyone who has been able to perform a *rakʿa* of the *ʿaṣr* prayer before sunset has caught the time of *ʿaṣr*, and anyone who has been able to perform a *rakʿa* of the morning prayer before sunrise has caught the right time of the morning prayer".

Those who preferred the tradition about the *imāma* of Jibrīl deemed the last permissible[90] timing to be the time when the shadow of a thing is twice its height (, while those who preferred Ibn ʿUmar's tradition deemed the final

[90] In contrast with the meritorious, preferable early part of the period of prayer.

permissible time to be when the sun turns yellow).[91] Those who decided to prefer Abū Hurayra's tradition said that the timing for *ʿaṣr* continues till the time for a *rakʿa* is left prior to sunset. These (last) are the Ẓāhirites, as we have stated. The majority adopted the method of reconciliation between the tradition of Abū Hurayra, on the one hand, and the traditions of Ibn ʿUmar and Ibn ʿAbbās on the other, as it clearly opposed the other two while the two traditions of Ibn ʿAbbās and Ibn ʿUmar state proximate limits. It is for this reason that Mālik formed one view on the basis of the first and another on the basis of the second. The tradition of Abū Hurayra, however, gives a widely separate limit; therefore they said that the tradition of Abū Hurayra applies to those who have an excuse (like a woman whose blood discharge (*ḥayḍ*) ends just before that time).

2.2.1.1.1.3. Issue 3

They disagreed about the evening prayer (*maghrib*), whether it has an extended time like all other prayers? A group of jurists held that it has a limited time that is not extendible. This is the best known report from Mālik and al-Shāfiʿī. Another group of jurists held that it has an extended time between sunset and the disappearance of the evening twilight (*shafaq*). This was the opinion of Abū Ḥanīfa, Aḥmad, Abū Thawr, and Dāwūd, and this opinion has also been related from Mālik and al-Shāfiʿī.

The reason for their disagreement over this arises from the conflict of the tradition of the *imāma* of Jibrīl with the tradition of ʿAbd Allāh ibn ʿUmar. The tradition about the *imāma* of Jibrīl states that he offered the *maghrib* prayer at the same time (at sunset) on both days, while the tradition of ʿAbd Allāh says, "It is time for the *maghrib* prayer till the disappearance of *shafaq*". Those who preferred the tradition about the *imāma* of Jibrīl determined a single (limited) time for it, while those who preferred ʿAbd Allāh's tradition determined an extended time for it. The tradition of ʿAbd Allāh has been recorded by Muslim, while the tradition of the *imāma* of Jibrīl has not been recorded by either of the two shaykhs (al-Bukhārī and Muslim), that is, the tradition of Ibn ʿAbbās, which says that he led the prayer for the Prophet (God's peace and blessings be upon him) in ten prayers that explained the prayer timings and then said, "The time is between these two". What is stated in ʿAbd Allāh's tradition about this is also found in the tradition of Burayda al-Aslamī that has been recorded by Muslim, and is the fundamental source for this topic. They (the jurists) said that the tradition of Burayda is preferable as it is a later tradition belonging to the era of Medina and was in response to a

[91] Editor's note: The parenthetical statement is an addition in the manuscript published at Fās. We included it as it was necessary.

question about the timings of prayer, while the tradition of Jibrīl belongs to the initial stipulation of the duty (of prayer) at Mecca.

2.2.1.1.1.4. Issue 4

They disagreed about the second evening prayer (*ʿishāʾ*) on two points. First, about the beginning of its timing and second, about its end. About the beginning of its timing, Mālik, al-Shāfiʿī, and a group of jurists held that it is the disappearance of the red evening twilight, while Abū Ḥanīfa said that it is the disappearance of the white twilight that comes after the redness.

The reason for their disagreement over this issue stems from the equivocality of the term "*shafaq*" in the Arabic language. Just as *fajr* (morning) is of two kinds, so is *shafaq*: red and white. The disappearance of the white *shafaq* necessarily implies that what follows is the beginning of the night.[92] There is no disagreement among them that it is established from the tradition of Burayda and the tradition about the *imāma* of Jibrīl that he offered the night prayer on the first day at the disappearance of the *shafaq*.

The majority preferred their opinion on the basis of the established report "that the Messenger of Allāh (God's peace and blessings be upon him) used to offer *ʿishāʾ* after the disappearance of the moon on the third night", while Abū Ḥanīfa preferred his opinion on the basis of what is established about delaying *ʿishāʾ* and the recommendation for delaying it in the words of the Prophet (God's peace and blessings be upon him), "If I had not feared hardship for my *umma*, I would have delayed this prayer up to midnight".

They disagreed over the end of its latest timing into three opinions. First, that it is the first third of the night. Second, that it is midnight. Third, that it is up to sunrise. The first opinion, that is, it is the first third of the night, was held by al-Shāfiʿī and Abū Ḥanīfa, and is the widely known view of Mālik. A second report from Mālik is also related, which holds it to be midnight. The third view is that of Dāwūd.

The reason for disagreement over this derives from the conflict of traditions. In the tradition about the *imāma* of Jibrīl it is stated that he prayed with the Prophet (God's peace and blessings be upon him) on the second day at the end of the first third of the night. In the tradition of Anas he says that "The Prophet (God's peace and blessings be upon him) delayed *ʿishāʾ* till midnight". This has been recorded by al-Bukhārī. It is also reported in the tradition of Abū Saʿīd al-Khudrī and that of Abū Hurayra from the Prophet (God's peace and blessings be upon him) that he said, "If I did not fear

[92] A few lines follow this in the original text and have been placed in parentheses by the editor of the original. He mentions in a note that they occur in the Egyptian manuscript and not in the Fās manuscript. The statement does not sit well with the rest of the text and complicates it. It appears to be a gloss that has crept into the text. This statement has not been included in the translation.

hardship for my *umma* I would have delayed *ʿishāʾ* up to midnight". In the tradition of Ibn Qatāda it is implied that neglecting sleep is not significant, but what is significant is delaying a prayer till it is time for the next.

Those who based their opinion on the preference of the tradition about the *imāma* of Jibrīl fixed it as the third of the night, while those who preferred the tradition of Anas said that it is the middle of the night. The Ẓāhirites relied upon the tradition of Abū Qatāda saying that it is general and later in time than the tradition about the *imāma* of Jibrīl, and, therefore, abrogates it. Had it not abrogated it the conflict would have led to dropping the *ḥukm*. It is, therefore, necessary to abide by the prevailing consensus, as they agreed that the time lapses after the coming of the *fajr* time (dawn), but they disagreed about what is before that. In addition, they related from Ibn ʿAbbās that the time, in his view, was up to *fajr*. Thus, it becomes obligatory that the prevailing *ḥukm* about the (latest) time continue, till agreement about its lapsing earlier is found. I believe that this is also upheld by Abū Ḥanīfa.

2.2.1.1.1.5. Issue 5

They agreed that the first timing for the morning prayer is true dawn (the appearance of the morning twilight) and it ends at sunrise, except what is related from Ibn al-Qāsim and some of the disciples of al-Shāfiʿī that the latest timing is when there is light (i.e. daybreak). They disagreed about its preferred timing. The Kūfīs, Abū Ḥanīfa, his disciples, al-Thawrī, and most of the jurists of Iraq maintain that the best time for it is when there is light (the beginning of daybreak), while Mālik, al-Shāfiʿī, his disciples, Aḥmad ibn Ḥanbal, Abū Thawr, and Dāwūd maintained that darkness preceding light is the preferred time for it.

The reason for their disagreement stems from their dispute over the method of reconciling the apparent meanings of the traditions on this issue. It is reported from the Prophet (God's peace and blessings be upon him) through Rāfiʿ ibn Khadīj that he said, "Perform the morning prayer at the time of the daybreak. The more frequently you do so the greater reward there is for it". Yet, the Prophet (God's peace and blessings be upon him) is reported to have said, when asked about the best acts, "Prayer at its first appointed timing". Moreover, it is established about the Prophet (God's peace and blessings be upon him) "that after he offered the morning prayer, women used to depart wrapped in their woolen garments, and could not be recognized due to the darkness". The apparent meaning of this tradition is that this was his usual practice.

Those who maintained that the tradition of Rāfiʿ is particular (*khāṣṣ*), while the saying of the Prophet (God's peace and blessings be upon him) "in its first appointed timing", is general (*ʿāmm*), held that the former restricted the latter according to the well-known rule that the particular restricts the general. In this way they exempted the morning prayer from the general implication and rendered the tradition of ʿĀʾisha as a report of an occasional, and not the usual, practice implying permissibility. Thus, they maintained that "praying into the light is preferable to prayer in the darkness". Those who preferred the general tradition, because it is explicit and evident and also agrees with ʿĀʾisha's tradition, while Rāfiʿ's tradition is subject to interpretation, as it can be interpreted as emphasizing the coming of *fajr* and as such there is no conflict between it and the tradition of ʿĀʾisha nor with the reported generality in this issue, said that the preferred timing is the early portion of the time.

Those who maintained that the latest timing for the morning prayer is the clear light of daybreak confined it to those under compulsion, in the tradition in which the prophet (God's peace and blessings be upon him) said, "He who has performed one *rakʿa* of the morning prayer before sunrise has captured the morning prayer". This resembles what the majority hold about *ʿaṣr*, and it is strange that they turned away from it on this issue (of the morning prayer) and agreed with the Ẓāhirites (on the other issue). The Ẓāhirites, therefore, have a right to question them about the difference between the two (similar situations).

2.2.1.1.2. *Division 2: Timings in case of necessity and excuse*

The jurists of the regions, as we have said have confirmed the special prayer timings for necessity and excuse, while the Ẓāhirites have denied them. The reason for their disagreement has already been mentioned. Those who confirmed them disagreed over three points. First, what are the prayers to which these timings are applicable? Second, what are the limits of these timings? Third, who are the persons with an excuse for whom an exemption has been made with respect to these timings and their *aḥkām*, that is, with respect to the obligation of prayer and its waiver.

2.2.1.1.2.1. Issue 1

Mālik and al-Shāfiʿī agreed that this special timing is applicable to four prayers: a timing common between *ẓuhr* and *ʿaṣr*, and a timing common between *maghrib* and *ʿishāʾ*. They differed about their common aspect, as will be coming up in what follows. Abū Ḥanīfa opposed them saying that this timing is for *ʿaṣr* alone, and there is no timing here that is common between them.

The reason for their disagreement over this is based on their dispute about the permissibility of combining of two prayers (*jamʿ*) during a journey at a time fixed for one prayer. This will be discussed later. Those who acted upon the text laid down for the *ʿaṣr* prayer, that is, the established saying of the Prophet (God's peace and blessings be upon him), "He who is able to observe a *rakʿa* of the *ʿaṣr* prayer prior to sunset has been able to perform *ʿaṣr* (in time)", understood this to imply a concession, and did not permit it as a common timing for combination, because of the words of the Prophet (God's peace and blessings be upon him), "The timing of a prayer does not pass till the coming of the timing for the next". They also used other arguments—that we shall mention under the topic of combination—to maintain that this timing was only for the *ʿaṣr* prayer. Those who permitted a common timing in combination during a journey, permitted it for those facing a necessity on its analogy, as the case of the traveller too is that of necessity and excuse. On this basis they determined a time common between *ẓuhr* and *ʿaṣr*, and another common between *maghrib* and *ʿishāʾ*.

2.2.1.1.2.2. Issue 2

Mālik and al-Shāfiʿī disagreed over the last common timing for two prayers. Mālik said that it continues from the declining of the sun, for *ẓuhr* and *ʿaṣr*, to an extent of four *rakʿa*s for a resident and two *rakʿa*s for the traveller till a time sufficient for four *rakʿa*s for the resident and two *rakʿa*s for the traveller is left of the daytime. Thus, he determined the time specific to *ẓuhr* as the time for four *rakʿa*s in the case of the resident, and two *rakʿa*s for the traveller after the declining of the sun. He determined the time specific to *ʿaṣr* as the time for four *rakʿa*s for the resident and two *rakʿa*s for the traveller prior to sunset. It follows that a person who catches only the specific portion of a the time of prayer is obliged for the prayer that is specific to this time, if prayer was not binding upon him prior to this time.[93] A person who has more time than this is to perform both prayers together. He fixed the last time for capturing the *ʿaṣr* prayer (*ʿadāʾ* not *qaḍāʾ*), as that of one *rakʿa* prior to sunset. He determined similar common timings for *maghrib* and *ʿishāʾ* prayers, except that on one occasion he made the time specific to *maghrib* to be an amount of time enough for three *rakʿa*s prior to the break of the dawn, and at another occasion he deemed it enough for the last prayer, as he did for *ʿaṣr*, saying that it is a time enough for four *rakʿa*s, which agrees with analogy. Moreover, he deemed the last timing for this (as *ʿadāʾ*) to be the time required for one *rakʿa* prior to the break of the dawn.

Al-Shāfiʿī fixed a single limit for these common timings, which is a stretch of time sufficient for one *rakʿa* prior to sunset, and this for *ẓuhr* and *ʿaṣr*

[93] For example, if a woman begins discharging menstrual blood after the declining of the sun by a time sufficient for four *rakʿas*, she has to pray *ẓuhr* when the *hayḍ* ceases. And if an adolescent boy or a girl reaches puberty before sunset by a time sufficient for four *rakʿas*, he or she must pray *ʿaṣr*.

together; and the time sufficient for a *rakʿa* prior to the breaking of the dawn in the case of *maghrib* and *ʿishāʾ* together. It is also related from him that he said it is a moment sufficient for pronouncing *takbīr*, that is, a person who is able to pronounce *takbīr* prior to sunset is under an obligation to pray *ẓuhr* and *ʿaṣr* for that day.

Abū Ḥanīfa agreed with Mālik in that the last timing for *ʿaṣr* for those under duress is equivalent to the time of one *rakʿa* prior to sunset, but he did not agree about the common timings nor about timings specific to prayers.

The reason for their disagreement, that is, Mālik's and al-Shāfiʿī's, is whether the assertion about the common timing for two prayers together implies that there are two types of timings, a timing specific for them and a timing common to them, or whether it implies that there is a single common timing alone. Al-Shāfiʿī's argument is that combining (two prayers) indicates only a common timing, and not a timing specific to each. Mālik, on the other hand, constructed an analogy basing the common timings in the case of necessity upon the common extended timings. This means that as the extended timing for *ẓuhr* and *ʿaṣr* has a common timing and an extended timing, it is necessary that the situation be the same in cases of necessity. Al-Shāfiʿī does not agree with him about a common extended timing for *ẓuhr* and *ʿaṣr*.

Their disagreement in this issue is based, Allāh knows best, on their disagreement over the prior issues, so ponder over it, as it is evident, Allāh knows best.

2.2.1.1.2.3. Issue 3

The jurists agreed that these timings, that is, the timings of necessity, pertain to four types of people: a menstruating woman entering the period of purity or who begins menstruating before she has prayed; the traveller who remembers prayer in these timings at a time when he is in a settlement, or a settler who remembers it when he is travelling; a minor who attains puberty during these timings; and a disbeliever who accepts Islam. They disagreed about the person who has fainted. Mālik and al-Shāfiʿī said that his *ḥukm* is like that of a menstruating woman and is entitled to these timings, for he is not obliged to make up (by way of *qaḍāʾ*) for the prayer that he misses because of fainting. According to Abū Ḥanīfa, however, he is obliged to make up for the prayer he has missed when the number of (lapsed) prayers is less than five. Thus, in his view, if he recovers from his fainting spell, he prays whenever he recovers. In the opinion of the others, if he recovers during the timings of necessity, he is obliged for the prayer within whose timing he recovers, but if he does not recover during such a time, the prayer is not binding upon him. The case of the person fainting will be treated in greater detail later.

They agreed that if the woman becomes pure within a prayer timing, this prayer alone is obligatory upon her. According to Mālik, if she becomes pure and enough time for four *rakʿas* is left prior to sunset, then she is obliged for *ʿaṣr* alone, but if the time left is enough for five *rakʿas*, she is under an obligation for both prayers, *ẓuhr* and *ʿaṣr*. In al-Shāfiʿī's view, if the time for a single *rakʿa* remains, she is obliged to observe both prayers together, as we have said, and according to his second opinion, she is to pray even when the time left is enough for a *takbīr*. The same is the case of the traveller, in Mālik's view, who has forgotten to pray and becomes a resident within these timings, or is a settler who is now travelling. Similarly, in the case of a disbeliever, who converts to Islam during these timings, that is, this prayer is obligatory upon him. The case of the minor is also similar.

The reason for Mālik's considering a *rakʿa* as a part of the last timing, and al-Shāfiʿī's considering a part of a *rakʿa*, like the *takbīr*, as the limit, is the saying of the Prophet (God's peace and blessings be upon him), "Whoever is able to perform a *rakʿa* of *ʿaṣr* prior to the setting of the sun has caught the prayer of *ʿaṣr* (in time)". This, in Mālik's view, is an indication of the minimum pointing to the maximum, while in al-Shāfiʿī's view it is the maximum indicating the minimum. He (al-Shāfiʿī) supported this with the report, "Whoever is able to perform one prostration prior to the setting of the sun has been able to perform *ʿaṣr* (in time)". Since a prostration is just one part of a *rakʿa*, he concluded that whoever is able to pronounce a *takbīr* prior to the setting or the rise of the sun has been able to perform his prayer in time.

Mālik maintains that the time for the menstruating woman is to be reckoned from the time when her period of purity terminates, so also the minor who attains puberty. If she is a disbeliever, her time is reckoned from the moment of conversion to Islam and not the termination of her period of purity, but there is disagreement over this. The person under a fainting spell is, in Mālik's view, like the menstruating woman, while he is like a disbeliever who has converted, in ʿAbd al-Malik's view. Mālik maintains that a menstruating woman, who begins to menstruate at a time before she has observed the prayer, her delayed performance (*qaḍāʾ*) is waived, while al-Shāfiʿī maintains that *qaḍāʾ* is obligatory upon her. *Qaḍāʾ*, in fact, is obligatory in the opinion of those who maintain that prayer becomes obligatory, with the coming of the prayer time Thus, if a woman menstruates after the start of the time for prayer and the passage of a period sufficient for the prayer, *qaḍāʾ* of this prayer is obligatory upon her. This, however, is not the view of those who maintain that prayer becomes obligatory not with the commencement of its time, but by the last part of it, which is Abū Ḥanīfa's view and not Mālik's. This, as you can see, is necessary in accordance with Abū Ḥanīfa's opinion, I mean, conforming with his principles, but not according to the principles of Mālik.

2.2.1.2. *Section 2: The Proscribed timings*

The jurists disagreed about the times during which prayer (*ṣalāh*) is forbidden. First, about their number, and second, about the types of prayers affected by the proscription.

2.2.1.2.1. Issue 1

The jurists agreed that there are three time-segments in which prayer is proscribed: the time of sunrise, the time of sunset, and the interval between the moment the worshipper has finished the dawn (*ṣubḥ*) prayer and sunrise. They disagreed about two timings: the time of the declining of the sun and the time after performing *ʿaṣr* prayer (up to sunset).

Mālik and his disciples maintained that the proscribed times are four: the times of sunrise, sunset, the time after the dawn prayer up to sunrise, and the time after *ʿaṣr* up to sunset. They permitted prayer at the declining of the sun. Al-Shāfiʿī maintained that all these five time-segments are proscribed, except the time of the declining of the sun on Friday, and he permitted prayer during this time. A group of jurists exempted from this (proscription) the time after *ʿaṣr*.

The reason for disagreement over this is one factor out of two. First, the conflict of a tradition with a tradition, and second the conflict of a tradition with practice, in the view of those who acknowledge practice, that is, the practice of the people of Medina, as is the principle of Mālik ibn Anas. When the proscription had been laid down and there was no opposition through words or acts, the jurists agreed upon it, but when a source of disagreement was found conflict occurred. Their disagreement over the time of the declining of the sun arises from the conflict of a tradition with practice. This is so as it has been established through the tradition of ʿUqba ibn ʿĀmir al-Juhanī that he said, "There were three times in which the Messenger of Allāh used to prohibit us from praying and burying our dead: when the sun begins to rise till it is fully risen, when the sun is at its height till it begins to decline, and when the sun begins to set till it sets completely". It has been recorded by Muslim. The tradition of Abū ʿAbd Allāh al-Ṣanābhī, which has been recorded by Mālik in his *al-Muwaṭṭaʾ*, conveys the same meaning, but its chain of transmission is incomplete.

Some of the jurists prohibited prayer during all these three periods, while others exempted from this (prohibition) the time of the declining of the sun, either always, in Mālik's opinion, or only for Friday, which is al-Shāfiʿī's view. Mālik, who regards the Medinan practice as a source of law, and found only two timings in practice, but not the third, that is, at the time of the declining of the sun, made an exemption for the prohibition and permitted prayer during that time deeming the proscription as abrogated by practice. Those who did not consider Medinan practice to be a source of law abided by the original principle of proscription. We have already talked about practice and its legal force in our book on juristic reasoning, which goes by the name of *uṣūl al-fiqh*.[94]

Al-Shāfiʿī based his opinion on the tradition related by Ibn Shihāb from Thaʿlabah from Ibn Abī Mālik al-Qaraẓī, which proved to be authentic in his view. It states that they used to pray on Fridays until ʿUmar came out (for the Friday prayer), and it is known that ʿUmar used to come out after the declining of the sun, as is established from the tradition about the carpet that was spread next to the western wall of the mosque; ʿUmar used to come out when it was completely covered with the shade of the wall. Further, he relied on what is related by Abū Hurayra "that the Messenger of Allāh (God's peace and blessings be upon him) prohibited prayer at noon till the sun declined, except for Friday". He, therefore, exempted prayer at the time of the declining of the sun on Fridays from this proscription.[95] This tradition was strengthened, in his view, by the practice during the days of ʿUmar, though the tradition itself was deemed weak by him. Those who preferred the established tradition on this issue followed the original proscription (of praying during the declining of the sun even on Fridays).

Their disagreement about prayer after the *ʿaṣr* prayer is based upon the conflict of established traditions, and there are two conflicting traditions about this. First is the tradition of Abū Hurayra that is agreed upon for its authenticity (by al-Bukhārī and Muslim) "that the Messenger of Allāh (God's peace and blessings be upon him) prohibited prayer after the *ʿaṣr* prayer till the sun had set, and prayer after the dawn prayer till the sun had risen (completely)". The second is the tradition of ʿĀʾisha who said, "The messenger of Allāh (God's peace and blessings be upon him) never relinquished two prayers in my house, neither secretly nor publicly, two *rakʿa*s before the dawn prayer and two *rakʿa*s after *ʿaṣr*". Those who preferred Abū Hurayra's tradition upheld prohibition, while those who preferred ʿĀʾisha's tradition, or held it to have abrogated the other, for it was an act that he (God's peace and blessings be upon him) used to undertake up to the time of his death, upheld permissibility. Umm Salama, however, relates a tradition that opposes ʿĀʾisha's tradition, as it states "that she saw the Messenger of Allāh (God's peace and blessings be upon him) praying two

[94] It has been difficult to ascertain whether this book of the author exists in published or manuscript form. If the manuscript does exist, it deserves to be published.

[95] The dispute here is not about the Friday prayer, which starts like *ẓuhr* prayer does, every day after the declining of the sun. The disagreement is about performing other prayers, like the *nāfila*, at the time of the declining of the sun.

*rakʿa*s after *ʿaṣr* and asked him about them. He said, 'Some people of ʿAbd al-Qays visited me and kept me from praying the two *rakʿa*s after *ẓuhr*, and these are those two *rakʿa*s' ".

2.2.1.2.2. Issue 2

The jurists disagreed about the prayers that are not permitted during these prohibited periods. Abū Ḥanīfa and his disciples maintained that prayers are not permitted in these periods at all, neither prescribed obligation, nor a *sunna* prayer, nor the supererogatory prayers, except the *ʿaṣr* prayer of the day. They further said that delayed performance (*qaḍāʾ*) of the *ʿaṣr* prayer is permitted at sunset if a person has forgotten it.

Mālik and al-Shāfiʿī agreed that delayed performance (*qaḍāʾ*) of obligatory prayers is permitted during these prohibited periods. Al-Shāfiʿī also held that the only prayers that are not permitted during these periods are the supererogatory prayers without a necessitating cause, but those with a cause, like the funeral prayer, are permitted during such periods. Mālik agreed with him about these prayers after *ʿaṣr* and after the dawn prayer, that is, with respect to all *sunna* prayers, but he exempted those that are observed due to a voluntary cause (pertaining to the worshipper himself), like the two *rakʿa*s upon entering the mosque, for al-Shāfiʿī permits these two *rakʿa*s after *ʿaṣr* and after the dawn prayer, while Mālik does not.

Mālik's opinion differed about the permissibility of *sunna* prayers at sunrise and sunset. Al-Thawrī maintained that the prayers not permitted during these times are those that are not obligatory (*farḍ*) prayers, and he did not make a distinction between the *sunna* and the supererogatory prayers.

Three opinions are thus arrived at in this issue. First, that prayer is not permitted at all (during these prohibited periods). Second, that these are *sunna* or supererogatory prayers, and are not the obligatory prayers. Third, that these are the supererogatory prayers and not the *sunan*. In pursuance of the narration, in which Mālik prohibited the funeral prayer during sunset, we arrive at a fourth opinion. This opinion prohibits the supererogatory prayers alone after the break of dawn and after *ʿaṣr*, and both supererogatory and *sunna* prayers during sunset and sunrise.

The reason for disagreement is their dispute over reconciling the conflicting general implications on this issue, that is, those occurring in the traditions, as to which is restricted by the other. For example, the general meaning of the words of the Prophet (God's peace and blessings be upon him), "When one of you forgets to perform a prayer, let him perform it when he remembers it", implies that he may do so at any time. Yet, the Prophet's saying in the traditions proscribing prayers in these (stated) periods, like "The Messenger of Allāh (God's peace and blessings be upon him) proscribed prayers during these times", implies the inclusion (in the prohibition) of all categories of prayers, obligatory, *sunan*, and supererogatory. When we construe the traditions in their general meanings a conflict occurs between them, which belongs to the category of conflict occurring between the general and particular words, either with respect to the time, or with respect to the term '*ṣalāh*'.

Those who decided to make the exception with respect to time, that is, the exception of the particular from the general, prohibited prayers absolutely during these times.[96] Those who made an exception for the obligatory prayers, whose *qaḍā'* is prescribed, did so from the general implication of the term *ṣalāh* that is applicable to the proscribed prayers, prohibiting what is besides the obligatory in these timings.[97]

Mālik preferred his opinion about the exception made for obligatory prayers from the general term *ṣalāh* on the basis of the reported saying of the Prophet (God's peace and blessings be upon him), "He who has been able to pray a *rak'a* of *'aṣr* prior to sunset has performed *'aṣr* (in time)". It is for the same reason that the Kūfī jurists made an exemption for the obligatory *'aṣr* prayer of the day out of other obligatory prayers, but it was binding upon them, consequently, to have made an exemption for the morning prayer too due to the existence of a text about it. They may not refute this on the basis of their opinion that one observing a *rak'a* prior to sunrise crosses over into the proscribed timing, while one observing a *rak'a* prior to sunset moves into a permissible timing. The Kūfīs, however, may respond to this by saying that this tradition does not indicate the exemption of the prescribed obligatory prayers from the general implication of the term *ṣalāh* to which the proscription is related in these periods, as the *'aṣr* prayer of the day is not implied in the meaning of the remaining obligatory prayers. Similarly, they could have said the same about the dawn prayer, even if they had conceded that its *qaḍā'* may be performed during the proscribed time.

The disagreement of the jurists, in the last analysis, refers to the question of whether the exception contained in the words belongs to a category of a particular word through which the particular is intended, or whether it belongs to a category of the particular word through which the general is implied? The reason is that those who held that the implication here is restricted to the *'aṣr* and the dawn prayers that have been mentioned in the text, considered it to be from the category of the particular word intended for a particular meaning, while those who said that the implication here is not for the *'aṣr* prayer alone, or for the dawn prayer, but extends to all the obligatory prayers, considered it

[96] By qualifying the first tradition with the second.

[97] By restricting the second tradition with the first, and by using the term *ṣalāh* in the first tradition to mean obligatory prayers.

to be a particular word implying the general. If this is the case, then there is no definitive evidence here that the obligatory prayers are exempted from the term "lapsed prayers", just as there is no evidence here, neither definitive nor probable, for the exemption of the particular time mentioned in the proscribing traditions, from the general implication of timings, laid down in the prescribing traditions, let alone the exemption of a particular prayer, mentioned in the prescribing traditions, from the general implication about prayer, laid down in the prohibiting traditions. This is evident, for when two traditions are in conflict and each carries a general and a particular implication, it is not required to give predominance to one of them without an evidence, I mean, exempting the particular implication of one tradition from the general implication of the other or vice versa. This is clear, Allāh knows best.

2.2.2. **Chapter 2** ***Adhān* and *Iqāma***

This chapter is also divided into two sections. The first is about *adhān* (the call for prayer). The second is about *iqāma* (the call for the commencement of prayer, or the second call for prayer).

2.2.2.1. *Section 1*: *Adhān*

This section is subdivided into five divisions. First about the description of the *adhān*. Second, about its *ḥukm*. Third, about its timing. Fourth, about its (prescribed) conditions. Fifth, about the response of the listener.

2.2.2.1.1. *Division 1*: *The description of* adhān

The jurists disagreed about *adhān* giving four widely known descriptions. The first prescribes the dual pronouncement of *takbīr*, four repetitions of the *shahāda*, and the dual pronouncement of the remaining (words). This is the opinion of the jurists of Medina, Mālik and the others. The later followers of Mālik preferred *tarjīʿ*, which requires the dual pronouncement of the *shahāda* in a lower tone followed by its dual pronouncement in a louder voice. The second is the Meccan version of the *adhān*, which was upheld by al-Shāfiʿī. It requires four pronouncements of the first *takbīr* and the two *shahāda*s, and the dual pronouncement of the remaining *adhān*. The third description is that of the Kūfīs. It involves four pronouncements of the first *takbīr* and the dual pronouncement of the remaining parts of the *adhān*. This was Abū Ḥanīfa's opinion. The fourth description is that of the *adhān* of the Baṣrans. It requires four pronouncements of the first *takbīr*, three pronouncements of *shahāda*, of *ḥayya ʿala'ṣ-ṣalāh*, and of *ḥayya ʿala'l-falāḥ*. The *muʾadhdhin* begins with *ashʾhadu an lā ilāha illaʾllāhu* till he reaches *ḥayya ʿalaʾl-falāḥ*, he then repeats them a second time, I mean, the four sentences, one after the other, and then repeats them a third time. This was the opinion of al-Ḥasan al-Baṣrī and of Ibn Sīrīn.[98]

The reason for the difference between these four descriptions is the conflict of the traditions and the communication of a differing practice to the jurists. The jurists of Medina argue for their opinion on the basis of the continuous practice prevailing in Medina. The same is the case with the Meccans, who argue on the basis of the practice reaching them, so also the Kūfīs and the Baṣrans. Each group has traditions that support their opinion.

The dual pronouncement of *takbīr* in the beginning, in accordance with the view of the jurists of Ḥijāz, is related through authentic chains from Abū Maḥdhūra and ʿAbd Allāh ibn Zayd al-Anṣārī, as is its fourfold pronouncement related from both of them through different chains. Al-Shāfiʿī said that these are additions that it is obligatory to accept, as they are supported by the communication of the practice at Mecca. With respect to *tarjīʿ* that was preferred by the later followers of Mālik, it is related through Abū Qudāma, although Abū ʿUmar said that Abū Qudāma is considered a weak narrator by them (the traditionists). As for the Kūfīs, they rely on the tradition of Ibn Abī Laylā, which says "that ʿAbd Allāh ibn Zayd saw a man in a dream who stood in the gap of a wall wearing two green garments; he made the call for prayer repeating twice, and then made the *iqāma*, repeating twice. He informed the Messenger of Allāh (God's peace and blessings be upon him) about it, after which Bilāl stood up and made the call repeating twice, and then made the *iqāma* repeating twice". The tradition reported by al-Bukhārī is from the report by Anas only, which says, "Bilāl was commanded to proclaim the *adhān* repeating twice and to make *iqāama* in single pronouncements, except the sentence 'prayer is about to commence', which is to be repeated twice". The version recorded by Muslim through Abū Maḥdhūra is in accordance with the description of the *adhān* of Hijāz.

It was due to the existence of this conflict about the versions of the *adhān* that Aḥmad ibn Ḥanbal and Dāwūd maintained that these differing descriptions have been prescribed by way of choice and not as an obligation to follow one of them, and that people have a choice in this matter.

They disagreed about the pronouncement by the *muʾadhdhin* for the morning prayer, "prayer is better than sleep", whether it is to be pronounced or not. The majority maintained that it is to be pronounced, while others held that it is not to be pronounced as it is not a part of the *adhān* practiced as a *sunna*. This was upheld by al-Shāfiʿī. The reason for their disagreement is

[98] Thus, according to their unanimous view, the *adhān* is to be concluded with the words *lā ilāha illaʾllāh*. This comes after the double *takbīr*.

their dispute whether it was pronounced in the days of the Prophet (God's peace and blessings be upon him), or whether it was added during the reign of ʿUmar.

2.2.2.1.2. *Division 2*: *The* ḥukm *of* adhān

The jurists disagreed about the *ḥukm* of *adhān*, whether it is obligatory or an emphatic *sunna*, and if it is obligatory whether it is a universal obligation or a communal one. It is related from Mālik that *adhān* is an obligation for congregational mosques, and it is related that it is an emphatic *sunna* (for them). He did not consider it an obligation for the individual, or even a *sunna*. Some of the Ẓāhirites said that it is a universal obligation, while others said that it is an obligation upon groups, whether on a journey or in a settlement. Some other Ẓāhirites maintained that it is obligatory for a group during travel. Al-Shāfiʿī and Abū Ḥanīfa agreed that it is a *sunna* for the individual and the group, except that it is emphatic in the case of the group. Abū ʿUmar said that there is complete agreement that it is an emphatic *sunna* or an obligation for persons in a settlement, because of the tradition "that the Messenger of Allah (God's peace and blessings be upon him) did not recite the *adhān* when he heard the call, but he did so when he did not hear it".

The reason for their disagreement is the conflict in understanding the apparent meanings of the traditions. It is established that the Messenger of Allah (God's peace and blessings be upon him) said to Mālik ibn al-Ḥuwayrith and his companion, "When you are on a journey, pronounce the *adhān* and the *iqāma*, and let the eldest among you lead the prayers". Similarly, it is related that this was the continuous practice of the Messenger of Allāh (God's peace and blessings be upon him) (when he was) in a congregation. Those who understood from this an absolute obligation said that it is obligatory (though they differed whether it is so only) upon groups or upon individuals as well. The first opinion is related by Ibn al-Mughallis from Dāwūd. Those who understood it to be an invitation to the group for prayer said that it is a *sunna* for the mosques or an obligation for those locations where the congregation assembles. The reason for disagreement is its (the *adhān's*) vacillation between being one of the pronouncements of prayer as its integral part or a means toward assembly.

2.2.2.1.3. *Division 3*: *Time for* adhān

The jurists agreed unanimously that *adhān* is not to be proclaimed before the (commencement of the) prescribed period of the prayer, except in the case of the morning prayer, over which they disagreed. Mālik and al-Shāfiʿī held that it is permitted to make the call before *fajr*, but Abū Ḥanīfa prohibited this. A group of jurists maintained that if the call is made before *fajr* another call is to be made after *fajr*, because the obligation in their view is for *adhān* after *fajr*. Abū Muḥammad ibn Ḥazm said that the call must be made after the commencement of the prescribed timing (for prayer), but if the call is made a short while before the timing it is permitted when the interval is short, just sufficient for the first *mu'adhdhin* to descend and the second to ascend.

The reason for their disagreement is that there are two conflicting traditions on this issue. The first is an authentic and widely known tradition, which is the saying of the Prophet (God's peace and blessings be upon him), "Bilāl makes the call when it is still night, so eat and drink till Ibn Umm Maktūm makes the call". Ibn Umm Maktūm was a blind man, who did not make the call till he was told that it is morning. The second tradition is related from Ibn ʿUmar "that Bilāl made the call before the break of dawn, so the Prophet (God's peace and blessings be upon him) ordered him to return and proclaim: 'The servant [of Allah] [that is, Bilāl] had slept'". The tradition of the jurists of Hijāz is more authentic, while the tradition of the Kūfīs has been related by Abū Dāwūd and declared authentic by many traditionists. The jurists decided with respect to these two traditions to adopt either the method of reconciliation or the method of preference. Those who adopted the method of preference were the jurists of Ḥijāz. They maintained that the tradition about Bilāl is more authentic and relying on it is more plausible. The Kūfī jurists adopted the method of reconciliation. They maintained that it is possible the call was made by Bilāl at a time that was mistakenly taken to be the time of *fajr*, as his eyesight was weak, while the call was made by Ibn Umm Maktūm when the time of dawn was certainly due. This is supported by what is related from ʿĀ'isha, who said, "The difference in time between their calls was a moment sufficient for one to descend and the other to ascend".

Those who combine the two, that is, making the call before *fajr* and after it, do so on the basis of the obvious implication of what is related specifically about the morning prayer, I mean, in the time of the Messenger of Allah (God's peace and blessings be upon him) two calls were made by two *mu'dhdhin*s, Bilāl and Ibn Umm Maktūm.

2.2.2.1.4. *Division 4: The conditions of* adhān

This division includes eight issues. The first is whether it is a condition that the person who makes the call be the same person who pronounces the *iqāma*? Second, whether it is a condition of *adhān* that it should not be interrupted by any conversation? Third, whether it is a condition that the *mu'adhdhin* be in a state of ritual purification? Fourth, is it a condition that the *mu'adhdhin* face the *qibla*? Fifth, whether it is a condition that the call be made while standing? Sixth, whether a call made while the *mu'adhdhin* is riding is deemed reprehensible (*makrūh*). Seventh, whether puberty is a condition for the person making the call? Eighth, whether it is a condition that no wages be taken for making the call?

About the issue of two men, one making the call and the other pronouncing the *iqāma*, the majority of the jurists of the regions maintain that this is permitted, while some maintained that this is not permitted. The reason for this disagreement is the existence of two conflicting traditions. First is al-Ṣudāʾī's tradition, who said, "I went up to the Messenger of Allāh, and when it was close to the dawn he ordered me to make the call. He then stood up for prayer and Bilāl came to pronounce the *iqāma*. The Messenger of Allāh said, 'The brother from Ṣudāʾ made the call, and he who makes the call is to pronounce the *iqāma*'". The second is the report that when ʿAbd Allāh ibn Zayd saw the *adhān* in a dream, the Messenger of Allāh ordered Bilāl to make the call. He then ordered ʿAbd Allāh, to pronounce the *iqāma*.

Those who adopted the method of abrogation maintained that ʿAbd Allāh ibn Zayd's tradition is earlier in time, while that of al-Sudāʾī is later. Those who adopted the method of preference said that ʿAbd Allāh ibn Zayd's tradition is more authentic, as al-Ṣudāʾī's tradition is an individual narration from ʿAbd al-Raḥmān ibn Ziyād al-Ifrīqī, who is not acceptable to them.

Their disagreement about (the permissibility of) wages for *adhān* is based on the dispute about the authenticity of the tradition relevant to this issue, that is, the tradition of ʿUthmān ibn Abī al-ʿĀṣ, who said, "One of the last instructions that the Messenger of Allāh gave me was to select a person for *muʾadhdhin* who would not take wages for making the call". Those who prohibited this also made the analogy for *adhān* upon prayer.

The reason for disagreement over the remaining conditions is based upon the analogy of *adhān* upon prayer. Those who constructed such an analogy imposed such conditions as are found for prayer, while those who did not construct the analogy did not impose them. Abū ʿUmar ibn ʿAbd al-Barr said that we have related from Abū Wāʾil ibn Ḥujr the tradition that "it is verified and is a practised *sunna* that no one makes the call unless he is standing, nor when he is ritually purified". He said that the words of Abū Wāʾil, who was one of the Companions, that "it is a *sunna*" moves it to the category of *musnad* (attributed to the Prophet), which is stronger than analogy.

The Qāḍī (Ibn Rushd) said that al-Tirmidhī has recorded (a tradition) from Abū Hurayra that the Prophet (God's peace and blessings be upon him) said, "No one is to make the call except after ablution".

2.2.2.1.5. *Division 5: What the listener says on hearing the* adhān

The jurists disagreed about the response of the listener to the *muʾadhdhin*. A group of jurists said that he repeats, word for word, what the *muʾadhdhin* says till the end of the call, while others said that he repeats what the *muʾadhdhin* says, except that when the *mu'adhdhin* says, "Come for prayer, come for salvation", the listener is to say, "There is no might and no power, but that with Allāh".

The reason for disagreement over this is the conflict of traditions. It is reported in a tradition from Abū Sa'īd al-Khudrī that the Messenger of Allāh (God's peace and blessings be upon him) said, "When you hear the *mu'adhdhin*, repeat what he says". It is reported by way of 'Umar ibn al-Khaṭṭāb and in a tradition from Mu'āwiya that the listener in response to "Come for prayer, come for salvation", should say: "There is no might and no power, but that with Allāh". Those who adopted the method of preference followed the general implication of Abū Sa'īd al-Khudrī's tradition, while those who qualified this general implication with the specific content (of the other tradition), reconciled the two traditions, and this is Mālik ibn Anas's opinion.

2.2.2.2. *Section 2*: Iqāma

They disagreed over *iqāma* on two points: its *ḥukm* and description. According to the jurists of the regions, its *ḥukm* is that of an emphatic *sunna* that is greater in strength than that for *adhān*, for individuals as well as for groups. In the Ẓāhirite view, it is an obligation, but I am not aware of whether it is an independent obligation or as one of the obligatory parts of prayer. The distinction is that according to the former opinion prayer does not become invalid if it is relinquished, but on the basis of the latter view it does. Ibn Kināna, one of the disciples of Mālik, said that if it is relinquished intentionally prayer is invalidated.

The reason for disagreement is their dispute about whether it comprises a part of the acts that were meant to be an unfolding of the unexplained command of performing prayer, and, therefore, it has to be construed as an obligation, because of the words of the Prophet (God's peace and blessings be upon him), "Pray as you see me praying", or whether it comprises acts that have to be construed as a recommendation. The apparent meaning of Mālik ibn al-Ḥuwayrith's tradition implies that it constitutes an obligation, either for the group or for the individual.

Its description, according to Mālik and al-Shāfi'ī, constitutes a *takbīr* in the beginning, which is twice, and the remaining is once, except the words, "Prayer is about to commence", which are pronounced once in Mālik's view and twice in al-Shāfi'ī's. According to the Ḥanafites, the *iqāma* is pronounced in pairs, while Aḥmad ibn Ḥanbal favoured an option between single and double pronouncement, in accordance with his opinion that there is a choice in making calls.

The reason for disagreement springs from the conflict of Anas's tradition about this issue with that of Ibn Abī Laylā, which has preceded. In the authentic tradition of Anas, Bilāl was ordered to call the *adhān* in a double pronouncement and the *iqāma* in a single pronouncement, except the words, "Prayer is about to commence". In Ibn Abī Laylā's tradition Bilāl was ordered to call the *adhān* as well as the *iqāma* in a double pronouncement.

The majority of the jurists maintain that women are under no obligation to pronounce the *adhān* or the *iqāma*. Mālik held that if they pronounce the *iqāma* it is better, while al-Shāfiʿī said that it is preferable if they pronounce both *adhān* and *iqāma*. Isḥāq was of the view that they are under an obligation to pronounce the *adhān* and *iqāma*. It is related from ʿĀʾisha, and recorded by Ibn al-Mundhir, that she used to pronounce the *adhān* as well as the *iqāma*. The disagreement refers to the dispute over whether a woman can lead the prayers. It is said that the original rule is that she has the same duties as a man, unless an evidence is adduced to qualify this, and it is also said that she has the same duties and it is only in some cases that a qualifying evidence is required.

2.2.3. **Chapter 3 The *Qibla***

The Muslim jurists agreed that turning toward the direction of the House is one of the conditions for the validity of prayer, because of the words of the Exalted, "And whencesoever thou comest forth [for prayer, O Muḥammad] turn thy face toward the Inviolable Place of Worship. Lo! it is the Truth from thy Lord".[99] If, however, the worshiper can see the House, then the obligation is to face the House itself, and there is no dispute about this. The jurists disagree about two issues, when the Kaʿba is not in sight. First, whether the obligation is to face the Kaʿba itself or to face in its direction. Second, whether the obligation is to be exact about it or estimate the direction, that is, being exact about the Kaʿba itself or about the general direction?

2.2.3.1. Issue 1

Some Jurists maintained that the obligation is for facing the Kaʿba itself, while others maintained that it is for facing its direction. The reason for their disagreement is whether in the words of the Exalted, "And whencesoever thou comest forth [for prayer, O Muḥammad] turn thy face toward the Inviolable Place of Worship", an implied word is to be assumed, so as to read, "And

[99] Qurʾān 2 : 149.

whencesoever thou comest forth [for prayer, O Muḥammad] turn thy face in the direction of the Inviolable Place of Worship", or whether the words are to be read as they are. Those who assumed an implied word maintained that the obligation is for facing in its direction, while those who did not assume an implied word here said that the obligation is to face the Kaʿba itself. It is necessary to interpret the words in their actual meanings, unless an evidence indicates their construction in the metaphorical meaning. It is, however, maintained that the evidence for an implied word here is to be found in the words of the Prophet (God's peace and blessings be upon him), "Whatever is between the east and the west is a *qibla*, if you take the direction of the House". They said that the agreement of the Muslim jurists about a long row of worshipers extending beyond the boundary of the Kaʿba is an evidence that the obligation is not to face the Kaʿba itself, that is when the Kaʿba is not in sight. What I would say is that if the obligation had been to aim at the Kaʿba itself it would have amounted to hardship, and the Exalted has said, "He hath chosen you and hath not laid upon you in religion any hardship".[100] Aiming directly at a thing is not possible without approaching it by the use of geometry and (astronomical) observation, and yet the result is approximate; then, how is it possible without these to determine the direction by way of *ijtihād*? We are not under the obligation of discovery by means of geometry based upon astronomical observation from which the whole length and breadth of the land may be derived.

2.2.3.2. Issue 2

Is the obligation of a person striving to determine the *qibla* (the attainment of) accuracy or is it just the exercise of effort to discover it? Thus, if we say that the obligation is to accurately determine it, he is to pray again if he discovers that he made a mistake (in determining the true direction). If we maintain that the obligation is only for exerting effort, he does not have to pray again if he makes an error, and also if he had prayed before an effort to discover the direction. Al-Shāfiʿī thought that the obligation was for accurate determination, and if it becomes obvious to the person that he had made a mistake, he was to pray again, always. A group of jurists said that he does not pray again if he has finished praying, unless he did so intentionally (that is, prayed in the wrong direction) or prayed without making an effort to discover the direction. This was the opinion of Mālik and Abū Ḥanīfa, except that Mālik recommended praying again if there was still time.

The reason for disagreement in this is the conflict between a tradition and analogy, along with a dispute over the authenticity of the tradition. The

[100] Qurʾān 22 : 78.

analogy is based on the similarity of (the obligation to face the) direction to time, that is, the timing for prayer. They agreed (about time) that the obligation was for the worshipper to hit the time accurately. If the subject realizes that he prayed before time his prayer becomes invalid, and he must pray again, invariably. There is, however, a slight deviation reported from Ibn ʿAbbās and al-Shaʿbī, as well as the report from Mālik that if a traveller is unaware of the timing and prays *ʿishāʾ* before the disappearance of twilight discovering later that he had prayed before this time, his prayer remains valid. The basis for the resemblance between them is that these are the bounds of timing just as those are the bounds of direction.

The tradition is found in the report of ʿĀmir ibn Rabīʿa, who said, "We were travelling with the Messenger of Allāh (God's peace and blessings be upon him) on a dark night, and the direction of the *qibla* became obscure to us. Each one of us prayed in a certain direction, as we guessed, but when it was morning we found that we had prayed in a direction other than that of the *qibla*. We asked the Prophet (God's peace and blessings be upon him) about it and he said, 'Your prayer was valid.' It was then that revelation came down with the verse, 'Unto Allāh belongeth the East and the West, and withersoever ye turn, there is Allāh's countenance'".[101] Thus, the implication of the verse stays confirmed, and it is concerned with the person who observes prayer and later discovers that he prayed in a direction other than the *qibla*. The majority of the jurists, however, maintain that it has been abrogated by the verse, "And whencesoever thou comest forth [for prayer, O Muḥammad] turn thy face toward the Inviolable Place of Worship".[102] Those for whom this tradition did not prove to be authentic constructed the analogy of the limits of direction upon the limits of timings. And those who accepted the tradition held that prayer was valid.

Within this topic is a widely known issue, namely the *ḥukm* of prayer inside the Kaʿba. The jurists disagreed about this. Some of them prohibited it absolutely, while others permitted it without qualification. There were others who made a distinction between supererogatory and obligatory prayers within it. The reason for their disagreement is based on the conflict of traditions related to the issue, and the question of whether a person facing one of its sides from within may be called "one facing the Kaʿba", as in the case of a person facing it from outside.

There are two conflicting traditions about the issue, and both are authentic. First is Ibn ʿAbbās's tradition, who said, "When the Messenger of Allāh (God's peace and blessings be upon him) entered the Kaʿba, he offered

[101] Qurʾān 2 : 115.
[102] Qurʾān 2 : 149.

supplication at each side, but he did not pray till he had come out. On coming out he offered two *rakʿas* besides the Kaʿba and said, 'This is the *qibla*'". The second tradition is that of ʿAbd Allāh Ibn ʿUmar "that the Messenger of Allāh (God's peace and blessings be upon him) entered the Kaʿba, along with Usāma ibn Zayd, ʿUthmān ibn Ṭalḥa, and Bilāl ibn Rabāḥ. The door was closed behind him and he stayed inside for some time. When he had come out, I asked Bilāl, 'What did the Messenger of Allāh (God's peace and blessings be upon him) do?' He said, 'He stood between two pillars, one on his left and one on his right, while three other pillars were behind him, and then prayed'".

Those who adopted the method of preference, or of abrogation, either maintained the absolute prohibition of prayer inside the Kaʿba, preferring Ibn ʿAbbās's tradition, or upheld its absolute permission, preferring Ibn ʿUmar's tradition. Those who adopted the method of reconciliation construed Ibn ʿAbbās's tradition to be concerned with obligatory prayers, and Ibn ʿUmar's tradition to mean supererogatory prayers. Reconciliation, however, between these two traditions is difficult, as the Prophet (God's peace and blessings be upon him) described the two *rakʿas* prayed by him outside the Kaʿba as supererogatory. Those who adopted the method of suspension of the conflicting traditions did not permit prayer inside the Kaʿba at all, when they extend the accompanying *ḥukm* of consensus and of agreement. Those who did not uphold the extension of the *ḥukm* of consensus, and reconsidered the application of the expression "one facing the Kaʿba" to the person praying inside it as well, they permitted such prayer, but when they did not permit such application of the expression, which is better, they did not permit prayer inside the House.

The jurists agreed upon the recommendation of having a curtain between the person praying and the *qibla*, when he is praying alone or as an *imam*. This is based on the words of the Prophet (God's peace and blessings be upon him), "If you were to place in front of you something like that on the back of a man, then, you may pray". They disagreed about the obligation to draw a line, in case a person not finding a curtain. The majority maintained that he is under no obligation to draw a line, while Aḥmad ibn Ḥanbal said that he is to draw a line in front of him.

The reason for their disagreement derives from their dispute over the authenticity of the tradition laid down on the issue. The tradition has been related by Abū Hurayra "that the Prophet said, 'When one of you prays he is to place something in front of his face. If he does not find anything then let him prop a staff in front of him. If he does not find a staff, let him draw a line in front of him. Thus, any one passing in front of him will not harm him'". It is recorded by Abū Dāwūd, and Aḥmad ibn Ḥanbal considered it as authentic, while al-Shāfiʿī did not. It is also related that "the Prophet (God's peace and blessings be upon him) prayed without a curtain". There is another authentic tradition that a staff with a pointed tip of iron used to be affixed for him. These, then, are the principles of this subject, incorporated in four issues.

2.2.4. **Chapter 4 Covering of Private Parts and the Dress for Prayer**

This chapter is divided into two sections. The first is about covering of the private parts (*satr al-ʿawra*), while the second is about the kinds of dress permitted for prayer.

2.2.4.1. *Section 1: Covering the* ʿawra

The jurists agreed that covering the private parts is an absolute obligation, but they disagreed on whether it is a condition for the validity of prayer? Similarly, they differed about the area of the body, for a woman and a man, that is delineated by the term *ʿawra*.

2.2.4.1.1. Issue 1

The preferred opinion in Mālik's school is that it (covering of the this area) is one of the *sunan* of prayer. Abū Ḥanīfa and al-Shāfiʿī said that it is one of the prerequisites of the validity of prayer. The reason for disagreement over this stems from the conflict of traditions and the differences among the jurists in their understanding of the meaning of the words of the Exalted, "O Children of Adam! Look to [take] your adornment at every place of worship",[103] whether the prescription is to be construed as an obligation or a recommendation.

Those who interpreted it as an obligation said that the implied meaning is the covering of the *ʿawra*. They argued for this on the basis of the context of the revelation of the verse that a woman used to circumambulate the Kaʿba naked, so the verse was revealed and "the Messenger of Allāh issued the command that from then on no polytheist be allowed to perform the pilgrimage, nor was anyone to make the circumambulation naked". Those who interpreted it to convey a recommendation said that the adornment mentioned is the external form of the dress or other clothes that constitute adornment. They argued for this on the basis of what is laid down in a tradition that some men used to join the Prophet in prayer with their wrappers tied to their necks, as is done for children, and the women were, therefore, advised not to raise their heads (from the *sujūd*) till the men straightened up into the sitting

[103] Qurʾān 7 : 31.

posture. They added that it was for this reason that there was no disagreement about whether a person who could not find anything to cover himself should pray, but there was a disagreement about one who could not purify himself, whether he could pray.[104]

2.2.4.1.2. Issue 2

The second issue is about the delineation of the *ʿawra* in the case of men. Mālik and al-Shāfiʿī said that the *ʿawra* in his case extends from the navel to the knees. This was also Abū Ḥanīfa's opinion. A group of jurists maintained that the *ʿawra* comprises the private parts alone (the male sex organ and the rear exit). The reason for their disagreement stems from the conflict of two traditions, and both are authentic. The first is the tradition of Jarhad that the Messenger of Allāh (God's peace and blessings be upon him) said, "The thighs are part of the *ʿawra*". The second is Anas's tradition "that the Messenger of Allāh (once) uncovered his thighs while he was sitting with his Companions". It is recorded by al-Bukhārī. Anas's tradition has a stronger chain, while the Jarhad's tradition is on the safer side. Some of the jurists have said that the *awra* comprises the buttocks, genitals, and the thighs.

2.2.4.1.3. Issue 3

The third issue relates to the limits of the *ʿawra* in the case of a woman. Most of the jurists maintained that her entire body constitutes *ʿawra*, except for the face and the hands. Abū Ḥanīfa maintained that her feet are not a part of the *ʿawra*. Abū Bakr ibn ʿAbd al-Raḥmān and Aḥmad said that her entire body is *ʿawra*.

The reason for their disagreement is based on the possible interpretations of the words of the Exalted, "And to display of their adornment only that which is apparent", that is whether the exemption relates to defined parts or to those parts that she cannot (help but) display? Those who maintained that the intended exemption is only for those parts that she cannot help but display while moving, said that her entire body is *ʿawra*, even her back. They argued for this on the basis of the general implication of the words of the Exalted, "O Prophet! Tell thy wives and thy daughters and the women of the believers to draw their cloaks close round them. That will make them recognizable and they will not be exposed to harm".[105] Those who held that the intended exemption is for what is customarily not covered, that is, the face and the hands, said that these are not included in the *ʿawra*. They (further) argued for this on the grounds that a woman does not cover her face during *ḥajj*.

[104] This is confusing. A person who cannot purify himself with water has to perform *tayammum* and pray.

[105] Quʾān 33 : 59. Pickthall's translation changed.

2.2.4.2. *Section 2: The dress permitted for prayer*

The source for this are the words of the Exalted, "O Children of Adam! Take your adornment at every place of worship",[106] along with the prohibition of certain forms of dress in prayer, such as wrapping oneself in clothes (for sleeping on the ground); that is, to use a garment as a support for the head, or to wrap oneself in a single piece of cloth (with its ends crossed) without there being anything covering the shoulders, or to wrap himself in a single garment without anything covering the private parts. All proscriptions laid down about it have as their aim the prevention of the means that lead to the uncovering of the private parts, and I do not know of anyone who said that prayer is not permitted in any of these forms of dress so long as the *ʿawra* is not uncovered. This, however, would be obligatory according to the principles of the Ẓāhirites.

They agreed that a man is permitted to pray in a single dress, because of the saying of the Prophet (God's peace and blessings be upon him) when he was asked: "Can a man pray in a single garment?" He said, "Do all of you have two garments?"

They disagreed about the case of a man praying with his back and the front part above the navel uncovered. The majority uphold the permission of such prayer, as the back and the chest are not part of the *ʿawra* for a man. A group of jurists deviated and said that his prayer is not permitted, because of the proscription from the Prophet (God's peace and blessings be upon him) about the prayer of a man with nothing of his dress on his shoulders. They also relied upon the words of the Exalted, "O Children of Adam! Take your adornment at every place of worship".[107]

The majority agreed that the dress permissible for a woman in prayer is a (long) shirt and a veil, because of what is related from Umm Salama "that she asked the Prophet (God's peace and blessings be upon him), 'In what kind of dress should a woman pray?' He said, 'In a veil and a long and loose-fitting garment that covers the upper part of her feet'". Further, it is related from ʿĀʾisha from the Prophet (God's peace and blessings be upon him) that he said, "Allah does not accept the pubescent woman's prayer, unless she wears a veil". It is also related from ʿĀʾisha, Maymūna, and Umm Salama, and they used to issue verdicts accordingly. All jurists say that if she prays without a covering, she is to repeat her prayer (when she realizes her error) either within its prescribed time or later, except that Mālik used to say that she is to repeat it only in its prescribed time.

[106] Qurʾān 7 : 31.
[107] Qurʾān 7 : 31.

The majority maintained that a slave-girl may pray with her head and feet uncovered, but al-Ḥasan al-Baṣrī deemed it obligatory for her to use the veil, while ʿAṭāʾ deemed it recommended. The reason for disagreement lies in the question of whether a (legal) communication addressed to either category of persons (sex) includes those who are free as well as those in bondage, or whether it includes only the free to the exclusion of slaves?

They disagreed about the case of a man praying while dressed in a silken garment. A group of jurists said that his prayer in it is valid (though prohibited), while another group said it is not. A third group recommended repeating the prayer in its prescribed time (without the silk dress). The reason for disagreement is over the question of whether avoidance of a thing prohibited absolutely is a condition for the validity of prayer? Those who maintained that it is a condition said that prayer in it is not permitted (nor valid), while those who maintained that he commits a sin because of his dress, but his prayer is permissible said that it is not a condition for the validity of prayer unlike purification, which is a condition. This issue is of the same nature as that of prayer in usurped property, dispute over which is widely known.

2.2.5. Chapter 5 Purification from Filth

It is unlikely for those who said that purification from filth is an emphatic *sunna* to say that it is an obligation for prayer, that is, a condition for its validity, while those who maintained that it is an absolute obligation would say that it is an obligation for prayer, but it is possible that they would not say this. Two opinions of the school (Mālik's) are related from ʿAbd al-Wahhāb. First, that removal of uncleanliness is a condition for the validity of prayer, when in possession of the means for doing so and in a state of remembering. The second opinion is that it is not a condition. The opinion that it is a condition does not conform with the better known opinion of the school that it is an emphatic *sunna*. It conforms more with the opinion that it is an obligation when the capacity to remove (the uncleanliness is available) and when in a state of remembrance. The issue had already preceded in the Book of Ritual Purification, and the reasons for disagreement were identified there.

The discussion relevant here is whether an absolute obligation that is related to prayer is necessarily an obligation of prayer also. The truth is that a thing that is an absolute requirement does not necessarily become a condition for the validity of another required thing, [even if it occurs during it, except by another command; similarly, an absolute command for a thing proscribed absolutely does not necessarily become a condition for the validity of another thing],[108] except by another command.

2.2.6. Chapter 6 Places Suitable for Prayer

The places in which prayer is permissible, in the opinion of some jurists, are all those that are free from uncleanliness. Some jurists exempted seven places out of these: the dunghill (garbage area), the slaughterhouse, the graveyard, the roadway, the public bath, the kneelingplace of camels, and the roof of the House of Allāh (Kaʿba). Others made an exemption for the graveyard alone, while some others exempted the graveyard and the public-bath. Some of them deemed praying in these undesirable places as merely abominable, but did not invalidate the prayer; this is one narration from Mālik. The permissibility of such prayer is also related from him, which is Ibn al-Qāsim's narration.

The reason for disagreement arises from the conflict of the apparent meanings of traditions on the issue. There are two traditions on the issue that are agreed upon, while two are disputed. The traditions agreed upon are the sayings of the Prophet (God's peace and blessings be upon him), "I have been granted seven things that were not granted to anyone before me . . . [He mentioned within this]: The earth has been made a mosque for me and a means of purification, so wherever the time of prayer overtakes me, I pray". The other tradition says, "Enliven your homes with your prayers in them occasionally, and do not convert them into graveyards". As to the disputed traditions, one report is "that the Prophet (God's peace and blessings be upon him) proscribed prayers in seven places: the dunghill, the place for slaughtering animals, the graveyard, the roadway, the public bath, the kneeling places of camels, and the roof of the House of Allāh". It has been recorded by al-Tirmidhī. The second is the report that Prophet (God's peace and blessings be upon him) said, "Pray in the resting places of cattle, but do not pray in the kneeling places of camels".

The jurists were divided over these traditions because of the employment of three methods. The first is the method of preference and abrogation. The second is the method of structuring, that is, structuring the particular upon the general. The third is the method of reconciliation. Those who adopted the method of preference and abrogation followed the widely known tradition, the words of the Prophet (God's peace and blessings be upon him), "The earth has been made a mosque for me and a means of purification". They maintained that this tradition abrogates those that conflict with it, as it counts the merits

[108] Editors note: The statement between the brackets does not appear in the Egyptian manuscript, but it does in the Fās manuscript.

granted to the Prophet (God's peace and blessings be upon him), and this cannot be abrogated, as abrogation belongs to the category of rules (*aḥkām*). Those who adopted the method of structuring the particular upon the general said that the tradition about permissibility is general whereas the proscribing tradition is particular; therefore it is necessary that the particular be structured upon the general. Some of these jurists (who apply this method) excluded the seven places, while some of them excluded only the public bath and the graveyard, saying that this is what is established from the Prophet (God's peace and blessings be upon him), as it is related that he also proscribed them independently. Some excluded only the graveyard due to the preceding tradition. Those who adopted the method of reconciliation, not excluding the particular from the general, said that the proscribing traditions are to be construed for abomination, and the others for permissibility.

They disagreed about praying in synagogues and churches. One group considered it as reprehensible, while another permitted it. A third group made a distinction on the basis of the existence of figures, which is Ibn ʿAbbās's opinion because of ʿUmar's statement, "We do not enter their churches because of the images". The underlying cause, however, for the opinion of those who considered it abominable is not the images, but the probability of the existence of uncleanliness (*najāsa*).

They disagreed about prayer on the (bare) ground and on carpets and other things used for sitting on the ground. The majority maintain the permissibility of prostrating on mats and other similar things made of material produced by the land, and deem the rest as abominable, which is Mālik ibn Anas's opinion.

2.2.7. Chapter 7 Conditions Stipulated for the Validity of Prayer

The jurists agreed that things stipulated to be relinquished in prayer include words as well as acts. The acts include all acts permissible outside prayer that are not part of prayer, except the killing of a scorpion or a snake during prayer, about which they disagreed due to the existence of a conflict between a tradition on the issue and analogy. They agreed, I think, about the permissibility of minor movements.

The words include all those that are not part of prayer. In this too, they agreed that they invalidate prayer, if uttered intentionally, because of the words of the Exalted, "And stand up with devotion to Allāh",[109] and also because of the report from the Prophet, "Allāh stipulates any command of His that He likes, and He stipulates that you should not speak during prayers".

[109] Qurʾān 2 : 238.

This is the tradition of Ibn Masᶜūd. The tradition of Zayd ibn Arqam reads, "We used to speak during prayer, till the words, "And stand up with devotion to Allāh", were revealed and we were commanded to maintain silence and prohibited from speaking". Further, there is the tradition of Muᶜāwiya ibn al-Ḥakam al-Sulamī, who said, "I heard the Messenger of Allāh (God's peace and blessings be upon him) saying, 'The speech of people is not suitable for our prayer, for prayer is praise (of Allāh), the repetition of the word of *tamhīd*, thanksgiving, and the recitation of the Qurʾān'". They disagreed, however, about this on two points. First, when a person speaks out due to forgetfulness, and second when he speaks out intentionally for correcting an error in prayer. Al-Awzāᶜī deviated from this saying that a person who speaks out in prayer for saving a life or for another serious matter may continue his prayer after that. Mālik's widely known opinion is that intentional speech with a view to rectification does not invalidate prayer. Al-Shāfiᶜī said that speech invalidates it, whatever its nature, except in the case of forgetfulness. Abū Ḥanīfa said that prayer is invalidated by speech without exception.

The reason for their disagreement stems from the conflict of the apparent meaning of the traditions. The preceding traditions imply the general prohibition of speech, and appear to conflict with Abū Hurayra's tradition, which says, "The Messenger of Allāh (God's peace and blessings be upon him) once concluded his prayer after two *rakᶜas*. Dhū al-Yadayn [a man so called] asked him, 'Has the prayer been shortened, or did you forget, O Messenger of Allāh?' The Messenger of Allāh (God's peace and blessings be upon him) said, 'Did Dhū al-Yadayn speak the truth?' They said, 'Yes'. The Messenger of Allāh (God's peace and blessings be upon him) stood up and prayed the remaining two *rakᶜas* and then concluded with the salutation'". The apparent meaning here is that the Messenger of Allāh (God's peace and blessings be upon him) spoke and so did the people with him, and they continued the prayer after this speech, which did not cut off their prayer. Those who followed this apparent meaning, and maintained that this speech was specific to the rectification of prayer, exempted it from the general implication (of prohibition). This is Mālik ibn Anas's opinion. Some maintained that there is no evidence in the tradition to indicate that they spoke intentionally during prayer, and said that it appears they spoke thinking that the prayer had been shortened, while the Prophet (God's peace and blessings be upon him) spoke thinking that the prayer had been completed. Further, they added that the report that the people spoke after the statement of the Prophet (God's peace and blessings be upon him), "The prayer has not been shortened nor did I forget", was not proved authentic in their view; therefore the tradition implies the permissibility of speech for a person who is not speaking intentionally. Thus, the reason for the disagreement between Mālik and al-Shāfiᶜī about the exemption from the general implication is their dispute over the meaning of this tradition, though al-Shāfiʿī also relied for this upon a general principle, which is the saying of the Prophet (God's peace and blessings be upon him), "Liability for mistake and forgetfulness has been removed from my *umma*". Abū Ḥanīfa, on the other hand, interpreted the proscribing traditions in their general meaning and held them to have abrogated the tradition of Dhū al-Yadayn, and as being preferred over it.

2.2.8. Chapter 8 *Niyya* and its Stipulation in Prayer

The jurists agreed about the stipulation of intention (*niyya*) for the validity of prayer, because prayer is the foremost form among the different kinds of ritual worship that have been ordained in the law without being assigned a rational interest (*maṣlaḥa*), that is, a tangible interest. They disagreed, however, about whether it is a condition that the *niyya* of the follower should conform with the *niyya* of the *imām*? In other words, is it permitted for a follower to pray *ẓuhr* when the *imām* is praying *ʿaṣr*? And, is it permitted for the *imām* to be praying supererogatory *ẓuhr* when the follower prays *farḍ*? Mālik and Abū Ḥanīfa maintained that it is obligatory that the intention of the follower conform with the intention of the *imām*, while al-Shāfiʿī held that it is not obligatory.

The reason for their disagreement is the conflict between the implication of the saying of the Prophet (God's peace and blessings be upon him), "The *imām* has been appointed so that he may be followed", and the tradition of Muʿādh that he used to pray with the Prophet (God's peace and blessings be upon him) and then lead his people in prayer. Those who maintained that this was specific to the case of Muʿādh and that the general implication of the words of Prophet (God's peace and blessings be upon him), "The *imām* has been appointed so that he may be followed", includes intention, stipulated the conformity of the *imām*'s intention with that of the follower. Those who maintained that the permission granted to Muʿādh extends to all the believers, which is the principle, said that there can be two possible interpretations of the other (former) tradition: first, that its general implication does not include intention, for its apparent meaning relates to (external) acts, in which case it would not conflict with Muʿādh's tradition; or it may include intention, in which case Muʿādh's tradition has restricted the generality.

Related to *niyya* are issues that have no concern with matters expressly stated in the law, and we decided to drop them, as our primary purpose is the discussion of issues that are directly related to matters expressly stated in the law.

2.3. Part 3: The Words and Acts of Prayer

This part covers the words and acts that constitute prayer, and these are the *arkān* (the elements). The obligatory prayers differ on the basis of an increase or decrease in these two elements, with respect to:

1. individual and congregational performance;
2. time, like the difference between the *ẓuhr* prayer on a Friday and the *ẓuhr* prayer for other days;
3. residence or travel;
4. security and fear; and
5. health and illness.

If it is desired that the discussion follow this classification and structure, it is necessary first to discuss what is common between these categories and then take what is specific to each. On the other hand, the discussion of each individual category may be taken up, which is easier, though this method of instruction leads to some repetition, but it was a method adopted by the *fuqahā*ʾ, and we will follow them in this.

We shall, therefore, divide this part into six chapters. The first chapter will cover the prayer of the individual who is resident, secure (from fear), and in good health. The second chapter will cover prayer in a congregation, that is, the *aḥkām* concerning the *imām* and the follower in prayer. The third chapter will deal with the *jumuʿa* prayer. Chapter 4 will deal with prayer during travel. Chapter 5 will discuss prayer in (a state of) fear. The sixth chapter will deal with the prayer of the sick.

2.3.1. Chapter 1 The Prayer of an Individual who is Resident, Secure, and in Good Health

There are two sections in this chapter. The first section is about the words of prayer, while the second is about its acts.

2.3.1.1. *Section 1: The words used in prayer*

The fundamental issues in this chapter are nine.

2.3.1.1.1. Issue 1: *Takbīr*

The jurists disagreed about *takbīr* (pronouncing the words: "*Allāhu Akbar*"—Allāh is Supreme) into three opinions. A group of jurists said that all pronouncements of *takbīr* in prayer are obligatory, while another group said that all pronouncements are not obligatory, which is a deviant opinion. The majority hold that the initial *takbīr* alone is obligatory.

The reason for disagreement among those who made all its instances obligatory and those who made only the *takbīr* of *iḥrām* obligatory stems from the conflict of the transmitted words of the Prophet (God's peace and blessings be upon him) with his transmitted acts. The transmitted saying of the Prophet (God's peace and blessings be upon him) is in the widely known tradition of Abū Hurayra that the Prophet (God's peace and blessings be upon him) said to a man, whom he was teaching how to pray, "When you resolve to pray, complete the ablution and face the *qibla*, then, pronounce the *takbīr* followed by recitation". The meaning here is that it is only the first *takbīr* that is obligatory, and had another *takbīr* been obligatory, he would have mentioned it to him, just as he mentioned the other obligations of prayer. The transmitted acts of the Prophet (God's peace and blessings be upon him) include Abū Hurayra's tradition "that he prayed pronouncing the *takbīr* each time he bowed or straightened up, and then said, 'I give you in my prayer a semblance of the prayer of the Messenger of Allāh (God's peace and blessings be upon him)'". Included (in the transmitted acts) is also the tradition of Muṭarrif ibn ʿAbd Allāh ibn al-Shikhkhīr, who said, ʿImrān ibn al-Ḥuṣayn and I followed ʿAlī ibn Abī Ṭālib, may Allāh be pleased with him, in prayer, and he pronounced *takbīr* when he prostrated, and when he raised his head after bowing. When he had completed the prayer, we went away and ʿImrān took hold of my hand and said, 'This reminds me of Muḥammad's prayer'".

Those who upheld its obligation, followed these acts transmitted in these traditions, and said that the principle is that all acts of the Prophet that have been described as an explanation of an obligatory act are to be construed as obligatory, as is justified by the words of the Prophet (God's peace and blessings be upon him), "Pray as you see me praying and acquire from me your acts of devotion".

The first group said that what is implicit in these traditions indicates that the acts of the Companions were for an affirmation (of the obligation) *takbīr*. Therefore, Abū Hurayra said, "I provide you with a semblance of the prayer of the Messenger of Allāh", while ʿImrān said, "I am reminded by this of Muḥammad's prayer". With respect to the opinion of those who deemed all instances of the *takbīr* as supererogatory, it is weak. Perhaps, they constructed an analogy for it from all those pronouncements of *dhikr* (remembrance) that are not obligatory, just as they constructed an analogy for the *takbīr* of *iḥrām* upon all other instances of *takbīr*.

Abū ʿUmar ibn ʿAbd al-Barr said that what supports the majority opinion is the report by Shuʿba ibn al-Ḥajjāj from al-Ḥasan ibn ʿImrān from ʿAbd

Allāh ibn ʿAbd al-Raḥmān ibn Abzī from his father, who said, "I prayed with the Prophet (God's peace and blessings be upon him) and he did not pronounce the *takbīr*, and I prayed with ʿUmar ibn ʿAbd al-ʿAzīz and he did not pronounce the *takbīr*". Further, the report by by Aḥmad ibn Ḥanbal from ʿUmar (God be pleased with him) that he did not pronounce the *takbīr* when he prayed alone. It appears that these jurists maintained that *takbīr* is meant to be an indication by the *imām* to the followers about his movements, and it also appears that those who considered it all supererogatory also held on to this reason.

2.3.1.1.2. Issue 2: The words of *takbīr*

Mālik said that it is not allowed to pronounce *takbīr*, except with the words *Allāhu Akbar*, while al-Shāfiʿī said that the forms *Allāhu Akbar* and *Allāhu al-Akbar* are both permitted. Abū Ḥanīfa said that *takbīr* is permitted with all those words that convey the same meaning, like Allāh is the Greatest (*al-Aʿẓam*) and Allāh is Greater (*al-Ajall*).

The reason for their disagreement is whether it is the words or their meaning that are prescribed for the opening. The Mālikites and the Shāfiʿites argued on the basis of the words of the Prophet (God's peace and blessings be upon him), "The key to prayer is purification, its sanctity starts with *al-takbīr*, and it is discharged with the salutation". They said that the definite article "*al*" is exhaustive and indicates that the *ḥukm* is confined to the thing expressed, and that it is not permissible without anything else. Abū Ḥanīfa does not agree with them about this principle, for such a meaning, in his view, arises from the literal category of *dalīl al-khiṭāb* (the indirect implication of the text), which requires the assigning of a meaning opposite that of the expressed subject to the unexpressed categories.[110] The *dalīl al-khiṭāb* is a method not used by Abū Ḥanīfa.

2.3.1.1.3. Issue 3: The post-*takbīr* words

A group of jurists said that *tawjīh* is obligatory in prayer. It is either the statement after *takbīr*, "I (have) turn(ed) (my face) to One Who created the heavens and the earth", which is al-Shāfiʿī's opinion, or it is the glorification of Allāh, which is Abū Ḥanīfa's opinion, or it is a combination of both, which is Abū Yūsuf's opinion, who was the disciple of Abū Ḥanīfa. Mālik said that *tawjīh* is not obligatory in prayer, nor is it a *sunna*.

[110] That is, maintaining it is not permitted with other words, which is something left unsaid by the tradition.

The reason for disagreement is the conflict of traditions about *tawjīḥ* with practice (of the people of Medina), in Mālik's view, or is based upon the dispute over the authenticity of the relevant traditions. The Qāḍī (Ibn Rushd) said that it is established in the *Saḥīḥayn* from Abū Hurayra "that the Messenger of Allah (God's peace and blessings be upon him) used to remain silent between *takbīr* and (later) recitation. So I said, 'O Messenger of Allāh, for you I would offer as ransom my father and mother. In this silence of yours between *takbīr* and recitation, what do you say?' He said, and I quote, 'O Allāh, distance me from my errors, as You have distanced the east from the west, O Allāh, cleanse me of errors like a white dress cleansed of filth, O Allāh, wash away my errors with water, snow, and the morning dew'".

A group of jurists preferred some occasions for silence during prayer, including the moment following the initial *takbīr*, after the recitation of the *umm al-Qur'ān*, and after the completion of recitation just before bowing. Some of those who upheld this are al-Shāfiʿī, Abū Thawr, and al-Awzāʿī. These were denied by Mālik, his disciples, and by Abū Ḥanīfa, and his disciples.

The reason for their disagreement arises from their dispute over the authenticity of Abū Hurayra's tradition, who said, "The Prophet (God's peace and blessings be upon him) observed three occasions for silence in his prayer: between his pronouncing the initial *takbīr* while beginning the prayer, before beginning the recitation of the *fātiḥat al-Kitāb*, and after he had finished reciting before bowing".

2.3.1.1.4. Issue 4: Prounouncing the *tasmiya*

The jurists disagreed about reciting the *basmala*, the words meaning, "In the name of Allāh, the Beneficent, the Merciful", before beginning recitation in prayer. Mālik prohibited this in the prescribed prayer, whether loudly or inaudibly, at the beginning of the *umm al-Qur'ān* or any other *sūra*, but he permitted it with supererogatory prayers. Abū Ḥanīfa, al-Thawrī, and Aḥmad said that it is to be pronounced inaudibly in each *rakʿa* with the *umm al-Qur'ān*. Al-Shāfiʿī said that it is to be pronounced aloud in case of audible recitation and in a whisper in case of the inaudible. In his view it is a verse of the *fātiḥat al-Kitāb*, which was also the opinion of Aḥmad, Abū Thawr, and Abū ʿUbayd. Al-Shāfiʿī, however, differed about whether it was a verse of every *sūra* or a verse of *sūrat al-Naml* and *fātiḥat al-Kitāb* alone? Both opinions are related from him.

The reason for disagreement in this refers to two factors. First is the conflict of traditions on the topic, while the second relates to the dispute whether *basmala* is a verse of *fātiḥat al-Kitāb*. The traditions relied upon by those who drop it include that of Ibn Mughaffal, who said, "My father heard me when I was reciting the *basmala*, and said, 'O my son, beware of innovation, for I have prayed with the Messenger of Allāh (God's peace and blessings be upon him), Abū Bakr, and ʿUmar, but I did not hear any of them reciting it'". Abū ʿUmar ibn ʿAbd al-Barr said that Ibn Mughaffal is an unknown narrator. They also include what is related by Mālik about the tradition of Anas, who said, "I prayed behind by Abū Bakr, ʿUmar, and ʿUthmān (God be pleased with them) and none of them recited the *tasmiya* at the beginning of the prayer". Abū ʿUmar said that in some versions he states: "Following the Prophet (God's peace and blessings be upon him) and he did not recite it". Abū ʿUmar said that the traditionists are of the view that the narrations of this tradition are confused, and it cannot be adduced as a persuasive evidence. The reason is that in one instance it has been related through a chain that can be traced back to the Prophet (God's peace and blessings be upon him) (*marfūʿ*), and on another occasion the chain did not extend to him, while some versions mention ʿUthmān and others do not. Some of its versions say that they used to recite it, while others say they did not. Some other versions say that they did not pronounce the *basmala* loudly.

The traditions opposing these include the tradition of Nuʿaym ibn ʿAbd Allāh al-Mujammir, who said, "I observed prayer led by Abū Hurayra and he recited the *basmala* before the *umm al-Qurʾān* and before the *sūra*, and he pronounced *takbīr* while bowing and while straightening up. He then said, 'I provide you with a semblance of the prayer of the Messenger of Allāh (God's peace and blessings be upon him)'". Included in these is the tradition of Ibn ʿAbbās "that the Prophet (God's peace and blessings be upon him) used to pronounce the *basmala* aloud". Another tradition is from Umm Salama, who said, "The Messenger of Allāh (God's peace and blessings be upon him) used to recite the *basmala* and the verse meaning, 'Praise be to Allāh, Lord of the Worlds'".

The conflict of these traditions is one factor giving rise to disagreement about the recitation of the *basmala* in prayer. The second reason, as we have said, is whether it is a verse only of the *umm al-Kitāb* or also of each *sūra*, or whether it is not a verse at all?

Those who deemed it a verse of the *umm al-Kitāb* made its recitation obligatory because of the obligation to recite the *umm al-Kitāb* in their view, while those who deemed it a verse at the beginning of each *sūra* made its recitation obligatory along with the *sūra* as well. There has been extensive disagreement over this issue, and the issue is subject to interpretation. The strangest thing that occurred in this issue is when they asked: What is the basis of their disagreement, is it that the *basmala* is a verse of the Qurʾān, even in cases other than the *sūrat al-Naml*, or is it a verse of the Qurʾān in *sūrat al-Naml* alone? They relate, as a rebuttal of al-Shāfiʿī's argument, that had it been a part of the Qurʾān in places other than *sūrat al-Naml*, the Prophet

(God's peace and blessings be upon him) would have explained it, as the Qur'ān has been transmitted through *tawātur*. This is what the Qāḍī[111] said and thought it was irrefutable. Abū Ḥāmid (al-Ghazālī) defended al-Shāfiʿī's position by saying that, had it been something other than the Qur'ān, it would have been obligatory upon the Prophet (God's peace and blessings be upon him) to explain it. All this is confused and meaningless for how is it possible to say about a single verse that it is a part of the Qur'ān on one occasion and that it is not a part of it on another? In fact, it may be said that it has been established to be a part of the Qur'ān wherever it is mentioned, and that it is a also a verse of *sūrat al-Naml*. Whether it is a verse of the *umm al-Qur'ān* and of each *sūra* used as a beginning, is disputed. The issue is subject to interpretation, as it is the opening for all the chapters, and is a part of *sūrat al-Naml*. Think over this for it is self-evident. Allāh knows best.

2.3.1.1.5. Issue 5: Prayer without recitation

The jurists agreed that prayer without recitation is not valid, whether the omission is intentional or out of forgetfulness, except what is related from ʿUmar (God be pleased with him) that he prayed and forgot to recite. He was told about this, and he asked how the bowing and prostrations go? When he was told that they were normal, he said, "Then there is no harm". But this is a solitary (*gharīb*) tradition in their view, although it is included by Mālik in his *al-Muwaṭṭa'*, in some versions of it. Further, there is the report from Ibn ʿAbbās that he did not recite in prayer not requiring audible recitation, and said, "The Messenger of Allāh (God's peace and blessings be upon him) recited in some prayers, but kept silent in others, so we recite where he recited and maintain silence where he kept silent". He was asked whether there was recitation in *ẓuhr* and *ʿaṣr* prayers, and he replied, "No!"

The majority followed the tradition of Khabbāb "that the Prophet (God's peace and blessings be upon him) used to recite in the *ẓuhr* and *ʿaṣr* prayers. He was asked: 'How did you come to know this?' He replied, 'By the movement of his beard'". The Kūfīs relied on Ibn ʿAbbās's tradition for relinquishing the obligation of recitation in the last two *rakʿa*s of prayer, because of the equivalence of audible and inaudible prayer with respect to the silence of the Prophet (God's peace and blessings be upon him) in these two *rakʿa*s.

Those who held that recitation is obligatory in prayer, disagreed as to what is to be recited. Some of them maintained that the obligation here is to recited

[111] The identity of this person is not clear, unless the title has been applied to the author's grandfather. On other occasions, the title is used for the author himself. He does however mention in the Book of Oaths a jurist by the name of Ismāʿīl al-Qāḍī, who was a disciple of Mālik.

the *umm al-Qurʾān* for one who has memorized it, and that there is no limitation about additional recitation. Some of them made it obligatory in each *rakʿa*, some for the major part of prayer, some for half the prayer, and others for one *rakʿa* in each prayer. The first opinion was held by al-Shāfiʿī, and it is also the widely known view of Mālik, but it is also related from him that if he recites it in two of a four-*rakʿa* prayer it would be valid. Al-Ḥasan al-Baṣrī and many jurists of Baṣra held that recitation in *rakʿa* is sufficient. The obligation according to Abū Ḥanīfa is for reciting any verse that the person may choose, while his disciples held that the minimum is three short verses or a lengthy verse, like that about *dayn* (debt). This was the case for the first two *rakʿa*s and for the remaining two he deemed as recommended (*mustaḥabb*) to recite *tasbīḥ*, "words glorifying the name of Allāh", and not recitation. This was upheld by the Kūfīs. The majority consider recitation as recommended (*mustaḥabb*) in all the *rakʿa*s.

The reason for this (disagreement) stems from the conflict of traditions on the topic, and the conflict of the apparent meaning of the Book with a tradition. One of the conflicting traditions is the authentic tradition of Abū Hurayra, "A man entered the mosque and prayed. He then came up to the Prophet (God's peace and blessings be upon him) and greeted him and the Prophet (God's peace and blessings be upon him) responded to the salutation and said, 'Go back and pray, for you have not prayed'. He prayed again and returned, but the Prophet ordered him to pray again. He did so three times, till the man said, 'By the One Who has sent you in truth, I cannot do better than this'. The Prophet (God's peace and blessings be upon him) said to him, 'When you arise for prayer, complete the ablution and face the *qibla*, then pronounce *takbīr*. After that recite what is convenient for you from the Qurʾān, and then bow and remain in that position for a while, then raise yourself till you are firmly erect, then prostrate for a while, then sit up for a while, then prostrate again for a while, then rise till you are erect and stable. Then, do this in your entire prayer" '. Conflicting with this are two confirmed traditions, which are recorded by al-Bukhārī and Muslim. First is the tradition of ʿUbāda ibn al-Ṣāmit that the Prophet (God's peace and blessings be upon him) said, "He has not prayed, the one who has not recited the *fātiḥat al-Kitāb*". The second is the tradition of Abū Hurayra that the Messenger of Allāh (God's peace and blessings be upon him) said, "When a person prays without reciting the *umm al-Qurʾān*, it is lost, lost, lost".

Abū Hurayra's former tradition apparently indicates that it is sufficient in a prayer for a worshipper to recite whatever is convenient for him from the Qurʾān, while the tradition of ʿUbāda ibn al-Ṣāmit and the latter tradition of Abū Hurayra imply that the *umm al-Qurʾān* is a condition for (the validity of) prayer. The apparent meaning of the words of the Exalted, "So recite of it whatever is easy (for you)",[112] also support Abū Hurayra's former tradition. The jurists disagreeing over this issue either decided to adopt the method of reconciliation for these traditions or they adopted the method of preference, and the same meaning emerges from both opinions. The reason is that those who maintained the obligation of reciting whatever is easy from the Qur'ān said that this is preferable, for the apparent meaning of the Book conforms with it, and they may also hold by way of reconciliation that the purpose of ʿUbāda's tradition is to deny perfection (of such prayer), not its validity, while the purpose of Abū Hurayra's (latter) tradition is to indicate its validity, as it imparts instruction about the obligations in prayer.

These jurists may also adopt these two methods (for the second opinion) by saying that the traditions (requiring any recitation) are greater in number and a widely known tradition from Abū Hurayra supports this view, and this is the tradition in which Allāh, the Exalted, says, "I have divided prayer in half between Myself and My servant, one-half is for Me and one-half for My servant, and My servant gets what he asks for. The servant says, 'Praise be to Allāh, the Lord of the worlds', and Allāh says, 'My servant has praised Me . . ' ". (till the end of the tradition). These jurists may also argue that the words of the Prophet, "recite whatever you can from the Qur'ān", are ambivalent, while the other traditions are explicit, and the explicit govern the ambivalent. There is a difficulty that arises from the meaning of the word "*mā*" (what) which signifies "whatever is easy". The other interpretation can be valid here if "what" indicates, in accordance with the usage of the Arabs, what is implied by the *lām al-ʿahd* (i.e., the "*al*" if it alludes to an already known thing), so that the text will be assumed to mean "recite what is easy for you from the Qur'ān", and its implication will be (recite) the *umm al-Qur'ān*, as the definite article "*al*" indicates the previously mentioned object. It is necessary to take this into consideration in the usage of the Arabs, and if you find that the Arabs do this, that is, make a concession in the implication of *mā* to indicate a determined object, then such an interpretation is to be adopted, otherwise there is no cause for it. The issue, as you can see, is ambiguous, and this ambiguity would be removed if abrogation is established.

The disagreement among those who deemed obligatory the recitation of *umm al-Kitāb* as to whether it is so in every *rakʿa* or in part of the prayer, is caused by the differences over the reference of the pronoun in the words of the Prophet (God's peace and blessings be upon him), "the one who has not recited the *fātiḥat al-Kitāb* in it *fīhā*", whether it is the whole prayer or every part of the prayer. Because, the person who has recited it as a whole (not in every *rakʿa*), or in some, that is in one *rakʿa* or more, cannot be included in

[112] Qur'ān 73 : 20. Pickthall's translation changed.

the ambit of the words of the Prophet (God's peace and blessings be upon him) about one who has not recited it (in every part). It was, in fact, this likelihood that led Abū Ḥanīfa to decide in favour of relinquishing recitation itself in part of the prayer, that is in the last two *rakʿa*s. Mālik preferred the recitation of *al-ḥamd* and a *sūra* in the first two *rakʿa*s of a four-*rakʿa* prayer, and *al-ḥamd* alone in the last two. Al-Shāfiʿī preferred that *al-ḥamd* and a *sūra* be recited in all four *rakʿa*s of the *ẓuhr* prayer, except that the *sūra* to be recited in the first two is to be longer. Mālik followed the authentic tradition of Abū Qatāda "that the Prophet (God's peace and blessings be upon him) used to recite the *fātiḥat al-Kitāb* and a *sūra* in the first two *rakʿa*s of *ẓuhr* and *ʿaṣr*, and the *fātiḥat al-Kitāb* only in the last two *rakʿa*s". Al-Shāfiʿī followed the apparent meaning of the authentic tradition of Abū Saʿīd "that he (the Prophet) used to recite in the first two *rakʿa*s of *ẓuhr* the length of about thirty verses, and in the last about fifteen verses". They did not disagree about *ʿaṣr* due to the agreement of the two traditions about it. The same tradition of Abū Saʿīd says "that in the first two *rakʿa*s of *ʿaṣr* he used to recite up to fifteen verses, and in the last two *rakʿa*s about half of that".

2.3.1.1.6. Issue 6: Recitation of the *Qurʾān* while bowing and prostrating

The majority agreed about the prohibition of the recitation of the Qurʾān while bowing and prostrating, because of the tradition of ʿAlī about it. According to this tradition, he (the Prophet) said, "Jibrīl prohibited me from reciting the Qurʾān while bowing and prostrating". Al-Ṭabarī said that it is an authentic tradition, and it was followed by the jurists of the various regions. Some of the Tābiʿūn decided to allow this, and it is also the opinion of al-Bukhārī, because the tradition did not prove to be authentic for him, Allāh knows best.

They disagreed on whether bowing and prostrating require determined words from the worshipper. Mālik said that there is nothing determined for them. Al-Shāfiʿī, Abū Ḥanīfa, Aḥmad, and a group of jurists said that the worshipper repeats the words, "Praise the name of thy Lord, the Tremendous",[113] three times while bowing, and the words "Praise the name of thy Lord, the Most High",[114] three times while prostrating, in accordance with the tradition of ʿUqba ibn ʿĀmir. Al-Thawrī maintained that it was preferable if the *imām* were to repeat these words five times, so that the follower would have time to repeat them thrice.

The reason for disagreement here stems from the conflict of Ibn ʿAbbās's tradition with the tradition of ʿUqba ibn ʿĀmir. In Ibn ʿAbbās" tradition the

[113] Qurʾān 56 : 74, 96.

[114] Qurʾān 87 : 1.

Prophet (God's peace and blessings be upon him) is reported to have said, "I have been prohibited from reciting the Qurʾān while bowing and prostrating. You should glorify the Lord while bowing and strive in making supplications while prostrating, for it is a deserving form for their being answered". In the tradition of ʿUqba ibn ʿĀmir, it is stated that when the verse "Praise the name of thy Lord, the Tremendous",[115] was revealed, the Prophet (God's peace and blessings be upon him) is reported to have said, "Recite this while bowing", and when the verse "Praise the name of they Lord, the Most High",[116] was revealed he said, "Recite this while prostrating".

Similarly, they disagreed about supplication when bowing, after they had agreed about glorification of Allāh. Mālik deemed this reprehensible because the Prophet (God's peace and blessings be upon him) said, "You should glorify the Lord while bowing and strive in making supplications while prostrating". A group of jurists said that supplication is permitted while bowing. They relied for this on traditions that state, "The Prophet (God's peace and blessings be upon him) used to make supplications while bowing". This is al-Bukhārī's opinion, who relied upon ʿĀʾisha's tradition. She said, "The Prophet (God's peace and blessings be upon him) used to say while bowing and prostrating, 'Glory to You O Allāh, our Lord, and all grateful praise for You. O Allāh, forgive me' ".

Abū Ḥanīfa does not permit supplication in prayer, using words other than the words of the Qurʾān, but Mālik and al-Shāfiʿī allow it. The reason for disagreement is based upon the dispute over whether it is (mundane) speech.

2.3.1.1.7. Issue 7: The obligation to recite the *tasshahhud*

They disagreed about *tashahhud* and its preferred text. Mālik, Abū Ḥanīfa, and a group of jurists held that *tashahhud* is not obligatory, while another group upheld its obligation, which was adopted by al-Shāfiʿī, Aḥmad, and Dāwūd. The reason for their disagreement arises from the conflict of analogy with the apparent meaning of traditions. Analogy requires its association with all other *arkān* (elements) that are not obligatory in prayer, because of their agreement over the obligation of (reciting) the Qurʾān (alone) in prayer, and that *tashahhud* is not a part of the Qurʾān so that it may be obligatory. In a tradition from Ibn ʿAbbās, he says, "The Messenger of Allāh (God's peace and blessings be upon him) used to teach us the *tashahhud* as he would teach us a *sūra* of the Qurʾān". This implies an obligation, along with the principle that the words and the acts of the Prophet (God's peace and blessings be upon him) must be construed to imply obligation till an evidence to the contrary is

[115] Qurʾān 56 : 74, 96.
[116] Qurʾān 87 : 1.

adduced. The principle followed by the others is contrary to this, which states that it is not obligatory to associate with matters whose obligation has been established by agreement or whose obligation has been expressly mentioned, unless their obligation has been expressly and explicitly mentioned (by the Prophet). These, as you can see, are two separate approaches.

In preferring the words of *tashahhud*, Mālik (God bless him) followed the words used by ʿUmar (God be pleased with him) for instructing people from the pulpit. The words are: "(All) greetings are for Allāh, righteous acts are for Allāh, good words and prayers are for Allāh. Peace on you O Prophet, and the mercy of Allāh and His blessings. Peace on us and on the righteous servants of Allāh. I testify that there is no god, but Allāh alone, without associates. I testify that Muḥammad is His servant and Messenger". The jurists of Kūfa, Abū Ḥanīfa and others, preferred the *tashahhud* used by ʿAbd Allāh ibn Masʿūd. Abū ʿUmar said that this was also preferred by Aḥmad and most of the traditionists, because of the authenticity of its transmission from the Messenger of Allāh (God's peace and blessings be upon him). The words are: "All salutations are for Allāh, as well as prayers and good words. Peace on you O Prophet, and the mercy of Allāh and His blessings. Peace on us, and on the righteous servants of Allāh. I testify that there is no god, but Allāh, and I testify that Muḥammad is His servant and Messenger". Al-Shāfiʿī and his disciples preferred the *tashahhud* used by Ibn ʿAbbās, which he related from the Prophet (God's peace and blessings be upon him), saying, "The Messenger of Allāh (God's peace and blessings be upon him) used to instruct us in *tashahhud* as he would in a *sūra* of the Qurʾān. He used to say, 'Salutations, blessed acts, prayers, and good words are (all) for Allāh. Peace on you O Prophet, the mercy of Allāh and His blessings. Peace on us and upon the righteous servants of Allāh. I testify that there is no god but Allāh and that Muḥammad is His Messenger'".

The reason for disagreement stems from their conviction about the preferred words. Those who were convinced about the preference of one of the three traditions followed it. Many jurists maintained that all this is a matter of choice, like words of *adhān* and *takbīr* in the case of funerals, the two *ʿĪd*s, and some other matters that have been attributed to the Prophet through *tawātur*. This appears to be the truth, Allāh knows best.

Al-Shāfiʿī stipulated blessings upon the Prophet (God's peace and blessings be upon him) as a condition of *tashahhud*, saying that it is an obligation because of the words of the Exalted, "Lo! Allah and His angels shower blessings on the Prophet. O ye who believe! Ask blessings on him and salute him with a worthy salutation".[117] He maintained that this salutation is the salutation in

[117] Qurʾān 33 : 56.

prayer.[118] The majority maintained that this is the salutation that is made after prayer.

A group of the Ẓāhirites said that it is obligatory for the worshipper reciting *tashahhud* to seek the refuge of Allāh from four things described in a tradition: the torment of the grave, the torment of Hell, the trial (*fitna*) of the Antichrist, and the trial of life and death. Because, it is established in the tradition "that the Messenger of Allāh (God's peace and blessings be upon him) used to seek refuge from them at the end of his *tashahhud*. Some versions of this tradition state: "When one of you completes the last *tashahhud*, he should seek refuge of Allāh from four things". The tradition has been recorded by Muslim.

2.3.1.1.8. Issue 8: Salutation concluding prayer

They disagreed about salutation after prayer. The majority upheld its obligation, while Abū Ḥanīfa and his disciples said that it is not obligatory. Some of those who maintained that it is obligatory said that it is obligatory upon the individual, and the *imām*, to make a single salutation, when others said that they make two (one to the right and one to the left).

The majority (who held that it is obligatory) followed the apparent meaning of ʿAlī's tradition, in which the Prophet (God's peace and blessings be upon him) said, "Its termination is the salutation". Those among them who said that the obligation is for making two salutations followed the established tradition that "the Prophet (God's peace and blessings be upon him) offered two salutations", and this is the case for those who construe his (God's peace and blessings be upon him) acts to imply obligation. Mālik preferred two salutations for the follower and a single salutation for the *imām*, though it is related from him that the follower offers three salutations, the first for termination, the second for (to greet) the *imām*, and the third for (to greet) the person on his left. Abū Ḥanīfa followed what was related by ʿAbd al-Raḥmān ibn Ziyād al-Ifrīqī that both ʿAbd al-Raḥmān ibn Rāfiʿ and Bakr ibn Sawādah related from ʿAbd Allāh ibn ʿAmr ibn al-ʿĀṣ who said, "If a man has taken the sitting posture at the end of his prayer and he passes wind before offering the salutation his prayer is complete". Abū ʿUmar ibn ʿAbd al-Barr said that the preceding tradition of ʿAlī is more authentic according to the traditionists, as the tradition of ʿAbd Allāh ibn ʿAmr ibn al-ʿĀṣ has been narrated only by al-Ifrīqī, a case that is considered weak by the traditionists.

The Qāḍī (Ibn Rushd) said: "If it is authentic by way of transmission, its text is subject to interpretation, because it does not indicate that completion of prayer is not possible without a salutation, except by way of the (indirect)

[118] The editor of the original text says: Attributing this to al-Shāfiʿī is subject to investigation. It appears, however, that the statement in the text is correct.

implication of the text (*dalīl al-Khiṭāb*), which is a construction that is considered weak by most. The majority, on the other hand, may say that the definite article, '*al*', which signifies inclusion is stronger than the (indirect) implication of the text in indicating the *ḥukm* of the unexpressed category, which is the opposite of the expressed *ḥukm*".

2.3.1.1.9. Issue 9: Supplication (*qunūt*)

They disagreed about the recitation of *qunūt*.[119] During the *iʿtidāl* in the last *rakʿa* Mālik maintained that *qunūt* is recommended for the dawn prayer, while al-Shāfiʿī said that it is a *sunna*. Abū Ḥanīfa held that reciting *qunūt* is not permitted in the dawn prayer, and its place is in the *witr* prayer. A group of jurists said that, in fact, *qunūt* is to be recited in every prayer. Some said that *qunūt* is recited only in the month of Ramaḍān, some said that it is recited in its second half, and others said that it is recited in the first half.

The reason for this disagreement is the conflict of traditions transmitted from the Prophet (God's peace and blessings be upon him) with analogy constructed upon other prayers, that is, analogy based upon those prayers in which *qunūt* is recited for those in which it is not. Abū ʿUmar ibn ʿAbd al-Barr said that recitation of *qunūt* was a prevailing practice among the first generation during the month of Ramaḍān, in which the disbelievers were cursed following the *sunna* of the Messenger of Allāh (God's peace and blessings be upon him), who made a supplication for cursing Waʿl and Dhakwān, and the group who killed the residents of Biʾr Maʿūna. Al-Layth ibn Saʿd said that for a period of forty-five years he had not offered *qunūt*, except behind an *imām* making such a supplication. He said that for this he had followed the tradition that was related from the Prophet (God's peace and blessings be upon him) that "he made supplications for a month or forty (days) pleading on behalf of one group and cursing others till Allāh, the Glorious and Exalted, censured him in the verse: 'It is no concern at all of thee (Muhammad) whether He relent toward them or punish them; for they are transgressors'".[120] The Messenger of Allāh (God's peace and blessings be upon him) gave up the supplication and did not repeat it till he met Allāh. Al-Layth said that since the time he bore this tradition with him, he did not make a supplication. This was also the opinion of Yaḥyāʾ ibn Yaḥyāʾ. The Qāḍī (Ibn Rushd) said: "The elderly scholars mentioned to me that this practice also prevailed among us at his mosque in Cordova, and it continued till our time or close to our time".

Muslim has recorded a report from Abū Hurayra "that the Prophet (God's

[119] It means the recitation of *duʿāʾ*.

[120] Qurʾān 3 : 128. Pickthall's translation changed.

peace and blessings be upon him) used to recite the *qunūt* in the dawn prayer, then information reached us that he relinquished this when the verse, 'It is no concern at all of thee (Muhammad) whether He relent toward them or punish them; for they are transgressors',[121] was revealed. He also recorded from Abū Hurayra that the Prophet (God's peace and blessings be upon him) used to supplicate during *ẓuhr*, *ᶜishā*ᵓ, and the dawn prayers. In addition, he has recorded a tradition from the Prophet (God's peace and blessings be upon him) that 'he continued to recite *qunūt* for one month during the dawn prayer invoking a curse upon Banū Uṣayya'".

They disagreed about the text of the *qunūt*. Mālik preferred that it be with the words: "O Allāh, we seek Your help, we seek Your forgiveness, we seek Your guidance, we believe in You, we bow and humble ourselves before You, we devote ourselves to You, and we shun him who denies You. O Allāh, You it is we worship, and for You we pray and prostrate ourselves, toward You we strive and hasten, seeking Your mercy, and fearing Your torment, for Your torment is about to chase the disbelievers". The jurists of ᶜIrāq call these the two *sūrahs*, and it is reported that they are to be found in the *muṣḥaf* of Ubayy ibn Kaᶜb. Al-Shāfiᶜī and Isḥāq said that the text of the *qunūt* is: "O Allāh, guide us with those You have guided, and deliver us with those You have delivered, guard us from the consequences of what You have decreed, You are the One Who decrees and there is no decree for You, You are the Glorious, our Lord, and the Exalted". This was related by al-Ḥasan ibn ᶜAlī through authentic channels that the Prophet (God's peace and blessings be upon him) had taught him this prayer to be used as a supplication in prayer. ᶜAbd Allāh ibn Dāwūd said: "Do not follow in prayer the person who does not supplicate using the two *sūrahs*". A group of jurists said that there is no special text prescribed for the *qunūt*.

2.3.1.2. *Section 2: The acts that constitute the elements* (arkān)

In this section there are eight fundamental issues:

2.3.1.2.1. Issue 1: Raising the hands (*rafᶜ al-yadayn*)

The jurists disagreed about raising of the hands in prayer on three points: first, about its *ḥukm*; second, about the occasions when the hands are raised; and third, about the extent to which they are to be raised.

Regarding the *ḥukm* the majority maintained that raising of the hands is a *sunna* of prayer, while Dāwūd and a group of his disciples maintained that it is an obligation. These jurists are further divided into sub-groups. Some of them

[121] Qurᵓān 3 : 128.

made it obligatory in the *takbīr* of *iḥrām* alone, some made it obligatory at the beginning of the prayer, while reciting the first words of *takbīr*, and at the time of bowing, that is, while lowering the body for *rukūʿ* and while raising it, some made it obligatory on these two occasions and at the time of prostration, and this in accordance with their disagreement about the occasions on which they are to be raised.

The reason for their disagreement is the conflict of the apparent meaning of Abū Hurayra's tradition, which contains instructions about the obligations of prayer, with the (reported) acts of the Prophet (God's peace and blessings be upon him). Abū Hurayra's contains the statement that the Prophet (God's peace and blessings be upon him) instructed him about *takbīr*, but he did not order him to raise his hands, while it is established from the Prophet (God's peace and blessings be upon him) through traditions reported by Ibn ʿUmar and others that "he used to raise his hands at the beginning of prayer".

About their disagreement over the occasions for raising the hands, the jurists of Kūfa, Abū Ḥanīfa, Sufyān al-Thawrī, and all their other jurists, said that the worshipper is not to raise his hands, except at the time of the first *takbīr*. This is also a narration of Ibn al-Qāsim from Mālik. Al-Shāfiʿī, Aḥmad, Abū ʿUbayd, Abū Thawr, the majority of the Ahl al-Ḥadīth, and the Ẓāhirites upheld the *ḥukm* of raising of the hands at the time of the first *takbīr*, and at the time of bowing, and while rising up from bowing. This is also related from Mālik, except that it is an obligation according to some of these jurists, while it is a *sunna* in Mālik's view. Some of the Ahl al-Ḥadīth upheld the raising of the hands at the time of prostration and on rising from it.

The reason for all this disagreement is related to the conflict of the traditions relevant to the issue, and the conflict of some of these with the practice at Medina. One of these traditions is that of ʿAbd Allāh ibn Masʿūd and al-Barāʾ ibn ʿĀzib "that the Prophet (God's peace and blessings be upon him) raised his hands once for the first *takbīr* and did not do so again". The second tradition is reported by Ibn ʿUmar from his father "that the Messenger of Allāh (God's peace and blessings be upon him) used to raise his hands up to the level of his shoulders at the beginning of prayer, and he also raised them when he straightened up after bowing and said, 'Allāh listens to one who praises Him, our Lord, all praise is for You', but he did not do this while prostrating". This is a tradition that is agreed upon for its authenticity (by al-Bukhārī and Muslim) and they believed that it was reported from the Prophet (God's peace and blessings be upon him) by about thirteen individuals from among his Companions. The third tradition is reported by Wāʾil ibn Ḥujr, which contains an addition over the tradition of Ibn ʿUmar "that he used to raise his hands while prostrating".

Among those who interpreted raising of the hands here to imply recommendation or obligation, there are some who restricted it to apply to the first *takbīr* by preferring the tradition of ʿAbd Allāh ibn Masʿūd and the tradition of al-Barāʾ ibn ʿĀzib, which is Mālik's opinion in conformity with practice (at Medina). Some of these jurists preferred the tradition of ʿAbd Allāh ibn ʿUmar and thus upheld raising of the hands on two occasions, that is while bowing and at the beginning because of its being widely known and because all of them agreed about it. Those among them who considered it to be an obligation interpreted it to be so, while those who deemed it to be a recommendation interpreted them to imply a recommendation. Those who adopted the method of reconciliation said that it is necessary to combine the additions with each other in accordance with what is contained in the tradition of Wāʾil ibn Ḥujr. Thus, the jurists adopted two methods with respect to these traditions: the method of preference or the method of reconciliation.

The reason for their disagreement over whether interpreting the raising of hands implies recommendation or obligation is the same reason that we have stated earlier that some of the jurists maintain that the principle about the acts of the Prophet (God's peace and blessings be upon him) is that they be construed as an obligation till an evidence is adduced to show the contrary, while others maintain that the principle is not to add to what has been established as an obligation of prayer through an authentic saying or through consensus, except on the basis of an explicit evidence. This explanation has already preceded in our description and there is no reason to repeat one single point many times.

The level to which the hands are to be raised has been determined by some to be up to the shoulders. This was the opinion of Mālik, al-Shāfiʿī, and a group of jurists. Some of them held it to be the level of the ears, which was upheld by Abū Ḥanīfa. Some jurists held that they be raised to the level of the chest. All this is related from the Prophet (God's peace and blessings be upon him), except that the most authentic of these reports is that they be raised up to the shoulders, and that is upheld by the majority. Raising them up to the ears is more authentic than raising them up to the chest, and is more widely known.

2.3.1.2.2. Issue 2: Rising straight from bowing

Abū Ḥanīfa maintained that *iʿtidāl* on rising from the *rukūʿ* and during it is not an obligation. Al-Shāfiʿī said it is obligatory. Mālik's disciples differed about whether the foremost opinion in the school implies that it is a recommendation or an obligation, as no explicit opinion is narrated from him on this.

The reason for disagreement here is whether the obligation is met by conforming with a part of that to which the term applies or by complying with the whole of it. Those for whom the obligation is met by complying with a part of that to which the term is applied, did not stipulate the maintenance of *iʿtidāl* while bowing. Those for whom the obligation is met by conformity with the whole stipulated rising to an erect position after *rukūʿ*, as this is established from the Prophet (God's peace and blessings be upon him). In a preceding tradition he said to a man whom he was instructing in the obligations of prayer, "Bow, resting a little in bowing, and raise yourself resting a while"; therefore, it is necessary to construe this as an obligation.

Those who maintain that the principle is not to construe the acts of the Prophet (God's peace and blessings be upon him) relating to his acts in prayer as obligatory unless an evidence indicates this, had recourse to this tradition; for this reason also they did not consider raising of the hands as obligatory nor even the other acts and pronouncements besides the first *takbīr* and recitation. Think over it for it is a principle that opposes the first principle (of interpreting the acts as obligatory), and is the cause of disagreement in most of these issues.

2.3.1.2.3. Issue 3: The sitting posture

The jurists disagreed about the sitting posture (in prayer). Mālik and his disciples said that the person is to lower himself on his buttocks toward the ground, with his right foot raised resting on the inside of its toes and his left leg bent under him and bend the left foot. In his view, the sitting posture for a woman is the same as that of a man. Abū Ḥanīfa and his disciples said that a man is to plant his right foot on the ground and seat himself on his left foot. Al-Shāfiʿī distinguished between the posture in the middle of the prayer and the posture at the end; for the posture during the middle he followed the same opinion as that of Abū Ḥanīfa, and for the last posture the same opinion as Mālik's.

The reason for their disagreement is the conflict of traditions. There are three traditions on the issue. The first, which is established by the agreement of all, is the tradition of Abū Ḥumayd al-Sāʿidī describing the prayer of the Prophet (God's peace and blessings be upon him). It contains the words, "When he sat down after two *rakʿa*s, he did so on his left leg and raised his right foot, but when he sat down at the end he bent his left leg and raised the right one sitting on his hips [on the left side]". The second is the tradition of Wāʾil ibn Ḥujr, which says, "When he sat down in prayer, he raised his right foot and sat on the left". The third tradition is related by Mālik from ʿAbd Allāh ibn ʿUmar, who said, "The *sunna* in prayer is that you raise your right foot and bend your left leg". It is a primary authority, because of his saying, "The *sunna* in prayer". In a report from al-Qāsim ibn Muḥammad he showed them the sitting posture during *tashahhud*, and raised his right foot and turned in the left, but he sat on his left hip not on his foot, saying "This is what ʿAbd Allāh ibn ʿAbd Allāh ibn ʿUmar showed me, and said that his father used to adopt this posture".

Mālik followed the method of preference on the basis of this tradition, while Abū Ḥanīfa favoured preference on the basis of Wāʾil's tradition. Al-Shāfiʿī adopted the method of reconciliation based on the tradition of Abū Ḥumayd. Al-Ṭabarī left it to the choice of the individual and said, "All these postures are permissible, and their adoption is commendable because they have been established through authentic reports from the Messenger of Allāh". This is a commendable opinion, as it is better to base the varying acts on selection rather than on conflict. This kind of conflict may often occur between acts as opposed to words, or in words opposed to words.

2.3.1.2.4. Issue 4: The *ḥukm* of the sitting postures

The jurists disagreed about the sitting postures in the middle of the prayer (that is, on rising from the second prostration of the second *rakʿa* and before standing up for the third) and at the end. Most of the jurists held that the posture in the middle of the prayer is *sunna* and is not an obligation. One group deviated from this and said that it is an obligation (*farḍ*). Likewise, the majority held that the sitting posture at the end of the prayer is obligatory, but some deviated and held that it is a *sunna*. The reason for their disagreement is the conflict of the implication of the text with analogy constructed upon one sitting posture over the other. This is so as in the preceding tradition of Abū Hurayra; the words are: "Then sit up and rest a little, while seated". According to the apparent meaning of this tradition the sitting posture is obligatory in the entire prayer. Those who adopted it said that all sitting postures are obligatory. It is however laid down in the confirmed tradition of Ibn Buhayna that "the messenger of Allah (God's peace and blessings be upon him) dropped the middle sitting posture and did not repeat it, and then prostrated on account of it". It is also established from him that he dropped two *rakʿas* but performed them again, as he did for one *rakʿa*. From this the jurists understood the difference between the *ḥukm* of the middle sitting posture and the *ḥukm* of a *rakʿa*. As a *rakʿa* was obligatory for them by consensus, it followed that the middle sitting posture was not obligatory. It is on this basis that the jurists differentiated between the two sitting postures and maintained the prostrations of forgetfulness are performed for *sunan* and not for obligations (*furūḍ*). Those who considered it to be an obligation maintained that the prostrations of forgetfulness are specific to the middle posture (if left out) as distinguished from the other obligations, and that cannot be counted as evidence that it (the middle posture) is not obligatory.

Those who maintained that both sitting postures are a *sunna* considered that the last sitting posture is to be so on the analogy of the middle sitting posture after having considered the middle sitting posture to be so on the basis of the evidence relied upon by the majority for considering it as *sunna*. Thus, the reason for their disagreement, in actual fact, refers to the conflict between reasoning and the implication of words or with the implication of acts. Some jurists, those who considered that the sitting postures are both obligatory, did so because for them the acts of the Prophet (God's peace and blessings be upon him) are the basis for declaring the acts of prayer as obligatory, unless there is an evidence indicating the contrary. Both bases taken together imply here that the last sitting posture is obligatory, for which reason the majority adopt this opinion. As there is only analogy opposing these two bases, that is, of words and acts, the weakest of the opinions is that which holds both sitting postures to be a *sunna*, Allāh knows best.

It is established from the Prophet (God's peace and blessings be upon him) that "he used to place his right hand on his right thigh and his left hand on his left thigh, and that he used to point with his finger [an indication of Divine Unity]". The jurists agree that this form of the sitting posture is to be preferred to others in prayer, but they differed about the movement of the finger because of the conflict of traditions in this, the established act being that he merely used to point it (not to shake it).

2.3.1.2.5. Issue 5: Placing one hand over the other in prayer (in the standing posture)

The jurists differed about placing one hand over the other in prayer. Mālik disapproved this in obligatory prayers, but permitted it in supererogatory prayers. A group of jurists, and these are the majority, maintained that this act is among the *sunan* of prayer. The reason for their disagreement is that confirmed traditions have been reported in which the description of the Prophet's prayer have been transmitted, but it has not been transmitted that he used to place his right hand over his left during prayer, while it has also been related that the people were commanded to do this. This has been related in the description of the prayer of the Prophet (God's peace and blessings be upon him) in the tradition of Abū Ḥumayd. A group of jurists, therefore, held that the traditions in which this is established imply an addition over those in which this addition has not been transmitted, and an addition has to be accepted. Another group said that it is necessary to adopt the traditions in which this addition has not been transmitted as these are more in number, and also because it (this practice) is not compatible with the acts of prayer for it belongs to the category of seeking support; therefore, Mālik permitted it in supererogatory and not in obligatory prayers. It appears that it depicts a posture of humility, which is appropriate for it.

2.3.1.2.6. Issue 6: Rising from prostrations after the odd *rakʿa* and leaning on the hands before prostrating

A group of jurists preferred that when a person is in the odd *rakʿa* of his prayer he should not stand up (after the second prostration) till he has straightened up in the sitting posture (for resting), while another group preferred that he rise up straight from the prostrations. The first was the opinion of al-Shāfiʿī and a group of jurists and the second was the opinion of Mālik and a group of jurists.

The reason for the disagreement is that there are two conflicting traditions in this. The first is the confirmed tradition of Mālik ibn al-Ḥuwayrith "that he saw the Messenger of Allāh (God's peace and blessings be upon him) pray, and when he was in the odd *rakʿa* of his prayer he did not stand up after the prostration till he had straightened up in the sitting posture". In the tradition of Abū Ḥumayd about the description of the prayer of the Prophet (God's peace and blessings be upon him) it is said "that when he raised up his head after the second prostration in the first *rakʿa*, he stood up and did not seat himself". Al-Shāfiʿī adopted the first tradition, while Mālik adopted the second.

They also differed about whether a person prostrating should place his hands on the ground before kneeling, or whether he should kneel before placing his hands. Mālik's view favours kneeling before the placing of hands. The reason for their disagreement is that in the tradition of Ibn Ḥujr, he said: "I saw that the Messenger of Allāh (God's peace and blessings be upon him) would kneel while prostrating before reaching for the floor with his hands, and would withdraw his hands before his knees while rising up". It is related from Abū Hurayra "that the Prophet (God's peace and blessings be upon him) said, 'When one of you is about to prostrate he should not kneel down like a camel, but should place his hands before kneeling'". ʿAbd Allāh ibn ʿUmar used to place his hands before his knees. Some of the traditionists have said that the tradition of Wāʾil ibn Ḥujr is more authentic than that of Abū Hurayra.

2.3.1.2.7. Issue 7: Prostration is on seven limbs

The jurists agreed that prostration is on seven limbs, the forehead, the (two) hands, the (two) knees, and the inside of the toes, because of the words of the Prophet (God's peace and blessings be upon him), "I have been commanded to prostrate on seven limbs". They differed about the person who prostrates and fails to employ one of these limbs: is his prayer invalidated? A group of jurists said that his prayer is not invalidated as the term "prostration" applies only to the face. Another group said that it is invalidated if he does not prostrate on the seven limbs stated in the tradition.

They did not differ, however, on the point that one who prostrates on his forehead and nose is considered to have prostrated on his face, but they disagreed on whether prostration on one or the other was permissible. Mālik said that if he prostrates on his forehead and not the nose it is permitted, but if he prostrates on his nose and not on his forehead it is not permitted. Abū Ḥanīfa said that this is allowed. Al-Shāfiʿī said that the prostration is not valid unless he prostrates on both.

The reason for their disagreement arised from the question of whether the obligation is to comply with part of that to which the term is applicable or to comply with the whole. This is so as the term face has been used in the tradition of Ibn ʿAbbās which says, "I have been commanded to prostrate on seven limbs". Those who maintained that the obligation is to comply with part of that to which the term is applicable said that it is sufficient if he prostrates on either the forehead or the nose. Those who maintained that the term prostration applies to the person who prostrates on his forehead only, but does not apply to one who prostrates on his nose only, permitted prostration on the forehead and not on the nose alone. This amounts to delineation of the part that achieves compliance with the obligation when such part is implied by the term, and it is based upon the opinion of those who distinguish between parts of a thing. They maintain that compliance with (the important) part of it fulfils the obligation, while compliance with another part (that is not important) does not. Think over this as it is one of the principles of this topic. (Had prostration on the nose alone been permitted) it would have been possible for one to say that even if the nose barely touches the ground prostration is valid. Those who maintain that the obligation is to comply with all that is included in the term make it obligatory for a person to prostrate on his forehead as well as his nose. Al-Shāfiʿī says that the ambiguity that is found in the words has been removed by the acts of the Prophet (God's peace and blessings be upon him) and has been explained, for he used to prostrate on his forehead and his nose as has been stated in a tradition that when he completed one of his prayers there were marks of dust and water on his forehead and nose, thus, his act has elaborated the unelaborated tradition.

Abū ʿUmar ibn ʿAbd al-Barr said that one of the *ḥadīth* authorities related the tradition of Ibn ʿAbbās and mentioned the face and the nose in it. The Qāḍī Abū al-Walīd (Ibn Rushd) said that some of them have mentioned only the forehead, and both narrations are in the compilation by Muslim, the latter being an evidence for Mālik.

They also disagreed on whether it is a condition for the prostrations that the hands be conspicuously placed on the prayer-mat on which the face rests? Mālik said that this is a condition of prostration, and I believe it is a condition of perfection. A group of jurists said that this is not a condition for prostration.

Within this topic is also their disagreement about prostrating on the bands of the turbans. The jurists are divided into three opinions about it. One opinion prohibits it, while another allows it. A third makes a distinction between prostrating on a small fraction of the band or on the major part of it, and whether or not a part of the forehead touches the ground. This disagreement is found all over the school and among the jurists of the regions. In al-Bukhārī there is a tradition to the effect that they used to prostrate on caps and turbans.

Those who did not uphold as obligatory to let the hands rest on the floor in prostration argued on the basis of Ibn ʿAbbās's opinion that "The Prophet (God's peace and blessings be upon him) ordered that we prostrate on seven limbs without folding back the clothes or hair", and also on analogy upon the knees in prayer and upon prayer in boots. It is possible to argue on the basis of the general implication here for prostrating on the band of the turban.

2.3.1.2.8. Issue 8: Prohibition of *iqʿāʾ* (sitting on the buttocks and folding up the knees) during prayer

The jurists agreed on the disapproval of *iqʿāʾ* during prayers on the basis of the prohibition (specified) in the tradition (which refers to) "a man sitting during prayer in the posture of a dog". They differed, however, about the implications of the term. Some of them maintained that the prohibited *iqʿāʾ* is the sitting posture of a man when he seats himself on his buttocks and folds up his thighs like posture of a dog or a lion. There is no disagreement among them that this is not one of the postures of prayer. Another group maintained that the *iqʿāʾ* that has been frowned upon is the resting of the buttocks on the ankles between the two prostrations while the feet are resting on the toes. This is Mālik's opinion as it is related that Ibn ʿUmar used to do this because his feet used to ache. Ibn ʿAbbās used to say that "sitting on the feet in this way is the *sunna* of your Prophet". It is recorded by Muslim.

The reason for their disagreement is the vacillation of the term *iqʿāʾ*, (frowned upon in prayers) between the literal meaning and the legal meaning, that is, the meaning to which this term has been restricted by the law. Those who said that it conveys a literal meaning identified it with the posture of a dog. Those who said that it conveys the legal meaning said that it indicates one of the postures prohibited during prayer, and as it is established from Ibn ʿUmar that the posture of a person sitting on his ankles letting his feet rest on their toes is not a *sunna* of prayer they were led to believe that it is this posture that has been prohibited. But this is a weak (argument) as terms for which no legal meaning has been established must be understood in their literal sense till such time that a legal meaning is established for them. This is unlike those terms for which legal meanings have been established, that is, these must be understood in their legal meaning till an evidence indicates their interpretation in the literal sense. Further, the tradition of Ibn ʿUmar has been contradicted by the tradition of Ibn ʿAbbās.

2.3.2. Chapter 2 Congregational Prayers and the Conditions of *Imāma*

The discussion of the rules in this chapter is covered in seven sections. The first is about the identification of the *aḥkām* of congregational prayers. The second is about the identification of the conditions of *imāma* and about the person who has precedence for *imāma* and the conditions specific to him. The third is about the position of the followers with respect to the *imām* and the *aḥkām* specific to the followers. The fourth is about the things in which a person follows the *imām* and those in which he does not follow him. The fifth is about the manner of following (the *imām*). The sixth is about the acts that the *imām* bears on behalf of the followers. The seventh is about the question of how far can the invalidation of the *imām*'s prayer be extended to the followers.

2.3.2.1. *Section 1*: *The* ḥukm *of congregational prayers*

In this section there are two issues. The first is whether prayer with the congregation is obligatory on the person who hears the call. The second issue relates to the following question: if a person enters the mosque and prays (separately before the congregational prayer is held), is it obligatory upon him to repeat the same prayers with the congregation?

2.3.2.1.1. Issue 1

The jurist disagreed about (the issue), with the majority maintaining that it is either a *sunna* or a communal obligation (*farḍ kifāya*). The Ẓāhirites maintained that prayer with the congregation is obligatory for each *mukallaf* (individual with legal capacity).

The reason for their disagreement arises from the conflict of the interpretations of the traditions on this issue. Thus, the apparent meaning of the words of the Prophet (God's peace and blessings be upon him), "Prayer with the congregation is superior to praying alone by twenty-five degrees or by twenty-seven degrees" conveys that congregational prayers belong to the category of recommended *aḥkām*. This means that it is a perfection over and above the obligatory prayer, as if the Prophet (God's peace and blessings be upon him) had said that prayer with the congregation is more perfect than the prayer of the (solitary) individual. Perfection is something additional to sufficiency. There is the well-known tradition about the blind man, who sought permission to stay away from congregational prayers as there was no one to lead him to it (the congregation). The Prophet (God's peace and blessings be upon him) granted him the exemption (at first), but then said to him, "Can you hear the call?" He said, "Yes". He said, "In that case I do not find any exemption for you". This is explicit about its obligation in the absence of a valid excuse. This is recorded by Muslim. Among those that strengthen this tradition is that related by Abū Hurayra, the authenticity of which is agreed upon and it states that the Messenger of Allāh (God's peace and blessings be upon him) said, "By Him in whose hands is my life, I had almost resolved to order the collection of firewood in bundles, order the call for prayer, then order a person to lead the people in prayers (on my behalf), and then chase reluctant men (in their houses) and to burn down their houses over them. By Him in whose hands is my life, if any of them had known that he would find a meaty bone or two good meat legs, he would be present at *ishā*ʾ". There is also the tradition of Ibn Masʿūd, in which he said, "The Messenger of Allāh (God's peace and blessings be upon him) taught us the paths of right guidance, and among these guided paths is prayer in a mosque where the call has been issued". In some of its versions it is said, "If you were to give up the practice of your Prophet you would be led astray".

Each group (of these jurists) followed the method of reconciliation by interpreting (in his own way) the tradition adopted by the contender and turning it toward the apparent meaning of the tradition adopted by them. Thus, the Ẓāhirites said that it is probable that grading can be found in things all of which are obligatory. Consequently, the obligatory congregational prayer has precedence, by the stated degrees, over the prayer of the solitary individual who has a valid excuse. They said that because of this there is no contradiction between the traditions. They also argued that this is similar to the case conveyed by the words of the Prophet (God's peace and blessings be upon him) that "the prayer of one sitting is half that of one standing (that is, though one is superior, both are obligatory)".

The others construed the tradition about the blind man to apply to the call for the Friday prayer as that is the call which it is obligatory by agreement to answer by one who hears it. This, however, is far-fetched, Allāh knows best. The text of the tradition states that Abū Hurayra said, "A blind man came up to the Prophet (God's peace and blessings be upon him) and said, 'O Messenger of Allāh, I have no one who can lead me to the mosque'. He then asked the Messenger of Allāh (God's peace and blessings be upon him) to exempt him so that he may pray in his house. The Prophet granted him the exemption. When the man turned around to go, he called him saying, 'Do you hear the call for prayer?' The man said, 'Yes'. He said, 'Then answer it' ". It is unlikely that this can be understood to mean the call for the Friday prayer. Moreover, going to the Friday prayer is obligatory upon everyone resident in the town even if he does not hear the call, and I am not aware of any disagreement over this. Further, this tradition is opposed by the tradition of ʿUtbān ibn Mālik mentioned in *al-Muwaṭṭaʾ*, which says that ʿUtbān ibn Mālik, a blind man who used to lead people in prayers, said to the Messenger of Allāh (God's peace and blessings be upon him), "It is (sometimes) dark and raining with flooding all around, and I am a man who has lost his sight. So come, O Messenger of Allāh, to pray in my house in a corner that I have set aside to be the place of prayer". The Messenger of Allāh (God's peace and blessings be upon him) came to him and said, "Where would you prefer that I pray?" He pointed out a spot in the house and the Messenger of Allāh (God's peace and blessings be upon him) prayed there.

2.3.2.1.2. Issue 2

The person who entered the mosque and prayed may have done it in one of two ways: he may have prayed alone, or he may have prayed with the congregation. If he has prayed alone, a group of jurists maintain that he is to repeat the prayer with the congregation, except in the case of the sunset prayer (*maghrib*) only. Those who upheld this opinion are Mālik and his disciples. Abū Ḥanīfa said that he is to repeat the prayer, except the sunset and the middle prayer (*ʿaṣr*), while al-Awzāʿī exempted the sunset and the morning prayers, and Abū Thawr exempted the middle and the morning prayers. Al-Shāfiʿī said that he is to repeat all the prayers.

They agreed generally about the repetition of the prayers (with the congregation) because of the tradition of Bishr ibn Muḥammad from his father "that the Messenger of Allāh (God's peace and blessings be upon him) said to him when he entered the mosque and did not pray with him, 'Why is it that you did not pray with the people, are you not a Muslim?' He said, 'Of course I am, O Messenger of Allāh, but I had prayed with my family.' The Prophet (God's peace and blessings be upon him) said to him, 'When you come you must pray with the people, even if you have already prayed'". The jurists disagreed due to the likelihood of the restriction of this general implication by means of analogy or an evidence. Those who interpreted it in its (unrestricted) general meaning made the repetition of all prayers obligatory, and this is the opinion of al-Shāfiʿī. Those who exempted from this only the sunset prayer, restricted the general meaning through *qiyās al-shabah*. This was done by Mālik (God bless him). He argued that repeating the sunset prayer, which is an odd number (of *rakʿas*), would make it an even number and it would no longer remain odd as the total would come to six *rakʿas*. Thus, it would be moved from its own category to the category of another prayer, which would invalidate it. There is weakness, however, in this analogy as the salutation has caused a separation between the two odd prayers, and adopting the general meaning is better than effecting a restriction by means of such analogy. Stronger than this argument is what is maintained by the Kūfīs, who argued that if he repeats the sunset prayer he has performed two odd prayers, and there is a tradition that "two odd numbered prayers cannot be performed in one night". Abū Ḥanīfa, on the other hand, said that the second prayer would be like supererogatory prayers. Thus, if a person repeats the middle prayer (*ʿaṣr*) he would be observing a supererogatory prayer after the *ʿaṣr* prayer, which is prohibited. He therefore exempted the middle prayer on the basis of this analogy and the sunset prayer because it is odd-numbered, and odd-numbered prayers are not to be repeated. This analogy is good if al-Shāfiʿī concedes to them that the repeated prayer is supererogatory. Those who made a distinction between the morning prayer and the middle prayer for this purpose did so because the traditions do not conflict about the prohibition of praying after the morning prayer, while they do conflict about prayer after the middle prayer, as has already been mentioned. This is al-Awzāʿī's opinion.

If a person has prayed in a congregation, is he to repeat the prayer with another congregation? Most of the jurists, including Mālik and Abū Ḥanīfa, maintain that he does not have to repeat such a prayer. Some of them said that he is to repeat it. Those who held this opinion are Aḥmad, Dāwūd, and the Ẓāhirites.

The reason for their disagreement stems from the conflict of the implications of the traditions on this issue. It is related from the Prophet (God's peace and blessings be upon him) that he said, "A prayer is not to be performed twice in a day". It is also related from him "that he ordered those persons, who had said their prayer in a congregation, to say it with another congregation about to start". Further, the apparent meaning of the tradition of Bishr requires repetition from each worshipper who comes into the mosque (when the congregational prayer is about to start), and the strength of this tradition is that of a general rule. Most of the jurists believe that if a general rule is based upon a particular cause, such rule is not to be restricted to its cause. In addition, there is the case of the prayer of Muʿādh with the Prophet (God's peace and blessings be upon him), who would then lead his own people for the same prayer, a fact which bears evidence for the permissibility of repeating a prayer (performed with a congregation) with another congregation.

The jurists adopted either the method of reconciliation or that of preference in these traditions. Those who adopted the method of preference accepted the general implication of the words of the Prophet (God's peace and blessings be upon him), "A prayer is not to be performed twice in a day", and they exempted from this the person who had prayed alone because of the agreement over his case. Those who adopted the method of reconciliation said that the meaning of the words of the Prophet (God's peace and blessings be upon him),

"A prayer is not to be performed twice in a day", is that a person should not repeat the same prayer believing that each one of them is obligatory (*farḍ*); on the contrary, he should believe that the second is an addition over the first, but it is commanded nevertheless. Another group said that the implication of this tradition is for the individual praying alone, that is, an individual should not say the same prayers twice (alone).

2.3.2.2. *Section 2: The conditions for* imāma *and issues of precedence*

This section is about the identification of the conditions for *imama*, identification of the person who has precedence, and about the *aḥkām* specific to the *imām*. In this section there are four issues.

2.3.2.2.1. Issue 1

They disagreed about the person who has precedence for *imāma*. Mālik said that he is the one most learned (about the rules of prayer), and not one who is the best reciter (of the Qur'ān). This was also al-Shāfi'ī's opinion. Abū Ḥanīfa, al-Thawrī, and Aḥmad said that the best reciter is to lead them.

The reason for their disagreement comes from the dispute over the meaning of the words of the Prophet (God's peace and blessings be upon him), "The person who recites the Book of Allāh best is to lead his people, and if two are equal in recitation then one who has greater knowledge of the *sunna*. If they are equal with respect to the *sunna* then the one who emigrated [to Medina] first. If they are equal with respect to emigration then the one who embraced Islam first. A man is not to lead another person who is under his authority, nor is he to take advantage of another person's hospitality without his permission". This is a tradition that is agreed upon for its authenticity, but the jurists differed about its meaning.

Among those who interpreted it through its apparent meaning is Abū Ḥanīfa. Some of them understood the words "best reciter" to mean the most learned in the law, as they believed that the need for *fiqh* in *imāma* is greater than that for recitation. Further, the best reciter among the Companions was necessarily the best in legal knowledge contrary to the situation that prevails today.

2.3.2.2.2. Issue 2

The jurists disagreed about the *imāma* of a minor who had not attained puberty but he could recite. A group of jurists permitted this due to the generality of this tradition[122] and due to the tradition of 'Amr ibn Salama

[122] According to the editor of the original, the words "this tradition" is an addition found in the Egyptian manuscript, though the word *athar* was not there.

that he used to lead his people in prayer when he was a minor. A group of jurists prohibited this absolutely, while another permitted it for supererogatory prayers, but not for obligatory prayers, which is a narration from Mālik.

The reason for the disagreement stems from the question of whether a person can lead another in prayer when such prayer is not obligatory for him, but is obligatory for the person being led. This is due to the difference in the *niyya* of the person leading and that of the follower.

2.3.2.2.3. Issue 3

They disagreed about the *imāma* of the disobedient (*fāsiq*). A group of jurists rejected it outright, while another permitted it without qualification. A third group made a distinction on the basis of the degree of certainty of his disobedience, and said that if his (the *imām*'s) disobedience is certain the worshipper is (obliged) to repeat his prayer always, but if it is probable, it is recommended that the worshipper repeat the prayer. This opinion was preferred by al-Abharī from among the opinions in the school. There were those who made a distinction according to whether there was a basis for his disobedience, like one who drinks *nabīdh* (a beverage of dates considered prohibited by some) and relies on the opinion of the jurists of Iraq for doing so; thus they permitted prayer behind a person (leader) who relies on some basis, but not behind one who does not have such a basis. The reason for their disagreement stems from the fact that it is something that is not expressly stated by the law, and the analogies are in conflict.

Those who maintained that as *fisq* (disobedience) does not invalidate prayer, and that the follower does not need more than the validity of the *imām*'s prayer—that is, according to the opinion of those who hold that the *imām* performs the prayer on behalf of the follower—permitted the *imāma* of the *fāsiq*. Those who compared *imāma* to the rendering of testimony and suspected the *fāsiq* of performing an invalid prayer, just as the (*fāsiq*) witness is suspected of rendering false testimony, did not permit his *imāma*. It is for this reason that some of the jurists made a distinction on the basis of whether his *fisq* is based on some legal justification. The distinction based on whether his disobedience is definitive or probable is almost similar to this, for when his *fisq* is certain it is as if he does not have a legal justification for it.

The Ẓāhirites preferred to permit the *imāma* of the disobedient on the basis of the general implication of the words of the Prophet (God's peace and blessings be upon him), "The best reciter is to lead them". They said that the disobedient has not been exempted from this. Arguing on the basis of a general implication, however, is deemed weak when the issue is not directly addressed by the text.

Some jurists made a distinction between the case where a person's disobedience is related to one of the conditions of the validity of prayer and where it is related to matters outside the ambit of prayer; this is so because it is a condition for the *imām* that his prayer be valid.

2.3.2.2.4. Issue 4

They disagreed about the *imāma* of a woman. The majority maintained that she cannot lead men, but they disagreed about her leading women (in prayer). Al-Shāfiʿī permitted this while Mālik prohibited it. Abū Thawr and al-Ṭabarī deviated (from the majority opinion) and permitted her *imāma* in absolute terms.

The majority agreed to prohibit her from leading men, because had this been permitted such permission would have been transmitted from the first generation (of Islam). Further, a known practice in prayer is that women should stand behind men; therefore it is obvious that their being at the front is not permitted. The Prophet (God's peace and blessings be upon him) said, "Keep them behind insofar as Allāh has kept them behind". It is for this reason that some jurists permitted them to lead women, as they have equal precedence for purposes of prayer. This has also been narrated from some members of the first generation.

Those who permitted her *imāma* argued on the basis of the tradition of Umm Waraqa recorded by Abū Dāwūd "that the Messenger of Allāh (God's peace and blessings be upon him) used to visit her at her house and appointed a *muʾadhdhin* for her to recite the *adhān* for her. He ordered her to lead the members of her household in prayer".

There are many issues under this topic of *imāma*, including their disagreement about the qualifications stipulated for the *imām*. We have left out their discussion as they are not expressly mentioned in the law.

The Qāḍī (Ibn Rushd) said: "What we have aimed for in this book is the discussion of issues that have been transmitted and of those that are closely related to the transmitted issues".

2.3.2.2.5. Issue 5: The *aḥkām* specific to the *imām*

There are four issues in this that are related to those expressly transmitted. The first is whether it is the *imām* who pronounces *āmīn* (amen) after he has completed the recitation of the *umm al-Qurʾān*, or is it the follower who does that. The second is when does he pronounce the *takbīr* of commencement. The third is whether he is to be led on if he waivers in the recitation. The fourth is whether his place of prayer is to be higher than that of the followers.

About the issue whether the *imām* is to pronounce *āmīn* (amen) once he has completed the recitation of the *umm al-Kitāb*, Mālik held, in the narrations of Ibn al-Qāsim and the Egyptians from him, that he is not to pronounce *āmīn*.

The majority maintained that he is to say *āmīn* just like the follower. This is also one narration from Mālik through the Medinites.

The reason for the disagreement are two traditions that have conflicting apparent meanings. First is the tradition of Abū Hurayra, which is agreed upon for its authenticity. He said, "The Messenger of Allāh (God's peace and blessings be upon him) said, 'When the *imām* pronounces *āmīn*, you should pronounce it too'". The second tradition is what is recorded by Mālik, also from Abū Hurayra, that the Prophet (God's peace and blessings be upon him) said, "When the *imām* says '*ghayr al-maghḍūbi ʿalayhim wa laʾḍḍālīn*', then you should say '*āmīn*'".

The first tradition is explicit about the pronouncing of *āmīn* by the *imām*. The second tradition indicates that the *imām* does not pronounce *āmīn*, for had he been required to pronounce *āmīn* why would the follower be asked to pronounce it after the completion of the recitation of the *umm al-Kitāb* and before the *imām*'s uttering of *āmīn*. The *imām* as the Prophet (God's peace and blessings be upon him) said, "has been appointed so that he be followed". (This holds true) unless the act in issue has been excluded from the words of the *imām*, that is, the follower may either say *āmīn* at the same time as the *imām* or before him. Thus there is no evidence in this tradition about *imām*'s pronouncing of *āmīn* and it only includes the *ḥukm* of the follower. It appears that Mālik adopted the method of preference for the tradition that he narrated because it is the listener who says *āmīn* and not the reciter. The majority preferred the first tradition because it was explicit and because there is nothing in it about the *ḥukm* of the *āmīn* of the *imām*. The difference between this tradition and the other is on the issue of the *āmīn* of the follower and not whether the *imām* is to say *āmīn*, so think over this.

It is possible that the first tradition be interpreted so as to say that the meaning of the words "When the *imām* pronounces *āmīn*, you should pronounce it too" is that (you should say it) when the *imām* reaches the point of *āmīn*. It is said that pronouncing *āmīn* is a form of prayer but this amounts to swerving from an apparent meaning to something that is not implied by the tradition, unless this is done through analogy, that is, the words of the Prophet should be read as saying, "When the *imām* says '*ghayr al-maghḍūbi ʿalayhim wa laʾḍḍālīn*", then you should say "*āmīn*" for the *imām* does not say "*āmin*".

About the point at which the *imām* is to pronounce *takbīr*, a group of jurists said that he is not to pronounce it except after the completion of the *iqāma* and the formation of the rows. This is the opinion of Mālik, al-Shāfiʿī, and a group of jurists. Another group said that the occasion for *takbīr* is prior to the completion of the *iqāma*, and they preferred that he should pronounce it when the *muʾadhdhin* says "*qad qāmatiʾṣ-ṣalāh*". This is the opinion of Abū Ḥanīfa, al-Thawrī, and Zufar.

The reason for disagreement over this stems from the conflict of the apparent meaning of the tradition of Anas with the tradition of Bilāl. In the tradition of Anas, he said that "the Messenger of Allāh (God's peace and blessings be upon him) turned toward us before pronouncing *takbīr* for the prayer and said, 'Form the rows and close up, for I can see you behind me' ". The apparent meaning of this is that these words were said after the completion of the *iqāma*. The same thing is related of ʿUmar, that after the completion of the *iqāma* he used to straighten up the rows and then pronounce *takbīr*. In Bilāl's tradition, he relates that "I used to pronounce the *iqāma* for the Prophet (God's peace and blessings be upon him) and used to say to him, 'O Messenger of Allāh, do not pre-empt me with *āmīn*' ". It is related by al-Ṭaḥāwī. They said that this indicates that the Messenger of Allāh (God's peace and blessings be upon him) used to pronounce the *takbīr* before the completion of the *iqāma*.

In the case of their disagreement about the admissibility of the *imām* to lead when he hesitates (in the recitation), Mālik, al-Shāfiʿī, and the majority of the jurists permitted that the *imām* be led on, but the Kūfīs prohibited this. The reason for their disagreement is based on the conflict of traditions. It is related "that the Messenger of Allāh (God's peace and blessings be upon him) hesitated while reciting a verse, and when he had finished said, 'Where is ʿUbayy (ibn Kaʿb)? Was he not among the people (worshipers)' ". Thus, he wanted to be led on. It is also related from the Prophet (God's peace and blessings be upon him) that he said, "The *imām* is not to be led on". The dispute over this exists from the first period, and it is well-known of ʿAlī that he prohibited it, while its permissibility is equally well known from Ibn ʿUmar.

A group of jurists permitted that the position of the *imām* be at a raised level with respect to the position of the followers, while another group prohibited this. Another group preferred that it be slightly higher, which was Mālik's opinion. The reason for disagreement is based on two conflicting traditions. First is the confirmed tradition that "the Prophet (God's peace and blessings be upon him) led the people (in prayer) from the pulpit so that he may teach them how to pray, but when he was about to prostrate he stepped down from the pulpit". The second is the tradition recorded by Abū Dāwūd that Hudhayfa led the people in prayer standing on (the raised platform of) a shop (or on a bench). Ibn Masʿūd took hold of his shirt and pulled him down. When he had finished praying he said, "Do you not know that they used to prohibit this or were prohibited from this?"

They disagreed about whether the *imām* should make a *niyya* for the *imāma*. A group of jurists said that this is not obligatory for him because of the tradition of Ibn ʿAbbās that he took up his position on one side of the

Messenger of Allāh (God's peace and blessings be upon him) after he had begun his prayer. A group of jurists said that this is probable; however, the *niyya* of *imāma* is necessary if the follower leaves out some of the acts of prayer, on the assumption that the *imām* bears it on behalf of the followers. This is so according to the opinion of those who maintained that the omissions by the follower are compensated by the *imām's* performance of the obligatory or supererogatory acts (of prayer).

2.3.2.3. *Section 3: The position of the follower with respect to the* imām, *and* aḥkām *specific to the followers*

In this section there are five issues as follows:

2.3.2.3.1. Issue 1

The majority of the jurists agreed that the practice for one person (male) is to stand on the right side of the *imām*, because of its being established through the traditions of Ibn ʿAbbās and others. If there are three persons besides the *imām* they are to stand behind the *imām*. They differed when there are two persons besides the *imām*. Mālik and al-Shāfiʿī said that they are to stand behind the *imām*, while Abū Ḥanīfa, his disciples, and the Kūfīs said that the *imām* is to stand between them.

Their disagreement is due to two conflicting traditions on this. The first is the tradition of Jābir ibn ʿAbd Allāh, who said, "I stood on the left of the Messenger of Allāh (God's peace and blessings be upon him), so he took hold of my hand and brought me around till I stood on his right side. Jābir ibn Ṣakhr then came, performed the ablution, and stood to the left of the Messenger of Allāh (God's peace and blessings be upon him). He took hold of our hands at the same time and pushed us till we stood behind him". The second tradition is Ibn Masʿūd's, that he prayed with ʿAlqama and al-Aswad while standing between them. He related this from the Prophet (God's peace and blessings be upon him). Abū ʿUmar said that the narrators of this tradition differed. Some of them stopped at Ibn Masʿūd, while others linked it up to the Prophet. The correct view is that it is *mawqūf* (stops at the Companion).

The practice for a woman is that she stands behind a male follower, when there is one man besides the *imām*, or she stands behind the *imām* if she is alone. I am not aware of a disagreement over this, because it is established from the tradition of Anas that has been recorded by al-Bukhārī "that the Prophet (God's peace and blessings be upon him) prayed with him and his mother or his aunt. He said, 'He made me stand on his right and made the woman stand behind us'". In that which is also related from him by Mālik, he says, "We formed a row, the orphan and I, behind the Prophet (God's peace and blessings be upon him) and the old woman stood behind us".

The practice for one single person is that he stands to the right of the *imām*, because of the tradition of Ibn ʿAbbās when he spent the night at Maymūna's place. A group of jurists said that he should stand on his left. There is no disagreement about a single woman standing behind the *imām*, and if she is praying together with another man, the man is to stand by the side of the *imām*, while the woman is to stand behind him.

2.3.2.3.2. Issue 2

The jurists agreed that the first row is to be desired; similarly standing close together and the straightening the rows, because of the confirmation of the command from the Messenger of Allāh (God's peace and blessings be upon him). They disagreed in ths case of a person standing alone behind a row. The majority of the jurists say that his prayer is valid, while Aḥmad, Abū Thawr, and a group of jurists said that his prayer is invalid.

The reason for their disagreement arises from the dispute over the authenticity of the tradition of Wābiṣa and its conflict with practice. The tradition of Wābiṣa is that the Prophet (God's peace and blessings be upon him) said, "No prayer (is counted) for the person standing alone behind a row". Al-Shāfiʿī said that this is contrary to the case of the old woman standing behind a row in the tradition of Anas. Aḥmad said that there is no legal force in this (argument) as it is the practice for women to stand behind men, and Aḥmad, as we have said, considered the tradition of Wābiṣa authentic. Others have said that it has wavering *isnād* and such a tradition cannot serve as a legal evidence. The majority argued on the basis of the tradition of Abū Bakra that he prayed alone, separately from the row, and the Messenger of Allāh (God's peace and blessings be upon him) did not order him to repeat the prayer. He said to him, "May Allāh increase your eagerness, but do not repeat that". If this (remark) is interpreted as recommendation (for praying alongside others in a line), there is no conflict between the traditions of Wābiṣa and Abū Bakra.

2.3.2.3.3. Issue 3

There was a dispute among the early jurists as to whether a person who hears the *iqāma* should increase his pace to reach the mosque for fear of missing part of the prayer. It is related from ʿUmar and Ibn Masʿūd that they used to walk rapidly upon hearing the *iqāma*. It is related from Zayd ibn Thābit, Abū Dharr, and other Companions that they did not deem it proper to rush to the mosque, rather they held that one should approach it with composure and tranquility. This is the opinion upheld by the jurists of the provinces, because of the confirmed tradition of Abū Hurayra, "If the *iqāma* has been pronounced do not approach it in a rush, but come to it in a tranquil state". It appears that the reason for disagreement over this arose either because this tradition had not reached them or because the Book contradicts it in the words of the Exalted, "So vie (*fa'stabiqū*: compete) with one another in good works",[123] "And the foremost in the race, the foremost in the race: Those are they who will be brought nigh",[124] "And vie (*sāriʿū*: rush forward) with one another for forgiveness from your Lord".[125] On the whole, the principles of the law bear testimony of competition in good works, but if the tradition is authentic it is necessary to make an exception for prayer from among other good works.

2.3.2.3.4. Issue 4

When is it considered recommended to stand up for prayer? Some prefer the time at the beginning of the *iqāma* on the principle that eagerness is desirable. Some prefer it when the words "*qad qāmati'ṣ-ṣalāh*" are being pronounced, while others prefer it on the pronouncement of the words "*ḥayya ʿalaʾl-falāḥ*". Some say that when people see the *imām* (it is time to get up), while others, like Mālik (God be pleased with him), have not fixed any (specific) time, for this depends on the capacity of the individual, and there is no transmitted evidence for it, except the tradition of Abū Qatāda that the Prophet (God's peace and blessings be upon him) said, "When the prayer is about to commence, do not get up till you see me". If this is proved authentic, it is necessary to act in accordance with it, but the issue remains indeterminate, I mean, there is no law for it, and whenever someone gets up then it is proper.

2.3.2.3.5. Issue 5

Mālik and the majority of the jurists maintain that a person who arrives when the *imām* is in the *rukūʿ* position, and fears that he will lose a *rakʿa*[126] if he hesitates or tries to reach the first row, he may bow behind the first row and then move forward while bowing. Al-Shāfiʿī considered this abominable, while Abū Ḥanīfa made a distinction between a group and an individual, considering it abominable for an individual, but permissible for a group. The position taken by Mālik is related from Zayd ibn Thābit and Ibn Masʿūd. The reason for their disagreement stems from their dispute over the authenticity of the tradition of Aū Bakr, which says that "he entered the mosque when the

[123] Qurʾān 2 : 148.
[124] Qurʾān 56 : 10,11.
[125] Qurʾān 3 : 133.
[126] The background is that if the follower joins while *imām* is bowing, or before this, a *rakʿa* is counted for him, but not if he joins after the *rukūʿ*.

Messenger of Allāh (God's peace and blessings be upon him) was leading the people in prayer and they were bowing. He bowed too and then moved towards the row. When the Messenger of Allāh had finished praying, he said, "Who moved?" Abū Bakr said, "It was I". He said, "May Allāh advance your eagerness, but do not repeat it".

2.3.2.4. *Section 4: Identification of things in which it is necessary for the follower to follow the* imām

The jurists agreed that it is obligatory on the follower to follow the *imām* in all his utterances and acts, except in reciting the words "*samiʿa Allāhu liman ḥamidah*" and when the *imām* is seated because of illness, according to those who permit *imāma* while sitting.

2.3.2.4.1. Issue 1

About their disagreement over the exception in reciting the words "*samiʿa Allāhu liman ḥamidah*", a group of jurists said that the *imām* pronounces only these words when he raises his head after bowing, and the follower, then, pronounces only the words "*rabbanā wa lakʾal-ḥamd*". Among in those who held this opinion are Mālik, Abū Ḥanīfa, and others. Another group of jurists maintained that the *imām* and the follower both say "*samiʿa Allāhu liman ḥamidah rabbanā wa lakʾal-ḥamd*", and that the follower follows the *imām* repeating with him as in the case of *takbīr*. It is related from Abū Ḥanīfa that when one person is praying with an *imām*, both should pronounce it together. There is no dispute about one single person and the *imām* reciting the whole (both parts of the statement) together.

The reason for disagreement over this (the former case) is based on two conflicting traditions. The first is the tradition of Anas that the Prophet (God's peace and blessings be upon him) said, "The *imām* has been appointed so that he may be followed. When he bows you must bow, and when he straightens up you must straighten up. When he says '*samiʿa Allāhu liman ḥamidah*,' you must say '*rabbanā wa lakʾal-ḥamd*' ". The second is the tradition of Ibn ʿUmar "that the Prophet (God's peace and blessings be upon him), when he began praying, would raise his hands to the level of the shoulders, and when he straightened up from bowing would say '*samiʿa Allāhu liman ḥamidah rabbanā wa lakʾal-ḥamd*' ".

Those who preferred the meaning of the tradition of Anas maintained that the follower is not to say "*samiʿa Allāhu liman ḥamidah*", and the *imām* is not to say "*rabbanā wa lakʾal-ḥamd*". This belongs to the category of the implication of the text (*dalīl al-khiṭāb*) for it assigns to the unexpressed case a *ḥukm* opposite that of the expressed case. Those who preferred the tradition of Ibn ʿUmar maintained that the *imām* does say "*rabbanā wa lakʾal-ḥamd*", and it is obligatory on the follower to follow the *imām* in saying "*samiʿa Allāhu liman ḥamidah*", because of the general application of the words of the prophet, "The *imām* has been appointed so that he may be followed". Those who reconciled the two traditions made a distinction between the *imām* and the follower, and the truth in this is that the tradition of Anas requires—through the implication of its text—that the *imām* does not say "*rabbanā wa lakʾal-ḥamd*", and that the follower does not say "*samiʿa Allāhu liman ḥamidah*", while the tradition of Ibn ʿUmar requires explicitly that the *imām* says "*rabbanā wa lakʾal-ḥamd*". It is not proper that an explicit text be given up because of an implication of the text, as the explicit text is stronger than its implication. The tradition of Anas requires, through its general application, that the follower is to say "*samiʿa Allāhu liman ḥamidah*", in conformity with the general implication of the words, "The *imām* has been appointed so that he may be followed", while it implies that he should not say these words. Thus it becomes necessary to make a choice between the general meaning and the implication of the text, and there is no dispute that the general meaning is stronger than the implication of the text, though the general meaning can also vary with respect to strength and weakness, and it is not unlikely that some implications can be stronger than the general meanings. The issue, then, upon my life, is one that is subject to interpretation, that is, with respect to the follower.

2.3.2.4.2. Issue 2

This relates to the prayer of one standing behind one who is seated. The gist of the opinions is that the healthy person is not to pray an obligatory prayer while seated when praying alone or as an *imām*, because of the words of the Exalted, "And stand up with devotion to Allāh".[127] There were three opinions about the case of the follower who was in sound health and prayed behind an *imām* who was not well and prayed while seated. The first opinion is that the follower is to pray behind him in the sitting posture. Included among those who upheld this opinion are Aḥmad and Isḥāq. The second opinion is that he should pray standing behind (the *imām*). Abū ʿUmar ibn ʿAbd al-Barr has said that this is the opinion of most of a body of jurists of the provinces: al-Shāfiʿī, his disciples, Abū Ḥanīfa, his disciples, the Ẓāhirites, Abū Thawr, and others. These jurists made an addition saying that the followers are to pray behind him while standing even if he is unable to bow and prostrate and merely makes a gesture (with his head). Ibn al-Qāsim has related that the

[127] Qurʾān 2 : 238.

imāma of a person seated is not permitted, and that if they pray behind him seated or standing, their prayer is void. It is related from Mālik that they are to repeat their prayers before the expiry of the time, but this has been based on the idea of disapproval not prohibition, though the first opinion is well-known from him.

The reason for their disagreement springs from the conflict of traditions over this (issue), and also the conflict of *ʿamal* with traditions, that is, the practice of the people of Medina according to Mālik. There are two conflicting traditions in this. The first is the tradition of Anas that the Prophet (God's peace and blessings be upon him) said, "If he prays while sitting then you should pray while seated". A tradition from ʿĀʾisha conveys the same meaning. Her tradition says that the Prophet (God's peace and blessings be upon him) prayed seated while complaining (he was not well). The people wanted to pray behind him while standing, but he gestured to them that they should be seated. When he had finished, he said, "The *imām* has been appointed so that he may be followed. If he bows, you must bow, and when he straightens up, you must straighten up too. If he is seated, then you must pray while seated". The second tradition is from ʿĀʾisha "that the Messenger of Allāh (God's peace and blessings be upon him) went out to the people when he was ill, an illness from which he [later] died. He reached the mosque and found Abū Bakr leading the people in prayer. Abū Bakr began to retreat, but the Messenger of Allāh (God's peace and blessings be upon him) gestured to him that he should stay where he was. The Messenger of Allāh (God's peace and blessings be upon him) sat down beside Abū Bakr, who then followed the Messenger of Allāh's in prayer and the people followed Abū Bakr in the prayer".

The jurists adopted two methods for interpreting these traditions: the method of abrogation (*naskh*) and the method of preference. Those who adopted the method of abrogation maintained that the apparent meaning of ʿĀʾisha's tradition is that the Prophet (God's peace and blessings be upon him) led the people in prayer and Abū Bakr was the transmitter, for it is not possible that there be two *imāms* for the same prayer. Further, the people were standing and the Prophet (God's peace and blessings be upon him) was sitting. Thus, this is necessarily an act of the Prophet (God's peace and blessings be upon him), and since it was later (shortly before the end of his life) it abrogates his prior acts (related to the same issue). Those who adopted the method of preference, preferred the tradition of Anas, for they said that the tradition of ʿĀʾisha has varying narrations over the question of who was the *imām*, the Messenger of Allāh (God's peace and blessings be upon him) or Abū Bakr. Mālik, however, has no basis for reliance in transmission, as both traditions agree on the permissibility of *imāma* while sitting, and they only differ about the standing or sitting of the follower. This led Abū Muḥammad ibn Ḥazm to say that in the tradition of ʿĀʾisha there is nothing to show whether the people prayed while standing or sitting, and it is not proper to relinquish the expressed rule in favour of a rule that has not been expressly stated.

Abū ʿUmar said that Abū al-Muṣʿab has recorded in his *Mukhtaṣar* from Mālik that he said, "The people are not to follow (in prayer) anyone who is sitting. If he leads them while sitting, their prayer and his prayer is invalid, because the Prophet (God's peace and blessings be upon him) has said, 'No one after me is ever to lead others while sitting'". Abū ʿUmar states that this tradition is not deemed authentic by the traditionists, for it has been narrated by Jābir al-Juʿfī as a *mursal* (the Companion supposed to have related the tradition is dropped). His tradition that he relates with a complete chain is not considered as sufficient proof, so how can his *mursal* tradition be accepted? It is related by Ibn al-Qāsim of Mālik that he used to argue on the basis of what was related by Rabīʿa ibn Abī ʿAbd al-Raḥmān "that the Messenger of Allāh (God's peace and blessings be upon him) went out to the people when he was ill, and Abū Bakr was praying as the *imām*. The Prophet prayed following the prayer of Abū Bakr and then said, 'No Prophet has died until he has prayed behind a man from his *umma*'". There is no evidence in this unless it is believed that he followed Abū Bakr in prayer as the prayer of an *imām* who takes up a sitting posture is not permitted. This is mere conjecture for which an explicit text cannot be relinquished; besides, the tradition is weak.

2.3.2.5. *Section 5: Description of the following*

This comprises two issues. First is the time of the initial *takbīr*, while the second is the *ḥukm* of the person who raises his head before the *imām* does so.

In their dispute over the initial *takbīr*, Mālik preferred that the follower should pronounce it after the *imām* has finished pronouncing it; if he pronounces it with the *imām* he (Mālik) still holds it to be valid, while some said that it is not so. But if he pronounces it before the *imām* it is not acceptable. Abū Ḥanīfa and others have said that he may pronounce the *takbīr* with the *imām*, but if he finishes the pronouncement before the *imām* it becomes invalid. There are two narrations from al-Shāfiʿī on this. First is like the opinion of Mālik and this is the better known opinion, and the second is that if the follower pronounces *takbīr* before the *imām* it becomes invalid.

The reason for disagreement is that there are two conflicting traditions on this issue. The first includes the words of the Prophet (God's peace and blessings be upon him), "If he pronounces *takbīr*, you should pronounce it too". The second is the narration "that the Prophet (God's peace and blessings be upon him) pronounced the initial *takbīr* in one of his prayers and then gestured to the people that they should wait. He went away and then returned with remnants of moisture on his head". The apparent meaning of this is that his *takbīr* was pronounced (again) after theirs, for his *takbīr* before this was not counted because of the absence of purification. This too is based upon his (al-Shāfiʿī's) principle that the prayer of the follower is not dependent upon the prayer of the *imām*. There is no indication in the tradition whether they renewed their *takbīr*. Thus, it is not proper to interpret it either way without evidence. The principle, however, is to follow (the *imām*), which can only be after the *imām's* pronouncement of *takbīr*.

About the person who raises his head (from the *rukūʿ* or bowing or *sujūd* or prostrating) before the *imām*, the majority are of the view that he has made an error, but his prayer is valid and it is obligatory on him to revert and follow the *imām*. Yet, a small group of jurists held that his prayer is nullified because of the proclaimed warning related to it, namely, the words of the Prophet (God's peace and blessings be upon him), "Is the person, who raises his head before the *imām*, not afraid that Allāh may turn his head into the head of donkey".

2.3.2.6. *Section 6: What the* imām *performs on behalf of the follower*

They agreed that that no exemption is granted to the follower from the obligations of prayer, except for the recitation. They disagreed about this (the recitation by the follower) holding three opinions. First, some held that the follower should undertake his recitation behind the *imām* in prayers with inaudible recitation, but he should not recite behind him when the recitation is audible to him. Second, that he should not recite behind the *imām* at all. Third, that he should recite the *umm al-Kitāb* and the rest in the case of prayers with inaudible recitation, and only the *umm al-Kitāb* in the case of prayers with audible recitation. Some made a distinction between the case of prayers with audible recitation when the follower can hear the *imām's* recitation and when he cannot hear him. Thus, they made recitation obligatory for him when he cannot hear the *imām*, but they prohibited him from doing so when he can hear him. The first view was held by Mālik, except that he preferred recitation in the case of inaudible recitation. The second opinion was held by Abū Ḥanīfa and the third by al-Shāfiʿī. Aḥmad ibn Ḥanbal made the distinction between the situation where the follower is able to hear the *imām's* recitation and the situation where he is not.

The reason for their disagreement stems from the conflict of traditions on this topic and the interpretation of some on the basis of others. There are four traditions on the topic. The first is the saying of the Prophet (God's peace and blessings be upon him), "There is no prayer, except with the *fātiḥat al-Kitāb*".

This is in addition to the traditions conveying the same meaning, which we have discussed under the issue of the obligation of recitation. The second is a tradition recorded by Mālik from Abū Hurayra that the Messenger of Allāh (God's peace and blessings be upon him) finished his prayer reciting in an audible voice, and said, "Did one of you recite with me just now". A man said, "Yes, I did O Messenger of Allāh". He said, "I say: How am I being challenged in the (recitation of the) Qurʾān". The people stopped reciting while praying behind the Messenger of Allāh (God's peace and blessings be upon him) when the recitation was made in an audible voice. The third is the tradition of ʿUbāda ibn al-Ṣāmit, who said that "the Messenger of Allāh (God's peace and blessings be upon him) led us in the morning prayer and the recitation became difficult for him. When he had finished he said, 'I see that you recite behind the *imām*'. We said, 'Yes.' He said, 'Do not do it, except for the *umm al-Qurʾān*'". Abū ʿUmar said that the tradition of ʿUbāda here is a narration from Makḥūl and other narrations have continuous chains and are authentic. The fourth tradition is that of Jābir from the Prophet (God's peace and blessings be upon him), who said, "The recitation of a person who has an *imām* leading him is undertaken by the *imām*". There is also a fifth tradition that has been declared authentic by Aḥmad ibn Ḥanbal. It is the narration that reports the Prophet (God's peace and blessings be upon him) as saying, "When the *imām* recites listen silently".

The jurists disagreed about the manner of reconciling these traditions. There were some who exempted the recitation of the *umm al-Qurʾān* alone from the proscription of recitation during audible recitation of the *imām*, on the basis of the tradition of ʿUbāda ibn al-Ṣāmit. There were those who exempted from the general implication of the words of the Prophet, "There is no prayer without the (recitation of) the *fātiḥat al-Kitāb*", only the case of the follower in a prayer with audible recitation, because of the prohibition of recitation in a prayer with audible recitation occurring in the tradition of Abū Hurayra. They supported this with the words of the Exalted, "And when the Qurʾān is recited, give ear to it and pay heed, that ye may obtain mercy".[128] They said that this was related to prayer. Some of them exempted (from the proscription) the obligatory recitation of the follower in group prayers, whether the prayer was with inaudible or audible recitation, and they confined the obligation of recitation to the cases of an *imām* and the single worshiper taking, into account the tradition of Jābir. This is the opinion of Abū Ḥanīfa. Thus, the tradition of Jābir became for him an evidence restricting the words of the Prophet (God's peace and blessings be upon him), "Recite whatever you can", for he does not specify the recitation of the *umm al-Qurʾān* in prayer,

[128] Qurʾān 7 : 204.

but he does prescribe the recitation of any Qurʾānic passage, as explained earlier. The tradition of Jābir, however, was related as *marfūʿ* (reaching the Prophet) only through the *isnād* of Jābir al-Juʿafī, and there is no force in a tradition related as *marfūʿ* through him alone. Abū ʿUmar said that it is a tradition that is not deemed authentic, except the *marfūʿ* narration of Jābir.

2.3.2.7. *Section 7: Things invalidating the prayer of the* imām *and extending the invalidity to the prayer of the follower*

They agreed that if he (the *imām*) is suddenly overcome by *ḥadath* (like releasing wind) during prayer and stops, the prayer of the followers is not invalidated (they continue individually or one of them steps forward and leads them). They disagreed over the case where the *imām* leads them in prayer in a state of ritual impurity, and they come to know of this after the prayer. A group of jurists said that their prayer is valid, while another group said that their prayer is invalid. A third group made a distinction on the basis of whether the *imām* was aware of his sexual defilement or was ignorant of it. They said that if he was aware of it their prayer is invalidated, but if he was unaware of it their prayer is not invalidated. The first opinion was held by al-Shāfiʿī and the second by Abū Ḥanīfa, while the third was held by Mālik.

The reason for their disagreement derives from their dispute over whether the validity of the follower's prayer is dependent upon the validity of the *imām's* prayer. Those who did not consider it to be dependent said that the prayer is valid, while those who considered it to be dependent said that their prayer is invalidated.

Those who made a distinction between forgetfulness and intentional silence took into account the apparent meaning of the preceding tradition, which says "that the Prophet (God's peace and blessings be upon him) pronounced the *takbīr* in one of his prayers and then (interrupting his prayer) gestured to the people that they should wait. He went away and on his return there were remnants of moisture on his body". The apparent meaning of this is that they continued their prayer (building upon the part they prayed before the Prophet interrupted his prayer). Al-Shāfiʿī (supporting this ruling) argued that had their prayer been dependent upon his prayer they would certainly have recommenced the prayer (with a fresh *takbīr*).

2.3.3. Chapter 3 The Friday Congregational Prayer (*Jumuʿa*)

The comprehensive discussion of the principles of this chapter is covered in four sections. The first section is about the obligation of *jumuʿa* prayer and about the person on whom it is obligatory. The second is about the conditions for *jumuʿa*. the third is about the elements (*arkān*) of *jumuʿa*. The fourth is about the *aḥkām* of *jumuʿa*.

2.3.3.1. *Section 1: The obligation of* jumuʿa *and the person on whom it is obligatory*

The majority of the jurists uphold the universal obligation of the *jumuʿa* (Friday) prayer, as a substitute for another obligation, which is the *ẓuhr* prayer, and also because of the apparent meaning of the words of the Exalted, "O ye who believe! When the call is heard for the prayer of the day of the congregation, haste unto remembrance of Allāh and leave your trading. That is better for you if ye did but know".[129] The command here necessitates an obligation. Further, because of the words of the Prophet (God's peace and blessings be upon him), "Let people desist from neglecting the Friday prayers, or Allāh will stamp their hearts". A group of jurists maintained that it is a communal obligation (*farḍ kifāyā*), and from Mālik there is an isolated opinion that it is a *sunna*.

The reason for this disagreement stems from its similarity to the *ʿĪd* prayer, because of the words of the words of the Prophet (God's peace and blessings be upon him), "This day has been determined to be an *ʿīd* by Allāh".

The person on whom it is obligatory is one who fulfils the conditions for the obligation of prayer, the discussion of which has preceded, and who meets four additional conditions, two of them are agreed upon and two are disputed. The two that are agreed upon are being a male, and being in sound health. Thus, it is not binding upon a woman, nor upon a sick person, but if they attend, their *jumuʿa* prayer would be valid. The disputed conditions are (not) being a traveller and (not) being a slave. The majority maintain that *jumuʿa* is not obligatory on them, while Dāwūd and his disciples maintained that it is obligatory.

The reason for disagreement arises from their dispute over the authenticity of the tradition related to this issue, which is the saying of the the Prophet (God's peace and blessings be upon him), "*Jumuʿa* is a duty that is obligatory upon each Muslim living among a group, except for four persons: an owned slave, a woman, a minor, and one who is sick". In another version the words are "except for five", and the words "a traveller" are added. The tradition has not been deemed authentic by most of the (*ḥadīth*) scholars.

[129] Qur'ān 62 : 9.

2.3.3.2. *Section 2: The conditions for* jumuʿa

They agreed that the conditions of the Friday prayer are the very conditions determined for obligatory prayers, that is, the eight preceding conditions, except for the time and the call for prayer, for they disagreed about these. Similarly, they disagreed about the conditions specific to the Friday prayer.

With respect to the time (of the *jumuʿa* prayer), the majority of the jurists maintained that it is the time for *ẓuhr* itself, that is, the time of the declining of the sun, and that it is not permitted before the declining of the sun. A group of jurists, including Aḥmad ibn Ḥanbal, maintained that it is permitted to observe it before the declining of the sun.

The reason for this disagreement stems from the dispute over the meaning of the traditions urging the early observance of the Friday prayer, like the one recorded by al-Bukhārī from Sahl ibn Saʿd, who said, "We did not take lunch or a midday nap, during the time of the Prophet (God's peace and blessings be upon him), until after the Friday prayer"; likewise another report says, "that they used to pray and return before the walls had cast their shade". Those who understood from these traditions that the prayer was observed before the declining of the sun permitted it, while those who only interpreted them to mean (just starting with the) *takbīr* did not permit it, so that the sources may not conflict with each other on this topic. The reason (for upholding this interpretation) is that it is established through the tradition of Anas ibn Mālik "that the Prophet (God's peace and blessings be upon him) used to pray when the sun had declined". Further, as the Friday prayer is a substitute for the (regular) *ẓuhr* prayer, it is necessary that its time be the time for *ẓuhr*. It therefore becomes necessary by way of reconciliation to construe those traditions so that they apply to *takbīr*, for they do not indicate explicitly that the time (for the Friday prayer) starts before the declining of the sun, and that is what the majority uphold.

The majority of the jurists agree that the time of *adhān* (for the Friday prayer) starts when the *imām* seats himself at the pulpit. They disagreed, however, on whether a single *muʾadhdhin* or more should make the call for prayer in front of the *imām*. Some of them maintained that only one *muʾadhdhin* is to make the call while facing the *imām*, and this is the call with which buying and selling are declared prohibited. Some other jurists said that there should be two *muʾadhdhins*, and not more, who are to make the call, while others have said that in fact three of them should make the call. The reason for the disagreement derives from the conflict of traditions about this. It is recorded by al-Bukhārī from al-Sāʾib ibn Yazīd that he said, "The call on Friday, during the time of the Prophet (God's peace and blessings be upon him) and also during the time of Abū Bakr and ʿUmar, was made when the *imām* had seated himself at the pulpit. When at the time of ʿUthmān the population had increased, a third call was instituted to be delivered from al-Zawrāʾ". It is also related from al-Sāʾib ibn Yazīd that he said, "In the time of the Messenger of Allāh (God's peace and blessings be upon him) there was only one *muʾadhdhin* for the Friday prayer". It is related from Saʿīd ibn al-Musayyab that he said, "The call for the Friday prayer during the periods of the Messenger of Allāh (God's peace and blessings be upon him) and Abū Bakr and ʿUmar used to be a single call when the *imām* came out, but when it was the time of ʿUthmān and the population increased he added to the one initial call in order to induce the people to get ready for the Friday prayer". Ibn Ḥabīb has related "that the *muʾadhdhins* during the time of the Messenger of Allāh (God's peace and blessings be upon him) used to be three".

A group of jurists followed the apparent meaning of the report by al-Bukhārī and maintained that on Friday two *muʾadhdhins* are to make the call. Some other jurists maintained that there should be a single *muʾadhdhin*. They said that the meaning of the words "When it was the time of ʿUthmān and the population increased, a third call was instituted", is that the second call was the *iqāma*. Others adopted what is reported by Ibn Ḥabīb, although the traditions of Ibn Ḥabīb are weak according to the traditionists, especially those that only he has related.

It is agreed upon by all, in the conditions of obligation and validity of the Friday prayer, that a condition for it is the congregation (*jamāʿa*), but they differed about the (minimum) number in the congregation. Some of them said that one person with the *imām* is sufficient. This is the opinion of al-Ṭabarī. Some said that there should be two persons besides the *imām*. Some said that there should be three persons besides the *imām*; this is the opinion of Abū Ḥanīfa. Some of them stipulated the presence of forty persons, which is the opinion of al-Shāfiʿī and Aḥmad, while some said there should be thirty. Some did not fix a number, but said that it should be a number sufficient to establish a settlement. Thus, according to this opinion, which was held by Mālik, it (Friday prayer) is not permissible with three or four persons.

The reason for their disagreement stems from their dispute over the minimum number that can be referred to in the plural whether this is three or four or two, and whether the *imām* is included in this number. Further, whether the plural for purposes of this prayer is the minimum that is applied in most cases, which is more than four or three. Those who maintained that the condition here is designation with the minimum to which the plural is applied—and for them the minimum for the plural was two—said that the *jumuʿa* is valid with two persons, the *imām* and another; this was the view of those who included the *imām* in the count, but if they were among those who did not include the *imām* in the count, they held that it is valid with two persons besides the *imām*. Those for whom the minimum for plurality was three, and they were not including the *imām* in the count, said that *jumuʿa* is valid with three persons besides the *imām*, but if they were among those who included the *imām* in the count, their opinion conformed with the opinion of those who said that the minimum for plurality was two while not counting the *imām* in the congregation. Those who took into account what is usually applied to a congregation by custom, said that it is not valid with two or with four, and they did not fix a minimum limit for this. As the condition for the (validity of) Friday congregation was that it be held in a permanent settlement, they fixed for this a number of people who are able to establish a permanent settlement by themselves. This is Mālik's opinion (God bless him). Those who fixed the number at forty did so relying on the report that this was the number of the group who held the Friday prayers for the first time (in Medina, just before the Hijra of the Prophet). This, then, is one of the conditions of the Friday prayer, that is, conditions of obligation and conditions of validity, as in the conditions for the Friday prayer, some are the conditions of obligation alone, while there are others that combine the two factors, I mean, they are the conditions of obligation as well as those of validity.

The second condition (of obligation and validity) is that it should be held in a (permanent) settlement (and the believer must be a resident there, not a traveller). The jurists agreed about this because of their agreement that the Friday prayer is not obligatory for a traveller. This is opposed by the Ẓāhirites who hold that the *jumuʿa* is obligatory for a traveller as well. Abū Ḥanīfa stipulated that there should be a permanent settlement and a (governing) authority along with it, but he did not stipulate a number.

The reason for disagreement in this matter arises from whether or not the circumstances prevailing at the time the Prophet (God's peace and blessings be upon him) held this prayer are to be considered as conditions for the validity or for the obligation of this prayer. It happened that the Prophet (God's peace and blessings be upon him) always observed this prayer in a congregation in a permanent settlement (village or town) and in a central mosque. Those who maintained that the linking of these surroundings with his prayer renders them conditions for the Friday prayer stipulated their existence as a condition. Those who linked (only) some of these (elements) with his Friday prayer stipulated (only) these as conditions to the exclusion of others. This is like the stipulation by Mālik of observing it in a mosque, and dropping the condition that it should take place in a permanent settlement and that there should be (a ruling) authority. In relation to this topic, we may add that the jurists disputed other points, like their disagreement over whether two or more Friday congregations could take place in one town.

The reason for their disagreement in stipulating some of these related circumstances and acts is that some of these circumstances are more suited to the acts of prayer than others. It is for this reason that they agreed upon the stipulation of performing it in a congregation as congregating is a legal feature of the Muslim prayer. For this reason also Mālik did not stipulate that the observance of the Friday prayer in a congregation should be conditional on the existence of a settlement and a supervising authority, because he did not consider these as either representative features of prayer or circumstances closely related to prayer. Yet he stipulated that the Friday congregation be held in a mosque as the mosque is closely related to prayer. His disciples, however, differed to the extent of whether the mosque should have a roof, and whether it is a condition that Friday prayers are regularly held in this mosque. Perhaps this amounts to too much probing, and the *Dīn* of Allāh requires ease. Someone may raise the objection that if all these were the conditions for the validity of prayer, the Prophet (God's peace and blessings be upon him) would not have remained silent about them and he would not have failed to give the explanation because of the words of the Exalted, "We have revealed unto thee the Remembrance that thou mayst explain to mankind that which hath been revealed for them",[130] and His words, "And We have revealed the Scripture unto thee only that thou mayst explain unto them that wherein they differ".[131] Allāh guides to what is right.

2.3.3.3. *Section 3: The elements* (arkān) *of* jumuʿa

The Muslim jurists agreed that the elements (major parts of the Friday prayer) are the *khuṭba* (sermon) and the two *rakʿas* after the *khuṭba*. Within this they agreed about five issues that are the principles of this topic.

2.3.3.3.1. Issue 1

Whether the *khuṭba* is a condition for the validity of this prayer and whether it is one of its elements (*arkān*). The majority maintained that it is a condition as well as an element. A group of jurists said that it is not obligatory, while the majority of the disciples of Mālik maintained that it is obligatory, except for Ibn al-Mājishūn.

The reason for their disagreement stems from the principle that has already been discussed, whether all things and circumstances existing at the time the Prophet used to hold the Friday prayer should necessarily constitute the

[130] Qurʾān 16 : 44.
[131] Qurʾān 16 : 64.

conditions for its validity. Those who maintained that the *khuṭba* is one of the circumstances specific to this prayer, especially when it is taken into account that it is a substitute for the two *rakʿas* that have been reduced from the (*ẓuhr*) prayer, said that it is an element of this prayer and one of the conditions of its validity. Those who maintained that its purpose is the usual exhortation that is the aim of all sermons, held that it is not a condition for this prayer. One group of jurists argued on the basis of the words of the Exalted, "haste unto remembrance of Allāh",[132] saying that this means the sermon.

2.3.3.3.2. Issue 2

Those who upheld that the sermon is an obligation differed about the minimum length of the sermon. Ibn al-Qāsim said that it is the minimum length that can be called a sermon in the usage of the Arabs, including a word of praise for Allāh (*al-Ḥamd*) at the beginning. Al-Shāfiʿī said that the permitted minimum requirement of a sermon is that it should be in two parts during which the speaker (*imām*) should be standing and that they should be separated by a short interval for sitting, and that at the beginning of each part he should pronounce words praising Allāh (*al-Ḥamd*), pray for the Prophet and preach piety. He should also recite a passage from the Qurʾān in the first part of the sermon and pray for the believers in the second part.

The reason for their disagreement over this issue is their dispute over the meaning of the minimum permissible length whether it is the literal or the technical meaning? Those who maintained that the permitted length is the literal minimum did not stipulate in it anything of the words that have been traced to the Prophet (God's peace and blessings be upon him) in his sermons. Those who maintained that the permitted length is the minimum to which the technical meaning applies stipulated that it should include words that were regularly included in the sermons of the Prophet (God's peace and blessings be upon him), that is, not just occasional words.

The reason for this disagreement is that the sermons that have been transmitted from him contained words regularly used and also occasional remarks. Those who took into account the occasional remarks and preferred the *ḥukm* emanating from them said that a sufficient length is the minimum to which the literal term applies, that is, the meaning of the term *khuṭba* in the usage of the Arabs. Those who took into account the regularly delivered speeches and gave predominance to their *ḥukm* said that the permitted length is the minimum to which the term *khuṭba* is applied in legal usage and practice.

Sitting down (between the two parts of the sermon) is not a condition for the *khuṭba* in Mālik's view, and it is a condition, as we have said, in al-

[132] Qurʾān 62 : 9.

Shāfiʿī's view. The reason is that those who attributed to it the ordinary meaning of being a rest for the *khaṭīb* (speaker) did not consider it to be a condition, while those who considered it to be a ritual deemed it a condition.

2.3.3.3.3. Issue 3

There are three different opinions about maintaining silence while the *imām* is delivering the sermon. Some of the jurists held that silence is obligatory under all circumstances and then it is a binding *ḥukm* of the sermon. These were the majority: Mālik, al-Shāfiʿī, Abū Ḥanīfa, Aḥmad ibn Ḥanbal, and all the jurists of the provinces. They are, however, divided into three groups. Some permitted the utterance of a blessing for a person who has sneezed, and also permitted responding to salutations; others distinguished between exclamation of a blessing and salutations, saying that one may respond to salutations, but not bless. The second view is the opposite of the first, that is, speech during any stage of the sermon is permitted, except when the Qurʾān is being recited during it. This is related from al-Shaʿbī, Saʿīd ibn Jubayr, and Ibrāhīm al-Nakhaʿī. The third opinion makes a distinction between the worshippers who can hear the sermon and those who cannot. The worshippers who can hear the sermon should maintain silence, but those who cannot hear it are permitted to occupy themselves in the remembrance of Allāh or to discuss religious issues. This was the opinion of Aḥmad, ʿAṭāʾ, and a group of jurists.

The majority maintain that if a person talks (during the sermon) his prayer is not invalidated, but it is related from Ibn Wahb that if a person indulges in idle talk he is obliged to pray the four *rakʿas* of *ẓuhr* (i.e. his Friday prayer is invalidated).

The majority upheld the obligation of maintaining silence because of the tradition of Abū Hurayra that the Prophet (God's peace and blessings be upon him) said, "If you say to your companion 'Be silent', during Friday prayer while the *imām* is delivering the sermon, then, you have indulged in idle talk'". Those who did not deem this obligatory, for them I do not recall an analogy, unless they were of the view that this matter is in conflict with the implication of the text in the words of the Exalted, "And when the Qurʾān is recited, give ear to it and pay heed, that ye may obtain mercy",[133] that is, there is no obligation to maintain silence for what is besides the Qurʾān, but this is weak, Allāh knows best. It is more probable that this tradition did not reach them.

In the case of their disagreement about responding to the salutation and about blessing the person sneezing, the reason for disagreement stems from the

[133] Qurʾān 7 : 204.

conflict between the general command to do so and the general command to maintain silence; the likelihood is that each is an exemption from the other. Thus, those who exempted from the general command to maintain silence during the *jumuʿa* sermon the command to respond to the salutation and to bless the person sneezing permitted them, while those who exempted from the general command to respond to the salutation, and to bless the person sneezing, the proscription of speaking during the Friday sermon, did not permit either. Among those who made a distinction between the two utterances, some exempted the response to a salutation from the proscription of speaking during the Friday sermon, and some exempted the expression of blessings for one who has sneezed. Each one of these two groups adopted one of these exemptions, about which it was convinced because of the strength in one general application and a weakness in the other. The reason is that the command for maintaining silence is general with respect to speech and particular with respect to time, while the command to respond to salutation and to utter blessings is general with respect to time and particular with respect to speech. Those who exempted the particular time from general speech did not permit, during the sermon, the response to salutation or blessing one who has sneezed, while those who exempted particular speech from the proscription of general speech permitted it.

The correct method is not to adopt an exemption of one of the general implications from one of the particular implications, except on the basis of an evidence. If this becomes difficult then a preference among the general and particular implications is to be investigated, and preference is to emphasize the commands. The discussion of all this is lengthy, but it should be known in brief that if the commands have equal strength and the general and particular implications are also equal in strength, and there is no evidence as to which is to be exempted from the other a dead end is inevitably reached, though this rarely happens. If this is not the case, then, the preference between general and particular meanings occurring in such cases involves an investigation of all kinds of relationships that exist between the particular and general meanings. These are four. Two general meanings possessing the same strength and two particular meanings having the same strength, are not to be exempted, one from the other, except on the basis of another evidence. The second case is the opposite of this, and this may be a particular meaning of extreme strength or a general meaning of extreme weakness. In such a case it is to be adopted, in fact it is necessary, that is, exempting the particular from the general. The third is the case of two particular meanings of the same category and a general meaning that is weaker than the other (general meaning). In this case it is necessary to restrict the weaker general meaning. The fourth case is that of two general meanings of the same category along with one particular meaning that is stronger than the other. In such a case it is necessary that the *ḥukm* be assigned to the stronger particular meaning. All this takes place when the commands are equal in emphasis. If that is different, the orders are all changed and the measures are applied equally to the implications of the words as well as to the commands. Because of the difficulty of ordering such matters, it is said that each *mujtahid* is correct or, at least, he is not at fault.[134]

2.3.3.3.4. Issue 4

They disagreed about whether a person who arrives in the mosque for Friday prayers when the *imām* is already at the pulpit, is to begin offering the (two required) *rakʿas*. Some of the jurists maintain that he is not to pray, and this is Mālik's opinion, while others maintained that he is to offer the *rakʿas*.

The reason for their disagreement arises from the conflict of analogy with the general implication of the tradition. The general implication of the words of the Prophet (God's peace and blessings be upon him), "When one of you arrives in a mosque, he is to offer two *rakʿas*", conveys that anyone entering a mosque on a Friday is to offer two *rakʿas* even if the *imām* is delivering the sermon. The evidence of the command of paying attention to the speaker in silence requires that the entrant is not to occupy himself with anything that distracts him from silent attention, even if such an activity is worship. The general meaning of this tradition is supported by the authentic tradition of the Prophet (God's peace and blessings be upon him), "When one of you enters the mosque when the imām is delivering the sermon, he should offer two short *rakʿas*". It is recorded by Muslim in some of its versions. Most versions of this tradition say, "The Prophet (God's peace and blessings be upon him) ordered a man who had entered the mosque that he should pray". He did not say, "When one of you enters the mosque . . ". This leads to a disagreement on

[134] The problem described by the author requires some understanding of the subject of *uṣūl al-fiqh*. A brief explanation might help. The *aḥkām* of Allāh are discovered or derived by the *mujtahid* from the commands occurring in the texts of the Qurʾān and *sunna*. These commands have two attributes. The first is that the commands may or may not be expressed in decisive terms. If the command is expressed decisively, the resulting *ḥukm* conveys an obligation (*wujūb*). If a command is not expressed decisively, the resulting *ḥukm* may convey a recommendation (*nadb*). Now the same command may be expressed in general terms – and this is the second attribute – in which case it will apply to all cases falling under it, or it may be expressed in specific terms and will apply to a particular case. This however is not the end of the matter. A command may be expressed decisively in general terms, but it may be opposed to or conflict with another command also expressed decisively and in general terms. Is one to restrict the other? If so, then on what grounds? In the discussion above the issue is highly complex. There are four commands, two general and two particular, that conflict with each other. The author is trying to explain how many combinations can arise, when some commands are to restrict the others, or when some are to be considered to be exemptions from the general rule contained in the others. He divides them into four cases, but assumes that all have the same attribute of decisiveness, that is all are conveying an obligation. He points out that if the assumption is changed, and we assume that some were expressed in decisive terms while others were not, then the order and relationships change and new priorities will have to be determined.

whether an addition by a single narrator, when he is opposed by the other narrators narrating through a common *shaykh*, is to be accepted. If the addition is proved authentic, it is necessary to act according to it, for it is explicit on a point of dispute, and an explicit text is not to be opposed by analogy. It appears that what Mālik has taken into account on this issue is *ʿamal* (practice of the jurists of Medina).

2.3.3.3.5. Issue 5

The majority of the jurists maintain that the recitation of the *sura* of *Jumuʿa*[135] in the first *rakʿa* of the Friday prayer is an established practice (*sunna*), for its repetition is observed in the acts of the Prophet (God's peace and blessings be upon him). Muslim has recorded from Abū Hurayra "that the Messenger of Allāh (God's peace and blessings be upon him) used to recite it in the first *rakʿa* during Friday prayers, and in the second (*rakʿa*) he used to recite *sūrat al-Munāfiqūn*".[136] Mālik has related that al-Ḍahhāk ibn Qays asked al- uʿmān ibn Bashīr what the Messenger of Allāh (God's peace and blessings be upon him) usually recited on a Friday after the *sūrat al-Jumuʿa*. He said, "He used to recite (the *sūra* beginning with the words), 'Hath there come unto thee the tidings of the Overwhelming?' "[137] Mālik preferred that the practice conform with this tradition, though it would be good, in his view, if (the *sūra* beginning with the words), "Praise the name of thy Lord the Most High"[138] was recited, for it is related from ʿUmar ibn ʿAbd al-ʿAzīz. Abū Ḥanīfa, on the other hand, did not specify anything in this respect.

The reason for their disagreement arises from the conflict between the reported practice and analogy. Analogy dictates that there should not be any *sūra* appointed for this purpose as is the case with the rest of the prayers, while the indication of practice requires that there an appointed *sūras*.

The Qāḍī said that Muslim has recorded from al-Nuʿmān ibn Bashīr "that the Messenger of Allāh (God's peace and blessings be upon him) used to recite on the occasion of the two *ʿĪds* and *Jumuʿa* (the *sūra* beginning with the words), 'Praise the name of thy Lord the Most High'[139] and also (the *sūra* beginning with the words), 'Hath there come unto thee the tidings of the Overwhelming?' "[140] He said that if the *ʿĪd* and *Jumuʿa* fell on the same day, they were recited in both prayers. This indicates that there is no appointed *sūra* for this and they were not always recited in the *Jumuʿa*.

[135] Qurʾān, chapter 62.
[136] Qurʾān,.chapter 63.
[137] Qurʾān 88 : 1.
[138] Qurʿān 87 : 1.
[139] Qurʾān 87 : 1.
[140] Qurʾān 88 : 1.

2.3.3.4. *Section 4: The* aḥkām *of* jumuʿa

This topic covers four issues. First, the *ḥukm* of purification for Friday prayers. Second, on whom it is obligatory from among those living outside the town. Third, the desired time for moving toward the Friday congregation. Fourth, the permissibility of trading on Friday after the call has been made.

2.3.3.4.1. Issue 1

They disagreed about purification (bathing) for Friday prayers. The majority maintained that it is a *sunna*, while the Ẓāhirites held that it is an obligation. There is no dispute, as far as I know, that it is not a condition for the validity of this prayer.

The reason for their disagreement stems from the conflict of traditions. On this subject, there is the tradition of Abū Saʿīd al-Khudrī, being the words of the Prophet (God's peace and blessings be upon him), "Bathing for the *jumuʿa* is obligatory on each adult, like bathing after sexual defilement". There is also the tradition from ʿĀʾisha, who said, "The people, who were mostly workers, used to come for Friday prayers in the condition that they were, and it was said to them, 'If only you had washed yourselves'". The first tradition is authentic by agreement, while the second has been recorded by Abū Dāwūd and Muslim. The apparent meaning of the tradition of Abū Saʿīd implies the obligation of bathing, while the apparent meaning of ʿĀʾisha's tradition conveys that it is only for purposes of cleanliness and is not a required ritual. It has been reported that "It is sufficient to perform ablution on a Friday, but if one takes a bath it is better". This is explicit in eliminating the obligation. It is, however, a weak tradition.

2.3.3.4.2. Issue 2

About the obligation of Friday prayers on one living outside a permanent settlement, a group of jurists have said that it is not obligatory on such a person, while another group has said that it is obligatory. These jurists differed extensively. Some said that if the distance between his place and the place of the congregation involves a journey of one day, it is obligatory on him to come to it. This is a deviant opinion. Some said that it is obligatory on him to come if the distance is within three miles. Others were of the view that it is obligatory on him to come to it from a distance up to which the call can normally be heard, and this is determined to be three miles from the place of the issuance of the call. The latter two opinions are related from Mālik. This issue is related to the conditions of obligation.

The reason for their disagreement on this topic arises from the conflict of traditions. It is reported that the people used to come for Friday prayers from the suburbs during the time of the Prophet (God's peace and blessings be upon him), which were up to three miles from Medina. Abū Dāwūd has reported that the Prophet (God's peace and blessings be upon him) said, "The Friday prayer is obligatory on one who hears the call". It is also reported that "Friday prayer is obligatory on one who can return to his family by nightfall", but this is a weak tradition.

2.3.3.4.3. Issue 3

Their disagreement about the preferred timings for setting off for the Friday prayer is based on the words of the Prophet (God's peace and blessings be upon him), "If one sets off in the first hour, it is as if he has made an offering of a camel. If one sets off in the second hour, it is as if he has made an offering of a cow. If one sets off in the third hour, it is as if he has made an offering of a horned ram. If one sets off in the fourth hour, it is as if he has made an offering of a chicken. If one sets off in the fifth hour, it is as if he has made an offering of an egg". Al-Shāfiʿī and a group of jurists believed that these hours are the hours of the day, and they recommended moving in the first hour of the day. Mālik maintained that these are the parts of the single hour prior to the declining of the sun and after it. A group of jurists said that these are the parts of the hour before the declining of the sun. This appears to be the prominent opinion, because there is an obligation of making haste after the declining of the sun, except for those who maintain that greater merit can also be attached to obligatory acts.

2.3.3.4.4. Issue 4

In their disagreement over buying and selling at the time of the call (and thereafter before the prayer), a group of jurists have said that the sale is rescinded if the call has been made, while another group said that it is not rescinded. The reason for their disagreement stems from their dispute on whether the proscription of a thing, which is essentially permissible, when associated with another attribute, renders void the thing proscribed?

The etiquette of Friday prayer covers three things: perfume, brushing the teeth (was done with a tooth-stick), and decent attire. There is no dispute about this because of the traditions related to the topic.

2.3.4. **Chapter 4 Prayers during a Journey**

In this chapter there are two sections. The first section is about curtailing the prayer and the second is about combining prayers.

2.3.4.1. *Section 1: Curtailing prayers (while travelling)*

Travelling is effective in curtailing (quadruple)[141] prayers, by agreement, and is effective in combining prayers, with disagreement.

The jurists agreed about the curtailment of prayers, except for a deviant opinion, which is the opinion of ʿĀʾisha, who maintained that curtailing prayers is not permitted, except for one in a state of fear, because of the words of the Exalted, "And when ye go forth in the land, it is no sin for you to curtail [your] worship if ye fear that those who disbelieve may attack you. In truth the disbelievers are an open enemy to you".[142] They said that the Prophet (God's peace and blessings be upon him) shortened his prayers for he was in a state of fear.

They (the majority) differed over this on five points. First, about the *ḥukm* of curtailing prayers. Second, about the length of the journey to which curtailment applies. Third, the kind of journey that justifies curtailment. Fourth, the point from which the traveller may commence shortened prayers. Fifth, the duration in time for which it is permissible for the traveller to continue curtailing prayers, if he has stayed on at one place.

With respect to the *ḥukm* of curtailing prayers, they held four different opinions. Some of them held that curtailing prayers is an obligation for the traveller and is determined for him. Some held that curtailing and completion are both obligatory for him by way of an option, like the option in case of expiation (*kaffāra*). Some held that curtailing of prayers is a *sunna*, while others were of the view that it is an exemption and offering complete prayers has greater merit. The first opinion was held by Abū Ḥanīfa, his disciples, and the Kūfīs as a whole, that is, it is a fixed obligation. The second opinion was held by some of the disciples of al-Shāfiʿī. The third, that it is *sunna*, was held by Mālik in the best known narration from him. The fourth, that it is an exemption, was held by al-Shāfiʿī in the best known narration from him and it is supported by his disciples.

The reason for their disagreement derives from the conflict between rational argument and the form of the command in the transmitted evidence, and also the conflict of the evidence from the acts with the rational argument and the form of the words used in the transmitted evidence. The (rational) meaning arising from the curtailing of prayers for a traveller is an exemption because of the existence of hardship, just as he has been exempted in the case of fasting and other things. This also is supported by the tradition of Yaʿlā ibn Umayya, who said, "I said to ʿUmar that Allāh has said 'if ye fear that those who disbelieve may attack you', intending thereby the curtailing of prayers during a

[141] That is, to pray two *rakʿas* instead of four, in the case of *ẓuhr*, *ʿaṣr*, and the *ʿishāʾ* prayers. Thus, the curtailment does not apply in the case of the morning and the *maghrib* prayers.

[142] Qurʾān 4 : 101.

journey. He said, 'I was also struck by what has struck you, so I asked the Messenger of Allāh (God's peace and blessings be upon him), and he replied, 'It is a charity that Allāh has granted to you, so accept the charity' ". This indicates an exemption. Further, there is the tradition of Abū Qalāba from a man from Banū ʿĀmir, who came to the Prophet (God's peace and blessings be upon him) and the Prophet (God's peace and blessings be upon him) said to him, "Allāh has lifted from the traveller the obligation for fasting and a part of prayer". These two traditions are found in the *Ṣaḥīḥ* compilations. All this indicates leniency, exemption, and the removal of hardship, and not that curtailing of prayer is obligatory or a *sunna*.

The tradition that contradicts, through the form of its words, the rational meaning and these traditions is the tradition of ʿĀʾisha, declared authentic by agreement, in which she said, "Prayer has been made obligatory two *rakʿas* at a time. The prayer during journey is this basic (unit), while the prayer within a settlement was increased". The evidence arising from the acts (of the Prophet) that conflicts with the rational meaning and with the meaning of the above transmitted traditions is what has been reported about the Prophet (God's peace and blessings be upon him) that he shortened his prayer in all his journeys, and it has never been proved authentically that the Prophet had ever offered the complete prayer during a journey. Those who maintained that it is a *sunna* or an obligation with an option (*wājib mukhayyar*), interpreted it to be so, for it did not prove to be authentic for them "that the Prophet (God's peace and blessings be upon him) completed his prayer, or did what was similar". It therefore follows that it is one of several types, that is, either it is an obligation with an option or it is a *sunna* or it is a determined obligation for the traveller. Its being a fixed obligation, however, conflicts with the rational meaning, while its being an exemption conflicts with the transmitted words. Thus, it is necessary that it be (either) an obligation with an option, or a *sunna*. This is a kind of reconciliation (of the evidences). They objected to the tradition of ʿĀʾisha for it is well-known of her that she used to offer the complete prayer. ʿAṭāʾ has related from her that she said, "The Prophet (God's peace and blessings be upon him) used to complete the prayer during a journey and he used to shorten it, he used to fast and give up fasting, he used to delay the *ẓuhr* prayer and hasten the middle prayer, and he used to delay *maghrib* and hasten *ʿishāʾ*". It is also opposed by the tradition of Anas and of Abū Najīḥ al-Makkī, who said "that the Companions of Muḥammad (God's peace and blessings be upon him) used to travel together, with some of them offering the full prayer and others curtailing it, with some of them fasting when others were not. They did not find fault with each other nor did they disagree about the offering of full prayer by ʿUthmān and ʿĀʾisha". This, then, is their disagreement on the first point.

In their disagreement on the second point, which concerns the length of the journey permitting curtailment of prayers, the jurists disagreed widely. Mālik, al-Shāfiʿī, Aḥmad, and a large group of jurists held that prayer is to be shortened during (a journey of) four *barīds*, which is a distance covered in one day moving at a medium pace. Abū Ḥanīfa, his disciples, and the Kūfīs said that the minimum for which prayer is to be shortened is a journey of three days, and curtailing is for a person who travels from one region to another. The Ẓāhirites said that curtailing prayers is permitted for each journey, whether to a near or distant place.

The reason for their disagreement stems from the conflict of the rational meaning with the words. Rationally speaking, the reason why travelling may occasion the curtailment of prayer is based on the hardship that exists, as in the case of fasting during travel. If this is the case, then, then curtailing is permissible whenever hardship is found. Those who take into account only the letter of the law maintain that the Prophet (God's peace and blessings be upon him) said, "Allāh has removed from the (liability of) traveller fasting and a part of prayer". Thus, anyone to whom the term traveller can be applied is permitted to curtail or to forgo (delay) fasting. They supported this with what has been recorded by Muslim from ʿUmar ibn al-Khaṭṭāb "that the Prophet (God's peace and blessings be upon him) used to curtail prayers during a journey of about seventeen miles".

A group of jurists, as we have said, adopted the fifth opinion maintaining that curtailing of prayers is not permitted, except to the person in a state of fear, because of the words of the Exalted, "And when ye go forth in the land, it is no sin for you to curtail (your) worship if ye fear that those who disbelieve may attack you. In truth the disbelievers are an open enemy to you".[143] It is said that this was ʿĀʾisha's opinion. They also maintained that the Prophet (God's peace and blessings be upon him) used to curtail his prayers as he was in a state of fear.

The basis for the disagreement of those who took into consideration the element of hardship stems from the disagreement of the Companions over this. Thus, the opinion about four *barīds* is related from Ibn ʿUmar and Ibn ʿAbbās, and has been reported by Mālik. The opinion about three days is related from Ibn Masʿūd, ʿUthmān, and others.

With respect to the third point that relates to the kind of journey for which curtailment is permissible, some of the jurists said that it is permitted in a journey undertaken to seek nearness to Allāh, like *ḥajj*, *ʿumra*, and *jihād*. Those who upheld this opinion include Aḥmad. Some of them permitted it in all permissible (*mubāḥ*) journeys, thus, excluding journeys undertaken for evil

[143] Qurʾān 4 : 101.

design. This was the opinion of Mālik and al-Shāfiʿī. Some of them allowed it in any kind of journey whether for seeking nearness, permissible, or for evil design. This was the opinion of Abū Ḥanīfa, his disciples, al-Thawrī, and Abū Thawr.

The reason for their disagreement springs from the conflict of the rational meaning, or the apparent meaning, with the evidence arising from the acts (of the Prophet). Those who took into account the element of hardship or the apparent meaning of the term "journey" did not differentiate between one kind of journey or another. Those who took into account the evidence arising from the acts said that it is not permitted, except in a journey undertaken to seek nearness to Allāh, as the Prophet (God's peace and blessings be upon him) did not ever curtail prayers, except during a journey undertaken to seek nearness to Allāh. Those who distinguished between a permissible journey and one undertaken with unlawful design in mind did so through an enhanced application of the rule. The rule pertains to whether exemptions are permitted in the pursuit of unlawful things. In this issue the rational meaning is in conflict with the apparent meaning, therefore the jurists differed over it.

On the fourth point that relates to the question of from which spot may the traveller commence to curtail prayers, Mālik stated in *al-Muwaṭṭaʾ* that prayers are not to be curtailed until the person has left the dwellings area on the outskirts of the village and he does not begin to offer full prayers till he reaches the first of such dwellings. It is also related from him that the person is not to curtail prayers in case of the well-populated village until he is at a distance of three miles from it and this, according to him in one narration, is the boundary for the area in which Friday prayers are obligatory on the persons living outside the centre of the town. The first opinion was adopted by the majority.

The reason for this disagreement stems from the conflict between the meaning of the term and the evidence arising from the acts. This is so as the word "traveller" is applied to a person the moment he commences his journey. Those who took into account the connotation of the term said that as soon as he goes beyond the houses of the village he is to curtail prayers. Those who took into account the evidence of acts, that is, the acts of the Prophet (God's peace and blessings be upon him), said that he is not to begin curtailing prayers, until he is at a distance of three miles from the houses of the village as this is established from the tradition of Anas, who said, "The Messenger of Allāh (God's peace and blessings be upon him) used to pray two *rakʿas* when he had travelled a distance of three miles or three *farāsikh*—Shuʿba doubted (which)".

In their disagreement over the time period for which a traveller may stop in a town (during his journey) and yet curtail his prayers there are many disputes;

Abū ʿUmar has related about eleven opinions, but the well-known ones are those that are held by the jurists of the provinces, and they have three different opinions. First is the opinion of Mālik and al-Shāfiʿī that if the traveller decides to stay for four days he is to offer complete prayers. The second is the opinion of Abū Ḥanīfa and Sufyān al-Thawrī that if he decides to stay for a period of fifteen days he is to offer complete prayers. The third is the opinion of Aḥmad and Dāwūd that if he decides to stay for more than four days he is to offer complete prayers.

The reason for disagreement arises from the fact that the matter is not expressly stated in the law, and using analogy for such prescription is deemed weak by all. All of them therefore strived to argue for their opinion on the basis of the reported circumstances in which the Prophet (God's peace and blessings be upon him) continued to curtail prayers while he stopped on the way or he continued to treat prayers with the *ḥukm* of a traveller.

The first group argued for their opinion on the basis of the report "that the Prophet (God's peace and blessings be upon him) stayed at Makka for three days and curtailed his prayer during his *ʿumra*". There is no evidence in this that this is the limit for curtailing prayers, in fact, it does furnish an evidence that the traveller is to curtail prayers when the stay is for three days or less. The second group argued for their opinion on the basis of the report that he (the Prophet) stayed at Makka and curtailed his prayers. This he did for about fifteen days in some versions, while it is also narrated (variously) as seventeen days, eighteen days, or nineteen days. This is recorded by al-Bukhārī. Each version was adopted by some group. The third group argued on the basis of the stay of the Prophet (God's peace and blessings be upon him) at Makka for his *ḥajj* during which he offered curtailed prayers for four days. The Mālikites supported their opinion with the report "that the Messenger of Allāh (God's peace and blessings be upon him) determined three days for the traveller at Makka after he had completed the rituals". This indicates in their view that a stay of three days does not stop the term "traveller" from being applicable to the person staying, and this is the point that was made by all. They strove to derive this from the acts of the Prophet (God's peace and blessings be upon him), that is, (the answer to the question of) when the term "traveller" is not applicable to the person who intends to stay. For this reason they agreed that if the term "traveller" is not lifted from him up to a certain period, on the basis of the opinion of one of them, the person will continue to curtail prayers if some impediment is preventing him (from resuming his journey) even if the stay is prolonged indefinitely (with the will of Allāh). Those who took into account the minimum period of his stay interpreted the maximum period of his stay, invoked by the rival, on the basis of this reasoning. Thus, the Mālikites, for example, said that the fifteen days for which the Prophet (God's peace and blessings be upon him) stayed after the conquest of Makka, he did so while constantly intending that he would not stay more than four days. The same argument can be valid against the time that they determined.

It is better for the *mujtahid* in such cases to follow one of two methods. He should assign the *ḥukm* to the maximum period of stay that has been reported during which the Prophet (God's peace and blessings be upon him) curtailed his prayers. He should fix this as the limit since not curtailing is the original principle and it is therefore necessary that this period not be increased except on the basis of an evidence. The alternative is to uphold that the original principle is based on the minimum period on which a consensus has taken place and the reports about the Prophet (God's peace and blessings be upon him) that he stayed for periods in excess of this minimum during which his prayers were curtailed; this is because it is likely that it is permitted to the traveller. Further, it is also likely that he stayed with the intention of staying for the (minimum) period permitted to the traveller, but that it occurred to him that he should stay longer. When there is an ambiguity, it is necessary to uphold the principle. The minimum that has been asserted on the issue is one day and night, and this is the opinion of Rabīʿa ibn Abī ʿAbd al-Raḥmān. It is related from al-Ḥasan al-Baṣrī that the traveller is always to curtail prayers, except when he stays at one of the cities. This is based on the assumption that the term "travelling" is applicable to him till he approaches one of the cities. These, then, are the governing issues related to curtailment of prayers.

2.3.4.2. *Section 2: Combining prayers* (jamʿ)

Three issues are related to the topic of combining prayers. First is its permissibility. Second, the manner of combining prayers. Third, things permissible in combining.

2.3.4.2.1. Issue 1: The permissibility of combining prayers

About the permissibility of combining prayers, the jurists agreed that combining *ẓuhr* and *ʿaṣr* at the time of *ẓuhr* at ʿArafa (by a pilgrim) is a *sunna*, and combining *maghrib* and *ʿishāʾ* at Muzdalifa at the time of *ʿishāʾ* is also a *sunna*. They disagreed about combining prayers on occasions other than these. The majority permitted it, but disagreed as to the occasions on which this is permitted and those on which it is not. Abū Ḥanīfa and his disciples prohibited this absolutely.

The reason for their disagreement arises from their dispute about the interpretation of the traditions that are cited in support of combining prayers and their employment as legal evidence for the permissibility of *jamʿ*. All of them comprise acts and not words, and acts are subject to wider interpretation, more than are words. Second, there is a dispute about the authenticity of the traditions. Third, there is a disagreement about the permissibility of employing analogy in this. Thus, there are three reasons for disagreement, as you can see.

The traditions about whose interpretation they disagreed, include the tradition of Anas, which is authentic by agreement and is recorded by al-Bukhārī and Muslim. He said, "When the Messenger of Allāh (God's peace and blessings be upon him) used to travel before the declining of the sun, he delayed *ẓuhr* till the time of *ʿaṣr*, when he used to descend (from his mount) and combine the two. If, however, the sun had declined before the commencement of the journey, he used to pray *ẓuhr* and then ride". They also include the tradition of Ibn ʿUmar, which too is recorded by the two Shaykhs (al-Bukhārī and Muslim). He said, "I have seen the Messenger of Allāh (God's peace and blessings be upon him), when he was hastening his journey (for some reason), delaying *maghrib* so that he would combine it with *ʿishāʾ*". The third is the tradition of Ibn ʿAbbās, recorded by Mālik and Muslim. He said, "The Messenger of Allāh (God's peace and blessings be upon him) prayed *ẓuhr* and ʿaṣr combined and *maghrib* and *ʿishāʾ* combined, in the absence of (a cause for) fear or journey". Those who uphold the permissibility of combining prayers interpreted this tradition to mean that he delayed praying *ẓuhr* till the time fixed for *ʿaṣr* and then combined the two. The Kūfīs maintained that he prayed *ẓuhr* in its last timing and *ʿaṣr* in its first timing in accordance with what is related about the *imāma* of Jibrīl. They said that it is proper that the tradition of Ibn ʿAbbās be interpreted this way as there is consensus on the point that without a valid excuse, two prayers are not to be offered in the time fixed for one of them. They also argued for their interpretation on the basis of the tradition of Ibn Masʿūd, who said, "By Him, besides Whom there is no god, the Messenger of Allāh (God's peace and blessings be upon him) did not offer a prayer, ever, other than in its appointed timing, except the two prayers that he combined: *ẓuhr* and *ʿaṣr* at ʿArafa, and *maghrib* and *ʿishāʾ* at Muzdalifa [*jamʿ*]". They also said, "It is possible to interpret these traditions to mean what we have said or to mean what you have said. The fixed timings of prayers and their performance within the timings, however, has been established, and it is not permitted to move away from an established principle to a matter that is subject to interpretation".

The tradition whose authenticity they differed about is related by Mālik from Muʿādh ibn Jabal: "They went out with the Messenger of Allāh (God's peace and blessings be upon him) on the day of (the expedition of) Tabūk, and the Messenger of Allāh (God's peace and blessings be upon him) used to combine *ẓuhr* and *ʿaṣr* and *maghrib* and *ʿishāʾ*. One day he delayed praying and then came out to pray *ẓuhr* and *ʿaṣr* combined, he went back (to his place of rest) and then came out to pray *maghrib* and *ʿishāʾ* combined". This tradition, if proved authentic, is clearer in meaning than those traditions that permit combining, as the apparent meaning here is that he advanced *ʿishāʾ* to the time of *maghrib*, though they would say that he prayed *maghrib* in its last timing and *ʿishāʾ* in its first appointed timing, as there is no definitive indication in the tradition about this; in fact, the words of the narrator are subject to interpretation.

Their disagreement about employing analogy in this relates to the association of all prayers during a journey with the prayers at ʿArafa and Muzdalifa, that combining is to be permitted on the analogy of these prayers. Thus, for example, it may be said: "These are prayers whose obligation has arisen during a journey, therefore, it is permitted to combine them, and the basis is the gathering of the people at ʿArafa and Muzdalifa". This is the opinion of Sālim ibn ʿAbd Allāh, I mean, the permissibility of this analogy, but the use of analogy in matters of worship is deemed weak.

These, then, are the causes of disagreement arising over the permissibility of combining prayers.

2.3.4.2.2. Issue 2: The method of combining prayers

Those who upheld the combining of prayer during a journey differed about its manner. Some of them said that it is preferable to delay the first prayer and offer it with the second prayer, however, if they are combined within the timing of the first this is also permitted. This is one narration from Mālik. Some of them deemed the two equal, that is, the second may be advanced to the timing of the first or it may be the other way round. This is al-Shāfiʿī's opinion and is a narration from Mālik through the jurists of Medina, while the first has been related by Ibn al-Qāsim from him. This kind of combination (delaying the first to the time of the second) is preferable according to Mālik, as it has been established through the tradition of Anas. Those who considered the two methods as equal relied on the principle that preference is not undertaken on the basis of *ʿadāla*, that is, one *ʿadāla* is not be preferred over another *ʿadāla* for determining the obligation of acting upon the tradition. This means that if the tradition of Muʿādh is proved authentic it is obligatory to act upon it, just as it is obligatory to act upon the tradition of Anas, if the *ʿadāla* of the transmitters of both traditions is established, and even if the *ʿadāla* of the transmitters of one tradition is stronger than that of the other.

2.3.4.2.3. Issue 3: The causes permitting the combining of prayers

Those who upheld the permissibility of combining prayers agreed that travel is one of the causes permitting the combining of prayers. They disagreed about combining prayers within a settlement and also about the conditions of travel that permits it, as some of them considered any kind of journey, whatever its nature, to be a valid cause for combining prayers, while others stipulated a particular form and a particular kind of prayer. Mālik is one of those who stipulate a particular form of journey, according to the narration of Ibn al-Qāsim from him. He said that the traveller is not to combine prayers unless the journey becomes cumbersome for him. Al-Shāfiʿī is among those who did not stipulate this, and this is also one narration from Mālik. Those who adopted this opinion (Mālik's) relied on the saying of Ibn ʿUmar "I have seen the Messenger of Allāh (God's peace and blessings be upon him), when he was hastening his journey (for some reason), delaying *maghrib* so that he would combine it with *ʿishāʾ*". Those who did not hold this opinion adopted the apparent meaning of the traditions of Anas and others.

Similarly, they disagreed, as we have said, about the kind of journey in which combining (of the prayers) is permitted. Some said that it is a journey motivated by piety, like *ḥajj* or war (*jihād*), and this is the apparent meaning of the narration of Ibn al-Qāsim. Some said that it is a journey that is permissible (motivated by piety or undertaken for any legitimate purpose), as against a journey undertaken for unlawful ends. This is al-Shāfiʿī's opinion and the apparent meaning of the narration of the Medinites from Mālik. The reason for their disagreement over this is the same as the reason for their disagreement over a journey during which prayer is curtailed, although in that case the meaning is general, as curtailment has been reported both through words and acts (of the Prophet), while combining has been reported through acts alone. Those who confined it to the kinds of journey in which the Messenger of Allāh (God's peace and blessings be upon him) combined his prayers did not permit it in other kinds of journeys, while those who considered it a kind of exemption (*rukhṣa*) for the traveller deemed it valid in other journeys as well.

Mālik and the majority of the jurists do not permit the combining of prayers within a settlement without an excuse, while a group of the Ẓāhirites and Ashhab, from among the disciples of Mālik, permitted it. The reason for their disagreement is based upon their dispute over the meaning of the tradition of Ibn ʿAbbās. Some of them interpreted it to apply to the case of rain, as did Mālik, while others adopted its absolute meaning. Muslim has recorded an addition in his report, namely, the words of the Prophet (God's peace and blessings be upon him) "in the absence of [a cause of] fear or journey or rain", and this was adopted by the Ẓāhirites.

Al-Shāfiʿī permitted the combining of prayers within a settlement when it rains, whether during the day or the night, while Mālik prohibited it during the day (because of rain) and permitted it during the night. He also permitted it during the night when there is slush (sludge) during the night in the absence of rain. Al-Shāfiʿī criticized Mālik for making a distinction between prayers during the day and prayers during the night, as he related the tradition and then diverted it (through interpretation), that is, restricted its general meaning on the basis of analogy. He commented on the words of Ibn ʿAbbās, "The Messenger of Allāh (God's peace and blessings be upon him) prayed *ẓuhr* and ʿaṣr combined and *maghrib* and *ʿishāʾ* combined, in the absence of [a cause of] fear or journey", saying that he considered this to have been at the time of rain. Al-Shāfiʿī said that he did not adopt the general meaning or its interpretation, that is, the restricted meaning, but he rejected part of it and interpreted (restricted) the rest. This is something that is not permitted by consensus, for he did not accept the words "prayed *ẓuhr* and *ʿaṣr* combined", but accepted the words "prayed *maghrib* and *ʿishāʾ* combined", and then interpreted them. I believe, however, that Mālik (God bless him) rejected part of the tradition as it was opposed by practice (*ʿamal*). He therefore adopted the part that was not opposed by practice, which is the combining of *maghrib* and *ʿishāʾ* within a settlement, for it is related that when those in authority used to combine *maghrib* and *ʿishāʾ*, Ibn ʿUmar used to combine these with them.

The investigation of this principle is based on the examination of the issue as to how practice (*ʿamal*) can be a legal evidence. The earlier Mālikites used to say that it is a category of the principle of consensus. There is, however, no basis for this as the consensus of a few is not to be relied upon. The later Mālikites used to say that it is a kind of communal transmission (*mutawātir*), and they argue for this on the basis of (the prevalent use of) a measure (*ṣāʿ*) and similar things that have been transmitted by the jurists of Medina from the predecessors. Practice is an act and acts do not convey *tawātur*, unless they are corroborated by words, for *tawātur* is a method of (oral) reports and not acts. To deem acts as exhibiting *tawātur* is difficult and perhaps not permissible. In my view, it is more likely to be a case of the general need of the people, a principle adopted by Abū Ḥanīfa, as it is not permissible to deem such recurring practices, along with their recurring causes, as unabrogated, when the people of Medina, who acted upon these *sunan* following their predecessors are oblivious of them. It is a stronger (evidence) than the (principle of) general need of the people adopted by Abū Ḥanīfa, for it is appropriate that the jurists of Medina not be oblivious of these as compared to those on whom Abū Ḥanīfa has relied for transmission. On the whole, *ʿamal* is corroborating evidence when it accompanies and conforms with something that is transmitted, in which case it conveys persuasive evidence, and when it is opposed by such transmission, it (still) conveys probable evidence. But the question, whether this corroborating evidence reaches a level with which authentic traditions transmitted through a single *isnād* (*āḥād*) can be rejected, needs investigation. It is possible that in certain cases it does reach such a level, while in others it does not because of the difference in the degree of the need of the people. The reason is that whenever the need for a *sunna* is acute and it is a matter that is constantly recurring for the subjects, the transmission of the *sunna* by way of *āḥād* that does not become widespread in reports and practice (despite the acute need of the people), exhibits weakness because it gives rise to one of two conclusions: that it is either abrogated, or that there is some discrepancy in its transmission. This has been elaborated by Mutakallimūn like Abū al-Maʿālī.

Mālik permitted the combining of prayers within a settlement by a sick person (*mariḍ*) when he was afraid that he would faint at the time of the other prayer, or when the person loses control of the excretion exits, but al-Shāfiʿī prohibited this. The reason for their disagreement stems from their dispute over extending the underlying cause of combining during a journey, that is, hardship. Those who applied the cause uniformly held that it is preferable and more appropriate in this case, as hardship for the *mariḍ* in observing separate prayers is greater than that for the traveller. Those who did not consider this (hardship) as the underlying cause and considered it, as they say, deficient, that is, specific to this *ḥukm* to the exclusion of others, did not permit it.

2.3.5. Chapter 5 Prayers under threat of attack (*Ṣalāt al-Khawf*)

The jurists disagreed about the permissibility and description of *ṣalāt al-khawf* after the time of the Prophet (God's peace and blessings be upon him). Most of the jurists maintain that *ṣalāt al-khawf* is permitted because of the general implication of the words of the Exalted, "And when ye go forth in the land, it is no sin for you to curtail (your) worship if ye fear that those who disbelieve may attack you. In truth the disbelievers are an open enemy unto you".[144] Further, it is also established through the practice of the Prophet (God's peace and blessings be upon him) and that of the Caliphs after him.

Abū Yūsuf, from among the disciples of Abū Ḥanīfa, deviated saying that *ṣalāt al-khawf*, after the time of the Prophet (God's peace and blessings be upon him), is not to be led by a single *imām*, and that after his time two *imāms* are to lead this prayer, with one of them leading a group in praying two *rakʿas* while another group maintains the watch, and then the other is to lead the second group while the first group having prayed maintains a watch.

The reason for their disagreement derives from their dispute of whether the *ṣalāt al-khawf* led by the Prophet (God's peace and blessings be upon him)

[144] Qurʾān 4 : 101.

amounts to worship or whether it is a special merit of the Prophet (God's peace and blessings be upon him). Those who maintained that it is a worship did not consider it to be a case specific to the Prophet (God's peace and blessings be upon him), while those who deemed it to be a special merit of the Prophet (God's peace and blessings be upon him) considered it to be something specific to him, and thus it would be possible for us to divide the people between two *imāms*, as their gathering behind one *imām* was one of the specific merits of the Prophet (God's peace and blessings be upon him). Such an interpretation is supported, in his (Abū Yūsuf's) view by the implication emerging from the words of the Exalted, "And when thou (O Muḥammad) art among them and arrangest (their) worship for them, let only a party of them stand with thee (to worship) and let them take their arms. Then when they have performed their prostrations let them fall to the rear and let another party come that hath not worshipped and let them worship with thee, and let them take their precaution and their arms".[145] The implication here is that if he is not among them the *ḥukm* is to be different.

A group of the jurists of Syria maintained that *ṣalāt al-khawf* is to be delayed from the time of fear to the time of security, just as the Prophet (God's peace and blessings be upon him) did on the day of the Battle of Khandaq. The majority of the jurists maintain that this act on the day of the Battle of Khandaq was prior to the revelation regarding *ṣalāt al-khawf* and was therefore abrogated by it.

The jurists disagreed extensively about the description of *ṣalāt al-khawf* because of the conflict of the traditions on this topic, that is, reports about the acts of the Prophet (God's peace and blessings be upon him) related to *ṣalāt al-khawf*. There are seven well-known descriptions. One of these is what is recorded by Mālik and Muslim about the tradition of Ṣāliḥ ibn Khawwāt from one who had observed the fear prayer with the Messenger of Allāh (God's peace and blessings be upon him) on the day of Dhāt al-Riqā. It says, "A group formed rows behind the Prophet (God's peace and blessings be upon him), while another group arrayed itself against the enemy. He led those with him for a *rakʿa* and then kept standing while they finished by themselves and departed to face the enemy. The other group then came and he led them for one *rakʿa* that was left of his prayer, after which he kept sitting while they completed their prayer and then made the salutation with them". Al-Shāfiʿī based his opinion on this tradition. Mālik related exactly the same tradition from al-Qāsim ibn Muḥammad from Ṣāliḥ ibn Khawwāt as a *mawqūf* tradition (attributed to a Companion) like that of Yazīd ibn Rūmān that when he had completed the *rakʿa* with the second group he made the salutation and did

[145] Qurʾān 4 : 102.

not wait for them to finish their prayer. Mālik preferred this description. Al-Shāfiʿī preferred the *musnad* over the *mawqūf*, while Mālik preferred the *mawqūf* as it conforms with the general principles, that is, the *imām* is not to sit down[146] so that the second group may complete their prayer, for it is the *imām* who is to be followed and he is not the follower.

The third description appears in the tradition of Abū ʿUbayda from ʿAbd Allāh ibn Masʿūd from his father. It is related by al-Thawrī and others and is recorded by Abū Dāwūd. He said, "The Messenger of Allāh (God's peace and blessings be upon him) offered *ṣalāt al-khawf* with one group while another group faced the enemy. He offered a *rakʿa* and two prostrations with them and they left to face the enemy without making the salutation. The other group then came and he offered a *rakʿa* with them and made the salutation. They stood up and offered the second *rakʿa* by themselves, made the salutation and went away to stand in the place of the others facing the enemy. The first group returned to their positions and offered a *rakʿa* by themselves and made the salutation". This description was adopted by Abū Ḥanīfa and his disciples, except for Abū Yūsuf as has preceded.

The fourth description occurred in the tradition of Abū ʿAyyāsh al-Zuraqī, who said, "We were with the Messenger of Allāh (God's peace and blessings be upon him) at ʿUsfān and Khālid ibn al-Walīd was leading the unbelievers. We offered the *ẓuhr* prayer. The unbelievers said: 'We have been negligent, we should have attacked them while they were praying.' Allāh then revealed the verse about shortening the prayer between the *ẓuhr* and *ʿaṣr* times. When it was time for the *aṣr* prayer, the Messenger of Allāh (God's peace and blessings be upon him) stood up facing the *qibla*, and the unbelievers were arrayed in front of him. Praying behind the Messenger of Allāh (God's peace and blessings be upon him) was one row and behind this was another row. When the Messenger of Allāh (God's peace and blessings be upon him) bowed [*rukūʿ*] all of them bowed with him, and when he made the prostration the row behind him prostrated, while those in the other row stood guard over them. When these people made the two prostrations and stood up, those behind them prostrated. The first row then stepped back taking the place of the second, while the second row advanced and took the place of the first. The Messenger of Allāh (God's peace and blessings be upon him) then bowed and all bowed with him, he then prostrated and the row behind him prostrated, while those [now] in the second row stood guard over them. When the Messenger of Allāh (God's peace and blessings be upon him) and the row behind him adopted the sitting posture those behind them prostrated and

[146] The editor of the original text notes that this should be "not to make the salutation" as in the previous lines.

finally all were seated. The Prophet then made the salutation and they all made the salutation after him". This prayer was offered at ʿUsfān and also at Banū Sulaym.

Abū Dāwūd said that this tradition has also been related from Jābir, from Ibn ʿAbbās, from Mujāhid, from Abū Mūsā and Hishām ibn ʿUrwa from his father from the Prophet (God's peace and blessings be upon him). He said that this is the opinion of al-Thawrī, and that it is the most cautious of all, implying thereby that there is not much in this description opposing the generally accepted practice. This description was upheld by a host of the disciples of Mālik and al-Shāfiʿī. Muslim has recorded it from Jābir. Jābir said: "Just as you do when you guard your leaders".

The fifth description occurs in the tradition of Ḥudhayfa. Thaʿlaba ibn Zahdam said, "We were with Saʿīd ibn al-ʿĀṣ in Ṭabaristān. He stood up and said, 'Which one of you has offered *ṣalāt al-khawf* with the Messenger of Allāh (God's peace and blessings be upon him)'. Ḥudhayfa said, 'I did' ". He then offered one *rakʿa* with one group and the second *rakʿa* with another group, and they did not offer any other *rakʿa*. This conflicts extensively with the original form of the prayer. A similar tradition is related from Ibn ʿAbbās, who said, "Prayer, through the tongue of your Prophet, in a settlement is four *rakʿas*, two while travelling, and a single *rakʿa* in *khawf*". Al-Thawrī permitted this description.

The sixth description occurs in the tradition of Abū Bakr and in the tradition of Jābir from the Prophet (God's peace and blessings be upon him) that he led each of the two groups in two *rakʿas* at a time. Al-Ḥasan (al-Baṣrī) issued his opinion in accordance with this. In this there is an evidence of the possible discrepancy between the *niyya* of the *imām* and the that of the followers, for he intends the full prayer while they are curtailing it. It has been recorded by Muslim from Jābir.

The seventh description occurs in the tradition of Ibn ʿUmar from the Prophet (God's peace and blessings be upon him) that when he was asked about *ṣalāt al-khawf* said, "The *imām* and one group of people step out and the *imām* leads them in one *rakʿa*, when a second group from among them that is facing the enemy has not prayed. When those with him have prayed a *rakʿa*, they move back to the positions of those who have not, but they do not make the salutation. Those who have not prayed as yet then step out and pray a *rakʿa* with him. The *imām* then moves away after having prayed two *rakʿas*, and each group then prays by itself a *rakʿa* after the departure of the *imām*. Thus each group prays two *rakʿas*. If the threat of attack is grave the men may pray while standing or while riding, facing the *qibla* or otherwise". Among those who upheld this description are Ashhab, Mālik, and a group of jurists. Abū ʿUmar said that the proof of those who adopted this tradition of Ibn

ʿUmar is that it has been reported through the transmission of the jurists of Medina, who are authorities in transmission against those who adopted an opposite view. In addition, it is also more in conformity with the principles, as the first and the second groups did not pray the second *rakʿa* except after the Messenger of Allāh (God's peace and blessings be upon him) had completed his prayer, and this is well-known in the practice of delayed performance that is agreed upon for all prayers.

Most of the jurists uphold what has been mentioned in this tradition about the gravity of the attack that it is permitted to pray while facing the *qibla* or without facing it, and without there being any indication of bowing or prostration. Abū Ḥanīfa opposed this saying: "One under an apprehension of attack is not to pray, except while facing the *qibla*, nor one in a state of intense absorption". The reason for disagreement over this stems from its conflict with the principles.

A group of jurists maintained that all of these descriptions are permissible, and the *mukallaf* (subject) may pray in accordance with the one he prefers. It is also said that this discrepancy is because of the difference of the location (of each battle).

2.3.6. Chapter 6 The Prayer of the Sick (*Ṣalāt al-Marīḍ*)

The jurists agreed that the communication of the performance of prayer is addressed to the *marīḍ*, and that the obligation to stand up (and pray) is waived for him only if he is unable to do so, in which case he prays while seated. Likewise, the obligation for bowing and prostrating is waived if he is unable to do either or both, and he may make a sign in their place. They disagreed about the condition of a person who may pray while seated, about the sitting posture, and about the posture of one who is unable to sit or stand.

A group of jurists said about the person who may pray while seated that he is one who is not able to stand at all. Another group of jurists said that he is a person for whom it is difficult to stand up because of illness. This is Mālik's opinion. The reason for disagreement stems from the question of whether the obligation to pray while standing is waived because of hardship (*mashaqqa*) or because of the inability to stand up. There is no explicit text on this.

About the sitting posture, which is a substitute for standing, a group of jurists said that the person is to sit on his buttocks with folded legs. Ibn Masʿūd disapproved of such a sitting posture. Those who upheld such a sitting posture (*tarabbus*) did not distinguish between this posture and that adopted for *tashahhud*, while those who disapproved it maintained that it is not a posture for prayer.

With respect to the manner of prayer for one who is not able to stand or sit, a group of jurists said that the person may pray while reclining on one side (facing the *qibla*), while another group said that he is to pray as is convenient for him, and a third group said that he is to pray with his legs (feet) pointed in the direction of the Kaʿba. One group maintained that if he is not able to sit, he is to pray reclined on one side, but if he is not able to recline on his side, he is to rest on his back with his legs (feet) pointing in the direction of the *qibla* to the extent that he is able to do so. This opinion has been selected by Ibn al-Mundhir.

2.4. Part 4: Repetition, Delayed Performance, and Prostrations for Forgetfulness

This part covers the acts of prayer that are not considered performed on time (*adāʾ*), and these are repetition (*iʿāda*), delayed performance (*qaḍāʾ*), and rectification (*jabr*) of excesses or shortfalls by means of prostrations (for forgetfulness). In this part there are thus three chapters. The first chapter is about *iʿāda* (repetition or re-performance). The second chapter is about *qaḍāʾ* (delayed performance). The third chapter covers rectification that is accomplished with prostrations.

2.4.1. Chapter 1 Repetition (*Iʿāda*)

The discussion in this chapter relates to the causes that require repetition of a prayer, and these are factors vitiating prayer. They agreed that a person who prays without purification, whether intentional or due to forgetfulness, is obliged to repeat his prayer (after purification). Similarly, one who prays in a direction other than the *qibla*, whether by intention or by mistake. On the whole, then, a person who violates one of the conditions of prayer is under an obligation of a repeat performance (in the correct way). (All this is by agreement of the jurists.) The jurists disagreed because of their dispute over the validating conditions.

2.4.1.1. Issue 1

There are disputed issues related to this topic that are beyond the basic elements of prayer. One of these is their agreement that the occurrence of a cause of *ḥadath* (losing the state of purification) terminates (invalidates) prayer. They disagreed, in this case, on whether it requires the repetition of prayer from the beginning, including a *rakʿa* or two completed prior to the occurrence of *ḥadath*, or to continue the prayer based on that already performed. The majority maintained that he is not to base it on continuation, neither in the case of *ḥadath* nor for another terminating cause (like making unauthorized movements), except in the case of a nosebleed alone. Some of them were of the view that he does not base it on continuation at all, either for *ḥadath* or for a nosebleed. This is al-Shāfiʿī's opinion. The Kūfīs maintained that he is to base the prayer on continuation in all kinds of *ḥadath*.

The reason for their disagreement is that there is no recorded tradition of permissibility from the Prophet (God's peace and blessings be upon him) in such a case (i.e. continuation), but it is established that Ibn ʿUmar had a nosebleed and based the (repetition of the) prayer on continuation (after washing away his blood and) without performing ablution. Those who maintained that this act on the part of a Companion amounts to a precedent, for he could not have based such an act upon analogy, permitted such an act. Those for whom a nosebleed does not amount to *ḥadath* permitted continuation in the case of a nosebleed only, and this is Mālik's opinion. Those for whom a nosebleed is a cause of *ḥadath* permitted continuation in all cases of *ḥadath* on the basis of analogy. And those who maintained that an act of a Companion is not to be relied upon unless it is a precedent from the Prophet (God's peace and blessings be upon him), did not permit continuation either in the case of *ḥadath* or a nosebleed, for there is consensus on the point that a worshipper praying in a direction other than the *qibla* has breached his prayer and also when he is making excessive movements.

2.4.1.2. Issue 2

The jurists disagreed on whether the passing of something in front of the worshipper terminates his prayer when he is praying without a curtain (*sutra*), or when the thing passes between him and the curtain. The majority maintain that none of these terminates the prayer, and there is no obligation for repetition on the worshipper. A group of jurists maintained that prayer is cut off by (the passing of) a woman, a donkey, or a black dog.

The reason for this disagreement is the conflict of a pronouncement with an act, as Muslim has recorded from Abū Dharr that the Prophet (God's peace and blessings be upon him) said, "A woman, a donkey, and a black dog [passing before a worshipper in prayer] cut off prayer". Muslim and al-Bukhārī, (on the other hand), have recorded from ʿĀʾisha that she said, "I found myself lying in front of the Messenger of Allāh (God's peace and blessings be upon him), when he was praying, in the same way as the body in a funeral is placed". Opinions similar to that of the majority have been related from ʿAlī and from Ubayy.

There is no dispute among the jurists about the abomination of something passing in front of a single worshipper (praying alone) or in front of the *imām* when praying without a *sutra*, or of passing between him and the *sutra*. They saw no harm, however, in passing anything behind the curtain. Likewise, they saw no harm in passing in front of the followers, because of the authenticated tradition of Ibn ʿAbbās, and of others. Ibn ʿAbbās said, "I came on the back of a donkey, when I was approaching puberty, and the Messenger of Allāh (God's peace and blessings be upon him) was leading the people in prayer. I passed in front of some of the rows. I dismounted, leaving the ass to graze, and joined one of the rows. No one objected to my act". This, in their view, resembles a *musnad* (i.e. a tradition attributed to the Prophet), but this is subject to scrutiny.

The majority agreed about the abomination of something passing before the praying worshipper because of the warning issued in this regard, and also because of the words of the Prophet (God's peace and blessings be upon him) "Push him away, for he is the devil".[147]

2.4.1.3. Issue 3

They disagreed about belching during prayer; there are three opinions. One group of jurists regarded it as an abomination, but did not impose repetition of prayer on the person who belched. Another group made repetition obligatory on a person belching. A third group made a distinction between that which was heard and that which was not. The reason for their disagreement stems from the vacillation of (the definition of) belching between being speech and non-speech.

2.4.1.4. Issue 4

They agreed that laughter cuts off prayer. They disagreed about smiling. Their disagreement about smiling is based on the question of whether it can take the ruling of laughter.

2.4.1.5. Issue 5

They disagreed about the prayer of the person suppressing the call of nature (*ḥāqin*). The majority of the jurists consider abominable that a person should pray while he is suppressing the call of nature, because of the tradition of Zayd ibn Arqam, who said, "I heard the Messenger of Allāh (God's peace and

[147] This is the tradition of Abū Saʿīd al-Khudrī that the Messenger of Allāh (God's peace and blessings be upon him) said, "When one of you is praying with a curtain between him and the people, and if another person attempts to pass in between, push him back. If he resists, fight him for he is a devil". Recorded in different versions by al-Bukhārī, Muslim, Abū Dāwūd and others.

blessings be upon him) saying, 'If one of you desires to go to the privy, he should do so before commencing prayer' ", and because of what is related from ʿĀʾisha from the Prophet (God's peace and blessings be upon him) that he said, "No one should pray in the presence of food, nor when he is suppressing the two dirts", that is, urination and defecation, and also because of the report of the proscription from ʿUmar.

A group of jurists maintained that prayer of such a person is not valid, and he has to repeat it. Ibn al-Qāsim's report from Mālik indicates that the prayer of a person suppressing the call of nature is invalid. The reason is that he reported from him that such a person must repeat the prayer before the expiry of the time, otherwise he has to do so as *qaḍāʾ*.

The reason for their disagreement arises from their dispute over the proscription whether it indicates the invalidity of the (performance of the) thing prohibited, or it merely indicates the sinfulness of the act in that condition, when the act so proscribed is originally obligatory or permissible. Those who upheld the invalidity of such a prayer relied on the tradition reported by the Syrians, with some reporting it from Thawbān, while others from Abū Hurayra from the Prophet (God's peace and blessings be upon him), who said, "It is not permitted for a believer to pray when he is forcibly suppressing the call of nature". Abū ʿUmar said that it is a tradition with a weak transmission, and it therefore has no legal force.

2.4.1.6. Issue 6

They disagreed about responding to the salutation by the praying worshipper. A group of jurists, among whom are Saʿīd ibn al-Musayyab, al-Ḥasan ibn al-Ḥasan al-Baṣrī, and Qatāda, permitted it. Another group disallowed responding in words, but permitted it with a gesture, and this is the opinion of Mālik and al-Shāfiʿī. Others prohibited responding by words or by gesture, and this is the opinion of Nuʿmām. One group permitted an inward (silent) response, while others said that he should respond when he has finished praying.

The reason for their disagreement stems from whether the response to a salutation is a kind of speech during prayer, which is proscribed. Those who maintained that it is a kind of speech prohibited in prayers, and restricted the verse, "When ye are greeted with a greeting, greet ye with a better than it or return it"[148] with traditions proscribing speech during prayer, said that it is not permitted to respond during prayer. Those who maintained that it is not included in the prohibited speech, and those who restricted the proscribing traditions with the command for responding to a greeting, permitted a

[148] Qurʾān 4 : 86.

response during prayer. Abū Bakr ibn al-Mundhir has said that those who say that the greeting is not to be responded to at all have opposed the *sunna*, for Ḥabīb has reported that the Prophet (God's peace and blessings be upon him) returned the greeting, with a gesture, of those who greeted him while he was praying.

2.4.2. Chapter 2 Delayed Performance (*Qaḍāʾ*)

The discussion in this chapter covers the identification of the person for whom *qaḍāʾ*[149] is obligatory, the description of the types of *qaḍāʾ*, and its conditions.

The Muslim jurists agreed that the person for whom *qaḍāʾ* is obligatory is one who forgets (to pray) or is asleep (till the expiry of the time). They disagreed about the case of one who delays praying intentionally and about one who faints. The Muslim jurists agreed about the obligation of *qaḍāʾ* for a person who misses prayer due to forgetfulness or sleep, because of the authentic reports about the words and acts of the Prophet (God's peace and blessings be upon him). By his words I mean the saying, "The Pen has been lifted on three counts", and here he mentioned one sleeping, and also his saying, "If one of you slept through [the time of] prayer or forgot it, then let him make up for it when he remembers". It is also reported that he himself overslept once till sunrise and then offered it as *qaḍāʾ*.

About the person who intentionally neglects prayer till its time is over, the majority hold that he is a sinner and *qaḍāʾ* is obligatory on him. Some of the Ẓāhirites have held that he is a sinner, but he is not to observe *qaḍāʾ*. One of the Ẓāhirites who held this was Abū Muḥammad ibn Ḥazm.

The reason for their disagreement is due to their dispute over two things. The first is the permissibility of employing *qiyās* (analogy) in the law. The second is the construction of analogy for the person who intentionally neglects to pray over one who forgets, once the validity of *qiyās* has been conceded. Those who made *qaḍāʾ* obligatory on him maintained that if *qaḍāʾ* has been imposed upon the person forgetting, whom the law has exempted in so many cases, it is appropriate that it be obligatory for the intentional forsaker who has no excuse. Those who did not permit the analogy of the person forgetting for the intentional relinquisher maintained that the person forgetting and the intentional relinquisher are opposites, and analogy cannot be undertaken for

[149] The term "atonement" is used by some to convey the meaning of *qaḍāʾ*. This appears to be incorrect insofar as atonement is achieved through the performance of some other act. *Qaḍāʾ*, on the other hand, requires the performance of the same act.

opposites, as the *aḥām* of the opposites are different, and that analogy is to be constructed for similar cases. The truth here is that if obligation (for *qaḍā'*) is considered as an enhanced liability (penalty) analogy would be true to form, but if it is considered as compassion for the person forgetting, for he has an excuse—and this benefit should not be denied to him—then the intentional relinquisher is the opposite of the person forgetting and the analogy is not formed since the person forgetting has an excuse while the intentional relinquisher does not. The principle is that *qaḍā'* is not obligatory because of the command of *adā'* (timely performance), but through a renewed command, as maintained by the Mutakallimūn, for the person forgetting lacks one of the conditions enabling him to perform the act in a valid manner, and this (condition) is time, which is one of the conditions of validity, and a delay in time amounts, in analogy, to a concession for him. There is a tradition, however, that settles the case of the persons forgetting and the persons sleeping; the case of the intentional relinquisher vacillates between being similar to their case and not being so. It is Allāh who guides to the truth.

For the person fainting, a group of jurists dropped *qaḍā'* altogether, while another group imposed *qaḍā'* upon him. Some of them stipulated *qaḍā'* of a specified number (of prayers) saying that he is to offer as *qaḍā'* five prayers or whatever is less. The reason for their disagreement arises from the vacillation of his case between that of one asleep and the insane person. Those who held him to be similar to one sleeping imposed *qaḍā'* on him, while those who compared him to an insane person waived *qaḍā'* in his case.

There are two kinds of *qaḍā'*: *qaḍā'* of the whole prayer, and *qaḍā'* in part. In the *qaḍā'* of the whole, the examination is of the description of *qaḍā'*, its conditions, and its time. The description of *qaḍā'* is identical to the description of *adā'*, if the two prayers have the same description with respect to the obligations. If, however, the circumstances of the two prayers are different, like remembering during a journey a prayer he missed when he was in a settlement, or remembering while in a settlement a prayer he missed during a journey, then, the jurists disagree about this, holding three opinions. A group of jurists said that he is to offer *qaḍā'* identical to the one he missed, disregarding his present condition. This is the opinion of Mālik and his disciples. Another group of jurists said that he is always to offer the prayer in its complete form, whether the prayer he missed was in a journey or in a settlement. Thus, according to their opinion if he remembers during a journey a prayer he missed in the settlement, he is to pray it as a prayer of the settlement, and if he remembers in a settlement a prayer he missed during a journey he is to pray it as a prayer of the settlement. This is al-Shāfi'ī's opinion. A third group of jurists said that he is always to pray *qaḍā'* as a prayer based on the present situation; thus, he is to offer *qaḍā'* during a journey as a curtailed prayer for a prayer missed in a settlement, and he is to offer in a settlement the prayer of a settlement for a prayer he missed during a journey. Those who likened *qaḍā*ʾ to *adā*ʾ took into account the time of the present situation and rendered the *ḥukm* according to it on the analogy of the sick person who remembers a prayer that he forgot while healthy, or that of the healthy person who remembers a prayer that he forgot during an illness, that is, his obligation is to pray the obligation of the prayer in the current situation. Those who compared *qaḍā*ʾ with debts imposed the obligation of praying as *qaḍā*ʾ a prayer identical to the one forgotten. Those, however, who imposed the obligation of always praying the prayer of the settlement took into account the description in one case and the circumstances in the other, that is, if he remembers a prayer of the settlement during a journey the description of the prayer offered as *qaḍā*ʾ is to conform with the description of the prayer missed, but if he remembers the prayer of a journey within a settlement the current situation is taken into account. This amounts to a disarray (of thought) outside the ambit of analogy, unless the opinion is based on the principle of precaution, which can be conceived particularly when curtailment (of prayer in a journey) is considered as an exemption.

2.4.2.1. *Section 1: The conditions of* qaḍāʾ *and its timing*

They differed over the order (of offering prayers), that is, they disagreed about the obligation of observing an order among the forgotten prayers, and between them and the *adā*ʾ prayer. Mālik maintained that observing a sequential order is obligatory for five prayers or whatever is less, and that the person is to begin with a forgotten prayer even if the time of the current prayer is to be missed. He went as far as saying that if he is occupied with the current prayer and remembers a forgotten prayer, the current prayer is invalidated for him. Similar views were expressed by Abū Ḥanīfa and al-Thawrī, except that they upheld the obligation of a sequential order only when the period for the current prayer is long enough (for the *qaḍā*ʾ and the *adā*ʾ prayers). These jurists agreed about the dropping of the obligation of order in the case of forgetfulness. Al-Shāfiʿī said that there is no obligation of maintaining an order, but if he does this and the time is long enough to accommodate the current prayer, it is commendable.

The reason for their disagreement stems from the conflict of the traditions on the issue, and also from their difference over the existence of a resemblance between *qaḍā*ʾ and *adā*ʾ. There are two conflicting traditions on the issue. The first is what is related from the Prophet (God's peace and blessings be upon him) that he said, "A person who has forgotten a prayer [and remembers it] while he is offering another with an *imām* should continue with the *imām*.

After he has offered this prayer, he should repeat [offer] the prayer he has forgotten and then repeat the prayer he offered with the *imām*". The disciples of al-Shāfiʿī consider this to be a weak tradition, while they authenticate the tradition of Ibn ʿAbbās that the Prophet (God's peace and blessings be upon him) said, "If one of you forgets a prayer and remembers it while he is offering another prescribed prayer, then, he should complete that which he is offering, and once he has finished it he should offer as *qaḍāʾ* the forgotten prayer". Yet, the authentic tradition on this topic is one that has preceded, where the words of the Prophet (God's peace and blessings be upon him) are: "If one of you slept through [the time of] prayer or forgot it, then let him observe the prayer when he remembers".

Their disagreement by way of comparing *qaḍāʾ* with *adāʾ* is that those who maintained that a sequential order in *adāʾ* (timely performance) is binding because the timings are specific to the prayer, and the prayers are ordered in themselves, as time cannot be conceived except as sequential, did not extend this obligation to *qaḍāʾ*, for there is no specific time for *qaḍāʾ*. Those who maintained that the order in prayers is sequential with respect to the act, even if the time is the same like the combining of two prayers in the time specific to one, held *qaḍāʾ* to be similar to *adāʾ*. The Mālikites were of the opinion that the sequential order be obligatory for the delayed prayer with respect to time and not with respect to the the act, because of the words of the Prophet (God's peace and blessings be upon him), "He should offer it when he remembers". They said that the time for the forgotten prayer is the time when it is remembered, therefore, it is necessary that the prayer he is currently offering be invalid at that time. This is meaningless, because if the time a prayer is remembered is the time for the forgotten prayer, then it is the time for the current prayer also, or of the forgotten prayers if there are more than one prayer. If the timing is the same then there is no question that the occurring disturbance in it is due to the sequence between the prayers, like the sequence of the different parts of one prayer, for one prayer is not more deserving of the time than its companion prayer, as the time is the same for both, unless an evidence of a sequence can be adduced. I am not in possession of anything here that I may render as a principle governing this topic with respect to a sequence in forgotten prayers except (the sequence in) combining, according to those who concede it. The sequential prayers have different timings and the sequence in *qaḍāʾ* is conceived essentially in a single time for two prayers taken together. Understand this, for there is some ambiguity here. I believe that Mālik, may Allāh have mercy on him, made an analogy for this from combining (*jamʿ*). All, however, adopted preference (*istiḥsān*) of sequence in forgotten prayers, when there is no apprehension of the current prayer being lost, because of the five prayers offered consecutively by the Prophet (God's peace and blessings be upon him) on the day of the Battle of Khandaq (Ditch). Those who make *qaḍā'* obligatory for the intentional relinquisher argued on the basis of this (case), but this has no strength for it (the precedent) stands abrogated, and further it was a forced delay with a legitimate excuse. As for the determination of the number five or whatever is less, there is no basis for it, unless it is said that it is consensus (*ijmā'*). This, then, is the *ḥukm* of *qaḍā'* that takes place for the whole prayer.

The *qaḍā'* that is offered for part of the prayer is either due to forgetfulness or it is due to the *imām* having advanced further than the follower, that is, the follower loses part of the prayer of the *imām*. In the case where the follower has lost part of the prayer, there are three fundamental issues. The first is when is a *rak'a* considered to be lost. Second, does the observance of what is lost, after the prayer of the *imām*, amount to *adā'* or *qaḍā'*? Third, when is the *ḥukm* of the prayer of the *imām* applicable to him and when is it not?

2.4.2.1.1. Issue 1

The question as to when a *rak'a* is deemed to be lost entails two issues. First, when the worshipper joins in when the *imām* has bent for the *rukū'*, and second, when he is praying with the *imām* and forgets to follow him in the *rukū'* or something in the nature of jostling occurs that prevents him from doing so.

2.4.2.1.1.1. Sub-issue 1

There are three opinions on this issue. The first, which is held by the majority, is that if he can catch up with the *imām* before he raises his head from the *rukū'* and is able to bow with him, then, he has caught the *rak'a* and there is no *qaḍā'* for him. These jurists differed on whether it is a condition for this person joining in that he pronounce two *takbīrs*, the initial *takbīr* and one for the *rukū'*, or is the *takbīr* of the *rukū'* to be sufficient for him, and if it is deemed compensated, is it a condition for it that he intends through it the initial *takbīr* also? Some of them said that a single *takbīr* would be sufficient if he includes in it the intention of the initial *takbīr*. This is the opinion of Mālik and al-Shāfi'ī but, the preference in their view is for two *takbīrs*. A group of jurists said that (pronouncing) two *takbīrs* is necessary. Another group said that one is sufficient even if he does not intend the initial *takbīr* through it.

The second opinion is that if the *imām* has gone into *rukū'*, the person has lost the *rak'a*, and that he cannot attain it unless he had done so after standing with the *imām*. This is attributed to Abū Hurayra. The third opinion is that if he approaches the last row when the *imām* has raised his head from the *rukū'*, but some of those in the row have not and he joins them in *rukū'*, he has gained the *rak'a*, for some are leading the others. This was upheld by al-Sha'bī. The reason for this disagreement derives from the vacillation of the meaning of the term *rakʿa* between the act of bowing alone, and the combined meaning of bowing and standing taken together. The Prophet (God's peace and blessings be upon him) has said, "One who has caught a *rakʿa* of the prayer has caught the prayer". Ibn al-Mundhir states that this tradition was established as authentic from the Messenger of Allāh (God's peace and blessings be upon him). Those for whom the term *rakʿa* is applied to mean both bowing and standing said that if the person has missed the standing posture with the *imām*, he has lost the *rakʿa*. Those for whom the term *rakʿa* is applied to bowing itself deemed the catching of bowing as the attainment of the *rakʿa*. The equivocality (*ishtarāk*) that is found in this term is its vacillation between the literal and the technical meanings, as the term in its literal sense applies to bowing only, but in its technical meaning it applies to standing, bowing, and prostrating. Those who maintained that the term *rakʿa* in the words of the Prophet (God's peace and blessings be upon him), "One who has caught a *rakʿa*", applies to the technical meaning, and also did not adopt the opinion of those who accept part of what is indicated by names, said that it is necessary for the person to observe all three acts with the *imām*, that is, standing bowing and prostrating. It is possible that those who were inclined to consider bowing only took into account the major part indicated by the term, as the person who has been able to participate in bowing has caught two parts, while the person who has missed bowing has been able to secure one part alone. On the basis of this, their disagreement refers to the dispute about accepting part of what is denoted by a term or by the entire denotation. It is possible to find disagreement with both views.

He who takes into account the bowing of the followers in the (last) row does so because the *rakʿa* of the prayer may be attributed to the *imām* alone or it may be attributed to the *imām* as well as the followers. The reason for disagreement, therefore, are the equal probabilities of such an association, that is, in the words of the Prophet (God's peace and blessings be upon him), "One who has caught a *rakʿa* of the prayer has caught the prayer", and the opinion of the majority here has a higher probability.

The reason for their disagreement over whether he is to pronounce one *takbīr* or two, that is, the follower joining the prayer when the *imām* is bowing, stems from whether it is a condition for the initial *takbīr* that it be pronounced while standing. Those who maintained that the posture in which it is pronounced is a condition for it, on the basis of the act of the Prophet (God's peace and blessings be upon him), and also on the grounds that every *takbīr* is an obligation, said that there must be two *takbīrs*. Those who maintained that the posture is not a condition for it on the basis of the general implication of the words of the Prophet (God's peace and blessings be upon him), "Its commencement is the *takbīr*", and also because, in their view, only the initial *takbīr* is obligatory, said it is permitted to him to pronounce that (the initial *takbīr*) alone. Those who permitted him to pronounce a single *takbīr* without intending the initial *takbīr* adopted, it is said, the opinion of those who do not consider the initial *takbīr* to be an obligation, and it is also said that they adopted the opinion of those who permit the delaying of the intention (*niyya*) of prayer till after the initial *takbīr*. This is because the intention of the initial *takbīr* has no meaning except in association with the intention of commencing prayer. As the initial *takbīr* has two attributes, associated intention and precedence, that is, its occurrence at the beginning of the prayer, they stipulated both attributes, and said that there should be an accompanying *niyya*. Those who were satisfied with a single attribute were also satisfied with a single *takbīr* even if it was not associated with intention.

2.4.2.1.1.2. Sub-issue 2

About the person forgetting to follow the *imām* in *rukūʿ* till the *imām* prostrates, a group of jurists said that if he has failed to observe the *rukūʿ* with him, he has lost the *rakʿa* and it is obligatory for him to offer it as *qaḍāʾ* (before his own *salām*). Another group of jurists said that he can count the *rakʿa* (as performed) if it is possible for him to complete the *rukūʿ* before the *imām* has commenced the next *rakʿa*. A third group of jurists said that he is to follow him and count the *rakʿa* as performed as long as the *imām* has not raised his head after bowing in the second *rakʿa*. This disagreement exists among the disciples of Mālik, and there is considerable dispute over details, along with disagreements among them relating to whether what was missed occurred due to forgetfulness or due to jostling, and whether it happened in a *jumuʿa* prayer or another, and whether this situation was faced by the follower in the first *rakʿa* or in another *rakʿa*.

Since our purpose is not to record the details of the opinions or to derive them, but only to indicate the fundamental issues and their (underlying) principles, we say the following:

The reason for the the disagreement in this issue arises from the dispute about whether it is a condition for the movements of the follower that they should accompany (or immediately follow) those of the *imām*, and whether this condition applies to all the three constituent acts of the *rakʿa*, that is, standing, bowing and prostrating, or is it a condition only for some of them? Further, when does his act go against him if this act does not (immediately) follow the act of the *imām*, that is, when he is performing one act and the *imām* is performing the next? Those who held that it is a condition for each constituent act of a single *rakʿa*—that is, the act of the follower should be concurrent with the same act of the *imām*, for otherwise this would amount to dissociating himself from the *imām*, and the Prophet (God's peace and blessings be upon him) has said, "The *imām* has been appointed so that he be followed, so do not go against him"—said that if he fails to accompany the *imām* in the *rukūʿ*, even though a small part of it, he would miss the *rakʿa*. Those who took into account only a part of it said that he collects the *rakʿa* if he collects a part of the *rakʿa* before the *imām* rises for the next *rakʿa*, and this does not amount to going against him. If the *imām* has risen into the second *rakʿa* and the follower is pursuing him (in the acts of the first), then, this amounts to going against him for the first *rakʿa*. Those who said that he may pursue his acts as long the *imām* has not bowed in the next *rakʿa*, held the opinion that it is not a condition for each segment of the act of the follower that it coincide with each segment of the act of the *imam* nor as a whole, but the condition is only that it take place after it. They agreed that if the *imām* has risen after bowing in the second *rakʿa*, then, the follower is not to count that *rakʿa* as performed, if he has been pursuing his acts in it, for these would be assigned the *ḥukm* of the first while the *imām* is subject to the *ḥukm* of the second, and this evidently amounts to going against him.

2.4.2.1.2. Issue 2

The second of the three fundamental issues that act as principles of the topic is whether the performance by the follower of the part of the prayer he has missed, from the *imām's* prayer, amounts to *adāʾ* or *qaḍāʾ*. There are three opinions on this issue.

A group of jurists said that the part he observes after the *imām's* salutation is *qaḍāʾ* and what he has observed with the *imām* is not the first part of his prayer. Another group said that what he observes after the salutation of the *imām* is *adāʾ* and what he observed with the *imām* is the first part of his prayer. A third group made a distinction between words and acts and said that he performs the words as *qaḍāʾ*, that is, the recitation, and continues on with the acts, meaning *adāʾ* thereby. Thus, according to the first opinion, the opinion which regards the missed part that the follower performs as *qaḍāʾ*, the person who is able to catch one *rakʿa* of the *maghrib* prayer will stand up when the *imām* ends his prayer with the salutation and offer two *rakʿas* reciting the *umm al-Qurʾān* and another *sūra* in each one of them, without adopting the sitting posture in between the two. In accordance with the second opinion, that is based on continuation, he will stand up for one *rakʿa* reciting in it the *umm al-Qurʾān* and another *sūra* and then adopt the sitting posture, after which he will rise for another *rakʿa* and recite in it only the *umm al-Qurʾān*. In accordance with the third opinion, he will stand up for a *rakʿa* reciting in it the *umm al-Qurʾān* and another *sūra* and then take the sitting posture, after which he will rise for the second *rakʿa* also reciting in it the *umm al-Qurʾān* and another *sūra*.

All three opinions have been attributed to the School (Mālik's) and the authentic opinion from Mālik is that he performs the words as *qaḍā*ʾ and continues in the acts, because there is no discrepancy in his opinion about the sunset prayer that if the person catches one *rakʿa* (with the *imām*) then he is to stand for the second *rakʿa* and then adopt the sitting posture; and there is no dispute about his opinion that the person is to recite the *umm al-Qurʾān* and another *sūra* as *qaḍā*ʾ. The reason for disagreement was that in some versions of the well-known tradition it is laid down: "Pray what you are able to catch and complete what you have lost", and completion implies that what he has been able to observe is the first part of his prayer. In other versions the words are, "Pray what you are able to catch and offer as *qaḍā*ʾ what you have lost", where *qaḍā*ʾ implies that what he has been able to observe (with the *imām*) is the last part of his prayer. Thus, those who adopted the opinion of completion said that what he has observed is the first part of his prayer. Those who adopted the opinion of *qaḍā*ʾ said that what he observed was the last part of his prayer. Those who adopted the method of reconciliation deemed the words to be *qaḍā*ʾ and the acts as *adā*ʾ. This, however, is weak, that is, part of the prayer should be *adā*ʾ and part *qaḍā*ʾ.

Their agreement on the obligation of a sequential order in the parts of the prayer, and on the occasion of pronouncing the initial *takbīr* is the commencement of prayer, implies the existence of a clear evidence that what he has been able to observe (with the *imām*) is the first part of the follower's prayer, but the intention of the *imām* and that of the follower have differed about the sequential order, so think over it. It appears that this is what was taken into account by those who maintained that his observance is the last part of the prayer.

2.4.2.1.3. Issue 3

The third of the three issues is the case in which the *ḥukm* of the prayer of the *imām* extends to the follower. This entails sub-issues. The first is when is he assumed to catch the *jumuʿa* prayer? The second is when is he liable for the *ḥukm* of the prostrations of forgetfulness along with the *imām*, that is, for the forgetfulness of the *imām*? The third is when is it binding for a traveller who joins up behind an *imām* (whose status is that of a resident) to complete his prayer (and not to curtail it) if he catches part of the prayer of the *imām*?

2.4.2.1.3.1. Sub-issue 1

A group of jurists said that if he is able to catch a *rakʿa* of *jumuʿa* then he has observed the *jumuʿa* prayer, and he is to perform the second *rakʿa* after the salutation of the *imām*, but if he catches less than a *rakʿa* he is to pray the four *rakʿas* as *ẓuhr*. This is the opinion of Mālik and al-Shāfiʿī. Another group of jurists said that he is to complete two *rakʿas* irrespective of what he has been able to catch of the prayer with the *imām*. This is Abū Ḥanīfa's opinion.

The reason for disagreement in this matter stems from what is supposed to be a conflict between the general implication of the words of the Prophet (God's peace and blessings be upon him), "Pray what you are able to catch (behind the *imām*), and complete what you have missed", and the meaning of his words, "He who has caught a *rakʿa* of a prayer (behind the *imām*) has caught the prayer". Those who decided on the basis of the words, "complete what you have missed", made it obligatory that the follower pray two *rakʿas* even if he has been able to catch (a little) less than two *rakʿas*. Those for whom there is an implied word in the words of the Prophet (God's peace and blessings be upon him), "he has caught the prayer", that is, he has caught the *ḥukm* of the prayer, said that the (indirect) indication of the text (*dalīl al-khiṭāb*) implies that one who has caught less than one *rakʿa* has not caught the *ḥukm* of the prayer. The implied word, however, in this text has multiple possibilities, for it is possible that it means the merit of the prayer, it is possible that it means the time of the prayer, and it is also possible that it means the *ḥukm* of the prayer. Perhaps the possible meaning in one of these is not more obvious than the other. If this is the case, then it belongs to the category of *mujmal* (unelaborated implication), which does not imply a *ḥukm*, and the other (text with a) general meaning becomes preferable. If, however, we concede that it is obvious in one of these implied meanings, for example, the *ḥukm* of the prayer in accordance with the opinion of those who hold this, then, this obvious meaning is not in conflict with the general meaning (in the other text), unless it is treated as a category of the indication of the text (*dalīl al-khiṭāb*), but the general meaning is stronger, unanimously, than the indication of the text, especially an indication based on several probabilities or on the obvious meaning. On the other hand, the opinion of those who maintain that the words of the Prophet (God's peace and blessings be upon him), "he has caught the prayer", include all the implied meanings, is weak and unknown in Arab usage, unless it is maintained that there is such a customary or technical meaning.

2.4.2.1.3.2. Sub-issue 2

On the issue of the follower following the *imām* in prostrations, that is, the prostrations of forgetfulness, a group of jurists fixed one *rakʿa* as the basis, that is, that he should catch at least a *rakʿa* with the *imām*; another group of jurists did not take this into account. Those who did not take this into account decided on the basis of the general implication of the words of the Prophet (God's peace and blessings be upon him), "The *imām* has been appointed so that he be followed". Those who took the *rakʿa* into account decided according to the meaning of the words of the Prophet (God's peace and blessings be upon him), "He has caught the prayer". It is for this reason that they also differed on the third sub-issue.

2.4.2.1.3.3. Sub-issue 3

A group of jurists said that if the traveller catches less than one *rakʿa* of the prayer of the *imām* (who is) in a settlement he is not to complete the rest of the prayer as one having the status of the resident, but if he catches one *rakʿa* completion is binding upon him.

This, then, is the *ḥukm* of *qaḍāʾ* for part of the prayer when the *imām* had started prayer before the follower.

The jurists agreed with respect to the *ḥukm* of *qaḍāʾ* for part of the prayer that occurs because of the forgetfulness of the *imām* or of the individual (praying independently), that he is to observe as *qaḍāʾ* whatever is an essential element (*rukn*) of the prayer, that is, an obligation, and it is not valid for him unless he performs this (part). There are, however, issues in it over which they disagreed, with some making *qaḍāʾ* (making up the missing parts) obligatory in them and the others imposing repetition, as in the case of the person who forgets to make four prostrations in four *rakʿas*, missing one prostration in each *rakʿa*. A group of jurists, thus, said that he rectifies the fourth by the prostrating and deems the earlier *rakʿas* as nullified and then repeats them. This is Mālik's opinion. Another group of jurists said that the prayer is nullified as a whole and repetition becomes binding upon him. This is one of the narrations from Aḥmad. A third group said that he performs four consecutive prostrations and his prayer stands completed. This was held by Abū Ḥanīfa, al-Thawrī, and al-Awzāʿī. A fourth group said that the fourth is rectified with two prostrations. This is al-Shāfiʿī's opinion.

The reason for the disagreement over this stems from the consideration of sequential order. Those who took it into account in the *rakʿas* and prostrations nullified the prayer. Those who took it into account for prostrations alone nullified the *rakʿas*, except the last on the analogy of what a follower misses of the prayer of the *imām*. Those who did not take sequential order into account permitted the prostrations of the (entire) prayer at one time in a single *rakʿa*, especially when they believed that a sequential order is not obligatory in an act that is repeated in each *rakʿa*, that is, in the prostrations, because each *rakʿa* comprises standing, bowing, and prostrating and the prostration is repeated. Thus, the disciples of Abū Ḥanīfa thought that as the prostrations are repeated it is not obligatory to take into account repetition in the sequential order. Of the same nature is a disagreement among the disciples of Mālik about the person who forgets to recite the *umm al-Qurʾān* in the first *rakʿa*. It is said that the *rakʿa* is not to be counted (as observed) and is to be performed as *qaḍāʾ*; it is said that he is to repeat the entire prayer, and it is also said that he is to make prostrations of forgetfulness for making his prayer complete.

There are a number of cases under this topic and all are not expressly stated in the texts, but our purpose here is to record those that are of the nature of principles.

2.4.3. **Chapter 3 Prostrations of Forgetfulness**

The prostrations transmitted in the law apply in one of two cases: first, in unintended excess or deficiency of acts or words; and second, in the case of doubt in the acts of the prayer. In the case of the prostrations resulting from forgetfulness, and not from doubt, the discussion is covered in six sections. The first section is about the identification of the *ḥukm* of the prostrations. The second is about their occasions in the prayer. The third relates to the identification of the species of the acts and the acts themselves because of which the prostrations are made. The fourth is about the description of the prostrations of forgetfulness. The fifth is about the identification of the person for whom the prostrations are obligatory. The sixth is about the means with which the follower alerts the *imām* about his forgetfulness.

2.4.3.1. *Section 1: Are the prostrations of forgetfulness an obligation or a* sunna?

They disagreed about the prostrations of forgetfulness, whether they are an obligation or a *sunna*. Al-Shāfiʿī held that they are a *sunna*, while Abū Ḥanīfa held them to be an obligation, but as one of the conditions of the validity of prayer. Mālik made a distinction between the prostrations of forgetfulness caused by forgetting words or forgetting some acts, and also those caused by an excess or a deficiency. He said that the prostrations of forgetfulness that are performed because of deficient acts are obligatory, and are, according to him, one of the conditions of the validity of prayer. This is the well-known report. It is also reported from him that prostrations on account of deficiency are obligatory and prostrations on account of excess are recommended.

The reason for their disagreement arises from their dispute about the interpretation of the acts of the Prophet (God's peace and blessings be upon him) related to this topic, whether they convey an obligation or recommendation. Abū Ḥanīfa interpreted the acts of the Prophet (God's peace and blessings be upon him) as obligatory, as that is the principle in his view, for they occur as an elaboration of an obligatory act. The Prophet (God's peace and blessings be upon him) said, "Pray as you see me praying". Al-Shāfiʿī interpreted his acts as conveying recommendation, and he deviated from the original meaning of the principle on the basis of analogy. He held that as prostrations, in the view of the majority, do not become a substitute for an obligation, but are a substitute for a recommended act; therefore, a substitute for something that is not obligatory cannot be obligatory. For Mālik there was greater emphasis on the acts as compared to the words, for they form the structure for the prayer more than the words, I mean, the obligations that are related to acts are more than those related to words. Thus, it was as if he held that there is greater emphasis for the acts as compared to words, even though the prostrations of forgetfulness become a substitute only for acts that are not obligatory. His distinction between prostrations made on account of deficiency and those made for excess, in accordance with the second narration, is based on the fact that the prostrations on account of deficiency are stipulated as compensation for what is dropped from the acts of the prayer, while prostrations on account of excess are like a repentance not a substitute.

2.4.3.2. *Section 2: The occasions for the prostrations of forgetfulness*

They disagreed about (the time) when the prostration of forgetfulness is to be made; there were five opinions. The Shāfiʿites held that the occasion for the prostrations of forgetfulness is always immediately before the salutation. The Ḥanafites maintained that the occasion for them is always after the salutation. The Mālikites made a distinction saying that if the prostrations are on account of a deficiency their occasion is before the salutation, but if they are on account of excess their occasion is after the salutation. Aḥmad ibn Ḥanbal said that the prostrations are made before the salutation for the occasions on which the Messenger of Allāh (God's peace and blessings be upon him) prostrated before the salutation and they are made after the salutation for occasions on which the Messenger of Allāh (God's peace and blessings be upon him) prostrated after the salutation. Those that are besides these occasions for them the prostrations are always before the salutation. The Ẓāhirites said that the prostrations are to be made only for the five occasions on which the Messenger of Allāh (God's peace and blessings be upon him) made them. Besides these cases, if the omission was for something obligatory he has to make them, but if they are recommended the person is under no obligation.

The reason for their disagreement stems from the established fact that the Prophet (God's peace and blessings be upon him) made prostrations at times before salutation and at others after it. Thus, it is established from the tradition of Buḥayna, who said, "The Messenger of Allāh (God's peace and blessings be upon him) led us in praying two *rakʿas* after which he stood up, not taking the sitting posture, and the people stood up with him. When he had performed the prayer, he made two prostrations while still seated". It is established from the tradition of Dhū al-Yadayn that has preceded where he had (first) made the salutation from the two *rakʿas*. Those who permitted analogy in the prostrations of forgetfulness—I mean, those who held the extension of the *ḥukm* for the occasions on which he (God's peace and blessings be upon him) prostrated to the cases similar to them in these authentic traditions—held three (differing) opinions. The first is based on the method of preference (*tarjīḥ*) and the second on the method of reconciliation (*jamʿ*). The third is based on the method or reconciliation between preference and (original) reconciliation.

Those who preferred the tradition of Ibn Buḥayna maintained that the prostrations are before the salutation. They argued for this on the basis of the authentic tradition of Abū Saʿīd al-Khudrī that the Prophet (God's peace and blessings be upon him) said, "If one of you is in doubt about his prayer and does not recollect how many he prayed, three or four, he should pray a *rakʿa* and prostrate twice while he is sitting prior to the salutation. If the *rakʿa* he prayed happens to be the fifth he will be converting it to an even count with these two prostrations, but if it is the fourth, the two prostrations are an affront to the devil". They said that in this are prostrations for an excess before the salutation, for it is possible for a fifth to occur. They also argued on the basis of what is related from Ibn Shihāb, who said, "One of the last commands from the Messenger of Allāh (God's peace and blessings be upon him) was about prostrations before the salutation".

Those who preferred the tradition of Dhū al-Yadayn said that the prostrations are after the salutation. They argued for the preference of this tradition that the tradition of Ibn Buḥayna had been opposed by the tradition of Mughīra ibn Shuʿba "that the Prophet (God's peace and blessings be upon him) stood up after the two *rakʿas* and did not sit down, he then made prostrations after the salutation". Abū ʿUmar said that this tradition is not equal in terms of transmission so that it may be opposed by it. They also argued for it on the basis of the authentic tradition of Ibn Masʿūd "that the Messenger of Allāh (God's peace and blessings be upon him) prayed a fifth *rakʿa* out of forgetfulness and made prostrations for his forgetfulness after the salutation".

Those who adopted the method of reconciliation said that these traditions do not contradict each other, as the prostrations in them that are after the salutation are due to excess, and the prostrations before salutation are due to deficiency; thus it is obligatory that the *ḥukm* of the prostrations in the remaining cases be like these cases. They said that this (reconciliation) is preferable to interpreting the traditions as being in conflict.

Those who adopted the method of reconciliation as well as preference said that prostrations are to be made in cases in which the Messenger of Allāh (God's peace and blessings be upon him) made the prostrations and in a manner in which he made them, for this is the *ḥukm* of those cases. The occasions on which the Messenger of Allāh did not make the prostrations, the *ḥukm* for them is that of prostrations prior to the salutation. It was as if they made analogy for these over those in which the Messenger of Allāh (God's peace and blessings be upon him) made prostrations before salutation, but not on the prostrations that he made after the salutation, while the original occasions on which he made the prostrations retained their rule. Thus, from one aspect they maintained the *ḥukm* of the occasions for which they occurred and assigned them differing *aḥkām*, this being a kind of reconciliation and the removal of conflict between the implications. From another aspect they extended the meaning of some to the exclusion of others, and attached those on which the law is silent to them, this being a kind of preference, that is, they made an analogy from those prostrations that were made before the salutation but not from those that were after the salutation.

As to those, and these are the Ẓāhirites, who did not understand from these cases a *ḥukm* existing outside of these cases, confined their *ḥukm* to the cases of their occurrence; thus they confined the prostrations in these cases to these cases alone. Aḥmad ibn Ḥanbal's view, on the other hand, is intertwined partially with the view of the Ẓāhirites and partially with that of those who made the analogy, because he confined the prostrations after the salutation, as we have said, to cases that occurred in the traditions and did not extend them, while he extended (by analogy) the cases of prostrations occurring before the salutation.

For each of these jurists there are evidences through which they come to prefer their opinions by means of analogy, I mean, for those upholding analogy. Our purpose in this book is not the copious recording of disagreement necessitated by analogy just as it is not our purpose to mention the issues on which the law is silent except to a minimum, and that too when they are well-known and serve as principles for cases besides them or when their occurrence is very frequent.

The five cases in which forgetfulness is associated with the Messenger of Allāh (God's peace and blessings be upon him) are: first, when he stood up after praying two *rakʿas* as in the tradition of Buḥayna; second, when he made the salutation after praying two *rakʿas*, as recorded in the tradition of Dhū al-Yadayn; third, when he prayed five *rakʿas*, according to what is in the tradition of Ibn ʿUmar, which is recorded by Muslim and al-Bukhārī; fourth, when he made the salutation after praying three *rakʿas* according to the tradition of ʿImrān ibn al-Ḥuṣayn; fifth, the prostrations on account of doubt according to what is in the tradition of Abū Saʿīd al-Khudrī, which will come up later.

They disagreed about the reason why prostrations of forgetfulness have been obligatory. It is said that they are obligatory because of an excess or deficiency (in the prayer), and this is the well-known view. It is also said that they are obligatory because of forgetfulness itself, and this was the view of the Ahl al-Ẓāhir and al-Shāfiʿī.

2.4.3.3. *Section 3: The words and acts leading to prostrations of forgetfulness*

The upholders of the prostrations of forgetfulness, whether for excess or deficiency that may occur in the prayer by way of forgetfulness, agreed that the prostrations are on account of (omission of) the *sunan* of the prayer and not the obligations nor on account of the desirable acts (*raghāʾib*) (lesser than *sunan*). There is no liability in their view for omission of this category, that is, if the person forgets one of them in prayer, unless they happen more than once. For example, Mālik is of the view that there is no obligation for prostrations on account of forgetting a single *takbīr*, but there is a prostration for leaving out more than one act of this category. There can be no validity with the omission of obligations. They are to be performed and undertaken. The consequence of forgetting them is the repetition of the prayer as a whole, as has preceded in the discussion of what leads to repetition and what leads to *qaḍāʾ*, I mean, like a person who may relinquish one of the constituent elements of prayer.

The prostrations of forgetfulness on account of an excess, on the other hand, occur due to an excess in the obligations as well as the *sunan*. In this statement, there is no dispute among them; they disagree only on the basis of their dispute as to what acts are obligations and what are not, what are *sunan* and what are not, and what is a *sunna* and what is a desirable act (*raghība*). An example of which is *qunūt*. According to Mālik the person is not to make prostrations for relinquishing *qunūt* for it is merely desirable (*mustaḥab*) (lesser than a *sunna*) in his view, but he is to make prostrations according to al-Shāfiʿī as it is a *sunna* in his view.

This is not unclear for you because of the discussion that has preceded about their disagreement over what is a *sunna*, an obligation (*farīḍa*), or a desirable act (*raghība*). According to Mālik and his disciples there are prostrations of forgetfulness for a minor excess in prayer, even if it is not from the category of prayer. It is necessary to know that *sunna* and *raghība*, in their view, both belong to the recommended (*nadb*) category. They differ, however, when in their view it is (a) higher or a lower (recommendation), that is, the emphasis in the command about them. This has reference to the surrounding circumstances of this form of worship. Their disagreement, therefore, becomes excessive in this category so much so that some of them hold that if certain *sunan* are relinquished intentionally or done intentionally if they were to be relinquished, their *ḥukm* becomes enhanced, that is, it becomes obligatory if it is a *sunna*, or a sin if it was a prohibition. This is to be found often with the disciples of Mālik. You therefore find them agreeing, except for the Ẓāhirites, that a person relinquishing *sunan* regularly as a whole is a sinner. Thus, a person relinquishing always the *witr* prayer or the two *rakʿas* of the morning prayer would be a *fāsiq* and a sinner. It is as if some forms of worship are obligatory in kind and in genus, like the five daily prayers, while some are *sunna* in kind and obligation in genus, like *witr* and the two *rakʿas* of the morning prayer and whatever is similar to them from among the *sunan*. Likewise, some of the desirable acts (*raghāʾib*) in their view are desirable in kind but *sunan* by genus, like what we have related from Mālik about the obligation of prostrations on account of (omission of) more than one *takbīr*, that is, for forgetting it. I do not think that they have a category that is *sunna* in kind as well as in genus.

The *sunan* according to the Ẓāhirites are *sunan* in genus alone, because of the words of the Prophet (God's peace and blessings be upon him) to the Bedouin who asked him about the obligations in Islam, "He will succeed if he speaks the truth, he will enter *janna* if he speaks the truth", and this after the man had said to him, "I swear by Allāh that I will not add to it or reduce from it", that is, to or from the obligations, and this tradition has preceded.

They agreed under this topic on the requirement of the prostrations of forgetfulness for the omission of the middle sitting posture, differing over it whether it is an obligation or a *sunna*. Similarly, they disagreed whether the *imām* may revert to it when he is reminded after rising from it. If he may revert to it, then at what stage? The majority said that he may revert to it as long as he has not stood up straight. A group of jurists said that he may revert to it as long as he has not commenced the third *rakʿa*. Another group of jurists said that he is not to revert to it if he has risen up to the measure of a spread out hand (*shibr*). If he reverts to it in the view of those who do not uphold that he should do so, his prayer is valid according to the majority, but a group of jurists said that it is nullified.

2.4.3.4. *Section 4: The description of the prostrations of forgetfulness*

They (the jurists) disagreed about the description of the prostrations of forgetfulness. Mālik was of the view that the *ḥukm* of the two prostrations of forgetfulness when they are after the salutation is that the person should recite the *tashahhud* and offer the salutation. This was Abū Ḥanīfa's opinion also as the prostrations in his view are after the salutation in each case. If the prostrations are before the salutation then he should recite the *tashahhud* alone, and the salutation of the prayer is the salutation for the prostrations. This was al-Shāfiʿī's opinion as such prostrations are always before the salutation in his view. It is also related from Mālik that he is not to recite *tashahhud* in the case of those that are before the salutation. This was also the opinion of a group of jurists. Abū ʿUmar has said that the salutation after those that follow (come after) the salutation (of the prayer) is established from the Prophet (God's peace and blessings be upon him), as for the *tashahhud*, I cannot trace it in an authentic narration.

The reason for this disagreement stems from their dispute over is the authenticity of what has been reported about it in the tradition of Ibn Masʿūd, that is, that the Prophet (God's peace and blessings be upon him) said, "Recite the *tashahhud* and then offer the salutation", and also the semblance between the prostrations of forgetfulness and the last two prostrations of the prayer. Those who compared the two did not make *tashahhud* obligatory, especially when both were within the same prayer. Abū Bakr ibn al-Mundhir has said that the jurists differed over this issue and had six opinions. One group said that there is no *tashahhud* in them and no salutation. This was the opinion of Anas ibn Mālik, al-Ḥasan, and ʿAṭāʾ. A second group said the opposite of this, that there is *tashahhud* as well as salutation in them. A third group said that there is *tashahhud*, but not salutation. This was the opinion of al-Ḥakam, Ḥammād, and al-Nakhaʿī. A fourth group said the opposite of this, that there is salutation in them, but not *tashahhud*. This is the opinion of Ibn Sīrīn. The fifth opinion is that it is up to the worshipper; if he likes he may recite the *tashahhud* and offer the salutation, but he is not obliged to do so. This is related from ʿAṭāʾ. The sixth opinion is that of Aḥmad ibn Ḥanbal that if the person is prostrating after the salutation he is to recite the *tashahhud*, but if he is prostrating prior to the salutation he is not to recite the *tashahhud*. This is what we related from Mālik. Abū Bakr said that it has been established from the Prophet (God's peace and blessings be upon him) that he pronounced a *takbīr* four times and then offered the salutation, but the authentication of his reciting *tashahhud* needs scrutiny.

2.4.3.5. *Section 5*: Ḥukm *of the prostrations of forgetfulness*

They agreed that performing the prostrations of forgetfulness is a *sunna* for the single worshipper as well as the *imām*. They disagreed about the follower who forgets while praying behind the *imām* whether he is he under an obligation to make the prostrations. The majority maintained that the *imām* bears the responsibility for forgetfulness on behalf of the follower, but Makḥūl made a deviant statement making the prostrations binding for his own forgetfulness.

The reason for their disagreement arises from their dispute over what constituent elements of prayer the *imām* bears on behalf of the follower. They agreed that if the *imām* forgets something the follower follows him in his prostrations of forgetfulness, even if he joined him after his forgetfulness.

They disagreed as to when the follower is to prostrate if he has missed part of the prayer with the *imām*, who has to make the prostrations. A group of jurists said that he makes the prostrations with the *imām* and then stands up to perform the part he had missed, whether the *imām* performed his prostrations before or after the salutation. This was upheld by ʿAṭāʾ, al-Ḥasan, al-Nakhaʿī, al-Shaʿbī, Aḥmad, Abū Thawr, and the upholders of *raʾy* (opinion). Another group of jurists said that he is to complete his prayer and then prostrate. This was held by Ibn Sīrīn and Isḥāq. A third group of jurists said that if the *imām* makes the prostrations before the salutation, he should prostrate with him, but if the *imām* makes the prostrations after salutation he is to complete his own prayer and then make the prostrations. This was upheld by Mālik, al-Layth, and al-Shāfiʿī. The fourth group of jurists said that he is first to make the prostrations with the *imām* and then to make them a second time after completing his prayer. This was held by al-Shāfiʿī.

The reason for their disagreement stems from their dispute over what is better and more meritorious. To follow the *imām* in the prostrations (of forgetfulness) at the same time or to prostrate after completing his own prayer? It was as if they agreed that following the *imām* is *wājib* because of the words of the Prophet (God's peace and blessings be upon him), "The *imām* has been appointed so that he be followed", but disagreed over whether the time of prostrating for the follower was its regular determined occasion, that is, at the end of his own prayer, or whether the time was that of the prostrations of the *imām*. Those who preferred the combining the follower's act with the act of the *imām* over the regular time of making the prostrations and held that it is a condition of the following, that is, that their acts should actually coincide, said that he should prostrate with the *imām* even if he did not prostrate at the time determined for the prostrations. Those who preferred the determined time of prostrations said that he should delay them till the end of his prayer. Those who made both forms obligatory placed an obligation on him for prostrating twice, but this is weak.

2.4.3.6. *Section 6: How to alert the person who forgets in prayer*

They agreed that the way to alert a person who forgets in his prayer is to pronounce *tasbīḥ* (saying *subḥāna Allāh*). This, however, is for men because of what is established from the Prophet (God's peace and blessings be upon him) that he said, "Why is it that I see you clapping hands (*taṣfīq*) frequently. One who is afflicted by something in his prayer should engage in the glorification of Allāh (*tasbīḥ*), for when he utters the *tasbīḥ*, he will attract attention. And clapping hands is for women".

They disagreed in the case of women. Mālik and a group of jurists said that *tasbīḥ* is both for men and women. Al-Shāfiʿī and a group of jurists said that *tasbīḥ* is for men, while *tasfīq* (striking the back of the left hand with the palm of the right) is for women.

The reason for their disagreement arises from their dispute over the implication of the words of the Prophet (God's peace and blessings be upon him), "*tasfīq* is for women". Those who held that the meaning of these words is that *tasfīq* is the *ḥukm* for women in case of forgetfulness, which is the apparent meaning, said that the women are to engage in *tasfīq* and not in *tasbīḥ*. Those who comprehended a derogation of *tasfīq* from this said that men and women are equal in terms of *tasbīḥ*, but there is some weakness in this view because it amounts to a departure from the apparent meaning without an evidence, unless an analogy with the case of men is drawn for women. The *ḥukm* for women is often different from that of men in the case of prayer, a fact which weakens the analogy.

With respect to performing the prostrations of forgetfulness that are occasioned by doubt, the jurists disagreed—holding three opinions—about the case of a person who feels doubt about (whether) his his prayer (was properly observed) and does not know how many *rakʿas* he has offered: whether one, two, three, or four *rakʿas*. A group of jurists said that he is to base the preceding part of the prayer on certainty, which is the least (number) for he is not to estimate, and after completing the prayer accordingly he should make the prostrations of forgetfulness. This is the opinion of Mālik, al-Shāfiʿī, and Dāwūd. Abū Ḥanīfa said that if this is the first occasion (of doubt in the prayer) his prayer becomes invalid, but if it recurs he is to make an estimation and act on the basis of the preponderant conviction in his mind (about the number), and then he is to make the prostrations of forgetfulness following the salutation. Another group of jurists said that if the person is in doubt he is neither to have recourse to certain conviction nor to estimation, but is simply obliged to make the prostrations of forgetfulness.

The reason for their disagreement is the conflict derives from the apparent meanings of the traditions laid down on the issue, and there are three traditions on the subject. The first is the tradition prescribing continuation on the basis of certainty (the lesser number). This is the tradition of Abū Saʿīd al-Khudrī, who said, "The Messenger of Allāh (God's peace and blessings be upon him) said, 'If one of you falls in doubt about his prayer and does not know how many (*rakʿas*) he has prayed, three or four, then he should relinquish his doubt and base his prayer on that of which he is certain, and thereafter make two prostrations before making the salutation. If he has prayed five they will even out his prayer, but if he has prayed to complete four, they will be an affront for the devil' ". It is recorded by Muslim. The second tradition is from Ibn Masʿūd that the Prophet (God's peace and blessings be upon him) said, "If one of you forgets while praying, then he should make an estimate and thereafter make two prostrations". Another version from him says, "He should make an inquiry into what appears to be the most correct [number], then make the salutation and thereafter make two prostrations, recite the *tashahhud* and make the salutation". The third is the tradition of Abū Hurayra, which is recorded by Mālik and al-Bukhārī, that the Messenger of Allāh (God's peace and blessings be upon him) said, "When one of you stands up to pray the devil comes and confuses him so that he does not recollect how many (*rakʿas*) he prayed, then, if one of you finds this he should make two prostrations while seated". Of the same implication is the tradition of ʿAbd Allāh ibn Jaʿfar, which has been recorded by Abū Dāwūd, that the Messenger of Allāh (God's peace and blessings be upon him) said, "One who is in doubt about his prayer should make two prostrations after it and then make the salutation".

In these traditions the jurists adopted either the method of reconciliation or that of preference. Some of those who adopted the method of preference ignored the conflicting text, and some interpreted the conflicting text and reconciled it with the preferred interpretation. There were also those who combined the two ways, that is, reconciled some of them and preferred some, reinterpreting the meaning not preferred to suit the preferred interpretation. Some of them reconciled some of them and dropped the *ḥukm* of the others.

Those who adopted the method of preference in part and that of reconciliation in part, along with the interpretation of the unpreferred directing it to the preferred meaning, include Mālik ibn Anas. He interpreted the tradition of Abū Saʿīd al-Khudrī to apply to the person who is not afflicted by doubt, and he interpreted the tradition of Abū Hurayra to apply to a person who is overcome by doubt and is afflicted by it. This (method) belongs to the category of reconciliation. He interpreted the tradition of Ibn Masʿūd so as to mean that the meaning of estimation here is having recourse to certainty. This acknowledged, in accordance with his methodology, all the traditions.

Those who adopted the method of reconciling part and dropping part, which is preference without interpreting the subordinated text (that is, not preferred text) include Abū Ḥanīfa. He said that the tradition of Abū Saʿīd implies a *ḥukm* for the person who has no preponderant basis to rely on, while the tradition of Ibn Masʿūd applies to one who does have such a basis to rely on. He dropped the *ḥukm* of the tradition of Abū Hurayra, and this by saying that the traditions of Abū Saʿīd and Ibn Masʿūd include an addition, and when there is an addition it must be accepted and followed. This too is a kind of reconciliation. Those who preferred part and dropped part are those who said that he is liable simply to prostrations. The reason is that they preferred the tradition of Abū Hurayra and dropped the traditions of Abū Saʿīd and Ibn Masʿūd. Thus, this is the weakest of the opinions.

This is what we thought of recording in this division of the two divisions of the Book of Prayer, and which is a discussion of the obligatory prayers. We now turn to a discussion of the second division of the prescribed prayers and these are prayers that do not impose a universal obligation.

III
THE SECOND BOOK OF PRAYER (ṢALĀH)

Prayers that are not prescribed as a universal obligation include prayers that are a *sunna*, or are supererogatory (*nafl*), or prayers that are prescribed as a communal obligation (*farḍ kifāya*). As (each of) these have *aḥkām*, some agreed upon and some disputed, we deemed it proper to take up the discussion of each prayer separately. These prayers together are ten in number: the two *rakʿas* of the morning prayer, the *witr* prayer, supererogatory prayers, the two *rakʿas* on entry into a mosque, prayers during Ramaḍān, the eclipse (*kusūf*) prayer, prayer for rain, the two *ʿīd* prayers, and the prostrations (on reciting certain parts) of the Qurʾān, which are also a kind of prayer. This book, therefore, comprises ten chapters. We shall be discussing funeral prayers separately under the chapter on the *aḥkām* of the dead, as is the practice of the jurists and that is what they compile under the title: "the book of *janāʾiz*".

3.1. Chapter 1 Discussion of the *Witr* Prayer

They disagreed about *witr* on five points: its *ḥukm*, its description, its time, the supplication (*qunūt*) during it, and its observance while travelling on a riding beast.

The discussion of its *ḥukm* has been covered in the discussion of obligatory prayers. Mālik (God bless him), in its description, preferred that it be offered as three *rakʿas* of *witr*, separated with a salutation.[150] Abū Ḥanīfa said that *witr* consists of three *rakʿas* without any separation between them by means of the salutation. Al-Shāfiʿī said that *witr* is a single *rakʿa*. For each group there are opinions coming down from the generations of the Companions and the Tābiʿūn.

The reason for their disagreement stems from the conflict of traditions on the subject. It is established from the Prophet (God's peace and blessings be upon him) through the tradition of ʿĀʾisha "that he used to pray eleven

[150] That is, two *rakʿas* ending with a salutation plus one *rakʿa*.

rakʿas at night, offering one as *witr*". It is established from Ibn ʿUmar that the Messenger of Allāh (God's peace and blessings be upon him) said, "The prayers during the night are (observed) two at a time, and if you find that the morning is going to overtake you, then, offer one *rakʿa* as *witr*". Muslim has reported from ʿĀʾisha "that the Prophet (God's peace and blessings be upon him) used to pray thirteen *rakʿas* at night, and offered five of these as *witr* without sitting in between, except at the end of the last". Abū Dāwūd has reported from Abū Ayyūb al-Anṣārī, "*Witr* is a prescribed duty for every Muslim, thus, he who prefers to observe it with five may do so, he who prefers to observe it with three may do so, and he who prefers to observe it with one may do so". Abū Dāwūd has recorded that the Prophet (God's peace and blessings be upon him) used to observe *witr* with seven, nine, and five *rakʿas*. He recorded (a tradition) from ʿAbd Allāh ibn Qays, who said, "I said to ʿĀʾisha, 'With how many (*rakʿas*) did the Messenger of Allāh (God's peace and blessings be upon him) observe *witr*?' She said, 'He used to observe *witr* with four and three, six and three, eight and three, ten and three, but he did not observe it with less than seven or with more than thirteen' ". There is also the tradition of Ibn ʿUmar from the Prophet (God's peace and blessings be upon him) that he said, "The sunset prayer (*maghrib*) is the *witr* of the prayers of the day".

The jurists adopted the method of preference in these traditions. Those who held that *witr* is a single *rakʿa* decided on the basis of the words of the Prophet (God's peace and blessings be upon him), "If you are apprehensive about the (approach of) dawn offer a single *rakʿa* as *witr*," and also on the basis of the tradition of ʿĀʾisha, "He used to observe *witr* with one *rakʿa*". Those who maintained that *witr* is three *rakʿas*, without there being a separation between them, and confined the *ḥukm* of *witr* to three only, have nothing to rely upon as proof in this matter, as all traditions imply a choice, except the tradition of Ibn ʿUmar that the prophet (God's peace and blessings be upon him) said, "The sunset prayer (*maghrib*) is the *witr* of the prayers of the day". Abū Ḥanīfa would say: "When one thing is compared with another and the *ḥukm* of both is made the same, it is appropriate that the things compared have the same description, thus, when *maghrib* is compared with the *witr* of the prayers of the day and as *maghrib* consists of three it follows that the *witr* of the night be also three".

Mālik, on the other hand, relied on the argument that the Prophet (God's peace and blessings be upon him) never observed *witr* unless it followed an even number (of *rakʿas*). He, therefore, held that this was the *sunna* of *witr* and that the minimum in this is two *rakʿas*. *Witr*, in his view, may in fact be a single *rakʿa* preceded by an even number of *rakʿas*, or that *witr*, which is prescribed has to include an even number along with it. Thus, if a *witr* is added to an even number of *rakʿas*, the whole becomes *witr* (an odd number). This opinion is supported by the tradition of ʿAbd Allāh ibn Qays—mentioned earlier—which describes *witr* prayers as comprising an even number of *rakʿas* and then an odd number. His belief that *witr* comprises a single *rakʿa* is revealed in his statement: "How can *witr* be observed when nothing precedes it, and for what is it a *witr* (odd number)?" The Messenger of Allāh (God's peace and blessings be upon him) has said, "What has been prayed before it makes it odd". The apparent meaning of this statement agrees with his view that the technical meaning of *witr* is the odd number itself, that is, something not consisting of an even number plus an odd number, because in such a case it is not an odd number in itself but because of the odd number besides it. This interpretation is better.

The truth, however, is that all these traditions imply a choice in the description of the *witr* prayer ranging from one to nine as has been reported in the acts of the Messenger of Allāh (God's peace and blessings be upon him). The inquiry (to be made) is whether it is a condition for the *witr* that it be preceded by an even number of *rakʿas*. It is possible to say that this is a condition as that was the case with the *witr* of the Messenger of Allāh (God's peace and blessings be upon him). It is also possible to say that it is not a condition for it as Muslim has recorded that the Prophet (God's peace and blessings be upon him) used to wake ʿĀʾisha up for her *witr* prayer when he had prayed up to the point of the *witr*. The apparent meaning of this is that she used to observe *witr* without it having been preceded by an even number. He (Muslim) has also recorded a tradition from ʿĀʾisha "that the Messenger of Allāh (God's peace and blessings be upon him) used to observe *witr* with nine *rakʿas*, sitting down in the eighth and ninth, and he did not offer the salutation except in the ninth. He then offered two *rakʿas* while seated. These are eleven *rakʿas*. When he grew older and put on some weight he used to observe *witr* with seven *rakʿas* sitting only in the sixth and the seventh, and not offering the salutation except at the end of the seventh. He then used to offer two *rakʿas* while seated, and these come to nine *rakʿas*". In this tradition the *witr* precedes the even number, and it contains a proof that it is not a condition for the *witr* that it be preceded by an even number, and that the term *witr* is applied to mean three. This is supported by what is related by Abū Dāwūd from Ubayy ibn Kaʿb, who said, "The Messenger of Allāh (God's peace and blessings be upon him) used to recite in the *witr* (the chapters) "Glorify the name of your Lord, the most High . . .", 'Say O disbelievers . . .', and 'Say, Allāh is One . . .' ".[152] There is a similar tradition from ʿĀʾisha where she says about the third recitation, "Say, Allāh is One

[151] That is, chapters 87, 109, and 112.

. . ., and the *muʿawwidhatān* ['Say, I seek refuge with the Lord of the daybreak . . .,' and 'Say, I seek refuge with the Lord of mankind . . .']"

The jurists agreed that the time of *witr* is after the *ishāʾ* prayer up to the break of the dawn, as this has been reported from the Prophet (God's peace and blessings be upon him) through a variety of channels. One of the most authentic of these is what is reported by Muslim from Abū Nuḍra al-ʿAwfī that Abū Saʿīd informed them that they had asked the Prophet (God's peace and blessings be upon him) about *witr*, and he said, "The *witr* is before the morning (prayer)". They disagreed about the permissibility of observing it after the dawn. A group of jurists prohibited this, while another group permitted it as long as the worshipper had not yet performed the morning prayer. The first opinion was held by Abū Yūsuf and Muḥammad, the disciples of Abū Ḥanīfa, and by Sufyān al-Thawrī. The second was held by al-Shāfiʿī, Mālik, and Aḥmad.

The reason for their disagreement derives from the conflict between the practice of the Companions in this regard and the traditions. The apparent meaning in the traditions about this (matter) is that it is not permitted to observe *witr* after dawn as in the tradition of Abū Nuḍra that has already been mentioned. Further, the tradition of Abū Ḥudhayfa is explicit about this as recorded by Abū Dāwūd, where it is said, "It has been prescribed for you (from the time) between the *ishāʾ* prayer till the break of the dawn". There is no dispute among the authorities on *uṣūl* (*al-fiqh*) that what occurs after the word *ilā* (till) has a *ḥukm* that is the opposite of what precedes it as it represents the limit. Though this belongs to one of the categories of the indirect indication of the text (*dalīl al-khiṭāb*), it is of a kind that is agreed upon as in the words of the Exalted, "Then strictly observe the fast till nightfall",[152] and in His words, "(Wash your hands) Up to the elbows".[153] There is no dispute among the jurists about (the propositon) that what is beyond the limit is the opposite of what is before the limit.

The conflict between practice and traditions is discernible from what is related from Ibn Masʿūd, Ibn ʿAbbās, ʿUbāda ibn al-Ṣāmit, Ḥudhayfa, Abū al-Dardāʾ, and ʿĀʾisha that they used to observe *witr* after the break of the dawn and before the morning prayers, and there was no opposition from the other Companions over this. A group of jurists held that such a case is within the category of consensus (*ijmāʿ*), but such a claim is not justified, as an opinion of one person about an issue cannot be attributed to another who is silent about it, that is to say, the opinion of a person on an issue should not to be ascribed to a consensual opinion when his opinion is not known. As to the

[152] Qurʾān 2 : 187.
[153] Qurʾān 5 : 6.

issue at hand, how is it correct to say that there is no reported dispute among the Companions over it. What dispute can be greater than the dispute of the Companions who related these (differing) traditions, I mean, their disagreement with those who permitted the *witr* prayer after the break of the dawn.

What I think of their practice on the issue, however, is that it does not go against the traditions reported on it, that is, the permissibility of praying *witr* after dawn. In fact, the permissibility in this regard belongs to the category of *qaḍāʾ* not to that of *adāʾ*. Their practice would go against the traditions if they considered praying *witr* after daybreak to be of the category of *adāʾ*. Think over this. The dispute over this issue actually relates to the question of whether *qaḍāʾ* in worship with determined timings is in need of a renewed command, that is, a command other than the command for *adāʾ*. Thus, such an interpretation ascribed to them is more suitable as the practice was reported from most of them that they were seen observing the *witr* as *qaḍāʾ* before the (morning) prayer, but after the break of the dawn. An opinion has been related from Ibn Masʿūd on this, that is, he used to say, "The time for *witr* is from the last time of *ishāʾ* up to the morning prayer". The existence of this opinion, however, does not necessarily mean that we should ascribe it to all of the Companions whom we have mentioned, that all shared that opinion because one Companion was seen praying *witr* after daybreak, and it is necessary to ponder over the nature of the transmission from them about this. Ibn al-Mundhir has reported five opinions about the timing of *witr* including the two well-known opinions that I have mentioned. The third opinion is that the worshipper should observe the *witr* even if he has offered the morning prayer. This is the opinion of Ṭāwūs. The fourth is that he should observe it even after sunrise. This was maintained by Abū Thawr and al-Awzāʿī. The fifth is that he may observe the *witr* of the previous night. This is the opinion of Saʿīd ibn Jubayr.

The reason for this disagreement stems from their dispute about the emphasis laid on observing *witr* and the degree of its nearness to the category of obligation (*farḍ*). Those who held it to be closer to obligation prescribed its *qaḍāʾ* in a period that is beyond that of the period determined for it. Those who held that it was not close to being an obligation prescribed *qaḍāʾ* in the shorter period. Those who held it to be a *sunna* like all the other *sunan* deemed *qaḍāʾ* to be weak in this case as *qaḍāʾ* is necessary in obligations. Hence, their disagreement about the *qaḍāʾ* of *īd* prayers for one who has missed it. It is necessary that no distinction be made in this between recommendation and obligation, that is, those who hold that *qaḍāʾ* of an obligation is through a renewed command should maintain the same about recommendation, and those who hold that it is obligatory through the original command should maintain the same about recommendation.

In their disagreement about the *qunūt* (supplication), Abū Ḥanīfa and his disciples maintained that the worshipper should recite it in the *witr* prayer. Mālik disallowed it, while al-Shāfiʿī permitted it during the second half of Ramaḍān. One group of jurists permitted it for the first half of Ramaḍān and a second group for the entire month of Ramaḍān.

The reason for their disagreement arises from the conflict of traditions. It has been related from the Prophet (God's peace and blessings be upon him) that he always recited the *qunūt*. It is also related that he permitted it for a month. Again, it is related that in his last days he did not recite *qunūt* in any part of the prayer. Finally, it is related that he prohibited it. This issue has been discussed earlier.

Observing the *witr* prayer while riding on a beast, whichever way it is facing, has been permitted by the majority as it has been established through the acts of the Prophet (God's peace and blessings be upon him), that is, he used to observe *witr* while riding. This is what they relied upon to prove that it is not an obligation, for it has been established from the Prophet (God's peace and blessings be upon him) that "he used to offer supererogatory prayers while riding", while it has not been established from him at all that he used to observe obligatory prayers while riding. In the view of the Ḥanafites, because of their agreement with the majority that on the premise that no obligatory prayer is to be observed while riding, and because of their belief that the *witr* prayer is obligatory, it must necessarily follow that it should not be prayed while riding, and they rejected the tradition on the basis of analogy, which is weak.

Most of the jurists held that if a person observes *witr* and then goes to sleep, he may not observe *witr* a second time if he wakes up to observe supererogatory prayers; this is because of the words of the Prophet (God's peace and blessings be upon him), "*Witr* is not observed twice in a night". It is recorded by Abū Dāwūd. Some of them held that he may make the first *witr* even by adding a *rakʿa* to it and then observe it a second time after offering an even prayer. This is an issue that they termed *naqḍ al-witr*. It is weak from two aspects: first, that *witr* cannot be converted to a supererogatory prayer by making it even; second, that observing a single *rakʿa* as a supererogatory prayer is not known in the law. Permitting it or not permitting it is the cause of disagreement on the issue. Those who took into account the underlying meaning in *witr*, which is the opposite of even, said that it is converted by making it even through the addition of a second *rakʿa*. Those who took into account the technical meaning said that it is not converted by making it even as the even prayer is supererogatory, while the *witr* is an emphatic *sunna* (*muʾakkada*) or it is obligatory.

3.2. Chapter 2 The two *Rakʿas* of the Morning Prayer

They agreed that the two *rakʿas* in the morning are *sunna* because of their being persistently observed by the Prophet (God's peace and blessings be upon him), more so than the *rakaʿas* of any other supererogatory prayer. He (God's peace and blessings be upon him) did so because he considered performing them as desirable and also because he performed them as *qaḍāʾ* after sunrise—when he had (once) overslept till after sunrise—thus praying the whole morning prayer as *qaḍāʾ*. They disagreed about it in (several) issues, one of which is the recommended (Qurʾānic) recitation in it.

According to Mālik it is recommended that only the *umm al-Qurʾān* be recited in it. Al-Shāfiʿī said that there is no harm if the *umm al-Qurʾān* is recited in it along with another short *sūra*. Abū Ḥanīfa said that there is no recorded precedent in it for recommended recital, and it is permitted that a person may recite from his nightly portion of Qurʾānic recitation.

The reason for their disagreement is the variation in the reported recitation by the Prophet (God's peace and blessings be upon him) in this prayer, and also their disagreement about the identification of recitation in the prayer. It is related about the Prophet (God's peace and blessings be upon him) "that he used to observe two light [short] *rakʿas* in the morning", and it is related from ʿĀʾisha, who said, "They [the two *rakʿas*] were so short that I wondered whether he had recited in them the *umm al-Qurʾān*". The apparent implication of this is that he used to recite only the *umm al-Qurʾān* in them. It is related through Abū Hurayra, as recorded by Abū Dāwūd, that "he [the Prophet] used to recite 'Say, God is One . . .', and 'Say, O disbelievers . . .', in them". Those who adopted ʿĀʾisha's tradition chose the recitation of the *umm al-Qurʾān* alone, while those who adopted the second tradition chose to recite the *umm al-Qurʾān* and a short *sūra*. Those who abided by their principle that no specific recitation is to be fixed for prayers, because of the words of the Exalted, "So recite of it that which is easy [for you]",[154] said that the person is to recite what he likes.

The second issue concerns the manner of the recitation that is recommended for it. Mālik, al-Shāfiʿī and most of the other jurists held that the recommendation is to recite it inaudibly. A group of jurists maintained that the recommendation is for audible recitation, while another group granted a choice (to the worshipper) between reciting it inaudibly and audibly.

The reason for disagreement in this stems from the conflict of the implied meanings of the traditions. In the (preceding) tradition of ʿĀʾisha the apparent implied meaning is that "the Prophet (God's peace and blessings be

[154] Qurʾān 73 : 20.

upon him) used to recite inaudibly in them". If this had not been the case ʿĀʾisha would not have had reason to doubt whether the Prophet recited the *umm al-Qurʾān* in them. The apparent meaning of what has been related from Abū Hurayra is that he used to recite "Say, O disbelievers . . .," and "Say, Allāh is One . . .", in them, and that the recitation of the Prophet (God's peace and blessings be upon him) used to be audible, for had this not been the case, Abū Hurayra would not have come to know what he was reciting in them. Those who adopted the method of preference in these two traditions either upheld the audible recitation, when the tradition of Abū Hurayra was preferred, or they upheld inaudible recitation, when the tradition of ʿĀʾisha was preferred. Those who upheld the method of reconciliation upheld a choice for the worshipper.

The third issue is about case of a person who has not offered the two *rakʿas* and finds the *imām* engaged in the (obligatory) prayer, or who enters the mosque to offer the two *rakʿas*, but finds that the obligatory prayer is about to commence. In such a case, Mālik held that if he enters the mosque and the obligatory prayer is being performed, then he is to pray with the *imām* and not to offer the two *rakʿas* in the mosque (when the *imām* is observing the obligatory prayer). If, however, he has not entered the mosque and he does not fear losing a *rakʿa* with the *imām*, he may offer the two *rakʿas* outside the mosque, but if he is afraid of losing a *rakʿa* he should pray with the *imām* and then offer them after sunrise. Abū Ḥanīfa agreed with Mālik in making the distinction between the case of a person having entered the mosque or not yet having done so, but he went against him in the detailed ruling. He said that the person may pray outside the mosque as long as he thinks that he will be able to offer one *rakʿa* of the morning prayer with the *imām*. Al-Shāfiʿī said that if the prescribed prayer has commenced he is not to offer the two *rakʿas* inside or outside the mosque. Ibn al-Mundhir has related that a group permitted the offering of the two *rakʿas* inside the mosque while the *imām* is observing the (obligatory) prayer, but this is a deviant opinion.

The reason for their disagreement arises from their dispute over the meaning of the words of the Prophet (God's peace and blessings be upon him), "If the prayer has commenced, then, there is no other prayer but the one prescribed". Those who adopted the general implication of this tradition did not allow the two morning *rakʿas*, either outside the mosque or inside it, if the prescribed prayer had commenced. Those who restricted this meaning to apply to praying inside the mosque permitted praying outside the mosque as long as the obligation is not lost, or if a part of the obligation is not lost. The underlying meaning (*ʿilla*) of the proscription, according to those who adopted the general meaning, is the occupation with supererogatory prayers to the neglect of the obligatory prayers. The underlying meaning according to those who restricted this to the mosque is the offering of two prayers at the same time as that would amount to going against the *imām*. It is related from Abū Salama ibn ʿAbd al-Raḥmān that he said, "Some people heard the prayer being undertaken so they stood up to pray. The Messenger of Allāh (God's peace and blessings be upon him) came out to them and said, 'Two prayers at one time? Two prayers at one time?' He said that this was during the time of the morning prayer and about the two *rakʿas* that are before the obligatory morning prayer".

Mālik and Abū Ḥanīfa disagreed over the portion of the obligatory prayer that is to be taken into account in determining whether a person should first engage in the two *sunna rakʿas* or join the *imām*. The dispute stems from their disagreement over the portion that ensures securing the merit of the congregational prayer. Further, there is disagreement over whether the congregational prayer is greater in merit than the two *rakʿas*. Those who maintained that by losing a *rakʿa* of the obligatory prayer the credit for the prayer with the congregation is lost said that he may remain occupied with the two *rakʿas* as long is a *rakʿa* of the obligatory prayer is not lost. Those who maintained that he secures the merit (of the congregation) as long he prays even a single *rakʿa* of the obligatory prayer (with the *imām*), said so because of the words of the Prophet (God's peace and blessings be upon him), "He who has caught a *rakʿa* of a prayer has caught the prayer", that is, he secures its merit. They interpreted this tradition so as to convey a general application covering one relinquishing the prayer intentionally or without exercising a choice, and thus said that he may remain occupied with it as long as he thinks that he can catch at least one *rakʿa* (with the *imām*). Mālik interpreted this tradition (Allāh knows best) to apply to a person who has missed the obligatory prayer intentionally. He therefore held that if he misses a single *rakʿa* from it he loses its merit.

The reason for the opinion of those who permitted the two morning *rakʿas* inside the mosque when the obligatory prayer had commenced is based on one of two reasons: either the tradition did not prove authentic in their view or it did not reach them. Abū Bakr ibn al-Mundhir has said that it is an authentic tradition, that is, the words of the Prophet (God's peace and blessings be upon him) "If the prayer has commenced, then, there is no other prayer but the one prescribed". Abū ʿUmar ibn ʿAbd al-Barr has also declared it authentic, and its authenticity is also related from ibn Masʿūd.

The fourth issue is about the time of their *qaḍāʾ* when they have been missed because of offering the morning (obligatory) prayer. A group of jurists said that the person is to offer them as *qaḍāʾ* after the (obligatory) morning prayer. This opinion was held by ʿAṭāʾ ibn Jurayj. Another group of jurists said that he is to offer them as *qaḍāʾ* after sunrise. Some of these jurists determined this inflexible time for it, while others declared it to be flexible saying that he may offer them from the time of the rising of the sun up to the time of its decline, but he is not to offer them after the declining of the sun. Some of these jurists, who upheld his offering them as *qaḍā'*, considered it a recommendation, while others granted the person a choice. The basis for praying them as *qaḍā'* is the Prophet's praying them as *qaḍā'* after sunrise when he overslept.[155]

3.3. Chapter 3 The Supererogatory Prayers (*Nawāfil*)

They disagreed about supererogatory prayers, whether they are to be observed as two *rakʿas*, four, or three. Mālik and al-Shāfiʿī said that voluntary prayers during the night or the day are to be offered as two *rakʿas* at a time with a salutation after every two *rakʿas*. Abū Ḥanīfa said that if the worshipper likes he may offer them as two at a time, or three, or four, or six, or eight, without offering a salutation in between. A group of jurists distinguished between prayers during the night and those during the day, saying that prayers during the night are two at a time while prayers during the day are four at a time.

The reason for their disagreement in this arises from the conflict of the traditions on the subject. A tradition from Ibn ʿUmar is related that a man asked the Prophet (God's peace and blessings be upon him) about prayers during the night, and he said, "The prayer during the night is two at a time, and if you find that the morning is going to overtake you, then, offer one *rakʿa* as *witr*". It is also established from the Prophet (God's peace and blessings be upon him) "that he used to pray two *rakʿas* before *ẓuhr* and two after it, two *rakʿas* after *maghrib*, two *rakʿas* after the Friday prayer, and two *rakʿas* before *ʿaṣr*". Those who adopted these two traditions said that prayers during the night as well as the day are two *rakʿas* at a time. It is established through a tradition of ʿĀ'isha in which she describes the prayer of the Messenger of Allāh (God's peace and blessings be upon him) by saying "He prayed four *rakʿas* and you cannot imagine how beautiful they were or how long! He then then prayed four and you cannot imagine how beautiful they were or how long! He then prayed three, and I said, 'O Messenger of Allāh, do you sleep before observing the *witr*?' He said, 'O ʿĀ'isha, my eyes go to sleep, but my heart does not'". It is also established, through a narration of Abū Hurayra, that the Prophet (God's peace and blessings be upon him) said, "He who prays after the *jumuʿa* should pray four". Al-Aswad has related from

[155] Once, on a journey, the Prophet asked Bilāl, before going to sleep, to wake them up for the morning prayer at the right time. Bilāl overslept, and the company continued to sleep until they were scorched by the heat of the sun. The Prophet and his company had to perform that morning prayer as *qaḍā'*.

ʿĀʾisha "that the Messenger of Allāh (God's peace and blessings be upon him) used to offer nine *rakʿas* during the night"—"but when he grew older, he prayed seven". Those who adopted the apparent meaning in these traditions permitted supererogatory prayers as four or three at a time without a break between them with the salutation. The majority maintained that supererogatory prayers are not offered through a single *rakʿa*, and I think there is some deviant disagreement in this.

3.4. Chapter 4 The two *Rakʿas* on Entering the Mosque

The majority maintain that the two *rakʿas* (to be offered) upon entry into a mosque are recommended and are not obligatory. The Ẓāhirites said that they are obligatory. The reason for the disagreement over this is whether the command, in the words of the Prophet (God's peace and blessings be upon him), "If one of you enters the mosque he should kneel for two *rakʿas*", is to be interpreted to imply a recommendation or an obligation. The tradition is agreed upon (by al-Bukhārī and Muslim) for its authenticity. Those who maintained with the majority that the rule is to construe absolute commands as implying obligation, unless an evidence indicates a recommendation and there is no objection against the evidence that transfers the *ḥukm* from being an obligation to that conveying a recommendation, said that these two *rakʿas* are obligatory. Those who raised an objection to the evidence converting the commands to recommendation, or for whom the rule is that the commands are to be construed to imply a recommendation, unless there is an evidence indicating an obligation, a rule which is held by one group, said that the two *rakʿas* are not obligatory.

The majority, however, construed the command in this case to indicate a recommendation owing to the existence of a conflict between this tradition and the traditions which we have mentioned at the beginning of this book, like the tradition of the desert dweller, (the traditions) that imply through their apparent, or explicit, meaning that the obligatory (daily) prayers are only five. The reason is that if the command here is construed to imply obligation it necessarily follows that the obligatory prayers become more than five. Those who made them obligatory maintain that the obligation here is related to the entry into a mosque and is not an absolute command like that for the five obligatory prayers. The (majority of the) jurists maintain that qualifying the command with respect to place is similar to qualifying it with respect to time.[156] The Ẓāhirites, however, hold that a specific place is not one of the

[156] Thus, treating them as an obligation will make the obligatory prayers more than five.

conditions of the validity of prayer, while time is a condition for the validity of the obligatory prayers.[157]

The jurists disagreed, under this subject heading, about the case of a person who enters a mosque and has already prayed the two *rakʿas* of the morning prayer in his house, whether he should offer the *rakʿas* on entering the mosque. Al-Shāfiʿī said that he should, and this is also a narration of Ashhab from Mālik. Abū Ḥanīfa said that he is not to offer them, and this is also a narration of Ibn al-Qāsim from Mālik. The reason for their disagreement stems from the conflict of the general implication of the Prophet (God's peace and blessings be upon him), "When one of you enters a mosque he is to offer two *rakʿas*", with the apparent meaning of his words, "There is no prayer after daybreak, except the two *rakʿas* of the morning". Here there are two general implications and two particular implications. The first is about time and the second about prayer. The reason is that the tradition prescribing prayer upon entry into a mosque is general with respect to time, but is particular with respect to prayer, while the tradition proscribing prayer after daybreak, except the two morning *rakʿas*, is particular with respect to time and general with respect to prayer. Those who exempted the particular case of prayer from the general upheld bowing (prayer) after the two morning *rakʿas*, while those who exempted the particular case of time from the general did not make this obligatory.

We have already said that if such a conflict arises, it is not binding to decide on the basis of either particular implication except on the basis of (further) evidence. Further, the proscribing tradition is not opposed by the tradition establishing the command, Allāh knows best. If the tradition is proved authentic then the evidence is to be sought from another quarter.

3.5. Chapter 5 Prayers during Ramaḍān

They (the jurists) agreed that the Ramaḍān night prayer is more desirable than the night prayer during any of the other months, because of the words of the Prophet (God's peace and blessings be upon him), "He who celebrates the Ramaḍān nights praying and worshipping because of his faith and only for Allāh's sake will be forgiven all prior sins that have issued forth from him". The (jurists agreed that the) *tarāwīh* prayers, the congregation in the mosque for which was started by ʿUmar, are desirable. They differed, however, on whether these (night prayers during Ramaḍān known as *tarāwīh*) have greater merit or the prayers during the later part of the night, that is, the prayer

[157] The analogy, therefore, on the basis of which the argument is made that considering them as obligatory makes the obligations more than five, is not valid.

preferred by the Messenger of Allāh (God's peace and blessings be upon him). The majority held that the prayers of the later part of the night have greater merit because of the words of the Prophet (God's peace and blessings be upon him), "The best prayer is the prayer in your houses, except the obligatory prayers". There is also ʿUmar's saying that "those for which you give up sleep have greater merit".

They disagreed about the preferred number of *rakʿas* that are to be undertaken by the people during the nights of Ramaḍān. Mālik, in one of his opinions, Abū Ḥanīfa, al-Shāfiʿī, Aḥmad, and Dāwūd preferred twenty *rakʿas* excluding *witr*. Ibn al-Qāsim has recorded from Mālik that he used to prefer offering thirty-six *rakʿas*[158] plus three of *witr*.

The reason for their disagreement comes from the conflict of transmission over this, as Mālik has related from Yazīd ibn Rūmān that he said, "The people, in the time of ʿUmar, used to pray twenty-three *rakʿas*. Ibn Abū Shayba has reported from Dāwūd ibn Qays, who said, 'I prayed with the people during the time of ʿUmar ibn ʿAbd al-ʿAzīz and Abbān ibn ʿUthmān and they used to pray thirty-six *rakʿas* and offered (another) three as *witr*'". Ibn al-Qāsim has reported from Mālik that this was the earlier directive, that is, praying thirty-six *rakʿas*.

3.6. **Chapter 6 Eclipse Prayer**

They agreed that the prayers for the solar eclipse are a *sunna* and that they are to be undertaken in a congregation. They disagreed about its description, about the description of the recitation during it, about the timings during which it is permitted, and also whether a sermon is one of its conditions. They also disagreed on whether the same sort of prayer is to be performed in the case of a lunar eclipse. There are thus five issues under this topic.

3.6.1. Issue 1

Mālik, al-Shāfiʿī, the majority of the jurists of Ḥijāz, and Aḥmad maintained that the eclipse prayer comprises two *rakʿas* with the *rukūʿ* (bowing) occurring twice in each. Abū Ḥanīfa and the Kūfīs held that the eclipse prayer is comprised of two *rakʿas* on the pattern of the *ʿīd* and Friday prayer.

The reason for their disagreement stems from the conflict of traditions on the issue and the conflict of analogy with some of them. This is so as it has been established in the tradition of ʿĀʾisha, in which she said, "A solar

[158] The reason behind this number, Allāh knows best, was that those in Mecca performed circumambulation around the Kaʿba between each set of four *rakʿas* of *tarāwīh*. Those in Medina, to compensate for this, added four *rakʿas* for each *ṭawāf*. This made sixteen (4 x 4) additional *rakʿas*, making it a total of thirty-six (20 + 16) of *tarāwīh*.

eclipse occurred during the period of the Messenger of Allāh (God's peace and blessings be upon him). He led the people in prayer, and stood praying for a long time after which he made the bow and bowed a long time. He then straightened up and prayed for a long time, but this was shorter than the first, after which he bowed for a long time, but this was shorter than the first bow. Thereafter he raised himself and prostrated once. He then sat up, then prostrated again. He then did the same in the second *rakʿa*. He then went away when the sun had brightened again". It is also established in the same manner through the tradition of Ibn ʿAbbās, that is, two bows in a *rakʿa*. Abū ʿUmar has said that these two are the most authentic traditions that have been related on the topic.

Those who relied on these two traditions and preferred them over the others on the basis of transmission said that the eclipse prayer comprises two *rukūʿs* in a single *rakʿa*. It has also been related in the traditions of Abū Bakr, Samura ibn Jundab, ʿAbd Allāh ibn ʿUmar, and al-Nuʿmān ibn Bashīr that the Prophet (God's peace and blessings be upon him) prayed two *rakʿas* during an eclipse like the prayer of *ʿīd*. Abū ʿUmar ibn ʿAbd al-Barr has said that all these are authentic and well-known traditions and the best of these is the tradition of Abū Qalāba from al-Nuʿmān ibn Bashīr, who said, "The Messenger of Allāh (God's peace and blessings be upon him) led us in prayer during an eclipse like your prayer where you bow and prostrate two *rakʿas* at a time, seeking the favour of Allāh till the brightening of the sun". Those who preferred these traditions, because of their large number and their conformity with analogy, that is, conformity with the other prayers said that the eclipse prayer is two *rakʿas*. The Qāḍī (Ibn Rushd) said that the tradition of Samura has been recorded by Muslim.

Abū ʿUmar said that on the whole each group adopted the traditions that had been reported by their predecessors, and for that reason some of the jurists have held that all this is a matter of choice. One of those who said this is al-Ṭabarī. The Qāḍī (Ibn Rushd) said that this is better, as reconciliation is better than preference. Abū ʿUmar said that in the case of the eclipse prayer ten *rukūʿs* in two *rakʿas*, eight in two, six in two, and four in two have been reported, but through channels that are unreliable. Abū Bakr ibn al-Mundhir and Isḥāq ibn Rahwayh have said that all this is mutually supportive and not conflicting as the consideration here is given to the brightening of the sun, and the excess in bowing occurred in accordance with variation in the brightening of the sun during the eclipse in which prayer was offered. It is related from al-ʿAlāʾ ibn Ziyād that in his view the worshipper should look at the sun when he raises his head from the bowing posture. If the sun has brightened he should prostrate and add to it a second *rakʿa*, but if it has not brightened in the first *rukūʿ* he should bow a second time and then look at the sun again, and if it has still not brightened he should bow a third time in the first *rakʿa* and continue this way till the sun brightens up. Isḥāq ibn Rahwayh used to say that this is not to exceed four *rukūʿs* in one *rakʿa*, as an excess beyond that has not been established from the Prophet (God's peace and blessings be upon him). Abū Bakr ibn al-Mundhir has said: "Some of our colleagues used to say that a choice in the matter of the eclipse has been established, and the choice lies with the worshipper, if he likes he may bow twice in one *rakʿa*, or thrice, or four times". He did not, however, consider this to be valid, but he maintained that these records imply that the Prophet (God's peace and blessings be upon him) prayed at length on a number of occasions during the eclipses. The Qāḍī (Ibn Rushd) said: "What he has mentioned has been recorded by Muslim and I do not know how Abū ʿUmar has said that these have been reported through weak channels. As for ten *rukūʿs* in a *rakʿa*, it has been reported by Abū Dāwūd alone".

3.6.2. Issue 2

They disagreed about the (nature of the) recitation in this prayer. Mālik and al-Shāfiʿī held that the recitation in it is to be inaudible. Abū Yūsuf, Muḥammad ibn al-Ḥasan, Aḥmad, and Isḥāq ibn Rahwayh maintained that the recitation in it is to be audible.

The reason for their disagreement arises from the conflict of traditions on the subject with respect to their implications and the form of words used. Thus, the implication of the authentic tradition of Ibn ʿAbbās is that the Prophet (God's peace and blessings be upon him) recited inaudibly in it, because of Ibn ʿAbbās's words about the Prophet, "that he prayed in it equal to the length of *sūrat al-Baqara*". The same is narrated from him expressly that he said, "I stood on one side of the Messenger of Allāh (God's peace and blessings be upon him) and I did not hear a word from him". It has been related through Ibn Isḥāq from ʿĀʾisha about the eclipse prayer that she said, "I listened intently to his recitation and guessed that he recited *sūrat al-Baqara*".

Those who preferred these traditions said that the recitation in it is to be inaudible, and because of what has been mentioned in these traditions, Mālik and al-Shāfiʿī considered it desirable to recite *sūrat al-Baqara* in the first *rakʿa*, *sūrat Āl ʿImrān* in the second, the length of one hundred and fifty verses of *sūrat al-Baqara* in the third, the length of fifty verses of *sūrat al-Baqara* in the fourth, and to recite the *umm al-Qurʾān* in each one of these *rakʿas*. They preferred their opinion also on the basis of what has been related from the Prophet (God's peace and blessings be upon him) that he said, "The prayers during the day are inaudible", but there are traditions that oppose this tradition. One of these is the report "that the Prophet (God's peace and blessings be upon him) in one of the *rakʿas* of the eclipse prayer recited *sūrat al-Najm*", and this means that he must have recited audibly. Aḥmad and Isḥāq used to support such an opinion through the tradition of Sufyān ibn al-Ḥasan from al-Zuhrī from ʿUrwa from ʿĀʾisha "that the Prophet (God's peace and blessings be upon him) recited audibly in a prayer of the solar eclipse". Abū ʿUmar has said that Sufyān ibn al-Ḥasan is not a reliable narrator. He maintained that his tradition was also narrated by others (by way of *mutābaʿa*) from al-Zuhrī from ʿAbd al-Raḥmān ibn Sulaymān ibn Kathīr and none of them is to be found in the tradition of al-Zuhrī. Further, the tradition of Ibn Isḥāq from ʿĀʾisha that has preceded opposes it. These jurists also supported their argument with *qiyās al-shabah*, saying that recitation in a *sunna* prayer that is observed in a congregation during the day must be audible, and the basis for this are the prayer for *ʿīd* and that for rain (*istisqāʾ*).

Al-Ṭabarī granted a choice in all this. This is the method of reconciliation, and we have already stated that it is preferable to the method of preference, if it is possible. There is no dispute about it that I know of among the experts on *uṣūl.*

3.6.3. Issue 3

They disagreed about the time in which it is to be observed. Al-Shāfiʿī said that it may be observed at all times, those in which prayer is prohibited and those in which it is not. Abū Ḥanīfa held that it is not to be observed in timings in which prayer is prohibited. Ibn Wahb has related from Mālik that he said: "Prayer for the solar eclipse is not to be observed except in timings in which supererogatory prayers are permitted". Ibn al-Qāsim has related that the established practice is to observe it from sunrise up to the decline of the sun.

The reason for their disagreement on this issue springs from their dispute over the categories of prayer that are not to be observed during the prohibited periods. Those who held that the prohibition applies to all categories of prayer during these periods did not permit the observance of the eclipse prayer or any other prayer in such timings. Those who maintained that these traditions are confined to the supererogatory prayers, and the eclipse prayer according to them is a *sunna*, permitted its observance (in such timings). Those who maintained that this prayer is supererogatory did not permit it either in the proscribed timings. The report of Ibn al-Qāsim from Mālik, however, has no basis except its semblance to the *ʿīd* prayer.

3.6.4. Issue 4

They also disagreed on whether delivering a sermon after the prayer is one of its conditions. Al-Shāfiʿī held that it is one of its conditions. Mālik and Abū Ḥanīfa maintained that there is to be no sermon after the eclipse prayer.

The reason for their disagreement stems from their dispute over the underlying cause for which the Messenger of Allāh (God's peace and blessings be upon him) addressed the people after he had completed the eclipse prayer, as is reported in ʿĀʾisha's tradition. She related "that when he had completed the prayer and the sun had brightened, he praised Allāh and glorified Him and then said, 'The sun and the moon are two signs from among the signs of Allāh, and they are not eclipsed for anyone's death nor for his life . . '".[159] Al-Shāfiʿī, therefore, believed that he delivered this sermon as a sermon is one of the practices of this prayer, as is the case with the *ʿīd* prayer and the prayer for rain. Some of those who adopted the opinion of the others believed that the sermon by the Prophet (God's peace and blessings be upon him) on that day was delivered because the people believed that the sun was eclipsed for the death of his son Ibrāhīm (God's peace and blessings be upon him).

3.6.5. Issue 5

They disagreed about the (kind of prayer that should be offered during a) lunar eclipse. Al-Shāfiʿī maintained that prayers for it are to be observed in a congregation in a manner similar to that for the solar eclipse. This was also held by Aḥmad, Dāwūd, and a group of jurists. Mālik and Abū Ḥanīfa maintained that prayers for it are not to be observed in a congregation and they recommended that people pray two *rakʿas* for it individually as is the case with all the other supererogatory prayers.

The reason for their disagreement arises from their dispute over the meaning of the words of the Prophet (God's peace and blessings be upon him), "The sun and the moon are two signs from among the signs of Allāh, and they are not eclipsed for anyone's death nor for his life, so when you see them eclipsed supplicate Allāh and pray till what has befallen you clears up, and then give alms". It has been recorded by al-Bukhārī and Muslim. Those who understood from this that the prescription for observing prayer in it is the same, which is the manner in which it is observed for the solar eclipse, held that prayer is to observed in a congregation. Those who comprehended a different meaning here, for it has not been related about the Prophet (God's peace and blessings be upon him) that he observed prayer for the lunar eclipse despite the frequency of its occurrence (during its lifetime), held that the meaning here is the minimum to which the term *ṣalāh* is applied in law and that is supererogatory prayer observed individually. The upholders of this opinion maintained that the principle here is to construe the term *ṣalāh* in the law, when it is prescribed, to imply the minimum that is covered by the term in the law, unless another evidence indicates the contrary. Thus, when the acts

[159] The author quotes the tradition in full a few paragraphs below.

of the Prophet (God's peace and blessings be upon him) with respect to the solar eclipse do not indicate it (i.e., prayer in a congregation) the meaning retains its (original) implication for the lunar eclipse in conformity with the principle. Al-Shāfiʿī, however, construes the acts of the Prophet (God's peace and blessings be upon him) with respect to the solar eclipse as an elaboration of an unelaborated (*mujmal*) meaning, and insofar as prayer for it has been prescribed it is necessary to rely on it. Abū ʿUmar ibn ʿAbd al-Barr believed that it has been related from Ibn ʿAbbās and ʿUthmān that both of them prayed two *rakʿas* with the congregation for the lunar eclipse, bowing twice in each *rakʿa*, just as is the opinion of al-Shāfiʿī.

A group of jurists recommended praying (on other occasions of natural occurances such as) earthquakes, storms, darkness (heavily overcast skies), and other such signs on the analogy of the lunar eclipse and the solar eclipse because of the Prophet's expressly stating the underlying cause for these, which is their determination as signs. This is one of the strongest categories of analogy in their view, for it is analogy on the basis of an underlying cause that is explicitly stated; but this was not the view of Mālik or al-Shāfiʿī, nor of any group of jurists. Abū Ḥanīfa said that if a prayer is observed on the occurance of an earthquake it is an excellent thing for there is no harm done anyway. It is related that Ibn ʿAbbās used to pray for it in the same way as for the eclipse prayer.

3.7. **Chapter 7 Prayer for Rain**

The jurists agreed that going out for seeking rain, moving away from the dwelling area, supplicating Allāh and entreating Him to sending down rain is a *sunna* established by the Messenger of Allāh (God's peace and blessings be upon him). They disagreed about prayer (*ṣalāh*) for rain. The majority maintain that this is one of the *sunan* when going out for seeking rain, except that Abū Ḥanīfa said that (formal) prayer itself is not one of its *sunan*.

The reason for disagreement stems from the conflict of traditions. It is related in some traditions that the Prophet (God's peace and blessings be upon him) made supplications for rain and also prayed, but in other traditions (formal) prayer is not mentioned. One of the best known traditions on the point that he did pray, and which was relied upon by the majority, is the tradition of ʿAbbād ibn Tamīm from his (paternal) uncle "that the Messenger of Allāh (God's peace and blessings be upon him) led the people out to make a supplication for rain and there he led them in a prayer of two *rakʿas* in which he recited audibly, raised his hands up to his shoulders, turned his cloak inside out, faced the *qibla*, and made a supplication for rain". It has been recorded by al-Bukhārī and Muslim. The traditions in which supplication is mentioned but prayer is not include the tradition of Anas ibn Mālik, which is recorded by Muslim, that he said, "A man came up to the Messenger of Allāh (God's peace and blessings be upon him) and said, 'O Messenger of Allāh, the animals are dying (of thirst), the paths have been blocked, so make a supplication to Allāh'. The Messenger of Allāh (God's peace and blessings be upon him) made a supplication, and then the rain poured from one Friday to the next". There is also, among them, the tradition of ʿAbd Allāh ibn Zayd al-Māzinī, in which he said, "The Messenger of Allāh went out and made a supplication for rain. He turned his cloak inside out when he faced the *qibla*". Prayer was not mentioned in this tradition. Those who adopted the apparent meaning of this tradition thought that this is related from ʿUmar ibn al-Khaṭṭāb, that is, he went out to the place of prayer and made a supplication, but did not pray. The argument of the majority is that because a tradition does not mention something, it cannot be used as evidence against that which does.

The implications of the conflict of the traditions is that prayer is not a condition for the validity of the supplication for rain, for it has been established that the Prophet (God's peace and blessings be upon him) "made a supplication for rain from the pulpit", but not that it (prayer) is not one of the *sunan* for rain, as has been held by Abū Ḥanīfa.

Those who maintained that prayer is one of the *sunan* for rain agreed that the sermon is also one of its *sunan*, because of its occurrence in a tradition. Ibn al-Mundhir said that it is established that the Messenger of Allāh (God's peace and blessings be upon him) observed the prayer for rain and delivered a sermon. They disagreed then on whether it should be delivered before the prayer or after it, because of the conflict of traditions on this point. One group maintained that it is after the prayer on the analogy of the two *ʿīd* prayers. This was upheld by Mālik and al-Shāfiʿī. Al-Layth ibn Saʿd said that the sermon is to be delivered prior to prayer. Ibn al-Mundhir has said that "it is related from the Prophet (God's peace and blessings be upon him) that he made a supplication for rain and delivered the sermon before prayer," and the same has been related from ʿUmar ibn al-Khaṭṭāb and that is what we accept. The Qāḍī (Ibn Rushd) said that this has been recorded by Abū Dāwūd through different channels, and those who mention the sermon state, to my knowledge, that it is delivered before the prayer.

They agreed that the recitation in it is to be audible, but they differed on whether the (the number of) *takbīrs* to be pronounced in it should be the same as that in the two *ʿīd* prayers. Mālik held that the *takbīrs* are to be pronounced in it as they are in the ordinary prayers, while al-Shāfiʿī maintained that the *takbīrs* are to be pronounced in it as they are in the *ʿīd* prayers. The reason for their disagreement arises from their dispute about its analogy over the two *ʿīd* prayers. Al-Shāfiʿī argued for his opinion by relying on what has been related from Ibn ʿAbbās "that the Messenger of Allāh (God's peace and blessings be upon him) observed two *rakʿas* in it as they are observed in the *ʿīd* prayers".

They agreed that one of its practices (*sunan*) is that the *imām* should face the *qibla* while standing, and he should make a supplication, turn his cloak inside out, and raise his hands, as has been related in the traditions. They disagreed, however, about the manner of doing this, and about the time when he should do it. With respect to the question as to how it is done, the majority maintain that he should turn his cloak from the right side on to his left (shoulder) and that on his left side to his right (shoulder). Al-Shafiʿī said that he should turn the lower part upward, what is on his right to his left, and what is on the left to his right. The reason for their disagreement derives from the conflict of traditions on the issue. It is reported in the tradition of ʿAbd Allāh ibn Zayd "that the Prophet (God's peace and blessings be upon him) went out to the place of prayer to make a supplication for rain. He faced the *qibla*, turned his cloak, and prayed two *rakʿas*". In some of its versions the tradition says, "I said: 'Did he place the left side toward the right and the right toward the left, or did he turn the lower part toward the top?' He said, 'In fact, he turned the left over to the right and the right over to the left'". Further, it is recorded in the tradition of this (person) ʿAbd Allāh that he said, "The Messenger of Allāh (God's peace and blessings be upon him) made a supplication for rain and (at that time) he was wearing a black shirt that he had. He tried to take hold of its lower part to turn it toward the top, but when this became difficult he placed it over his shoulders".

As to when the *imām* is required to do this, both Mālik and al-Shāfiʿī said that he does this after delivering the sermon. Abū Yūsuf held that he turns his cloak when the early part of the sermon is over. This has also been related from Mālik. All of them maintain that if the *imām* turns his cloak while standing the people are to turn theirs while sitting, because of the words of the Prophet (God's peace and blessings be upon him), "The *imām* has been appointed so that he be followed". The exception are Muḥammad ibn al-Ḥasan, al-Layth ibn Saʿd, and some of the disciples of Mālik. The followers (behind the *imām*) in their view are not to turn their cloaks because of the *imām's* turning his, as this has not been reported in the traditions about the Prophet's prayer when he led them.

A group of jurists held that the time of departure for this prayer is the same as that of the *ʿīd* prayers, except for Abū Bakr ibn Muḥammad ibn ʿAmr ibn Ḥazm, who said that the time for departure for it is at the declining of the sun. It is reported by Abū Dāwūd from ʿĀʾisha "that the Messenger of Allāh

(God's peace and blessings be upon him) departed for the supplication for rain when the rim of the sun had appeared".

3.8 Chapter 8 Prayer on the two *ʿĪds*

The jurists agreed upon the religious merit of bathing for (each of) the two *ʿīd* prayers and that they are observed without the call for prayers and (without) the pronouncement of the *iqāma*, as this was the established practice of the Messenger of Allāh (God's peace and blessings be upon him), except for the innovation in this practice by Muʿāwiya as recorded in a most authentic statement according to Abū ʿUmar. Likewise, they agreed that the *sunna* is to observe the prayer before the sermon, as that too has been established from the Messenger of Allāh (God's peace and blessings be upon him), except what is related from ʿUthmān ibn ʿAffān that he delayed the prayer and advanced the sermon so that the people should not disperse prior to the *khuṭba*. They also agreed that there is no time limit set for the recitation in the *ʿīd* prayers. Most of them recommended that *sūrat al-Aʿlā* be recited in the first *rakʿa* and *sūrat al-Ghāshiya* in the second as this is transmitted through *tawātur* (by the whole community) from the Messenger of Allāh (God's peace and blessings be upon him). Al-Shāfiʿī recommended that *sūrat Qāf* and *sūrat al-Qamar* be recited, because it was established from the Prophet (God's peace and blessings be upon him).

They disagreed in this over (several) issues, the foremost of which is their disagreement over *takbīr*. Abū Bakr ibn al-Mundhir has narrated close to twelve opinions about this, though we will mention only those that rely upon the statement of a Companion or upon transmission. Thus we say:

Mālik held that the *takbīrs* in the first *rakʿa* of the *ʿīd* prayers are seven, including the initial *takbīr* prior to recitation, and are six in the second *rakʿa*, including the *takbīr* for rising up from the prostrations. Al-Shāfiʿī said that in the first they are eight[160] and in the second they are six along with the *takbīr* for rising up from the prostrations. Abū Ḥanīfa said that in the first *rakʿa* he is to pronounce three *takbīrs* raising his hands in each after the initial *takbīr*, then he is to recite the *umm al-Qurʾān* followed by another *sūra* after which he is to bow pronouncing the *takbīr*, but without raising hands. When he rises for the second *rakʿa*, he is to pronounce the *takbīr* without raising his hands and recite the *Fātiḥat al-Kitāb* and another *sūra*. He is then then to pronounce three *takbīrs* with the raising of hands after which he pronounces a *takbīr* for

[160] Note by the editor of the original text: That is, the initial *takbīr* is included in them.

the bow but does not raise his hands. A group of jurists said that there are nine (*takbīrs*) in each *rakʿa*. This is related from Ibn ʿAbbās, al-Mughīra ibn Shuʿba, Anas ibn Mālik, Saʿīd ibn al-Musayyab, and it was also upheld by al-Nakhaʿī.

The reason for their disagreement derives from the conflict of the traditions transmitted on the issue from the Companions. Mālik, may Allāh have mercy on him, relied on what is related from Ibn ʿUmar, who said, "I witnessed (celebrated) *al-aḍḥā* and *al-fiṭr* [the two *ʿīds*] with Abū Hurayra and he pronounced seven *takbīrs* in the first *rakʿa* prior to recitation and five in the other *rakʿa*, prior to recitation". Further, the practice (*ʿamal*), in his view, in Medina was in accordance with this. This tradition was relied upon by al-Shāfiʿī, except that he interpreted the seven as excluding the initial *takbīr*, just as in the five *takbīrs* in the second *rakʿa* he excluded the *takbīr* for rising up. It appears that what led Mālik to conclude that the initial *takbīr* is to be counted among the seven and the *takbīr* for rising up is to be counted as an addition to the reported five is the prevailing practice. This appears, in his view, to be a kind of reconciliation between the tradition and (prevailing) practice. Abū Dāwūd has recorded the contents of Abū Hurayra's tradition in reports going up to ʿĀʾisha and ʿAmr ibn al-ʿĀṣ. It is related that Abū Mūsā al-Ashʿarī and Ḥudhayfa ibn al-Yamān were asked as to how the Messenger of Allāh (God's peace and blessings be upon him) pronounced the *takbīrs* during *al-aḍḥā* and *al-fiṭr*. Abū Mūsā said, "He used to pronounce four *takbīrs* (just as he did) on the funerals". Ḥudhayfa said, "He has spoken the truth". Abū Mūsā then added, "This is what I used to do at Baṣra when I was appointed (governor) over them". A group of jurists upheld this opinion. Abū Ḥanīfa and the rest of the Kūfians relied for this upon Ibn Masʿūd, for it is established from him that he used to teach them to observe the *ʿīd* prayer in the manner that has preceded.

All of them decided this by adopting the opinions of Companions on the issue as nothing has been established from the Prophet (God's peace and blessings be upon him) on this, and it is known that the act of a Companion in such a case serves as a precedent, for analogy has no role in such an issue (of worship).

Likewise, they disagreed about the raising of hands while pronouncing each *takbīr*. Some of them recommended that practice, and this is the opinion of al-Shāfiʿī. Some held that the raising of hands was applicable only at the time of commencement, while others granted a choice in this.

They disagreed about the person on whom the *ʿīd* prayer is obligatory, that is, obligation as a *sunna*. A group of jurists said that it is to be observed by a resident as well as a traveller, and this was upheld by al-Shāfiʿī and al-Ḥasan al-Baṣrī. Al-Shāfiʿī also maintained that it is to be observed by the people living in the countryside and the desert, and even those who do not gather for prayer like women in their houses. Abū Ḥanīfa and his disciples held that the Friday congregation and the *ʿīd* prayer are obligatory only on the residents of towns and cities. It is reported from ʿAlī that he said that there is no Friday prayer and no *tashrīq* except in the city where people congregate. It is related from al-Zuhrī that he said: "There is no *aḍḥā* or *fiṭr* prayer for the traveller".

The reason for this disagreement stems from their dispute about its analogy with the Friday prayer. Those who made the analogy with the Friday prayer held the same view about it as they did about the Friday prayer. Those who did not draw such an analogy held that the command is addressed to each subject unless an exemption for such a communication is proved in his case, because it is established that "the Prophet (God's peace and blessings be upon him) ordered the women to go out for observing the two *ʿīd* prayers, but he did not do so in the case of the Friday congregation".

They also differed about the location from which it was necessary to go for the prayer just as they disagreed about the (obligation of the) Friday prayer—from up to three miles to a distance of a whole day's journey.

They agreed that the time for *ʿid* prayer extends from the rising of the sun up to its decline. They disagreed about the obligation of those whom information has not reached that the day of *ʿīd* has come, until after the time of the declining of the sun. A group of jurists said that they are not obliged to pray that day or the next. This was the opinion of Mālik, al-Shāfiʿī, and Abū Thawr. Some other jurists said that they are to go and pray on the second day of *ʿīd*. This was the opinion of al-Awzāʿī, Aḥmad, and Isḥāq. Abū Bakr ibn al-Mundhir said that this is what we uphold on the basis of the tradition that we have related from the Prophet (God's peace and blessings be upon him) "that he ordered them to break the fast, and on the next morning to go to their place of prayer". The Qāḍī (Ibn Rushd) said that this is recorded by Abū Dāwūd, but that it is from an unknown Companion, and the principle in their case, may Allāh be pleased with them (the Companions), is to assume *adāla* (moral probity).

If the *ʿīd* day falls on a Friday, should the *ʿīd* (prayer) replace the Friday congregation? They disagreed over this. A group of jurists said that *ʿīd* acts as a substitute for the Friday prayer and the subject is not under an obligation for anything (during the rest of the afternoon) except the *ʿaṣr* prayer. This was upheld by ʿAṭāʾ and has been related from Ibn al-Zubayr and ʿAlī. Another group of jurists said that this is only an exemption for the people living in the countryside (with widely scattered dwellings)[161] who come to the cities

[161] When a settled community forms a congregation it becomes like a village or town and its inhabitants are then bound by all congregational obligations.

specifically for *ʿīd* and the Friday congregation. It has been related from ʿUthmān that he addressed the people on an *ʿīd* that was a Friday and said: "Those from the countryside who like to wait for the Friday congregation may do so, and those who wish to return may return. It is recorded by Mālik in *al-Muwaṭṭaʾ*". He also related a tradition similar to it attributed to ʿUmar ibn ʿAbd al-ʿAzīz, and this opinion was adopted by al-Shāfiʿī. Mālik and Abū Ḥanīfa said that if the *ʿīd* falls on a Friday the subject remains under an obligation for both, *ʿīd* as a *sunna* and the Friday congregation as an obligation, and one cannot be a substitute for the other. This is the principle unless an evidence is established to which recourse is necessary. Those who adopted ʿUthmān's view did so not because it is an opinion, but because his statement is based on a precedent,[162] and it is not totally inconsistent with the principles. As to the dropping of the obligation of *ẓuhr* or *jumuʿa* (which is its substitute) due to the existence of the *ʿīd* prayer, it falls far beyond the ambit of the principles, unless there is established an evidence to which recourse is necessary.

They disagreed about the case of a person who has lost the prayer with the *imām*. A group of jurists said that he is to pray four *rakʿas*. This was upheld by Aḥmad and al-Thawrī, and it was related from Ibn Masʿūd. Another group of jurists said that he is to offer two *rakʿas* as *qaḍāʾ* in the same way as the prayer of the *imām*, pronouncing the *takbīrs* in it like those of the *imām* and reciting audibly like him. This was upheld by al-Shāfiʿī and Abū Thawr. A third group said that he observes two *rakʿas* without pronouncing the *takbīrs* in it or reciting audibly. A fourth group said that if the *imām* observed the prayer in the place of prayer the person is to observe two *rakʿas* else he is to observe four *rakʿas*. A fifth group of jurists said that there is no *qaḍāʾ* for him. This is the opinion of Mālik and his disciples. Ibn al-Mundhir has related from him an opinion similar to that of al-Shāfiʿī.

Those who maintained that he is to observe four *rakʿas* compared it (the *ʿīd* prayer) to the Friday congregation, but this is a weak comparison. Those who held it to be two *rakʿas* like those observed by the *imām* did so on the basis of the principle that *qaḍāʾ* must be performed in the same way as the *adāʾ*. Those who disallowed *qaḍāʾ* maintained that it is a prayer that has stipulated conditions of a congregation and an *imām* like the Friday prayer; therefore, they did not prescribe the *qaḍāʾ* of either two or four *rakʿas* for they do not substitute for anything. These two opinions are those around which the issue revolves, that is, the opinion of al-Shāfiʿī and the opinion of Mālik. As for the other opinions, they are weak and meaningless, for the

[162] That is, such an opinion is assumed to be based upon an earlier precedent from the Prophet (God's peace and blessings be upon him) about which the Companion has knowledge.

Friday prayer is a substitute for *ẓuhr*, but these prayers do not form a substitute for anything. How, then, can we draw an analogy from one with the other for *qaḍā'*? In fact, the *ẓuhr* prayer of the person who has missed the Friday congregational prayer is not *qaḍā'* rather it is *adā'*, because on missing the substitute this becomes obligatory. Allāh is the Grantor of truth.

They disagreed about supererogatory prayers before the *ʿīd* prayer and after it. The majority maintain that he (the worshipper) is not to offer supererogatory prayers either before it or after it. This is related from ʿAlī ibn Abī Ṭālib, Ibn Masʿūd, Ḥudhayfa, and Jābir, and it is also upheld by Aḥmad. It is said, however, that he is to offer supererogatory prayers both before it and after it. This is the opinion of Anas and ʿUrwa, and it has been upheld by al-Shāfiʿī. There is a third opinion in this that he is to offer supererogatory prayers after it but not before it. This was upheld by al-Thawrī, al-Awzāʿī, and Abū Ḥanīfa, and it is also related from Ibn Masʿūd. A group of jurists made a distinction between whether the prayer was in a place of prayer (for *ʿīd*) or in the mosque, and this is the well-known opinion of Mālik's school.

The reason for their disagreement is that it has been established "that the Messenger of Allāh (God's peace and blessings be upon him) went out on the day of *fiṭr* or on the day of *aḍḥā* and prayed two rakʿas without praying before them or after them". On the other hand, it is related that the Prophet (God's peace and blessings be upon him) said, "When one of you enters a mosque he should bow in two *rakʿas*". The ambiguity also arises from the aspect of its being prescribed, that is, whether the recommendation of supererogatory prayers both before and after it arises from its *ḥukm* of being a prescribed prayer. Those who considered the relinquishment of prayer before it and after as belonging to the category of relinquishment of prayer before the *sunan* and after them, and in whose view the term "mosque" did not apply to the place of prayer (for *ʿīd*), did not prescribe supererogatory prayers before it or after it. It was for this reason that the opinion of the School vacillated with respect to prayers before it when the *ʿīd* is observed inside the mosque, as the implication of the act is in conflict with the words. I mean, it is recommended that the person should pray insofar as he has entered the mosque, but insofar as he is about to observe the *ʿīd* prayer (at the place of *ʿīd* prayer) it is recommended that he should refrain from praying (prior to it) on the analogy of the act of the Prophet (God's peace and blessings be upon him). Those who maintained that it belongs to the category of exemptions, and also held that the term "mosque" applies to the place of prayer, approved of supererogatory prayers being offered before it. Those who compared it to the obligatory prayers deemed it recommended that he pray before it and after it, as we have said. A group of jurists held that supererogatory prayers before it and after it belong to the permissible (*mubāḥ*) category and not the recommended category nor the disapproved (*makrūh*) category. This has minimum ambiguity, if the term "mosque" does not encompass the place of (*ʿīd*) prayer.

They disagreed about the time of *takbīr* during *ʿīd al-fiṭr*, after the majority had agreed upon its recommendation, because of the words of the Exalted, "He desireth not hardship for you; and (He desireth) that ye should complete the period, and that ye should magnify Allāh for having guided you".[163] The majority said that the worshipper should start pronouncing the *takbīrs* from the time of departure for the prayer. This is the opinion of Ibn ʿUmar and a group of Companions and the Tābiʿūn, and was also upheld by Mālik, Aḥmad, Isḥāq, and Abū Thawr. A group of jurists said that he should start pronouncing the *takbīrs* from the night of *ʿīd al-fiṭr* when the moon has been sighted till the departure for the prayer and the emergence of the *imām*. The same, in their view, is the rule for the night of *aḍḥā* if they are not *ḥajj* pilgrims. The complete denial of pronouncing *takbīrs* is related from Ibn ʿAbbās, unless the *imām* pronounces it.

They agreed about the pronouncement of *takbīr* immediately after each prayer during the days of *ḥajj*, but they disagreed extensively over the time set for this. A group of jurists said that he is to pronounce *takbīrs* from the morning prayer on the day of ʿArafa till the time of *ʿaṣr* on the last of the (three) days of *tashrīq*.[164] This was upheld by Sufyān, Aḥmad, and Abū Thawr. It is said that he is to pronounce *takbīrs* from the time after the *ẓuhr* prayer on the day of sacrifice up to the morning prayer on the last day of *tashrīq*. This is the opinion of Mālik and al-Shāfiʿī. Al-Zuhrī said that a *sunna* has prevailed that the *imām* should pronounce *takbīr* in the cities after the *ẓuhr* prayer on the day of sacrifice up to *ʿaṣr* of the last day of *tashrīq*.

On the whole, there is extensive disagreement over this, and Ibn al-Mundhir has related ten opinions in it. The reason for their disagreement over this stems from the fact that it has been based on acts and that no determinable saying has been transmitted in this regard. When the Companions disagreed among themselves over this, their followers likewise disagreed. The basis for this subject are the words of the Exalted, "Remember Allāh through the appointed days".[165] The majority maintained that this command, even if it is primarily directed at the pilgrims, applies generally to others, and this has been derived from practice, even though there is disagreement about the time set for it. Perhaps, the fixing of a time for *takbīr* is a matter of choice for all of them agreed about the fixing of time while they differed over the act itself. A group of jurists said that the *takbīr* after prayer on these days applies only to the

[163] Qurʾān 2 : 185.
[164] That is, the three days following the *aḍḥā* day.
[165] Qurʾān 2 : 203.

person praying with the congregation. They also differed about the description of the *takbīr* during these days. Mālik and al-Shāfiʿī said that the worshipper is to pronounce it three times: *Allāhu Akbar*, *Allāhu Akbar*, *Allāhu Akbar*. And it is said that the words *lā ilāha illallāhu waḥdahu lā sharīka lah*, *lahu ʾl-mulk wa lahu ʾl-ḥamd*, *wa huwa ʿalā kulli shayʾin qadīr*, are to be added after this. It is related from Ibn ʿAbbās that he used to say, *Allāhu Akbar Kabīra*, three times and then with the fourth he would say *wa lillāhi ʾl-ḥamd*. A group of jurists said that there is nothing determined for this.

The reason for their disagreement over this arises from the absence of a determination in the law along with their understanding from the law that there is such a determination, that is, according to the understanding of most. This is the cause of their disagreement about the fixing of a time for *takbīr*, that is, comprehending such fixing in the absence of a text for it.

They agreed that it is recommended that the worshipper eat something on the day of *ʿīd al-fiṭr* before departing for the place of (*ʿīd*) prayer, and that he should not eat anything on the day of *ʿīd al-aḍḥā* except after the completion of prayer. They also held that it is recommended that he should return by a path different from the one he treaded (while going for prayer), because this practice has been established through the act of the Prophet (God's peace and blessings be upon him).

3.9. Chapter 9 Prostrations of the Qurʾān

The discussion of this topic is covered in five sections: the *ḥukm* of the prostrations; the number of prostrations that are obligatory, that is, those (occasions) for which the person is to prostrate; the times during which he may prostrate; the person who is under an obligation to prostrate; and the description of the prostrations.

About the *ḥukm* of the prostrations of recitation, Abū Ḥanīfa and his disciples said that they are obligatory. Mālik and al-Shāfiʿī said that they are prescribed as a *sunna* and are not obligatory. The reason for disagreement arises from their dispute about the implication of the commands requiring prostrations and the traditions that convey the meaning of commands. For example, whether the (following) words of the Exalted, "When the revelations of the Beneficent were recited unto them, they fell down, adoring and weeping",[166] are to be interpreted as an obligation or a recommendation. Abū Ḥanīfa interpreted them in their apparent meaning of obligation, while Mālik and al-Shāfiʿī followed the (interpretation of) the Companions, for they were

[166] Qurʾān 19 : 58.

the ones best grounded in the meaning of the commands of law. Thus, it has been established that ʿUmar ibn al-Khaṭṭāb recited *sūrat al-Sajda* on a Friday. He descended (from the pulpit) and made a prostration, and the people prostrated with him. On the next Friday, he recited it again and the people prepared for the prostrations, so he said, "Wait! Wait! Allāh has not prescribed it for us, unless we want to do it". They said that this occurred in the presence of the Companions, and no disagreement was transmitted from any of them. They were the ones who best knew the essence of the law. This is used in support of that view by those who rely on the opinion of a Companion when there is no other conflicting evidence. The disciples of al-Shāfiʿī argued on the basis of the tradition of Zayd ibn al-Thābit, who said, "I used to read out the Qurʾān for the Messenger of Allāh (God's peace and blessings be upon him). Once I recited *sūrat al-Ḥajj* and he did not prostrate, and neither did we". These jurists also argued on the basis of the report "that the Prophet (God's peace and blessings be upon him) did not prostrate during (the recitation of) *al-Mufaṣṣal sūrahs*", and also on the reports that he did prostrate during their recitation; a reconciliation between these implies that the prostrations are not obligatory. Each one of them reported what he saw, that is, those who said that he prostrated and those who said that he did not.

Abū Ḥanīfa, on the other hand, relied in this on the argument that the principle is to construe the commands as implying an obligation, and also those reports that amount to commands. Abū al-Maʿālī has said that the argument of Abū Ḥanīfa on the basis of the prescribed commands has no validity, as the absolute obligation of prostrations does not imply their obligation in a qualified sense at the time of recitation, that is, the recitation of the verses of prostration. He said that had the position been as is believed by Abū Ḥanīfa, prayer would have become obligatory on the recitation of the verses that contain the commands for prayer, and as this is not obligatory the prostrations too are not obligatory upon recitation of the verses in which the commands for prostration have been laid down. Abū Ḥanīfa, however, would say that the Muslims (jurists) have agreed that the reports about prostrations during the recitation of the Qurʾān are in the form of a command, and this is for most occasions. If this is the case, then, the command prescribing prostrations applies to the time of recitation, and as the command also occurs in an absolute sense it is necessary to construe the absolute in the qualified sense. The case of prostrations in not the same as prayer as the obligation of prayer has been qualified through other restrictions. Further, the Prophet (God's peace and blessings be upon him) did prostrate on such occasions, so the meaning of commands occurring on these occasions becomes obvious to us, that is, they apply to the time of recitation. Thus, it is necessary to construe the implication of the command as an obligation.

With respect to the number of requirements of prostrations, Mālik says in *al-Muwaṭṭa*ʾ: "The position, in our view, is that the prescription regarding the prostrations of the Qurʾān is for eleven prostrations that do not include anything from the *Mufaṣṣal sūrahs*". His disciples said that the first of these is at the end of *al-Aʿrāf*;[167] the second is in *al-Raʿd* after the words, "And unto Allāh falleth prostrate whosoever is in the heavens and the earth, willingly or unwillingly, as do their shadows in the morning and the evening hours";[168] the third is in *al-Naḥl* after the words, "And unto Allāh maketh prostration whatsoever is in the heavens and whatsoever is in the earth of living creatures, and the angels (also), and they are not proud. They fear their Lord above them, and do what they are bidden";[169] the fourth is in *Banī Isrāʾīl* after the words, "They fall down on their faces, weeping, and it increaseth humility in them";[170] the fifth is in *Maryam* after the words, "When the revelations of the Beneficent were recited unto them, they fell down, adoring and weeping";[171] the sixth is in *al-Ḥajj* being the first one after the words, "Hast thou not seen that unto Allāh payeth adoration whosoever is in the heavens and whosoever is in the earth, and the sun, and the moon, and the stars, and the hills, and the trees, and the beasts, and many of mankind, while there are many unto whom doom is justly due. He whom Allāh scorneth, there is none to give him honour. Lo! Allāh doeth what He will";[172] the seventh is in *al-Furqān* after the words, "And when it is said unto them: Adore (prostrate to) the Beneficent! they say and what is the Beneficent? Are we to adore (prostrate to) whatever thou (O Muhammad) biddest us? And it increaseth aversion in them";[173] the eighth is in *al-Naml* after the words, "So that they worship not (prostrate not to) Allāh, Who bringeth forth the hidden in the heavens and the earth, and knoweth what ye hide and what ye proclaim, Allāh: there is no God save Him, the Lord of the tremendous Throne";[174] the ninth is in *al-Sajda* after the words, "Only those believe in our revelations who, when they pray are reminded of them, fall down prostrate and hymn the praise of their Lord, and they are not scornful";[175] the tenth is in *Ṣād* after the words, "And David guessed that We had tried him, and he sought forgiveness of his Lord, and he bowed himself and fell down prostrate and repented";[176] and the eleventh is

[167] Qurʾān 7 : 206.
[168] Qurʾān 13 : 15.
[169] Qurʾān 16 : 49, 50.
[170] Qurʾān 17 : 109.
[171] Qurʾān 19 : 58.
[172] Qurʾān 22 : 18.
[173] Qurʾān 25 : 60.
[174] Qurʾān 27 : 25, 26.
[175] Qurʾān 32 : 15.
[176] Qurʾān 38 : 25.

in *Fuṣṣilat* after the words, "And of His portents are the night and the day and the sun and the moon. Adore not (prostrate not to) the sun nor the moon; but adore (prostrate to) Allāh Who created them, if it is in truth Him whom ye worship", and it is said that it is after the words, "But if they are too proud—still those who are with thy Lord glorify Him night and day and tire not".[177]

Al-Shāfiʿī said that there are fourteen prostrations. Three of these are in the *Mufaṣṣal sūrahs*, that is, in *al-Inshiqāq*, *al-Najm*, and *al-ʿAlaq*, but he did not believe that there was a prostration in *Ṣād*, the occasion there, in his view, being that of thankfulness. Aḥmad said that there are fifteen prostrations adding a second one in *al-Ḥajj* and including the prostration in *Ṣād*. Abū Ḥanīfa said that there are twelve prostrations. Al-Ṭaḥāwī said that this (the number in Abū Ḥanīfa's opinion) includes every prostration that is expressed in the form of a report.

The reason for their disagreement stems from their choice of source regarding the number of prostrations. Some of them relied upon the practice of the jurists of Medina, some relied on analogy, and some relied on transmission. Those who relied upon practice (*ʿamal*) are Mālik and his disciples. Those who relied upon analogy are Abū Ḥanīfa and his disciples, as they maintained that all the prostrations that they agreed upon were found to be expressed in the form of a report—and these were the prostrations in *Aʿrāf*, *al-Naḥl*, *al-Raʿd*, *al-Isrāʾ*, *Maryam*, the first occasion in *al-Ḥajj*, *al-Furqān*, *al-Naml*, and *al-Sajda*—and this made it necessary to link with them the remaining prostrations expressed in the form of reports, which are in *Ṣād* and *al-Inshiqāq*. The three that occur in the form of a command were dropped, and these occur in *al-Najm*, the second occasion in *al-Ḥajj*, and in *al-ʿAlaq*. Those who relied upon transmission decided on the basis of what has been established from the Prophet (God's peace and blessings be upon him) about the prostrations in *al-Inshiqāq*, *al-ʿAlaq*, and *al-Najm*. This has been recorded by Muslim.[178] Al-Athram said that Aḥmad was asked about the prostrations in *al-Ḥajj*, and he replied that there were two prostrations. He declared the tradition of ʿUqba ibn ʿĀmir from the Prophet (God's peace and blessings be upon him) as authentic, and in which he said, "In *al-Ḥajj* there are two prostrations". This is also the opinion of ʿUmar and that of ʿAlī. The Qāḍī (Ibn Rushd) said: "This has been recorded by Abū Dāwūd".

Al-Shāfiʿī decided upon dropping the prostration in *Ṣād* on the basis of what has been related by Abū Dāwūd of the tradition of Abū Saʿīd al-Khudrī

[177] Qurʾān 41 : 37, 38.

[178] The reference to this tradition occurs a few paragraphs below, where another similar tradition is deemed a ***munkar*** by Abū ʿUmar.

"that the Prophet (God's peace and blessings be upon him) was reciting the verse of prostrations in *sūrat Ṣād*, while on the pulpit, when he descended and prostrated. When he recited it on another day the people prepared themselves for the prostrations, so he said, 'This is repentance for a Prophet, but as I had seen you preparing for a prostration I came down and prostrated'". In this there is a kind of evidence for Abū Ḥanīfa in upholding the obligation of prostrations, for he (the Prophet) declared the underlying cause of relinquishment of prostrations in this prostration to be a cause that is absent in the other occasions of prostration. Thus, it becomes necessary that the *ḥukm* in which an underlying cause is absent be different from that in which the underlying cause is established. This is a kind of demonstrative proof, and there is disagreement over it, as it belongs to the category of assigning a metaphorical meaning to the indirect indication of the text (*dalīl al-khiṭāb*).

Some jurists, who did not uphold the occurrence of prostrations in the *Mufaṣṣal sūrahs*, argued on the basis of the tradition of ʿIkrima from Ibn ʿAbbās, which has been recorded by Abū Dāwūd, "that the Messenger of Allāh (God's peace and blessings be upon him) did not prostrate in any of the *Mufaṣṣal sūrahs* from the time that he migrated to Medina". Abū ʿUmar said that it[179] is a *munkar* (inconsistent) tradition, as Abū Hurayra who has related the prostrations of the Prophet in the *Mufaṣṣal sūrahs* did not become a Companion of the Prophet (God's peace and blessings be upon him) except in Medina. Trustworthy narrators have related from him "that the Prophet (God's peace and blessings be upon him) prostrated in *al-Najm*".[180]

They disagreed about the time of the prostrations. A group of jurists prohibited the prostrations during a period of time that is proscribed for prayer. This is the opinion of Abū Ḥanīfa in accordance with his principle of prohibiting the obligatory prayers in these timings.[181] Mālik has also disallowed these in the *Muwaṭṭaʾ*, as these are supererogatory in his view, and supererogatory worship is prohibited during these timings according to him. Ibn al-Qāsim has related from him that the prostrations may be made after *ʿaṣr* as long as the sun has not turned yellow or changed in colour. Likewise after the morning prayer. This was upheld by al-Shāfiʿī. This is based on the view that the prostrations are a *sunna*, and the *sunan* may be observed in these timings as long as the sun is not about to set or about to rise.

About the person towards whom the *ḥukm* is directed they agreed

[179] This apparently refers to a tradition attributed to Abū Hurayra about the *Mufaṣṣal sūrahs*. This tradition has not been reproduced by the author in the discussion; however, it appears to be similar in content to, and could be a version of, the tradition following it, which has also been referred to above. It is also possible that some text before this sentence is missing.

[180] This is the authentic tradition referred to in the paragraph before last above.

[181] These prostrations are also obligatory in his view.

unanimously that it is directed towards the person reciting, whether in prayer or otherwise. They disagreed about whether the listener is obliged to prostrate. Abū Ḥanīfa said that he is under an obligation to prostrate, and he did not differentiate between a man or a woman. Mālik said that the listener is to prostrate on two occasions: first, when he has sat down to listen to the Qur'ān, and second, when the reciter himself prostrates, and that the latter can validly be an *imām* for the listener. Ibn al-Qāsim has related from Mālik that the listener is to prostrate himself once he has sat down to listen to the reciter even if the reciter is not qualified to be an *imām*.

The majority of the jurists said about the description of the prostrations that when the person reciting prostrates he should pronounce the *takbīr* on lowering himself and upon rising. Mālik's opinion has differed on the issue when the person is not observing prayer, but when he is praying he is to pronounce *takbīr* without a dispute.

IV

THE BOOK OF THE *AḤKĀM* OF THE DECEASED

The discussion in this book, which relates to the rights of the dead over the living, is divided into six chapters. The first chapter is about the recommended acts to be undertaken when the time of death approaches and the acts after death. The second is about bathing the deceased. The third is about enshrouding him. The fourth is about carrying him (to the grave) and walking in his funeral. The fifth is about the prayer over him. The sixth is about his burial.

4.1. Chapter 1 The Recommended Acts on the Approach of Death and the Acts after Death

It is recommended that on the approach of death the affirmation (credo) "*lā ilāha illallāh* [There is no god but Allāh]" be whispered into the ear of the dying person, because of the words of the Prophet (God's peace and blessings be upon him), "Whisper to those of you who are dying the affirmation, 'There is no god but Allāh' ", and because of his words, "The person whose last words are, 'There is no god but Allāh,' will enter *janna* [Paradise]".

They disagreed about whether to turn him in the direction of the *qibla*. A group was of the view that he should be turned, while another group was not. It is related from Mālik that he said about turning the dead person toward the *qibla*: "This is not an earlier practice". It is related from Saʿīd ibn al-Musayyab that he denied this, and it has not been related from any of the Companions nor from the Tābiʿūn, that is, the command to turn the body in the direction of the *qibla* (*tawjīh*).

When the person dies his eyes are to be closed. Hastening the burial is recommended because of the traditions laid down in this regard, with the exception of the drowned person in which case delay in burying him is recommended (in the School) for fear that he might still be alive and that excessive water in his body may have made the signs of life in him less obvious. The Qāḍī (Ibn Rushd) said: "If this is said about the drowned person, then, it is more appropriate in the case of many sicknesses, which cause the person to become motionless and appear dead, as is well known to the physicians. The physicians have recommended that burial of those who fall into a coma should be delayed for at least three days until death has been ascertained".

4.2. **Chapter 2 Bathing the Deceased**

This chapter is covered in four sections: the *ḥukm* of bathing; which of the dead are to be bathed; who is to undertake the bathing and the *ḥukm* of the person bathing him; and the description of bathing.

4.2.1. *Section 1: The* ḥukm *of bathing the deceased*

It is said that the *ḥukm* of bathing the dead conveys a communal obligation.[182] It is also said that it is a communal *sunna*. Both views exist in the School. The reason for this (disagreement) is that it has been transmitted through acts and not through words, and acts do not have a form from which obligation can or cannot be derived. ʿAbd al-Wahhāb has argued for its obligation on the basis of the command of the Prophet (God's peace and blessings be upon him) (to the women around) about his daughter (who had died), "Bathe her three or five times", and (his command) about one (who had died) in the (state of) *iḥrām*, "Bathe him". Those who held that these words were said by way of instruction about the description of bathing and not by way of commands to do so, did not uphold its obligation. Those who said that they include both a command and description upheld its obligation.

4.2.2. *Section 2: The deceased who are to be bathed*

The jurists agreed that the dead whose bathing is necessary are Muslims who have not been killed on the battlefield during a war with the disbelievers. They disagreed about bathing the *shahīd* (martyr) and about praying over him, and

[182] A communal obligation undertaken by some members of the community is regarded as having been completely fulfilled on behalf of the entire community.

also about the bathing of the polytheist. With respect to the *shahīd*, that is, one who has died in combat with the polytheists, the majority uphold the relinquishment of bathing, because of the report "that the Messenger of Allāh (God's peace and blessings be upon him) directed that the dead (of the battle) of Uḥud[183] be buried with their clothes, and he did not pray over them". Al-Ḥasan and Saᶜīd ibn al-Musayyab used to say that each Muslim is to be bathed as each dead person becomes defiled. Perhaps they were of the view that what the Prophet directed about those slain at Uḥud was due to necessity, that is, the hardship involved in bathing them. Among the jurists of the provinces who upheld their opinion is ᶜUbayd ᶜAllāh ibn al-Ḥasan al-ᶜAnbarī. Abū ᶜUmar was asked about the narration from Ibn al-Mundhir about the bath of the *shahīd* and he said: ᶜUmar was bathed, placed in a shroud, embalmed, and prayed over, and he was a *shahīd*,[184] May Allāh have mercy upon him".

Those who agreed that the *shahīd* in a war with the polytheists is not to be bathed differed about the case of persons who are martyred by robbers or who die in a war with people other than the polytheists. Al-Awzāᶜī, Aḥmad, and a group of jurists said that their *ḥukm* is the same as that of the persons slain by the polytheists. Mālik and al-Shāfiᶜī said that they are to be bathed. The reason for their disagreement stems from the question of whether the cause for the removal of the *ḥukm* of bathing is absolute martyrdom or martyrdom at the hands of the disbelievers. Those who maintained that the cause is absolute martyrdom said that all those persons from among those slain about whom the Prophet (God's peace and blessings be upon him) has explicitly said that they are martyrs are not to be bathed. Those who maintained that the underlying cause is martyrdom at the hands of the disbelievers restricted the *ḥukm* to such persons alone.

About the bathing of a disbeliever by a Muslim, Mālik said that a Muslim is not to bathe his disbelieving father nor is he to make a grave for him unless he fears the decay of his body in which case he may bury him. Al-Shāfiᶜī said that there is no harm if a Muslim bathes and buries his next of kin who are polytheists. This was also held by Abū Thawr and Abū Ḥanīfa and his disciples. Abū Bakr ibn al-Mundhir has said that there is no precedent about the bathing of a dead polytheist that may be followed. It is related, however, "that the Prophet (God's peace and blessings be upon him) ordered the bathing of his uncle when he died". The reason for disagreement is whether bathing belongs to the category of worship or to that of cleanliness. If it is

[183] A battle fought between the polytheists of Mecca and the Prophet. It took place near Medina in the third year of the Hijra.

[184] He is considered as such though the mu.

worship, the bathing of a disbeliever is not permitted, but if it is cleanliness his bathing is permitted.

4.2.3. *Section 3: The person permitted to bathe the dead*

With respect to the person for whom it is permitted to bathe the dead, they agreed that men are to bathe men and women are to bathe women. They had three different opinions about the case of a woman dying among men or a man dying among women when there is no spouse. A group of jurists said that a person (of the opposite sex) is to bathe his or her companion from over the clothing. A group of jurists said that the companion is to rub the person's limbs with clean soil (*tayammum*). This was the opinion of al-Shāfiʿī, Abū Ḥanīfa, and the majority of the jurists. Another group of jurists said that the companion is not to bathe the person or to rub the limbs with soil but is to bury the person. This was the opinion of al-Layth ibn Saʿd.

The reason for disagreement stems from the superimposing of the proscription over the command or of the command over the proscription, as bathing has been commanded while a man's looking at the body of a woman or a woman's looking at the body of a man is proscribed. Those who let the proscription govern absolutely, that is, who did not make an analogy for the dead over the living with reference to purification with clean soil as a substitute for water because of the obstacle related to (bathing with) water, said that neither is to bathe the companion or to rub his or her limbs with soil. Those who let the command govern the proscription, that is, let the command dominate the proscription absolutely, said that each person is to bathe his or her companion. Those who permitted *tayammum* did so with the idea that there is no conflict between the command and the proscription, as looking at the objects of *tayammum* is permitted to the opposite sex. It was for this reason that Mālik held that a man may perform *tayammum* only on the hands and face of the woman as these are not her private parts (*ʿawra*), and for a woman to perform *tayammum* on the man's face and hands up to the elbows as the private parts of a man are, in his view, from the navel to the knees. It was as if the necessity that moved the (*ḥukm* of the) dead person from bathing to *tayammum*, according to those who upheld it, was the conflict between the command and the proscription. It appears that he (Mālik) held this necessity to be similar to the necessity that permits the living to perform *tayammum*, but it is a similarity that is far-fetched, yet that is what is maintained by the majority.

Mālik's opinion, however, has differed on this issue. On one occasion he said that each person is to perform *tayammum* on the companion without qualification. On another occasion he made a distinction between persons who are *maḥram* (spouse or relative with whom marriage is precluded on the basis of consanguinity) and those who are not. A third time he made a distinction, within the *maḥram* category, between men and women. Thus, three views are available from him for the *maḥram* category. The best known is that each companion is to bathe the other from over the clothing. Second, none of them is to bathe the other, but is to perform *tayammum* as in the opinion of the majority for the non-*maḥram* category. The third is based on a distinction between men and women, that is, a woman may bathe a man (with his clothes on), but a man is not to bathe a woman. The reason for disallowing this is that it is not permitted to either to look at the objects of bathing of the companion as is the case with strangers, and the reason for permitting it is that it is a point of necessity the basis for excuse in their case being greater than that in the case of the stranger. The reason for the distinction is that a man's looking at a woman is more grievous than a woman's looking at a man, on the evidence that women are concealed from the eyes of men, but men are not concealed (to such an extent) from them.

They agreed under this topic on the permissibility of a woman bathing her (dead) husband, but they disagreed on his bathing her. The majority permit this. Abū Ḥanīfa said that a man is not to bathe his wife. The reason for their disagreement is the similarity between death and divorce. Those who considered death similar to divorce said that it is not permitted to him to look at her after death. Those who did not hold it to be similar to divorce, and these are the majority, said that what is permitted for him to see before death is permitted for him after it. Abū Ḥanīfa equated death with divorce for he held that if a man's wife dies it is permitted to him for marry her sister, as is the case when she is divorced, but this is far fetched, for the underlying reason for the prohibition of marrying two sisters at the same time is removed between the living and the dead. This is the reason why she (the second sister) becomes permitted to him for marriage, unless it is said that the underlying reason of the prohibition of marrying two sisters is not rational, and is merely a ritual prohibition that cannot be rationalized. In this case Abū Ḥanīfa's view is strengthened.

Similarly, they agreed that an irrevocably divorced wife is not to bathe her former (dead) husband. They disagreed about the woman whose divorce was retractable, and it is related from Mālik that she may bathe him, which is also upheld by Abū Ḥanīfa and his disciples. Ibn al-Qāsim said that she is not to bathe him even if the divorce was retractable, and this is an analogy drawn from Mālik's opinion, namely that it is not permitted for him to, look at her. This was upheld by al-Shāfiʿī. The reason for their disagreement is whether it is permitted for a husband to look at his divorced wife whose divorce is revocable.

They disagreed about the *ḥukm* of the person giving the bath as to what is obligatory upon him. A group of jurists said that one who bathes a dead person is under an obligation to take a bath. Another group said that he is not obliged to bathe. The reason for their disagreement arises from the conflict of the tradition of Abū Hurayra with that of Asmāʾ. Abū Hurayra has related from the Prophet (God's peace and blessings be upon him) that he said, "One who bathes a dead person should bathe, and one who carries him should perform ablution". It has been recorded by Abū Dāwūd. The tradition of Asmāʾ is that when she bathed Abū Bakr, may Allāh be pleased with him, she went out and asked those of the Muhājirūn and the Anṣār who were present saying, "I am fasting and this is a very cold day, so do I have to bathe?" They said, "No". The tradition of Asmāʾ is authentic, while the tradition of Abū Hurayra, according to most of the scholars as reported by Abū ʿUmar, is not authentic. Yet, in actual fact, the tradition of Asmāʾ does not conflict with it, for it is possible that if a person denied something he does so as the *sunna* on that issue has not reached him. The question raised by Asmāʾ reflects the disagreement over this among the first generation (the Companions). Allāh knows best. Therefore, what al-Shāfiʿī, may Allāh be pleased with him, has said, that there is no obligation of bathing on one who bathes a dead person, is in accordance with his practice of adopting the safer course and relying on the traditions, unless the tradition of Abū Hurayra is proved authentic.

4.2.4. *Section 4: Description of bathing*

There are (three) issues in this section.

4.2.4.1. Issue 1

The first issue is about whether the dress of the dead person is to be removed or whether the bath is to be given from under the dress. They disagreed about this. Mālik said that when a dead person is being bathed the dress is to be taken off and the private parts are to be covered. This was upheld by Abū Ḥanīfa. Al-Shāfiʿī said that bathing is to be done from under the dress. The reason for their disagreement stems from the vacillation of the (implication of the) bathing of the Prophet (God's peace and blessings be upon him) from under his dress (when he died) between being something specific to him or being a *sunna*. Those who said that it was specific to him and that looking at a dead person is not prohibited, except what was prohibited when he was living, said that he is to be bathed without a covering with the exception of the private parts which it was prohibited to see when the person was living. Those who maintained that it is a *sunna* rely on consensus or on a divine act, for it is related in a tradition that they heard a voice saying, "Do not take off his dress", or that they were subjected to sleep; thus they said that it is better if the dead person is bathed from under his dress.

4.2.4.2. Issue 2

Abū Ḥanīfa said that ablution is not to be performed on the dead person. Al-Shāfiʿī said that it is. Mālik said that it is better if ablution is performed. The reason for disagreement over this derives from the conflict of analogy with a tradition. Analogy implies that there is to be no ablution for the dead person, as ablution is a purification prescribed for the purpose of worship (by the living). If the the obligation of worship is dropped in the case of the dead, the condition is to be dropped too, which is ablution, and had bathing not occurred in a tradition that too would not be obligatory. The apparent meaning of the authentic tradition of Umm ʿAṭiyya is that ablution is a condition in the bathing of a dead person, as according to this tradition the Messenger of Allāh (God's peace and blessings be upon him) said about the bathing of his daughter, "Begin with her right side and the limbs of ablution". This authentic addition is recorded by al-Bukhārī and Muslim. Thus it is necessarily in conflict with the traditions in which bathing is laid down in an unqualified form, and the qualified form governs the absolute as is held by many for it contains an addition. It appears that one of the reasons for disagreement over this also stems from the conflict of the absolute with the qualified meaning, as many traditions have been reported in which bathing occurs without the qualification of ablution. Thus, these jurists preferred the absolute meaning over the qualified, because of its conflict with analogy on this point, while al-Shāfiʿī held on to the principle of construing the absolute in the light of the qualified meaning.

4.2.4.3. Issue 3

They disagreed about the number of times the body is to be washed. Some of them made a fixed number of washings obligatory, while others merelycon-sidered it desirable. Some of those who made the fixing of the number obligatory deemed it to be an odd number. This was the opinion of Ibn Sīrīn. Some fixed it at three, and this was done by Abū Ḥanīfa. Some determined the minimum odd number for this and said that it should not be less than three, but they did not fix a maximum limit. This was the opinion of al-Shāfiʿī. Some determined a maximum limit for it and said that it should not exceed seven. This was done by Aḥmad ibn Ḥanbal. Those who considered an odd number to be desirable, but did not fix a limit for this, include Mālik ibn Anas and his disciples.

The reason for disagreement among those who stipulated fixing a number as a condition and those who did not stipulate a number but considered this desirable, stems from the conflict between analogy and a tradition. This is so as the apparent meaning of the tradition of Umm ʿAṭiyya implies the fixing of a number, as it says, "bathe her three or five times or more than this if you deem it proper", and in some versions it is "or seven". The analogy, on the other hand, drawn for the dead from the living with reference to purification implies that there is no fixed number in this just as there is no fixed number in the purification of a living person. Those who preferred the tradition over reasoning upheld fixing. Those who preferred reconciliation between the tradition and reasoning saw fixing as desirable.

The reason for disagreement between those who differed over fixing a number stems from the contradiction between the various versions related from Umm ʿAṭiyya. Al-Shāfiʿī held the opinion that it should not be less than three times as that is the minimum odd number expressed in the tradition of Umm ʿAṭiyya. He maintained that what is above this is permissible because of the words of the Prophet (God's peace and blessings be upon him), "If you deem it proper". Aḥmad upheld the maximum odd number expressed in some versions of the tradition, and this is in the words of the Prophet (God's peace and blessings be upon him) "or seven". Abū Ḥanīfa, when restricting the number to three, based his decision on the report that Ibn Sīrīn upheld the report from Umm ʿAṭiyya about bathing to be thrice, twice with lotus and the third time with camphor water. In addition, the odd number in law, in his view, is applied to mean three only. Mālik preferred the first bathing to be with pure water, the second with lotus, and the third with camphor water.

They disagreed (about the case) where impure matter was excreted from the dead person's body, whether bathing had to be repeated. It is said that bathing is not to be repeated (only the excretion is to be washed away), and this was upheld by Mālik. It is also said that it is to be repeated. Those who maintained that it is to be repeated disagreed over the number of repetitions that is obligatory if the impure matter is excreted repeatedly. It is said that bathing is to be repeated only once. This was al-Shāfiʿī's opinion. It is said that it is to be repeated thrice, and it is said that the repetition is seven times. They agreed, however, that it is not to exceed seven times.

They disagreed about the clipping of nails of the dead person and about the shaving of hair. A group of jurists said that the nails are to be clipped and hair shaved, while another group said that the nails are not to be clipped nor the hair to be shaved. There is no tradition on this matter. The reason for disagreement over this emanates from the disagreement extending from the first generation, and it also appears that the disagreement results from the drawing of an analogy for the dead over the living. Those who made such an analogy deemed the clipping of nails and shaving of the pubic region as obligatory, for that is a *sunna* for the living by agreement. Similarly, they disagreed about the squeezing of the abdomen before bathing. There were those who upheld this and those who did not. Those who upheld it maintained that in this there is a kind of removal of impure material at the commencement of purification, which is required for the dead person as it is for the living. Those who did not uphold it said that it is an occupation with a duty that has not been laid down by the law, and the case of the living differs from the dead in this.

4.3. Chapter 3 The Shroud for the Dead

The source for this topic is (the tradition) "that the Messenger of Allāh (God's peace and blessings be upon him) was shrouded in three white garments from the Yemen (coastal region) and their was no shirt or turban". Abū Dāwūd has recorded from Laylā bint Qāʾif al-Thaqafiyya, who said, "I was among those who bathed Umm Kulthūm, the daughter of the Messenger of Allāh (God's peace and blessings be upon him). The first thing that the Messenger of Allāh (God's peace and blessings be upon him) gave me was the lower garment, then the upper garment, then the head covering, then the cloak, and then later she was placed in another garment". She said, "The Messenger of Allāh (God's peace and blessings be upon him) was sitting by the door and had with him her shroud. He gave us the garments one by one".

There were some jurists who adopted the apparent meaning of these traditions and said that a man is to be enshrouded in three garments and a woman in five. This was the opinion of al-Shāfiʿī, Aḥmad, and a group of jurists. Abū Ḥanīfa said that the minimum shroud for a woman is three garments, but the *sunna* is five, and the minimum shroud for a man is two garments, but the *sunna* is three. Mālik maintained that there is no limit in this, and even a single garment is valid for both, except that he preferred an odd number.

The reason for their disagreement over the fixing of a number stems from their dispute over the meaning of these two traditions. Those who understood from them the meaning of permissibility did not fix a number though they preferred an odd number, as the traditions agree upon that, and they did not differentiate in this between a woman and a man. It appears that they derived permissibility from these two traditions, except for fixing a number, and thus derived from it a rule on the basis of compatibility with the law. Those who understood from the number a stipulation of permissibility upheld the fixing of a number, either by way of obligation or by way of desirability. There is a wide latitude in all this, God willing, and there is no determined law on this. Perhaps it would amount to imposition of a rule in something for which there is no law. Musʿab ibn Umayr was enshrouded during the battle of Uḥud with a woollen garment. When they tried to cover his head with it his feet stuck out, and when they covered his legs with it his head was uncovered. The Messenger of Allāh (God's peace and blessings be upon him) said, "Cover his head with it and place some grass on his feet".

They agreed that the head of the dead person is to be covered and some fragrance is to be applied, except for the person in the ritual state of *iḥrām*, about whom they differed. Mālik and Abū Ḥanīfa said that a person in a state of *iḥrām* is no different from one who is not. Al-Shāfiʿī said that the head of the person in a state of *iḥrām* is not to be covered nor is fragrance to be used on him. The reason for the disagreement derives from the conflict of the general meaning with the particular. The particular rule is to be found in the tradition of Ibn ʿAbbās, who said, "A man whose riding beast threw him over and he died was brought to the Prophet (God's peace and blessings be upon him). He was in a state of *iḥrām*. So the Prophet said, 'Enshroud him in two garments and bathe him with water and lotus leaves, but do not cover his head or apply any perfume, for he will be raised on the day of Judgment pronouncing the *talbiya*'". The general meaning is to be found in the absolute command for bathing. Those who exempted, according to this tradition, the person in a state of *iḥrām* from the general *ḥukm* for the dead, as they did in the case of the martyrs of Uḥud, applied the *ḥukm* of the Prophet (God's peace and blessings be upon him) issued for one person to all, saying that the head of the person in a state of *iḥrām* is not to be covered nor is perfume to be applied to him. Those who adopted the method of reconciliation and not the method of exemption and restriction said that the tradition of villager is restricted to his case and is not to be extended to others.

4.4. Chapter 4 Walking with the *Janāza* (Body of the Dead Person; Funeral Procession)

They disagreed about the *sunna* of walking with the body of the dead person.[185] The jurists of Medina held that one of its *sunan* is to walk in front of it. The Kūfians, Abū Ḥanīfa, and all the rest said that walking behind it is better.

The reason for their disagreement stems from the conflict of the traditions that each group related from their predecessors and acted upon. Mālik related

[185] The use of the term "bier" for *janāza* is being avoided as that is the stand on which the coffin is placed and does not convey the meaning of the Islamic term *janāza*. The word *janāza* as used in this discussion at times conveys the meaning of the body of the dead person while at other times it indicates the funeral procession.

from the Prophet (God's peace and blessings be upon him) as a *mursal* tradition,[186] and also from Abū Bakr and ʿUmar, that one is to walk in front of the body. This was also the opinion of al-Shāfiʿī. The jurists of Kūfa relied on what they related from ʿAlī ibn Abī Ṭālib through ʿAbd al-Raḥmān ibn ʿAbzī, who said, "I was walking with ʿAlī in a funeral procession and he was holding on to my arm. He was walking behind the *janāza*, while Abū Bakr and ʿUmar were walking in front of it. I asked him about this and he said, 'The person walking behind it has precedence over the person walking in front of it, like the precedence of the obligatory prayers over the supererogatory prayers. Both of them know this but they are trying to make it easy for the people to do so'". It is also related from him, may Allāh be pleased with him, that he said, "Keep it in front of you and fix your gaze on it, for it is a warning, a remembrance, and a lesson". It is also related that Ibn Masʿūd used to say, "We asked the Messenger of Allāh (God's peace and blessings be upon him) about walking with the *janāza* and he said, 'The *janāza* is to be followed and does not follow. He who is ahead of it is not with it'". In the tradition of al-Mughīra ibn Shuʿba from the Prophet (God's peace and blessings be upon him) he said, "The rider goes in front of the *janāza*, and those on foot go behind it, in front of it, on its right, and on its left, staying close to it". The tradition of Abū Hurayra also conveys the same meaning "Walk behind the *janāza*". These traditions were relied upon by the Kūfians, and they are traditions authenticated by them, but declared weak by the others.

The majority of the jurists maintain that standing up for the *janāza* is abrogated by what was related from ʿAlī ibn Abī Ṭālib "that the Messenger of Allāh (God's peace and blessings be upon him) used to stand up for the *janāʾiz* and then sat down (that is, later he used to remain seated)". A group of jurists upheld the obligation of standing up, and they relied in this upon what is related about the commands issued by the Prophet (God's peace and blessings be upon him) about rising for it, like the tradition of ʿĀmir ibn Rabīʿa, who said, "The Messenger of Allāh (God's peace and blessings be upon him) said, 'When you see the *janāʾiz*, rise up [in respect] till they leave you behind or are laid on the ground'". Those who held the view that rising up is abrogated disagreed about standing by the grave at the time of burial. Some of them held that this is not included in the proscription, while others held that it is included in the apparent meaning of the proscription. Those who excluded it from this argued on the basis of the act of ʿAlī in this, for he related the abrogation. He stood on the grave of Ibn Mukaffaf when it was said

186 This is a tradition from the *isnād* of which the name of the Companion, who is supposed to have related the tradition, is missing.

to him, "Will you not sit down, O Amīr al-Muʾminīn?" He replied, "Our standing on the grave of our brother is a minor thing for him".

4.5. Chapter 5 Prayer over the *Janāza*

This chapter is covered in sections, after the identification of the obligation of the act. The first is about the description of the prayer. The second is about the person over whose body prayers are offered, and who has precedence for prayer. The third is about the time of this prayer. The fourth is about the location of the prayer. The fifth is about the conditions of the prayer.

4.5.1. *Section 1: The description of prayer over the* janāza

There are several issues related to the description of the prayer.

4.5.1.1. Issue 1

They first Muslim generation (the Companions of the Prophet) (may Allāh be pleased with them) disagreed extensively over the number of *takbīrs*, but the jurists of the provinces maintained that there are four *takbīrs*, except for Ibn Abī Laylā and Jābir ibn Zayd, for they used to maintain that they are five.

The reason for their disagreement arises from the conflict of the traditions over the issue. It is related in the tradition of Abū Hurayra "that the Messenger of Allāh (God's peace and blessings be upon him) announced the death of al-Najjāshī (Negus, emperor of Ethiopia) on the day that he died. He went out with the people to the place of prayer and made them form rows and pronounced four *takbīrs*". This is a tradition whose authenticity was agreed upon (by al-Bukhārī and Muslim) and because of it the majority of the jurists of the Provinces relied upon it. With the same implications is another tradition "that the Prophet (God's peace and blessings be upon him) prayed over the grave of a poor woman and pronounced four *takbīrs*". Muslim has related from ʿAbd al-Raḥmān ibn ʿAbī Laylā that he said, "Zayd ibn Arqam used to pronounce four *takbīrs* over the *janāʾiz*. He pronounced five *takbīrs* over a *janāza* and we asked him about it. He replied, 'The Messenger of Allāh (God's peace and blessings be upon him) used to pronounce them' ". It is related from Abū Khyathama from his father, who said, "The Prophet (God's peace and blessings be upon him) used to pronounce four, five, six, seven, or eight *takbīrs* over dead persons till the death of the Negus, when he made the people form rows behind him and pronounced four *takbīrs*. The Prophet (God's peace and blessings be upon him) then persisted with four till his death". In this there is evident proof for the majority.

The jurists agreed on the raising of hands at the time of the first *takbīr* pronounced over a dead person, but they differed over the remaining *takbīrs*. A group of jurists said that hands are to be raised in them, while another said they are not. Al-Tirmidhī has related from Abū Hurayra "that the Messenger of Allāh (God's peace and blessings be upon him) pronounced a *takbīr* over a dead person and raised his hands. He then placed his right hand over the left". Those who adopted the apparent meaning of this tradition, and their view about prayer was that hands are to be raised only in the first *takbīr*, said that raising of hands is for the first *takbīr* alone. Those who maintained that hands are to be raised in every *takbīr* held the second *takbīr* to be the same as the first, as that is what is done for each *takbīr* pronounced while standing or rising up.

4.5.1.2. Issue 2

The jurists differed about recitation in the prayer over the dead. Mālik and Abū Ḥanīfa said that there is no recitation in it, it is merely supplication. Mālik said: "The recitation of *Fātiḥat al-Kitāb* in it is not practised in our land under any circumstances". He maintained that after the first *takbīr* Allāh is to be praised and glorified, then the second *takbīr* is to be pronounced and blessings are to be offered for the Prophet (God's peace and blessings be upon him), then the third *takbīr* is to be pronounced and salvation is to be sought for the dead person, then the fourth *takbīr* is to be pronounced after which the salutation is made. Al-Shāfiʿī said that the *Fātiḥat al-Kitāb* is to be recited after the first *takbīr* and the same is to be done in the remaining *takbīrs*. This was upheld by Aḥmad and Dāwūd.

The reason for their disagreement arises from the conflict of traditions with the practice (*ʿamal*) (at Medina), and also from the question of whether the term *salāh* includes prayer over the dead. The practice is that related by Mālik about his land. The tradition is what is related by al-Bukhārī from Ṭalḥa ibn ʿAbd Allāh ibn ʿAwf, who said, "I prayed behind Ibn ʿAbbās over a dead person and he recited the *Fātiḥat al-Kitāb* in it. He then said, 'You must know that this is the *sunna*'". Those who preferred this tradition over practice, and in whose view the term *salāh* included the prayer over the dead bearing in mind the fact that the Prophet (God's peace and blessings be upon him) has said that "There is no prayer without the *Fātiḥat al-Kitāb*", held that the *Fātiḥat al-Kitāb* is to be recited in it. It is possible to argue for Mālik's opinion on the basis of the apparent meaning of the traditions in which the supplication by the Prophet (God's peace and blessings be upon him) over the dead persons has been transmitted and it is not transmitted that he recited in it. In this way these traditions would be said to conflict with the tradition of Ibn ʿAbbās and would restrict the words of the Prophet (God's peace and blessings be upon him), "There is no prayer without the *Fātiḥat al-Kitāb*". Al-Ṭahāwī has related from Ibn Shihāb from Abū Umāma ibn Sahl ibn Ḥanīf, who was one of the leading Companions, a jurist among them, and a descendant of one of those who participated in the Battle of Badr, that he said, "One of the Companions of the Prophet (God's peace and blessings be upon him) informed me that the *sunna* in the prayer over the dead is that the *imām* pronounces the *takbīr* and then recites the *Fātiḥat al-Kitāb* inaudibly to himself, he then supplicates after the remaining three *takbīrs*". Ibn Shihāb said, "I mentioned what had been reported by Abū Umāma to Muḥammad ibn Suwayd al-Fahrī and he said, 'I heard al-Daḥḥāk ibn Qays narrate from Ḥabīb ibn Maslama the same about prayer over the dead as has been related to you by Abū Umāma'".

4.5.1.3. Issue 3

They disagreed about the salutation at the end of the prayer over the dead person, whether it is a single salutation or double. The majority maintain that it is a single salutation. A group of jurists, including Abū Ḥanīfa, said that two salutations are to be made, and this is what was preferred by al-Muzanī one of the disciples of al-Shāfiʿī. It is also one of the opinions from al-Shāfiʿī.

The reason for their disagreement stems from their dispute about salutation after *ṣalāh*, and the analogy of the prayer over the dead drawn from the obligatory prayer. Those who maintained that there is a single salutation at the end of the obligatory prayer, and who derived an analogy for the prayer over the dead from it, held that there is a single salutation. Those who maintained that there are two salutations after the obligatory prayer held that there are two salutations in this case too, if both were *sunna* according to them, or both were obligatory. Likewise, the school differed over whether the salutation is to made in a loud voice.

4.5.1.4. Issue 4

They disagreed about where the *imām* is to stand with respect to the (body of the) dead person. A group of jurists said that he is to position himself in front of the waist of the dead person, whether the dead person is male or female. Another group said that he is to stand facing the waist in the case of a female, and by the head in the case of the male. Those who said that he is to stand for both male and female facing the waist include ibn al-Qāsim, and it is also the opinion of Abū Ḥanīfa. There is no specification for this by Mālik and al-Shāfiʿī. Another group said that he is to stand wherever he likes with respect to the dead person.

The reason for their disagreement comes from the conflict of traditions on the topic. Al-Bukhārī and Muslim have recorded the tradition of Samura ibn Jundub, who said, "I prayed behind the Messenger of Allāh (God's peace and blessings be upon him) over Umm Kaᶜb, who had died of childbirth. The Messenger of Allāh (God's peace and blessings be upon him) stood for prayer opposite her waist". Abū Dāwūd has recorded the tradition of Humām from Abū Ghālib, who said, "I prayed with Anas ibn Mālik over a dead man and he stood near his head. Thereafter, they brought a dead woman and said, 'O Abū Ḥamza, pray over her'. He (then) stood near the middle of the cot. Al-ᶜAlāʾ ibn Zayd then said, 'This is how I saw the Messenger of Allāh (God's peace and blessings be upon him) praying over the dead, pronouncing four *takbīrs*, and standing near a dead woman where you stood and (also) standing near the man where you stood'. He said, 'Yes'".

The jurists disagreed about the meaning of these acts. Some of them maintained that the Prophet's standing at one of these positions or at other different positions indicates permissibility and the absence of fixation. Some maintained that his standing at one of these places indicates that it is law, and it indicates fixation. These latter jurists are divided into two groups. One of these groups relied on the tradition of Samura ibn Jundub, because of the agreement over its authenticity, and said that a woman and a man are the same for this purpose, as the principle is that their *ḥukm* is the same, unless a legal distinction is established. Some of them declared the tradition of Abū Ghālib to be authentic and said that there is in it an addition over the tradition of Samura ibn Jundub reliance upon which is obligatory, and that there is essentially no conflict between them. For the opinion of Ibn al-Qāsim and Abū Ḥanīfa, however, I do not know of any transmitted evidence, except what is related from Ibn Masᶜūd about it.

4.5.1.5. Issue 5

They disagreed about the arrangement of praying over the bodies of men and women, when they are present at the same time. Most of the jurists said that the bodies of men are to be placed near the *imām* and the bodies of women nearer the *qibla*. Another group said the opposite of this, that is, the women nearer the *imām* and the men nearer the *qibla*. There is a third opinion which says that each group is to be prayed over separately, men alone and women alone.

The reason for the disagreement stems from what (to the jurist) appears most convincing taking into account the state of the law, as it was necessary that there be a definite law for this, yet there is no law laid down on this that can be relied upon. Thus, a large number of jurists held that there is no law in such cases that can be relied upon, for had there been a law it would have been known to the people. Most of them adopted the view that we have stated of giving precedence to men over women, because of what Mālik has related in *al-Muwaṭṭa'* that Uthmān ibn ʿAffān, ʿAbd Allāh ibn ʿUmar, and Abū Hurayra used to pray in Medina over the dead, both men and women together, and they used to place the bodies of men nearer the *imām* and those of women nearer the *qibla*. ʿAbd al-Razzāq has related from Ibn Jurayj from Nāfiʿ from Ibn ʿUmar that he prayed in the same manner over dead persons, and also present were Ibn ʿAbbās, Abū Hurayra, Abū Saʿīd al-Khudrī, and Abū Qatāda, and the *imām* that day was Saʿīd ibn al-ʿĀṣ (the Umayyad governor of Medina). He asked them about it, or ordered someone to ask them, and they said, "It is a *sunna*". It belongs to the category of *musnad* in their view. It appears that those who maintained that men be placed nearer the *imām* determined their position in front of the *imām* on the basis of their position behind him, because of the words of the Prophet (God's peace and blessings be upon him), "Make them stay at the back insofar as Allāh has put them next to men". Those who maintained the precedence of women over men (putting them closer to the *imām*) believed, it appears, that those in the first position (with respect to the *qibla* away from the *imām*) had precedence and they did not determine precedence on the basis of nearness to the *imām*. Those who made a distinction (and upheld separate prayers for each group) did so on the basis of the apprehension that it could make lawful something prohibited, as there is no *sunna* that expressly permits combined prayers. It is likely that it retains its original permissibility and it is likely that it is disallowed by the law. When an equal probability exists, it is better to refrain from making a rule if a way can be found to do so.[187]

4.5.1.6. Issue 6

They disagreed on certain points about the case of a person who has missed some of the *takbīrs* in a prayer over a dead person. The first point is: does he join the prayer with a *takbīr*? Second, does he pronounce the *takbīrs* that he has missed as *qaḍā'*? Third, if he does perform it as *qaḍā'*, does he make a supplication between the *takbīrs*? Ashhab has related from Mālik that he is to pronounce the first *takbīr* for joining the prayer. This is also one opinion from al-Shāfiʿī. Abū Ḥanīfa said that he is to wait till the *imām* pronounces the *takbīr*, and it is then that he is to pronounce it. This is also a narration of Ibn al-Qāsim from Mālik. This is analogy drawn from the person joining in on obligatory prayer.

Mālik, Abū Ḥanīfa, and al-Shāfiʿī agreed that he is to pronounce as *qaḍā'* the *takbīrs* missed by him, except that Abū Ḥanīfa maintained that he is to

[187] Apparently, the way out is to pray separately for each group.

make a supplication in between *takbīrs*, while Mālik and al-Shāfiʿī said that he is to pronounce as *qaḍāʾ* the *takbīrs* missed uninterrupted by supplication. They agreed upon *qaḍāʾ* because of the general implication of the words of the Prophet (God's peace and blessings be upon him), "Pray what you can catch of the prayer and complete what you have missed". Those who maintained that this general implication includes *takbīrs* and supplication said that he is to pronounce the *takbīr* as *qaḍāʾ* and make the supplications missed. Those who excluded supplication from this, as there is nothing fixed for it, said that he is to pronounce only the *takbīr* as *qaḍāʾ* as that is fixed. The exclusion of supplication from this general implication belongs to the category of restriction of the general implication through analogy. Abū Ḥanīfa adopted the general and the other jurists the restricted meaning.

4.5.1.7. Issue 7

They disagreed about praying over the grave by the person who has missed the prayer over the dead person (*janāza*). Mālik said that he is not to pray over the grave. Abū Ḥanīfa said that no one is to pray over the grave except the *walī* of the person if he has missed the *janāza* and a person other than a *walī* has prayed over the dead person. Al-Shāfiʿī, Aḥmad, Dāwūd, and a group of jurists said that a person who has missed the *janāza* may pray over the grave. Those who permitted prayer over the grave agreed that a condition for it is that burial should have been accomplished, but they disagreed over the period after which prayer can be said for the dead. The maximum, however, is a month.

The reason for their disagreement arises from the conflict of *ʿamal* (practice) with tradition. With respect to the tradition opposing practice, Ibn al-Qāsim said to Mālik that there is a tradition that the Prophet (God's peace and blessings be upon him) prayed over the grave of a woman. Mālik replied that this tradition had been laid down, but it is not practised. Prayer over a grave, however, is established by agreement of the traditionists. Aḥmad ibn Ḥanbal has said that prayer over the grave has been related from the Prophet (God's peace and blessings be upon him) through six channels and all of them are *ḥasan* (sound). Some other traditionists have added three more channels and this makes it nine. As for al-Bukhārī and Muslim, they have related this from Abū Hurayra. Mālik recorded it from Abū Umāma ibn Sahl.

Ibn Wahb has related an opinion from Mālik that is the same as al-Shāfiʿī's. Abū Ḥanīfa, on the other hand, followed his usual method, as far as I know, that is, of rejecting *āḥād* traditions the subject matter of which is related to general public need, if these traditions have not become well-known and are not widely practised. The reason is that the lack of being widespread, when the subject-matter of this report is of a nature that it be well known, becomes circumstantial evidence weakening the report that moves it from a category of overwhelming conviction of truth to one of overwhelming conviction of falsehood or of its abrogation. The Qāḍī (Ibn Rushd) said: "We have already discussed in what has preceded in this book the mode of proof on the basis of *ʿamal* (practice), and also this form of demonstrative proof which the Ḥanafites call *umūm al-balwā*, and we have already said that they belong to the same category".

4.5.2. *Section 2: Who is to be prayed over and who has precedence*

Most of the jurists agreed about the permissibility of praying over a person who has pronounced "*la ilāha illallāh*". There is a tradition about this that the Prophet (God's peace and blessings be upon him) said, "Pray over one who has pronounced *la ilāha illallāh*", irrespective of the person's having committed major sins or of his being an innovator. Mālik, however, disapproved of the idea that meritorious people should pray over innovators, and he also did not require that the *imām* (ruler) pray over a person whom he has executed for a *ḥadd* penalty. They disagreed about the case of a person who commits suicide. A group of jurists maintained that he is not to be prayed over, while others permitted the prayer. There are jurists who did not permit prayer over persons who had committed major sins, nor over those who were guilty of insurrection or innovation.

The reason for their disagreement over such prayer in the case of innovators stems from their disagreement over the imputation of disbelief (*kufr*) to them because of their innovation. Those who imputed *kufr* to them because of their implausible interpretations did not permit prayer over them, while those who did not impute *kufr* to them because in their view disbelief results from accusing the Messenger of falsehood and not from the interpretation of the sayings of the Prophet (God's peace and blessings be upon him), held that prayer over them is permitted.

The jurists agreed about the relinquishment of prayer over the hypocrites even if they have pronounced the testimony (that there is no god but Allāh), because of the words of the Exalted, "And never (O Muḥammad) pray for one of them who dieth, nor stand by his grave. Lo! they disbelieved in Allāh and His messenger, and they died while they were evil-doers".[188] Their disagreement over those guilty of major sins (*kabāʾir*) cannot possibly have a cause except by way of their imputing them with *kufr* because of their sins, but this is not the doctrine of the Ahl al-Sunna. It is, therefore, not proper that the jurists should disallow prayer over those guilty of major sins.

[188] Qurʾān 9 : 84.

Mālik's disapproval of offering prayer over the innovators is by way of a deterrence and punishment for them, but Mālik's view about the *imām* (ruler)not praying over those whom he has executed through a *ḥadd* penalty derives from the fact that "the Messenger of Allāh (God's peace and blessings be upon him) did not pray over Māʿiz and did not disallow prayer over him". This is recorded by Abū Dāwūd.

They disagreed about the case of a person who commits suicide because of the tradition of Jābir ibn Samura "that the Messenger of Allāh (God's peace and blessings be upon him) refused to pray over a person who had killed himself". Those who authenticated this tradition said that the person killing himself is not to be prayed over, but those who did not consider it authentic said that the *ḥukm* for him is the same as that for all other Muslims, even if he is one of the residents of the Fire as laid down in a tradition, but he would not reside there forever for he is one of those who believe. The Prophet (God's peace and blessings be upon him) said as a narration from his Lord (commanding the angels), "Take out of the Fire every person who has a shred of faith in his heart".

They also disagreed about prayer over martyrs who had fallen in battle. Mālik and al-Shāfiʿī said that a martyr who has fallen in battle is not to be prayed over or bathed. Abū Ḥanīfa said that he is to be prayed over but not bathed. The reason for their disagreement arises from the conflict of the traditions on the issue. Abū Dāwūd recorded from Jābir "that the Prophet (God's peace and blessings be upon him) ordered the martyrs of Uḥud to be buried with their clothes, and he did not pray over them or have them bathed". It is related as a *musnad* from Ibn ʿAbbās "that the Prophet (God's peace and blessings be upon him) prayed over those slain at Uḥud and over Ḥamza, and they were not bathed or given *tayammum*". This is also related as a *mursal* tradition from Abū Mālik al-Ghifārī. Similarly, it is related that when a dweller of the desert was hit by an arrow in his throat and died the Prophet (God's peace and blessings be upon him) prayed over him and said, "This is a servant who went out to strive in Your way. He has fallen as a martyr, and I stand witness over him".

Both groups prefer the traditions that they could rely upon. The Shāfiʿites considered the tradition of Ibn ʿAbbās as defective and said that it was related by Ibn Abū al-Zinād who used to contradict himself in his later years, and also that Shuʿba used to doubt its accuracy. The *mursal* traditions are not persuasive proof in their view.

They disagreed about the age at which an infant is to be prayed over when it dies. Mālik said that the infant is not to be prayed over unless it was heard crying at the time of birth. This was also upheld by al-Shāfiʿī. Abū Ḥanīfa said that it is to be prayed over when life has been breathed into it, and this happens when it is in its mother's womb at least for four months. This was also the opinion of Ibn Abī Laylā. The reason for their disagreement arises from the conflict of the absolute with the qualified meaning. Al-Tirmidhī has related from Jābir ibn ʿAbd Allāh from the Prophet (God's peace and blessings be upon him) that he said, "An infant is not to be prayed over, nor is he to inherit or be inherited from, unless he was heard crying at birth". It is related from the Prophet (God's peace and blessings be upon him) in a tradition from al-Mughīra ibn Shuʿba that he said, "The infant is to be prayed over". Those who based their opinion on the tradition of Jābir said that this is general and that is explanatory, and it is necessary to interpret the general in terms of the explanatory tradition. Thus, the meaning of the tradition of al-Mughīra turns out to be: "The infant is to be prayed over if it is heard crying at birth". Those who based their opinion on the tradition of al-Mughīra said that it is known that the prerequisite for prayer is *ḥukm* of Islam and life; thus, if the infant moves he is alive and his *ḥukm* is the *ḥukm* of the Muslims, and any living Muslim when he dies is to be prayed over. They preferred this general meaning over the qualified meaning of the other (tradition), because of its conformity with analogy. Some of the jurists deviated and said that infants are not to be prayed over at all. It is related by Abū Dāwūd "that the Prophet (God's peace and blessings be upon him) did not pray over his son Ibrāhīm though he was eight months old". It is also related "that he prayed over him and he was seventy nights old".

They disagreed about praying over the children of (non-Muslim) captives. Mālik, in a narration from him by the Baṣrans, held that a child of the enemy (*ḥarbī*) is not to be prayed over unless he can comprehend Islam, whether he became a captive with his parents or otherwise, and that his *ḥukm* is the same as that of his parents, except when the father accepts Islam, as his status is dependent on the status of the father but not that of the mother. Al-Shāfiʿī agreed with him in this, except that the child's status depends on whichever parent accepts Islam, not on that of the father alone as is maintained by Mālik. Abū Ḥanīfa said that the captive children are to be prayed over and their *ḥukm* is the same as those who captured them. Al-Awzāʿī said that if the Muslims come to own them they are to be prayed over, that is, if they are bought in captivity. He added that this was the practice at the military front (border) and that is the legal verdict. They agreed unanimously that if they were accompanying their parents who had not come into the ownership of a Muslim nor had either of the parents converted to Islam, their *ḥukm* is the *ḥukm* of their parents.

The reason for their disagreement stems from their dispute over whether children of the polytheists would go to heaven or to hell. This is so as it has been laid down in some traditions that they join their parents, that is, their *ḥukm* is the same as the *ḥukm* of their parents. On the other hand, the saying of the Prophet (God's peace and blessings be upon him) that "Each child is born according to *fiṭra* (Islam)" is evidence that their *ḥukm* is that of the believers.

Who has the prior right to pray over the dead person? It is said that it is the *walī* (the next of kin) and it is said that it is the *wālī* (ruler). Those who upheld that it was the ruler held that this prayer is to be similar to the Friday prayer insofar as it is a congregational prayer. Those who maintained that the next of kin had the prior right compared it to all other rights for which the guardian has precedence, as in protection and burial. Most of the jurists maintain that the ruler has a prior right. Abū Bakr ibn al-Mundhir said that al-Ḥusayn ibn ʿAlī asked Saʿīd ibn al-ʿĀṣ, who was the governor of Medina, to come forward and pray over al-Ḥasan ibn ʿAlī (his brother). He said: "Had it not been a *sunna* I would not have come forward". Abū Bakr said: "This is what I uphold".

The majority of the jurists maintain that prayer over the dead is not to be performed in absentia. The body of the dead person must be present. Some said that an absent dead person may be prayed over following the tradition of the Negus. The majority maintain that this was an exceptional case specific to the Negus alone. They disagreed on whether one may pray over a part of the body. The majority maintained that prayer is to be said over a greater part of the body as that falls under the term "dead person". Those who maintained that one may pray over a part of the body said that the sanctity of a part is like the sanctity of the whole, especially when that part is vital for life. These were the jurists who also permitted prayer over an absent body.

4.5.3. *Section 3: The time for prayer over the dead*

They disagreed about the time during which prayer over the dead is permissible. A group of jurists said that one is not to pray over the dead person during the three timings in which prayer has been proscribed, and these are the timings of sunset, sunrise, and the declining of the sun in accordance with the apparent meaning of the tradition of ʿUqba ibn ʿĀmir, "There are three timings in which the Messenger of Allāh (God's peace and blessings be upon him) prohibited us to pray or to bury our dead". A group of jurists said that it is only sunrise and sunset during which this prayer is not to be observed and that it may be observed after the start of the period of the *ʿaṣr* prayer as long as the sun has not turned yellow, and also after dawn, before daybreak. A group of jurists said that prayer is not to be said over a dead person during five timings in which prayer has been proscribed. This was maintained by ʿAṭāʾ, al-Nakhaʿī, and others, and it can be derived analogically from the views of Abū Ḥanīfa. Al-Shāfiʿī said that a dead person may be prayed over at any time as the proscription, in his view, is applicable to prayers having no special cause, not the *sunan* as has previously been discussed.

4.5.4. *Section 4: The location for the prayer*

They disagreed about praying over the dead in a mosque. Some of the jurists permitted it while some disapproved of it and these include Abū Ḥanīfa and some of the disciples of Mālik. This (disapproval) is also related from Mālik, and the implication of this in practice is that the dead person is placed outside the mosque when the people are inside it.

The reason for disagreement over this derives from the difference between the tradition of ʿĀʾisha and that of Abū Hurayra. The tradition from ʿĀʾisha is the one related from Mālik that she requested that the body of Saʿd ibn Abī Waqqāṣ to be taken past her in the mosque so that she may make a supplication for him. The people objected to her doing that, so ʿĀʾisha said, "How quickly people forget! The Messenger of Allāh (God's peace and blessings be upon him) did not pray over Sahl ibn Bayḍāʾ but in the mosque". The tradition of Abū Hurayra is that "the Messenger of Allāh (God's peace and blessings be upon him) said, 'He who prays over the dead in a mosque gains nothing'". The tradition of ʿĀʾisha is authentic, while that of Abū Hurayra is not, or at least its authenticity is disputed. The objection raised by the Companions against ʿĀʾisha's request indicates, however, that the usual practice with them was different. This is also supported by the Prophet's going out of the town to the place of prayer for the Negus.

Some of them claimed that the reason for this is that the corpse of the sons of Adam are like carrion, but this is weak, as the *ḥukm* for the impurity of carrion is a legal determination (not rational), and the *ḥukm* of carrion is not established for the sons of Adam in the absence of an evidence.

Some of the jurists disapproved of prayer over the dead among the graves, because of the proscription of such prayer, while most of the jurists permitted this on the general implication of the words of the Prophet (God's peace and blessings be upon him), "The earth has been deemed a mosque for me and a means of purification".

4.5.5. *Section 5: The conditions of prayer over the dead*

The majority agreed that one of its conditions is purification, just as all of them agreed that one condition is facing the *qibla*. They disagreed about the permissibility of *tayammum* when it is feared that the prayer might be missed. A group of jurists said that one may perform *tayammum* and observe the prayer if he fears that he might miss it. This was the opinion of Abū Ḥanīfa,

Sufyān, al-Awzāʿī, and a group of jurists. Mālik, al-Shāfiʿī, and Aḥmad said that one is not to observe this prayer with a *tayammum.*

The reason for their disagreement stems from the analogy with the obligatory prayer. Those who held that it is similar to that permitted *tayammum* in it, I mean, those who compared (the apprehension of missing) the prayer over the dead to the missing it (the obligatory prayer) due to the passage of time. Those who did not hold it to be similar did not permit *tayammum*, for this prayer, in their view, is a communal obligation or is a communal *sunna*, in accordance with their respective differences. One group gave a deviant opinion and said that it is permitted to pray over the dead without purification. This is the opinion of al-Shaʿbī. These jurists thought that the term "*ṣalāh*" does not include prayer over the dead, but is included in the meaning of supplication for there is no bowing or prostration in it.

4.6. **Chapter 6 Burial**

They agreed unanimously about the obligation of burial. The source for this are the words of the Exalted, "Have We not made the earth a receptacle, both for the living and the dead".[189] and His words, "Then Allāh sent a raven scratching up the ground, to show him how to hide his brother's naked corpse".[190]

Mālik and al-Shāfiʿī disapproved of plastering graves (with gypsum), but Abū Ḥanīfa permitted it. Likewise, a group of jurists disapproved of sitting on the graves, while another group permitted it saying that sitting is a need of human beings. The traditions that have been laid down proscribing these things include the tradition of Jābir ibn ʿAbd Allāh, who said, "The Prophet (God's peace and blessings be upon him) prohibited the plastering of graves, writing on them, sitting on them, and building structures over them". There is also the tradition of ʿAmr ibn Ḥazm, who said, "The Messenger of Allāh (God's peace and blessings be upon him) saw me (sitting) on a grave and said, 'Step down from the grave, do not chastise the person in the grave and you will not be chastised by him'".

Those who permitted sitting on the graves relied on what is related from Zayd ibn al-Thābit, who said, "The Messenger of Allāh (God's peace and blessings be upon him) prohibited sitting on the graves for purposes of impurity, defecation, or urination". They said that this is supported by what is related from Abū Hurayra, who said, "The Messenger of Allāh (God's peace

[189] Qurʾān 77 : 25, 26.
[190] Qurʾān 5 : 31.

and blessings be upon him) said, 'One who sits on a grave and urinates or defecates, sits, as it were, on a firebrand'". This was upheld by Mālik, Abū Ḥanīfa, and al-Shāfiʿī.

V
THE BOOK OF *ZAKĀT*

A comprehensive discussion[191] of this form of worship, after the determination of its obligation, is covered in five chapters. The first chapter is about the persons on whom it is obligatory. The second chapter deals with the identification of the kinds of wealth on which it is imposed. The third chapter is about the identification of the rates and the amounts on which it is levied. The fourth chapter is about the identification of the periods during which it is levied and the periods in which it is not. The fifth chapter is about the identification of the persons for whom it is to be paid and of the amounts due to them.

The determination of its obligation through the Qur'ān, the *sunna*, and from *ijmāʿ* (consensus) is well-known, and there is no dispute about this.

5.1. Chapter 1 The Persons on whom *zakāt* is Obligatory

They agreed that it is obligatory upon every Muslim who is free, *bāligh*, sane, and who owns wealth equal to the (minimum) prescribed scale (*niṣāb*) through a complete (unencumbered) ownership. They disagreed about its obligation upon the orphan, the insane, the slaves, the *ahl al-dhimma*, and the person with deficient (encumbered) ownership like a person who is in debt or is a creditor, or when for example the capital (of the wealth) is held in a trust (*ḥabs, waqf*).

With respect to minors, one group said that *zakāt* is obligatory on their wealth. This was the opinion of ʿAlī, Ibn ʿUmar, Jābir, and ʿĀ'isha from among the Companions, and of Mālik, al-Shāfiʿī, al-Thawrī, Aḥmad, Isḥāq, Abū Thawr, and others from among the jurists of the provinces. Another

[191] Editor's note: The manuscript we are using deals with the Book of *Zakāt* before the Book of Fasting; therefore, we are following the same order, although the Egyptian manuscript deals with the Book of Fasting first.

group said that there is no *zakāt* at all on the wealth of the minor. This was the opinion of al-Nakhaʿī, al-Ḥasan, and Saʿīd ibn Jubayr from the Tābiʿūn. One group of jurists made a distinction between the yield of the land and wealth not derived from the land. They said that there is *zakāt* on the yield from the land, but there is no *zakāt* on what is besides this like cattle, liquid assets, goods (chattel). This was the opinion of Abū Ḥanīfa and his disciples. Yet another group distinguished between liquid assets and other things saying that there is *zakāt* on the wealth except on liquid assets.

The reason for their disagreement over the persons on whom *zakāt* is obligatory arises from their dispute over the nature of the legal form of *zakāt*, whether it is a kind of worship like prayer and fasting or whether it is an obligatory right of the poor over the rich. Those who said that it is worship stipulated *bulūgh* of the person as a condition (for the obligation), while those who said that it is an obligatory right of the poor and the needy over the wealth of the rich did not take into account *bulūgh* of the person, among other things. Those who made a distinction between the yield of the land and what is not derived from it, and also between visible and invisible wealth, for them I am not aware at this time of the evidence relied upon.

Most of the jurists agree that there is no *zakāt* on all categories of the *ahl al-dhimma*, except what is related by a group about the imposition of *zakāt* for the Arab Christians of Banū Taghlab, I mean, for example, that an amount should be taken from them equal to what is taken from the Muslims on all things. Those who held this opinion include al-Shāfiʿī, Abū Ḥanīfa, Aḥmad, and al-Thawrī. There is no narration of an opinion from Mālik on this. These jurists came to this decision on the basis of what ʿUmar ibn al-Khaṭṭāb decided for these people, and it appears that they considered this to be a precedent, but the principles conflict with it.

The jurists are divided on the question of the obligation of *zakāt* on slaves. There are three opinions. One group said that there is no *zakāt* at all on their wealth. This is the opinion of Ibn ʿUmar and Jābir from among the Companions and of Mālik, Aḥmad, and Abū ʿUbayd from among the jurists. Another group said that, in fact, *zakāt* on the wealth of the slave is levied on the master. This was al-Shāfiʿī's opinion as related by Ibn al-Mundhir, and of al-Thawrī, Abū Ḥanīfa, and his disciples. A third group imposed *zakāt* on the slave for his wealth. This is related from Ibn ʿUmar (again) from among the Companions, and it was the opinion of ʿAṭā" from among the Tābiʿūn, and of Abū Thawr, the Ẓāhirites, and some others from among the jurists. The majority of those who said that there is no *zakāt* on the wealth of the slave also maintained that there is no *zakāt* on the wealth of the *mukātab* until he is free. Abū Thawr, however, held that there is *zakāt* on the wealth of the *mukātab*.

The reason for their disagreement over *zakāt* on the wealth of the slave is based on their dispute over whether the slave owns his wealth through a complete ownership or whether this is deficient. Those who maintained that his ownership is deficient and it is the master who is the owner, as his wealth cannot be separated from that of the master, said that the *zakāt* is due from the master. Those who maintained that *zakāt* is to be imposed on one of the two persons who owns it through a complete ownership said that this person is not the master for the wealth is in the possession of the slave not in that of the master, and it is also not the slave's for the master has the right to take it away from him. They, therefore, held that there is no *zakāt* at all on the wealth of the slave. Those who maintained that possession of the wealth determines the incidence of *zakāt*, because of the right of disposal in it on the analogy of the right of disposal of a free man, said that the *zakāt* is to be imposed on the slave, especially in the view of those who held that the general communication of the law includes both free men and slaves and that the payment of *zakāt* is a worship that relates to the subject (*mukallaf*) because of his right of disposal in the wealth.

The jurists disagreed about those owners (of wealth) who are in debt, and whose debts are greater than their wealth, or they cover an amount on which *zakāt* can be levied while they have in hand wealth on which *zakāt* is due. A group of jurists said that there is no *zakāt* on the wealth, whether it is in the form of grain or something else, unless the debts are deducted from it. If the remaining amount (after payment of debts) reaches the minimum amount which is subject to *zakāt*, it is to be paid otherwise not. This was the opinion of al-Thawrī, Abū Thawr, Ibn al-Mubārak, and a group of jurists. Abū Ḥanīfa and his disciples said that debts do not ward off *zakāt* on grain, but they do prevent it on other kinds of wealth. Mālik said that debts prevent *zakāt* on liquid assets alone, unless these include goods that can pay off the debt, in which case *zakāt* is not prevented. A group of jurists maintained, in contrast to the first view, that debts do not prevent *zakāt* at all.

The reason for their disagreement (again) stems from their dispute on whether *zakāt* is a form of worship or a right assessed on the wealth for the needy. Those who maintained that it is a right due to needy said that there is no *zakāt* on the wealth of a person who is burdened with debt, as the right of the creditor is prior, with respect to time, to the right of the needy, for the wealth in reality is owned by the creditor and not the person who has possession over it. Those who maintained that it is worship said that it is to be levied on the person who has possession of it, as that is the basis of liability (*taklīf*) and a criterion for imposing the obligation on the subject irrespective of his being in debt. Further, there is a conflict here between two kinds of rights, the right of Allāh and the right of man, and the right of Allāh has a higher priority for being met. Yet the dropping of *zakāt* in the case of the debtors is closer to the purposes of the (divine) law, because of the words of the Prophet (God's peace and blessings be upon him), "(It comprises) a charitable donation that is acquired from the wealthy and granted to the poor", and debtors are not wealthy. Those who distinguished between grain and other kinds of wealth, and between liquid assets and tied assets, for them I cannot find a clear analogy. Abū ʿUbayd used to say that if it cannot be known whether the person has a debt, except by his own claim, he is not to be considered truthful, but if it can be known (through other means) *zakāt* is not to be levied on him. This does not contradict the opinion of those who maintain that *zakāt* is to be dropped because of debt, in fact, it contradicts those who maintain that he is to be considered truthful for claiming a debt just as he is deemed truthful in stating the amount of his wealth.

The wealth that exists as a liability, that is, as a liability upon someone else (credit), and is not in the possession of the owner, is also a debt, and about this too they differed. A group of jurists said that there is no *zakāt* on this even when it returns to the hands of its owner until the conditions of *zakāt* are met while it is with the possessor, and this is the passage of a year (*ḥawl*) while it is in his possession. This is one of the two opinions of al-Shāfiʿī, and it was maintained by Abū Thawr or is derivable by analogy from his views. Another group of jurists said that if he comes to possess it he is to be charged for the past years (for which it stood unpaid). Mālik said that he is to be charged *zakāt* for a single *ḥawl* (year), even if it has stayed with the debtors for a number of years, in case the principal has been given in return for compensation. If it was not linked to compensation, like inheritance, then the *ḥawl* begins from the moment of possession. There are a number of details about this in the School (Mālik's).

In this topic there is also their dispute about *zakāt* on fruit when the trees belong to a trust, and about the land held on a tenancy, as to who is liable for the *zakāt* on the yield, whether it is owed by the landlord or the tenant. There is also their disagreement over *kharāj* land when it is transferred from those liable for *kharāj* to the Muslims, who are liable for *ʿushr*. Then there is the dispute over *ʿushr* land when it is converted to *kharāj* land, that is given to the *ahl al-dhimma*. It appears that the reason for dispute over all this is due to the fact that these are deficient forms of ownership.

5.1.1. Issue 1

This issue relates to fruit from trees, when the trees are the property of a trust. Mālik and al-Shāfiʿī used to impose *zakāt* on them, while Makḥūl and Ṭāwūs used to say that there is no *zakāt* on them. A group of jurists used to make a distinction when the trees were a trust for the needy generally or for a specified group. They imposed *zakāt* on them when the beneficiaries were a determined (specified) group, but they did not do so when the beneficiaries were the needy generally. There is no justification in imposing the *zakāt* on the needy as two disqualifying factors operate in this: first, it amounts to a deficient ownership, and second, the needy are an indeterminate category of people on whom the *zakāt* funds are to be spent and not those from who it is due.

5.1.2. Issue 2

The second issue relates to land given out on rent. It deals with the question as to who is liable for *zakāt* on the yield of this land. A group of jurists said that the *zakāt* is to be levied on the tenant, who is the owner of the plants. This was the opinion of Mālik, al-Shāfiʿī, al-Thawrī, Ibn al-Mubārak, Abū Thawr, and a group of jurists. Abū Ḥanīfa and his disciples maintained that *zakāt* is due from the owner of the land and the person who rents it from him does not owe anything.

The reason for their disagreement arises from the question of whether *ʿushr* is a duty related to the land or to cultivation or to both. o one has said that it is a duty related to both when, in fact, it is a duty related to both. They agreed that it is a duty incumbent upon one of the two, but they disagreed on which one has precedence for being associated with a point on which there is agreement, and that is the occasion when the crop as well as the land belong to a single owner. The majority maintained that it is related to the thing from which *zakāt* is to be paid, and that is grain (or the yield). Abū Ḥanīfa maintained, however, that it is related to the thing that is the basis of the obligation, and that is land.

With respect to their dispute over *kharāj* land, when it is transferred to the Muslims, as to whether *ʿushr* is imposed on it along with *kharāj* or whether there is no *ʿushr*, the majority maintained that there is *ʿushr*, that is, *zakāt*, while Abū Ḥanīfa and his disciples held that there is no *ʿushr* on it. The reason for their disagreement stems, as we have said, from the question of whether *zakāt* is a duty related to the land or to the crop. If we maintain that it is a duty related to the land, then, two duties cannot be linked to it at the same time, and these are *ʿushr* and *kharāj*. If we maintain that *zakāt* is linked to the crop, then, *kharāj* would be assigned to the land and *zakāt* to the crop. This dispute arises because the ownership is deficient as we have stated and it was because of this that the jurists disagreed over the sale of *kharāj* land. If, however, *ʿushr* land is transferred to a *dhimmī* who cultivates it, the majority maintain that there is no liability on him. Al-Nuʿmān held that when the *dhimmī* buys *ʿushr* land it is converted into *kharāj* land. It appears that he considered *ʿushr* to be a duty owed on Muslim land and he considered *kharāj* to be a duty owed on the land of the *dhimmīs*, but on the basis of this rule it was necessary for him to say that if the *kharāj* land was transferred to the Muslims it would be converted to *ʿushr* land, just as in his view if the *ʿushr* land was transferred to a *dhimmī* it would be converted to *kharāj* land.

5.1.3. Issue 3: Issues related to the owner of wealth

There are sub-issues related to the owner of wealth the discussion of which is suitably placed is this section. The first of these is (the situation) when a man sets aside *zakāt* but it is lost. Second, when the setting aside of *zakāt* is possible but when part of the wealth is destroyed before *zakāt* is set aside. Third, where the owner was under an obligation to pay *zakāt*, but died before paying it. Fourth, who is to pay *zakāt* if he sells off the crop or fruit on which *zakāt* was due, and similarly when he gives it away as a gift.

5.1.3.1. Sub-issue 1

This (issue) deals with the problem where the owner sets aside *zakāt* and it is lost. A group of jurists said that he is to be given credit for it. Another group said that he is liable for it till he delivers it to its location. A third group made a distinction between his setting it aside later than when it was possible to do so and between setting it aside (promptly) at the beginning of the time when the obligation arises and when it is possible to do so. Some of these jurists said that if he sets it aside some days after the time at which the obligation arises and the possibility to do so, then he is liable but if he sets it aside at the first moment obligation arises and there was no negligence on his part he is not liable. This is a well-known opinion in Mālik's school. A fourth group of jurists said that if there was negligence on his part he is to compensate for it, but if he was not negligent he is to pay *zakāt* on the remainder alone. This was the opinion of Abū Thawr and al-Shāfiʿī. A fifth group said that what has been lost is to be counted as a loss for all parties, and the needy people as well as the owner are to be considered co-owners in proportion to their shares in the remaining wealth, as (is the case) with two partners when part of the common capital is lost but remain partners in the residue in the same ratio. Thus, we arrive at five opinions on the issue: first, that he is not to compensate for the loss at all; second, that he always compensates; third, that he compensates if he was negligent, but does not if he was not negligent; fourth, that he compensates if he was negligent and pays *zakāt* on the residue if he was not; and fifth, that they (the owner and the needy) become partners in the remaining wealth.

5.1.3.2. Sub-issue 2

When part of the wealth is lost after the commencement of the obligation and before it was possible to set aside *zakāt*, a group of jurists said that he pays *zakāt* on the residue, while another group held that the needy and the owner of the wealth are treated as partners part of whose capital has been lost.

The reason for their disagreement stems from the comparison between *zakāt* and debts, that is, the duty is associated with liability and not with the substance of the wealth, or it is its comparison with duties that are related to the substance of the property not with the liability of the person who is in possession of the wealth, as in the case of trustees and others. Those who considered the owners of wealth to be similar to the trustees said that if he sets it aside and it is lost there is nothing due from him. Those who considered them similar to debtors said that they are to compensate (for the loss). Those who made a distinction on the basis of negligence, and the absence of it, associated them with trustees from all aspects, as the trustee compensates (for the loss) in case of negligence. Those who maintained that if he was not negligent he is to pay *zakāt* on the residue compared the person who had lost part of his wealth after setting aside *zakāt* with one who had lost part of his wealth before the commencement of the obligation; just as that person pays *zakāt* at the time of the obligation on what exists with him, this person will pay *zakāt* on what exists with him. The reason for the disagreement arises from the variation in the association of the owner with a debtor, a trustee, a partner, and with one who has lost part of his wealth before the obligation.

If, however, *zakāt* became due and he was able to set it aside but did not do so till part of his wealth was lost, the jurists agreed, as far as I know, that he is liable except in the case of cattle, according to those who hold that the condition for their obligation is the arrival of the *zakāt* collector after the *ḥawl*, and this is Mālik's opinion.

5.1.3.3. Sub-issue 3

This relates to the person who dies after the commencement of the obligation of *zakāt*. A group of jurists said that it is to be taken out from his capital.[192] This was the opinion of al-Shāfiʿī, Aḥmad, Isḥāq, and Abū Thawr. Another group said that *zakāt* is to be paid only if he leaves a testament to the effect that it is to be paid from his estate. In that case, it is to be taken out from the third of the estate. Otherwise nothing is due. Some of these jurists said that *zakāt* is to be satisfied first if it is as much as the third or is less than that, while others said that it is not to be satisfied first. Both opinions are narrated from Mālik, but the well-known opinion is that it is to be treated as a bequest.

5.1.3.4. Sub-issue 4

With respect to their disagreement about wealth that is sold after *zakāt* has become due on it, a group of jurists said that the person from whom *zakāt* is due (the seller) may take the *zakāt* from the wealth itself, and the buyer is to have recourse to the seller for its value. This was the opinion of Abū Thawr.

[192] That is, from his estate after payment of the cost of his funeral and before distribution among his heirs.

Another group of jurists said that the sale is rescinded, and this was al-Shāfiʿī's opinion. Abū Ḥanīfa said that the buyer has an option between the execution of the sale or its revocation, and the *ʿushr* is to be taken from the fruit or from the grain on which *zakāt* was due. Mālik said that the seller is liable for the payment of *zakāt*.

The reason for their disagreement arises from the comparison of the sale of the property with its loss and destruction. Those who considered them similar said that *zakāt* is the liability of the person destroying the property or causing its loss. Those who maintained that sale does not amount to destruction of the substance of the wealth nor its loss, but amounts to sale by a person of what does not belong to him said that *zakāt* is linked to the substance of the wealth. Whether the sale is to be rescinded is a separate discussion that will be taken up in the section on sales, God willing. Their dispute about *zakāt* on wealth that has been alienated by a gift is of a similar nature.

In some of these issues that we have mentioned there are detailed discussions in the School that we have not deemed proper for presentation here, as that is not compatible with our aim. Further, it becomes difficult to give the reasons for these distinctions, because most of them are based on *istiḥsān*, like their discussion of the details of debts that are liable for *zakāt* and those that are not, and debts that cause a waiver of *zakāt* and those that do not. This, then, is what we considered should be mentioned in this chapter and it relates to the identification of the person from whom *zakāt* is due, to the conditions of ownership with which it becomes due, and to the *aḥkām* of the person from whom it is due.

One well-known *ḥukm* from among the *aḥkām* of such a person remains and that relates to the question as to what is the *ḥukm* of the person who refuses to pay *zakāt*, but does not deny its obligation.

Abū Bakr (God be pleased with him) said that his *ḥukm* is that of the apostate. This is how he ruled in the case of those Arabs who refused to pay *zakāt* (after the death of the Prophet), and he fought with them and made their children captive. He was opposed in this by ʿUmar (God be pleased with him) who freed those of them who had been made captive. The majority adopted ʿUmar's view. A group decided to impute disbelief to those who refused to perform any of the religious obligations although they did not deny their being obligatory.

The reason for the disagreement stems from whether the term "faith (*īmān*)", which is the opposite of disbelief, can be applied to mean belief alone without practice, or whether the existence of accompanying practice is one of its conditions. Some of them held that one of its conditions is accompanying practice. Some did not stipulate this even when the person did not render verbal testimony (*shahāda*) for it. If he merely considered it to be true, he was considered to be a believer (*muʾmin*) in the sight of Allāh. The majority, and these are the Ahl al-Sunna, maintained that acts (practice) are not to be stipulated in it, that is, for the conviction of faith the opposite of which is disbelief, except the pronouncement of *shahāda*, because of the words of the Prophet (God's peace and blessings be upon him), "I have been commanded to fight the people until they say *lā ilāha illallāh,* and then believe in me". Thus, he stipulated speech with knowledge (of faith), which is a kind of act. Those who held the remaining obligatory acts to be similar to speech said that all the obligatory acts are a condition for the knowledge that is faith. Those who considered speech to be the same as the remaining acts, about which the majority agreed that they are not a condition for the knowledge that is faith, said that confirmation (by words) alone is a condition for faith, and with that his *ḥukm* becomes, in the sight of Allāh, the *ḥukm* of a believer (*muʾmin*). The (other) two views are deviant, and the exemption from all the acts by two pronouncements of the *shahāda* is what the majority uphold.

5.2. **Chapter 2 The Kinds of Wealth Subject to *Zakāt***

They agreed about some of the categories in which *zakāt* is obligatory and disagreed about others. The categories which they agreed upon include two kinds of minerals, namely, gold and silver that are not moulded into jewelry, three categories of animals, namely, camels, cows and sheep, two categories of grains namely wheat and barley, and two categories of fruit, namely dates and raisins. There is some dispute about olives.

They disagreed about gold only when it is in the form of jewelry. This is so as the jurists of Ḥijāz, Mālik, al-Layth, and al-Shāfiʿī, maintained that there is no *zakāt* on it if it is intended for adornment and wearing. Abū Ḥanīfa and his disciples said that *zakāt* is to be levied on it. The reason for disagreement stems from its vacillation between being goods and being gold and silver that are used primarily as a medium of exchange for all other things. Those who held them to be similar to goods, whose primary purpose is utility, said that there is no *zakāt* in it (jewelry). Those who considered them similar to gold and silver, the primary purpose of which is to facilitate exchange, said that it is subject to *zakāt*. There is also another reason for their disagreement, and that is the conflict of traditions on the issue. It is related from Jābir from the Prophet (God's peace and blessings be upon him) that he said, "There is no *zakāt* in jewelry". ʿAmr ibn Shuʿayb has related from his father from his grandfather "that a woman came up to the Messenger of Allāh (God's peace and blessings be upon him) accompanied by her daughter, who was wearing (two) gold bracelets on her hands. He said to her, 'Do you pay *zakāt* on these?' She said, 'No!' He said, 'Would it please you if Allāh were to put on your hands, on the Day of Judgment, two bracelets of fire?' She took them off and placing them before the Prophet (God's peace and blessings be upon him) and said, 'They are for Allāh and His Messenger'". Both traditions are weak, particularly the tradition of Jābir.

Another major reason for their disagreement stems from the vacillation of jewelry acquired for adornment between its being gold and silver, the primary purpose of which is facilitating trade and not utility, and between being goods, whose primary purpose is the opposite of gold and silver, that is, use and not facilitating exchange. I mean by exchange their existence as currencies. Mālik's opinion differed about jewelry that is acquired for renting. He held it once to be similar to jewelry that is acquired for adornment, and on another occasion held it to be similar to gold metal that is used for transactions.

Their disagreement over animals includes their dispute over species and their dispute over categories. The disagreement about species relates to horses, as the majority maintain that there is no *zakāt* in horses. Abū Ḥanīfa maintained that if they pasture freely and their purpose is breeding there is *zakāt* on them, that is, when they are male and female. The reason for the disagreement arises from the conflict of analogy with the text as well as what is believed to be a conflict of one text with another. The text implying that there is no *zakāt* on them is the saying of the Prophet (God's peace and blessings be upon him), "There is no *ṣadaqa* (*zakāt*) for a Muslim on his horse and on his slave". The analogy that conflicts with this general meaning is that the purpose (of keeping) pasturing horses is growth and breeding because of which they resemble cows and sheep. The text that is assumed to conflict with this general meaning is the saying of the Prophet (God's peace and blessings be upon him) when "he mentioned horse and did not forget the right of Allāh in the horses themselves [as animals subject to *zakāt*], as well as in their growth as wealth". Abū Ḥanīfa held that the right of Allāh here means the payment of *zakāt* on them, and this is to be applied to the pasturing horses among them. The Qāḍī (Ibn Rushd) said: "It is better if this text is treated as unelaborated (*mujmal*) rather than general, so that it may be used as an argument for *zakāt*". Abū Ḥanīfa was opposed by his two disciples, Abū Yūsuf and Muḥammad on this issue. It is, however, established from ʿUmar, may Allāh be pleased with him, that he used to assess *zakāt* on them. It is, therefore, said that this was done as a voluntary contribution by the payees.

Their disagreement over categories (of animals) relates to (freely) pasturing camels, cows, and sheep as distinguished from the non-pasturing animals. A group of jurists imposed *zakāt* on these three categories irrespective of their being pasturing or non-pasturing animals. This was the opinion of al-Layth and Mālik. The remaining jurists of the provinces held that there is no *zakāt* on the non-pasturing animals in these three categories.

The reason for their disagreement comes from the conflict of an absolute meaning with a qualified meaning, and the conflict of analogy with the general implication of a text. The absolute meaning is in the saying of the Prophet (God's peace and blessings be upon him), "In forty sheep is [the *zakāt* of] one sheep". The qualified meaning is in the saying of the Prophet (God's peace and blessings be upon him), "On pasturing sheep there is *zakāt*". Those who gave predominance to the absolute implication over the qualified said that there is *zakāt* in pasturing as well as non-pasturing (animals), while those who gave predominance to the qualified meaning said *zakāt* is levied on the pasturing animals alone. It is possible to say that the reason for disagreement stems also from the conflict of the indirect indication of the text (*dalīl al-khiṭāb*) with the general implication. The indirect indication of the text in the saying of the Prophet (God's peace and blessings be upon him), "On pasturing sheep there is *zakāt*", implies that there is no *zakāt* on a non-pasturing sheep, while the general meaning in the saying of the Prophet, "In forty sheep is one sheep", implies that pasturing sheep here have the same status as the non-pasturing sheep, but the general meaning (as a rule) is stronger than the indirect indication of the text, just as the predominance of the qualified meaning over the absolute meaning is better known. Abū Muḥammad ibn Ḥazm, however, held that the absolute meaning governs the qualified meaning, and that on sheep, pasturing or non-pasturing, there is *zakāt*, so also on camels, because of the saying of the Prophet (God's peace and blessings be upon him), "There is no *ṣadaqa* on what is less than five camels", and as there is no established tradition about cows it is necessary to rely upon consensus which says that *zakāt* is levied on pasturing cows alone. Thus, with the distinction of cows from the rest this becomes a third opinion.

The analogy that is in conflict with the general implication of the saying of the Prophet (God's peace and blessings be upon him), "In forty sheep is one sheep", implies that it is the pasturing animal whose purpose is growth and profit, which is present here to the maximum. Moreover, *zakāt* is levied on surplus wealth and surplus is usually found in pasturing wealth (animals), and it is because of this that *ḥawl* (passage of one year) has been prescribed for it. Those who restricted the general meaning with this analogy did not impose *zakāt* on animals other than pasturing animals, but those who did not restrict it and held that the general meaning is stronger imposed it equally on both categories.

This, then, is what they differed over in the case of animals on which *zakāt* is levied. They agreed unanimously that there is no *zakāt* on what is derived from animals, except in the case of honey, over which they differed. The majority maintained that there is no *zakāt* on it. A group of jurists said that *zakāt* is levied on it. The reason for their disagreement stems from their dispute over the authentication of the tradition regarding on this subject, and that is the saying of the Prophet (God's peace and blessings be upon him), "For every ten bags is one bag". It is recorded by al-Tirmidhī and others.

The crops (vegetation) over which they disagreed, after their agreement over the four categories we have mentioned, relates to the species of crops. Some of them did not uphold *zakāt* on anything besides these four categories. This was the opinion of Ibn Abī Laylā, Sufyān al-Thawrī, and Ibn al-Mubārak. Some of them maintained that *zakāt* is to be levied on any vegetation (crop) that can be stored as food. This is the opinion of Mālik and al-Shāfiʿī. Some said that *zakāt* is to be levied on all that is produced from the land, except for grass, wood, and cane. This was Abū Ḥanīfa's the opinion.

The reason for disagreement among those who restricted *zakāt* to the categories agreed upon and those who extended it to storable food, is related to their dispute over whether *zakāt* on these four categories is specific to their substance or is due to an underlying cause they represent, which is that they are used as food. Those who maintained that it is for the categories in themselves restricted the obligation to them, and those who said that it is because of the underlying cause that they are food extended the obligation to all kinds of food. The reason for disagreement among those who restricted the obligation to food and those who extended it to everything produced from land, except those over which there is consensus, like grass, wood, and cane, is based on the conflict of analogy with a general text. The text implying a general application is the saying of the Prophet (God's peace and blessings be upon him), "There is *ʿushr* in what is watered by the sky, but in that which is irrigated by the watering-can there is one-half of *ʿushr*". *Mā* (what), a relative pronoun like the term *alladhī*, implies generality. The other text implying the general meaning are the words of the Exalted, "He it is Who produceth gardens trellised and untrellised, and the date-palm, and crops of divers flavour, and the olive and the pomegranate, like and unlike. Eat ye of the fruit thereof when it fruiteth, and pay the due thereof upon the harvest day".[193] Analogy implies that the purpose of *zakāt* is the elimination of need, and this is usually done through what is food. Those who restricted the general meaning with this analogy waived *zakāt* on what is other than food, but those who gave predominance to the general implication extended it to what is besides it, except the things excluded by consensus.

Those who agreed about food differed over certain things with reference to their dispute over whether these are in the category of food, and whether

[193] Qurʾān 6 : 142.

analogy can be constructed upon that which is agreed upon. This is like the disagreement of Mālik and al-Shāfiʿī over olives. Mālik upheld the obligation of *zakāt* on them, while al-Shāfiʿī disallowed this in his later opinion rendered in Egypt. The reason for disagreement is based on their dispute over whether olives are storable food. Of the same nature is the disagreement of Mālik's disciples about the obligation of *zakāt* on figs. Some of them held that *zakāt* is to be levied on fruits but not vegetables, and this is the opinion of Ibn Ḥabīb, because of the words of the Exalted, "He it is Who produceth gardens trellised and untrellised, and the date-palm, and crops of divers flavour, and the olive and the pomegranate, like and unlike. Eat ye of the fruit thereof when it fruiteth, and pay the due thereof upon the harvest day".[194] Those who distinguished between fruit and olives through the interpretation of the verse have no basis, except a very weak one.

They agreed that there is no *zakāt* on goods (chattel includes slaves) that are not intended for trade, but they disagreed about the imposition of *zakāt* on goods that are employed in trade. The jurists of the provinces upheld its obligation, but the Ẓāhirites disallowed it. The reason for their disagreement arises from their dispute about the imposition of *zakāt* through analogy, and also their dispute over the authenticity of the tradition of Samura ibn Jundub, who said, "The Messenger of Allāh (God's peace and blessings be upon him) used to order us to set aside *zakāt* on goods that we included in trade". It is also related from the Prophet (God's peace and blessings be upon him) that he said, "Pay *zakāt* on wheat". The analogy on which the majority relied is that the goods acquired for trade have growth as their purpose and therefore resemble the three species on which *zakāt* is levied by agreement, that is, crops, cattle, and gold and silver. Al-Ṭaḥāwī believed that *zakāt* on goods is established from ʿUmar and from Ibn ʿUmar and none of the Companions opposed them. Some thought that such a situation amounts to a consensus of the Companions, that is, when an opinion is transmitted from one of them, and nothing is transmitted from another Companion against it, but this is weak.

5.3. Chapter 3 The *Niṣāb* and Rates of *Zakāt*

This chapter deals with the identification of the *niṣāb* of each category of wealth on which *zakāt* is levied, and that is the quantity on which *zakāt* is charged for those items reaching the *niṣāb*. It also deals with the identification of the amount due on an item, that is, on itself and its quantity. We shall

[194] Qurʾān 6 : 142.

mention those things that they agreed upon and those over which they differed for each of the species, whether agreed upon or disputed. We will divide the discussion into sections. The first section is about gold and silver. The second is about camels. The third is about sheep. The fourth is about cows. The fifth is about crops. The sixth is about goods.

5.3.1. *Section 1: The* niṣāb *and rates for gold and silver*

They agreed that the quantity of silver on which *zakāt* is levied is five *awqiya* [ounces], because of the authentic saying of of the Prophet (God's peace and blessings be upon him), "There is no *ṣadaqa* in what is less than five *awqiya* [ounces] of silver". They disagreed about the stipulation of a *niṣāb* for minerals other than silver, and also about the amount due on them. An *awqiya*, in their view, was equal to five *dirhams* by weight. They agreed that the amount due on this is one-fourth of a tenth. This applies to gold as well, that is, *zakāt* is one-fortieth. This is so as long as they are in a state when they do not cease to be minerals.

Under this topic they disagreed over five points: first, the *niṣāb* for gold; second, does *waqṣ* apply to them, that is, is there no increase in *zakāt* with an increase in an amount above the *niṣāb*;[195] third, can one category be added to another for purposes of *zakāt* so that they are considered as an independent category, that is, at the time of the fixation of the *niṣāb*, or are they two separate categories; fourth, is it a condition for the *niṣāb* that there be a single owner for it and not two; and fifth, the consideration of the *niṣāb* for minerals, their *ḥawl*, and the amount due on them.

5.3.1.1. Issue 1

The first issue deals with their disagreement over the *niṣāb* of gold. The majority of the jurists maintain that *zakāt* is to be levied on twenty *dīnārs* by weight as it would be in two hundred *dirhams*. This is the opinion of Mālik, al-Shāfiʿī, Abū Ḥanīfa, their disciples, Aḥmad, and a group of the jurists of the provinces. A group of jurists, including al-Ḥasan ibn Abī al-Ḥasan al-Baṣrī and most of the disciples of Dāwūd ibn ʿAlī, held that there is nothing to be paid on gold until it reaches an amount of forty *dīnārs*, and in that the amount due is one-fourth of a tenth – one *dīnār*. A third group said that there is no *zakāt* on gold until its market rate equals two hundred *dirhams*[196] or it has that

[195] *Waqṣ* is to be imagined in the *zakāt* on animals. For example, if one sheep is to be paid for five camels and someone has eight camels, that is, less than ten or two units of the *niṣāb*, it will be a case of *waqṣ*. The excess over one unit of the *niṣāb* is disregarded until the next unit of the *niṣāb* is complete. Here the author raises the question whether this could be applicable in the case of gold and silver.

[196] ote that the rate of gold is being worked out in silver *dirhams*.

value. If it reaches that value one-fourth of a tenth is due on it, whether its weight is twenty *dīnārs* or less or more. This applies to an amount that is less than forty *dīnārs*, but when it reaches an amount of forty *dīnārs* its own weight is to be taken into account and not its value in *dirhams* or its market rate or value.

The reason for their disagreement over the *niṣāb* of gold is that nothing has been established about it from the Prophet (God's peace and blessings be upon him), in the manner of the *niṣāb* of silver. The tradition related from al-Ḥasan ibn ʿUmāra through ʿAlī that the Prophet (God's peace and blessings be upon him) said, "Bring forth the *zakāt* on gold at [the rate of] one-half *dīnār* for every twenty *dīnārs*" is not, according to most, a tradition that can be acted upon, because of its being an isolated tradition narrated by al-Ḥasan ibn ʿUmāra alone. Those for whom this tradition was not authentic relied upon consensus, which is their agreement about the obligation of *zakāt* on forty *dīnārs*. Mālik, however, relied upon *ʿamal* (practice at Medina) and for that reason he said in *al-Muwaṭṭaʾ*: "The *sunna* over which there is no dispute among us is that *zakāt* is due on twenty *dīnārs* as it is due on two hundred *dirhams*". Those who determined that *zakāt* is due on what is less than forty did so on the basis of *dirhams*. As both gold and silver belonged to the same species, in their view, they deemed silver to be the basis, because a text has proved authentic for it. They, therefore, determined that (the value of) gold is to be dependent on that of silver by value and not on the basis of weight. This applies in the absence of consensus. In addition, in some traditions the words are, "There is no *ṣadaqa* in less than five *awqiya* (ounces) of *riqa*", and it is said that the term *riqa* applies to both gold and silver.

5.3.1.2. Issue 2

They disagreed over what is in excess of the value of the *niṣāb* (of gold and silver). The majority maintained that the weight in excess of two hundred *dirhams* is to be assessed in the same ratio, that is, one-fourth of a tenth. Those who upheld this opinion include al-Shāfiʿī, Abū Yūsuf and Muḥammad, the disciples of Abū Ḥanīfa, Aḥmad ibn Ḥanbal, and a group of jurists. Another group of jurists, mostly from Iraq, maintained that there is nothing due on what is in excess of two hundred *dirhams* until the excess reaches an amount of forty *dirhams*. If it does reach an amount of forty *dirhams*, one-fourth of a tenth is due on it, which is one *dirham*. This was the opinion of Abū Ḥanīfa, Zufar, and a group from among their disciples.

The reason for disagreement arises from their dispute about the authenticity of the tradition of al-Ḥasan ibn ʿUmāra, the conflict between the indirect indication of the text with it the tradition and also their vacillation between two bases in this context, each carrying a different *ḥukm*, and these bases are cattle and grains. Al-Ḥasan ibn ʿUmāra related his tradition from Abū Isḥāq from ʿĀṣim ibn Ḍumra from ʿAlī from the Prophet (God's peace and blessings be upon him), "I have waived the *ṣadaqa* on horses and slaves, but pay on gold and silver at (the rate of) one-fourth of a tenth from every two hundred *dirhams* being five *dirhams*, (and pay) one-half *dīnār* for every twenty *dīnārs*. There is nothing due on two hundred *dirhams* until a year has passed over them and then five *dirhams* are due on them, and what is in excess of this there is due a *dirham* for every forty *dirhams*, and for every four *dīnārs* in excess of the (first) twenty *dīnārs* is a *dirham* until the excess reaches forty *dīnārs*, and then for every forty *dīnārs* is a *dīnār* and for every twenty-four *dīnārs* is one-half *dīnār* and a *dirham*". The indirect indication of the text (*dalīl al-khiṭāb*) that is in conflict with it arises from the saying of the Prophet (God's peace and blessings be upon him), "There is no *ṣadaqa* on less than five *awqiya* of silver", as it means that what is in excess of this is subject to *ṣadaqa*. As to their vacillation between the two bases, which are cattle and grain, the text about *waqṣ* has been laid down for cattle, and they agreed that there is no *waqṣ* in grain. Those who held silver and gold to be similar to cattle said that *waqṣ* operates in it, while those who held them to be similar to grains said that there is no *waqṣ* in them.

5.3.1.3. Issue 3

The third issue deals with the adding of gold to silver for purposes of *zakāt*. According to Mālik, Abū Ḥanīfa, and a group of jurists *dirhams* may be added to *dīnārs*, and if the *niṣāb* is attained by combining them *zakāt* becomes due on it. Al-Shāfiʿī, Abū Thawr, and Dāwūd said that gold is not to be added to silver nor is silver to be added to gold.

The reason for their disagreement stems from whether *zakāt* is levied on each of these categories for a reason inherent in (each of) them or for an underlying reason that is common to all, and that is, as is maintained by the jurists, the attribute of their being sources of capital (currencies) and a means of valuating consumable things. Those who maintained that the consideration in each is the inherent substance, because of which the *niṣāb* for each is different, said that these are two separate species, as is the case with cows and sheep and, therefore, one is not to be added to the other. Those who maintained that the consideration in them is for the common attribute that we have mentioned, permitted the adding of one category to the other. It appears that the differences should be taken into account due to the variation in *aḥkām* insofar as the names are different and insofar as the commodities themselves are different, although the goal of making profit provides a common basis, and that is what was taken into account by Mālik (God bless him) in this topic, and also in the case of *ribā*.

Those who permitted adding of the categories together differed over the description of addition. Mālik held that they are to be combined on the basis of a determined currency (rate), and this is to be done by converting one *dīnār* into ten *dirhams*, as was held by him earlier. Thus, a person who has ten *dīnārs* and one hundred *dirhams* is under an obligation to pay *zakāt* on both, in his view. He permitted that any one of them may be converted into the other. Some other jurists, out of these, said that the addition is to be done on the basis of value at the time of *zakāt*. If, therefore, a person has one hundred *dirhams* and nine *mithqāls* having a value of one hundred *dirhams* he is under an obligation to pay *zakāt* on them. If the person has one hundred *dirhams* that are equal to eleven *mithqāls* and he also has nine *mithqāls*, then, he too is obliged to pay *zakāt* on them. Those who held this opinion include Abū Ḥanīfa, and a similar opinion was expressed by al-Thawrī, except that he preferred being careful in favour of the needy, that is, in the use of value or a determined rate (of conversion) for addition. Some of these jurists maintained that a category lesser in quantity should be (converted and) added to the one greater in quantity, and the category greater in quantity should not be added to the one lesser in quantity. Some other jurists said that it is always the *dīnārs* that are (converted and) added by value, whether they are less in number than the *dirhams* or more, and that the *dirhams* are not to be added to the *dīnārs*, as it is *dirhams* that are the basis and *dīnārs* are dependent on them, for there is no established tradition or consensus about *dīnārs* until they reach the number of forty. Some maintained that if the person possessed the *niṣāb* in one category, the other category is to be added to it whether it is less or more. They did not attempt to make a *niṣāb* through addition when neither reaches the *niṣāb* alone.

The reason for such entanglement was their desire to render the *niṣāb* of two separate things having different weights into a single *niṣāb*. All this is meaningless. Perhaps, those who desired to add one category to the other created a new *ḥukm* in the law where there is no *ḥukm*, for they came up with a *niṣāb* that is neither the *niṣāb* of gold nor that of silver. It is difficult, in practice relating to the imposition of liability and the issuance of injunctions, to lay down specific *aḥkām* for such probable cases. The *sharᶜ*, therefore, remains silent on them and this silence leads to disagreement to such an extent. The Lawgiver had sent the Prophet (God's peace and blessings be upon him) for the removal of disputes.

5.3.1.4. Issue 4

According to Mālik and Abū Ḥanīfa, two partners are not under an obligation to pay *zakāt* individually until each one of them possesses the *niṣāb*. According to al-Shāfiᶜī, combined wealth has the *ḥukm* of a single individual.

The reason for disagreement stems from the consensus upon the saying of the Prophet (God's peace and blessings be upon him), "There is no *ṣadaqa* on less that five *awqiya* (ounces) of silver". It is possible to understand from this that this is its *ḥukm* when there is one owner, and it is also possible to understand that this *ḥukm* applies to it when it is owned by one or more, except that as the purpose of the stipulation of *niṣāb* is relief from burden it is deemed necessary this *niṣāb* be for one owner. This is a better interpretation, Allāh knows best. Al-Shāfiʿī, it appears held it to be similar to the mixing of the two capitals,[197] but the effectiveness (in law) of mixing the capitals for purposes of *zakāt* is not agreed upon, as will be coming up later.

5.3.1.5. Issue 5

This relates to their disagreement about consideration of the *niṣāb* in minerals (in the form of ore) and the amount due on them. Mālik and al-Shāfiʿī did take the *niṣāb* into account in the case of minerals. The disagreement between the two is that Mālik did not stipulate the passage of one year for them, while al-Shāfiʿī did stipulate that, as we will discuss in the fourth chapter. Likewise, their views did not differ on the point that the amount due on them is one-fourth of a tenth. Abū Ḥanīfa did not stipulate a *niṣāb* in minerals nor the passage of a year. He said that the amount due is a fifth. The reason for disagreement is whether the term *rikāz* (treasure) includes minerals as well. The Prophet (God's peace and blessings be upon him) is reported to have said, "In the treasure-trove there is a fifth". Ashhab has related from Mālik that minerals found without effort are treated as *rikāz* and it is in these that there is a fifth. The reason for their disagreement over this derives from "the connotation of a word" (*dalālat al-lafẓ*), which is a basis for the common disputes that we have mentioned.

5.3.2. *Section 2: The* niṣāb *and the* zakāt *due on camels*

The Muslim jurists agreed that on every five camels there is a sheep, up to twenty-four. If there are twenty-five camels the *zakāt* due is one *bint makhāḍ* up to thirty-five camels, but if a *bint makhāḍ* is not available the *zakāt* due is one *ibn labūn* male. If the number of camels is thirty-six the *zakāt* due is one *bint labūn* up to forty-five camels. When the camels are forty-six the *zakāt* is on *ḥiqqa* up to sixty. If the camels are sixty-one the *zakāt* due is one *jadhaʿ* up to seventy-five camels. If the camels are seventy-six the *zakāt* due is two *bint labūn* up to ninety. When the camels are ninety-one the *zakāt* due is two *ḥiqqas*

[197] Al-Shāfiʿī holds the view that in a partnership the capital of two or more partners be mixed in a such a way that the capital of one partner cannot be distinguished from that of the other. This is normally the case in co-ownership. See the section on *sharika*.

up to one hundred and twenty camels. All this is prescribed because it is established in the book of *ṣadaqa* laid down by the Prophet (God's peace and blessings be upon him), and which was followed after him by Abū Bakr and ʿUmar.

They disagreed about it on certain points. These include: the issue of the number of camels over one hundred and twenty; the *ḥukm* in the case of lack of a camel of the required age when the person possesses one that is older than it or one that is younger; and the question whether *zakāt* is levied on very young camels, and if it is then what is due?

5.3.2.1. Issue 1

This relates to their disagreement about camels in excess of one hundred and twenty. Mālik said that if they exceed one hundred and twenty the collector has the choice of acquiring three *bint labūns* or two *ḥiqqas* up to one hundred and thirty camels, in which case there will be one *ḥiqqa* and two *bint labūns*. Ibn al-Qāsim, from among his disciples, said that he is to pay three *bint labūns* without a choice till the total is one hundred and eighty camels when the required payment is one *ḥiqqa* and two *bint labūns*. This was also al-Shāfiʿī's opinion. ʿAbd al-Malik ibn al-Mājishūn, one of the disciples of Mālik, said that the official collector is to take only two *ḥiqqas* without having a choice, up to one hundred and thirty camels.

The Kūfīs, Abū Ḥanīfa, his disciples, and al-Thawrī, said that if the camels are in excess of one hundred and twenty the assessment of what is due is to begin afresh. This means that there is one sheep due on every five camels in their view. If the total number of camels is one hundred and twenty-five, the *zakāt* due will be two *ḥiqqas* and a sheep, the two *ḥiqqas* being due on one hundred and twenty and the sheep on the five camels. If the total reaches one hundred and thirty there are two *ḥiqqas* and two sheep on them, and if it is one hundred and thirty-five the *zakāt* due is two *ḥiqqas* and three sheep up to one hundred and forty, in which case there will be four sheep and two *ḥiqqas* up to one hundred and forty-five. If the figure of one hundred and forty-five is reached the *zakāt* is two *ḥiqqas* and one *bint makhāḍ*, the two *ḥiqqas* being for one hundred and twenty camels and the *bint makhāḍ* for the twenty-five (excess) camels, as was the case in the initial assessment, and this up to one hundred and fifty camels. If the total reaches that figure there are three *ḥiqqas* due on it. If the figure exceeds one hundred and fifty the assessment is to revert to the initial ratios until the figure reaches two hundred camels, in which case the *zakāt* will be four *ḥiqqas*, when it is to revert to the initial assessment again. The jurists other than the Kūfians agreed that for whatever exceeds one hundred and thirty there is one *bint labūn* for every forty and one *ḥiqqa* for every fifty.

The reason for their disagreement in reverting the assessment to the original or not reverting it, arises from the conflict of traditions on the issue. It is established in the book of *ṣadaqa* that the Prophet (God's peace and blessings be upon him) said, "In a number exceeding one hundred and twenty, for every forty there is one *bint labūn* and for every fifty a *ḥiqqa*". It is related through Abū Bakr ibn ʿAmr ibn Ḥazm from his father from his grandfather from the Prophet (God's peace and blessings be upon him) that he caused the book of *ṣadaqa* to be written and it says, "If the camels are in excess of one hundred and twenty, the imposition of the obligation is to commence anew". The majority preferred the first tradition since it is more authentic. The Kūfians decided to prefer the tradition of ʿAmr ibn Ḥazm as this was proved authentic through the transmissions of ʿAlī and Ibn Masʿūd. They said that it is not proper that such a thing be anything but a precedent, for such a thing cannot be expressed on the basis of analogy (opinion).

The reason for disagreement between Mālik and his disciples on the one hand and al-Shāfiʿī on the other over what is in excess of one hundred and twenty up to one hundred and thirty is that they had no uniform method with which they could accommodate the forties and fifties. Those who maintained that what is between one hundred and twenty and up to the point where the calculation can be accommodated is *waqṣ*, said that there is nothing to be levied until the figure reaches one hundred and thirty (two forties plus one fifty), and this, they said, is according to the apparent meaning of the tradition. Al-Shāfiʿī and Ibn al-Qāsim held that there are three *bint labūns* in this case, as it is related from Ibn Shihāb that in the book of *ṣadaqa* it is stated that if the figure reaches one hundred and twenty-one the levy is three *bint labūns*, and if the figure reaches one hundred and thirty the levy is two *bint labūns* and one *ḥiqqa*. The reason for disagreement between Ibn al-Mājishūn and Ibn al-Qāsim stems from the conflict between the apparent meaning of an established tradition and an explanatory text that occurs in this tradition. Ibn al-Mājishūn preferred the apparent meaning, because of the agreement about its authenticity, while Ibn al-Qāsim and al-Shāfiʿī placed a construction upon the *mujmal* (obscure) meaning through the explanatory text. It appears that by granting an option to the official collector, Mālik tried to reconcile the two traditions, Allāh knows best.

5.3.2.2. Issue 2

This issue deals with the case when a camel of the right age is not available among the camels, but the assessee has camels of an age that is either higher or is lower. Mālik said that he is to be obliged to buy a camel of that age. A group of jurists said that he is to deliver the camel that he possesses along with a payment of twenty *dirhams* if the age of the camel that he has is less (than the prescribed age), or he may give two sheep. If the age of the camel that he has is greater, the collector of the *ṣadaqa* is to pay him either twenty *dirhams* or two sheep. This is established in the book of *ṣadaqa*, so there is no purpose in arguing over it. Perhaps this tradition did not reach Mālik. Al-Shāfiʿī and Abū Thawr based their opinions on this tradition. Abū Ḥanīfa said that the obligation is to pay the value, and this on the basis of his principle of assessing values for the purpose of *zakāt*. Another group of jurists said that he is to deliver the camel that he has and adjust the value of the difference.

5.3.2.3. Issue 3

The third issue is whether *zakāt* is levied on very young camels, and if it is due then what is the liability? A group of jurists said that *zakāt* is levied on them, while another group said that it is not.

The reason for their disagreement arises from whether the term used for the species includes very young camels. Those who maintained that there is no *zakāt* on them, and these are Abū Ḥanīfa and a group of jurists from Kūfa, argued on the basis of the tradition of Suwayd ibn Ghafla, who said, "The collector appointed by the Prophet (God's peace and blessings be upon him) came over to us and I sat with him when I heard him say, 'It is my mandate that I do not take one of the suckling baby camels and that I do not combine distinctive categories nor do I separate combined things.' He [Suwayd] said, 'A man came up to him with a camel with a mounting hump (*kawmāʾ*), but he refused to accept it'". Some of those who made *zakāt* obligatory on young camels said that he is to be obliged to buy a camel of the right age due on them, while others said he may take one out of them, which is closer to analogy. They disagreed in the same way over calves and kids.

5.3.3. *Section 3: The* niṣāb *for cows and the* zakāt *due on them*

The majority of the jurists maintain that for every thirty cows *zakāt* in the form of a one-year-old cow (*tabīʿ*) is due and for every forty cows a two-year-old cow (*musinna*). A group of jurists said that for every ten cows one sheep is due, and this rate applies to up to thirty for which a one-year-old cow is due. It is said that when the number reaches twenty-five there is one cow due on them up to seventy-five, and two cows are due when they exceed this number. If the number reaches one hundred and twenty, then, for every forty one cow is due, and this is related from Saʿīd ibn al-Musayyab. The jurists differed over the number between forty and sixty. Mālik, al-Shāfiʿī, Aḥmad, al-Thawrī, and a group of jurists held that there is nothing due on the cows that exceed forty until the number reaches sixty. If the number reaches sixty there are two one-year-old cows for them up to seventy. At seventy there is one two-year-old cow and one one-year-old cow up to eighty. At eighty there are two two-year-old cows up to ninety. At ninety there are three one-year-old cows up to one hundred. At hundred there are two one-year-old cows and one two-year-old cow and so on for whatever goes beyond that. Thus, for every thirty there is a one-year-old cow and for every forty a two-year-old cow.

The reason for their disagreement over the *niṣāb* stems from the fact that the tradition of Muʿādh is not agreed upon for its authenticity, for which reason it has not been recorded by al-Bukhārī or Muslim. The reason for disagreement amongst the jurists of the provinces over *waqṣ* in cows is that it is reported in this tradition of Muʿādh that he had suspended judgment in the case of *waqṣ* and had said that he would decide after asking the Prophet (God's peace and blessings be upon him). But when he had reached him he had found that he (God's peace and blessings be upon him) had died. As there was no text in this the *ḥukm* was sought by analogy. Those who constructed the analogy upon camels and sheep did not consider anything to be due in *waqṣ*, while in the case of those who maintained that the principle for *waqṣ* was the imposition of *zakāt*, unless exempted from it by an evidence, it was necessary that there be no operation of *waqṣ* in cows, as there is no evidence from consensus or from any other source.

5.3.4. *Section 4: The* niṣāb *for goats and the* zakāt *due on them*

They agreed under this topic that for sheep reared on (free) grazing one sheep is due if the number reaches forty sheep, up to one hundred and twenty. For the excess over one hundred and twenty there are two sheep up to a number of two hundred. If the number exceeds two hundred, three sheep are due up to three hundred, and if it exceeds three hundred, then, for every hundred sheep there is one sheep. This is the opinion of the majority, except al-Ḥasan ibn Ṣāliḥ, who said that if the number of sheep reaches three hundred and one the number of sheep due on them are four, and if the number is four hundred and one, five sheep are due on them. This opinion has been related from Manṣūr from Ibrāhīm. The authentic traditions related from the book of *ṣadaqa* support the opinion of the majority.

They agreed that goats are to be combined with sheep, but they differed about the category (species) from which the collector is to take *zakāt*. Mālik said that he is to take the *zakāt* from the category which has the greater number (of animals), and if they are equal the collector has a choice. Abū Ḥanīfa said that if the categories differ the collector is given a choice. Al-Shāfiʿī said that he is to take average quality animals from the different categories because of an opinion related from ʿUmar (God be pleased with him) that "we assess them for young lambs that are tended by the shepherd, but we do not take them, nor do we take sheep fattened for consumption, nor those that have given birth to offspring or those about to do so, nor the rams. We do take sheep that are six months and those that are one or two-year-old". This ensures a balance between choice and an average quality.

The jurists of the provinces agreed that male (billy) goats and animals that are very old or blind in one eye are not to be accepted for *ṣadaqa*, because this has been established from the book of *ṣadaqa*, unless the collector considers them to be in the interest of the needy. They disagreed about animals that are totally blind or have a defect whether they are to be included in the count of the owner's flock. Mālik and al-Shāfiʿī held that they are to be counted, while it is related from Abū Ḥanīfa that he did not hold that they be counted. The reason for disagreement stems from whether the unqualified term should be considered to include both the physically sound and those that are not so.

They disagreed under this topic on whether the offspring are to be counted with the mothers in order to complete the *niṣāb*, if the flock is falling short of the *niṣāb*. Mālik said that they are to be counted with them, while al-Shāfiʿī, Abū Ḥanīfa, and Abū Thawr said that they are not to be counted with the lambs, unless the mothers are completing the *niṣāb*. The reason for their disagreement is the saying of ʿUmar (God be pleased with him) when he ordered that they be counted with the lambs and nothing should be taken from them as *ṣadaqa*. A group of jurists understood that this is to be done when the mothers are completing the *niṣāb*. Another group of jurists understood this in unqualified terms. I believe that the Ẓāhirites do not impose *zakāt* on young lambs nor do they count them irrespective of the mothers completing the *niṣāb*, as the unqualified term for the species does not include them.

Most of the jurists maintained that co-ownership has an affect on the amount of *zakāt* due. Those who upheld this disagreed over whether it affects the *niṣāb*. Abū Ḥanīfa and his disciples did not consider co-ownership to have any effect, either on the amount due or on the amount of *niṣāb*. An explanation for this is that Mālik, al-Shāfiʿī, and the majority of the jurists of the provinces maintained that co-owners are to pay *zakāt* as a single owner. They disagreed about this on two points. First, whether the *niṣāb* of co-owners is to be treated as the *niṣāb* for one owner even if the share of each reaches the *niṣāb* separately, or are they to pay *zakāt* on the *niṣāb* for each owner separately if they own the *niṣāb* individually. Second, about the description of the co-ownership that is effective in this case.

The reason for their disagreement, first, over whether co-ownership is effective in the *niṣāb* and in the amount due, is their dispute over the meaning of what is established about the saying of the Prophet (God's peace and blessings be upon him) through the book of *ṣadaqa* that "distinguishable categories are not to be combined nor are combined categories to be distinguished under the apprehension of *zakāt*, and those composed of two mixed categories are to be settled jointly (or equally)". Each group interpreted the meaning of this tradition in accordance with their own assumptions.

Those who maintained that mixed categories were effective in the determination of the *niṣāb* and the amount due, or in the determination of the amount due alone, said that the words of the Prophet (God's peace and blessings be upon him), "those composed of two mixed categories are to be settled jointly (or equally)" and "distinguishable categories are not to be combined and combined categories are not to be distinguished" indicate clearly that co-ownership in combined property is like the ownership of a single individual. This tradition restricts the words of the Prophet (God's peace and blessings be upon him), "There is no *ṣadaqa* in less than five camels".[198] This applies either for purposes of *zakāt* alone, according to Mālik and his disciples, or both for purposes of the determination of *zakāt* and *niṣāb*, according to al-Shāfiʿī and his disciples. Those who did not uphold this view of co-ownership said that the partners are sometimes referred to as co-owners, and it is likely that the words of the Prophet (God's peace and blessings be upon him), "distinguishable categories are not to be combined and combined categories are not to be distinguished" amount to a proscription for the collector not to divide up the property of one individual in such a way that he becomes liable to excessive *zakāt*, as in the case of the individual who has one hundred and twenty sheep and whose property is divided up into units of forty thrice, or by combining his property with that of another so that the combined number yields more *zakāt*. They said that if these probabilities exist in this tradition, it is better not to restrict the established and agreed upon principles with it, that is, the rule that the *niṣāb* and the amount due are to be worked out on the basis of individual ownership. Those who upheld the view based on mixing said that the term "mixing" is better understood in terms of mixing itself rather than in the meaning of partnership, and if this is the case, then, the words of the Prophet (God's peace and blessings be upon him), "are to be settled jointly (or equally)" indicate that the duty owed by both has the *ḥukm* of a single individual, and also that these words, "are to be settled jointly (or equally)", imply that the mixing of two things does not imply two partners, as settlement between partners is not to be conceived here, because *zakāt* is being taken from the capital of the partnership. Thus, those who limited their view to this meaning and did not draw an analogy for the *niṣāb* said that co-owners are to be subjected to the *zakāt* of a single individual if each one of them possesses the *niṣāb*. Those who considered the *ḥukm* of the *niṣāb* to be dependent upon

[198] So that it applies to individual ownership of five or more camels, but not to joint ownership.

the *ḥukm* of the *zakāt* due said that their *niṣāb* is the *niṣāb* of a single individual, just as their *zakāt* is the *zakāt* of a single individual.

Each group interpreted the words of the Prophet (God's peace and blessings be upon him), "distinguishable categories are not to be combined and combined categories are not to be distinguished", in accordance with his own views. Mālik (God be pleased with him) said that the meaning of the words of the Prophet (God's peace and blessings be upon him), "combined categories are not to be distinguished", is that if there are two co-owners each with a share of one hundred and one sheep, their total liability would be three sheep, but if they separate each will pay one sheep. The meaning of his words, "distinguishable categories are not to be combined," he said, is that if there are three individuals each having forty sheep, they would pay one sheep if they combined their flocks. In his opinion, then, the proscription is directed toward those co-owners each of whom possesses the *niṣāb* independently. Al-Shāfiʿī, on the other hand, said that the meaning of the words of the Prophet (God's peace and blessings be upon him), "combined categories are not to be distinguished", is that if there are two persons who jointly own forty sheep, their separating their flocks would cause them not to be liable for *zakāt*, as the *niṣāb*, in his view, is that of the co-owners, which is in its *ḥukm* like that of an individual.

Those who upheld the view based on mixing differed as to what kind of mixing is effective in the determination of *zakāt*. Al-Shāfiʿī said that the condition of mixing is that they mix their flocks together so that they tend them jointly, gather the milk in one place, make them graze jointly, drink jointly, and that their offsprings are also mixed up together. There is no difference, in his view, as a whole between mixing (property) and partnership, and he, therefore, considers the *niṣāb* as belonging to each of the partners, as has preceded. In Mālik's view the co-owners are those who participate in terms of contribution, drinking, grazing, shepherding, and offspring. His disciples disagreed about the observance of some of these conditions or of all of them. The reason for their disagreement stems from the equivocality in the term "mixing", and for that reason a group of jurists did not uphold the effectiveness of mixing in the determination of *zakāt*. This was the opinion of Abū Muḥammad ibn Ḥazm al-Andalusī.

5.3.5. *Section 5: The* niṣāb *for crops (grains) and fruits and the* zakāt *due on them*

They agreed that the obligation of *zakāt* for crops of rain-fed land is one-tenth (*ʿushr*), while the *zakāt* for crops of irrigated land is one-half of one-tenth, as this has been established from the Prophet (God's peace and blessings be upon him).

They disagreed about the stipulation of a *niṣāb* for this category of *zakāt*-wealth. The majority decided to impose a *niṣāb* in it, which was held to be five *awsuq*. One *wasq* is equal to sixty *ṣā*ʿ by consensus, and one *ṣā*ʿ is equal to four *mudd*, in accordance with the *mudd* used by the Prophet (God's peace and blessings be upon him). The majority maintain that the *mudd* used by him is one and one-third rotl (*raṭl*), which is slightly more than the one used in Baghdād. This is what was conceded by Abū Yūsuf when he was confronted by Mālik on the basis of the opinion of the jurists of Iraq and the testimony of the jurists of Medina about it. Abū Ḥanīfa used to say about the *mudd* that it is equal to two rotls, and about the *ṣā*ʿ that it is equal to eight rotls. Abū Ḥanīfa also said that there is no *niṣāb* for crops and fruits.

The reason for their disagreement arises from the conflict between the general meaning and the particular meaning. The general meaning is in the saying of the Prophet (God's peace and blessings be upon him), "That which is watered by the sky is liable to one-tenth, while that irrigated by the water-can [human effort] is liable to one-half of one-tenth". The particular meaning is found in the words of the Prophet (God's peace and blessings be upon him), "There is no *ṣadaqa* in what is less than five *awsuq*". Both traditions are authentic. Those who maintained that the general meaning is to be construed in terms of the particular said that there is a *niṣāb* and that is the renowned opinion. Some other jurists held that the general and the particular meanings conflict with each other here, as the one revealed prior or later in time is not known, for the particular may be abrogated by the general in their view and the general may be abrogated by the particular, and because anything that can be acted upon may be abrogated, which may be abrogation in part or abrogation in full. When these jurists preferred the general meaning they said that there is no *niṣāb*. The construction of the general in terms of the particular by the majority, in my view, belongs to the category of preferring the particular meaning over the general for that part in which they were in conflict, because the general meaning is apparent while the particular is explicit. So think over this as this is the cause which has been eliminated by the majority by saying that the general is to be construed in terms of the particular, whereas, in fact, this is not the case. The conflict between them does exist, unless the particular were to follow the general immediately, in which case it would amount to an exemption. There is, however, a weakness in the argument of Abū Ḥanīfa relating to (the absence of) the *niṣāb* on the basis of the general meaning, as the tradition here has been laid down as an explanatory text for the quantity due (and not as one imposing an initial rule).

They disagreed in this topic over *niṣāb* on three issues. The first issue is about adding some of the grains to the others for completing the *niṣāb*. The second issue is about the permissibility of calculating the *niṣāb* for grapes and dates by estimation. The third issue is whether the quantity of his fruit or crop consumed by the owner prior to harvesting and threshing is to be taken into account for the *niṣāb*.

5.3.5.1. Issue 1

They agreed that one category of good grain may be added[199] to a lower category of grain, and *zakāt* is to be taken from the whole in proportion to the quantity of each, that is, from the good as well as the bad quality grain. If fruit is of different quality, the *zakāt* is to be taken from the average quality.

They disagreed about the addition of lentil of different quality one to the other and about the addition of wheat and barley and wheat extract. Mālik said that lentil of different quality is to be seen as one category, as are wheat, barley, and wheat extract. Al-Shāfiʿī, Abū Ḥanīfa, Aḥmad, and a group of jurists said that lentil comprises different categories, in accordance with their names, and one category is not to be added to another for the calculation of the *niṣāb*. Similarly, wheat, barley, and wheat extract are three different categories, and one of these is not to be added to the other for the completion of the *niṣāb*.

The reason for disagreement is whether consideration is to be given to the common benefit that is to be derived or to the common names. Those who maintained that common names are to be taken into account said that they are different categories if their names differ. Those who maintained that the common benefit is to be taken into account said that as long the benefit to be derived is the same, they form one category, even if the names are different. Each group sought to affirm its rule by an empirical counting of the cases provided in the law, that is, one group argued for its opinion on the basis of things in which the law has taken into account the names of categories, while the other sought support from those in which the benefits have been given importance. It appears that the law bears testimony to the consideration of names more than it does for the common benefit for purposes of *zakāt*, though both considerations are present in the law, Allāh knows best.

5.3.5.2. Issue 2

This issue relates to the calculation of the *niṣāb* by estimation and accepting it without using a measure. The majority of the jurists uphold the permission of estimation in the case of dates and grapes, when they have begun to ripen, because of the necessity of releasing them for consumption to the owners when they are still moist (fresh). Dāwūd said that there is to be no estimation, except in the case of dates. Abū Ḥanīfa and his two disciples said that estimation is invalid and it is up to the owner of the wealth to render one-tenth of the yield, whether it is in excess of the estimated amount or less.

199 Addition here does not mean actual physical combination but merely in calculation.

The reason for their disagreement comes from their dispute about the permissibility of estimation because of the conflict between the principles and the traditions reported on the issue. The tradition laid down on this is the one relied upon by the majority, in which it is related "that the Messenger of Allāh (God's peace and blessings be upon him) used to send ʿAbd Allāh ibn Rawāḥa and others to Khaybar to estimate the yield of dates". The principles that oppose this are that relying on estimation belongs to the category of (the forbidden) *muzābana*, which is the sale of fruit on trees in exchange for other measured fruit, and also because it amounts to the sale of ripe dates with fresh dates with a delay, circumstances which introduce a proscription on account of excess and delay, both of which are the bases of *ribā*. When the jurists of Kūfa took this into account along with the fact that the estimation in the case of the people of Khaybar was not for the purpose of *zakāt* for they were not obliged to pay *zakāt*, said that it is possible that it was an estimate to know the quantity of dates that would be available to each group of people.

The Qāḍī (Ibn Rushd) said: The apparent implication of Mālik's tradition is that it (estimation) was for purposes of division, because of the report that ʿAbd Allāh ibn Rawāḥa, when he had finished estimating, said: "If you like this part is for me and if you like it is for you", that is, it was in the case of fruit not grains. The tradition of ʿĀʾisha, on the other hand, which has been related by Abū Dāwūd, states that the estimation was for purposes of the share that they were obliged to pay. The tradition is that she said, while mentioning the case of Khaybar, "that the Prophet (God's peace and blessings be upon him) used to send ʿAbd Allāh ibn Rawāḥa to the Jews of Khaybar, and he estimated the dates for them when they began to ripen and before they began to consume them". Estimation, however, has not been recorded by the two shaykhs, al-Bukhārī and Muslim. In whichever way estimation is established, it would be an exemption from these principles, and this if it is established that it was a *ḥukm* from the Prophet (God's peace and blessings be upon him) for the Muslims, for if the *ḥukm* is established for the Ahl al-Dhimma it does not raise the obligation of a *ḥukm* for the Muslims, except on the basis of an evidence, Allāh knows best. If the tradition of ʿAttāb is authentic, the *ḥukm* of estimation would be clear, Allāh knows best. The tradition of ʿAttāb ibn Usayd is that he said, "The Messenger of Allāh (God's peace and blessings be upon him) ordered me to estimate the grapes and to collect *zakāt* in the form of raisins, just as the *zakāt* of dates on trees is taken in the form of *tamr* (dried dates)". The tradition of ʿAttāb ibn Usayd has been objected to on the ground that one of the narrators in it is Saʿīd ibn al-Musayyab, and he could not (possibly) transmit from him. This was the reason that Dāwūd did not permit the estimation of grapes.

Those who imposed *zakāt* on olives differed about the permissibility of estimation of olives. The reason for their disagreement stems from their dispute about the analogy drawn for them from dates and grapes. The category in which *zakāt* is to be paid, in the case of fresh dates, is preserved dates (*tamr*) and not fresh dates. Similarly, the payment for grapes is in the form of raisins, not in grapes themselves. Likewise, the payment, in the view of those who uphold *zakāt* on olives, is to be made in olive oil and not in the fruit on the basis of the analogy with *tamr* and raisins. About those categories of grapes that cannot be dried and those olives that cannot be pressed Mālik has maintained that payment be taken in the form of the fruit.

5.3.5.3. Issue 3

Mālik and Abū Ḥanīfa said that the person who consumes from his fruit or from his crops before harvest is to be held accountable for the amount consumed for purposes of *zakāt*. Al-Shāfiʿī said that this is not to be included against him and the estimator is to set aside a part that may be consumed by the owner and his family.

The reason for disagreement arises from the conflict of a tradition with what is in the Qurʾān and also with analogy. The *sunna* in this is in what is related by Sahl ibn Abī Ḥathma "that the Prophet (God's peace and blessings be upon him) sent Abū Ḥathma as an estimator. A man later came and said, 'O Messenger of Allāh, Abū Ḥathma has left me an excess.' The Messenger of Allāh (God's peace and blessings be upon him) said, 'The son of your uncle believes that you have left him an excess?' He said, 'O Messenger of Allāh, I left him an amount that will be given out by his family, an amount from which he will feed the needy, and an amount that will be wasted by the wind.' He said, 'The son of your uncle has left you an excess and has done justice to you'". It has also been related that the Messenger of Allāh (God's peace and blessings be upon him) said, "When you make an estimate leave a third, and if you cannot do that, then, leave a fourth". It is related from Jābir that the Messenger of Allāh (God's peace and blessings be upon him) said, "Be lenient in estimation, as the wealth (orchard) contains the *ʿariyya*, the *ākila* (birds and insects consuming fruit), the *waṣiyya* (rights pertaining to bequests), the right of workers and the deputies, and the claims that are made on the fruit". The text of the Qurʾān that may appear to conflict with this tradition and analogy, are the words of the Exalted, "Eat ye of the fruit thereof when it fruiteth, and pay the due thereof upon the harvest day".[200] The analogy (from this) is that it is wealth that is liable to *zakāt* and the basis for this is the remaining wealth (after consumption).

These, then, are the well-known issues related to the amount that is due in *zakāt* and to the three categories that are liable to it, from which the payment

[200] Qurʾān 6 : 142.

is to be made in their own kind. They did not disagree that if *zakāt* is paid in the same kind it is valid, but they disagreed on whether it was permitted to make the payment with a substitute for the original by value.

Mālik and al-Shāfiʿī said that payment according to value is not permitted in *zakāt* as a substitute for that expressly stated in the texts. Abū Ḥanīfa said that it is permitted, irrespective of the owner's ability to make the payment in the expressly mentioned categories. The reason for their disagreement stems from the dispute as to whether *zakāt* is a form of worship or a right due to the needy. Those who maintained that it is a form of worship said that if the person makes the payment with something other than the substance of the category his act is not valid, because worship performed in a way different from the one prescribed is invalid. Those who maintained that it is a right of the needy saw no difference between the thing itself and its value. The Shāfiʿites said that even if the right of the needy is conceded the Lawgiver has suspended the claim upon the thing itself and which is satisfied by joint participation of the poor and the rich in the thing itself. The Ḥanafites say: "The things constituting the wealth have been specified as a convenience for the owners of wealth, as it is easy for each owner of wealth to make payment from the kind of wealth that he possesses". It is for this reason that in some of the traditions it is laid down that he (the Prophet) determined that the payment of *diya* (blood-money) be made in the form of credits for those who possess them, as will be coming up in the book of *ḥudūd*.

5.3.6. *Section 6: The* niṣāb *for* ʿurūd *(goods)*

The *niṣāb* for goods, according to the opinion of those who uphold it, is constituted by the goods acquired for sale especially what is held prior to the payment of *zakāt*. The *niṣāb* for them is based on the commodities as it is these that represent the value of consumable things and the capital. Likewise, the *ḥawl* (passage of a year) for goods, according to those who imposed *zakāt* on goods. Mālik said that if a person sells goods he is liable for *zakāt* once a year, as is the case with debts. This is for traders who record the timings for the purchase of their goods. The traders who do not record the timings for what they sell and buy, and who are referred to by the term *mudīr* (the active trader like the shopkeeper). The *ḥukm* in Mālik's view is that when a period of one year passes from the time of the commencement of their trade they should determine the value of the goods they hold (inventories). To this is added the value of the things they possess (assets) and their wealth in terms of loans they hope will be repaid (accounts receivable), that is, if they do not have similar debts that they owe (accounts payable), and this is different from his opinion about the *mudīr*. If the sum of all this that they possess reaches the *niṣāb* they are to pay *zakāt* on it, whether during the year they were able to convert a thing to liquid assets (cash) or whether such conversion amounted to the *niṣāb*. This is the narration of Ibn al-Mājishūn from Mālik. Ibn al-Qāsim has related from him that if he does not have liquid assets (cash) and he trades with goods (barter), there is nothing to be paid on the goods.

Thus, some of the jurists did not stipulate the existence of liquid assets in his possession, while some did stipulate it. Those who stipulated this considered a *niṣāb* for the goods, while those who did not stipulate it did not take the *niṣāb* into account. Al-Muzanī said that *zakāt* on goods is based on the things themselves (cost) not on their prices. The majority—al-Shāfiʿī, Abū Ḥanīfa, Aḥmad, al-Thawrī, al-Awzāʿī, and others—said that the *ḥukm* for the *mudīr* and others is the same, and that the person who purchases goods for the purpose of trade evaluates his goods after the passage of the *ḥawl* and pays *zakāt* on them accordingly. Some said that he is to pay *zakāt* on the basis of the price at which he purchased the goods (cost price) and not on their value (book value or market value).

The majority did not stipulate anything for the *mudīr* as the *ḥawl* has been stipulated for the things and not for their species. Mālik, however, compared the species to the things themselves so that the liability for *zakāt* is not removed entirely from the *mudīr*. This amounts to additional law, and it appears to be derived from the established law. Cases like this are referred to as *qiyās mursal*, which is a law that does not rely on an evidence that is expressly stated in the law, but is understood from the jurisprudential interests found in it. Mālik, may Allāh have mercy on him, used to consider interests (*maṣāliḥ*) even when they were not based on a specific text.

5.4. Chapter 4 The Time for the Payment of *Zakāt*

The majority stipulates for the obligation of *zakāt* on gold, silver, and cattle, the passage of the *ḥawl*, because this is established from the four caliphs, was known widely among the Companions, was practised widely, and because of their belief that its being so widely known and practised without any opposition is not possible, unless there was an earlier precedent (from the Prophet). It is related from Ibn ʿUmar from the Prophet (God's peace and blessings be upon him) in a (*marfūʿ*) tradition that he said, "There is no *zakāt* on wealth unless one *ḥawl* (year) has passed over it". This is agreed to unanimously by the jurists of the provinces. There is no disagreement about it in the first generation, except what is related from Ibn ʿAbbās and Muʿāwiya. The reason for the disagreement is that there is no established tradition about it.

In this topic they disagreed about eight well-known issues. The first issue is whether a *ḥawl* is to be stipulated for minerals, if we maintain that the amount due on them is one-fourth of a tenth. Second, the consideration of a *ḥawl* in the case of profits on capital. Third, the passage of a *ḥawl* on the additions to things that are liable to *zakāt*. Fourth, the consideration of the passage of a *ḥawl* on loans, if we maintain that *zakāt* is levied on them. Fifth, the consideration of a *ḥawl* for goods, if we maintain that there is *zakāt* on them. Sixth, the *ḥawl* on the benefits derived from cattle. Seventh, the *ḥawl* on the offspring of sheep, if we maintain that they are to be added to the mothers, either according to the opinion of those who stipulate that the mothers should complete the *niṣāb*, and these are al-Shāfiʿī and Abū Ḥanīfa, or according to the opinion of those who do not stipulate this, which is Mālik's opinion. Eighth, the permissibility of setting aside *zakāt* prior to the *ḥawl*.

5.4.1. Issue 1

This issue relates to minerals. Al-Shāfiʿī took into account the *ḥawl* as well as the *niṣāb* in minerals, while Mālik took into account the *niṣāb*, but not the *ḥawl*.

The reason for their disagreement arises from the vacillation of their resemblance between what is derived from the land and between owned gold and silver. Those who held them to be similar to what is derived from the land did not stipulate a *ḥawl* for them, while those who held them to be similar to gold and silver stipulated the *ḥawl*. The resemblance with gold and silver is clearer, Allāh knows best.

5.4.2. Issue 2

The jurists disagreed about the *ḥawl* for profit on capital holding three opinions. Al-Shāfiʿī held that its *ḥawl* is to be calculated from the day it accrues, irrespective of the capital itself amounting to the *niṣāb*. This is related from ʿUmar ibn ʿAbd al-ʿAzīz, who gave the instructions that the profits from trade should not be liable for *zakāt* until a *ḥawl* has passed. Mālik said that the *ḥawl* of the profits corresponds with the *ḥawl* of the capital, that is, when the year has passed for the capital the profit becomes subject to *zakāt* at the same time, whether the principal amounts to a *niṣāb* on its own or reaches the *niṣāb* by adding the profits to it. Abū ʿUbayd said that this was not followed by any of the other jurists, except his own disciples. One group of jurists made the distinction of whether the capital undergoing the *ḥawl* amounts to a *niṣāb*. They said that if it does amount to the *niṣāb* on its own the profit becomes subject to *zakāt* along with it, but if it does not amount to the *niṣāb*, *zakāt* is not levied on it (even if it amounts to the *niṣāb* by the addition of profits to it). Those who held this opinion include al-Awzāʿī, Abū Thawr, and Abū Ḥanīfa.

The reason for their disagreement arises from the vacillation of profit between the *ḥukm* of wealth derived as a benefit and the *ḥukm* of the capital. Those who held it to be similar to an accruing benefit said that it has to independently undergo a *ḥawl*, while those who held it to be similar to capital said that it takes the *ḥukm* of the capital, except that one of the conditions of such comparison is that *zakāt* should be due on the capital, and this does not happen unless it amounts to the *niṣāb*. It is for this reason that the analogy for profit over capital is considered weak in Mālik's school. It appears that what Mālik (God be pleased with him) relied upon is the similarity between profit from capital and the offspring of sheep, but the case of the offspring of sheep is also disputed. An opinion like that of the majority is also related from Mālik.

5.4.3. Issue 3

This issue deals with the *ḥawl* of additions (*fawāʾid*).[201] They agreed that if the wealth is less than the *niṣāb* and some addition other than the profit accrues to the owner thus completing the *niṣāb*, then, the *ḥawl* is to be commence independently for the total from the day of accrual. They disagreed over when the addition accrues to him when he already has wealth that is equal to the *niṣāb* on which the *ḥawl* is complete. Mālik said that the addition is to be liable for *zakāt* according to its own *ḥawl*, if it amounts to the *niṣāb*, and it is not to be added to the wealth on which *zakāt* is now due. The same opinion about additions is expressed by al-Shāfiʿī. Abū Ḥanīfa, his disciples, and al-Thawrī said that all additions are to be subjected to *zakāt* on the basis of the *ḥawl* of the capital, if that amounts to the *niṣāb*. The same is the case for profit in their view.

The reason for their disagreement is whether the fresh addition takes the *ḥukm* of wealth on which the addition has occurred or it takes the *ḥukm* of wealth that has not accrued upon other wealth. Those who maintained that its *ḥukm* is the *ḥukm* of the original wealth that is independent of other wealth, that is, wealth upon which *zakāt* is due, said that there is no *zakāt* on the addition. Those who determined for it the *ḥukm* of wealth on which *zakāt* is due and who consider it to be the same wealth because *zakāt* is due upon this wealth as it amounts to a *niṣāb*, considered its *ḥawl* in accordance with the *ḥawl* of wealth on which *zakāt* is due. The general meaning in the words of the Prophet (God's peace and blessings be upon him), "There is no *zakāt* on wealth unless one *ḥawl* has passed over it", implies that newly acquired wealth should not be added to the wealth in hand except on the basis of an evidence. It appears that Abū Ḥanīfa relied in this upon the analogy of liquid assets over cattle. One of his principles, on which he relies in this topic, is that it is not a

[201] It appears that this category would fall under the modern term known as "capital gains".

condition for the *ḥawl* that all the constituent parts of the wealth should comprise the *niṣāb* throughout the year, and it is enough that the *niṣāb* can be found at both ends of the year, and the *hawl* in one of the parts of the wealth. Thus, in his view, if the wealth constituted the *niṣāb* at the beginning of the *ḥawl* after which parts of it were lost or destroyed making it less than the *niṣāb*, but at the end of the *ḥawl* there were additions to it that completed the *niṣāb*, *zakāt* would be levied upon it. This situation exists for him in this kind of wealth as the *ḥawl* has not been completed, yet it is in essence the same wealth in all its constituent parts; in fact, it is more but it had shed the *niṣāb* at different stages of the *ḥawl*.

It is obvious that the *ḥawl*, which has been stipulated for *zakāt* on wealth, is for some determined wealth, irrespective of the increase or decrease in it, either by profit or by additions or by anything else, as the purpose of the *ḥawl* is to ensure that the wealth is a surplus that is beyond the (normal) needs. This is based on the assumption that what has remained throughout the *ḥawl* without change must be beyond the needs of the owner. On this account *zakāt* has been imposed on it, and *zakāt* is imposed only on surplus wealth. For those who maintain that the stipulation of the *ḥawl* is to determine the growth in wealth, it becomes obligatory to say that the gains, in addition to the profit, are to be merged with the capital and the completion of the *niṣāb* is to be taken into account at both ends of the *ḥawl*. Think over this for it is evident, Allāh knows best. It was for this reason that Mālik held the view that a person who had cattle that were liable to *zakāt* at the beginning of the *ḥawl* then sold them off and substituted for them at the end of the *ḥawl* other cattle of the same species, *zakāt* would be levied on them. It appears that he also took into account both ends of the *ḥawl* in accordance with the opinion of Abū Ḥanīfa. He also adopted the analogy, relied upon by Abū Ḥanīfa, for additions to liquid assets over cattle, as we have already stated.

5.4.4. Issue 4

This issue deals with the consideration of the *ḥawl* for loans (given to others),[202] if we maintain that *zakāt* is levied upon them. A group of jurists said that the *ḥawl* is to be considered for it from the time of its commencement (as a loan) imposing *zakāt* on it for its duration. If it is spread over one *ḥawl*,

[202] This passage deals with loans made out to others. It becomes easy to understand by first distinguishing between debts and credits, or accounts receivable. The discussion relating to debts owed to others has preceded in the earlier part of this section, that is, the book on *zakāt*, where the issue was whether debts prevent the imposition of *zakāt*. Here the discussion is about loans given to others, and which are due to be repaid. The person on whom *zakāt* is to be levied is the creditor. The question is when will *zakāt* be imposed? How many past years are relevant to the calculation? The author discussed the problem briefly in the previous discussion and mentioned that there are a number of details in Mālik's school. The details are provided here.

then, it is for one *ḥawl*, but if it is spread over a number of *ḥawls*, then, it is for such a number of *ḥawls*. This means that if it is a single *ḥawl* a single levy of *zakāt* is imposed, but if it is spread over several years the *zakāt* is levied for such number of years. A group of jurists said that it is to be subjected to *zakāt* for a single year, even if the loan stays outstanding for a number of years with the person who owes the debt. A group of jurists said that the *ḥawl* is to be postponed because of it. Those who said that the *ḥawl* is to be postponed because of the debt from the day the loan was made, did not uphold the imposition of *zakāt* on a loan, while those who maintained that *zakāt* is to be levied upon it for the number of years it stayed outstanding decided on the basis of the resemblance of a loan with wealth in hand. For those who said that *zakāt* is to be levied on it for a single year even if it stays outstanding for a number of years, I do not know of their reliance at the present moment, because as long as it remains a loan they may either say that *zakāt* is levied on it or they may say that it is not, and if they say that there is no *zakāt* on it then there is no point in discussing it; rather we start all over again. If there is *zakāt* on it, then, the *ḥawl* is either stipulated for it or it is not. If we stipulate it, it becomes obligatory to take into account the number of years, unless it is said that each time the *ḥawl* is completed and he is not able to pay *zakāt* for it (due to non-payment by the debtor), this obligatory right against him is dropped for that year. As *zakāt* is imposed with two conditions, the presence of the substance of the wealth and the completion of the *ḥawl*, then in this case only the *zakāt* due for the last year remains. This is held to by Mālik to be similar to goods acquired for trade. In his view, *zakāt* is not to be imposed on them until the person sells them off, even if they remained with him for a number of years.

There is another factor in it that resembles the case of cattle that are not visited by the collector for years. When he finally arrives and finds that they have decreased in number, he is to impose *zakāt* on the remainder on the basis of what he finds there, according to Mālik's opinion. The reason is that as the *ḥawl* passed and the owner was not able to set aside the *zakāt*, the coming of the collector being a condition with Mālik for setting it aside after the passage of the *ḥawl*, the claim against him for that *ḥawl* lapsed and he is to be assessed for the previous years, whether the amount due is more or less. This is something that contradicts analogy, and Mālik relied upon *ʿamal* for it. Al-Shāfiʿī, on the other hand, considers such an owner to be liable, as the coming of the collector is not a condition for the obligation. Related to this is the fact that some jurists maintain that it is not obligatory for the owner to set aside *zakāt* on his wealth, unless he can deliver it to the *imām*. In case of the absence of the *imām* or of an *ʿādil imām*—if the owner believes that *ʿadāla* is one of the conditions for the *imām*—if the wealth is destroyed after the *ḥawl* has passed and prior to his ability to deliver the *zakāt*, the owner is not liable for anything.

Loans for (purposes of) *zakāt* are divided, in Mālik's view, on the basis of these three situations, that is, some of the debts according to him are liable for *zakāt* for a single year, like the loans in trade; for some debts the *ḥawl* is postponed, like the loans of inheritance; and the third case relates to the loans of the *mudīr*.[203] A complete discussion of his views on loans is beyond our purposes.

5.4.5. Issue 5

This relates to the *ḥawl* for goods and its discussion has preceded under the topic of the *niṣāb* for goods.

5.4.6. Issue 6

This issue relates to gains in cattle. The opinion of Mālik in this case is the opposite of what it is in the case of liquid assets. The reason is that he bases the gains on the capital,[204] if that capital amounts to a *niṣāb*, just as Abū Ḥanīfa does it in the cases of *dirhams* and gains in cattle. Abū Ḥanīfa's opinion on gains is that there is a common *ḥukm*, that is, it is based upon the capital if it amounts to a *niṣāb*, whether the gain is in sheep or in liquid assets. The profits and increase in offspring, in his view, are like gains. For Mālik profits and offspring have a common *ḥukm*, but he distinguishes between the gains in liquid assets and those in cattle. For al-Shāfiʿī profits and gains have a common *ḥukm* through the consideration of an independent *ḥawl* for them, and also the gains in cattle and offspring have a common *ḥukm* through the consideration of their *ḥawl* along with the capital if that amounts to the *niṣāb*.

This is the summary of the opinions of these three (leading) jurists. It appears that Mālik distinguished between cattle and liquid assets following ʿUmar, otherwise the analogy is the same for both cases, that is, profit being similar to (a growth in) offspring and gains (on capital) being similar to gains (in stock). The tradition of ʿUmar here is that he ordered them to count the young lambs (in the *niṣāb*), but not to take anything from them as *zakāt*. The tradition has preceded in the section on *niṣāb*.

5.4.7. Issue 7

This issue is about the consideration of a *ḥawl* in the case of the offspring of sheep. Mālik said that it is the same *ḥawl* that applies to the mothers, irrespective of their constituting a *niṣāb*, as was his opinion about profits on

[203] The word in the original is *mudabbar*; however, it appears that it should be *mudīr*, the retail trader mentioned in the previous discussions.

[204] The word capital is being used here to mean both monetary capital in the case of liquid assets or the original stock in the case of cattle.

liquid assets. Al-Shāfiʿī, Abū Ḥanīfa, and Abū Thawr maintained that the *hawl* of the offspring is not the same as that for the mothers, unless the mothers constitute a *niṣāb*. The reason for their disagreement is the same reason for their disagreement about profits.

5.4.8. Issue 8

This issue is about the payment of *zakāt* prior to the completion of the *ḥawl*. Mālik disallowed this, while Abū Ḥanīfa and al-Shāfiʿī permitted it. The reason for their disagreement is whether *zakāt* is a form of worship or a duty owed to the needy. Those who said that it is a form of worship, and they compared it to prayer, did not permit paying it prior to the time set for it. Those who held it to be similar to delayed obligatory duties permitted paying it prior to the end of the period like voluntary donations. Al-Shāfiʿī argued for his opinion on the basis of the tradition of ʿAlī "that the Prophet (God's peace and blessings be upon him) borrowed the *ṣadaqa* of al-ʿAbbās prior to its time".

5.5. **Chapter 5 The Persons to whom *Zakāt* is Due**

The discussion of this topic is covered in three sections. The first is about the number of categories for whom *zakāt* is due. The second is their description that requires such a duty. The third is about the amount due to them.

5.5.1. *Section 1: The number of categories to whom* zakāt *is due*

The number of categories for whom *zakāt* is due is eight, and they have been mentioned in the Qurʾān in the words of the Exalted, "The alms are only for the poor and the needy, and those who collect them, and those whose hearts are (to be) reconciled, and to free the captives and the debtors, and for the cause of Allāh, and (for) the wayfarers; a duty imposed by Allāh. Allāh is Knower, Wise".[205]

They disagreed about their number on two issues.

5.5.1.1. Issue 1

First, whether it is permissible that the entire *ṣadaqa* (*zakāt*) be spent on one category out of these categories, or whether they are partners in the *ṣadaqa* and it is not permitted to single out one category for it. Mālik and Abū Ḥanīfa held that it is allowed to the *imām* to spend it on one category or on more than one

[205] Qurʾān 9 : 61.

category, if he thinks that there is need for it. Al-Shāfiʿī said that this is not permitted and that he is to spend it on the eight categories mentioned in the words of Allāh.

The reason for their disagreement arises from the conflict between the literal meaning and the implication (of the words of Allah). The literal meaning requires that it be divided among all of them. The implication requires that he should place greater emphasis on the needy (at the time), as the purpose of *zakāt* is the elimination of want. Thus, the enumeration of these categories in the verse that has been laid down, in the view of these jurists, is because of distinguishing the categories, that is, the persons entitled to the *zakāt* and not their partnership in it. The first view is obvious by way of the literal meaning, while this (latter) implication is clearer in terms of the implication. One of the supporting evidences for al-Shāfiʿī is what is related by Abū Dāwūd from al-Ṣudāʾī that a man asked the Prophet (God's peace and blessings be upon him) that he be given from the *ṣadaqa*. The Messenger of Allāh (God's peace and blessings be upon him) said to him, "Allāh did not leave the *ṣadaqāt* to the *ḥukm* of a prophet or of anyone else, but He has laid down a *ḥukm* Himself. He has divided the persons entitled into eight categories, so if you are in one of these categories I will give you your right".

5.5.1.2. Issue 2

Does the right of the *muʾallafat qulūbuhum* still subsist up to this day? Mālik said that there are no such persons today. Al-Shāfiʿī and Abū Ḥanīfa maintained that the right of the *muʾallafat qulūbuhum* does subsist till today if the *imām* considers it to be so, and they are the people who are to be induced and encouraged to abide by Islam.

The reason for their disagreement is whether this was a right specific to the Prophet (God's peace and blessings be upon him) or it was available generally and to the rest of the *umma*. The apparent meaning is that it is a general right, but is it permitted to the *imām* to exercise it under all circumstances or only under certain circumstances and not in others, that is, in a state of weakness and not in that of strength. It is for this reason that Mālik said that there is no need for them today due to the strength of Islam. This, as we have said, is recourse on his part to jurisprudential interests (*maṣāliḥ*).

5.5.2. *Section 2: The qualifications for entitlement to* zakāt

The foremost qualification, because of which they are entitled to *ṣadaqa*, or the opposite attribute, because of which they are excluded from it, is poverty, which is the opposite of affluence, on the basis of the words of the Exalted,

"The alms are only for the poor and the needy".[206] They disagreed about the kind of affluence in which *ṣadaqa* is permissible and that in which it is not.

With respect to affluence in which *ṣadaqa* is not permitted, the majority of the jurists maintained that it is not permitted for all the wealthy persons, except the five that have been mentioned by the Prophet (God's peace and blessings be upon him) in his saying, "*Ṣadaqa* is not permitted to a wealthy person, except five types: the warrior fighting in the path of Allāh; the worker who collects it; a debtor; (the person who buys it with his money;)[207] and a person who has a poor neighbour to whom he gives charity and the poor man gives a gift to this rich man". Ibn al-Q̄āsim has related that it is not permitted to the warrior or the collector to take from the *ṣadaqa* at all. Those who permitted it to the collector, even if he is wealthy also permitted it for the *qāḍīs* and other persons who work for the public benefit of the Muslims. Those who did not permit this did so on the analogy that it is not permitted to the wealthy at all.

The reason for their disagreement is whether the underlying cause giving rise to *ṣadaqa* for the mentioned categories is merely need or it is need as well as public benefit. Those who took into account only the persons in need, who have been mentioned in the verse, said that the cause is need alone. Those who maintained that the underlying cause is need as well as public benefit took into account the benefit in the case of the worker and need in the case of the remaining enumerated categories.

With respect to the amount of wealth that precludes the entitlement to *ṣadaqa*, al-Shāfiʿī said that the limit preventing *ṣadaqa* is the minimum to which the name can be applied. Abū Ḥanīfa held that a wealthy person is one who owns the *niṣāb*, as it is these persons whom the Prophet (God's peace and blessings be upon him) termed as wealthy in his words addressed to Muʿādh in his tradition, "Inform them that Allāh has made *ṣadaqa* obligatory for them, which is to be taken from the wealthy amongst them and is to be given to their poor". As the rich here were those who owned the *niṣāb* it follows that the poor should be their opposites. Mālik said that there is no limit in this and it is a matter referred to *ijtihād*.

The reason for their disagreement is whether affluence, which is an obstacle to receiving *zakāt*, is based on a legal or a literal meaning. Those who maintained that it has a legal meaning said that the existence of the *niṣāb* proves wealth. Those who maintained that it is based on the literal meaning said that it is the minimum amount to which the term is applied. Those who maintained that it is the minimum amount to which the term is applied, and

[206] Qur'ān 9 : 61.

[207] The sentence in parentheses is missing from the original text.

who also held that it is limited at all times and for all individuals, fixed such a limit for this, while those who maintained that it is not limited and that it differs with circumstances, needs, persons, locations, and times left it undetermined and to be a subject of *ijtihād*. Abū Dāwūd has recorded a tradition from the Prophet (God's peace and blessings be upon him) about wealth where it is (determined as) the ownership of fifty *dirhams*, and there is another tradition where it is determined as possession of one *awqiya*, which comes to forty *dirhams*. I believe that one group based their opinion on these traditions.

They disagreed in this topic about the description of the poor and the needy and about the distinction between them. A group of jurists said that a poor person (*faqīr*) is better off than the needy (*miskīn*), and this was upheld by the disciples of Mālik from Baghdād. Another group said that the needy person is in a better condition than the poor. This was the opinion of Abū Ḥanīfa, his disciples, and al-Shāfiʿī in one of his two opinions. In another opinion al-Shāfiʿī said that both terms indicate the same meaning, and this was the opinion of Ibn al-Qāsim. This is a literal view even though there is no legal connotation. It appears more likely, on an empirical examination of the language, that both terms indicate slightly different meanings.

They disagreed about the term *fī al-riqāb*. Mālik said that these are slaves who are to be set free by the *imām*, ensuring that their loyalty is to the Muslims. Al-Shāfiʿī and Abū Ḥanīfa said that these are the *mukātab* slaves. The wayfarer is one who in their view is a traveller performing a religious duty, but his provision has been exhausted and he has nothing to spend. Some of the jurists have stipulated that the traveller should be in close proximity to the source of the *ṣadaqa*. With respect to striving in the way of Allāh, Mālik said that this applies to the occasions of *jihād* or being stationed to guard the Muslim frontier. This was also Abū Ḥanīfa's opinion. Other jurists said that this category includes (needy) pilgrims and those undertaking *ʿumra*. Al-Shāfiʿī said that he is a fighter who is close to the source of the *ṣadaqa*. The proximity to the source of *zakāt* was stipulated because most of them did not permit that the *ṣadaqa* be transferred from one place to another, except on the basis of necessity.

5.5.3. *Section 3: The amount of the entitlement*

With respect to the amount that is to be given to each category, the debtor is to be given the amount that he owes if his debt was incurred for a legitimate cause, not for extravagance, in fact, because of necessity. Likewise, the traveller is to be given an amount that will enable him to get home. It appears that for the warrior, in the view of those who consider the wayfarer to be a warrior, it is an amount that will take him to the battle front. They disagreed about the amount of *ṣadaqa* that is to be given to a single needy person. Mālik did not put a limit on this and left the matter to *ijtihād*. This was also al-Shāfiʿī's opinion, who said that it does not matter if the person is given an amount equal to the *niṣāb* or less than the *niṣāb*. Abū Ḥanīfa disapproved of giving a person an amount equal to the *niṣāb*. Al-Thawrī said that no one is to be given more than fifty *dirhams*. Al-Layth said that he is to be given an amount with which he can employ a servant, in case the person has a family and the *zakāt* is enough. Most of them agreed that it is not proper to give the person a grant with which he becomes a person for whom *ṣadaqa* is not permissible, for by virtue of the amount received by him of this wealth, that is, over and above the amount on the basis of which he is entitled to *ṣadaqa*, he moves into the first grade of affluence and it becomes prohibited for him. They disagreed over this issue in accordance with their dispute over the limit of the amount (of the first degree of affluence). This issue, it appears, is structured on the first grade of affluence. There is no dispute among the jurists about the collector of *zakāt* that he takes from it (an amount) in proportion to the work that he does.

This is what we sought to establish in this book, and if we should recall something that is relevant to our purpose, we will incorporate it, God willing.

VI

THE BOOK OF *ZAKĀT AL-FIṬR*

The discussion in this book is covered in sections. The first is about the identification of the *ḥukm* of *zakāt al-fiṭr*. The second is about the identification of the person on whom it is obligatory. The third relates to the amount that is due and in what kinds of commodities. The fourth is about the time when it is due. The fifth is about the person entitled to receive it.

6.1. *Section 1: The identification of its* ḥukm

The majority of the jurists maintain that *zakāt al-fiṭr* is an obligation. Some of the later jurists in Mālik's school held that it is a *sunna*, and this was also the opinion of the jurists of Iraq. One group of jurists said that it stands abrogated by the injunction of *zakāt* (on wealth).

The reason for their disagreement arises from the conflict of the traditions on the issue. This is so as in the authentic tradition of ʿAbd Allāh ibn ʿUmar, in which he says, "The Messenger of Allāh (God's peace and blessings be upon him) declared *zakāt al-fiṭr* as prescribed for the people at the end of Ramaḍān, one *ṣāʿ* of dates or one *ṣāʿ* of barley for each freeman or slave, male or female, from among the Muslims". The apparent implication of this is an obligation in accordance with the opinion of those who follow the opinion of a Companion in comprehending it as an obligation, or it implies a recommendation in the command of the Prophet (God's peace and blessings be upon him) as his exact words have not been stated for us. It is also established that the Messenger of Allāh (God's peace and blessings be upon him) in the well-known tradition about the Bedouin mentioned *zakāt*; the man asked: "Is there another obligation on me besides this?" The Messenger of Allāh (God's peace and blessings be upon him) replied, "No! unless you pay voluntarily". The majority maintained that this *zakāt* is included in the prescribed *zakāt* (that is, it takes the same *ḥukm* of obligation), while others held that it is not. They argued on the basis of what is related from Qays ibn Saʿd ibn ʿUbāda that he said, "The Messenger of Allāh (God's peace and blessings be upon him) used to order us to pay it prior to the revelation of the verse of *zakāt*. When the verse of *zakāt* was revealed he did not command us to pay it nor did he prohibit us from doing so, and we still pay it".

6.2. *Section 2: The person on whom it is obligatory and the persons on whose behalf it is to be paid*

They agreed unanimously that the Muslims are the addressees in the command, whether male or female, minor or major, slave or freeman, because of the preceding tradition of Ibn ʿUmar, except the deviation by al-Layth, who exempted the residents of the capital from the obligation to pay *zakāt al-fiṭr*, and restricted it to the residents of the villages, but he has no evidence for this. Another deviation is found in the opinion of those who do not make it obligatory on behalf of the orphans. As to the persons on whose behalf it is obligatory, they agreed that it is obligatory on each person who is able to pay it on his own behalf, for it is a *zakāt* on the person and not on wealth. It is also obligatory on the person to pay it on behalf of his minor children if they do not own independent wealth, and also for slaves if they do not own any wealth. They differed over what is besides this.

The summary of Mālik's opinion is that a person is obliged to pay *zakāt al-fiṭr* on behalf of all persons whose maintenance is obligatory on him. Al-Shāfiʿī agreed with him on this, but they differ with reference to their dispute over whom a man is obliged to maintain if he is in difficult straits. Abū Ḥanīfa opposed him with respect to a wife and said that she is to pay for herself. Abū Thawr opposed them in the case of a slave who owns wealth. He said that if he has wealth he is to pay for himself, and his master is not to pay on his behalf. This was also upheld by the Ẓāhirites. The majority maintain that a man is not obliged to pay on behalf of his minor children if they have their own wealth sufficient for *zakāt al-fiṭr*. This was the opinion of al-Shāfiʿī, Abū Ḥanīfa, and Mālik. Al-Ḥasan said that the liability is upon the father, and if he pays it out of the wealth of his son (child) he is to compensate it.

Affluence is not a condition for this kind of *zakāt*, according to most of the jurists, and there is no *niṣāb*, but they only stipulated that this *zakāt* be a surplus over his need for food for himself and for his family. Abū Ḥanīfa and his disciples said that it is not obligatory on a person entitled to claim *ṣadaqa*, as it is not possible that a person should be liable for it as well as entitled to it. This is evident, Allāh knows best.

The majority maintain that this *zakāt* is not dependent on the prerequisite of being a *mukallaf* (that is, a person responsible for the performance of worship), as is the case with other forms of worship. The obligation, therefore, applies to minors and slaves (and to the insane person). (It is to be paid on their behalf by their guardian or maintainer.) Those who understood from this that the underlying cause of the *ḥukm* is *wilāya* said that the *walī* is under an obligation to pay the *ṣadaqa* (*zakāt al-fiṭr*) for all those who are under his guardianship. Those who understood the cause to be maintenance said that it is the maintainer who is to pay the *zakāt al-fiṭr* for all those whom he is obliged to maintain under the law. This disagreement arose because they agreed over the minor and the slave, and it is these two cases that point out that this *zakāt* is not linked to the person of the *mukallaf* alone, but is owed on behalf of others if guardianship and the obligation to maintain exist. Mālik, then, maintained that the underlying cause is the obligation to maintain, while Abū Ḥanīfa held that the cause here is *wilāya*, and for that reason they differed over the wife. It is related as a *marfū*ᶜ tradition that: "Pay the *zakāt al-fiṭr* on behalf of all those whose burden of maintenance has been placed upon you". It is, however, not well-known.

They disagreed over the case of slaves on a number of issues. The first, as we have mentioned, is the obligation of his *zakāt* on his master if he (the slave) has wealth. This is based on the point of whether he can or cannot own something. The second case is about the slave who is a disbeliever, whether he (the master) should pay *zakāt* on his behalf. Mālik, al-Shāfiᶜī, and Aḥmad said that there is no obligation of *zakāt* on the master for his disbelieving slave. The Kūfīs said that he is liable for *zakāt* on his behalf. The reason for their disagreement stems from their dispute over the addition on the issue laid down in the tradition of Ibn ᶜUmar. This relates to his words "the Muslims", over which Nāfiᶜ has been opposed, as Ibn ᶜUmar being the narrator of the tradition also held the opinion that *zakāt* is to be paid on behalf of disbelieving slaves. There is another reason for the disagreement and that is whether the obligation of *zakāt* on the master for his slave is due to the fact that the slave is a *mukallaf* or whether he is property. Those who maintained that it is due to his being a *mukallaf* stipulated that being a believer is a condition, while those who said that it is due to his being property did not stipulate it. These latter jurists said that this is indicated by the consensus of the jurists that if the slave is freed and the master has not paid *zakāt al-fiṭr* on his behalf, it is not obligatory for him to pay as in the case in expiation. The third issue is about the *mukātab*. Mālik and Abū Thawr said that the master is to pay *zakāt al-fiṭr* on his behalf. Al-Shāfiᶜī, Abū Ḥanīfa, and Aḥmad said that he is not obliged to pay on his behalf. The reason for the disagreement emanates from the vacillation of the case of the *mukātab* between a freeman and slave. The fourth is the case of slaves acquired for trade. Mālik, al-Shāfiᶜī, and Aḥmad held that the master is obliged to pay *zakāt al-fiṭr* on their behalf, while Abū Ḥanīfa and others besides him said that there is no *ṣadaqa* payable for slaves owned for purposes of trade. The reason for the disagreement arises from the conflict of analogy with the general implication (in the tradition). This is so as the general implication of the word slave (used in the preceding tradition) implies the obligation of *zakāt* for slaves owned for trade as well as others. In Abū Ḥanīfa's view this general implication is restricted by analogy, and that is due to the convergence of two kinds of *zakāt* in a single type of wealth. They disagreed, likewise, in the case of slaves owned by slaves and the cases under this topic are many.

6.3. *Section 3: The categories (of wealth) from which it is obligatory*

From what kind of wealth is it due? A group of jurists held that it is due either in wheat, or dates, or barley, or in *aqiṭ* (cheese made from sour milk), and that this is a choice of the person on whom it is obligatory. Another group of jurists held that it is obligatory upon him in the staple food of the land, or in the food of the *mukallaf* if he does not possess the dominant staple food. This is what ʿAbd al-Wahhāb has related as the opinion of the School (Mālik's).

The reason for their disagreement stems from their dispute over the meaning of the tradition of Abū Saʿīd al-Khudrī, who said, "We used to pay *zakāt al-fiṭr* during the period of the Messenger of Allāh (God's peace and blessings be upon him) as a *ṣāʿ* of food or a *ṣāʿ* of barley or a *ṣāʿ* of *aqiṭ* or a *ṣāʿ* of dried dates". Those who understood a choice from this said that any of these things he pays in is sufficient. Those who understood from it that the variety in payment is not a basis of permissibility, but is the consideration of the food of the person paying or of the staple food of the land, upheld the second opinion.

How much is obligatory? The jurists agreed that the *zakāt al-fiṭr* paid in the form of dried dates or barley is not to be less than one *ṣāʿ*, because that has been established in the tradition of Ibn ʿUmar. They disagreed about the quantity the person may pay in wheat. Mālik and al-Shāfiʿī said that less than one *ṣāʿ* would not be sufficient, while Abū Ḥanīfa and his disciples said that one-half *ṣāʿ* is sufficient.

The reason for their disagreement stems from the conflict of traditions. It is related in the tradition of Abū Saʿīd al-Khudrī, who said, "We used to pay *zakāt al-fiṭr* during the period of the Messenger of Allāh (God's peace and blessings be upon him) as a *ṣāʿ* of food or a *ṣāʿ* of barley or a *ṣāʿ* of *aqit* or a *ṣāʿ* of dried dates or a *ṣāʿ* of raisins". The apparent meaning is that by food he meant wheat. Al-Zuhrī has also related from Abū Saʿīd from his father that the Messenger of Allāh (God's peace and blessings be upon him) said, "For the *ṣadaqa* of *fiṭr* is one *ṣāʿ* of wheat shared by two persons or a *ṣāʿ* of barley or one of dates for each person". It is recorded by Abū Dāwūd. It is related from Ibn al-Musayyab that he said, "The *ṣadaqa* of *fiṭr* in the period of the Messenger of Allāh (God's peace and blessings be upon him) was one-half *ṣāʿ* of wheat or one *ṣāʿ* of barley or one *ṣāʿ* of dried dates". Those who adopted these traditions said that the obligation is for one-half *ṣāʿ* of wheat, while those who adopted the apparent meaning of the tradition of Abū Saʿīd made an analogy for wheat upon barley and held them to be similar for the obligation.

6.4. *Section 4: When is* zakāt al-fiṭr *due?*

When does *zakāt al-fiṭr* become (immediately)[208] due? They agreed that it becomes obligatory at the end of Ramaḍān, because of the tradition of Ibn ʿUmar that "The Messenger of Allāh (God's peace and blessings be upon him) declared *zakāt al-fiṭr* as prescribed for the people at the end of Ramaḍān". They disagreed over the determination of a specific time. Mālik, in a narration from him by Ibn al-Qāsim, makes it obligatory with the breaking of the dawn on the day of *fiṭr*. Ashhab has related from him that he considers it obligatory at sunset on the last day of Ramaḍān. The first opinion was also held by Abū Ḥanīfa and the second by al-Shāfiʿī. The reason for their disagreement is whether it is a worship associated with the day of *ʿīd* or with the passing of the month of Ramaḍān,[209] as the night of *ʿīd* is not part of Ramaḍān. The application of this dispute is to be seen in the case of a child born before morning on the day of *ʿīd*, but after sunset (of the last day of Ramaḍān). Is *zakāt al-fiṭr* obligatory on behalf of this child?[210]

6.5. *Section 5: Avenues of expenditure*

To whom is it to be paid? They agreed that it is to paid to the poor, because of the saying of the Prophet (God's peace and blessings be upon him), "Make them free from want on this day". They disagreed whether it is permissible for the poor of the Ahl al-Dhimma. The majority maintain that it is not permitted for them, while Abū Ḥanīfa said that it is permissible.

The reason for their disagreement is whether the basis for its entitlement is poverty alone, or it is poverty as well as being a Muslim. Those who maintained that it is poverty as well as being Muslim did not permit it for the *dhimmiyūn*, while those who maintained that it is poverty alone permitted it for them. One group, however, stipulated for the Ahl al-Dhimma that they be monks.

[208] Otherwise, its payment may be voluntarily advanced any time during the month of Ramaḍān, which is good for the poor who may have to prepare food for consumption.

[209] This happens at sunset on the last day of Ramaḍān.

[210] It is not according to the first ruling, but it is according to the second opinion.

The Muslim jurists agreed unanimously, however, that the *zakāt* on wealth is not permitted for the Ahl al-Dhimma, because of the saying of the Prophet (God's peace and blessings be upon him): "It is a *ṣadaqa* acquired from their rich and bestowed on their poor".

VII

THE BOOK OF *ṢIYĀM* (FASTING)

This book is divided into two books. The first is about obligatory fasting and the other about recommended fasting. The study of obligatory fasting is divided into two parts. The first is about fasting and the other about breaking the fast. The first part, fasting, is divided into two chapters. The first is about the kinds of obligatory fasts and the other is about the identification of its elements (*arkān*). The part that includes the study of breaking the fast is divided into the identification of things which break (annul) the fast and the *aḥkām* related to persons who break it.

7.1. BOOK I: OBLIGATORY FASTS

We begin with the first book in this (main) book.

7.1.1. **Part 1: Fasting (*Ṣawm*)**

We begin with the first chapter that covers the identification of the kinds of fasting.

7.1.1.1. **Chapter 1 The Kinds of Obligatory Fasts**

We Say: Fasting prescribed by law is obligatory and recommended. Obligatory fasting is of three kinds. The first is obligatory during a fixed time, and this is fasting during the month of Ramaḍān itself. The second is prescribed due to a reason, and this is fasting for expiation (*kaffāra*). The third is fasting that a person imposes on himself; this is fasting after a vow (*nadhr*). The discussion in this book about the kinds of obligatory fasting is related to fasting during the month of Ramaḍān alone. Fasting for expiation will be discussed on those occasions where expiation is an obligatory consequence. Similarly, fasting due to a vow will be discussed in the Book of Vows.

Fasting during the month of Ramaḍān is obligatory on the basis of the Qur'ān, the *sunna*, and consensus. In the Qur'ān the basis are the words of the Exalted, "O ye who believe! Fasting is prescribed for you, even as it was prescribed for those before you, that ye may ward off [evil]".[211] In the *sunna* it is the saying of the Prophet (God's peace and blessings be upon him), "Islam is structured on five things"—and he mentioned "fasting"; and also his words to the Bedouin, "And the fast of the month of Ramaḍān". He asked, "Am I obliged for something else besides (all) this". He replied, "No! Unless it is voluntary". Consensus is found as there is no disagreement that has been attributed to any of the *imāms* over this.

The person on whom it is obligatory without a choice is the believer who is a major and a sane person, who is not on a journey, is in sound health, and is free of a relieving factor, which is menstruation for women. There is no dispute over this because of the words of the Exalted, "And whosoever of you is present [living through the month], let him fast the month".[212]

7.1.1.2. Chapter 2 The (Integral) Elements (*Arkān*) of Fasts

There are three elements. Two of them are agreed upon, and these are duration and abstinence from acts breaking the fast, while the third is disputed, which is formulation of the intention.

7.1.1.2.1. The first element: duration

The first element, which is duration, is divided into two kinds. The first is the period of obligation, which is the month of Ramaḍān, while the other is the period of abstinence from acts that break the fast, and this covers day-time of the the days of this month, thus, excluding the nights. To each of these periods are related fundamental issues over which they disagreed. We begin with those that relate to the period of the obligation. The first of these is the determination of the two ends of this period. The second relates to the identification of the method by which a knowledge of the limiting signs is attained with respect to each individual and to the various horizons.

[211] Qur'ān 2 : 183.

[212] Qur'ān 2 : 185. Statement in parentheses added to Pickthall's translation.

With respect to the two ends of the period (of obligatory fasting), the jurists agreed that the Arabic month spans over twenty-nine days that are sometimes thirty, and that the criterion for the determination of the month of Ramaḍān is the sighting of the new moon, because of the saying of the Prophet (God's peace and blessings be upon him), "Fast with its [the moon's] sighting and break it with its sighting". By sighting here is meant the first appearance of the new moon after the declining of the sun. They disagreed about the *ḥukm* when there are factors that conceal sighting and make it impossible. They also disputed the proper time for sighting the new moon. As to their disagreement when the moon is concealed (in clouds), the majority maintain that the *ḥukm* in such a case is to complete the period of the preceding month (Shaʿbān), thirty days. If the moon is concealed at the (probable) beginning of the month, the month before it is to be counted as having thirty days. Thus, the first day of the Ramaḍān would be the next day. If the moon is concealed at the end of the month (of Ramaḍān), the people will fast for thirty days. Ibn ʿUmar held a different opinion, that is, if the concealed moon is that of the beginning of the month of Ramaḍān, the next day which is called the Day of Doubt is to to be observed as a fast. It is related from some of the predecessors (early jurists) that if the moon is concealed recourse is to be had to astronomical calculation, and this is the opinion of Muṭarrif ibn al-Shikhkhīr, one of the leading Tābiʿūn. In a narration by Ibn Surayj from al-Shāfiʿī he said that if a person is proficient in astronomy, and according to his calculation the new moon could be sighted had it not been for the obstruction he may (should) commence fasting and his fast would be valid.

The reason for their disagreement arises from the lack of detail (*ijmāl*) in the saying of the Prophet (God's peace and blessings be upon him), "Fast on sighting it and break the fast on sighting it. If it is concealed, make an assessment about it (*fa ʾqdurū lahu*)". The majority maintained that this means "complete the period of thirty days". One group of jurists said that the meaning of *taqdīr* here is to fix its time by reckoning. Some of them even said that the believer should wake up fasting, which is the opinion of Ibn ʿUmar, as we have mentioned. This, however, is a remote interpretation. The majority decided upon their interpretation due to the authentic tradition of Ibn ʿAbbās that the Prophet (God's peace and blessings be upon him) said, "If it is concealed from you, then, complete the count of thirty days". The former (tradition) lacks detail (they said) and this is its explanation, thus, it is necessary to construe the unelaborated through its explanation. This is a method over which there is no dispute among the experts on *uṣūl*, as there is in fact no conflict at all between the *mujmal* and the *mufassar*. The opinion of the majority on this point is more convincing, Allāh knows best.

In their disagreement about the legitimate time of sighting, they first agreed that if it is sighted in the evening the month begins on the next day (starting after sunset). They disagreed when it was sighted during the daytime on the last day of Shaʿbān, that is, the first time of its sighting. The opinion of the majority is that if the first sighting of the moon is during the day, it is the moon of the next day, just like its sighting in the evening. This opinion was held by Mālik, al-Shāfiʿī, Abū Ḥanīfa, and the majority of their disciples. Abū Yūsuf, the disciple of Abū Ḥanīfa, al-Thawrī, and Ibn Ḥabīb one of the disciples of Mālik held that if the moon is sighted before the declining of the sun it belongs to the previous night, but if it is sighted after the declining of the sun it belongs to the coming night.

The reason for their disagreement is the relinquishment of experience, where experience provides a way out, and having recourse instead to reports on the issue. There is no tradition on this issue from the Prophet (God's peace and blessings be upon him) to which recourse can be had. There are, however, two traditions from ʿUmar (God be pleased with him). One of them is general and the other is explanatory. One group relied upon the general report, while the other relied upon the explanatory. The report with the general implication is related by al-Aʿmash from Abū Wāʾil, the brother of Ibn Salama, who said, "A letter from ʿUmar came to us, when we were at Khaniqayn that the crescent moon appears in different sizes. Sometimes it looks large and it may look small. (The letter said:) 'If you sight the moon during day-time, do not stop fasting till two men testify that they have seen the new moon during the (previous) evening'". The tradition with the particular implication is what is related by al-Thawrī from him that a report reached ʿUmar that some people had sighted the new moon after the declining of the sun and had broken their fast. He wrote to them reprimanding them for it and said: "If you sight the moon during the day before the declining of the sun, break your fast, but if you see it after the declining of the sun do not break it".

The Qāḍī (Ibn Rushd) said: "What is dictated by analogy and experience is that the moon cannot be seen when the sun has not gone down, unless it is far away from it, for at that time it is greater than the arc of vision, though it varies growing greater or lesser, but it is unlikely, Allāh knows best, to be so large as to be seen when the sun has not gone down yet. The best reliance in this matter is on experience, as we have said. There is no difference here whether it is before the declining of the sun or after it, and the thing to be considered is the disappearance of the sun".

As far as their disagreement about the legitimate knowledge of sighting is concerned, there are two methods for it. One of these is based upon the senses (perception) and the other upon reports. The jurists agreed that a person, who alone sights the moon, is under an obligation to fast, except for ʿAṭāʾ ibn Abī Rabāḥ, who said that he is not to fast unless another person besides him has sighted it too. They disagreed about whether he can stop fasting on the basis of his own sighting. Mālik, Abū Ḥanīfa, and Aḥmad held that he is not to cease fasting. Al-Shāfiʿī said that he is to stop fasting, and this was also the opinion of Abū Thawr. This dispute has no meaning, as the Prophet (God's peace and blessings be upon him) made fasting and breaking the fast dependent upon sighting, and sighting is by perception. Had there been no consensus about fasting on the basis of a report of sighting, because of the apparent meaning of this tradition, the imposition of an obligation of fasting on the basis of reports would be far-fetched. Those who made a distinction between the moon of fasting and that of terminating the fast did so for the prevention of improper claims that may be made falsely by the devious, who may cease fasting illegitimately, claiming they have seen the moon when in actual fact they have not. Al-Shāfiʿī, therefore, said that if he fears accusations he should abstain from eating and drinking and consider himself as having ceased fasting. Mālik deviated from this and said that the person who sights the moon alone and breaks his fast is liable to *qaḍāʾ* as well as expiation. Abū Ḥanīfa said that he is only liable for *qaḍāʾ*.

They disagreed regarding certain questions related to the report of moon sighting. First, over the number of reporters whose reports must be accepted, and then about their qualifications. Mālik said that it is not permitted to commence fasting or to cease fasting on the testimony of less than two trustworthy men. Al-Shāfiʿī, in a narration by al-Muzanī, said that fasting is to commence on the testimony of one man about sighting, but fasting is not to be stopped with the testimony of less than two men. Abū Ḥanīfa said that if the sky is overcast the testimony of one person is accepted, but if it is clear in a large city only the testimony of a large number of persons is acceptable. It is also related from him that he would accept the testimony of two morally upright persons when the sky was clear. It is related from Mālik that he would not accept the testimony of two witnesses when the sky was overcast. They agreed that for breaking the fast not less than two witnesses are acceptable, except for Abū Thawr who did not make a distinction between fasting and breaking the fast, unlike al-Shāfiʿī.

The reason for their disagreement stems from the conflict of traditions on the subject, and the vacillation of a tradition between falling under the category of testimony and the category conveying no stipulated number (for witnesses). The traditions include what has been related by Abū Dāwūd from ʿAbd al-Raḥmān ibn Zayd ibn al-Khaṭṭāb that he addressed the people on a Day of Doubt and said, "I used to mix with the Companions of the Messenger of Allāh (God's peace and blessings be upon him) and asked them, and all of them related to me that the Messenger of Allāh (God's peace and blessings be upon him) said, 'Commence fasting on sighting it and cease fasting on sighting it. If it is concealed from you, then, complete a period of thirty (days). If two witnesses render testimony (of sighting the moon), commence fasting or cease fasting'". They also include the tradition of Ibn ʿAbbās that he said, "A Bedouin came up to the Prophet (God's peace and blessings be upon him) and said, 'I sighted the moon tonight.' He said, 'Do you testify that there is no god but Allāh and that Muḥammad is his servant and messenger?' He replied, 'Yes'. He (the Prophet) said, 'Bilāl, announce to the people that they are to fast tomorrow'". This is recorded by al-Tirmidhī, who stated that there is a dispute about its *isnād* as a group has reported it as *mursal.* There is also the tradition of Ribʿī ibn Khirāsh (Ḥirāsh?) that is recorded by Abū Dāwūd from Ribʿī ibn Khirāsh from one of the Companions of the Prophet (God's peace and blessings be upon him), who said, "The people were fasting on the last day of Ramaḍān, when two Bedouins stood up and testified to the Prophet (God's peace and blessings be upon him) that they had sighted the moon the previous evening. The Messenger of Allāh (God's peace and blessings be upon him) ordered the people to break the fast and to go to the place of [*ʿīd*] prayer".

The jurists adopted the methods of preference or the method of reconciliation for these traditions. Al-Shāfiʿī reconciled the traditions of Ibn ʿAbbās and Ribʿī ibn Khirāsh through their apparent meanings and, thus, deemed the commencement of fasting obligatory on the testimony of one person and its cessation on the testimony of two. Mālik preferred the tradition of ʿAbd al-Raḥmān ibn Zayd on the basis of analogy, that is, holding it to be similar to testimony in other claims. It appears that Abū Thawr did not see a conflict between the traditions of Ibn ʿAbbās and that of Ribʿī ibn Khirāsh. This is so as he (the Prophet) decided on the testimony of two witnesses according to the tradition of Ribʿī ibn Khirāsh, and in the tradition of Ibn ʿAbbās he decided on the the testimony of one witness. This (Abū Thawr said) indicates the permissibility of both, and not that there is a conflict. Nor is there an indication that the decision in the first was specific to the commencement of fasting and that in the second to its cessation, for such an opinion would be based on the assumption of a conflict. The same appears to be true for the conflict between the traditions of ʿAbd al-Raḥmān ibn Zayd and Ibn ʿAbbās, unless the conflict is claimed on the basis of the indirect indication of the text, which is weak as the text opposes it. Thus, we see that the opinion of Abū Thawr, despite its deviation (from the majority view), is more evident, although comparing sighting to narration is closer than comparing sighting to testifying. The reason is that in testimony the stipulation of a number (for witnesses) may either be guidance by revelation, and thus it cannot be subjected to intellectual interpretation as it is not permitted to draw an analogy from it, or it may be said that the stipulation of number is due to the litigation that accompanies claims and the doubt that is associated with the testimony of a person by the litigants. Thus, a multiplicity of witnesses is stipulated so that the conviction becomes predominant and the inclination toward the claims of one litigant is strengthened. The number did not go beyond two so that adducing evidence does not become difficult thereby vitiating claims. There is no accompanying doubt due to an opponent in the case of the sighting of the moon that should necessitate its clarification through an increase in number.

It appears that al-Shāfiʿī made a distinction between the moon of fasting and the moon of cessation of fasting on the basis of the suspicion that is associated with people in the sighting of the moon of cessation of fasting, but is not present in the case of the moon of fasting. The opinion of Abū Bakr ibn al-Mundhir is the same as the opinion of Abū Thawr, and I believe it is also that of the Ẓāhirites. Abū Bakr ibn al-Mundhir argued on the basis of this tradition for the occurrence of a consensus for the obligation of breaking the fast and abstaining from eating on the testimony of one person. It therefore becomes necessary that the matter be the same for entering into the month and moving out of it, as both are signs separating the period of non-fasting from the period of fasting.

If we say that sighting is established for those who have not sighted it on the basis of a report, then, can this be extended from one land to the other, I mean, is it obligatory upon the people in one region, if they have not sighted the moon, to adopt the sighting in another land, or is sighting necessary for every land? There is disagreement over this. Ibn al-Qāsim and the Egyptian jurists (who follow Mālik) have related from Mālik that if it is established for the people of one town that the people in another have sighted the moon, they are under an obligation of *qaḍāʾ* for the day observed by others and missed by them. This was also the opinion of al-Shāfiʿī and Aḥmad. The Medinites have related from Mālik that sighting on the basis of a report is not binding upon people not living in the land in which sighting occurred, unless the *imām* requires the people to do so. This was the opinion of Ibn al-Mājishūn and of al-Mughīra from among the disciples of Mālik. They agreed that this is not to be taken into account for lands distant from each other, like al-Andalus and al-Ḥijāz.

The reason for this disagreement comes from the conflict of traditions and reasoning. The reasoning is that if the timing of the rising of the sun and the stars in different lands does not differ very much, it is necessary that one should follow the other, as by reason they have the same horizon. If it does differ much, however, then it is not binding upon one region to follow the other. The tradition is what is related by Muslim from Kurayb that Umm al-Faḍl bint al-Ḥārith sent him to Muʿāwiya in Syria. He said, "I reached Syria and did what she had required. The moon of Ramaḍān came upon me while I was in Syria, and I sighted it on the night before Friday. Near the end of the month I moved to Medina where ʿAbd Allāh ibn ʿAbbās questioned me and then mentioned the moon, saying, 'When did you sight the moon (in Syria)?' I said, 'We saw it on the night before Friday.' He asked, 'Did you, yourself, see it?' I said, 'Yes, and so did the people. They fasted and Muʿāwiya fasted too'. He said, 'But we sighted it on the night before Saturday, and we continue to fast till we either complete thirty days or sight it'. I said, 'Do you not consider Muʿāwiya's fasting as sufficient?' He replied, 'No! This is what the Prophet (God's peace and blessings be upon him) ordered us to do'". The apparent meaning in this tradition implies that each land, near or distant, must sight the moon. Investigation, however, reveals a difference between distant and near lands, especially those that are at a great distance in terms of longitude and latitude. If the report (about sighting) reaches the level of *tawātur* there is no need to support it with testimony. These, then, are the issues related to the duration of the obligation.

On the issues related to the duration of abstinence they agreed that it is terminated by the setting of the sun, because of the words of the Exalted, "Then strictly observe the fast till nightfall".[213] They disagreed about the time of its commencement. The majority said that it is at the appearance of the second dawn, the white line (horizon), the appearance of the true morning twilight, because it is established from the Messenger of Allāh (God's peace and blessings be upon him), who defined it as the spreading white line (horizon), and also because of the words of the Exalted, "Eat and drink until the white thread becometh distinct to you from the black thread of the dawn".[214] One group deviated saying that it is the red dawn that appears after the white and it is a replica of the red dusk (the evening twilight). This is related from Ḥudhayfa and Ibn Masʿūd.

The reason for disagreement emanates from the conflict of traditions on the issue and the equivocality of the term "dawn", that is, it is applied to mean either the white or the red. The traditions on the basis of which they argued include the tradition of Zarr from Abū Ḥudhayfa, who said, "I had meals with the Prophet (God's peace and blessings be upon him) before daybreak, and had I liked I could have said it was daytime, yet the sun had not risen". Abū Dāwūd had recorded from Qays ibn Ṭalq from his father that the Prophet (God's peace and blessings be upon him) said, "Eat and drink, and let not the rising white light intimidate you. Eat and drink, until you see the red light spreading across [the horizon]". Abū Dāwūd stated that this tradition was narrated by the people of Yamāma alone, and this is deviation, for the words of the Exalted, "Eat and drink until the white thread becometh distinct to

[213] Qurʾān 2 : 187.
[214] Qurʾān 2 : 187.

you",[215] are explicit, or almost explicit, in this. Those who held that it is the spreading white line of the dawn, and these are the majority, who are on firmer ground, disagreed about the exact limit for abstention from such things as eating (and drinking). A group of jurists said that it is the breaking of the dawn in itself. Another group said that it is its awareness for the person looking at it. If he does not become aware of it, then, observance of abstention is not obligatory, even if it is already daybreak. The significance of the distinction is that if the person discovers that it was daybreak before he became aware of it, then, according to those for whom the limit is the break of the dawn itself, he is liable for *qaḍā'*. Those who consider the limit to be the person's own awareness of it, hold that *qaḍā'* is not obligatory for him.

The disagreement over this is caused by the possible interpretations of the words of the Exalted, "Eat and drink until the white thread becometh distinct to you from the black thread of the dawn".[216] Is abstinence to commence when the distinction becomes evident to the person or as soon as it actually happens? Arabs employ the term figuratively for the occurrence of a phenomenon to denote another that follows it. It was thus as if it was said, "Eat and drink until the white thread becomes distinct to *you* from the black thread". If it becomes evident in itself it becomes evident to us, thus, attributing its becoming evident to us is the reason for the dispute, because it may have become evident and distinct in itself and still not be evident to us. The apparent meaning necessitates the linking of abstinence to actual knowledge, while analogy associates it with the actual fact. I mean, analogy drawn from the *ḥukm* of the sunset prayer and from all the other religious obligations attached to time-limits, like the *ẓuhr* prayer starting at the declining of the sun, as well as others. The consideration in all of these is attached to the actual realities themselves, not to their knowledge. The well-known opinion from Mālik, which is also held by the majority, is that engagement in acts like eating may go up the beginning of daybreak (dawn). It is said, however, that abstinence should be prior to dawn. The evidence for the first view is what is related in the *Ṣaḥīḥ* of al-Bukhārī, and I believe in some versions of the tradition, that the Prophet (God's peace and blessings be upon him) said, "Eat and drink until Ibn Umm Maktūm makes the call [for the dawn prayer], for he does not make the call unless it is the break of the dawn".[217] This is explicit on the point of dispute, or almost explicit, and conforms with the words of the Exalted, "Eat and drink until the white thread becometh distinct to you from the black thread of the dawn".[218] Those who maintained that abstinence is to

[215] Qur'ān 2 : 187.
[216] Qur'ān 2 : 187.
[217] The background is that Bilāl used to recite the dawn *adhān* earlier to wake up the believers.
[218] Qur'ān 2 : 187.

commence prior to the dawn did so as a precaution and for the prevention of means (to violation). This is a more conservative opinion, but the other is more in line with analogy, Allāh knows best.

7.1.2.2. The second element: Abstinence

They agreed that abstinence from food, drink, and sexual intercourse is obligatory, on the person fasting, during the period of the fast due to the words of the Exalted, "So hold intercourse with them and seek that which Allāh hath ordained for you, and eat and drink until the white thread becometh distinct to you from the black thread of the dawn".[219] They differed in this over issues some of which are not expressly stated in the law while others are. Those that are not expressly stated include the question of things entering the stomach but are not food, that of things entering the stomach from other than the passage for food and drink, like enema, and the problem of things entering some parts of the body other than the stomach, like those entering the brain but not reaching the digestive tract.

The reason for their disagreement over these things stems from the analogy drawn from food for those that are not food. This is so as things expressly mentioned are food. Those who thought that the purpose of fasting has a rational meaning did not link non-food with food. Those who maintained that it is a worship that does not have a rational meaning and that the aim of fasting is abstinence alone from things that reach the stomach held food and non-food to be the same (for this purpose). The summary of Mālik's opinions is that it is obligatory to abstain from things that reach the gullet through any opening, whether they are food or non-food.

With respect to things other than food and drink that break the fast, all of them agreed, except for Mālik, that a person who kisses and ejaculates has broken the fast, but one who passes pre-seminal fluid does not. They disagreed over kissing by the person fasting. Some of them permitted this. Some disapproved (frowned upon) it for a young man but permitted it for the elderly. Some prohibited it absolutely. Those who granted an exemption for it did so because of what is related of the traditions of ʿĀʾisha and Umm Salama "that the Prophet (God's peace and blessings be upon him) used to kiss when he was fasting". Those who disapproved of it did so as kissing may lead to sexual intercourse. One group deviated and said that a kiss breaks the fast. They argued for this on the basis of what is related from Maymūna ibn Saʿd, who said, "The Messenger of Allāh (God's peace and blessings be upon him) was asked about kissing by one fasting. He said, 'Both are to break the fast' ".

[219] Qurʾān 2 : 187.

Al-Ṭaḥāwī recorded this tradition but declared it as weak. Those acts, that occur as a result of an overpowering emotion or forgetfulness, their discussion will be taken up under the discussion of things breaking the fast and their *aḥkām*.

The things that are expressly mentioned and over which they disagreed are cupping and vomiting. There are three opinions about cupping. A group of jurists said that cupping breaks the fast and abstaining from it is obligatory. This was the opinion of Aḥmad, Dāwūd, al-Awzā'ī, and Isḥāq Ibn Rāhwayh. Another group of jurists said that it is disapproved (deprecated) for the person fasting, but it does not break the fast. This was the opinion of Mālik, al-Shāfi'ī, and al-Thawrī. A third group said that it is neither frowned upon nor does it annul the fast. This was the opinion of Abū Ḥanīfa and his disciples.

The reason for their disagreement comes from the conflict of traditions that have been reported on the issue. There are two traditions on the issue. The first is related through Thawbān and through Rāfi' ibn Khadīj that the Prophet (God's peace and blessings be upon him) said, "The person cupping and the one being cupped have broken the fast". This tradition of Thawbān was considered authentic by Aḥmad. The second is the tradition of 'Ikrima from Ibn 'Abbās "that the Messenger of Allāh (God's peace and blessings be upon him) was cupped when he was fasting". This tradition of Ibn 'Abbās is authentic.

The jurists, in their treatment of these traditions, adopted three methods. The first is the method of preference. The second is the method of reconciliation. The third is the giving up of the conflicting traditions and having recourse to the original rule of no liability, as the abrogated text cannot be distinguished from the abrogating text. Those who adopted the method of preference argued on the basis of the tradition of Thawbān, as it imposes a *ḥukm* while the tradition of Ibn 'Abbās removes it, and that imposing it is to be preferred over one removing it. If the *ḥukm* is established in a manner that it is obligatory to act upon it, it cannot be removed except by way of an obligation of not acting upon it. The tradition of Thawbān necessitates that it be acted upon. The tradition of Ibn 'Abbās has two probabilities; namely, it is the abrogated or the abrogating tradition. This invokes doubt and doubt does not necessitate action nor does it remove a conviction necessitating action. This is in accordance with the method of those who do consider doubt to be operative against conviction. Those who sought to reconcile the two traditions interpreted the proscribing tradition to mean disapproval and the tradition depicting cupping to imply the removal of prohibition. Those who dropped the traditions due to conflict upheld the permissibility of cupping for the person fasting.

With respect to vomiting, the majority of the jurists maintained that one who vomits involuntarily has not broken his fast, except Rabīʿa who said that he has. The majority, except Ṭāwūs, also maintain that the person who vomits voluntarily has broken his fast. The reason for their disagreement stems from the assumed conflict between the traditions that are laid down on the issue, and also their dispute about the authenticity of these traditions. There are two traditions on the topic. The first is the tradition of Abū al-Dardāʾ "that the Messenger of Allāh (God's peace and blessings be upon him) vomited and broke his fast". Maʿdān said, "I met Thawbān in the mosque of Damascus and said to him that Abū al-Dardāʾ told me 'that the Messenger of Allāh (God's peace and blessings be upon him) vomited and broke his fast.' He said, 'He spoke the truth, and I poured out water for his ablution'". This tradition of Thawbān has been declared authentic by al-Tirmidhī. The other tradition is from Abū Hurayra and is recorded by al-Tirmidhī and Abū Dāwūd. It says that the Prophet (God's peace and blessings be upon him) said, "One who is overcome by vomiting when he is fasting is not under an obligation for *qaḍāʾ*, but one who causes himself to vomit is under the obligation for *qaḍāʾ*". This has also been related as *mawqūf*[220] from Ibn ʿUmar. Those for whom both traditions did not prove to be authentic said that there is no breaking of the fast at all in this case. Those who adopted the apparent meaning of the tradition of Thawbān and preferred it over the tradition of Abū Hurayra upheld the obligation of (*qaḍāʾ* for) breaking the fast after vomiting without qualifications, that is, they did not distinguish between deliberate and non-deliberate vomiting. Those who reconciled the two traditions maintained that the tradition of Thawbān lacks detail, while the tradition of Abū Hurayra is explanatory, and it is necessary to construe the concise tradition through the explanatory. They, therefore, distinguished between vomiting and self-induced vomiting, and this is the opinion of the majority.

7.1.1.2.3. The third element: intention

The discussion of intention is undertaken from different aspects. These include whether it is a condition for the validity of this worship, and if it is a condition, then, what kind of determination is considered valid? Further, whether its renewal every day of Ramaḍān is obligatory or is the intention expressed on the first day sufficient? If the subject makes the resolve, what is the time of this resolve that makes the fast valid, so that if it is not expressed at such time it is nullified? Does failure to form the intention necessitate breaking the fast, and what if the person does not break the fast? The jurists differed on each of these questions.

[220] The tradition is attributed to a Companion, but his disciple through whom the tradition is supposed to be narrated is dropped from the *isnād*.

The opinion of the majority of the jurists is that intention is a condition for the validity of the fast, but Zufar deviated and said that the month of Ramaḍān does not require intention, unless the person happens to have reason to be relieved from the obligation of fasting, such as being on a journey, but wishes to fast. The reason for their disagreement stems from their notion about the nature of fasting whether it is a worship having a rational meaning or it has no such meaning. Those who maintained that it is a worship having no rational purpose made intention obligatory, while those who maintained that it is a worship with rational purpose said that the purpose is attained even if the person does not form an intention. The confining of this reasoning by Zufar to only some kinds of fasting presents some weakness. It appears that he formed his opinion on the grounds that it is not permitted to cease fasting during the days of Ramaḍān and that any fast kept during these days of the month fulfils this form of prescribed fasting, and this is something specific to these days.

With respect to their dispute over the specification of the kind of fasts through the formulation of a valid intention, Mālik said that it is necessary to identify the fast of Ramaḍān in the intention, and it is not sufficient in Ramaḍān to have a general intention to fast, nor an intention specifying another fast. Abū Ḥanīfa (held the opposite view, and) said that if the person forms an absolute (unqualified) intention, or an intention specifying another fast other than the fast of Ramaḍān it is valid and the fast turns into a fast of Ramaḍān. This is so, unless the person is on a journey for, in his view, if the traveller during Ramaḍān makes an intention for fasts other than the fast of Ramaḍān his intention will apply to the intended fast. The reason is that while travelling he is not under an obligation to observe the fast of Ramaḍān. His two (renowned) disciples did not distinguish between one travelling and the resident. They said that each fast intended during Ramaḍān is converted into a fast of Ramaḍān.

The reason for their disagreement stems from the dispute as to whether it is sufficient for the fasts of Ramaḍān that the category of fasting be identified generally or that it has to be specified. Both forms (of intention) exist in the law. An example of the general intention is the intention of ablution in which it is sufficient to intend the removal of impurities. The worshipper may then perform any kind of worship whose validity depends on ablution (prayers, *ṭawāf*, carrying a copy of the Qurʾān, etc.). Thus, ablution is not specific to one kind of worship. This is different from the intention for prayer, in which it is necessary to specify the particular prayer that is about to be performed. It is, therefore, necessary to specify the prayer as *ʿaṣr*, if it is *ʿaṣr*, and *ẓuhr* if it is *ẓuhr*. All this is well-known to the jurists. Fasting, therefore, vacillates between these two general rules in the view of these jurists. Those who associated it to one genus said that it is sufficient to make a resolve for fasting alone. Those who associated it with the second genus stipulated the specification of the fast.

They also disagree over the issue that if he makes an intention, during the days of Ramaḍān, for another kind of fast whether this is converted (to the fast of Ramaḍān). The reason for this is that some kinds of worship are converted due to the fact that the time in which it occurs is specific for the worship to which they are converted. There are some kinds of worship that are not converted, and this applies to most forms of worship. Those, however, that are converted include *ḥajj*, by agreement. They said that if a person on whom *ḥajj* is obligatory commences it as a voluntary form of worship during the *ḥajj* season, the voluntary form is converted to the obligatory form. They did not say this for prayer or other forms of worship. Those who held fasting to be similar to *ḥajj* said that it is converted, while those who held it to be similar to other forms said that it is not.

In their disagreement over the time of forming the intention, Mālik said that fasting is not valid except by an intention formed before the break of the dawn, and this applies to all kinds of fasting. Al-Shāfiʿī said that intention formed after dawn is valid in supererogatory fasting, but it is not in obligatory fasts. Abū Ḥanīfa held that intention formed after dawn is sufficient for all kinds of fasting whose obligation is linked to a particular time, like those of Ramaḍān, those linked to specific days or dates after a vow, and also those that are supererogatory, but it is not for the fasts that exist as a liability.

The reason for their disagreement arises from the conflict of traditions on the issue. The first of these traditions is the one recorded by al-Bukhārī from Ḥafṣa that the Prophet (God's peace and blessings be upon him) said, "One who does not form the intention to fast during the night has no fast". It has also been related as *mawqūf* by Mālik. Abū ʿUmar said that there is some discrepancy in the *isnād* of Ḥafṣa's tradition. The second is recorded by Muslim from ʿĀʾisha, who said, "The Messenger of Allāh (God's peace and blessings be upon him) said to me one day, 'ʿĀʾisha, do you have something (to eat)?' I said, 'O Messenger of Allāh, we have nothing'. He said, 'Then I am fasting'". In the tradition of Muʿāwiya, he said on the pulpit, "O people of Medina, where are your learned men? I heard the Messenger of Allāh (God's peace and blessings be upon him) saying, 'Today it is the day of ʿĀshūrāʾ and its fast has not been prescribed for us. I am fasting, so those of you who wish to fast may do so and those who like may continue to eat'".

Those who adopted the method of preference relied on Ḥafṣa's tradition, while those who adopted the method of reconciliation distinguished between supererogatory and obligatory fasting, that is, they construed the tradition of Ḥafṣa as implying obligatory fasts and the traditions of ʿĀʾisha and Muʿāwiya as implying supererogatory fasts. Abū Ḥanīfa made a distinction between universal obligation and an obligation that is a liability, as the universal obligation has a determined time that takes the place of intention for specification, while the fast that is a liability has no fixed time; thus, he made it obligatory that it be specified with an intention.

The majority of the jurists maintain that freedom from *janāba* is not a condition for the validity of the fast, because of what is established from the traditions of ʿĀʾisha and Umm Salama, the two wives of the Prophet (God's peace and blessings be upon him), who said, "The Messenger of Allāh (God's peace and blessings be upon him) used to arise in the morning during Ramaḍān in a state of major impurity from sexual intercourse, not a wet dream, and then kept the fast". An evidence for this is that a wet dream during the day does not invalidate the fast. It is, however, related from Ibrāhīm al-Nakhaʿī, ʿUrwa ibn Zubayr, and Ṭāwūs that if the person does this intentionally (induces ejaculation) the fast is invalidated.

The reason for their disagreement comes from what is related from Abū Hurayra, who used to say, "One who arises in the morning during Ramaḍān in a state of major impurity has broken his fast". Mālik has related that a menstruating woman who reaches the period of purity before dawn, but delays bathing is not to fast on that day. The opinions of these jurists are deviant and rejected by the well-known and established *sunan*.

7.1.1.3. Chapter 3 Breaking the Fast and Not Fasting and the *Aḥkām*

This chapter discusses breaking the fast (and not fasting) and its *aḥkām*. Those who may break the fast (or not fast) are, in the law, of three kinds: a category in which it is permitted, by consensus, to fast or not to fast; a category in which it is obligatory not to fast, along with the accompanying disagreement among Muslim jurists; and a category in which it is forbidden not to fast. For each of these there are related *aḥkām*.

Those to whom both things are permitted are the the sick person, by agreement, the traveller, with disagreement, the pregnant woman, the wet-nurse, and the old person. This division is agreed upon in its entirety, except the traveller whose problem is examined from various aspects. These include the point: that if he fasts, whether his fast is considered to be valid. If it is valid, whether it is better for the traveller to fast or not to fast, or whether he has a choice between the two. Whether breaking the fast is permitted to him for a limited type of journey or for any journey to which the term "journey" is applied in usage. When may the traveller stop fasting? When does he begin fasting (again)? If he initiates a journey during Ramaḍān, does he have the right to break the fast after the passage of a portion of the month? Finally, if he does not fast, what is the *ḥukm* for him? The case of the sick person involves the discussion of the identification of the sickness which entitles him not to fast, and also the *ḥukm* while not fasting.

7.1.1.3.1. Issue 1

This relates to the question of the sick person and the traveller if they fast, whether their fast is considered valid as an obligatory fast. The jurists disagreed over this. The majority maintain that if they fast their fast is in order and valid. The Ẓāhirites maintain that their fasts are not valid and their obligation is to perform *qaḍā*ʾ on other days (not in Ramaḍān).

The reason for the disagreement is based on the interpretation of the words of the Exalted, "And whosoever of you is sick or on a journey, (let him fast the same) number of other days",[221] whether they are to be read as they are so that no implied word is assumed, or whether they are to be construed metaphorically and an implied word is to be read into them so as to read, "and he does not fast then (let him fast the same) number of other days". This kind of absence of words in speech is known to the experts of the language as *laḥn al-khiṭāb* (style of Arabic). Those who read the verse as it is and not metaphorically said that the obligation for the traveller is to fast the same number of other days, because of the words of the Exalted, "number of other days". Those who assumed the implied words "and he does not fast" said that his obligation is a number of other days if he does not fast. Both groups support their interpretation on the basis of traditions that testify to the correctness of their understanding, though the principle is to read a text as it is, unless another evidence indicates that it be read in its metaphorical meaning.

The majority argue for their opinion on the basis of the established tradition of Anas, who said, "We travelled with the Messenger of Allāh (God's peace and blessings be upon him) during Ramaḍān and he did not find fault with the person fasting in preference to the person not fasting nor did he find fault with the person not fasting in preference to the one fasting". It is also established from him that he said, "The Companions of the Messenger of Allāh (God's peace and blessings be upon him) used to travel together with some of them fasting when others were not". The Ẓāhirites argue for their opinion on the basis of what is established from Ibn ʿAbbās "that the Messenger of Allāh (God's peace and blessings be upon him) travelled to Mecca in the year of its conquest during Ramaḍān. He continued to fast up to al-Kadīd after which he stopped fasting and so did the people", and they used to act upon the most recent of the commands of the Messenger of Allāh (God's peace and blessings

[221] Qurʾān 2 : 185.

be upon him). They said that this indicates the abrogation of fasting (during travel). Abū ʿUmar said that the argument against the Ẓāhirites is their consensus that if the sick person keeps the fast his fast is considered to be valid.

7.1.1.3.2. Issue 2

This relates to the question whether fasting is better than not fasting (during travel). If we say, according to the opinion of the majority, that the traveller is entitled not to fast, then we must add that the jurists had three different opinions (within this general agreement). Some of them held that fasting has greater merit. Those who held this opinion include Mālik and Abū Ḥanīfa. Some maintained that not fasting is better. Those who held this opinion include Aḥmad and a group of jurists. Some maintained that this was a matter of choice, none is better.

The reason for their disagreement arises from the conflict of an interpretation with the apparent meaning of some transmitted texts, and the conflict of some transmitted texts with other transmitted texts. This is so as the understandable meaning of the permission of not fasting for a person is an exemption intended to remove hardship for him, and when an exemption is provided it is meritorious to relinquish the exemption. This is testified to by the tradition of Ḥamza ibn ʿAmr al-Aslamī, recorded by Muslim, that he said, "O Messenger of Allāh, I find in myself the strength to fast during a journey, would I then be sinning?" The Messenger of Allāh (God's peace and blessings be upon him) said, "It is an exemption from Allāh, so he who acts upon it does good, but there is no sin on the person who wishes to fast". The saying of the Messenger of Allāh (God's peace and blessings be upon him), however, that "It is not an act of piety to fast during a journey", along with the fact that one of his last acts was not to fast, gives the impression that it is better not to fast. Not fasting, though, is not the *ḥukm*, but a permissible act, and it was difficult for the majority to deem the permissible act as being better than the prescribed. Those who gave a choice in the matter did so because of the tradition of ʿĀʾisha, who said, "Ḥamza ibn ʿAmr al-Aslamī asked the Messenger of Allāh (God's peace and blessings be upon him) about fasting during a journey and he said, 'Fast if you like, and if you like do not' ". It is recorded by Muslim.

7.1.1.3.3. Issue 3

Whether the permissibility of not fasting for the traveller is limited to journeys of a minimum determined distance. The jurists disagreed about it. The majority said that he may not fast in a journey for which prayer is to be curtailed, and that varies in accordance with their disagreement on that issue.

A group of jurists maintained that he may cease fasting in every journey to which the term "journey" is applied. These are the Ẓāhirites.

The reason for their disagreement stems from the conflict of the apparent meaning of the text with an interpretation. The apparent meaning is that the person may not fast in any journey to which the term is applicable, because of the words of the Exalted, "And whosoever of you is sick or on a journey, (let him fast the same) number of other days".[222] Yet, the understandable meaning of the permission of not fasting during a journey is (relief from) hardship. As hardship is not to be found in every journey it becomes necessary that not fasting be permitted in that journey that entails hardship, and because the Companions were apparently agreed upon a limit for this, it follows that an analogy be drawn upon the limit for the curtailment of prayer.

7.1.1.3.4. Issue 4

They also disagreed about the sickness during which not fasting is permitted. A group of jurists said that it is a sickness in which hardship and duress become associated with the fast. This was Mālik's opinion. Another group of jurists said that it is an overwhelming sickness. This was Aḥmad's opinion. A third group of jurists said that if the term "sick" could be applied to such a person he is not to fast. The reason for their disagreement is the very reason that is assigned for the limit of the journey.

7.1.1.3.5. Issue 5

When does the traveller stop fasting and when does he fast? A group of jurists said that he is to cease fasting the very day that he begins his journey. This was the opinion of al-Shaʿbī, al-Ḥasan, and Aḥmad. Another group said that he is not to cease fasting the day he commences his journey. This was upheld by the jurists of the provinces. A group of jurists considered it desirable for the person who knows that he will reach a city on the first day of his journey should enter it while fasting. Some of them were more strict in this than others, but all of them did not impose expiation on a person who entered when he was not fasting. They disagreed about the person who entered a city when only part of the day had past. Mālik and al-Shāfiʿī said that he is to continue eating and drinking. Abū Ḥanīfa and his disciples said that he is to abstain from eating, just as the menstruating woman, in their view, refrains from eating when she enters the period of purity.

The reason for their disagreement about the time at which the traveller is to stop fasting arises from the conflict of traditions with reasoning. It is

[222] Qurʾān 2 : 185.

established through the tradition of Ibn ʿAbbās "that the Messenger of Allāh (God's peace and blessings be upon him) kept the fast until he reached al-Kadīd when he stopped fasting and so did the people with him". The apparent meaning of this tradition is that he stopped fasting after he had formed the intention for fasting. In the case of the people, however, there is no doubt that they broke the fast after they had formed the intention for it the previous night. Implying the same is the tradition of Jābir ibn ʿAbd Allāh "that the Messenger of Allāh (God's peace and blessings be upon him) travelled to Mecca in the year of its conquest. He continued to travel up to Karāʿ al-Ghamīm, where he asked for the drinking bowl, when the people were fasting, and raised it so the people could see him. He then drank from it. It was later said to him that some of the people continued to fast. He said, 'They are the disobedient. They are the disobedient'". Abū Dāwūd has recorded from Abū Buṣra al-Ghifārī that he had barely gone beyond the houses when he asked for the dining sheet. Jaʿfar, the narrator of the tradition, said, "I said to him, 'Do you not see the houses?' He replied, 'Do you shy away from the *sunna* of the Messenger of Allāh (God's peace and blessings be upon him)'". Jaʿfar said, "He then ate". The reasoning here is that as the traveller is permitted only to form the intention for his fast on the previous night it is not permitted that he annul his fast, because he formed the intention on the basis of the words of the Exalted, "O ye who believe! Obey Allāh and obey the messenger and render not your actions vain".

The reason for their disagreement about abstaining from eating, or not abstaining, on the part of the person entering a city during the day is their dispute about its similarity with the person not fasting on the Day of Doubt (and who abstains) when it is proved to him that it is the first day of Ramaḍān. Those who held this case to be similar to it said that he is to abstain from eating (to fast), while those who did not hold it to be similar said that he is not to abstain as that case is based on a lack of knowledge while this is based upon a cause permitting or giving rise to eating. The Ḥanafites said that both are causes giving rise to abstinence from eating following the permission to eat.

7.1.1.3.6. Issue 6

This relates to the question of whether it is permitted for a person fasting during Ramaḍān to begin a journey and then stop fasting while travelling. The majority maintain that he is permitted to do so. It is related from some, and these are ʿUbayda al-Salmānī, Suwayd ibn Ghafla, and Ibn Majāz, that if he has been fasting during Ramaḍān and begins a journey in it he is not permitted to cease fasting.

The reason for their disagreement arises from their dispute over the meaning of the words of the Exalted, "And whosoever is present let him fast the month".[223] This can be interpreted to mean that one who is present (resident) for part of the month is under an obligation to fast for the whole month. It is also possible to understand from it that the person who has witnessed part of the month (as a resident) should fast for that part, as the meaning by agreement is that the person who has witnessed the whole month should fast for the whole month, it should also mean that one who has witnessed part of the month (as a resident) should fast for that part. The opinion of the majority is supported by the fact that the Prophet began his journey during Ramaḍān.

The *ḥukm* for the traveller if he ceases to fast (during Ramaḍān) is *qaḍā*ʾ, by agreement, and the same holds for the sick person, because of the words of the Exalted, "(Let him fast the same) number of other days".[224] The exceptions are persons who are sick due to fainting or insanity, but the jurists disagreed about the two cases. The jurists of the provinces maintain the obligation of *qaḍā*ʾ for the person who faints, but differ about the insane. In Mālik's opinion he is under an obligation for *qaḍā*ʾ, but it is weak because of the words of the Prophet (God's peace and blessings be upon him), "The pen (liability) has been lifted in the case of three persons . . ., and the insane person until he recovers". Those who imposed the obligation on both disagreed about the existence of fainting and insanity as vitiating factors for fasting. One group said that they do vitiate fasting, while another group said that they do not. A third group of jurists made a distinction between the fainting spell occurring before dawn or after dawn. One group said that if it occurs after the passage of the greater part of the day the person's fast is valid, but if it occurs in the first part of the day he is to fast as *qaḍā*ʾ, and this is Mālik's opinion.

All this is weak, as fainting and insanity are causes because of which liability (*taklīf*) is removed, especially in the case of insanity. When the liability is removed the person cannot be described as one fasting or not fasting. How, then, can it be said about an attribute removing liability altogether that it invalidates the fast, for it would amount to saying about a dead person or one all of whose acts are invalid that his fast and his acts have been nullified.

7.1.1.3.7. Sub-issues related to *qaḍā*ʾ

There are certain sub-issues related to the *qaḍā*ʾ of the traveller and the sick person including the questions: do they perform consecutively? What is required from them as *qaḍā*ʾ? What is their duty if they delay, without excuse, the performance of *qaḍā*ʾ until the next Ramaḍān? If they die without performing the required *qaḍā*ʾ, does the guardian (*walī*) fast on their behalf?

[223] Qurʾān 2 : 185.
[224] Qurʾān 2 : 185.

Some of the jurists made it obligatory that *qaḍā*ʾ be performed consecutively like *adā*ʾ, while others did not. Some of these jurists gave the person a choice, with some considering consecutive performance to be desirable, but the greater majority stands for the relinquishment of the obligation of consecutive performance.

The reason for their disagreement arises from the conflict of the apparent meaning of the text with analogy. Analogy, in this case, requires that *qaḍā*ʾ performance be the same as *adā*ʾ, the basis for this being prayer and *ḥajj*. The apparent meaning of the words of the Exalted, "(Let him fast the same) number of other days",[225] implies that the obligation exists for the same number alone and not for consecutive performance. It is related from ʿĀʾisha that she said, "The verse was revealed as 'consecutive number of days', but the word 'consecutive' was dropped".

With respect to delaying *qaḍā*ʾ until the next Ramaḍān has started, a group of jurists said that the obligation upon such a person is *qaḍā*ʾ after the new Ramaḍān as well as expiation (*kaffāra*). This was the opinion of Mālik, al-Shāfiʿī, and Aḥmad. Another group of jurists said that there is no obligation of expiation upon him. This was the opinion of al-Ḥasan al-Baṣrī and of Ibrāhīm al-Nakhaʿī.

The reason for their disagreement is whether analogy can be used for extending one expiation to another? Those who did not permit analogy for expiation said that he is only liable for *qaḍā*ʾ. Those who permitted analogy in expiation said that he is obliged to make expiation on the analogy of the person who breaks his fast intentionally as both violate the sanctity of the fast. This person does it by relinquishing *qaḍā* at its proper time whereas the other does it by eating during a day on which eating is not permitted. Analogy here would be well grounded had it been established explicitly by the Lawgiver that there is a determined time for *qaḍā*ʾ, because the timings for ʿ*adā*ʾ have been determined by the Lawgiver. One group of jurists deviated saying that if the illness of the person continues up to the next Ramaḍān there is no *qaḍā*ʾ for him. This opposes the text.

A group of jurists said that if the person dies having missed an obligatory fast, no one else is to fast on his behalf. Another group of jurists said that his *walī* is to fast on his behalf. Those who did not make fasting obligatory on the guardian said that he is to feed (the needy) on his behalf. This was al-Shāfiʿī's opinion. Some said that there is no obligation for fasting or for feeding unless the person leaves a testament to the effect. This was Mālik's opinion. Abū Ḥanīfa said that the guardian is to fast. If he is not able to do this he is to feed (the needy). One group of jurists made a distinction between (fasting due to) a

[225] Qurʾān 2 : 185.

vow (*nadhr*) and the regular obligatory fasting, saying that his guardian is to fast on his behalf for a vow, but not for obligatory fasting.

The reason for their disagreement stems from the conflict of analogy with traditions. It is established from the Prophet (God's peace and blessings be upon him) through a tradition from ʿĀʾisha that he said, "If a person dies when he owed a duty to fast, his *walī* is to fast on his behalf". It is related by Muslim. It is also established from him (God's peace and blessings be upon him) through the tradition of Ibn ʿAbbās, who said, "A man came up to the Prophet (God's peace and blessings be upon him) and said, 'O Messenger of Allāh, my mother has died owing the fast for a month. Should I, then, fast on her behalf?' He said, 'Had there been a debt against your mother would you have paid that on her behalf?' He replied, 'Yes'. He said, 'The debt of Allāh has a prior claim for payment'". Those who maintained that the principles oppose this, because as no one prays for another or performs ablution for another then no one is to fast for another, said there is no obligation of fasting for the guardian. Those who adopted the text for this said that he is obliged to fast. Those who did not employ the text for this confined it to the case of (a fast due to) a vow. Those who constructed an analogy from this (vow) said that he is to fast on his behalf for Ramaḍān (missed).

Those who imposed the feeding of the needy decided on the basis of the verse, "(Fast) a certain number of days; and (for) him who is sick among you, or on a journey, (the same) number of other days; and for those who can afford it there is ransom: the feeding of a man in need".[226] Those who granted a choice in this reconciled the verse and the tradition.

These, then, are the *aḥkām* of the traveller and the sick person to whom it is permitted not to fast or to fast.

7.1.1.3.8. Sub-issues relating to the pregnant woman, the wet-nurse, and old persons

The remainder of this chapter is devoted to the discussion of the wet-nurse, the pregnant woman, and the old person. There are two well known issues related to this. The first is if the pregnant woman and wet-nurse do not fast, what is their duty? The jurists have four opinions on this issue. The first is that both feed the needy and there is no *qaḍāʾ* for them. This is related from Ibn ʿUmar and ibn ʿAbbās. The second opinion, which is the counterpart of the first, is that they only perform *qaḍāʾ* and they are not obliged for feeding the needy, and this is the opinion of Abū Ḥanīfa, his disciples, Abū ʿUbayd,

[226] Qurʾān 2 : 184.

and Abū Thawr. The third opinion is that they perform *qaḍā᾽* as well as feed the needy. This was al-Shāfiʿī's opinion. The fourth opinion is that the pregnant woman performs *qaḍā᾽* but does not feed the needy, while the wet-nurse performs *qaḍā᾽* as well as feeds the needy.

The reason for their disagreement derives from the vacillation of their cases between resemblance with those for whom fasting is difficult and between the sick person. Those who regarded them to be similar to the sick person said that they are only to perform *qaḍā᾽*. Those who regarded them to be similar to those for whom fasting is exhausting said that they are only obliged to feed the needy; this view rests on the evidence of the recitation, recited by some, of the verse, "And those for whom it is overwhelming is ransom: feeding the needy (*masākīn*)".[227] Those who considered both factors for them, it appears, formed their opinion on the basis of both resemblances. Thus, they said that they are obliged for *qaḍā᾽* insofar as they resemble the sick person, and they are obliged for ransom insofar as they resemble those for whom fasting is difficult. Holding them similar to a person of sound health who does not fast, however, is weak as there is no permission for the healthy person not to fast. Those who made a distinction between the pregnant woman and the wet-nurse associated the pregnant woman with the sick person, and they rendered the *ḥukm* of the wet-nurse to be a combination of the *ḥukm* of the sick person and the *ḥukm* of the person for whom fasting is difficult, or they held her to be similar to the person in sound health. Those who singled out one *ḥukm* for them have a better opinion, Allāh knows best, as compared to those who combined the two, just as those who singled out the *ḥukm* of *qaḍā᾽* for them have a better opinion than those who singled out the *ḥukm* of feeding for them, as the reading of the verse on the basis of which they assigned it is not *mutawātir* (and is variant). So ponder over it, for it is evident.

The jurists agreed that the old man and woman who are not able to fast may not fast, but they disagreed about their obligation if they do not. A group of jurists said that they are under an obligation to feed the needy, while another group said that they are not. The first view was held by al-Shāfiʿī and Abū Ḥanīfa, and the second was held by Mālik, except that he considered it (feeding) desirable. The majority of those who uphold feeding say that it is an amount of one *mudd* for each day. It is, however, said that even if they dole out handfuls, as Anas used to do, it is considered sufficient for them.

The reason for their disagreement derives from the variant recitation that we mentioned, that is, "And those for whom it is overwhelming is ransom: feeding the needy (*masākin*)".[228] Those who considered acting upon a verse, which is

227 A variant reading in place of Qur᾽ān 2 : 184.

228 A variant reading in place of Qur᾽ān 2 : 184.

not established in the *muṣḥaf*, as obligatory when it has been transmitted as an individual narration by *ʿadl* narrators, said that the old man (*shaykh*) is covered by it. Those who did not consider this to be obligatory maintained that the *ḥukm* of the old person is that of a sick person whose illness continues up to his death.

These are the *aḥkām* of the category of persons to whom it is permitted not to fast, that is, the well-known *aḥkām* that are either explicitly stated in the law or are related to those that are stated with respect to persons who are allowed not to fast.

7.1.1.3.9. Violation of the fast

The examination of the category of persons to whom it is permitted not to continue the fast if they have broken their fast is taken up with reference to breaking the fast through sexual intercourse or through some other way, and with reference to an act that is agreed upon or that which is disputed, that is, an act based on doubt and one that is not. Each of these two cases occurs either due to forgetfulness or due to intention or due to choice or due to duress.

The majority of the jurists maintained that a person who breaks his fast through intentional sexual intercourse is under an obligation of *qaḍāʾ* as well as expiation, because of what is established through the tradition of Abū Hurayra, who said, "A man came up to the Messenger of Allāh (God's peace and blessings be upon him) and said, 'I am ruined, O Messenger of Allāh'. He said, 'And what has ruined you?' He said, 'I had sexual intercourse with my wife during Ramaḍān.' He said, 'Do you have a slave that you can set free?' He replied, 'No'. He said, 'Are you able to fast for two months consecutively?' He replied, 'No'. He said, 'Do you have food with which you can feed sixty needy persons?' He replied, 'No'. He then waited. The Prophet (God's peace and blessings be upon him) received as a gift a *faraq* [fifteen *ṣāʿs*, sixty *mudds*] of dates and said to him, 'Give these as alms'. The man said, 'To someone who is poorer than I? There is no household between the boundaries of the town more in need of it than ours'. The Prophet (God's peace and blessings be upon him) smiled so that his canine teeth were noticeable, and said, 'Go, feed it to your family'". They differed over this on several points including: whether breaking a fast intentionally by eating or drinking carries the same *ḥukm* as that for breaking the fast through sexual intercourse involving *qaḍāʾ* and expiation? If the person has sexual intercourse out of forgetfulness, what is his obligation? What is the obligation for the woman if she was not forced into it? Is expiation obligatory in the listed order or is it a matter of choice? What is the amount that is to be given to each needy person, if he makes expiation by feeding the needy? Does expiation recur with the recurrence of sexual intercourse? If feeding is deferred when he is in difficult straits, does it become binding when his situation improves?

One group of jurists deviated (from the majority opinion) and did not impose anything on a person breaking his fast intentionally through sexual intercourse, except *qaḍāʾ*. They maintained this either because this tradition did not reach them or because (they thought that) the matter did not amount to a determined decision in this tradition, for had it been so the person would be under an obligation to fast when he was not able to manumit a slave or to feed the needy, and this indeed was a must, according to the apparent meaning of this tradition, if he was in sound health. Further, had this been a determined ruling the Prophet (God's peace and blessings be upon him) would have informed him that fasting was obligatory on him once he could afford it. Likewise, another group deviated and said that there is no liability for this offence except expiation alone, as *qaḍāʾ* has not been mentioned in the tradition, and the *qaḍāʾ* mentioned in the Qurʾān applies to persons to whom breaking the fast is allowed, or to those to whom fasting is not permitted. We may recall here the disagreement over this, which we have already stated. As there is no text for the obligation of *qaḍāʾ* on the person who breaks his fast intentionally, the dispute surrounding the *qaḍāʾ* of such a person was linked with the *qaḍāʾ* of a person who intentionally relinquishes prayer until its prescribed time is over. The dispute over these two issues is deviant. The well-known dispute, however, is over the issues we have listed.

7.1.1.3.9.1. Sub-issue 1

Is expiation obligatory for intentionally breaking the fast by eating or drinking? Mālik, his disciples, Abū Ḥanīfa, his disciples, al-Thawrī, and a group of jurists maintained that the person who intentionally breaks his fast by eating or drinking is liable to *qaḍāʾ* and expiation mentioned in this tradition. Al-Shāfiʿī, Aḥmad, and the Ẓāhirites held that liability for expiation arises in the case of breaking the fast through sexual intercourse alone.

The reason for their disagreement arises from their dispute over drawing an analogy between the person breaking the fast through sexual intercourse and one breaking it by eating and drinking. Those who maintained that they have a common basis, which is the violation of the sanctity of the fast, determined that the *ḥukm* should be the same for them both. Those who maintained that though expiation is a punishment for the violation of sanctity, it is more suitable by its intensity for the person breaking the fast through sexual intercourse as compared to others, and (thus, they said that) because the purpose of punishment is deterrence a greater punishment is laid down for the act for which there is a more powerful desire. This act, they said, is more powerful than other offences, though the degrees of the offences are close and the aim of the imposition of expiation is to make people abide by the laws and be pious and upright, as in the words of the Exalted, "O ye who believe! Fasting is prescribed for you, even as it was prescribed for those before you, that ye may ward off (evil)". This enhanced form of expiation, they said, is therefore specific to sexual intercourse. These views are expressed by those who uphold analogy in this case.[229] The opinion of those who do not uphold analogy here is obvious, they do not extend the *ḥukm* for (violation through) sexual intercourse to eating and drinking.

The report by Mālik in *al-Muwaṭṭaʾ*, that a person broke his fast during Ramaḍān and the Prophet (God's peace and blessings be upon him) ordered him to make the listed expiation, is not persuasive as the statement of the narrator that the person "broke his fast" is *mujmal* (unelaborated), and the *mujmal* does not have a general implication that can be adopted. It does, however, give an opinion as the narrator reported expiation to be a consequence for breaking the fast. Had this not been the case he would not have mentioned these words, and he would have mentioned one of the ways in which the fast is broken.

7.1.1.3.9.2. Sub-issue 2

When the person fasting has sexual intercourse out of forgetfulness, al-Shāfiʿī and Abū Ḥanīfa maintain that there is no *qaḍāʾ* for the person nor is there any expiation. Mālik said that he is liable for *qaḍāʾ*, but there is no expiation. Aḥmad and the Ẓāhirites maintained that he is liable for both *qaḍāʾ* and expiation.

The reason for their disagreement over *qaḍāʾ* of the person acting out of forgetfulness stems from the conflict of the apparent meaning of the tradition with analogy. The analogy holds one forgetting prayer to be similar to the person forgetting his fast. Those who held him to be similar to one forgetting prayer held him liable for *qaḍāʾ* as the person forgetting prayer has been held liable by the text. The tradition conflicting with the apparent implication of this analogy is what has been recorded by al-Bukhārī and Muslim from Abū Hurayra, who said, "The Messenger of Allāh (God's peace and blessings be upon him) said, 'One who forgets while fasting and eats or drinks should complete his fast, for indeed it is Allāh who has given him to eat and made him drink'". This tradition is supported by the general implication of the saying of the Prophet (God's peace and blessings be upon him), "Liability for mistake, forgetfulness, and what they did under duress has been lifted from my *umma*".

[229] The Ẓāhirites have been mentioned among these jurists, but they reject analogy altogether. Logically, their opinion should be the one that follows.

Within this topic their disagreement about whether there is *qaḍāʾ* for the person who (mistakenly) believes that the sun has gone down and breaks his fast, but the sun appears thereafter. The reason is that such a person has made a mistake, and the *ḥukm* of one making a mistake is the same as that for one forgetting. In whatever way we express it, the effectiveness of forgetfulness in dropping (the obligation) of *qaḍāʾ* is evident, Allāh knows best. The argument is that if we were to maintain the principle that *qaḍāʾ* is not binding on the person forgetting until an evidence indicates this, it becomes necessary to hold that forgetfulness in fasting is not liable to *qaḍāʾ* as there is no evidence to indicate this, as against the situation in prayer. If, on the other hand, we were to hold that the principle is that *qaḍāʾ* is obligatory until an evidence indicates its removal from the liability of the person forgetting, then, we can say that an evidence has indicated its removal from the liability of the person forgetting in the tradition of Abū Hurayra. Unless one were to maintain that the evidence which exempted the case of the person forgetting the fast from the rule of forgetfulness for the other forms of worship, where all liability is removed by the text from one relinquishing it, is analogy to the case of fasting constructed upon the case of prayer. The imposition of obligation of *qaḍāʾ* by means of analogy, however, is weak. And *qaḍāʾ* in the opinion of the majority is obligatory through a renewed command.

The opinion of those who imposed *qaḍāʾ* as well as expiation upon the person committing sexual intercourse in forgetfulness is weak. The effectiveness of forgetfulness in the waiving of punishments is evident in the law, and expiation is a kind of punishment. What led them to decide this is their reliance upon the unelaborated (*mujmal*) text transmitted in the tradition; I mean, it was not mentioned in that text whether the person committed the act intentionally and not out of forgetfulness. Yet, those who imposed expiation on the hunter of prey (in the prohibited months) in forgetfulness did not maintain this principle of theirs along with the fact that the text relates to the person acting intentionally. It was more becoming for the Ẓāhirites to adopt the tradition that was authentic by agreement, which imposes expiation upon the person acting intentionally until an evidence indicated its applicability to forgetfulness, or they should have adopted the general implication of the saying of the Prophet (God's peace and blessings be upon him), "Liability for mistake, forgetfulness, and what they did under duress has been lifted from my *umma*", until an evidence indicated the restriction. Both groups did not abide by their principle, and in the unelaborated implication transmitted in the tradition about the Bedouin there is no persuasive force. Those experts of *uṣūl* who maintained that the lack of detail from the Lawgiver in varying circumstances stands in the position of a general implication arising from sayings is weak. The Lawgiver has not laid down any rule at all that is not elaborated, and lack of elaboration belongs to us.

7.1.1.3.9.3. Sub-issue 3

This issue is about their disagreement over the obligation of expiation upon the woman who has been coaxed into having sexual intercourse (while fasting). Abū Ḥanīfa and his disciples, and Mālik and his disciples made expiation obligatory for her. Al-Shāfiʿī and Dāwūd said that there is no expiation for her.

The reason for the disagreement stems from the conflict of the apparent meaning of the tradition with analogy, because the Prophet (God's peace and blessings be upon him) did not order the woman in the tradition to make expiation. The analogy is that she is like the man as both are under the liability.

7.1.1.3.9.4. Sub-issue 4

Is there an order for the making of the expiation, as in the case of *ẓihār* (injurious assimilation), or is there a choice? By order I mean that the subject is not to move from one obligation to the other unless he is unable to perform the previous one; and by choice I mean that he is permitted to make a choice of one without being unable to perform the other. They disagreed about this. Al-Shāfiʿī, Abū Ḥanīfa, al-Thawrī, and all the Kūfīs said that there is an order. Thus, the person is to manumit a slave first, and if he is unable to do this he is to fast, and if he is unable to do that then he is to feed the needy. Mālik said that it is based on choice. Ibn al-Qāsim has related from him that he considered feeding the needy more desirable than manumission and fasting.

The reason for their disagreement in imposing an order derives from the conflict of the apparent meanings of the traditions and the various analogies. The apparent meaning of the tradition about the Bedouin implies an order, as the Prophet (God's peace and blessings be upon him) asked him about his ability to perform acts in a definite order. The apparent meaning of what is related by Mālik that "A man broke his fast during Ramaḍān and the Messenger of Allāh (God's peace and blessings be upon him) ordered him to set free a slave, or to fast for two consecutive months, or to feed sixty needy persons", indicates a choice, as the word *ʿaw* (or), in the usage of the Arabs implies a choice, even though this occurred in the words of the narrator, one of the Companions, who were best acquainted with the context and the implications of the words.

The conflicting analogies, on the other hand, are based on holding it to be similar, once, with the expiation in *ẓihār* and, another time, with the expiation for an oath, though it resembles more the expiation for *ẓihār* rather than that for an oath, and also by deriving an order from the statement of the narrator.

The desirability of commencing with feeding the needy, in Mālik's view, is in conflict with the apparent meaning of the traditions. He decided this on the basis of analogy as he saw that feeding of the needy had been mentioned as a substitute for fasting on a number of occasions in the law, and that it is more compatible with it than the others on the evidence of the variant recitation, "And those for whom it is overwhelming is ransom: feeding the needy".[230] It was for the same reason that he, and a group of jurists, deemed it desirable for a person who has died with a pending duty to fast that expiation through feeding be made on his behalf. This appears to belong to the category of preferring analogy, which is supported by principles, over a tradition that is not supported by the principles.

7.1.1.3.9.5. Sub-issue 5

This relates to their disagreement over the quantity of food to be given to the needy. Mālik, al-Shāfiʿī, and their disciples said that he is to give one *mudd* of food to each needy person in accordance with the *mudd* used by the Prophet (God's peace and blessings be upon him). Abū Ḥanīfa and his disciples held that less than two *mudds*, in accordance with the *mudd* used by the Prophet (God's peace and blessings be upon him) would not be sufficient, and this comes to one-half *ṣāʿ* for each needy person.

The reason for their disagreement arises from the conflict of analogy with a tradition. The analogy is based upon the similarity of this ransom with that in the case of not shaving the head (at the close of the pilgrimage) due to an ailment, which is expressly stated. The tradition is what is related in different versions of the traditions about expiation that a *faraq* (a large measure) comprised of fifteen *ṣāʿs*. Its comprising fifteen *ṣāʿs*, however, does not indicate its obligation for each needy person in this case, except through a very weak indication, but it does indicate that the substitute for fasting in this expiation is this amount.

7.1.1.3.9.6. Sub-issue 6

This is about the recurrence of expiation with a recurrence of the violation of the fast. They agreed that a person who has sexual intercourse during Ramaḍān and makes an expiation, and then has sexual intercourse on another day has to make another expiation. They agreed that the person who commits sexual intercourse a number of times on the same day is only obliged to make a single expiation. They disagreed about the case of a person who has intercourse on one day during Ramaḍān and does not make the expiation until he has intercourse on another day. Mālik, al-Shāfiʿī, and a group of jurists said that he is to make an expiation for each of these day. Abū Ḥanīfa and his disciples said that he is to make a single expiation as long as he has not made an expiation for the first intercourse.

The reason for the disagreement stems from the similarity of these expiations with those in the *ḥudūd*. Those who held them to be similar to the

[230] A variant reading in place of Qurʾān 2 : 184.

ḥudūd said that one expiation is sufficient in this on account of a number of acts, just as the person committing unlawful sexual intercourse is subjected to one penalty of stripes even if he has committed the act a thousand times (before that) when he has not been subjected to *ḥadd* for any of those occasions. Those who did not consider them to be similar to the *ḥudūd* determined a separate *ḥukm* for each of the days in which the fast has been violated, and therefore imposed one expiation for each day. They maintained that the distinction is based upon expiation being a way of attaining nearness to Allāh, while the *ḥudūd* are a form of pure deterrence.

7.1.1.3.9.7. Sub-issue 7

Does a person, who committed the offence of copulation during the fast of Ramaḍān and could not afford the cost of expiation at the time, have to offer it when his financial condition improves? Al-Awzāʿī said that he owes nothing if he was hard up at the time of the offence. Al-Shāfiʿī hesitated over this question.

The reason for their disagreement is that it is a *ḥukm* not expressly stated in the law, and it is, therefore, likely to be similar to debts, in which case the obligation reverts if his financial position improves, and it is equally likely to say that if this had been obligatory the Prophet (God's peace and blessings be upon him) would have explained it.

These, then, are the *aḥkām* of the cases in which the jurists agreed that the fast was broken by deliberate action. In disputed cases those who held that the fast had been broken differed as to whether *qaḍā*ʾ alone should be imposed, or *qaḍā*ʾ as well as expiation. Examples for these are: cupping, vomiting, swallowing a stone, and the traveller breaking his fast on departing the first day, in the opinion of those who maintain that he should not do so.

Mālik made *qaḍā*ʾ and expiation obligatory on such a traveller, but he was opposed in this by the remaining jurists of the provinces and the majority of his disciples. Those who considered *qaḍā*ʾ and expiation obligatory in the case of deliberate vomiting include Abū Thawr and al-Awzāʿī, but the remaining jurists who maintain that vomiting breaks the fast impose only *qaḍā*ʾ for it. The jurist who imposed *qaḍā*ʾ and expiation in the case of cupping, from among those who maintained that cupping breaks the fast, is ʿAṭāʾ alone.

The reason for this disagreement derives from the existence of similarity of disputed factors breaking the fast with undisputed factors breaking it, and with acts that do not break it by agreement. Those who granted predominance to one of these resemblances made obligatory the *ḥukm* assigned to it. These two kinds of resemblances that are to be found in them are what gave rise to the disagreement, I mean, whether the person is considered to have broken the fast or he is not considered to have done so. As breaking the fast is doubtful, expiation is not obligatory according to the majority, only *qaḍā*ʾ is obligatory.

On account of this, Abū Ḥanīfa felt that the person who breaks the fast intentionally and then something occurs on that day permitting the breaking of the fast for that person, there is no expiation for him. This is like the case of a woman who breaks the fast intentionally and then starts menstruating during the rest of the day. Another example is when a person in sound health breaks the fast intentionally and then falls ill. A third is when a resident breaks his fast and then goes on a journey. Thus, those who considered the ultimate development that legitimized breaking of his fast said that there is no expiation for him. The reason is that to each of these persons it was revealed by the eventual development that breaking his fast on that day was permitted to him. Those who paid more attention to the violation of the law imposed expiation upon this person, as at the time when he broke the fast he did not have knowledge of the permissibility arising afterwards. This is the opinion of Mālik and al-Shāfiʿī.

Within this topic is the imposition of *qaḍāʾ* alone by Mālik upon a person who broke his fast when he was still doubtful about the dawn, and also the imposition of *qaḍāʾ* and expiation upon the person who breaks the fast when he is doubtful about sunset, in accordance with the distinction between them that has preceded.

The majority agreed that there is no expiation for breaking the fast on a day of *qaḍāʾ* for Ramaḍān, because it does not possess the same sanctity as that of *adāʾ*, that is, of Ramaḍān. The exception was Qatāda, who imposed *qaḍāʾ* as well as expiation in this case. It is related by Ibn al-Qāsim and Ibn Wahb that such a person is under an obligation to fast for two days on the analogy of an invalid *ḥajj*.

They agreed that one of the *sunan* of fasting is the delay of the meal before dawn, and haste in the breaking of the fast, because of the saying of the Prophet (God's peace and blessings be upon him), "The people will continue to enjoy blessings (of Allāh) as long as they hasten the breaking of the fast and delay the meal before dawn". He also said, "Have the meal before dawn for it bears a blessing". The Prophet (God's peace and blessings be upon him) said that "The difference between our fast and that of the People of the Book is having the pre-dawn meal".

The majority of the jurists also maintain that one of the *sunan* of Ramaḍān and one of its desirable practices is the restraining of the tongue from uttering obscenities and nonsense, because of the saying of the Prophet (God's peace and blessings be upon him), "The fast is a shield, so when one of you arises in the morning with a fast he should not utter obscenities and foolish things. If another person hurls abuses at him he should say: I am fasting". The Ẓāhirites held that uttering obscenities breaks the fast. This, however, is a deviant opinion.

These then are the well-known issues related to obligatory fasting. The discussion of recommended fasting remains, and that is the second part of this book.

7.2. BOOK II: RECOMMENDED FASTS

The discussion of recommended fasting is about the three elements and about the *ḥukm* of breaking the fast. The days on which recommended fasting is undertaken, which is the first element, are divided into three types: desirable days, prohibited days, days about which there is silence. Some of these are disputed and some are agreed upon. The fasts that are considered desirable and are agreed upon are the fasts of the *ʿĀshūrā*. Those that are disputed are the fast on the day of *ʿArafa*, six days of Shawwāl, and the *ghurar* in each month, and these are the thirteenth, fourteenth, and the fifteenth.

The fast of the day of *ʿĀshūrā* is established, because "The Messenger of Allāh (God's peace and blessings be upon him) kept a fast on this day and ordered that it be observed as a fast", and he said about it "that one who wakes up without fasting should complete the rest of the day fasting". They disagreed whether it is the ninth or tenth day (of Muḥarram). The reason for their disagreement is the conflict of traditions. Muslim recorded from Ibn ʿAbbās that he said, "When you see the moon of Muḥarram, then, count the days and wake up on the ninth day fasting". I asked him (the narrator from Ibn ʿAbbās), "This was the way that Muḥammad, the Messenger of Allāh (God's peace and blessings be upon him) kept the fast?" He said, "Yes". It is also related that "When the Messenger of Allāh (God's peace and blessings be upon him) kept a fast on the day of *ʿĀshūrā* and ordered that it be observed as a fast, they said, 'O Messenger of Allāh, it is a day that is held sacred by the Jews and the Christians'. The Messenger of Allāh (God's peace and blessings be upon him) said, 'Next year, by the will of Allāh, we shall fast on the ninth day.' He said before ʿĀshūrā of the next year arrived, the Messenger of Allāh (God's peace and blessings be upon him) passed away".

Their disagreement about the day of *ʿarafa* is based upon the reason that the Prophet (God's peace and blessings be upon him) did not fast on the day of *ʿarafa*, but he is also reported to have said about it: "The fast of the day of *ʿarafa* absolves [the sins of] the previous year and of the one to come". The jurists disagreed because of this. Al-Shāfiʿī decided upon not fasting for pilgrims on this day and fasting for the others by way of reconciliation between the two traditions. Abū Dāwūd has recorded that the Messenger of Allāh (God's peace and blessings be upon him) proscribed the fast of *ʿArafa* at *ʿArafa*.

About the six days of Shawwāl it is established that the Messenger of Allāh (God's peace and blessings be upon him) said, "One fasting during Ramaḍān and then following it up with six days of Shawwāl is like fasting through Time (perpetual fasting)". Mālik, however, considered this to be disapproved, either because people might associate with Ramaḍān what is not a part of it, or either because the tradition had not reached him or it did not prove to be authentic for him, which is more likely. Likewise, Mālik considered as disapproved the pursuit of the fasts of the *ghurar*, despite the tradition laid down in it, for fear that the unlettered might consider them to be obligatory. It is established "that the Messenger of Allāh (God's peace and blessings be upon him) used to fast each month for three undetermined days, and that he said to ʿAbd Allāh ibn ʿAmr ibn al-ʿĀṣ, because of his excessive fasting, 'Are three days in each month not sufficient for you?'" He said, "I said, 'O Messenger of Allāh, I am able to fast more than that'. He said, 'Five?' I said, 'O Messenger of Allāh, I am able to fast more than that.' He said, 'Seven?' I said, 'O Messenger of Allāh, I am able to fast more than that.' He said, 'Nine?' I said, 'O Messenger of Allāh, I am able to fast more than that.' He said, 'Eleven?' I said, 'O Messenger of Allāh, I am able to fast more than that'. The Prophet (God's peace and blessings be upon him) then said, 'There is no fast beyond the fast of Dāwūd. Fasting one day and not fasting the other is fasting to the brink of Time (perpetual)'". Abū Dāwūd has recorded that "he used to fast on Mondays and Thursdays". It is established that he never observed fasting for the whole month, except for Ramaḍān, and that most of his fasts were during the month of Shaʿbān.

The proscribed days also include those that are agreed upon and those that are disputed. Those agreed upon are the day of *fiṭr* and the day of *aḍḥā*, because of the established proscription about them. Those disputed are the days of *tashrīq*, the Day of Doubt, Friday, Saturday, the second half of Shaʿbān, and perpetual fasting.

The Ẓāhirites did not permit fasting on the days of *tashrīq*, while another group of jurists permitted this. A third group considered this as disapproved, and this is the opinion of Mālik, except that he permitted fasting during these days for the person for whom the obligation arose out of *ḥajj*, and this is for one performing *tamattuʿ*. These days are the three days following the day of the sacrifice.

The reason for their disagreement derives from the vacillation of the saying of the Prophet (God's peace and blessings be upon him) that "these are the days of eating and drinking" between being construed as an obligation and a recommendation. Those who interpreted this to imply an obligation said that fasting is prohibited (during these days), while those who interpreted it to mean a recommendation said that fasting is disapproved. It appears that those who interpreted it as a recommendation decided this by giving it prominence over the principle of (initial) interpretation as (always) implying obligation, because they saw that if they construed it as an obligation it would be opposed by the authentic tradition of Abū Saʿīd al-Khudrī through the indication of its text. In this tradition he said, "I heard the Messenger of Allāh (God's peace and blessings be upon him) saying, 'Fasting is not valid on two days, the day of *fiṭr* after Ramaḍān and the day of sacrifice'". The indication of the text implies that fasting is valid on days other than these two days, otherwise specifying them would be futile, having no purpose.

A group of jurists did not disapprove of fasting on a Friday. These include Mālik, his disciples, and a group of jurists. Another group disapproved of fasting on this day, unless a fast was kept before it or after it. The reason for their disagreement stems from the conflict of traditions over this. One of these is the tradition of Ibn Masʿūd "that the Prophet (God's peace and blessings be upon him) used to fast on three days of each month". He said: "I have not seen him not fasting on a Friday". This is an authentic tradition. There is also the tradition of Jābir "that a questioner asked Jābir, 'I have heard that the Messenger of Allāh (God's peace and blessings be upon him) prohibited that Friday be singled out for fasting.' He replied, 'Yes, by the Lord of this House'". It is recorded by Muslim. Included in these is also the tradition of Abū Hurayra, who said, "The Messenger of Allāh (God's peace and blessings be upon him) said, 'None of you should fast on a Friday, unless he fasts before it or after it'". This too is recorded by Muslim. Those who adopted the apparent meaning of the tradition of Ibn Masʿūd permitted fasting on a Friday without qualifications. Those who adopted the apparent meaning of Jābir's tradition disapproved it absolutely. Those who followed Abū Hurayra's tradition reconciled the two tradition, that is, Jābir's tradition and that of Ibn Masʿūd.

The majority of the jurists uphold the prohibition of fasting on the Day of Doubt considering it a part of Ramaḍān on the apparent meaning of the traditions that link fasting to the sighting, or with the completion of the number of the days of Shaʿbān (thirty), except what we have related from Ibn ʿUmar. They disagreed about pursuing voluntary fasting on this day. Some of the jurists disapproved this on the apparent meaning of the tradition of ʿAmmār, "He who fasts on the Day of Doubt has defied Abū al-Qāsim". Those who permitted it did so on the report "that the Prophet (God's peace and blessings be upon him) kept the fasts for the whole of Shaʿbān", and also because of the report that the Prophet (God's peace and blessings be upon him) said, "Do not advance Ramaḍān by a day or by two days, unless that is the day on which one of you is accustomed to fasting, in which case he may do so".[231] Al-Layth ibn Saʿd used to say that if the person fasts on the assumption that it is a day of Ramaḍān and then it is established that it is Ramaḍān his fast is considered to be valid. This provides an evidence that intention to fast becomes effective after dawn, as the intention of a voluntary fast is converted to that of an obligatory fast.

The reason for their disagreement about fasting on Saturday arises from their dispute about the authenticity of the report from the Prophet (God's peace and blessings be upon him) that he said, "Do not fast on a Saturday, except (the occasion) when it is obligatory for you". It is recorded by Abū Dāwūd. They said that this tradition has been abrogated by the tradition of Juwayriya bint al-Ḥārith "that the Prophet (God's peace and blessings be upon him) came up to her on a Friday, when she was fasting, and said, 'Did you fast yesterday?' She said, 'No'. He said, 'Do you wish to fast tomorrow?' She said, 'No'. He said, 'Then break your fast'".

The proscription for fasting perpetually was laid down, but Mālik saw no harm in this, and he could have thought that the proscription was based on the apprehension of weakness or illness.

Fasting during the second half of Shaʿbān was disapproved by one group of jurists and permitted by another. Those who disapproved it did so on the basis of the report that the Prophet (God's peace and blessings be upon him) said, "There is no fast after the middle of Shaʿbān up to Ramaḍān". Those who permitted it did so on the basis of the report from Umm Salama, who said, "I have not seen the Messenger of Allāh (God's peace and blessings be upon him) fasting for two consecutive months, except for Shaʿbān and Ramaḍān", and also on the basis of what is related from Ibn ʿUmar, who said, "The Messenger of Allāh (God's peace and blessings be upon him) used to combine Shaʿbān with Ramaḍān". These traditions have been recorded by al-Ṭaḥāwī.

The second element (of fasts) relates to intention and I do not know of anyone who did not stipulate intention for voluntary fasting, but they did differ over the time of forming the intention in accordance with what has preceded.

The third element is abstinence from things that break the fast, and that is exactly the same as abstinence in obligatory fasting. The disagreement that exists there is carried over here.

With respect to the *ḥukm* of breaking the fast in voluntary fasting they agreed that a person who commences a voluntary fast and then cuts it off due to a legitimate reason is not liable to *qaḍāʾ*. They disagreed when he cuts it off intentionally and without an excuse. Mālik and Abū Ḥanīfa imposed *qaḍāʾ*

[231] This is like someone accustomed to fasting on some specific day, like Monday and Thursday each week, and the Day of Doubt falls on one of them.

upon him. Al-Shāfiʿī and a group of jurists said that there is no *qaḍāʾ* for him.

The reason for their disagreement stems from the conflict of traditions about this. Mālik has related that Ḥafṣa and ʿĀʾisha, the two wives of the Prophet (God's peace and blessings be upon him) kept a voluntary fast together. A gift of food was brought to them and they broke their fast. The Messenger of Allāh (God's peace and blessings be upon him) said, "Fast another day in its place". This is opposed by the tradition of Umm Hānī, who said:[232] "On the day of the conquest, the conquest of Mecca, Fāṭima came and sat to the left of the Messenger of Allāh (God's peace and blessings be upon him) when Umm Hānī was to his right. She said: A maid came with a utensil containing a beverage. She gave it to him and he drank from it. He then gave it to Umm Hānī who also drank from it. She said: O Messenger of Allāh, I have broken my fast, for I was fasting. The Prophet (God's peace and blessings be upon him) said to her: Were you observing *qaḍā* for something? She said: No. He said: Then it does not harm you, if it was voluntary". Al-Shāfiʿī argued, for a similar implication, on the basis of the tradition of ʿĀʾisha. She said, "The Messenger of Allāh (God's peace and blessings be upon him) entered upon me and I said to him, 'I have hidden something for you'. He said, 'I had intended to fast, but bring it over'". The traditions of ʿĀʾisha and Ḥafṣa are not *musnad*.

Their disagreement over this issue has another reason. It is the vacillation of the voluntary fast between its resemblance with voluntary prayer and with voluntary *ḥajj*. This is so as they agreed that the person who commences *ḥajj* or *ʿumra* on a voluntary basis and then moves out of it is liable for *qaḍāʾ*. They also agreed that the person who leaves a voluntary prayer is not liable for *qaḍāʾ* as far as I know. Those who made an analogy for fasting on the basis of prayer thought that it resembles prayer more closely than it does *ḥajj*, as *ḥajj* has a specific *ḥukm* in this case, which is that it is binding upon one who has invalidated it to continue moving in it up to the end.

If the person breaks a voluntary fast out of forgetfulness, the majority hold that there is no *qaḍāʾ* for him. Ibn ʿUlayya said that he is liable to *qaḍāʾ* on the analogy of *ḥajj*. Perhaps, Mālik construed the tradition of Umm Hānī to apply to forgetfulness. The tradition of Umm Hānī has been recorded by Abū Dāwūd. Likewise, he recorded the tradition of ʿĀʾisha with almost similar words that we have stated. He recorded the tradition of ʿĀʾisha and Ḥafṣa in the exact same words.

232 It appears from the text that the words are of some other narrator. Quotation marks avoided.

VIII

THE BOOK OF *IʿTIKĀF* (SECLUSION IN A MOSQUE)

Iʿtikāf is recommended in the law and is obligatory after a vow. There is no dispute about this, except what is related from Mālik that he disapproved undertaking it under the apprehension that its conditions would not be met. It has greater merit in Ramaḍān than at other times, especially during its last ten days, as that was when the last *iʿtikāf* of the Prophet (God's peace and blessings be upon him) took place. It generally consists of specific tasks, at a specific location, at a particular time, with special conditions, and with specific kinds of abstention.

There are two opinions about the acts that are specific to it. It is said that prayer, remembrance of Allāh [by heart and by tongue], and the recitation of the Qurʾān are the only acts required for piety and nearness to Allāh. This is the opinion of Ibn al-Qāsim. It is also said that it includes all the acts required for seeking nearness to Allāh and for piety and that are specific to the hereafter. This is the opinion of Ibn Wahb. In accordance with this opinion the worshipper may attend funerals, visit the sick, and be engaged in studies, but not in accordance with the first opinion. This is also the opinion of al-Thawrī, while the first is the opinion of al-Shāfiʿī and Abū Ḥanīfa.

The reason for their disagreement is that this is something not expressed in the law, that is, there are no legal definitions laid down for it. Those who understood *iʿtikāf* to mean the dedication of the self to acts that are specific to mosques said that only prayer and recitation are permitted to the *muʿtakif* (person retiring to the mosque). Those who understood it to mean the devotion of the self to all acts seeking spiritual nearness permitted him to engage in other acts that we have mentioned. It is related from ʿAlī (God be pleased with him) that he said, "The person who retires to a mosque is not to indulge in obscenities or exchange abuses, he is to attend the Friday congregation prayer as well as funerals, he is to communicate with his family members if the need arises, but he is to do this while standing and not seated". This has been mentioned by ʿAbd al-Razzāq. The opposite of this has been related from ʿĀʾisha, which is that the *sunna* for the *muʿtakif* is not to attend funerals or visit the sick. This is also one of the factors that led to a disagreement over its meaning.

They disagreed about the locations at which *iʿtikāf* is to be practised. One group of jurists said that there is no *iʿtikāf*, except in three mosques: the House of Allāh (al-Masjid al-Ḥarām, Mecca), the mosque at Jerusalem, and the mosque of the Prophet (God's peace and blessings be upon him) at Medina. This was the opinion of Ḥudhayfa and Saʿīd ibn al-Musayyab. Others maintained that *iʿtikāf* is unrestricted, and can be undertaken in all mosques. This was the opinion of al-Shāfiʿī, Abū Ḥanīfa, and al-Thawrī, and it is the well-known opinion from Mālik. Some other jurists said that there is no *iʿtikāf* except in a mosque where the Friday congregational prayers are held. This is a narration by Ibn ʿAbd al-Ḥakam from Mālik. All of them agreed, however, that a condition for *iʿtikāf* is that it be undertaken in a mosque, except what is related from Ibn Lubāba that it is valid in places other than the mosque. They also agreed that intercourse with women is prohibited for the *muʿtakif* if he retires to a mosque. Abū Ḥanīfa, however, maintained that a woman is to undertake *iʿtikāf* in the place of worship in her house.

The reason for their disagreement over the stipulation of a mosque or the dropping of this stipulation stem from the probabilities of interpretation in the words of the Exalted, "And touch them not while you are undertaking *iʿtikāf* in the mosques",[233] as to whether there is an indication of the text here. Those who maintained that there is an indication of the text said that there is no *iʿtikāf*, except in a mosque, and a condition of the *iʿtikāf* is the avoidance of intercourse. Those who maintained that there is no (indirect) indication of the text said that the meaning here is that *iʿtikāf* is permitted in places other than the mosque where there is no restriction upon intercourse, because if one were to say, "Do not give such and such person anything while he is inside the house", the (indirect) implication of the text would be that he be given the thing if he is outside the house. It is, however, a deviant opinion, and the majority held that mosques have been associated with *iʿtikāf* as that is one of its conditions.

The reason for their disagreement about restricting or not restricting it to some mosques arises from the conflict of the general meaning with analogy that restricts it. Those who preferred the general implication said that it is valid in all mosques according to the apparent meaning of the verse. Those who subjected it to restriction through analogy specifying some mosques included in the general meaning, stipulated that it be in a mosque where Friday prayers are held so that the *muʿtakif's* devotion is not interrupted by going out for the Friday prayer, or that it should be one of the three mosques to which

[233] Qurʾān 2 : 187. Pickthall's translation has not been followed in this case.

journeying is a pious act, like the mosque of the Prophet (God's peace and blessings be upon him) where his *iʿtikāf* was undertaken.[234] They did not extend it by analogy to the remaining mosques because they are not equal in terms of their sanctity.

The reason for their disagreement over the *iʿtikāf* undertaken by a woman also arises from the conflict of analogy with a tradition. It is established that Ḥafṣā, ʿĀʾisha, and Zaynab (bint Jaṣh) the wives of the Prophet (God's peace and blessings be upon him) sought permission from the Messenger of Allāh (God's peace and blessings be upon him) for *iʿtikāf* in the mosque, he permitted them after which they set up their curtained spaces in it. This tradition is an evidence for the permissibility of a woman's *iʿtikāf* in the mosque. The analogy that conflicts with this is the one constructed from prayer. As the prayer of a woman in her residence [or house] is better than her prayer in the mosque, as is laid down in a report, it is necessary that her *iʿtikāf* be preferable in her room. They said that it is permitted for a woman to undertake *iʿtikāf* in a mosque only with her husband in the manner that has been described about the *iʿtikāf* of the wives of the Prophet (God's peace and blessings be upon him) with him, just as a wife is to travel only with her husband and not alone. It appears to be a kind of reconciliation between the tradition and analogy.

There is no limit, in their view, for the maximum amount of time to be assigned for *iʿtikāf*, even though all of them consider it as having greater merit during the last ten days of Ramaḍān. Thus, perpetual *iʿtikāf* is permitted, either without qualifications by those who do not consider fasting to be one of its conditions, or for days other than those in which fasting is not allowed in the view of those who consider fasting to be one of its conditions.

They disagreed over the minimum time-limit for it. Likewise, they disagreed about the time when the *muʿtakif* commences his *iʿtikāf* and about the time when he terminates it. There is no limit for the minimum duration of the *iʿtikāf* in the view of al-Shāfiʿī, Abū Ḥanīfa, and the majority of the jurists. There are different views from Mālik. It is said it is three days, and it is said that it is one day and a night. Ibn al-Qāsim has related from him that the minimum is ten days. His disciples from Baghdād said that ten days is desirable, but the minimum is one day and one night.

The reason for their disagreement stems from the conflict of analogy with a tradition. The analogy is that those who considered fasting to be one of its conditions said that *iʿtikāf* is not permitted during the night, and if it is not permitted during the night, then, it cannot be for less than a day and a night, for the forming of intention for the fast has to be during the night. The

[234] The other two are al-Masjid al-Ḥarām at Mecca and the mosque at Jerusalem.

tradition opposing it is recorded by al-Bukhārī that "Umar, may Allāh be pleased with him, made a vow for undertaking *iʿtikāf* for a night. The Messenger of Allāh (God's peace and blessings be upon him) ordered him to abide by his vow". Reasoning in the face of an opinion based upon an established tradition is meaningless.

With respect to their disagreement about the time when the *muʿtakif* is to commence his *iʿtikāf*, if he has made a vow for a determined number of days or for one day, Mālik, al-Shāfiʿī, and Abū Ḥanīfa agreed that the person who has made a vow for an *iʿtikāf* of one month must enter the mosque before sunset. About the person who has made a vow for one day al-Shāfiʿī said that the person who intends to undertake *iʿtikāf* for one day should enter the mosque before dawn and should come out after sunset. Mālik's opinion is exactly the same whether it is for one day and for one month. Zufar and al-Layth said that he is to enter before dawn; but whether for one day or one month for them it is the same. Abū Thawr made a distinction between vows made for the night and those for the day. He said: "If he makes a vow that he will undertake *iʿtikāf* for ten days, he should enter before dawn, but if he makes a vow for ten nights he should enter before sunset". Al-Awzāʿī said that he should commence the *iʿtikāf* after the morning prayer.

The reason for their disagreement emanates from the conflict of analogies, some with the others, and the conflict of a tradition with all of them. This is so as those who thought that a month begins with a night, and they took into consideration the nights, said that he is to begin before the disappearance of the sun. Those who did not take the nights into account said that he is to enter before dawn. Those who said that the term *yawm* is applied to mean both night and day together made it obligatory that if the vow is for a *yawm* he should enter prior to sunset. Those who maintained that this term is applied to mean day made the entry before dawn obligatory. Those who said that the term *yawm* is applicable to the day and the term *layl* to night made a distinction between vows made for the night and those made for the day. The truth is that the term *yawm* in the usage of the Arabs is sometimes applied to day alone and sometimes to the day and the night together, but it appears that its primary application is specific for the day, and its implication for the night is consequential.

The tradition that opposes all these analogies is what is recorded by al-Bukhārī and other compilers of the *ṣaḥīḥ* traditions from ʿĀʾisha, who said, "The Messenger of Allāh (God's peace and blessings be upon him) used to undertake *iʿtikāf* during Ramaḍān, and after observing the morning prayer he would enter the place where is undertook *iʿtikāf*".

About the time of coming out from *iʿtikāf*, Mālik held that the person who was undertaking *iʿtikāf* in the last ten days of Ramaḍān should come out of the mosque for the *ʿīd* prayer, and this was desirable, but if he came out after sunset (on the last day) his act is valid. Al-Shāfiʿī and Abū Ḥanīfa said that he is to come out after sunset. Saḥnūn and Ibn al-Mājishūn said that if he goes to his house first prior to the *ʿīd* prayer his *iʿtikāf* becomes invalid. The reason for disagreement is whether the remaining night is included in the ten days.

The conditions for *iʿtikāf* are three: intention, fasting, and avoidance of mixing with women. I do not know of any disagreement in the case of intention. They disagreed about fasting. Mālik, Abū Ḥanīfa, and a group of jurists said that there is no *iʿtikāf* without fasting, while al-Shāfiʿī said that *iʿtikāf* is permitted without fasting. An opinion similar to Mālik's was expressed by Ibn ʿUmar and Ibn ʿAbbās, with some dispute, from among the Companions, and one similar to al-Shāfiʿī's was expressed by Ibn Masʿūd and ʿAlī. The reason for their disagreement is "that the *iʿtikāf* of the Messenger of Allāh (God's peace and blessings be upon him) occurred during Ramaḍān". Those who maintained that the fasting accompanying his *iʿtikāf* is a condition for the *iʿtikāf*, even though the fasting was not observed because of the *iʿtikāf*, said that fasting is a must with *iʿtikāf*. Those who maintained that this was a mere coincidence and it does not mean that it was the aim of the Prophet (God's peace and blessings be upon him) in his *iʿtikāf* said that fasting is not a condition for it. There is another reason for this, which is its association with fasting in the same verse. Al-Shāfiʿī argued on the basis of the tradition of ʿUmar that has preceded where the Prophet (God's peace and blessings be upon him) ordered him to undertake *iʿtikāf* for a night, and the night is not the time for *siyām*. The Mālikites argued on the basis of what is related by ʿAbd al-Raḥmān ibn Isḥāq from ʿUrwa from ʿĀʾisha that she said, "The *sunna* for the *muʿtakif* is that he should not be interrupted by such things as visiting the sick and attending a funeral. He is not to touch a woman nor have intercourse with her nor go out for anything that is not extremely necessary, and there is no *iʿtikāf* without fasting and no *iʿtikāf* except in a congregational mosque". Abū ʿUmar ibn ʿAbd al-Barr said: "No one has used the words the 'the *sunna*' in the tradition of ʿĀʾisha, except ʿAbd al-Raḥmān ibn Isḥāq, and such a narration is not valid in their view, unless it is related by al-Zuhrī. If that is the case it is no longer valid to hold it similar to a *musnad*".

They agreed about the third condition, which is about the prohibition of sexual intercourse, that if the *muʿtakif* has intercourse intentionally his *iʿtikāf* is invalidated, except what is related from Ibn Lubāba in the case of locations other than the mosque. They disagreed about the situation when he has intercourse out of forgetfulness. They also disagreed about the effect on *iʿtikāf* resulting from of acts other than intercourse, like kissing or touching. Mālik held that all this invalidates the *iʿtikāf*. Abū Ḥanīfa said that there is no invalidity through *mubāshara*, unless he ejaculates. Al-Shāfiʿī had two opinions: the first is the same as the opinion of Mālik, and the second like that of Abū Ḥanīfa.

The reason for their disagreement is whether the word vacillating between its actual and figurative application has a general implication. This is one kind of the equivocal word. Those who maintained that it does have a general implication said that the term *mubāshara* (touching) in the words of the Exalted, "And touch them not while you are undertaking *iʿtikāf* in the mosques",[235] is applied to mean sexual intercourse or what is less than that. Those who maintained that it does not have a general implication, which is the better known and usual application, said that it sometimes indicates sexual intercourse and at other times what is less than that. If we were to say that it indicates sexual intercourse by consensus all other indications would be invalidated, because a single term cannot denote its actual application and the figurative meaning at the same time. Those who deemed ejaculation to be the same as intercourse did so as it is covered by the meaning, while those who did the opposite of this did so as the term in its actual application does not indicate this.

They disagreed about the liability of the person who does have intercourse (during *iʿtikāf*). The majority said that he is not liable for anything, while a group of jurists said that he is liable for expiation. Some of the latter jurists said that it is the expiation offered by one having had sexual intercourse during Ramaḍān. This was the opinion of al-Ḥasan. One group said that he is to give two *dīnārs* as alms. This was the opinion of Mujāhid. Another group said that he is to manumit a slave, and if he does not have a slave that he is to sacrifice a she-camel, if he does not have one he should make alms to the amount of twenty *ṣāʿs* of dried dates. The basis for the dispute is whether analogy is permitted in cases of expiation. The better opinion is that it is not permitted.

They disagreed about a vow made for an undetermined *iʿtikāf*, whether it should be consecutive (without interruption). Mālik and Abū Ḥanīfa said that it is a condition for it, while al-Shāfiʿī said that it is not. The reason for their disagreement stems from the analogy drawn for it from a vow for undetermined fasting.

They agreed that the acts proscribed for *iʿtikāf* are all those that are besides the integral acts of *iʿtikāf*, and that it is not permitted to him to go out of the mosque except for answering the call of nature or for those that have the same intent and that are required due to necessity. This is because of what is established from the tradition of ʿĀʾisha, who said, "The Messenger of Allāh (God's peace and blessings be upon him) when he performed *iʿtikāf* would

[235] Qurʾān 2 : 187. Pickthall's translation has not been followed in this case.

move his head near me and I used to comb it [his hair], and he did not enter the house unless it was to answer the call of nature". They disagreed about the length of the period which invalidates *iʿtikāf*, if the person came out without a (permitted) need. Al-Shāfiʿī said that his *iʿtikāf* is terminated as soon as he steps out. Some made an exemption for one hour, while others made it for a day.

They disagreed about whether he should enter a room other than a room in his mosque (for sleeping). Some made an exemption for him in this, and these are the majority—Mālik, al-Shāfiʿī, and Abū Ḥanīfa—while others held that this invalidates his *iʿtikāf*. Mālik permitted him to buy and sell and to supervise a marriage, but others opposed him in this. The reason for their disagreement arises from the fact that there is no determination on these things except *ijtihād* and a comparison of things that they agreed upon with those they disputed.

They also disagreed over whether it is permitted to the *muʿtakif* to stipulate an act that is prevented by the *iʿtikāf* in order that his stipulation may benefit him in making it permissible, like the stipulation of attending a funeral or some other thing. The majority of the jurists maintain that such stipulation is of no avail, and if he commits that act his *iʿtikāf* is nullified. Al-Shāfiʿī said that his stipulation does benefit him. The reason for their disagreement comes from the similarity between *iʿtikāf* and *ḥajj*, as both are kinds of worship that prevent the undertaking of many permissible acts. Stipulations in *ḥajj* were decided upon, by those who upheld them, on the basis of the tradition of Ḍabāʿa that the Messenger of Allāh (God's peace and blessings be upon him) said to her, "Form the *niyya* of *ḥajj* and stipulate to free yourself from the *ḥajj* restrictions where you encountered me". But the (operation of the) principle is disputed in *ḥajj*. Thus, there is weakness in this analogy in the view of the opposing contender.

They disagreed when the person stipulates continuity in the vow or when continuity itself is binding. In an unqualified vow, for those who uphold it, what are the things by which the *iʿtikāf* is interrupted and is either renewed or is continued, for example, illness. Some of them said that if illness cuts off the *iʿtikāf* the *muʿtakif* can resume it (from the point of interruption). This is the opinion of Mālik, Abū Ḥanīfa, and al-Shāfiʿī. Some of them said that he is to start the *iʿtikāf* from the beginning, and this is the opinion of al-Thawrī. There is no disagreement, as fas as I know, that a menstruating woman continues (from the point of interruption). They disagreed on whether she is to move out of the mosque. Similarly, they disagreed on when the *muʿtakif* suffers a fit of insanity or faints, whether he is to continue (later) or to start again on recovering. The reason for their disagreement on this topic is that there is nothing determined on it through transmission. Thus, disputes arise on the basis of their comparisons between what they agreed upon and what they disputed, that is, what they agreed upon in this worship or in those kinds of worship in which continuing after interruption is stipulated like the fast of one attaining the period of purity and others like it.

The majority maintain that if a voluntary *iʿtikāf* is cut off without an excuse *qaḍāʾ* is obligatory in it, because of the tradition "that the Messenger of Allāh (God's peace and blessings be upon him) intended to observe *iʿtikāf* in the last ten days of Ramaḍān, but he did not, and, therefore, observed *iʿtikāf* in ten days of Shawwāl". In the case of an obligatory *iʿtikāf* due to a vow, there is no dispute about its *qaḍāʾ*, as far as I think.

The majority maintain that the *iʿtikāf* of a person who commits a grave sin is cut off.

This is all that we sought to establish about the principles and rules of this subject, Allāh is the Grantor of success and support, and prayers and blessings upon our master Muḥammad, his family, and his companions.

IX

THE BOOK OF *ḤAJJ* (PILGRIMAGE TO MECCA)

The discussion in this book is related to three categories. The first category comprises things that form the preliminaries of this worship, and whose identification is necessary for practising this worship. The second category is about things that constitute the elements (*arkān*), and these are prescriptions to be acted upon themselves and things that are to be relinquished. The third category is about things that relate to associated matters, and these are the *aḥkām* for the acts. In fact, each worship can be found to be constituted by these three categories.

9.1. The First Category

This category comprises two things: the identification of the obligations and the conditions, and the person for whom it is obligatory and when.

There is no dispute about its obligation, because of the words of the Exalted, "And pilgrimage to the House is a duty unto Allāh for mankind, for him who can find a way thither".[236] The conditions of the obligation are of two kinds: conditions of validity and the conditions of obligation. There is no dispute among the jurists that the conditions of validity include (professing the faith of) Islam, as pilgrimage by a person who is not a Muslim is not valid. They disagreed about its validity when performed by a minor (*ṣabī*). Mālik and al-Shāfiʿī maintained that it is permissible (and valid), while Abū Ḥanīfa prohibited it.

The reason for the disagreement stems from the conflict of a tradition with the principles. Those who permitted it acted on the basis of the well known tradition of Ibn ʿAbbās, which is recorded by al-Bukhārī and Muslim, and it contains the words, "A woman raised a young boy toward the Prophet (God's peace and blessings be upon him) and said, 'Is there *ḥajj* for him, O Messenger of Allāh?' He said, 'Yes, and there is reward for you'". Those who disallowed

[236] Qurʾān 3 : 97.

this relied on the principle that worship is not valid if performed by one lacking discretion.

Mālik's disciples also differed about the validity of its performance on behalf of an infant. There is no dispute about the validity of its performance by one whose performance of prayer is valid, which corresponds to what the Prophet (God's peace and blessings be upon him) said, "From seven to ten".

The conditions of obligation include being a Muslim, in accordance with the opinion that the disbelievers are addressed by the laws of Islam.[237] There is no dispute about the stipulation of ability (both physical and financial) for this, because of the words of the Exalted, "For him who can find a way thither".[238] Though there is a disagreement over the details of this (ability) it is generally considered to be of two kinds: direct and by delegation. In direct ability there is no disagreement among the jurists that its conditions are bodily ability, financial ability, and security. They disagreed about the details of bodily and financial ability. Al-Shāfiʿī, Abū Ḥanīfa, and Aḥmad, and this was the view of Ibn ʿAbbās and ʿUmar ibn al-Khaṭṭāb, held that the conditions for these are food provisions and the availability of transportation. Mālik said that for the person who is able to walk the availability of a riding animal (a means of transportation) is not a condition of obligation and pilgrimage is obligatory for him. Likewise, surplus is not a condition for ability, in his view, if the person is able to earn a living on the way even if he has to beg.

The reason for this disagreement arises from the conflict between the tradition (which is) laid down for the elaboration of ability and the general implication of its words. This is so as a tradition from the Prophet (God's peace and blessings be upon him) is laid down that "he was asked, 'What is the ability (to perform the pilgrimage)?' He said, 'Food provisions and a riding animal'". Abū Ḥanīfa and al-Shāfiʿī interpreted this to apply to everybody, while Mālik interpreted it to apply to a person who was not able to walk and also did not have the strength to eke out a living on the way. Al-Shāfiʿī formed this opinion as it is his method that if an unelaborated text occurs in the Qurʾān and then a *sunna* is laid as an elaboration of this unelaborated word it is not possible to avert the elaboration.

With respect to its obligation through ability by delegation, Mālik and Abū Ḥanīfa maintain that delegation is not binding, even when that ability is there, if the inability for direct performance exists. Al-Shāfiʿī maintains that it is binding, thus, for a person who possesses sufficient wealth with which someone other than he can perform the pilgrimage, if he himself cannot perform it physically, then that person must perform it on his behalf. But if

[237] The apparent meaning here is that though the disbelievers are subject to all the laws of Islam, they have been excluded from this worship by the stipulation of Islam as a condition.

[238] Qurʾān 3 : 97.

someone is found who can perform it on his behalf with his own wealth and physical ability, like a brother or next of kin, his liability is dropped. This is an issue that they termed *maʿḍūb* (incapacitated person), who is a person who cannot be seated on the riding animal. In his view, if a person dies without performing the pilgrimage, it is binding upon his heirs to set something from his estate with which some person can perform the pilgrimage on his behalf.

The reason for disagreement over this arises from the conflict of analogy with a tradition. Analogy dictates that acts of worship cannot be performed by one person on behalf of another by delegation, thus, no one prays on behalf of another nor does one pay *zakāt* in another's place. The tradition opposing this is the well-known tradition of Ibn ʿAbbās recorded by the two shaykhs (al-Bukhārī and Muslim), and it reads "that a woman from Khathʿam said to the Messenger of Allāh (God's peace and blessings be upon him), 'O Messenger of Allāh, *ḥajj* is an obligation prescribed for His servants, but I find my father an old man who cannot sit firmly on a riding animal. Should I then perform the *ḥajj* for him?' He said, 'Yes'". This was the case of a living person. In the case of a dead person there is a tradition that was recorded by al-Bukhārī, which is also from Ibn ʿAbbās, who said, "A woman from Juhayna came up to the Prophet (God's peace and blessings be upon him) and said, 'O Messenger of Allāh, my mother made a vow to perform *ḥajj*, but she died, so should I perform it on her behalf?' He said, 'Perform the pilgrimage for her. Do you think that if she had a debt would you not pay it off? The debt of Allāh has a prior claim for satisfaction'". There is no dispute among the Muslim jurists that it is voluntary when performed for another, the disagreement is about its performance as an obligation.

In this topic, they disagreed about the person who performs *ḥajj* for someone else, who may be living or dead, as to whether it is a condition for him that he should have performed *ḥajj* himself. Some of the jurists held that this is not a condition, but if he has performed the obligation for himself that would be better. This was Mālik's opinion for the person who performed *ḥajj* on behalf of a dead person, for in his view *ḥajj* for a person who is living is not valid. The other jurists held that it is a condition that he should have performed the obligation for himself. This was the opinion of al-Shāfiʿī and others besides him, and if a person, who had not performed *ḥajj* for himself, did perform *ḥajj* for another it would be converted to a personal performance. The reliance of these jurists is upon the tradition of Ibn ʿAbbās "that the Prophet (God's peace and blessings be upon him) heard a man pronouncing the *talbiya* on behalf of someone called Shubrama. He said, 'And who is this Shubrama?' The man replied that he was his brother or (he said) his close relative. He said, 'Have you performed *ḥajj* for yourself?' The man said, 'No'. He said, 'Perform *ḥajj* for yourself first and then for Shubrama'". The first group of jurists objected to this tradition as it was narrated as *mawqūf* up to Ibn ʿAbbās (i.e. the *isnād* (chain) did not contain the name of the Companion's disciple).

They also differed, in this topic, about a person who offers himself for a wage to perform *ḥajj* on behalf of someone else. Mālik and al-Shāfiʿī disapproved of this, but said that if it happens it is permissible. Abū Ḥanīfa did not permit it. He relied on the argument that the purpose was to seek nearness to Allāh and wages are not allowed for that. The argument of the first group was the consensus about the permissibility of earning wages for writing the *muṣḥaf* and for the construction of mosques, which are also one way of seeking nearness to Allāh. Hiring during *ḥajj*, in Mālik's view, is of two kinds. The first is what his disciples called the *balāgh*, whereby a person offers his services for a wage that would be enough to provide the (required) provision and a riding animal. If that wage falls short of the *balāgh* he is to be paid what would be enough, and if an excess is left over he is to return it. The second is the customary hiring whereby something falling short is to be made up by him and if there is an excess it belongs to him. The majority maintain that *ḥajj* is not binding upon a slave until he is manumitted, but some of the Ẓāhirites make it obligatory for him.

This is all about the person on whom this worship is obligatory and about the person whose performance is valid.

With respect to the time when it becomes obligatory, they disagreed whether the command necessitates immediate or delayed compliance?[239] Both opinions are attributed to Mālik and his disciples. The apparent opinion of the later jurists of his school is that it is delayed, but his disciples from Baghdād said that it is immediate. Reports from Abū Ḥanīfa and his disciples differ, but their preferred opinion is that it is immediate. Al-Shāfiʿī said that it is spread out over a period of time. The reliance of those who say that it spreads over a span of time (is not immediate) is that *ḥajj* became obligatory years before the Prophet (God's peace and blessings be upon him) performed the *ḥajj*. If it required immediate compliance the Prophet (God's peace and blessings be

[239] This issue appears to be based on the discussion in *uṣūl al-fiqh* whether an unqualified command requires immediate or delayed compliance. The author after discussing the details of the issue asserts that it is not actually based on this, but a little explanation of the discussion in *uṣūl al-fiqh* might help. The question becomes somewhat technical in legal theory and it is better to give one example to clarify it. Take the case of the *ẓuhr* prayer that may be observed during a period of time that is longer than the time required for the performance of the prayer, unlike the *maghrib* prayer for which the time span is just sufficient for prayer. If the time of the *ẓuhr* prayer has commenced and, say, that half an hour later there is a person, who has not yet prayed, goes on a journey. The question is whether the *ahkām* of the traveller will apply to this person for this particular prayer? If we say that the command requires immediate compliance, the person becomes liable for the full prayer as soon as it was time for the prayer, but if the compliance is delayed the *aḥkām* of the traveller would apply.

upon him) would not have delayed the performance of his *ḥajj*. If he had done so because of an excuse he would have explained it. The argument of the other group is that if it is specific to a particular time, the principle would be to attribute sin to the person who relinquishes it till the time passes, the basis (for the analogy) being the time of prayer. The distinction between this and the command for prayer, in the view of the second group, is that its obligation is not renewed from moment to moment and in prayer it is renewed every moment. On the whole, those who held the initial time of obligation in *ḥajj*, as applicable to an individual who has the ability (for performance), to be similar to the initial time of prayer said that compliance is delayed, while those who held it to be similar to the last time of prayer said that compliance is immediate. The reason for holding it to be similar to the last portion of the time of prayer is that it is terminated with the advent of the time in which his act is not valid, just as the time of prayer is terminated with the advent of time in which the worshipper is not considered to be offering his prayer as *ʿadāʾ*. These jurists also argue on the basis of the risk that becomes associated with the postponement to another year because of the greater possibility of death occuring during a longer period. They maintain that this is different from the case of delay in prayer from its first time to its last, as the likelihood of the person's death within that short time is far less than it is within a year. Perhaps they may add that delaying prayer within its fixed period does not separate the worshipper from the chance to perform the prayer as *ʿadāʾ*, but delay in this case of *ḥajj* leads to the expiry of its period and the start of a much longer period in which the performance of this worship is not valid. This is not similar to the case of the unqualified command, because in the unqualified command, in the view of those who maintain that it implies liberty of delayed compliance, a delay in performance does not lead to the advent of a time in which the required worship is not valid, as it does in the case of *ḥajj* when it is time for it and the subject postpones it to the future. The disagreement, then, on this issue does not belong, as has been assumed, to the category of their dispute whether an unqualified command necessitates immediate or delayed compliance.

They disagreed, within the topic, whether it is a condition for the obligation of *ḥajj* on a woman that she must have a husband or a *dhū maḥram* (a relative of the prohibited degree for marriage) who is willing to accompany her on the journey for *ḥajj*. Mālik and al-Shāfiʿī said that this is one alternative condition for the obligation. The other alternative is for a woman to go for *ḥajj* with a trustworthy female companion. Abū Ḥanīfa, Aḥmad, and a group of jurists said that the availability of a willing husband or a *maḥram* is a condition for the obligation.

The reason for the disagreement arises from the conflict of the command for *ḥajj* and of taking up travel for it with the proscription about a woman's travelling alone without her husband or a *maḥram*. This is so as it is established from the Prophet (God's peace and blessings be upon him) through Abū Saʿīd al-Khudrī, Abū Hurayra, Ibn ʿAbbās, and ʿUmar, that he said "It is not permitted for a woman, who believes in Allāh and the Last Day to travel without a *dhū maḥram*". Those who gave predominance to the generality of the command of *ḥajj* said that she may travel for *ḥajj* even when she is not accompanied by a *dhū maḥram* (but with a trustworthy group of women). Those who restricted the general implication with this tradition, or held that it is an elaboration of "ability", said that she is not to travel for *ḥajj*, unless she is accompanied by a *dhū maḥram*.

We have now spoken about this rite, which is called *ḥajj*, regarding the basis due to which it becomes obligatory, and for who and when. In this section there remains the discussion of the rite known as *ʿumra*. A group of jurists said that it is obligatory. This was the opinion of al-Shāfiʿī, Aḥmad, Abū Thawr, Abū ʿUbayd, al-Thawrī, al-Awzāʿī, and it was the opinion of Ibn ʿAbbās and Ibn ʿUmar from among the Companions, and also of a group of the Tābiʿūn. Mālik and a group of jurists said that it is a *sunna*. Abū Ḥanīfa said that it is voluntary, which was also the opinion of Abū Thawr[240] and Dāwūd. Those who maintained that it is obligatory argued on the basis of the words of the Exalted, "Perform the pilgrimage and the *ʿumra* for Allāh,"[241] and also on the basis of the reported traditions. One of these is the report from Ibn ʿUmar from his father, who said, "A Bedouin, who had a fair countenance and was wearing white clothes came up to the Messenger of Allāh (God's peace and blessings be upon him) and said, 'What is Islam, O Messenger of Allāh?' He replied, 'That you testify that there is no god but Allāh, that Muḥammad is His messenger, and you establish prayer, pay the *zakāt*, fast the month of Ramaḍān, perform the pilgrimage and the *ʿumra*, and wash yourself free of impurities'". ʿAbd al-Razzāq has mentioned that "Maʿmar informed us on the authority of Qatāda, who used to relate that when the verse 'And pilgrimage to the House is a duty unto Allāh for mankind, for him who can find a way thither',[242] was revealed the Messenger of Allāh (God's peace and blessings be upon him) said, 'The two, the *ḥajj* and the *ʿumra*, anyone who performs them has fulfilled the obligation'". It is related from Zayd ibn Thābit from the Prophet (God's peace and blessings be

[240] There appears to be an error here as the author mentions the name of Abū Thawr among those who consider it to be obligatory. This cannot be confused with the name of al-Thawrī, as his name is mentioned in that opinion too.

[241] Qurʾān 2 : 196. Pickthall's translation has been changed here slightly as he translates it as, "Perform the pilgrimage and the visit (to Mecca) for Allāh". This version does not place enough emphasis on the word *ʿumra* which is important for the discussion.

[242] Qurʾān 3 : 97.

upon him) that he said, "The *ḥajj* and the *ʿumra* are two obligations, and there is no harm for you with whichever you commence". It is related from Ibn ʿAbbās that *ʿumra* is obligatory, and some have attribute this statement through an *isnād* to the Prophet (God's peace and blessings be upon him).

The argument of the other group of jurists, who hold that it is not obligatory, is based on authentic and well-known traditions that have been laid down about the number of the obligations in Islam and that do not mention the *ʿumra*. An example is the tradition of Ibn ʿUmar, "Islam is structured upon five things", in which he mentioned the pilgrimage alone. There is also the tradition of the one asking what Islam is, and in some of its versions are the words, "that you perform the pilgrimage to the House". Perhaps, these jurists also said that a command implying completion (as it appeared in the Qurānic verse 2 : 196 quoted above) does not give rise to an obligation, as it means that once an obligation or a *sunna* act is started, it should be completed and not cut off. The jurists who maintained that it is a *sunna*, also argued on the basis of traditions. These include the tradition of al-Ḥajjāj ibn ʿArṭā from Muḥammad ibn al-Munkadir from Jābir ibn ʿAbd Allāh, who said, "A man asked the Prophet (God's peace and blessings be upon him) about the *ʿumra*, whether it was obligatory? He replied, 'No, but if you perform the *ʿumra* it is better for you'". Abū ʿUmar ibn ʿAbd al-Barr said that this is not persuasive insofar as he was the sole narrator.

Perhaps, those who maintained that it was voluntary argued on the basis of what is related from Abū Ṣāliḥ al-Ḥanafī, who said, "The Messenger of Allāh (God's peace and blessings be upon him) said, '*Ḥajj* is obligatory and *ʿumra* is voluntary'". This, however, is a *munqaṭiʿ* tradition.

The reason for the disagreement stems thus from the conflict of traditions on the subject, and the vacillation of the command requiring completion between whether or not it gives rise to an obligation.

9.2. The Second Category

This covers the identification of the acts of this worship (*ḥajj*), namely its basic elements, as well as the discussion of acts to be avoided during the period of its performance. This worship, as we have said, is of two types: *ḥajj* and *ʿumra*. *Ḥajj* itself is of three types: *ifrād*,[243] *tamattuʿ*,[244] and *qirān*.[245] All these

[243] That is, to start with *ḥajj* and perform the *ʿumra* afterwards.

[244] To start with the *ʿumra*, then wait for the start of *ḥajj*, enjoying the acts prohibited during *ḥajj* in the meantime.

[245] To combine both *ḥajj* and *ʿumra*.

consist of determined acts (to be performed) at determined locations and at determined times. Some of these are obligatory, while some are not, along with things to be avoided during these acts, each one of which has determined *aḥkām* (to be applied) either at the time of a breach or on the occurrence of an obstacle.

This category is, therefore, divided first into a discussion of the acts (to be performed) and a discussion of the things to be avoided. The third category will include the discussion of the *aḥkām*.

We begin, then, with the acts (of this worship). Some of these acts are stipulated for these four kinds of rites, that is, for the three types of *ḥajj* and for *ʿumra*, while some are specific to individual types. We begin the discussion with the acts common to them and will then move to what is specific to the individual types. We say: The first of the acts in *ḥajj* and *ʿumra* is the act known as the *iḥrām*.

9.2.1. Chapter 1 Discussion of the Conditions of Iḥrām

The first condition for the *iḥrām*[246] is that of location and time. The locations are what are called the *mawāqīt* of *ḥajj*. We will begin the discussion with these. The jurist generally agree that the *mawāqīt* are where the *iḥrām* (intention to start the *ḥajj* as well as wearing the *ḥajj* attire) is to be formulated. For the people of Medina the location is Dhū al-Ḥulayfa, for the people of Syria it is al-Juḥfa, for the people of Najd it is Qarn, and for the people of Yemen it is Yalamlam, because all this is established from the Messenger of Allāh (God's peace and blessings be upon him) in the tradition of Ibn ʿUmar and others. They disagreed about the *mīqāt* for the people of Iraq. The majority of the jurists of the provinces maintain that the *mīqāt* for them is Dhāt ʿIrq. Al-Shāfiʿī and al-Thawrī said that if they adopt the *iḥrām* at al-ʿAqīq it would be preferable. They disagreed as to who had determined this location for them. A group of jurists said that it was ʿUmar ibn al-Khaṭṭāb. Another group of jurists said that, in fact, it was the Messenger of Allāh (God's peace and blessings be upon him) himself who determined the location for the people of Iraq to be Dhāt ʿIrq or al-ʿAqīq. This has been related in traditions from Jābir, Ibn ʿAbbās, and ʿĀʾisha.

[246] *Iḥram* is the ceremonial status of the pilgrim from the moment he starts the *niyya* for *ḥajj*—meaning the *ḥajj* attire—until he completes all the pilgrimage rites and is released from the *ḥajj* restrictions. In this state he is described as a *muḥrim*. *Iḥrām* also denotes the forming of the *niyya* for *ḥajj* in addition to denoting the *ḥajj* attire.

The majority of the jurists maintain that the person who misses these points, though he has in mind to go through the *iḥrām* and does so after crossing them is liable for atonement by slaughtering (of an animal) (*dam*). Some of these jurists said that if he returns to the *mīqāt* and performs the *iḥrām* there the liability for atonement is dropped. Al-Shāfiʿī is one of these jurists. Some of them said that the liability for atonement is not dropped even if he returns. This was Mālik's opinion. One group said that there is no atonement for him. Another group said that if he does not return to the *mīqāt* his *ḥajj* becomes invalid and that he should return and begin the rites of the *ʿumra*. This is discussed fully in the chapter dealing with the *aḥkām*.

The majority of the jurists maintain that the person whose residence is nearer (Mecca) than the *mīqāt*, the *mīqāt* for his *iḥrām* is his residence. They disagreed whether there is greater merit for the pilgrims to begin the process of *iḥrām* from their residences or from the *mīqāt* if their residences are nearer to Mecca than the *mīqāt*. A group of jurists said that it is better for such a person to start from his residence, and that to start from the *mīqāt* in their case is an exemption. This was the opinion of al-Shāfiʿī, Abū Ḥanīfa, al-Thawrī, and a group of jurists. Mālik, Isḥāq, and Aḥmad said that to start from the the *mawāqīt* is better. The reliance of these jurists is on the preceding traditions and (on the argument) that it is a *sunna* established by the Messenger of Allāh (God's peace and blessings be upon him) and is therefore better. The reliance of the other group is on the argument that the Companions—Ibn ʿAbbās, Ibn ʿUmar, Ibn Masʿūd, and others—started the process of the *iḥrām* from the *mīqāt*. They said that they (the Companions) knew better the *sunna* of the Prophet (God's peace and blessings be upon him). The principles of the Ẓāhirites imply that it is not permitted to commence the *iḥrām* from any place other than the *mīqāt*, unless an authentic consensus indicates the contrary.

They disagreed about the person who does not commence the *iḥrām* from the *mīqāt* assigned to his region and starts instead from another *mīqāt*, like a resident of Medina relinquishing Dhū al-Ḥulayfa and starting from al-Juḥfa. A group of jurists said that he is liable for atonement by slaughtering an animal (*dam*). Those who held this opinion are Mālik and some of his disciples. Abū Ḥanīfa said that there is no liability for him. The reason for the disagreement is whether it is one of the rites the relinquishment of which makes a person liable for atonement by slaughtering an animal (*dam*).

There is no disagreement that it is binding upon a person who passes by these locations, when he intends to perform the *ḥajj* or the *ʿumra*, to commence the *iḥram* there. In the case of persons who do not intend to perform these rites, but pass by the locations, a group of jurists said that it is binding on them to adopt the *iḥrām*, except those who do so very frequently, like woodcutters and other similar people. This was Mālik's opinion. Another group of jurists said that this is not binding on any person except those who intend to perform the *ḥajj* or the *ʿumra*. All this is in the case of persons who are not residents of Mecca.

The residents of Mecca adopt the *iḥrām* from their residences, in case of the *ḥajj*. In the case of the *ʿumra*, they go outside the boundaries of the *Ḥaram* (*ḥill*), and that is necessary. With respect to the time when the residents of Mecca are to adopt the *iḥrām*, it is said that they do so when they sight the new moon (of Dhū al-Ḥijja), and it is said when the pilgrims start moving toward Minā (on the eighth of Dhū al-Ḥijja). This is the (discussion of the) *mīqāt* with reference to location, which is stipulated for the different types of this worship.

9.2.2. Chapter 2 Discussion of the *Mīqāt* of Time

The *mīqāt* of time is also determined for the the three types of *ḥajj*. It is the period comprising Shawwāl, Dhū al-Qaʿda, and the first nine days of Dhū al-Ḥijja, by agreement. Mālik said that it is a total of three months. Al-Shāfiʿī said that it consists of the two first months and the first nine days of Dhū al-Ḥijja. Abū Ḥanīfa said that it is the two months plus the first ten days of Dhū al-Ḥijja.

The evidence for Mālik's opinion is the generality of the words of the Exalted, "The pilgrimage is (in) the well-known months",[247] implying that this applies to all the days of Dhū al-Ḥijja as it does to all the days of Shawwāl and Dhū al-Qaʿda. The evidence of the second group is the termination of the ritual state of *iḥrām* before the completion of the third month by the completion of all its obligatory acts. The implication of the dispute is the (permissibility of) delaying of the of the *ṭawāf al-ifāḍa* (the obligatory final circumambulation of the Kaʿba) till the end of the month.

Mālik disapproves a person's commencing the *iḥrām* before the months of *ḥajj*, but such commencing of the *iḥrām* is valid in his view. Other jurists maintain that the *iḥrām* of this person is not valid. Al-Shāfiʿī said that his *iḥrām* is to be converted to the *iḥrām* for *ʿumra*. Those who held this to be similar to the time for prayer said that it is not effective before time. Those who relied upon the general implication of the words of the Exalted, "Complete the performance of the pilgrimage and the *ʿumra* for Allāh",[248] said that whenever he starts the *iḥrām* it takes effect, for he is commanded to

[247] Qurʾān 2 : 197.
[248] Qurʾān 2 : 196. Pickthall's translation changed.

complete (the pilgrimage). Perhaps, they held *ḥajj* in this context to be similar to *ʿumra* and held the *mīqāt* of time to be similar to those of *ʿumra*. Al-Shāfiʿī's opinion is based upon the argument that whoever undertakes an act of worship in a time that pertains to an identical worship the worship is converted to the identical form, like one fasting after a vow during Ramaḍān. There is disagreement over this principle in the School (Mālik's).

The jurists agreed that *ʿumra* is permissible at any time of the year, as in the days of *jāhiliyya* it was not performed during the days of *ḥajj* (but during the rest of the year), which is the meaning of the saying of the Prophet (God's peace and blessings be upon him), "*ʿUmra* stands merged in the *ḥajj* up to the Day of Judgment". Abū Ḥanīfa said that it is permitted throughout the year, except on the day of *ʿArafa*, the day of sacrifice, and the days of *tashrīq* when it is considered disapproved.

They disagreed about its repetition in a single year. Mālik considered one *ʿumra* as desirable every year but disapproved the performance of two or three in one year. Al-Shāfiʿī and Abū Ḥanīfa held that there is no abomination in this.

This, then, is the discussion of the conditions of the *iḥrām* pertaining to time and location. It is necessary after this to move to the discussion of the *iḥrām*, but before that it is essential to talk about the things to be avoided by the person in the ritual state of the *iḥrām*. Thereafter, we will talk about the specific acts of the person in a ritual state of the *iḥram* until he is released from it and these are all the acts that are to be observed or are to be shunned relinquishments of *ḥajj*. We shall then take up the *aḥkām* of vitiation due to the commission of a prohibited act or the relinquishment and abuse of a required act. We, therefore, begin with the relinquishments.

9.2.3. **Chapter 3 Discussion of the Acts to be Avoided**

These are ordinarily permissible acts that are not permitted to a person in the ritual state of *iḥrām*. The source for this topic is what is established through the tradition of Mālik from Nāfiʿ from ʿAbd Allāh ibn ʿUmar "that a man asked the Messenger of Allāh (God's peace and blessings be upon him), 'What kind of clothes does a person in a ritual state of *iḥrām* wear?' The Messenger of Allāh (God's peace and blessings be upon him) said, 'You should neither wear shirts, nor turbans, nor trousers, nor hooded cloaks, nor shoes, unless a person does not find sandals for then he may wear shoes after cutting them below the ankles. And do not wear any clothing which has been touched (dyed) by saffron or *wars* (yellow dye)' ".

The jurists agreed upon some of the *aḥkām* laid down in this tradition and they disagreed about some. Those that they agreed upon are that the person in the ritual state of *iḥrām* should not wear a shirt or any other thing mentioned in this tradition nor anything that is similar, that is, stitched clothing. This is specific for men, that is, wearing stitched clothing, and there is no harm if a woman wears a shirt, coat, trousers, shoes, and a head-cover.

They differed about the person who does not find anything other than trousers. Is he to wear them? Mālik and Abū Ḥanīfa held that he is not permitted to wear trousers and if he does so he atones for it. Al-Shāfiʿī, al-Thawrī, Aḥmad. Abū Thawr, and Dāwūd said that there is no liability upon him if he cannot find a loin-cloth. The reliance in Mālik's opinion is upon the apparent meaning of the preceding tradition of Ibn ʿUmar. He said that had there been some exemption in this the Messenger of Allāh (God's peace and blessings be upon him) would have expressed it as he did in the case of shoes. The reliance of the other group is upon the tradition of ʿAmr ibn Dīnār from Jābir and Ibn ʿAbbās, who said, "I heard the Messenger of Allāh (God's peace and blessings be upon him) saying, 'Trousers are for the person who does not find a loin-cloth and shoes for one who cannot find sandals'".

The majority of the jurists permit the wearing of shoes that have been cut down for a person who cannot find sandals. Aḥmad said that it is permitted to a person who cannot find sandals to wear shoes that have not been cut, and this by relying upon the unqualified implication in the tradition of Ibn ʿAbbās. ʿAṭāʾ said that in cutting them down there is waste and Allāh does not like waste. They differed about the person who wears cut down shoes when sandals are available. Mālik said that he has to make atonement, and this was also the opinion of Abū Thawr. Abū Ḥanīfa said that there is no atonement for him. Both views are related from al-Shāfiʿī, and we shall mention this in the discussion of the *aḥkām*.

The jurists agreed unanimously that the person in the state of *iḥrām* is not to wear clothing that is dyed with *wars* or saffron, because of the words of the Prophet (God's peace and blessings be upon him) in the tradition of Ibn ʿUmar, "And do not wear any clothing which has been touched [dyed] by saffron or *wars* [yellow dye]". They disagreed about clothing dyed with safflower. Mālik said that there is no harm in that as it is not a perfume. Abū Ḥanīfa and al-Thawrī said that it is a perfume and there is ransom (*fidya*) for using it. The evidence for Abū Ḥanīfa is what Mālik has recorded from ʿAlī "that the Prophet (God's peace and blessings be upon him) prohibited the wearing of *qassīy* (a silk striped garment) and a garment dyed with safflower".

They agreed that the *iḥrām* of a woman pertains to her face. She is to cover her head and hair and that she should let her head covering hang a little in front of her face so that she is veiled from the view of men, in accordance with what is related from ʿĀʾisha, who said, "We were accompanying the

Messenger of Allāh (God's peace and blessings be upon him) and were in the ritual state of *iḥrām*. When a rider would pass by us we would pull down our head-garments a little in front of our faces from over the head, and when the rider had passed we would lift it". There is no narration about the covering of their faces, except what has been related by Mālik from Fāṭima bint al-Mundhir, who said, "We used to veil our faces while wearing the *iḥrām* along with Asmā' daughter of Abū Bakr al-Ṣiddīq".

They disagreed about the covering of the face by a man in a state of *iḥrām* after they agreed unanimously that he is not to cover his head. Mālik has related from Ibn ʿUmar that the part of the head above the chin is not to be covered by a man in the state of *iḥrām*. This was the opinion of Mālik. It is also narrated from him that if he does this and does not uncover it up to its proper place he is to pay ransom. Al-Shāfiʿī, al-Thawrī, Aḥmad, Abū Dāwūd, and Abū Thawr said that a person wearing the *iḥrām* may cover his face up to the eyebrows. This is related from the Companions: from ʿUthmān, Zayd ibn Thābit, Jābir, Ibn ʿAbbās, and Saʿd ibn Abī Waqqāṣ.

They disagreed about the wearing of gloves by a woman. Mālik said that if a woman wears gloves she is liable for ransom. Al-Thawrī made an exemption in this, which is related from ʿĀʾisha. The evidence for Mālik is what has been related by Abū Dāwūd from Prophet (God's peace and blessings be upon him) "that he proscribed the wearing of veils and gloves". Some of the narrators report it with the chain stopping at Ibn ʿUmar, and some narrators report it with a complete chain, that is narrate it from the Prophet (God's peace and blessings be upon him).

These are their well-known agreements and disagreements over (the pilgrim's) clothing. The basis of all this is their dispute over the analogies constructed for the unexpressed cases from those that are expressly mentioned, their dispute over the possible interpretations of the text, and whether or not such text is authentic.

The second item in the things to be avoided is perfume. The jurists agreed that all kinds of perfume are to be avoided during *ḥajj* and *ʿumra* by the pilgrim so long as he is in a state of *iḥrām*. They disagreed about its permissibility for the *muḥrim* at the time when he is about to form the *niyya* the *iḥrām*, so that its effect may remain after he has entered into the state of *iḥrām*. Some jurists disapproved of it, while others permitted it. Included in those who disapproved it is Mālik, who related it from ʿUmar ibn al-Khaṭṭāb. It is also the opinion of ʿUthmān, Ibn ʿUmar, and a group of the Tābiʿūn. Those who permitted it include Abū Ḥanīfa, al-Shāfiʿī, al-Thawrī, Aḥmad, and Dāwūd. The evidence for Mālik, by way of transmission, is the tradition of Ṣafwān ibn Yaʿlā that has been recorded in the *Saḥīḥayn*, and it includes the words, "A man came to the Prophet (God's peace and blessings be upon him) donning a tunic and wearing perfume. He said, 'O Messenger of Allāh, what do you think about a man in a state of *iḥrām* for the *ʿumra* who wears a tunic and has applied perfume?' It was then that a revelation was sent down to the Messenger of Allāh (God's peace and blessings be upon him), and when he had recovered he said, 'Where is the questioner who asked about the *ʿumra* a short while ago?' The man was found and brought to him. The Prophet (God's peace and blessings be upon him) said, 'As for the perfume that you have on, wash it away from yourself three times. The tunic you should take off, and then do for the *ʿumra* what you do for your *ḥajj*'". I have summarized the tradition and have mentioned its essential meaning.

The reliance of the other group is on what is related by Mālik from ʿĀʾisha, who said, "I used to apply perfume to the head of the Messenger of Allāh (God's peace and blessings be upon him) for his *iḥrām* before he had started the process of the *iḥrām*, and also when he was not in a state of *iḥrām* and was about to perform the circumambulation of the House". The first group relied on the tradition related from ʿĀʾisha, who having heard about the rejection by Ibn ʿUmar of the use of perfume prior to the *iḥrām* said, "May Allāh have mercy on the father of ʿAbd al-Raḥmān, I perfumed the Messenger of Allāh (God's peace and blessings be upon him) and he visited his wives and then arose in the morning in a state of *iḥrām*". They responded arguing that if he visited his wives, then, he must have taken a bath (afterwards), and only the smell of perfume remained upon him, not its substance. As a consensus occurred (they added) that all things not permitted to the *muḥrim* initially, like the wearing of clothing and killing of game, are not permitted to him during the state of *iḥrām*, it becomes necessary that the *ḥukm* of its continuity be the same, that is, it should be true for perfume. The reason for disagreement, therefore, stems from the conflict of traditions on the topic.

The third thing to be avoided is sexual intercourse. This is so as the Muslim jurists agreed that sexual intercourse with women is prohibited to the person performing the pilgrimage from the time that he assumes the state of *iḥrām*, because of the words of the Exalted, "There is (to be) no lewdness nor abuse nor angry conversation on the pilgrimage".[249]

The fourth thing prohibited is the removal of dirt, cutting hair, and killing lice, but they agreed that it is permitted for the person to wash his head because of a major impurity. They disagreed about the disapproval of washing his head due to a reason other than a major impurity. The majority said that there is no harm if he washes his head. Mālik upheld the disapproval and his

[249] Qurʾān 2 : 197.

reliance is on the fact that ʿAbd Allāh ibn ʿUmar did not wash his head while he was a *muḥrim*, except after a nocturnal emission. The reliance of the majority is on what is related by Mālik from ʿAbd Allāh ibn Jubayr "that Ibn ʿAbbās and al-Miswar ibn Makhrama disputed at al-Abwāʾ (the washing of the head by a *muḥrim*). ʿAbd Allāh said that a *muḥrim* may wash his head, while al-Miswar ibn Makhrama said that a *muḥrim* is not to wash his head. He said, ʿAbd Allāh ibn ʿAbbās sent me to Abū Ayyūb al-Anṣārī. I found him (he said) bathing between two props curtained with a cloth. I greeted him. He said, 'Who is that?' I said, "ʿAbd Allāh ibn Jubayr. ʿAbd Allāh ibn ʿAbbās sent me to you to ask you how the Messenger of Allāh (God's peace and blessings be upon him) used to wash his head when he was in the state of *iḥrām*'. Abū Ayyūb then slapped on the cloth till I could see his head. He said to the person who was pouring water on him to pour it over his head. The person poured it over his head and he moved his head with his hands, taking them forwards and backwards. He then said, 'This is how I saw the Messenger of Allāh (God's peace and blessings be upon him) doing it'". ʿUmar also used to wash his head when he was in a state of *iḥrām* and said, "It will only make it (hair) more ruffled". It is recorded by Mālik in *al-Muwaṭṭaʾ*. Mālik interpreted the tradition of Abū Ayyūb al-Anṣārī to apply to (a bath because of a) major impurity. The evidence for him is their consensus that the *muḥrim* is prohibited from killing lice, trimming hair, or removal of *tafath*, which is dirt, and the person who washes his head does all or some of these things. They agreed about the prohibition of the *muḥrim* washing his head with marsh mallow. Mālik and Abū Ḥanīfa said that if he does this he has to pay ransom. Abū Thawr said that he is under no liability.

They disagreed about entering a public bath. Mālik disapproved this and held that whoever does this has to pay ransom. Abū Ḥanīfa, al-Shāfiʿī, al-Thawrī, and Dāwūd said that there is no harm in this. It is related through two channels from Ibn ʿAbbās that he entered the public bath when he was in a state of *iḥrām*. It is better to disapprove entry into the bath as the *muḥrim* is prohibited from removing dirt.

The fifth thing that is prohibited is hunting. This is also agreed upon because of the words of the Exalted, "To hunt on land is forbidden you as long as ye are on pilgrimage",[250] and His words, "Kill no wild game while ye are on the pilgrimage".[251] They agreed that the person in a state of *iḥrām* is not permitted to hunt nor to eat what he has hunted. They disagreed about whether it is permitted to the *muḥrim* to eat game when someone not in the state of *iḥrām* hunts it. There are thre opinions. According to one opinion it is

[250] Qurʾān 5 : 96.
[251] Qurʾān 5 : 95.

permitted for him to eat it without restriction. This was expressed by Abū Ḥanīfa, and it is also the opinion of ʿUmar ibn al-Khaṭṭāb and al-Zubayr. One group said that it is prohibited for him under all circumstances. This is the opinion of Ibn ʿAbbās, ʿAlī, and Ibn ʿUmar, and it was also the opinion of al-Thawrī. Mālik said that as long as it has not been hunted for a *muḥrim* or for those in *iḥrām* generally it is permissible for him, but if it has been hunted for a *muḥrim* it is prohibited for each *muḥrim*.

The reason for disagreement emanates from the conflict of traditions about this. One of these is a tradition recorded by Mālik from Abū Qatāda "that he was with the Messenger of Allāh (God's peace and blessings be upon him) when they were on one of the ways leading to Mecca when Abū Qatāda stayed behind with some of the Prophet's Companions who were in a state of *iḥrām*, while he was not. He noticed a wild ass and mounting on his horse asked his company to hand him his whip. They refused to do this so he asked them for his spear, which they also refused. He, then, took it himself and charging the wild ass killed it. Some of the Companions of the Messenger of Allāh (God's peace and blessings be upon him) ate of it while others did not. When they caught up with the Messenger of Allāh (God's peace and blessings be upon him) they asked him about it and he said, 'It was food that Allāh fed you with'". Implying the same is the tradition of Ṭalḥa ibn ʿUbayd Allāh that is recorded by al-Nasāʾī that ʿAbd al-Raḥmān al-Tamīmī said, "We were with Talḥa ibn ʿUbayd Allāh and in a state of *iḥrām*. A gazelle was brought as a gift for him when he was sleeping. Some of us ate of it and when Ṭalḥa woke up he approved of eating, and said, 'We ate it along with the Messenger of Allāh (God's peace and blessings be upon him)'". The second tradition is from Ibn ʿAbbās and has also been recorded by Mālik that "a wild ass was brought for the Messenger of Allāh (God's peace and blessings be upon him) at al-Abwāʾ" or at Waddān. He returned it to the person and said, 'We would not wish to decline it, it is only that we are in a state of *iḥrām*'".

There is another reason for the disagreement and that is whether the proscription is linked to eating the game itself, as distinct from whether the *muḥrim* killed it or it was killed for him, or to the act of killing by the *muḥrim*, or to a combination of both. Those who relied upon the tradition of Abū Qatāda said that the proscription is related to eating along with the act of killing. Those who acted upon the tradition of Ibn ʿAbbās said that the proscription is related to each individual action. Those who adopted the method of preference in these traditions either acted upon the tradition of Abū Qatāda or on the tradition of Ibn ʿAbbās. Those who reconciled the traditions upheld the third opinion. They said that reconciliation is better and they supported this with the tradition related from Jābir from the Prophet (God's peace and blessings be upon him) that he said, "Game from the land is permitted to you when you are in a state of *iḥrām* as long as you have not hunted it and it has not been hunted for you".

They disagreed about the case of the person under duress whether he is to consume carrion or is to hunt in the state of *iḥrām*. Mālik, Abū Ḥanīfa, al-Thawrī, Zufar, and a group of jurists said that if he is under duress he may eat carrion or swine flesh without hunting. Abū Yūsuf said that he is to hunt and eat, and he is obliged to make reparation. The first view is better for the blocking of the means (to seek an unlawful end), while the view of Abū Yūsuf reflects a better analogy, because this (carrion) is prohibited for itself and hunting is (temporarily) prohibited for some reason, and what is prohibited temporarily for a reason is lesser in gravity than what is perpetually prohibited in itself.

The Muslim jurists agreed that these five things are prohibitions of the *iḥrām*, but they differed about the marriage of the *muḥrim*. Mālik, al-Shāfiʿī, al-Layth, and al-Awzāʿī said that a *muḥrim* is not to marry nor give someone away in marriage. If he does that the marriage is void. This is also the opinion of ʿUmar, ʿAlī ibn Abī Ṭālib, Ibn ʿUmar, and Zayd ibn Thābit. Abū Ḥanīfa and al-Thawrī said there is no harm if the *muḥrim* marries himself or gives someone away in marriage.

The reason for their disagreement arises from the conflict of traditions on the subject. One of these is related as a tradition from ʿUthmān ibn ʿAffān, who said, "The *muḥrim* is not to marry nor give someone away in marriage, nor is he to make a marriage proposal". The tradition that opposes this is from Ibn ʿAbbās "that the Messenger of Allāh (God's peace and blessings be upon him) married Maymūna when he was in a state of *iḥrām*". It is recorded by the compilers of the authentic traditions, except that it has been opposed by a number of traditions from Maymūna (herself), who said "that the Messenger of Allāh (God's peace and blessings be upon him) married her when he was not in the state of *iḥrām*". It has been related from her through various channels from Abū Rāfiʿ, from Sulaymān ibn Yassār, who was her *mawlā* (client), and from Zayd ibn al-Aṣamm. It is possible to reconcile the traditions by interpreting one to imply disapproval and the other to indicate permissibility.

These are the well-known issues about what is prohibited to the *muḥrim*. As to when he is to be released from the status of *iḥrām*, when the proscribed acts become permissible again, we shall mention it when discussing the acts of *ḥajj*. The state of *iḥrām* for the person performing the *ʿumra* ceases after he has made the *ṭawāf* and the *saʿy*, and had his head shaved. They differed about the termination of this state for those performing *ḥajj*, as will be coming up later. And now, as we have discussed the things to be avoided by the *muḥrim*, we move to a discussion of his acts.

9.2.4. **Chapter 4 Discussion of the Rites of Pilgrimage**

The persons in the ritual state of *iḥrām* either perform the *ʿumra* separately and the *ḥajj* separately (*mufrid*) or they combine the *ḥajj* and the *ʿumra*. He who intends to do both may begin with the *ḥajj*, in which case he is called a *mufrid*, or with the *ʿumra*, in which case he is a *mutamattiʿ*, or he may combine both, and then he is known as a *qārin*. It is necessary, initially, to separate the three types of these rites and then to discuss what the *muḥrim* does in each one of these, and discuss what is specific to each of these types, if there is something specific to them. We shall do the same thing after discussing the *iḥrām* with the acts of *ḥajj*.

9.2.4.1. *Section 1: Detailed discussion of the rites*

We say: *ifrād* (the method by which the pilgrim begins with *ḥajj*) is the type stripped of the characteristics of *tamattuʿ* and *qirān*. It is, therefore, necessary that we first begin with a description of *tamattuʿ* and then follow it up with the description of *qirān*.

9.2.4.1.1. Discussion of *tamattuʿ*

We say: The jurists agreed that this is the kind of rite[252] that is implied in the words of the Exalted, "Then whosoever enjoyed freedom from the restriction of the *iḥrām* by commencing with the *ʿumra* before the *ḥajj*, (shall give) such gifts as can be had with ease".[253] This means that the pilgrim pronounces the *talbiya* for the *ʿumra* from the appointed locations (*mīqāt*) during the months of *ḥajj*. This is the case if his residence is beyond the *Ḥaram* (otherwise he does so from his residence). He moves from there until he reaches the House (the Sacred Mosque) and makes the circuits around the Kaʿba, performs the *saʿy*, and then has his hair shaved (or shortened) within these months. He is then no longer in the state of *iḥrām* though he is in Mecca. He will begin his *ḥajj* in the very same year and in these appointed months without going back to his homeland, except what is related from al-Ḥasan. He said that he is to be considered a *mutamattiʿ* even if he goes back to his homeland without performing the *ḥajj*, that is, he is liable for the sacrifice of the *mutamattiʿ* that is mentioned in the words of the Exalted, "such blood sacrifice as can be had with ease".[254] He (al-Ḥasan) used to maintain that a *ʿumra* during the days of

[252] *Tamattuʿ* means that the *mutamattiʿ*, after finishing the *ʿumra* and while waiting in Mecca to begin the *ḥajj*, can enjoy doing things that are forbidden to the *muḥrim*.

[253] Qurʾān 2 : 196.

[254] Qurʾān 2 : 196.

ḥajj amounts to *tamattuʿ*. Ṭāwūs maintained that the person who performs *ʿumra* before the months of *ḥajj* and then stays on (in Mecca) till the *ḥajj* and performs it in the same year is also to be considered a *mutamattiʿ*.

The jurists agreed that a person who is not residing (permanently) in the (vicinity of) *al-Masjid al-Ḥarām* is eligible for being a *mutamattiʿ*. They disagreed about the resident of Mecca whether he is eligible for *tamattuʿ*. Those who maintained that he is eligible agreed that there is no (obligation of) atonement , because of the words of the Exalted, "That is for him whose folk are not present in the vicinity of *al-Masjid al-Ḥarām*".[255] They disagreed as to who is resident in *al-Masjid al-Ḥarām*. Mālik said that they are the residents of the town of Mecca and those of Dhū Ṭuwa, as well as others whose residence is as far from Mecca as Dhū Ṭuwa. Abū Ḥanīfa said that they are the persons who live withing the *mawāqīt* and within Mecca. Al-Shāfiʿī said, at Egypt, that these are the persons who live up to a distance of two nights travel from Mecca, and this is the maximum distance of the *mawāqīt*. The Ẓāhirites said that they are those who live within the boundaries of the Ḥaram, while al-Thawrī said that they are the residents of Mecca alone.

Abū Ḥanīfa said that *tamattuʿ* does not apply to the persons present at *al-Masjid al-Ḥarām*. Mālik considered this to be disapproved. The reason for their disagreement stems from their dispute over the minimum and maximum implication of "those present at *al-Masjid al-Ḥarām*", therefore, there is no doubt that the residents of Mecca are among "those present at *al-Masjid al-Ḥarām*", just as there is no doubt that those living outside the *mawāqīt* are not among them.

This then is the well-known form of the method known as *tamattuʿ*. The meaning of *tamattuʿ* is that the pilgrim benefited from the removal of the prohibitions of *iḥrām* between the two rites and by the elimination of the need for making another journey for the *ḥajj*.

There are two other kinds of *tamattuʿ* over which the jurists disagreed. The first is the conversion of *ḥajj* into *ʿumra*, which is the changing of the intention of the *iḥrām* for *ḥajj* into to one for *ʿumra*. The majority of the jurists from the first generation, as well as the jurists of the provinces, disapprove of this. Ibn ʿAbbās held this to be permissible, and it was also upheld by Aḥmad and Dāwūd, and they all agreed that the Messenger of Allāh (God's peace and blessings be upon him) ordered his Companions in the year he went for *ḥajj* to convert their *ḥajj* into *ʿumra*, and this is according to the saying of the Prophet (God's peace and blessings be upon him), "If I were to start off again, I would not drive the sacrificial animals, and I would change it to *ʿumra*". Moreover, he directed those of his Companions who had not

[255] Qurʾān 2 : 196. Pickthall's translation changed.

brought sacrificial animals to convert their declared intention of *ḥajj* into that for *ʿumra*. This is what the Ẓāhirites relied upon. The majority maintained that this is specific to the Companions of the Messenger of Allāh (God's peace and blessings be upon him). They also argued for this on the basis of what is related from Rabīʿa ibn Abī ʿAbd al-Raḥmān from al-Ḥārith ibn Bilāl ibn al-Ḥārith al-Madanī from his father, who said, "I said, 'O Messenger of Allāh, Is the cancellation for us specifically, or for those who come after us?' He said, 'It is specific to us' ". This has not reached the required level of authenticity for the Ẓāhirites insofar as it is opposed by the earlier practice. It is related from ʿUmar that he said, "I have forbidden two kinds of *mutʿa* that existed in the days of the Messenger of Allāh (God's peace and blessings be upon him), and I will award punishment for them; namely, the *mutʿa* with women and the *mutʿa* of *ḥajj*". It is related from ʿUthmān that he said, "The *mutʿa* of *ḥajj* was for us and is not for you". Abū Dharr said: "It was not proper for anyone after us to pronounce the *talbiya* for *ḥajj* and then convert it to *ʿumra*". All of this conforms with the words of the Exalted, "Perform the pilgrimage and the *ʿumra* for Allāh",[256] The Ẓāhirites maintain that the principle is to act upon the practice of the Companions until an evidence from the Qurʾān or the authentic *sunna* indicates that it has been restricted. The reason for the disagreement stems from whether the practice of the Companions is to be construed as implying a general or a specific rule.

The second kind of *tamattuʿ* is the one that was explained by Ibn al-Zubayr to the effect that the *tamattuʿ* mentioned by Allāh is where one is overwhelmed by a disease or besieged by the enemy.[257] This happens when a person departs for the pilgrimage but is hampered by a disease or an incident because of which he is prevented from completing *ḥajj* until the days of *ḥajj* have passed. He, therefore, goes up to the House, makes the circumambulation, performs the *saʿy* between al-Ṣafā and al-Marwa. and then removes his *iḥrām*. After this, he can enjoy what was prohibited by the *iḥrām* until the next *ḥajj* season when he performs the *ḥajj* and makes the sacrifice. Accordingly, the well-known form of *tamattuʿ* is not upheld by consensus. Ṭāwūs also deviated (from the majority view) and said that if a resident of Mecca performs *tamattuʿ* from another town he is liable for the sacrifice.

The jurists disagreed about the case of a person who commences his *ʿumra* before the months of *ḥajj* and then carries it forward to the months of *ḥajj* performing the *ḥajj* thereafter in the same year. Mālik said that his *ʿumra* pertains to the month in which he completed it. If he does this in the months

[256] Qurʾān 2 : 196. Pickthall's translation has been changed.

[257] There is a detailed discussion about what this means in the third category dealing with the *aḥkām* of *ḥajj*.

of *ḥajj* he is considered a *mutamattiʿ*, but if he does it before the months of *ḥajj* he is not a *mutamattiʿ*. Almost the same opinion as his was expressed by Abū Ḥanīfa, al-Shāfiʿī, and al-Thawrī, except that al-Thawrī stipulated that his entire circumambulation should occur during Shawwāl, and that was upheld by al-Shāfiʿī. Abū Ḥanīfa said that if he performs three circuits in Ramaḍān and four in Shawwāl he is to be considered a *mutamattiʿ*, but if the matter is the other way round he is not a *mutamattiʿ*, I mean, if he performs four circuits in Ramaḍān and four in Shawwāl. Abū Thawr said that if he commences the *ʿumra* before the months of *ḥajj* he is not to be considered a *mutamattiʿ* irrespective of his having performed the circuits during the months of hajj or before that.

The reason for the disagreement stems from the question of whether he becomes a *mutamattiʿ* by pronouncing the *talbiya* for *ʿumra* during the months of *ḥajj* alone or by the performance of the circumambulation along with it. Further, if it is with the occurrence of the circumambulation, then, is it through the complete circuits or through most of them? Thus, Abū Thawr says that he does not become a *mutamattiʿ* except with the *iḥrām* of *ʿumra* during the *ḥajj* months, as the *ʿumra* is constituted by its *iḥrām*. Al-Shāfiʿī said that the circuits are the major element of the *ʿumra*, and it is, therefore, necessary that he should become a *mutamattiʿ* because of them. The majority of the jurists thus maintain that one who has performed part of it during the *ḥajj* months is the same as one who has performed it entirely in these months.

The conditions of *tamattuʿ*, in Mālik's view, are six. The first is that he should perform the *ḥajj* and *ʿumra* in a single month. The second is that this should occur in the same year. The third is that he perform part of the *ʿumra* in the *ḥajj* months. The fourth is that he should perform the *ʿumra* before *ḥajj*. The fifth is that he should commence the *ḥajj* after completing the *ʿumra* and after his release from its *iḥrām*. The sixth is that his place of residence should be other than Mecca.

This, then, is the form of *tamattuʿ* with the well-known disagreement over it as well as the agreement.

9.2.4.1.2. Discussion of the *qārin*

Qirān is the pronouncing of the *iḥrām* (intention) for performing the *ḥajj* and the *ʿumra* together, or it is the pronouncing of the *iḥrām* for the *ʿumra* during the *ḥajj* months and then commencing with the *ḥajj* before his release[258] from the *iḥrām*.

[258] The text uses the word for wearing the *iḥrām* and declaring the intention. Obviously, the release from the *iḥrām* is intended.

The disciples of Mālik differed about the time when the pilgrim can do this (i.e. combining *ḥajj* with *ʿumra*). It is said that he has a right to do this as long as he has not commenced the circumambulation (of the *ʿumra*), not even a single circuit. It is also said that as long as he has not completed the circuits and bowed (offered the post-*ṭawāf sunna* prayer) after that. It is considered disapproved after the circumambulation and even before the *ʿīd ṭawāf* prayer, but if he does so it becomes binding upon him. It is also said that he has a right to do this as long as some part of the *ʿumra* is still left, either the circuits or the *saʿy*. They agreed, however, that if he pronounces the *iḥrām* (intention) of *ḥajj* and none of the acts of the *ʿumra* is left, except the clipping of the hair, he cannot be considered a *qārin*.

The *qārin* on whom the same sacrifice as the *mutamattiʿ*s is binding is not one of those who are permanently resident in the vicinity of *al-Masjid al-Ḥarām*. Ibn al-Mājishūn, one of the disciples of Mālik, said that a *qārin*, even on who is a resident of Mecca, is in his view under an obligation for the sacrifice.

Ifrād is a kind (of *ḥajj*) that is devoid of these attributes and is performed by one who is neither a *mutamattiʿ* nor a *qārin*, and he begins by pronouncing the *iḥrām* (the intention) of *ḥajj* alone.

The jurists disagreed over which form is better: *ifrād*, *qirān*, or *tamattuʿ*. The reason for their disagreement arises from their dispute over the form of *ḥajj* performed by the Messenger of Allāh (God's peace and blessings be upon him). It is related about him that he performed it as a *mufrid*, as a *mutamattiʿ*, and as a *qārin*. Mālik chose *ifrād*, and for this he relied upon what is related from ʿĀʾisha that she said, "We accompanied the Messenger of Allāh (God's peace and blessings be upon him) on the Farewell Pilgrimage and with us were those who began with the *ʿumra*, those who combined *ḥajj* and *ʿumra*, and the Messenger of Allāh (God's peace and blessings be upon him) started with *ḥajj*". This tradition has been related from ʿĀʾisha through many channels. Abū ʿUmar ibn ʿAbd al-Barr said: "*Ifrād* as performed by the Prophet (God's peace and blessings be upon him) was reported by Jābir ibn ʿAbd Allāh through various channels that are *mutawātir* and authentic". This (the greater merit of *ifrād*) was also the opinion of Abū Bakr, ʿUmar, ʿUthmān, ʿĀʾisha, and Jābir.

Those who maintained that the Prophet (God's peace and blessings be upon him) performed it as a *mutamattiʿ* argued on the basis of what is related by al-Layth from ʿUqayl from Ibn Shihāb from Sālim from Ibn ʿUmar, who said, "The Messenger of Allāh (God's peace and blessings be upon him) performed *tamattuʿ* during the Farewell Pilgrimage by commencing with the *ʿumra* and [later] moving on to *ḥajj*. He drove the sacrificial animals with him from Dhū al-Ḥulayfa". This was the view of ʿAbd Allāh ibn ʿUmar, Ibn ʿAbbās, Ibn al-Zubayr, and the report from ʿĀʾisha varies between *ifrād* and *tamattuʿ*.

Those who maintain that the Prophet (God's peace and blessings be upon him) performed as *qārin* rely on a large number of traditions, including the tradition of Ibn ʿAbbās from ʿUmar ibn al-Khaṭṭāb, who said, "I heard the Messenger of Allāh (God's peace and blessings be upon him) saying when he was at the valley of al-ʿAqīq, 'The previous night a revelation came to me from my Lord instructing me: "Proclaim the *iḥrām* in this blessed valley, and let the *ʿumra* be included in the *ḥajj*" ' ". It has been recorded by al-Bukhārī. There is also the tradition of Marwān ibn al-Ḥakam, who said, "I witnessed ʿUthmān and ʿAlī, when ʿUthmān was prohibiting the *mutʿa* or to combine the two (*ḥajj* and *ʿumra*). When ʿAlī saw this he pronounced the *talbiya* for both: *labbayk* for the *ʿumra* and *ḥajj*. He said, 'I was not about to give up the *sunna* of the Messenger of Allāh (God's peace and blessings be upon him) for anyone's opinion' ". It has been recorded by al-Bukhārī. Moreover, in the tradition of Anas, which has also been recorded by al-Bukhārī, he also said, "I heard the Messenger of Allāh (God's peace and blessings be upon him) saying: *labbayk*, *ʿumra* and *ḥajj*". And in the tradition of Mālik from Ibn Shihāb from ʿUrwa from ʿĀʾisha, she said, "We accompanied the Messenger of Allāh (God's peace and blessings be upon him) on the Farewell Pilgrimage and we pronounced the *talbiya* for the *ʿumra*. The Messenger of Allāh then said, 'The person who has his sacrificial animal with him should pronounce the *talbiya* for *ḥajj* with the *ʿumra*, and he will not be released from the *iḥrām* until he has completed both' ". They argued saying that it is known that he (God's peace and blessings be upon him) had the sacrificial animals with him, and it is unlikely that he should order the person who had his sacrificial animal to perform *qirān*, and then not perform *qirān* himself when he had the sacrificial animals. In another tradition of Mālik also from Nāfiʿ from Ibn ʿUmar from Ḥafṣa from the Prophet (God's peace and blessings be upon him), he said, "I have garlanded my sacrificial animal and matted my hair, so I will not take off my *iḥrām* until I sacrifice my animal". Aḥmad said: "I have no doubt that the Messenger of Allāh (God's peace and blessings be upon him) was a *qārin*, but *tamattuʿ* is dearer to me. He argued for choosing *tamattuʿ* on the basis of the saying of the Prophet (God's peace and blessings be upon him), 'If I were to start off again, I would not drive the sacrificial animals, and I would change it to *ʿumra*' ".

Those who maintained that *ifrād* is better argued by way of reason that *tamattuʿ* and *qirān* are prescribed as exemptions, because of which atonement (a blood sacrifice) has been made obligatory in them.

We have now discussed the obligation of this rite, on whom it is obligatory, what are the conditions of its obligation, when it becomes obligatory, for what time, and from which location. After this we discussed what the *muḥrim* is to avoid followed by the different forms of this rite that become obligatory. It is necessary that we now discuss the first act of the pilgrim or of one performing the *ʿumra*, and that is the *iḥrām*.

9.2.5. Chapter 5 Discussion of the *Iḥrām*

The majority of the jurists agreed that bathing is a *sunna* for commencing with the *iḥrām*, and it is one of the acts of the *muḥrim*, so much so that Ibn Nawāz said: Bathing for the *iḥrām* has greater significance, for Mālik, than bathing for the Friday prayer. The Ẓāhirites said that it is obligatory. Abū Ḥanīfa and al-Thawrī said that performing the ablution is sufficient.

The evidence of the Ẓāhirites is the *mursal* report by Mālik in the tradition of Asmāʾ bint ʿUmays "that she gave birth to Muḥammad ibn Abī Bakr at al-Baydāʾ. Abū Bakr mentioned this to the Messenger of Allāh (God's peace and blessings be upon him), who said, 'Tell her to bathe and then wear the *iḥrām*' ". The command in their view implies an obligation. The reliance of the majority is upon the principle that the original rule is freedom from liability until an obligation is established by an irrefutable command.

Further, ʿAbd Allāh ibn ʿUmar used to bathe for his *iḥrām* before commencing it, and for entering Mecca, and on the evening prior to the his stationing at ʿArafa. Mālik held these three baths to be the acts of the *muḥrim*.

They agreed that (the ritual state of) *iḥrām* cannot be assumed without forming an intention. They disagreed on whether the intention is enough without the pronouncement of the *talbiya*. Mālik and al-Shāfiʿī said that intention without the *talbiya* is sufficient. Abū Ḥanīfa said that *talbiya* in *ḥajj* is like the initial *takbīr* in prayers, except that any words used as a substitute for the *talbiya* are sufficient, just as all words used in the place of the *takbīr* on the commencement of prayer are enough, when they indicate exaltedness.

The jurists agreed that the words of the *talbiya* of the Messenger of Allāh (God's peace and blessings be upon him) were "*labbayk Allāhumma labbayk, labbayka lā sharīka laka labbayk, inna ʾl-ḥamda wa ʾn-niʿmata laka wa ʾl-mulk, lā sharīka lak* (At Your command, O Allāh, at Your command; at Your command, You have no partner, at Your command; all praise and grace are Yours, and Yours the dominion; You have no partner). It is the narration of Mālik from Nāfiʿ from Ibn ʿUmar from the Prophet (God's peace and blessings be upon him) and it carries the highest degree of authenticity. They disagreed on whether the *talbiya* has to be in these words. The Ẓāhirites said that it is obligatory that it be said in these words. There is no disagreement among the majority of the jurists about the desirability of these words, but they differed about the additions to them or about substitutions. The Ẓāhirites also considered the raising of the voice with the *talbiya* as obligatory, which is desirable according to the majority, because of what is related by Mālik "that the Messenger of Allāh (God's peace and blessings be upon him) said, 'Jibrīl came to me and directed me to order my companions and those who are with me that they should raise their voices with the *talbiya* and in forming the intention'". The jurists agreed that (the manner of) a woman's *talbiya*, as related by abū ʿUmar, is that she should be able to hear herself pronouncing it.

Mālik said that the *muḥrim* is not to raise his voice in congregational mosques, and it is enough to let the person next to him hear him, except for *al-Masjid al-Ḥarām* and the mosque at Minā, for he is to raise his voice there. The majority considered the raising of voice desirable on encountering a company and on approaching elevated places. Abū Ḥāzim said: The voices of the Companions of the Messenger of Allāh (God's peace and blessings be upon him) became hoarse by the time they reached al-Rawḥāʾ.

Mālik did not hold *talbiya* to be an element (*rukn*) of *ḥajj*, and held the person who neglects it is to be liable for atonement by slaughtering a sacrificial animal. The other jurists besides him considered it to be a *rukn*. The evidence of those who deemed it obligatory is that if the acts of the Prophet (God's peace and blessings be upon him) occur as an elaboration of an obligatory act they are to be construed as implying an obligation until another evidence indicates the contrary. And this is so because of the saying of the Prophet (God's peace and blessings be upon him), "Acquire your rites from me (my actions)". This is the tradition relied upon by those who consider the words of the *talbiya* to be obligatory. Those who do not consider the words to be obligatory relied upon what is related of the tradition of Jābir, who said, "the Messenger of Allāh (God's peace and blessings be upon him) pronounced the *talbiya*". After this he repeated the words that are in the tradition of Ibn ʿUmar and said, "The people used to add words *labbayka dhā ʾl-maʿārij*[259] and similar phrases. The Prophet (God's peace and blessings be upon him) listened to them and did not say anything". Further, it is related from Ibn ʿUmar that he used to add to the *talbiya*, which is also related from ʿUmar ibn al-Khaṭṭāb, Anas, and others.

The jurists considered it desirable that the *muḥrim* begin reciting the *talbiya* after the prayer (two *rakʿas* of *iḥrām*) that he should observe. Mālik used to consider it desirable that it follow the supererogatory prayers, because of his *mursal* report from Hishām ibn ʿUrwa from his father "that the Messenger of Allāh (God's peace and blessings be upon him) used to observe two *rakʿas* at the mosque at Dhū al-Ḥulayfa, and when his mount rose he pronounced the

[259] This means: "Here we come, Lord of the Ascending Stairways".

talbiya". The traditions differ about the location from where the Messenger of Allāh (God's peace and blessings be upon him) commenced the *iḥrām* with the implication in the traditions that he did so from the area around Dhū al-Ḥulayfa, but a group said that he did so from the mosque at Dhū al-Ḥulayfa after praying in it. Another group said that he adopted the *iḥrām* when he approached al-Baydāʾ. Yet another group said that he pronounced the *iḥrām* and *talbiya* when his mount rose up with him. Ibn ʿAbbās was asked about their disagreement over this and he said: "Each has related not his (God's peace and blessings be upon him) first *talbiya* but the one he heard for the first time. The people used to arrive with some following the others and because of that there is no conflict, and the *talbiya* follows the prayer".

The jurists agreed that adopting the *iḥrām* (intention) is not binding upon a resident of Mecca until he departs for Minā to perform the acts of *ḥajj*. Their reliance is upon what is related by Mālik on the authority of Ibn Jurayj, who said to ʿAbd ʿAllāh ibn ʿUmar, "I have seen you doing four things here that I have not seen anyone else doing". He mentioned one of these saying, "I have seen you when you were at Mecca delaying the *iḥrām* until the day of *tarwiya* (the eighth day of Dhū al-Ḥijja), when the other people did so on sighting the moon". Ibn ʿUmar replied saying, "As to the assumption of the *iḥrām*, I have not seen the Messenger of Allāh (God's peace and blessings be upon him) commencing it until his mount rose up with him". He meant thereby until the commencement of the acts of *ḥajj* (on the day of *tarwiya*). Mālik has related from ʿUmar ibn al-Khaṭṭāb that he used to direct the residents of Mecca to begin the *iḥrām* on sighting the moon. There is no disagreement that when the resident of Mecca is performing the pilgrimage he is only to pronounce the *iḥrām* from within Mecca, but if he is performing the *ʿumra* they agreed that it is binding upon him to move to the outskirts of the Ḥaram and form the *iḥrām* (intention), and traverse the external area and the Ḥaram as the others pilgrims do, I mean, because they go to *ʿArafa*, which is outside the boundary of the Ḥaram. They agreed, generally, that this is the *sunna* for one performing the *ʿumra*. They disagreed on when he does not do so. A group of jurists said that his performance is to be considered valid, but he has to make atonement by sacrificing an animal. This was upheld by Abū Ḥanīfa and Ibn al-Qāsim. Another group said that this is not sufficient for him. This was the opinion of al-Thawrī and Ashhab.

With respect to the time when the *muḥrim* stops pronouncing the *talbiya*, it is related by Mālik from ʿAlī ibn Abī Ṭālib (God be pleased with him) that he stopped pronouncing the *talbiya* when the sun went down on the day of *ʿarafa*, and Mālik said that this is the practice still followed by the learned in our land. Ibn Shihāb has said that the Imāms Abū Bakr, ʿUmar, ʿUthmān, and ʿAlī used to stop pronouncing the *talbiya* after the declining of the sun on the day of *ʿArafa*. Abū ʿUmar ibn ʿAbd al-Barr has said that reports from ʿUthmān and ʿĀʾisha differ about this. The majority of the jurists of the provinces, the traditionists, Abū Ḥanīfa, al-Shāfiʿī, al-Thawrī, Aḥmad, Isḥāq, Abū Thawr, Dāwūd, Ibn Abī Laylā, Abū ʿUbayd, al-Ṭabarī, and al-Ḥasan ibn Yaḥyā maintain that the *muḥrim* is not to stop reciting the *talbiya* until he throws pebbles at the first pillar at Minā (*Jamrat al-ʿAqaba*), because of what is established that "the Messenger of Allāh (God's peace and blessings be upon him) continued to pronounce the *talbiya* until he threw pebbles at the *Jamrat al-ʿAqaba*". They disagreed about the exact time when he is to discontinue it. A group of jurists said that this is when he has finished throwing the pebbles and this is because of what is related from Ibn ʿAbbās that al-Faḍl ibn ʿAbbās, who was riding behind the Messenger of Allāh (God's peace and blessings be upon him) on his riding beast, when he was pronouncing the *talbiya* while throwing the pebbles at the *Jamrat al-ʿAqaba* and he stopped when he had cast the last pebble. A group of jurists said that he is to stop when he throws the first pebble and this is related from Ibn Masʿūd. There are other opinions besides these that have been related about the termination of the *talbiya*, but these two opinions are better known.

They disagreed about when to stop the *talbiya* during *ʿumra*. Mālik said that he is to stop pronouncing it upon reaching the Ḥaram. This was also upheld by Abū Ḥanīfa. Al-Shāfiʿī said that he does this on commencing the circumambulation. Mālik followed Ibn ʿUmar and ʿUrwa in this, while the reliance of al-Shāfiʿī is upon the argument that the meaning of *talbiya* is a response for returning to the circumambulation of the House, so it should not be stopped until the act is commenced. The reason for the disagreement stems from the conflict of analogy with the practice of some of the Companions.

The majority of the jurists agree about the conversion of *ḥajj* into *ʿumra*, but they disagree about the conversion of *ʿumra* into *ḥajj*. Abū Thawr said that *ḥajj* cannot be converted into *ʿumra* nor can *ʿumra* be converted into *ḥajj*, just as one prayer cannot be converted into another.

These are the acts of the *muḥrim* insofar as he is a *muḥrim*, and it is the first act of *ḥajj*. The act that follows this is the circumambulation upon entry into Mecca. We, therefore, move to the circumambulation.

9.2.6. **Chapter 6 Discussion of the Circumambulation of the House**

This discussion is about the circumambulation of the House, its description, its conditions, the *ḥukm* of its obligation or recommendation, and about the number of the circuits.

9.2.6.1. *Section 1: Description of the circumambulation*

The majority agree unanimously that the form of the circumambulation, whether obligatory or recommended, is that the worshipper begins at *al-ḥajar al-aswad* (the Black Stone). If he is able to kiss the stone he should do so, or touch it with his hand if possible and then kiss it. He then turns, with the House on his left, and he walks around it. He makes seven circuits, adopting the *ramal* (rythmic trot while shrugging the shoulders; marking time but moving ahead) for the first three circuits. He then walks in the remaining four circuits. This is for the circumambulation of greeting (*ṭawāf al-qudūm*) on entering Mecca and it is for those performing *ḥajj* or *ʿumra* (as well as those who are simply visiting the House of Allāh) to the exclusion of the *mutamattiʿ*. There is no *ramal* for women. The worshipper is to make a salutation to *al-rukn al-yamānī*, which is the corner (of the House) before *al-rukn al-aswad* (the corner with the Black Stone) (by raising both hands toward it), because this has been established as an act of the Prophet (God's peace and blessings be upon him).

They disagreed about the *ḥukm* of *ramal* in the first three circuits for the person coming into Mecca, whether this is a *sunna* or an act of merit. Ibn ʿAbbās said that it is a *sunna*, and this was the opinion of al-Shāfiʿī, Abū Ḥanīfa, Isḥāq, Aḥmad, and Abū Thawr. The opinions of Mālik and those of his disciples vary on the point. The difference between the two opinions is that those who deem it to be a *sunna* made its relinquishment liable to atonement (*dam*), while those who did not consider it a *sunna* did not impose any duty. Those who did not consider *ramal* to be a *sunna* argued on the basis of the tradition of Ibn al-Ṭufayl from Ibn ʿAbbās that he said, "I said to Ibn ʿAbbās that some people are under the impression that the Messenger of Allāh (God's peace and blessings be upon him) adopted *ramal* when he made the circumambulation of the House, and that this is a *sunna*. He said, 'They spoke in truth and they lied'. I said, 'What was the truth and what was the lie?' He said, 'They were truthful about the *ramal* adopted by the Messenger of Allāh when he circumambulated the House, and they lied about saying it is a *sunna*. The Quraysh, during the time of Ḥudaybiya, while they were stationed on the Quʿayqiyān (mountain) watching the Prophet (God's peace and blessings be upon him) and his Companions, said, 'He and his companions are emaciated'. When this was communicated to the Prophet (God's peace and blessings be upon him) he said to his Companions, 'Adopt the *ramal* and let them see that you have strength'. The Messenger of Allāh (God's peace and blessings be upon him) adopted the *ramal* from the Black Stone to *al-rukn al-yamānī*, but when he was concealed from their view he walked". The evidence of the majority is based upon the tradition of Jābir "that the Messenger of Allāh (God's peace and blessings be upon him) adopted the *ramal* in the (first) three circuits during the Farewell Pilgrimage and walked in (the remaining) four". It is an authentic tradition related by Mālik and others. The majority maintained that the versions related by Abū al-Ṭufayl from Ibn ʿAbbās have varied; thus it is related from him "that the Messenger of Allāh (God's peace and blessings be upon him) adopted the *ramal* from the Black Stone up to the Black Stone", which is different from the first narration. *Ramal* is obligatory in accordance with the principles of the Ẓāhirites, because of the saying of the Prophet (God's peace and blessings be upon him), "Acquire your rites from me", and that was their opinion or it is the opinion of some of them now, as far as I know.

They agreed that there is no *ramal* for the person who begins the *iḥrām* of *ḥajj* from Mecca, other than its residents, and these are the persons who are performing *tamattuʿ*, as they have already performed *ramal* when they entered Mecca and performed the initial circumambulation. They disagreed about the residents of Mecca whether they are to adopt *ramal* if they perform *ḥajj*. Al-Shāfiʿī said that in each (session of) circumambulation made before the day of *ʿarafa*, and which is followed by the *saʿy*, there is *ramal*. Mālik considered this desirable, while Ibn ʿUmar did not consider them to be subject to *ramal* when they made the circumambulation, in accordance with the report from him by Mālik.

The reason for the disagreement arises from the question of whether *ramal* was adopted for an underlying reason or whether it pertains to the traveller. The background for this is that when the Prophet (God's peace and blessings be upon him) performed the *ramal* he had travelled to Mecca.

They agreed that one of the *sunan* of the circumambulation is the salutation of the two corners, the corner of the Black Stone and *al-rukn al-yamānī*, and that this is for men and not the women. They disagreed on whether the salutation was to be made on all corners. The majority maintained that the salutation is made at only two corners, because of the tradition of Ibn ʿUmar "that the Messenger of Allāh (God's peace and blessings be upon him) did not make the salutation except at two corners". Those who upheld the salutation at all corners argued on the basis of what is related by Jābir, who said, "When we circumambulated we made the salutation at all corners". Some of the predecessors deemed it necessary to make the salutation at two corners, except for the odd-numbered circuits.

They agreed, likewise, that the kissing of the Black Stone in particular was one of the practices of the circumambulation, and if the worshipper was not able to reach it he was to kiss his hand. This is based upon the tradition of ʿUmar ibn al-Khaṭṭāb, which has been related by Mālik, that he said, "You are a stone, and if I had not seen the Messenger of Allāh kissing you I would not kiss you". He then kissed it.

They agreed that one of the *sunan* of the circumambulation is the observance of two *rakʿas* of prayer after the completion of the circuits. The majority maintain that the worshipper observes them at the end of each week if he performs the circumambulation (a number of times) for more than a (period of one) week. Some of the predecessors permitted that he should not make a distinction on the basis of weeks and he should not separate them by praying and then he should observe two *rakʿas* for every week. This is related from ʿĀʾisha that she did not separate three weeks and then observe six *rakʿas*. The evidence for the majority is "that the Messenger of Allāh (God's peace and blessings be upon him) made the circumambulation of the House in seven circuits and then observed two *rakʿas* behind the station [of Ibrāhīm], and then said, 'Acquire your rites from me'". Those who permitted the combining (of the *rakʿas*) said that the object is the observance of two *rakʿas* every week, and circumambulation has no fixed time nor *rakʿas* after it that have been established as a practice; therefore, it is permissible to combine more than two *rakʿas* for more than two weeks. Those who considered it desirable to distinguish between (a block of) three weeks did so as the Messenger of Allāh (God's peace and blessings be upon him) observed the *rakʿas* after an odd number of circumambulations. Thus the person who has performed the circuits for a number of weeks that are not odd and then observes the *rakʿas* is not doing so after an odd-numbered circumambulation.

9.2.6.2. *Section 2: Discussion of its conditions*

Its conditions include the delineation of its boundary. The majority of the jurists maintain that the *ḥijr* (northern wall) is part of the House, and whoever circumambulates the House is bound to include the *ḥijr* in it, and that it is a condition for the *ṭawāf al-ifāḍa* (the post-ʿArafāt circumambulation, after throwing the pebbles). Abū Ḥanīfa and his disciples said that it is a *sunna*. The evidence of the majority is what is related by Mālik from ʿĀʾisha that the Messenger of Allāh (God's peace and blessings be upon him) said, "Were it not for the fact that disbelief is a recent memory of your people I would have demolished the Kaʿba and erected it on the foundations laid by Ibrāhīm". They had left seven *dhirāʿ* of the *ḥijr* due to shortage of funds and wood. This was the opinion of Ibn ʿAbbās. He argued relying on the words of the Exalted, "And go around the ancient House",[260] and said that the Messenger of Allāh (God's peace and blessings be upon him) made the circumambulation

[260] Qurʾān 22 : 29.

beyond the *ḥijr*. The evidence for Abū Ḥanīfa is the apparent meaning of the verse.

They disagreed about the time of its permissibility holding three opinions. The first is the permissibility of circumambulation after the morning prayer and after *ʿaṣr*, and its prohibition at the time of sunrise and sunset. This is the opinion of ʿUmar ibn al-Khaṭṭāb and Abū Saʿīd al-Khudrī. This was upheld by Mālik, his disciples, and a group of jurists. The second opinion is about its abomination after the morning prayer and *ʿaṣr*, and its prohibition at sunrise and sunset. This was the opinion of Saʿīd ibn Jubayr, Mujāhid and a group. The third opinion permits it at all times. This was upheld by al-Shāfiʿī and a group of jurists.

The roots of their disagreement can be found in the prohibition or permissibility of prayer during these times. The traditions are unanimous about the prohibition of prayer at sunrise and sunset. Whether circumambulation is linked to prayer for this purpose is a matter of dispute. The evidence relied upon by the Shāfiʿites is the tradition of Jubayr ibn Muṭʿim that the Prophet (God's peace and blessings be upon him) said, "O sons of ʿAbd Manāf—or he said O sons of ʿAbd al-Muṭṭalib—if you come to supervise anything from this affair do not prevent anyone circumambulating this House from praying at any hour of the day or night". It is related by al-Shāfiʿī and others from Ibn ʿUyayna with its chain reaching up to Jubayr ibn Muṭʿim.

They disagreed about the permissibility of circumambulation without purification after their agreement that purification is a *sunna* for it. Mālik and al-Shāfiʿī said that it is not valid to circumambulate without purification, whether it is done intentionally or due to forgetfulness. Abū Ḥanīfa said that this is valid and he considered its repetition desirable. He also held the person liable for atonement (*dam*). Abū Thawr said that if he performs the circumambulation without ablution his act is to be considered valid if he was not aware of it, but it is not valid if he did know. Al-Shāfiʿī stipulates the purification of the dress of the person making the circumambulation, as he does for one praying.

The reliance of those who stipulate purification for circumambulation is upon the words of the Prophet (God's peace and blessings be upon him) to a menstruating woman, who was Asmāʾ bint ʿUmays, "Do what the pilgrims are doing but do not make the circumambulation of the House". This is an authentic tradition. They also argue on the basis of the saying of the Prophet (God's peace and blessings be upon him), "Circumambulation is prayer, except that Allāh has permitted speech in it, so do not utter anything but what is good". The reliance of those who permitted circumambulation without purification is upon the consensus of the jurists about the permissibility of *saʿy* between al-Ṣafā and al-Marwa without purification. They argue that purity from menstruation is stipulated for a type of worship, and it does not follow that purity from *ḥadath* would also be stipulated. Fasting is a good example (purity from menstruation is a condition for fasting, but purity from *janāba* is not).

9.2.6.3. *Section 3: Discussion of its types and their* aḥkām

The jurists agreed that circumambulation is of three types: the circumambulation of greeting (*ṭawāf al-qudūm*) on arrival in Mecca, *ṭawāf al-ifāḍa* after throwing pebbles at the first pillar (*Jamrat al-ʿAqaba*) on the day of sacrifice, and the farewell circumambulation (before departure from Mecca). They agreed that the obligatory circumambulation among these, without which the *ḥajj* is lost, is the *ṭawāf al-ifāḍa*, and that is the one intended in the words of the Exalted, "Then let them make an end of their unkemptness and pay their vows and go around the ancient House".[261] Further, no atonement is acceptable in its place. The majority also maintain that the initial circumambulation is not a valid substitute for the *ṭawāf al-ifāḍa* if the pilgrim forgets the latter, because of its being before the day of sacrifice. One group, from among the disciples of Mālik, maintained that the initial circumambulation is a valid substitute for the *ṭawāf al-ifāḍa*, and it appears that they considered the obligation to be for only one type of circumambulation. The majority of the jurists maintain, however, that the farewell circumambulation is a valid substitute for the *ṭawāf al-ifāḍa*, if the pilgrim has not performed the latter, as the former is a circumambulation performed during the period of the obligatory circumambulation, which is the *ṭawāf al-ifāḍa*, as against the initial circumambulation that is performed before the time of the *ṭawāf al-ifāḍa*.

They agreed, according to what has been related from Abū ʿUmar ibn ʿAbd al-Barr, that the initial and the farewell circumambulation are part of the *sunan* for the pilgrim, except for the person who fears losing the *ḥajj* (due to shortage of time), for in his case the *ṭawāf al-ifāḍa* is sufficient. A group of the jurists considered it desirable for a person faced with such a situation to adopt the *ramal* in the first three circuits of the *ṭawāf al-ifāḍa*, in accordance with the practice in the initial circumambulation.

They agreed that a resident of Mecca is only obliged to perform the *ṭawāf al-ifāḍa*, just as they agreed that for the person performing the *ʿumra* the only obligation is for the initial circumambulation. They also agreed that the person who has benefited from the performance of the *ʿumra* (in the *tamattuʿ* form of *ḥajj*) before beginning the *ḥajj* is under the obligation to perform two circumambulations, one for the *ʿumra* and another for *ḥajj* on the day of

[261] Qurʾān 22 : 29.

sacrifice, in accordance with the well-known tradition of ʿĀʾisha. The person performing *ḥajj* as a *mufrid* is obliged for only one circumambulation, as we have said, on the day of the sacrifice. They disagreed about the *qārin*. Mālik, al-Shāfiʿī, Aḥmad, and Abū Thawr maintained that one circumambulation and one *saʿy* are sufficient for the *qārin*, which was also the opinion of ʿAbd Allāh ibn ʿUmar and Jābir. Their reliance for this is on the tradition of ʿĀʾisha that has preceded. Al-Thawrī, al-Awzāʿī, Abū Ḥanīfa, and Ibn Abī Laylā maintain that the *qārin* is under an obligation of performing two circumambulations and two *saʿys*. They related this from Ibn Masʿūd, as they are two rites with each having a condition, if performed separately, that the circumambulation be performed with the *saʿy*; thus, it is necessary that it be the same when they are performed together.

This, then, is the discussion about the obligation of this act, its description, conditions, types, time, and description of the time period. The act of *ḥajj* that follows this, I mean the initial circumambulation, is the *saʿy* between al-Ṣafā and al-Marwa. It is the third act in the state of *iḥrām* and we now move to it.

9.2.7. Chapter 7 Discussion of the *Saʿy* between al-Ṣafā and al-Marwa

The discussion of the *saʿy* covers its *ḥukm*, its description, conditions, and its order.

9.2.7.1. *Section 1: Discussion of its* ḥukm

Mālik and al-Shāfiʿī said that it is obligatory by its *ḥukm*, and if the pilgrim does not perform it, *ḥajj* would (still) be obligatory upon him in the next season. This was also the opinion of Aḥmad and Isḥāq. The Kūfīs said that it is a *sunna*, and if he returns to his homeland without performing it he is liable to atonement by slaughtering an animal. Some of the jurists said that it is voluntary and there is no obligation upon the person who relinquishes it.

The reliance of those who made it obligatory is upon the report "that the Messenger of Allāh (God's peace and blessings be upon him) used to perform the *saʿy* and say, 'Perform the *saʿy* for Allāh has prescribed the *saʿy* for you'". This tradition has been related by al-Shāfiʿī from ʿAbd Allāh ibn al-Muʾmil. Further, the principle is that the acts of the Prophet (God's peace and blessings be upon him) in this worship are to be construed as conveying obligation, except those excluded by a transmitted evidence, consensus, or analogy in the view of those who uphold analogy to be a valid principle. Those who did not consider it obligatory relied on the words of the Exalted, "Lo! (the mountains) as-Ṣafā and al-Marwa are among the indications of Allāh. It is therefore no sin for him who is on pilgrimage to the House (of God) or visiteth it, to go around them".[262] They said that the meaning here is that he may "not go round them", which is the (variant) reading of Ibn Masʿūd, just as the words of the Exalted, "Allāh expoundeth unto you, so that ye err (not)",[263] mean "lest ye err". They also considered the tradition of Ibn al-Muʾmil to be weak. ʿĀʾisha said that the verse is to be understood in its obvious meaning, and it was revealed in the case of the Anṣār who shunned running between al-Ṣafā and al-Marwa in the way they used to during the period of the *jāhiliyya* as it served as a place for the slaughtering of animals for the polytheists. It is also said that they used not to run between al-Ṣafā and al-Marwa out of veneration for some of the idols (Manāt). They inquired about this, and the verse was revealed validating their hesitation.

The majority decided that it is one of the acts of the *ḥajj*, because it is described as an act of the Prophet (God's peace and blessings be upon him) by way of *tawātur* in these traditions, I mean the linking of *saʿy* with circumambulation.

9.2.7.2. *Section 2: Discussion of its description*

In describing it, the majority of the jurists maintained that a *sunna* of the *saʿy* between al-Ṣafā and al-Marwa is that the worshipper having ascended al-Ṣafā is to go down its slope after completing the supplication. He is then to walk at his normal pace till he reaches the bottom of the *masīl* (valley, bed of the stream).[264] He is (now) to adopt the *ramal* through it until he traverses it getting closer to al-Marwa from where he moves at his normal gait till he arrives at al-Marwa. He ascends it until he can see the House, then he makes a supplication and pronounces the *takbīr* in a manner similar to what he said at al-Ṣafā. If he stops at the base of al-Marwa (and does not climb it) it is considered valid in their collective view. He then descends from al-Marwa and proceeds at his normal pace until he reaches the bottom of the valley. When he reaches it he is to adopt the *ramal* until he crosses over to the side of al-Ṣafā. He is to do this seven times, beginning at al-Ṣafā and ending at al-Marwa. If he begins at al-Marwa before going to al-Ṣafā, that journey is annulled, because of the saying of the Messenger of Allāh (God's peace and blessings be

[262] Qurʾān 2 : 158. the word "visiteth" in Pickthall's translation here stands for *ʿumra*.

[263] Qurʾān 4 : 177. The parenthesis have been placed around the word "not" to bring into focus what the author is saying.

[264] Today this is represented by lines at some distance from each other on the paved floor of the tract between al-Ṣafā and al-Marwa.

upon him), "We begin with that with which Allāh began, so we begin with al-Ṣafā", and by this he meant the words of the Exalted, "Lo! (the mountains) as-Ṣafā and al-Marwa are among the indications of Allāh. It is therefore no sin for him who is on pilgrimage to the House (of God) or visiteth it, to go around them".[265] ʿAṭāʾ said that if he does not know and begins at al-Marwa, his act is to be considered as valid.

They agreed unanimously that there is no determined opinion about the time for the *saʿy*, as it is a case of supplication. It is established in the tradition of Jābir "that the Messenger of Allāh (God's peace and blessings be upon him), when he stood at al-Ṣafā, pronounced the ***takbīr*** three times and said, 'There is no god but Allāh alone, and He has no partner, His is the dominion and for Him is all praise, and He has power over all things'. He did this three times, and he made a supplication at al-Marwa and did the same thing".

9.2.7.3. *Section 3: Discussion of its conditions*

They agreed that one of its conditions is purity from menstruation, as is the case with the circumambulation, because of the saying of the Prophet (God's peace and blessings be upon him) in the tradition of ʿĀʾisha, "Do what all the pilgrims do, but do not circumambulate the House and do not perform the *saʿy* between al-Ṣafā and al-Marwa". Yaḥyā was alone in relating this addition from Mālik as compared to the others who have related this tradition from him. There is no dispute among them that ablution is not one of its conditions, except for al-Ḥasan as he held it to be similar to the circumambulation.

9.2.7.4. *Section 4: Discussion of its order*

The jurists agreed that in the order of performance the *saʿy* comes after the circumambulation, and that the person who performs the *saʿy* before circuiting the House is to go back and perform the circumambulation even if he has moved out of Mecca. If he did not realize this, in the case of the ***ʿumra*** or the *ḥajj*, until he has cohabited with women, he is under the obligation for *ḥajj* in the next season and for the sacrifice or for *ʿumra* (as the case may be). Al-Thawrī said that if he does this he is not liable for anything. Abū Ḥanīfa said that if he leaves Mecca he is not obliged to return, but he is liable for atonement.

[265] Qurʾān 2 : 158.

This was the discussion of the *ḥukm* of *saʿy*, its description, well-known conditions, and the order (of performance).

9.2.8. Chapter 8 Moving Out to ʿArafa

The act of the pilgrim that follows this act (*saʿy*) is moving out on the Day of *Tarwiya* (eighth of Dhū al-Ḥijja) to Minā and staying there the eve of ʿArafa. They agreed that the *imām* leads the people in prayer on the eighth of Dhū al-Ḥijja at Minā, and *ẓuhr* and *ʿaṣr* and *maghrib* and *ʿishāʾ* are curtailed over there. They agreed, however, that this act is not a condition for the validity of *ḥajj* for the person who is short of time. When the sun rises on the Day of ʿArafa (ninth Dhū al-Ḥijja) the *imām* walks with the people from Minā up to ʿArafa, and they take up station there.

9.2.9. Chapter 9 The Station at ʿArafa

The discussion of this act includes the identification of its *ḥukm*, its description, and its conditions. The jurists agreed about the *ḥukm* of stopping at ʿArafa that it is one of the essential elements (*arkān*) of *ḥajj*. In the opinion of the majority of the jurists the person who misses this is under an obligation to perform *ḥajj* in the next season and to make the sacrifice, because of the saying of the Prophet (God's peace and blessings be upon him), "The *ḥajj* is ʿArafa".

Its description is that the *imām* leads the people in prayer at ʿArafa on the Day of ʿArafa (ninth Dhū al-Ḥijja) before the declining of the sun. If the sun has declined he is to address the people and then combine *ẓuhr* and *ʿaṣr* in the first timing of *ẓuhr*, and thereafter they stay stationed there until the sun goes down.

They agreed upon this as this is the description that is agreed upon unanimously in the acts of the Prophet (God's peace and blessings be upon him). There is no dispute among them that the establishing of the *ḥajj* (leading the prayer) is the right of the sultan with the highest authority, or of a person whom the sultan has appointed, and also that the people are to pray behind him whether he is pious, sinful, or and innovator. The *sunna* for this is that he should come to the mosque at ʿArafa on the Day of ʿArafa along with the people. When the sun has declined he should address the people, as we have said, and he should combine the *ẓuhr* and *ʿaṣr* prayers.

They disagreed about the time for the call to the prayer by the *muʾadhdhin* for the *ẓuhr* and *ʿaṣr* prayers. Mālik said that the *imām* is to address the people and when the major part of his sermon is over the *muʾadhdhin* should make the call for prayer while he (the *imām*) is addressing the people. Al-Shāfiʿī said that he is to make the call when the *imām* begins the second sermon. Abū Ḥanīfa said that when the *imām* ascends the pulpit he should order the *muʾadhdhin* to make the call, who is to make the call as is the case in the Friday congregational prayer. When the *muʾadhdhin* has finished making the call the *imām* is to begin his sermon, after which he is to descend and the *muʾadhdhin* will announce the *iqāma* (the call for the commencement of prayer). This was also the opinion of Abū Thawr, who held it to be similar to the Friday prayer. Ibn al-Mundhir has related from Mālik that he said: "The call for prayer is to be made after the *imām* sits down for the sermon. The words in the tradition of Jābir are 'that when the sun had declined the Prophet (God's peace and blessings be upon him) ordered al-Qaṣwāʾ to be brought and riding on it he reached the middle of the valley and addressed the people. Bilāl then made the call for prayer. After this he stood up and prayed *ẓuhr*. He then rose up and prayed *ʿaṣr* without anything intervening between the two prayers. He then returned to where he was stationed'".

They disagreed whether these two prayers are to be combined with two calls for prayer and two calls for commencement, or with one call for prayer and two calls for commencement. Mālik said that they are to be combined with two calls for prayer and two calls for the commencement. Al-Shāfiʿī, Abū Ḥanīfa, al-Thawrī, Abū Thawr, and a group of jurists said that they are to be combined with one call for prayer and two calls for commencement. An opinion like theirs has also been related from Mālik. It is also related from Aḥmad that they are to be combined with two calls for commencement. The evidence for al-Shāfiʿī is the lengthy tradition of Jābir about the description of the *ḥajj* of the Prophet (God's peace and blessings be upon him), in which he says, "He observed *ẓuhr* and *ʿaṣr* with one call for prayer and with two calls for commencement", as we have said. The opinion of Mālik has been related from Ibn Masʿūd, and hie evidence is the principle that each prayer is to be individually preceded by a call for prayer and a call for commencement.

There is no dispute among the learned that if the *imām* does not deliver the sermon the prayer is valid, as against the Friday prayer. They also agreed that the recitation in this prayer is inaudible, and the prayer is curtailed if the *imām* has travelled (to this place). They disagreed when the *imām* is a resident of Mecca, whether he is to curtail the prayer on the eighth of Dhū al-Ḥijja at Minā, at ʿArafa on the Day of ʿArafa, and at Muzdalifa on the eve of the day of sacrifice, if he is a resident of one of these places. Mālik, al-Awzāʿī, and a group of jurists said the *sunna* for occasions is curtailment whether or not he is a resident. Al-Thawrī, Abū Ḥanīfa, al-Shāfiʿī, Abū Thawr, and Dāwūd said that it is not permitted to curtail the prayer if he is a resident of one these places. The evidence for Mālik is that no one has related that some person completed his prayer while praying with the Prophet (God's peace and blessings be upon him), after he had made the salutation. The argument of the other group is the retention of the well-known principle that curtailment of prayer is not permitted to anyone other than a traveller, unless another evidence restricts it.

The jurists disagreed about the obligation of Friday prayer at Minā and at ʿArafa. Mālik said that the Friday congregational prayer is not obligatory at ʿArafa nor at Minā, except during the days of *ḥajj*, neither for the residents of Mecca nor for others, unless the *imām* himself is a resident of ʿArafa. Al-Shāfiʿī held the same opinion, except that he stipulated for the obligation of the Friday congregational prayer that there be present at least forty men, in accordance with his opinion about the stipulation of this number for Friday. Abū Ḥanīfa said that if the leader of the *ḥajj* is a person whose prayer cannot be curtailed at Minā or at ʿArafa, he is to lead them in the Friday prayer if this happens by chance. Aḥmad said that if it is the governor of Mecca he is to lead the assembly. This was also the opinion of Abū Thawr.

The (first) condition for it is the assumption of the station at ʿArafa after the prayer, and there is no disagreement among the jurists "that the Messenger of Allāh (God's peace and blessings be upon him), after he had observed *ẓuhr* and *ʿaṣr* at ʿArafa, arose and stopped close to the mountain making supplications to Allāh, the Exalted. All those who were with him also stayed up to sunset. When the setting of the sun was ascertained and it became obvious to him he proceeded toward Muzdalifa". There is no dispute among them that this is the *sunna* of the stationing at ʿArafa. They agreed that the person who stops at ʿArafa prior to the declining of the sun and moves from there before the declining of the sun, his stationing there is of no account. If he does not return and stop there till after the declining of the sun or on this night before the rise of the dawn, his *ḥajj* is lost. It is related from ʿAbd Allāh ibn Maʿmar al-Daylī, who said, "I heard the Messenger of Allāh (God's peace and blessings be upon him) saying, 'The *ḥajj* is ʿArafāt, thus he who makes it to ʿArafa before the rise of the dawn has made it'". It is a tradition which is related by this person alone from among the Companions, except that it is agreed upon.

They disagreed about the person who stays at ʿArafa after the declining of the sun and then leaves before sunset. Mālik said that he is liable for *ḥajj* in the next season, unless he returns before dawn. If, however, he leaves before the *imām*, but after sunset, his act is considered to be valid. On the whole, the condition for the validity of stationing, in his view, is that he should stay the night. The majority of the jurists said that the person who stays on at ʿArafa till after the declining of the sun his *ḥajj* is complete, even if he leaves before sunset, except they differed about the obligation of atonement for him. The reliance of the majority is on the tradition of ʿUrwa ibn Muḍarris, which is agreed upon for its authenticity, that he said, "I went up to the Messenger of Allāh (God's peace and blessings be upon him) at Muzdalifa (Jamʿ) and said to him, 'Have I completed the *ḥajj*?' He replied, 'The person who observes this prayer with us and stops at this station and he arose and moved before this from ʿArafāt, by night or by day, has completed his *ḥajj* and has done away with the dirt on his body' ". They agreed that the meaning of his words, "by day", in this tradition imply that it is after the declining of the sun. Those who stipulated the night argued on the basis of his (God's peace and blessings be upon him) being stationed at ʿArafa when the sun was setting, but the majority may reply that his being stationed at ʿArafa up to sunset has been indicated by the tradition of ʿUrwa ibn Muḍarris to the effect that it is better if the person has a choice.

It is related from the Prophet (God's peace and blessings be upon him) through different channels that he said, "All of ʿArafa is a station, but keep away from the middle of ʿUrana. All Muzdalifa is a station, except the middle of Muḥassir. All of Minā is the place of sacrifice. The road to Mecca is a place of sacrifice and a stop for the night". The jurists differed about the person who moves from ʿArafa and stays (again) at ʿArafa. It is said that his *ḥajj* is complete, but he is liable for atonement. This was Mālik's opinion, while al-Shāfiʿī said that there is no *ḥajj* for him. The reliance of those who nullify his *ḥajj* is the proscription laid down about this in a tradition. The reliance of those who do not invalidate it is the principle that staying at any place in ʿArafa is permitted, unless the contrary is indicated by an evidence. They said that the proscription is not laid down in the tradition in a manner that makes its evidence binding and the giving up of the principle necessary.

This, then, is the discussion about the *sunan* of the day of ʿArafa. The act, from among the acts of *ḥajj*, that follows the stationing at ʿArafa is the movement toward Muzdalifa after sunset and what is done there.

9.2.10. **Chapter 10 Discussion of the Acts at Muzdalifa**

A general discussion of this too is covered by the identification of its *ḥukm*, description, and time.

The existence of this act as one of the constituent elements of *ḥajj* is based on the words of the Exalted, "But, when ye press on in the multitude from

ʿArafāt, remember Allāh by the sacred monument. Remember Him as He hath guided you, although before this you were astray".[266] They agreed that the person who after stationing at ʿArafa spends the eve of the day of sacrifice at Muzdalifa, combining the *maghrib* and *ʿishāʾ* prayers that night with the *imām*, and stays up to the morning light, his *ḥajj* is complete. They also argued that this was the description of the act of the Messenger of Allāh (God's peace and blessings be upon him). They disagreed, however, as to whether staying at Muzdalifa till after the morning prayers and spending the night there is a *sunna* of *ḥajj* or one of its obligations. Al-Awzāʿī and a group of the Tābiʿūn said that it is an obligation of *ḥajj*, and the person who misses this is under an obligation to perform *ḥajj* in the next season and along with the sacrifice. The jurists of the provinces maintain that it is not an obligation of *ḥajj*, and the person who misses the stay at Muzdalifa during the night is liable for atonement by sacrifice. Al-Shāfiʿī said that the person who spends the first half of the night there and then leaves not spending the whole night is liable to atonement.

The reliance of the majority is upon the authentic tradition from the Prophet (God's peace and blessings be upon him) that he sent the weak members of his family during the night and they did not stay to witness the morning there with him. The reliance of the first group is on the saying of the Prophet (God's peace and blessings be upon him) in the tradition of ʿUrwa ibn Muḍarris, which is agreed upon (by al-Bukhārī and Muslim) for its authenticity, that "the person who observes this prayer with us", that is, the morning prayer at Muzdalifa, "and stops at this station and he arose and moved before this from ʿArafāt, by night or by day, has completed his *ḥajj* and has done away with the dirt on his body". They also rely on the words of the Exalted, "But, when ye press on in the multitude from ʿArafāt, remember Allāh by the sacred monument. Remember Him as He hath guided you, although before this you were astray".[267] The other group argue that the Muslim jurists agreed unanimously on relinquishing the adoption of all that is in this tradition. Thus, most of them maintain that the person who stops at Muzdalifa during the night and leaves before the morning prayer his *ḥajj* is complete, and so also the person who stays the night there and kept on sleeping without praying. They also agreed that the person who stays at Muzdalifa without engaging in the remembrance of Allāh his *ḥajj* is complete. Their reliance upon the verse is also weak in the light of its apparent meaning.

Muzdalifa and Jamʿ are the two names for this place and the *sunna* of *ḥajj* for it, as we have said, is that the person spend the night there combining

266 Qurʾān 2 : 198.
267 Qurʾān 2 : 198.

maghrib and *ʿishāʾ* in the early part of the time for *ʿishāʾ*, and then stay up to the morning there.

9.2.11. **Chapter 11 Discussion of Throwing Pebbles at the *Jamras***

The act that follows it (the stay at Muzdalifa) is the throwing of pebbles at the pillars (*jimār*), because the Muslim jurists agreed that "the Prophet (God's peace and blessings be upon him) stopped at *al-mashʿar al-ḥarām*, which is Muzdalifa, till after he had observed the morning prayer. He then departed from there before sunrise toward Minā. It was on this day, which was the day of sacrifice, that he threw stones at the *Jamrat al-ʿAqaba* after sunrise". The Muslim jurists also agreed that the person who throws stones at it on this day at this time, that is, after sunrise up to the declining of the sun, has thrown them during the prescribed time. They agreed that the Messenger of Allāh (God's peace and blessings be upon him) did not throw pebbles at the other *jamarāt* besides it on the day of the sacrifice.

They disagreed about the case of the person who throws pebbles at the *Jamrat al-ʿAqaba* before sunrise. Mālik said: "No report has reached us that the Messenger of Allāh (God's peace and blessings be upon him) made an exemption for anyone to throw the pebbles before sunrise, and this is not permitted. If he throws the pebbles before dawn he is to repeat the act". This was also the opinion of Abū Ḥanīfa, Sufyān, and Aḥmad. Al-Shāfiʿī said there is no harm in this, although it is desirable that he do it after sunrise.

The evidence of those who prohibited this is the act of the Prophet (God's peace and blessings be upon him) along with his saying, "Acquire your rites from me". Further, it is related from Ibn ʿAbbās "that the Messenger of Allāh (God's peace and blessings be upon him) sent the weak among his family members (from Muzdalifa) and said, 'Do not throw pebbles at the *jamra* until the sun rises'". The reliance of those who permitted stoning before dawn is the tradition about Umm Salama, which has been recorded by Abū Dāwūd and others, "that ʿĀʾisha said, 'The Messenger of Allāh (God's peace and blessings be upon him) sent Umm Salama on the day of sacrifice and she threw pebbles before dawn, after which she hastened on and performed the *ṭawāf al-ifāḍa*'. This was a day when the Messenger of Allāh (God's peace and blessings be upon him) was with her". There is also the tradition of Asmāʾ that she threw pebbles at the *jamra* during the night and said: "We used to do this during the days of the Messenger of Allāh (God's peace and blessings be upon him)".

The jurists agreed that the desirable time for throwing pebbles at the *Jamrat al-ʿAqaba* is from the rising of the sun up to its decline, but if a pilgrim throws the pebbles before the setting of the sun on the day of sacrifice his act is valid and does not incur a liability (for atonement). Mālik, however, said that it is desirable for such a person to atone by sacrifice. They disagreed about the case of a person who does not throw the pebbles till after the setting of the sun, and does it during the night, or on the next day. Mālik said that he is liable for atonement by slaughtering an animal. Abū Ḥanīfa said that if he throws the pebbles during the night he does not incur any liability, but if he delays it till the next day he is liable to atonement by slaughtering an animal. Abū Yūsuf, Muḥammad, and al-Shāfiʿī said that there is no liability for him if he delays it till the night or up to the next day. Their evidence is "that the Messenger of Allāh (God's peace and blessings be upon him) made an exemption for those tending the camels to throw the pebbles during the night", and also the tradition of Ibn ʿAbbās "that the Messenger of Allāh (God's peace and blessings be upon him) was asked by a questioner, 'O Messenger of Allāh, I threw the pebbles after sundown.' He said to him, 'No harm done' ". Mālik's reliance is on the argument that this time, which is agreed upon, during which the Messenger of Allāh (God's peace and blessings be upon him) threw the pebbles is the *sunna*, and the person who violates one of the *sunan* of *ḥajj* is liable for atonement by slaughtering an animal, in accordance with what is related from Ibn ʿAbbās. This opinion was adopted by the majority.

Mālik said that the underlying meaning of the exemption for the persons tending the camels is this that if the day of sacrifice had passed and they had thrown pebbles at the *Jamrat al-ʿAqaba* and then the third day would arrive, which was the first day of departure, the Messenger of Allāh (God's peace and blessings be upon him) made an exemption for them that they may throw pebbles for that day (the second) and for the day following it, and they may depart as they have finished or stay behind with the people till the next day, the day of final departure, and then leave. The meaning of the exemption for the persons tending the animals in the view of a group of jurists is the combining of two days in one, except that combining in Mālik's view is possible for what has become due, like combining in the third day and thus throwing pebbles for the second and the third day, because delayed performance is not possible in his view except for what has become due. Many jurists, however, made an exemption for combining two days into one, whether the day being added to the other has passed or is yet to come, and they did not draw a similarity with *qaḍāʾ*.

It is established "that the Messenger of Allāh (God's peace and blessings be upon him) threw pebbles during his *ḥajj* at the *jamra* on the day of sacrifice, he then sacrificed a she-camel, then had his head shaved, and thereafter performed the *ṭawāf al-ifāḍa*". The jurists agreed that this was the *sunna* of *ḥajj*. They disagreed over the case of someone who advances an act over the sequence maintained by the Prophet (God's peace and blessings be upon him) or delays it. Mālik said that the person who shaves his head before throwing pebbles at the *Jamrat al-ʿAqaba* is liable for redemption (*fidya*; ransom). Al-Shāfiʿī, Aḥmad, Dāwūd, and Abū Thawr said that there is no liability for him. Their reliance is upon what was related by Mālik of the tradition of ʿAbd Allāh ibn ʿUmar, who said, "The Messenger of Allāh (God's peace and blessings be upon him) stopped for the people at Minā, when they were asking him questions. A man came up and said, 'O Messenger of Allāh, I did not realize it and shaved my head before making the sacrifice'. The Prophet (God's peace and blessings be upon him) said, "'ake the sacrifice, there is no harm'. Another man then came forward and said, 'O Messenger of Allāh, I did not know and made the sacrifice before throwing the pebbles'. The Prophet (God's peace and blessings be upon him) said, 'Throw the pebbles, there is no harm'. Whenever, on this day, the Messenger of Allāh (God's peace and blessings be upon him) was asked about advancing or delaying an act over the sequence he replied, 'Do it, there is no harm'". This has (also) been related on the authority of Ibn ʿAbbās from the Prophet (God's peace and blessings be upon him).[268] Mālik's reliance is upon the argument that the Messenger of Allāh (God's peace and blessings be upon him) laid down the *ḥukm* of redemption for a person shaving his head earlier due to a necessity; so how can this be for a person who does it when there is no necessity, along with the fact that the tradition does not mention the shaving of the head before the throwing of pebbles.

In Mālik's view, the person who shaves his head before slaughtering the animal is under no liability, and also the person who slaughters the animal before throwing the pebbles. Abū Ḥanīfa said that if the person shaves his head or throws the pebbles before he makes the sacrifice, he is liable for atonement by slaughtering an animal, and if he is a *qārin* he has to atone twice. Zufar said that he is liable for atoning three times, once for *qirān*, and twice for shaving his head before the sacrifice and before throwing the pebbles.

They agreed unanimously that the person who makes the sacrifice before throwing the pebbles is not liable for anything as that is explicitly mentioned in the text, except for Ibn ʿAbbās who used to say that the person who advances or delays anything in his *ḥajj* has to sacrifice an animal, and the person who advances the *ṭawāf al-ifāḍa* over throwing of pebbles and shaving of the head is bound to repeat the circumambulation. Al-Shāfiʿī, and those who followed him, said that he is not obliged to repeat it. Al-Awzāʿī said that if he performs the *ṭawāf al-ifāḍa* before throwing pebbles at the *Jamrat al-*

[268] See two paragraphs above.

ʿAqaba and then has intercourse with his wife he is to atone by sacrificing an animal.

They agreed that the total number of pebbles that the pilgrim is to throw is seventy including seven at the *Jamrat al-ʿAqaba* on the day of sacrifice. The pilgrim is to throw these pebbles at the *Jamrat al-ʿAqaba*, from whichever spot is convenient, striking the lower part, the upper, and the middle, and there is freedom in this. The place of choice for the position taken is the middle of the valley in accordance with what is laid down in the tradition of Ibn Masʿūd that he sought the middle of the valley and said: "By Him, besides Whom there is no god, I saw the one to whom the *sūrat al-Baqara* was revealed throwing the pebbles in this way". They agreed that the pilgrim is to throw a pebble again if it does not strike the *Jamrat al-ʿAqaba*. He is to throw pebbles each day during the days of *tashrīq* (11th, 12th, and 13th of Dhū al-Ḥijja) on all the three *jamarāt*, twenty-one pebbles in all with seven for each *jamra*. It is permitted to him to throw the pebbles on two days and leave on the third day, because of the words of the Exalted, "Remember Allāh through the appointed days. Then whoso hasteneth (his departure) after two days, it is no sin for him, and whoso delayeth, it is no sin for him".[269]

The size of the stones, in their view, is similar to the size of date stones, because of what is related in the traditions of Jābir, Ibn ʿAbbās, and others that the Prophet (God's peace and blessings be upon him) threw stones at the *jimār* that were similar in size to date stones.

The *sunna* for the throwing of stones at the *jamarāt* on each day of the days of *tashrīq*, in their view, is that the pilgrim throw stones at the first *jamra* halting there for a while and and making a supplication. He is to do the same at the second *jamra* and prolong his stay. He is then to throw stones at the third and is not to stay, because of what is related about this from the Messenger of Allāh (God's peace and blessings be upon him), and "this is what he used to do in his throwing of the pebbles". It is preferable in their view to pronounce the *takbīr* while throwing pebbles at each *jamra*, as that is related from the Prophet (God's peace and blessings be upon him). They agreed that one *sunna* for throwing pebbles at the three *jamarāt* during the days of *tashrīq* is that it be undertaken after the declining of the sun. They disagreed when a pilgrim throws the pebbles before the declining of the sun during the days of *tashrīq*. The majority of the jurists maintained that the person who throws the pebbles before the declining of the sun is to repeat the performance after its decline. It is, however, related from Abū Jaʿfar Muḥammad ibn ʿAlī that he said, "The throwing of pebbles is undertaken any time from moment of the rising of the sun until it sets".

[269] Qurʾān 2 : 203.

They agreed unanimously that the person who did not throw pebbles at the *jimār* during the days of *tashrīq* up to the time when the sun sets on the last of these days is not permitted to do so after these days. They disagreed about the obligation for this in terms of expiation. Mālik said that the person who relinquishes the throwing of pebbles at the *jimār* in part or completely or even at one of them, he is liable to atonement by slaughtering an animal. Abū Ḥanīfa said that if he relinquishes this completely he is liable for atonement by slaughtering an animal, but if he misses one pillar or more he is liable to feed needy person with half a *ṣāʿ* of wheat for each pillar missed until the amount reaches the sacrifice of an animal. This, however, does not apply to the *Jamrat al-ʿAqaba* and the person who misses it has to sacrifice an animal. Al-Shāfiʿī said that for each pebble missed he is liable for one *mudd* of food, for two pebbles it is two *mudds*, but for three he is liable for sacrificing an animal. Al-Thawrī held the same opinion, except that he imposed the sacrifice of an animal on the fourth pebble. A group of the Tābiʿūn made an exemption for missing one pebble and imposed no penalty for it, and their evidence is the tradition of Saʿd ibn Abī Waqqāṣ, who said, "We accompanied the Messenger of Allāh (God's peace and blessings be upon him) during his *ḥajj*, and some of us said, "We threw seven," while others said, "We threw six". We did not, however, find fault with each other". The Ẓāhirites said that there is no atonement in all this.

The majority maintained that the *Jamrat al-ʿAqaba* (throwing pebbles at it) is not an one of the elements (*arkān*) of *ḥajj*. ʿAbd al-Malik, one of the disciples of Mālik, said that it is an element of *ḥajj*.

These, then, are all the acts of *ḥajj* from the time of assuming the state of *iḥrām* up to the time of release from it. Release from the *iḥrām* is of two types: major, which is the *ṭawāf al-ifāḍa*, and minor, which is the throwing of stones at the *Jamrat al-ʿAqaba*. We will mention the disagreement surrounding these in what follows.

9.3. The Third Category

This category includes the discussion of the *aḥkām*. We shall discuss fully the *ḥukm* of certain incidents that occur during *ḥajj*. The greatest of these relates to the pilgrim who commences *ḥajj*, but is prevented (from completing it) by an illness, or by being besieged by the enemy, or he misses some rite at its prescribed time, which is a condition for the validity of *ḥajj*, or his *ḥajj* stands nullified by his commission of certain forbidden acts that vitiate *ḥajj* or his commission of acts whose relinquishment is required. We begin, out of these, with the factors mentioned explicitly in the law; namely, the *ḥukm* of the person obstructed, the *ḥukm* of the person killing game, the *ḥukm* of the person shaving his head before the occasion arises, and of getting rid of his dirt before the removal of the *iḥrām*. Included in this topic is the *ḥukm* of the *mutamattiʿ* and the *ḥukm* of the *qārin* on the basis of the opinion that the obligation of sacrificing an animal is imposed on them because of this exemption.

9.3.1. **Chapter 1 Discussion of the Person Prevented**

The source for (the *aḥkām* of) confinement are the words of the Exalted, "And if ye are prevented, then send such gifts as can be obtained with ease",[270] up to His words, "And if ye are in safety, then whosoever enjoyed freedom from the restriction of the *iḥrām* by commencing with the *ʿumra* before the *ḥajj*, (shall give) such gifts as can be had with ease".[271] The jurists disagreed extensively over the meaning of this verse, the cause of which is the *ḥukm* of the person prevented due to disease or by the enemy.

The first point of their disagreement over this verse is whether the person prevented is besieged by the enemy or he is prevented by disease. A group of jurists said that here it means the person besieged by the enemy. Some other jurists said that in fact it is the person prevented by disease. Those who maintained that the person prevented here is one besieged by the enemy argued on the basis of the words of the Exalted, "And whoever among you is sick or hath an ailment of the head must pay a ransom of fasting or alsmgiving or offering". They asserted that if (in the first case) he was prevented by disease, what was the point of mentioning disease once again? They also argued on the basis of the words of the Exalted, "And if ye are in safety, then whosoever enjoyed freedom from the restriction of the *iḥrām* by commencing with the *ʿumra* before the *ḥajj*, (shall give) such gifts as can be had with ease". This is very clear evidence.

Those who maintained that the verse was laid down for the person prevented by disease argued that *al-muḥṣar* is the passive participle of the fourth form, that is, "to be obstructed by illness", and this form by itself is not

[270] Qurʾān 2 : 196.

[271] The complete verse reads: "Perform the pilgrimage and the Visit (to Mecca) for Allāh. And if ye are prevented, then send such gifts as can be obtained with ease, and shave not your heads until the gifts have reached their destination. And whoever among you is sick or hath an ailment of the head must pay a ransom of fasting or alsmgiving or offering. And if ye are in safety, then whosoever enjoyed freedom from the restriction of the *iḥrām* by commencing with the *ʿumra* before the *ḥajj*, (shall give) such gifts as can be had with ease. And whosoever cannot find (such gifts), then a fast of three days while on the pilgrimage, and of seven when ye have returned; that is, ten in all. That is for him whose folk are not present at the Inviolable Place of Worship. Observe your duty to Allāh, and know that Allāh is severe in punishment."

used (in Arabic) to denote one besieged by the enemy. What may be used in case of prevention by the enemy is the first form of the verb "*ḥaṣara*". Thus, the correct usage is to say "*ḥaṣarahu al-ʿaduww*" (the enemy besieged him) and "*aḥṣarahu al-maraḍ*" (he is prevented by disease). They said that disease has been mentioned again in the verse as disease is of two types: disease that prevents and disease that does not prevent. They added that the meaning of the words of the Exalted, "And if ye are in safety", is safety from disease. The first group maintained the opposite of this. They said that the fourth and the first forms of the verb, while they share the root meaning, convey separate shades of meaning. The first form is used when one does something to another, while the fourth form is employed to convey the idea of being exposed to suffer that action. Thus, it is said "he killed him" when the object, the sufferer, is the victim directly, and the other form simply means that he exposed him to harm. If this is the case then the fourth form "*aḥṣara*" is more likely used to convey the idea of being besieged by the enemy, and the first form *ḥaṣara* is more suitable for sickness, as the enemy is merely the cause of the confinement while disease is the direct actor in prevention. They also added that the word "*amn*" (safety) is never used except for the absence of fear of the enemy and when it is used in the case of disease it is a figurative application, but figurative use is not to be resorted to except for something that necessitates the departure from the literal application. Further, the mentioning of the *ḥukm* of the diseased person after giving the *ḥukm* of *al-muḥṣar* shows that *al-muḥṣar* is not the diseased person. This is the opinion of al-Shāfiʿī. The second opinion is that of Mālik and Abū Ḥanīfa. Another group of jurists said that the person besieged in this case is one who is prevented from *ḥajj* by any reason, either by disease or by the enemy or by an error in counting or by anything else besides these. The majority, however, maintain that the person prevented is of two types: the person prevented by disease, and the person besieged by the enemy.

The majority of the jurists agreed that the person prevented by the enemy is to relinquish the state of *iḥrām* for the *ʿumra* or *ḥajj* where and when he is besieged. Al-Thawrī and al-Ḥasan ibn Ṣāliḥ held that he is not to do so except on the day of sacrifice. Those who maintained that he is to resume his normal state when and where he was stopped, differed about his obligation to sacrifice an animal and about the place of sacrifice if he is obliged to make a sacrifice. They disagreed on whether he is to repeat what he has been prevented from, whether that is *ḥajj* or *ʿumra*. Mālik held that he is not under an obligation to make a sacrifice, but if he has a sacrificial animal with him he is to sacrifice it where he relinquishes the state of *iḥrām*. Al-Shāfiʿī upheld the obligation of sacrifice upon him, and that was also the opinion of Ashhab. Abū Ḥanīfa stipulated the slaughter of the animal at the Ḥaram, while al-Shāfiʿī said he is to do it wherever he was intercepted. With respect to repetition, Mālik held that there is no repetition for him, while a group of jurists maintained that he is to repeat the worship. Abū Ḥanīfa said that if he was undertaking the *ḥajj* he is under an obligation of performing *ḥajj* as well as *ʿumra*, but if he was a *qārin* then he is under an obligation for *ḥajj* and two *ʿumras*. If, on the other hand, he was undertaking *ʿumra*, he is to perform his *ʿumra* as *qaḍāʾ*. There is no obligation of shaving or shortening his hair in the view of Abū Ḥanīfa and Muḥammad ibn al-Ḥasan, but Abū Yūsuf differed on that.

Mālik's reliance for maintaining that *al-muḥṣar* is not under an obligation to repeat the worship he has missed is "that the Messenger of Allāh (God's peace and blessings be upon him) and his Companions released themselves from the *iḥrām* at al-Ḥudaybiya where they sacrificed their animals, shaved off their heads and became free of all restrictions before they could reach Mecca to make the circumambulation of the House, and before the sacrifice reached the House. Further, it was never heard that the Messenger of Allāh (God's peace and blessings be upon him) ordered any of the Companions or any of those who were with him to perform any rite as *qaḍāʾ* or to repeat it".

The reliance of those who made repetition obligatory is "that the Messenger of Allāh (God's peace and blessings be upon him) performed the *ʿumra* in the next year after the year of al-Ḥudaybiya as *qaḍāʾ* for the *ʿumra* he had missed". It is, therefore, called the *ʿumrat al-qaḍāʾ*. Further, they arrived at a consensus that the person prevented by illness or something similar is under an obligation to perform it as *qaḍāʾ*. The reason for their disagreement is whether the Messenger of Allāh (God's peace and blessings be upon him) performed the *ʿumra* as *qaḍāʾ*, and whether *qaḍāʾ* can be established through analogy. The majority of the jurists maintain that *qaḍāʾ* can become obligatory because of a command different from the command for *ʿadāʾ*.

Those who made the sacrificing of animals obligatory (on *al-muḥṣar*) did so on the basis that the verse deals with the person prevented by the enemy, or that it is a general command for that all causes of obstruction, and the order of sacrificing an animal is explicitly laid down in the verse. They also argued on the basis of the slaughter of animals by the Prophet (God's peace and blessings be upon him) and his Companions in the year of al-Ḥudaybiya when they were prevented (by the Quraysh). The other group replied with the argument that the sacrifice by the Prophet and his Companions then was not the means for release from the status of *iḥrām*, but because sacrificial animals had been brought along already. The reliance of these jurists is on the principle that there is no obligation on such a person for sacrificing an animal, unless an evidence were to indicate this.

The basis of their disagreement over the place of sacrifice, in accordance with the opinion of those who made it obligatory, stems from the dispute over the place where the Messenger of Allāh (God's peace and blessings be upon him) sacrificed his animals in the year of al-Ḥudaybiya. Ibn Isḥāq (author of the Prophet's biography) said that he sacrificed them (or had them sacrificed) in the Ḥaram. Some others reported that he sacrificed them outside it (*ḥill*), and argued on the basis of the words of the Exalted, "These it was who disbelieved and debarred you from the Inviolable Place of Worship, and debarred the offering from reaching its goal".[272]

Abū Ḥanīfa maintained that anyone who is prevented from performing *ḥajj* is under an obligation for performing the *ḥajj* and the *ʿumra* as the pilgrim had annulled his *ḥajj* while he was involved with the *ʿumra*, and he did not perform either. This, then, is the *ḥukm* of the person prevented by the enemy, in the view of the jurists.

With respect to the person prevented due to illness, it is the opinion of al-Shāfiʿī and the jurists of al-Ḥijāz that he can be released from the restrictions of the *iḥrām* only by undertaking the circumambulation of the House and the *saʿy* between al-Ṣafā and al-Marwa. In other words, he can be freed from the restrictions of the *iḥrām* by undertaking the *ʿumra*, because the loss of his *ḥajj*, having missed the rites at *ʿArafa* due to a prolonged illness converts the *ḥajj* into *ʿumra*. This is the opinion of Ibn ʿUmar, ʿĀʾisha, and Ibn ʿAbbās. The jurists of Irāq opposed this and said that he is freed from the *iḥrām* where he is and his *ḥukm* is the same as that of the person prevented by the enemy, that is, he is to send his sacrificial animal to the Ḥaram and is to watch for the Day of Sacrifice and then be fully free from the *iḥrām* on the third day (of Dhū al-Ḥijja). This was the opinion of Ibn Masʿūd. They argued on the basis of the tradition of al-Ḥajjāj ibn ʿAmr al-Anṣārī, who said, "I heard the Messenger of Allāh (God's peace and blessings be upon him) saying, 'A person [on pilgrimage] who breaks a bone or becomes lame moves out of the ritual state of *iḥrām* and is under an obligation to perform another *ḥajj*' ". Further, they argued on the basis of their consensus that circumambulating the House is not a condition for moving out of the state of *iḥrām* for a person prevented by the enemy.

The majority of the jurists maintain that a person prevented by disease is under an obligation for making a sacrifice. Abū Thawr and Dāwūd maintained, relying upon the apparent *ḥukm* of such a prevented person, that there is no obligation for him to sacrifice an animal. They also claimed that the verse was laid down for the person prevented by the enemy, but they did uphold the obligation of *qaḍāʾ* for him.

The person who misses his *ḥajj* due to an error in counting the days of *ḥajj* because the moon was concealed from his view or who has some other excuse,

[272] Qurʾān 48 : 25.

his *ḥukm* is the same, in Mālik's view, as that of the person prevented by disease. Abū Ḥanīfa said that the person who has missed the *ḥajj* due to an excuse other than disease moves out of the ritual state of *iḥrām* by undertaking *ʿumra* and he is under no obligation to sacrifice an animal, but he is under an obligation to repeat the *ḥajj*. A resident of Mecca prevented by disease is, in Mālik's view, like a person who is not a resident of Mecca, and is freed from the *iḥrām* by undertaking the *ʿumra* and is under an obligation to sacrifice an animal. Al-Zuhrī said that it is necessary that he undertake the *wuqūf* (at ʿArafa) in *ʿumra* even if he has to be carried upon a cot (bier).[273] The principle in Mālik's opinion is that if the person prevented by disease were to stay in the state of *iḥrām* until the next year when he would perform his *ḥajj* as *qaḍāʾ* there would be no sacrifice for him, but if he frees himself from the *iḥrām* by undertaking *ʿumra* he would be under an obligation to sacrifice an animal.

All those who interpreted the words of the Exalted, "And if ye are in safety, then whosoever enjoyed freedom from the restriction of the *iḥrām* by commencing with the *ʿumra* before the *ḥajj*, (shall give) such gifts as can be had with ease",[274] to mean that it is a communication for the person prevented (by the enemy) are bound to rule on the grounds of the apparent meaning of the text that he is obliged to make two offerings: a sacrifice for shaving his head while moving out of the state of *iḥrām* prior to the sacrifice on account of the *qaḍāʾ ḥajj*, and a sacrifice for benefiting through the *tamattuʿ* by advancing the *ʿumra* before the *ḥajj*. If he moves out of the state of *iḥrām* of the *ʿumra* during the months of *ḥajj* a third sacrifice is obligatory upon him, which is the sacrifice due to *tamattuʿ*, and this offering is one of the rites of *ḥajj*. Mālik, may Allāh have mercy on him, used to interpret the verse, because of this complication, to mean that the person prevented is under an obligation for making one sacrifice. He used to say that the sacrifice mentioned in the words of the Exalted "And if ye are prevented, then send such gifts as can be obtained with ease",[275] is the same sacrifice that is mentioned in the words of the Exalted, "And if ye are in safety".[276] This interpretation, however, is not plausible. A more obvious interpretation of the words of the Exalted, "And if ye are in safety, then whosoever enjoyed freedom from the restriction of the *iḥrām* by commencing with the *ʿumra* before the *ḥajj*, (shall

[273] The editor of the original manuscript points out that this is how the statement appears in most of the manuscripts, while in some it reads, "He must repeat", and the rest is a blank. The contradiction, it appears, arises in the use of the text of "*wuqūf*" which is peculiar to *ḥajj*, and so far it is alright, but why does he say *bi-ʿumra*? The solution is to interpret the word *yaqifa* to mean "undertake *ʿumra*".

[274] Qurʾān 2 : 196.

[275] Qurʾān 2 : 196.

[276] Qurʾān 2 : 196.

give) such gifts as can be had with ease",[277] would be that they do not apply to the person prevented but to the person who is actually performing *ḥajj* through the *tamattuʿ* form. Thus, the words would appear to mean, "And if you are not in a state of fear, but have released yourself from the *iḥrām* by undertaking the *ʿumra* before the *ḥajj*, then, such gifts as can be had with ease". This meaning is indicated by the words of the Exalted, "That is for him whose folk are not resident in the vicinity of the Sacred Mosque",[278] because the persons who are resident there as well as others are on the same footing with respect to prevention (by the enemy), by consensus.

9.3.2. Chapter 2 Discussion of the *Aḥkām* of Reparation for Game

We say: The Muslim jurists agreed unanimously that the words of the Exalted, "O ye who believe! Kill no wild game while ye are on the pilgrimage. Whoso of you killeth it of set purpose he shall pay its forfeit in the equivalent of that which he hath killed, of domestic animals, the judge to be two men among you known for justice, (the forfeit) to be brought as an offering to the Kaʿbah; or, for expiation, he shall feed poor persons, or the equivalent thereof in fasting, that he may taste the evil consequences of the deed",[279] explicitly govern the issue. They disagreed over the details of the *aḥkām* in the verse, and over what kinds of analogies are to be based upon its implications.

One of these disagreements is whether the obligation for killing game is payment of its value or payment with a similar animal (*mithl*). The majority of the jurists maintained that the obligation is for a similar animal. Abū Ḥanīfa held that the person has a choice to pay by value, that is, to pay the value or to buy an animal with the value. They also disagreed about issuing a new ruling for a person killing game with reference to cases already decided by the predecessors from among the Companions. For example, their ruling that if a person kills an ostrich he is liable for a she-camel, and the person who kills a gazelle is liable for a goat, and the person who kills a wild buffalo is liable for a domesticated cow. Mālik said that a new ruling is to be issued in each case that occurs under this rule. This was also Abū Ḥanīfa's opinion. Al-Shāfiʿī said that if the decision is arrived at in accordance with the precedents of the Companions it is permitted.

Another disagreement is whether the verse implies an order or whether there is a choice. Mālik said that it implies a choice, which was also the opinion of Abū Ḥanīfa. He meant thereby that the two arbitrators (estimators) are to

[277] Qurʾān 2 : 196.
[278] Qurʾān 2 : 196.
[279] Qurʾān 5 : 95.

grant the person who has to make the reparation a choice. Zufar said that the verse implies an order.

They disagreed on whether the value is to be that of the game killed or that of the substitute animal, if the person chooses to feed needy persons, so that he may purchase food in the value, and this in accordance with the opinion that permits such an obligation. Mālik said that he is to procure the valuation of the animal killed, while al-Shāfiʿī said that he is to obtain the valuation of the substitute animal.

They did not disagree in general over the determination of the equivalence of fasts with food, even though they did disagree on details. Mālik said that he is to fast one day for each *mudd* of food, and that is the amount to be given to each needy person in their view. This was also the opinion of al-Shāfiʿī and the jurists of al-Ḥijāz. The jurists of Kūfa maintained that he is to fast one day for every two *mudds* of food, and that is the quantity of food to be given to each needy person in their view.

They disagreed about the killing of game by mistake, whether that entails reparation. The majority of the jurists maintained that reparation is to be paid for it, while the Ẓāhirites said that there is no reparation.

They also disagreed about a group participating in the killing of the animal. Mālik said that if a group of people in a ritual state of *iḥrām* participate in killing game, then, on each person is the obligation of making a full reparation. This was also the opinion of al-Thawrī and a group of jurists. Al-Shāfiʿī said that they are liable for one reparation as a group. Abū Ḥanīfa made a distinction between those who are in a state of *iḥrām* and those who are not when they participate in killing game withing the Ḥaram. He said that each person in the state of *iḥrām* is liable for a full reparation, while those who are not in the state of *iḥrām* are liable for one as a group.

They disagreed whether one of two estimators can be the person who has killed game. Mālik said that this is not permitted, while al-Shāfiʿī said that it is. The disciples of Abū Ḥanīfa differed on this issue.

They disagreed about the place where the needy are to be fed. Mālik said that this is the location where the game was hunted, if the food is sufficient for that place, otherwise it is to be in locations adjacent to it. Abū Ḥanīfa said that this may be any place. Al-Shāfiʿī said that only the needy of Mecca are to be fed.

The jurists agreed unanimously that if a person in a state of *iḥrām* kills game he is under an obligation to make reparation, because of the text, but they differed about the person who is not in the state of *iḥrām* who kills game within the Ḥaram. The majority of the jurists of the provinces said that he is liable for reparation. Dāwūd and his disciples said that there is no reparation for him.

The Muslim jurists did not differ about the prohibition of killing game within the Ḥaram, but they disagreed about the expiation to be made for it, and this because of the words of the Exalted, "Have they not seen that We have appointed a sanctuary immune (from violence), while mankind are ravaged all around them?"[280] and also because of the saying of the Messenger of Allāh (God's peace and blessings be upon him), "Allāh made Mecca a sanctuary the day He created the heavens and the earth". The majority of the jurists of the provinces maintain that if a person in the state of *iḥrām* kills an animal and eats it he is liable for one expiation. It is related from ʿAṭāʾ and a group of jurists that there are two expiations for it.

These are the well-known issues related to this verse.

With respect to the reasons that led them on to this dispute, we shall indicate some of them, therefore, we say:

Those who stipulated, for the obligation of reparation, that the killing should be intentional argue that such stipulation is mentioned in the verse. Further, intention is a cause for penalty and expiation is a kind of punishment. Those who made reparation obligatory in the case of forgetfulness have no (valid) evidence, unless they hold the killing of the hunted animal to be similar to the destruction of wealth, as wealth in the view of the majority is to be compensated even when destroyed by mistake or through forgetfulness. This analogy is opposed by the stipulation of intention for the obligation of reparation. Some of these jurists answered this point by saying: "Intention is stipulated as being related to penalty in His words, 'That he may taste the evil consequences of the deed'".[281] This argument, however, is meaningless as tasting the evil consequences relates to penalty, so whether he kills an animal by mistake or intentionally, he has to taste the evil of the consequences (of his deed). There is no dispute, however, that a person acting in forgetfulness is not to be punished, and this argument is binding to the utmost for those who maintain the principle that expiation is not established by analogy. Thus, those who establish it against the person acting in forgetfulness have no evidence, except analogy.

The reason for their disagreement over *mithl* (similar), whether it entails similarity in resemblance or similarity in value, is that the term *mithl* is applied to that thing which is similar in appearance and also to that similar in value. The argument, however, of those who maintain that it is similarity in appearance is stronger from the aspect of the implication of the text, because the application of the term *mithl* to similarity in appearance, in the usage of the Arabs, is evident and well-known as compared to its application to value.

[280] Qurʾān 29 : 67.

[281] Qurʾān 5 : 95.

There are, on the other hand, reasons that moved those who apply it to value to adopt such a belief. The first is that *mithl* is the equivalence that is explicitly mentioned in the text in the case of feeding and fasting. Further, if *mithl* is interpreted here to mean equivalence it becomes generally applicable to all kinds of game, as there is a certain kind of game for which an equivalent cannot be found. In addition, *mithl* in the case of animals for which one similar in appearance cannot be found is equivalence. In fact a similar animal for a wild animal cannot be found except in genus, and it has been stated in the text that the *mithl* due in its place is from a different species, thus, it becomes necessary that it be *mithl* in the sense of equivalence and value. Beyond this, there is no difficulty in deciding upon an animal similar in appearance, but the *ḥukm* of equivalence is something that differs with a change in seasons and because of that it is always in need of two arbitrators (valuers) mentioned in the text. On the basis of this the verse becomes subject to interpretation (though it was explicit [*muḥkam*] before this).[282] It would appear to say: "Those of you who intentionally kill wild game are under an obligation to pay its value, or an equivalent value in the shape of food or an equivalent of that in fasting".

With respect to their disagreement over whether the valuation is to be based on the hunted animal or on a similar animal when an equivalence for food is being determined, those who maintained that the basis of valuation is the hunted animal argued that if a similar animal is not to be found then the (value of the) hunted animal is to be ascertained (anyway) to detere the equivalence in food. Those who maintained that the basis is the animal offered as reparation said that the valuation of a thing is to be carried out if a similar animal is not found, that is, one that resembles it. Those who maintained that the verse indicates a choice had recourse to the word *aw* (or) as its implication in the usage of the Arabs is choice. Those who attached significance to the order of expiation in it held it to be similar to other cases of expiation where a sequence is followed by agreement, and these are the expiations in imprecation and homicide.

The reason for their disagreement over the issue of whether a new ruling is to be given each time for every single wild animal for which a ruling has already been laid down by the Companions is whether the *ḥukm* is legal without a rational underlying basis or whether it does have a rational underlying cause. Those who maintained that it does have an underlying reason said that what has been decided may not be based on the availability of a similar animal at that time, like the ostrich for which no similar animal can be found, thus, they held that there is no point in reviewing the ruling. Those

[282] See the beginning of this chapter on reparation.

who maintained that it is an act of worship (that is deciding through valuation by two persons each time) maintained that the process should be repeated, and that this is obligatory. This was Mālik's opinion.

In their disagreement about the case of a group of persons participating in killing a single wild animal, the basis is whether the cause of reparation is the tort itself or whether it is tort against a corpus of the animal. Those who said that it is the delict itself made reparation obligatory on each member of the group that killed the animal. Those who said that it is the delict against the corpus of the animal said that they are liable to a single reparation. This issue is similar to the assessment of *niṣāb* (the minimum scale for liability) in theft and with *qiṣāṣ* in the case of limbs and life, which will be coming up in its proper place in this book, God willing. The distinction drawn by Abū Ḥanīfa between those in the state of *iḥrām* and those who kill the animal in the Ḥaram but are not in the state of *iḥrām* is by way of enhancing the penalty for those who are in the state of *iḥrām*. Those who made reparation obligatory on each person did so for blocking the legal means to an illegal end (*sadd al-dharāʾiʿ*). If the penalty was to be dropped against them completely those who wished to hunt animals within the Ḥaram without penalty would have done it in a group. If we maintain that the reparation is expiation for a sin, then it appears that the sin for killing the wild animal should not be split up by participation in it; it then becomes necessary to say that the reparation should also not be split up and each one of them should be liable for expiation.

The reason for their disagreement over whether a person killing a wild animal can himself be one of the two persons evaluating stems from the conflict of the meaning arising from an obvious interpretation and the meaning arising from a legal principle. This is so as they did not stipulate any condition for the arbitrators, except *ʿadāla* (probity). Thus, in accordance with this apparent meaning it is permissible that the arbitrator be a person in whom this condition is met, wether he is the killer of game or someone else. The meaning arising from the principle of the law is that a litigant cannot be a judge in his own cause.

Their disagreement about the location is based upon its being unqualified (in meaning), that is, no condition has been stipulated for the location. Those who held it to be similar to *zakāt* insofar as it is a right of the needy persons said that it is not to be transferred from its location. Those who maintained that the purpose of this (law) is compassion for the needy persons of Mecca said that only the needy of Mecca are to be fed with it. Those who relied upon the apparent unqualified meaning said that he may use it to feed persons wherever he likes.

Their disagreement over whether the person who kills game in the Ḥaram, while not in the state of *iḥrām*, is liable to expiation is based on the question of whether analogy can be drawn for cases of expiation, in accordance with the opinion of those who uphold *qiyās* as a principle, and on whether *qiyās* is a principle of interpretation in the law, for those who dispute this. The Ẓāhirites deny the application of analogy to the case of the person in the state of *iḥrām*, who kills game in the Ḥaram, because of their rejection of analogy as a principle in the law. It proves true also on the principle of Abū Ḥanīfa who denies the application of analogy to cases of expiation. There is no dispute among them, however, about attributing sin to such persons, because of the words of the Exalted, "Have they not seen that We have appointed a sanctuary immune (from violence), while mankind are ravaged all around them?"[283] and also because of the saying of the Messenger of Allāh (God's peace and blessings be upon him), "Allāh made Mecca a sanctuary the day He created the heavens and the earth".

In their disagreement over the case of a person who kills it and then consumes it as to whether he is liable to one or two reparations, arises from whether his eating it is an additional tort, besides the tort of killing the animal. Further, if it is a tort, then, is it equal to the first tort? This is so as they agreed that he sins if he eats it.

As the expiation through reparation comprises four elements—identification of the obligation, identification of the person upon whom it is obligatory, identification of the act because of which it is obligatory, and the identification of the subject-matter of the obligation—and as a discussion of most of these has been undertaken, two things remain. The first is the disagreement over some of the things due from among the animals similar to those hunted. The second is about the creature killed, which does not amount to a wild animal. We must, therefore, examine what remains.

One of the sources of this topic is what has been related from ʿUmar ibn al-Khaṭṭāb that he awarded a *kabsh* (ram) for a *ḍabʿ* (hyena) and an *ʿanz* (goat) for a gazelle, a *jafra* (four month old goat) for a rabbit and a gerbil. A gerbil (*yarbūʿ*) is a creature with four legs that moves (haltingly) like a goat, and it belongs to the genus of rodents. An *ʿanz*, according to the learned, is a goat that has given birth to offspring or is one of the same age. The *jafra* and *ʿanāq* are goats, with the *jafra* being a young goat that has started eating and is past the age of weaning, while the *ʿanāq* is said to be older than the *jafra*, and it is also claimed that it is younger. Mālik opposed this tradition saying that in the case of a gerbil and rabbit, there is to be no valuation for less than what is given as an offering and sacrifice. This would be a *jadhaʿ* (two year old goat) and what is above that from sheep, and *thanīy* (two years for cows and five years for camels, and above) from camels and cows. The evidence for Mālik is

[283] Qurʾān 29 : 67.

in the words "to be brought as an offering to the Kaʿba".[284] They agreed that the person who imposes on himself the making of an offering is not considered to have met the requirement with less than a *jadhaʿ* or what is older in sheep and a *thanīy* in what is besides them. The rule is the same for young game as it is for game older in years. Al-Shāfiʿī said that the ransom for a younger wild animal is its equivalent in younger cattle and older for older. This is also related from ʿUmar, Uthmān, Alī, and Ibn Masʿūd. His argument is that this reflects exact similarity. Thus, in his view, for a large ostrich is a she-camel or a cow, and for a smaller ostrich a young camel separated (due to its age) from its mother. Abū Ḥanīfa abides by his principle of determining the value.

They disagreed under this topic about the pigeons in Mecca and things besides them. Mālik held that in the case of a pigeon of Mecca there is to be one goat, while there is to be damage assessment (*ḥukūma*) in the case of pigeons on the outskirts (*ḥill*) of Mecca. The opinion of Ibn al-Qāsim differs in the case of the pigeons of the Ḥaram, other than those of Mecca. He said once that there is a goat for each, as in the case of the pigeons of Mecca, while he said another time that there is *ḥukūma* like that for the pigeons of the outskirts of Mecca. Al-Shāfiʿī said that for each pigeon there is a goat, but for pigeons outside the Ḥaram the value is to be paid. Dāwūd said that there is no reparation for any wild animal for which a similar animal cannot be found, except for the pigeons for which there is a goat for each. Perhaps, he thought that this was based upon consensus. It is related from ʿUmar ibn al-Khaṭṭāb and none of the Companions opposed him in this. It is related from ʿAṭāʾ that he said: "For each bird there is a goat".

They differed under this topic about the eggs of an ostrich. Mālik said that he held an ostrich egg to be compensated with one-tenth value of a camel or a cow. Abū Ḥanīfa abides by his principle of valuation, and al-Shāfiʿī agreed with him on this issue. This was also the opinion of Abū Thawr. Abū Ḥanīfa maintained that if there was a dead offspring in the egg the person is liable for reparation, that is, reparation for an ostrich. Abū Thawr stipulated here that the offspring should come out alive and then die (for such reparation). It is related from ʿAlī that he ruled in the case of an ostrich egg that a male and female camel be allowed to mate and if the female is impregnated the offspring is to be designated as compensation for the egg—the narrator said: this would be equal to a sacrificial animal—and if the fetus is lost there is to be no reparation in this case. ʿAṭāʾ said that for the person who owns camels the opinion of ʿAlī is to be followed, otherwise two *dirhams* are to be paid for each egg. Abū ʿUmar said that it is related from Ibn ʿAbbās from Kaʿb ibn ʿUjra

[284] Qurʾān 5 : 95.

from the Prophet (God's peace and blessings be upon him) that "for the egg of an ostrich a person in the state of *iḥrām* is charged its price", but this is not authentic from some aspects. It is related from Ibn Masʿūd that the value of the egg is to be paid, and he said there is a weak tradition about this.

The majority of the jurists maintained that for locust, among the creatures on land, there is an obligation for reparation on the person in the state of *iḥrām*. They disagreed about the extent of the obligation in this. ʿUmar, may Allāh be pleased with him, said that it is a handful of food. This was also Mālik's opinion. Abū Ḥanīfa and his disciples said that is a dried date given as charity for each locust. Al-Shāfiʿī said that there is to be valuation for the locust, which was also the opinion of Abū Thawr, except that he said that whatever is given as charity whether a handful of food or dates becomes its value. It is related from Ibn ʿAbbās that there is a liability for a date for a locust, as in Abū Ḥanīfa's opinion. Rabīʿa said that there is one *ṣāʿ* of food for it, however, that is a deviant opinion. It is related from Ibn ʿUmar that there is a small goat for this, but this too is deviant.

These are the well-known issues in which they agreed about the imposition of reparation, but disagreed about what is the (exact) reparation.

In their disagreement about what is game and what is not, and about what is catch from the sea (or rivers) and what is not, they agreed that wild animals on the land are prohibited to the person in the state of *iḥrām*, except for five offending creatures that have been mentioned in the text, and they disagreed what can be linked to these and what cannot. Likewise, they agreed that all of the catch from the sea (or rivers) is permitted to the person in the state of *iḥrām*, but they disagreed about the description of such catch from the sea (or rivers). This disagreement arises from the differences in the understanding of the the words of the Exalted, "To hunt and to eat the fish of the sea is made lawful for you, a provision for you and for seafarers; but to hunt on land is forbidden you so long as you are on the pilgrimage".[285] We shall discuss the well-known issues from those agreed upon and those disputed in these two categories.

We say: It is established from the traditions of Ibn ʿUmar and others that the Messenger of Allāh (God's peace and blessings be upon him) said, "There are five creatures for the killing of which there is no sin upon the *muḥrim*: the crow, the kite, the scorpion, the rat, and the biting dog". The jurists agreed in their opinions about (the implications of) this tradition, and the majority of them maintain the permissibility of killing what it includes, because it is not wild game, even though some of them stipulated some additional characteristics for these things. They disagreed over whether this was the category of a

[285] Qurʾān 5 : 96.

specific (*khāṣṣ*) implying a specific, or it was the specific category conveying a general (*ʿāmm*) meaning. Those who said that it was the specific category implying generality disputed what kind of general meaning was intended. Mālik said that the biting dog mentioned in the tradition implies every aggressive predatory animal, but any animal that is not aggressive is not to be killed by the *muḥrim*, and he also did not uphold the killing of their young offspring nor of those that were not aggressive.

There is no disagreement among them about the killing of a snake, the viper, and the python. This is related from the Prophet (God's peace and blessings be upon him) in the tradition of Abū Saʿīd al-Khudrī, who said, "The Messenger of Allāh (God's peace and blessings be upon him) said, 'The viper and the python are to be killed' ". Mālik said that he did not uphold the killing of ants. The reports about killing them are *mutawātir*, but generally not in the Ḥaram, therefore, Mālik suspended judgment in the case of the Ḥaram. Abū Ḥanīfa said that biting dogs are not to be killed, unless they are pets, and also wolves (are to be killed). A group of jurists deviated and said that nothing is to be killed except the spotted crow. Al-Shāfiʿī said that each thing that is prohibited for eating is linked to the five things. Al-Shāfiʿī's reliance is on the argument that only those things permissible for consumption to the non-*muḥrim* have been prohibited for the *muḥrim*, and the killing of things permitted for eating is not permitted by consensus based upon the proscription by the Messenger of Allāh (God's peace and blessings be upon him) of hunting animals. Abū Ḥanīfa, on the other hand, did not understand a biting dog to mean a pet alone, but every wild wolf. They disagreed about wasps, with some of them holding them to be similar to scorpions and considering their sting to be weaker.

On the whole, the specifically mentioned categories imply different kinds of injury. Those who thought that these are specific cases to be extended generally associated similar things with each one of them, if a similarity existed, while those who did not uphold this confined the cases to the expressly stated categories. A group of jurists deviated saying that only the spotted crow is to be killed, thus, they restricted the general term (crow) stated in the tradition with what is related from ʿĀʾisha that the Prophet (God's peace and blessings be upon him) said, "five things are to be killed in the Ḥaram", and he mentioned among these "the spotted crow". Al-Nakhaʿī deviated from all this and prohibited the *muḥrim* from killing any wild animal except the rat.

With respect to their disagreement over what is catch from the sea (or rivers) and what is not, they agreed that fish is included in it. They disagreed about what is besides fish, and this is based on their belief that out of these the things that need to be slaughtered are not game from the sea (or rivers), and most of these are prohibited (for eating). There is no disagreement among those who believe that all things found in the sea (or rivers) are permitted for eating that their hunting is allowed. These jurists differed about the *ḥukm* to be applied to things that live in the sea as well as in water. The conclusion to be drawn from the opinions of most jurists is that the *ḥukm* of the place where they live usually is to be assigned to them, which is where they are born.

The jurists agreed that birds living on water are governed by the *ḥukm* of animals living on the land. It is related from ʿAṭāʾ that he maintained about the birds of water that the *ḥukm* of the place where they normally thrive is to be applied to them.

They disagreed about the vegetation in the Ḥaram whether there is reparation for it? Mālik said that there is no reparation, but there is sin in destroying it, because of the proscription laid down for it. Al-Shāfiʿī said that there is reparation for it: a cow for a tall branching tree and a goat for what is less than that. Abū Ḥanīfa said that anything that is the result of human plantation has no reparation for it, but whatever is naturally growing vegetation is to be assessed by value. The reason for disagreement arises from whether an analogy for vegetation can be drawn from animals, because of the common proscription laid down for both in the saying of the Prophet (God's peace and blessings be upon him), "Its animals are not to be driven away nor are its trees to be cut down".

This is the discussion of the well-known issues in this category (section). We now move to the *ḥukm* of a person shaving off his head before the time appointed for it.

9.3.3. Chapter 3 Discussion of Ransom for Ailment and the *Ḥukm* of the Person Shaving his Head before the Appointed Time

The ransom for ailment (in the head) is also agreed upon because of its being laid down in the Book and in the *sunna*. In the Book it is the words of the Exalted, "And whoever among you is sick or hath an ailment of the head must pay a ransom of fasting or almsgiving or offering".[286] The *sunna* is in the authentic tradition of Kaʿb ibn ʿUjra, "That he was with the Messenger of Allāh (God's peace and blessings be upon him) in a state of *iḥrām*, and he was afflicted with lice in his head. The Messenger of Allāh (God's peace and blessings be upon him) ordered him to shave off his head and said, 'Fast for three days, or feed six needy persons with two *mudds* for each person, or make a sacrifice of a goat, whichever you do will be sufficient for you'".

[286] Qurʾān 2 : 196.

The discussion of this verse deals with (the following): the person who is liable to pay ransom and the person who is not; if it becomes due then what is the amount of the ransom and what is its form; and the person for whom it becomes due, when, and where?

With respect to the person on whom it is obligatory, the jurists agreed that it is every person who removes the cause of the ailment due to necessity, because of the existence of the text about this. They disagreed about the person who removes it without necessity. Mālik said that he is liable for ransom stated in the text. Al-Shāfiʿī and Abū Ḥanīfa maintained that if he does it without necessity he liable for atonement by slaughtering an animal (*dam*) alone.

They disagreed about whether it is a condition for the person who becomes liable for ransom due to the removal of the ailment that he should have done it intentionally or whether the person doing it out of forgetfulness and one doing it intentionally are equal (in the eyes of the law). Mālik said that the person doing it intentionally and one doing it out of forgetfulness are equal. This is also the opinion of Abū Ḥanīfa, al-Thawrī, and al-Layth. Al-Shāfiʿī, in one of his opinions, and the Ẓāhirites said that there is no ransom for one doing it out of forgetfulness.

Those who stipulated necessity for the imposition of ransom have the text as their evidence. Those who imposed it upon the person not acting out of necessity argue that if it is obligatory for the one acting out of necessity, then, its obligation is more appropriate for the person not acting out of necessity. Those who made a distinction between the person acting intentionally and the person forgetting did so as this distinction is found on many occasions in the law, and they also held this because of the general implication of the words of the Exalted, "And there is no sin for you in the mistakes that ye make unintentionally but what your hearts propose (that would be a sin for you),[287] and because of the saying of the Prophet (God's peace and blessings be upon him), "Liability for mistake and forgetfulness has been lifted from my *ʿumma*". Those who did not make a distinction between them did so on the analogy of a number of acts of worship in which the law has not made a distinction between intention and forgetfulness.

With respect to the question what is the liability in the ransom of ailment, the jurists agreed that it comprises three things with a choice between them—fasting, feeding, and sacrifice—because of the words of the Exalted, "pay a ransom of fasting or almsgiving or offering".[288] The majority maintain that feeding is for six needy persons, and the minimum sacrifice is a goat. It is related from al-Ḥasan, ʿIkrima, and Nāfiʿ that they said: Feeding is of ten

[287] Qurʾān 33 : 5.
[288] Qurʾān 2 : 196.

needy persons and fasting is for ten days. The evidence of the majority is the authentic tradition of Kaʿb ibn ʿUjra. Those who said that fasting is for ten days did so by drawing an analogy from the fasts of *tamattuʿ* and by equating fasts with feeding, and also because of what is reported about the reparation for hunting in the words of the Exalted, "or the equivalent thereof in fasting".[289]

How much food is to be given to each needy person, out of the six mentioned in the text? The jurists disagreed about this because of the conflict of traditions about feeding in the cases of expiation. Mālik, al-Shāfiʿī, Abū Ḥanīfa, and their disciples maintained that the food to be given to each needy person is two *mudds*, in accordance with the *mudd* used by the Prophet (God's peace and blessings be upon him). It is related from al-Thawrī that he said: "for wheat it is one-half *ṣāʿ*, and for dried dates, raisins, and barley it is one *ṣāʿ*". The same opinion is also related from Abū Ḥanīfa, and that is his principle in the cases of expiation.

For what act does ransom become obligatory? The jurists agreed that it becomes obligatory upon a person who shaves off his head due to necessity arising from disease or due to an injury caused in the head by an animal (insect). Ibn ʿAbbās said: "A disease is that he have sores in his head and an ailment is that he have lice or other such things". ʿAṭāʾ said: "Disease means a headache and ailment means lice and other such problems".

The majority of the jurists maintain that anything that is not allowed to the *muḥrim* like (wearing) stitched garments, shaving of the head, clipping of nails, if he permits it to himself he is liable for ransom, that is, atonement by slaughtering an animal, in accordance with the dispute they have over it, or feeding of the needy. They did not make any distinction in these things on the basis of hardship. They hold the same in case of using fragrance. One group of jurists said that there is no liability for clipping nails, while another group said that there is atonement by slaughtering an animal for it. Ibn al-Mundhir has related that there is consensus on the prohibition of clipping nails for the *muḥrim*. They disagreed about the person who clips some of his nails. Al-Shāfiʿī and Abū Thawr said that the person who clips one nail should feed one needy person, and if he clips two he is to feed two needy persons, but if he clips three at one place (time) he is liable to atonement by slaughtering an animal. Abū Ḥanīfa, in one of his opinions, said that there is no liability on him unless he clips them all. Abū Muḥammad ibn Ḥazm said that the *muḥrim* may clip his nails and trim his whiskers, but this is a deviant opinion, and in his view there is no ransom but for the person who shaves off his head because of the excuse laid down in the text.

[289] Qurʾān 5 : 95.

They agreed about the prohibition of shaving hair from the head, but they disagreed about shaving them from the rest of the body. The majority of the jurists maintain that this entails ransom, while Dāwūd said that there is no ransom for this. They disagreed about the person who plucks a hair or two from his head, or who pulls them out from his body. Mālik said that there is no liability upon the person who plucks out a small number of hair unless he has eliminated an ailment thereby, in which case there is atonement by slaughtering an animal. Al-Ḥasan said that for one hair there is one *mudd* (of food) and two *mudds* for two hair, and for three hair there is atonement by sacrifice. This was also the opinion of al-Shāfiʿī and Abū Thawr. ʿAbd al-Malik, the disciple of Mālik, said that in a small amount of hair there is feeding and for a larger number there is atonement. Those who understood the prohibition of shaving hair to be a mode of worship held a small number (of hair) and a large number to be the same, while those who understood it to mean cleanliness, adornment, and the ease that comes with shaving them made a distinction between small and large numbers, as in the removal of a small quantity of hair there is no elimination of an ailment.

They disagreed about the place of ransom. Mālik said that he may do what he likes in this case, if he prefers to do it in Mecca he may do so, and if he likes he may do it in his own land. Slaughter of an animal, fasting, and feeding are the same for him for this purpose. This was also the opinion of Mujāhid. In Mālik's view this is only a sacrifice and not an offering, as an offering only takes place inside Mecca or Minā. Abū Ḥanīfa and al-Shāfiʿī maintained that atonement by slaughtering an animal and feeding are not valid outside Mecca, but fasting may be undertaken wherever he likes. Ibn ʿAbbās said that atonement by slaughtering an animal is to take place in Mecca, while feeding and fasting may be undertaken wherever he likes. There is an opinion from Abū Ḥanīfa identical to this. Al-Shāfiʿī maintained consistently that atonement by feeding is not valid except for the needy persons within the Ḥaram.

The reason for disagreement arises from analogy for atonement by slaughtering an animal drawn from an offering. Those who drew an analogy for it from the offering imposed in it the conditions of the offering with respect to slaughter, a particular spot, and the needy of the Ḥaram, though Mālik used to hold that the offering may be used for feeding the needy outside the Ḥaram. The thing that is common between this sacrifice and the offering is its purpose of benefiting the needy around the House of Allāh. The opponents (of this opinion) maintain that as the law has made a distinction by naming one of them *nususk* and the other *hady* it follows that their *ḥukm* must be different.

With respect to the time, the majority of the jurists maintain that this expiation cannot occur except after the removal of the ailment, an it is not unlikely that there be a disagreement over this on the analogy of the expiation for oaths. This, then, is the discussion about the expiation for the removal of the ailment.

They disagreed about the shaving of the head whether it is a rite of *ḥajj*, or it is an act with which the person removes the *iḥrām*. There is no disagreement among the majority of the jurists that it is one of the acts of *ḥajj*, and that shaving the head has greater merit than clipping the hair, as has been established through the tradition of Ibn ʿUmar "that the Messenger of Allāh (God's peace and blessings be upon him) said, 'O Allāh, have mercy upon those who shaved their heads'. They said, 'And those who clip their hair, O Messenger of Allāh'. He said, 'O Allāh, have mercy upon those who shaved their heads'. They said, 'And those who clip their hair, O Messenger of Allāh'. He said, 'O Allāh, have mercy upon those who shaved their heads.' They said, 'And those who clip their hair, O Messenger of Allāh'. He said, 'And those who clip their hair'".

The jurists agreed that women do not shave their heads and the *sunna* for them is clipping their hair. They disagreed over whether it is a rite that is primarily for the pilgrims and those performing the *ʿumra*. Mālik said that shaving is primarily for the pilgrims and those performing *ʿumra* and it has greater merit than clipping the hair, and it is also obligatory on a person who has missed his *ḥajj*, having been prevented by the enemy or by disease or by any excuse. This is also the opinion of a group of jurists, except in the case of prevention by the enemy, for Abū Ḥanīfa said that such a person is not obliged to shave his head or clip his hair. On the whole, those who held shaving or clipping to be a rite made atonement by sacrificing an animal obligatory, while those who did not consider it to be a rite did not impose any liability for it.

9.3.4. Chapter 4 Discussion of Expiation for the *Mutamattiʿ*

There is no dispute about the obligation of expiation for the *mutamattiʿ*, which is explicitly laid down in the words of the Exalted, the Glorious, "Then whosoever enjoyed freedom from the restriction of the *iḥrām* by commencing with the *ʿumra* before the *ḥajj*, (shall make) such offering as can be had with ease".[290] The disagreement, in fact, is about the *mutamattiʿ* as to who is the *mutamattiʿ*? The discussion of of the disagreement over this point has preceded, and of the discussion of this expiation also refers to the same

[290] Qurʾān 2 :196. Pickthall's translation has been changed somewhat to bring it in line with the terminology used in the discussion. His translation reads: "Then whosoever contenteth himself with the Visit for the Pilgrimage (shall give) such gifts as can be had with ease".

categories: on whom is it obligatory? What is due? When does it become obligatory, for whom, and at what location?

There is agreement that it is obligatory on the *mutamatti*ʿ, and the details of the disagreement as to who is the *mutamatti*ʿ have preceded. With respect to their disagreement about the obligation, the majority of the jurists maintain that the offering that can be had with ease is a goat. Mālik argued that the term *hady* is applied to mean a goat in accordance with the words of the Exalted in the reparation for killing game, "(the forfeit) to be brought as an offering (*hady*) to the Kaʿba",[291] and it is known by consensus that the obligation of reparation for killing game is a goat. Ibn ʿUmar maintained that the term *hady* is not applied to anything but camels and cows, and the words of the Exalted, "such offering as can be had with ease",[292] mean a cow of a lower quality than another cow and a *badana* (she-camel) of a lower quality than another *badana*.

They agreed that this expiation maintains an order, that is, only a person who is unable to make an offering is under an obligation to fast. They disagreed about the time during which he may move for the performance of his obligation from an offering to fasting. Mālik said that if he begins fasting he has transferred his obligation to fasting, even if he is able to make an offering during the period of fasting. Abū Ḥanīfa said that if is able to make the offering during the first three days of the period of fasting it becomes binding upon him, but if he finds it during the next seven days of fast it is not binding upon him (to make the offering). This issue is a parallel of the issue in which water becomes available to a person during his prayer when he has already performed *tayammum*.

The reason for disagreement stems from whether a condition stipulated initially for the worship continues to hold throughout its performance. Abū Ḥanīfa made a distinction between the first three days (of fasts) and the last seven, as three days of fasting, in his view, are a substitute for the offering, while the seven do not constitute a substitute (with equivalence). They agreed that if he fasts for three days in the first ten days of Dhū al-Ḥijja, he has complied with the obligation in its prescribed time, because of the words of the Exalted, the Glorious, "And whosoever cannot find (such gifts), then a fast of three days while on the pilgrimage".[293] And, there is no dispute that the first ten days of Dhū al-Ḥijja are a part of the period of *ḥajj*.

They disagreed about the person who undertakes these fasts during his occupation with the rites of the ʿ*umra* and before he forms the *iḥrām* (*niyya*) for the *ḥajj*, or if he undertakes them during the days spent at Minā. Mālik

[291] Qurʾān 5 : 95.
[292] Qurʾān 2 :196.
[293] Qurʾān 2 : 196.

permitted the fasts of this expiation during the days of Minā, while Abū Ḥanīfa disallowed them saying that if he loses the first days (of the month) the offering becomes due from him as a liability. Mālik prohibited them (immediately) before the commencement of the rites of *ḥajj*, while Abū Ḥanīfa allowed them. The reason for disagreement is whether these disputed days belong to the period of *ḥajj*. If they do, then, is it a condition of the expiation that the fasts must be undertaken after the occurrence of their cause? Those who maintained that expiation is not valid except after the occurrence of its cause said that fasting is not valid except after the commencement of *ḥajj*. Those who drew an analogy for it from the expiation of oaths said that it is valid. They agreed that if he fasts for seven days when he is (back home) with his family his act is valid. They disagreed over when he fasts on the way back. Mālik said that the fasts are valid, while al-Shāfiʿī said that they are not. The reason for disagreement is based upon the probabilities of interpretation of the words of the Exalted, the Glorious, "And of seven days when ye have returned",[294] as the term *rājiʿ* is applied to the person who has completed his return journey and also to one who is in the middle of the journey. This is the expiation that is established through the transmitted texts, and is agreed upon.

There is no dispute about the case of a person who loses the *ḥajj* after he commenced it, either because of missing one of its elements (*arkān*), or because of a miscalculation of time, or because of his ignorance, or because of forgetfulness, or because of the commission of an act during *ḥajj* that renders it invalid, that he is under an obligation for *qaḍāʾ* if it was an obligatory *ḥajj*. But is he under an obligation for an offering along with *qaḍāʾ*? They disagreed about this. Further, if the *ḥajj* was voluntary, is he under an obligation of *qaḍāʾ*? There is a disagreement in all this, but the majority of the jurists maintain that he is liable for an offering because of the occurrence of a shortcoming that seems to denote the obligation of making an offering. A group of jurists deviated and said that there is no obligation for the offering or for *qaḍāʾ*, unless it is an obligatory *ḥajj*.

What is unique about an invalid *ḥajj* as compared to the remaining forms of worship is that the person continues to complete it even when he has invalidated it (due to some reason), and he is liable for atonement by slaughtering an animal. One group deviated and said that it is like the other forms of worship. The reliance of the majority is upon the words of the Exalted, "Complete the Pilgrimage and the Visit (*ʿumra*) (to Mecca) for Allāh".[295] The majority considered this to be a general (command), while the

[294] Qurʾān 2 : 196.

[295] Qurʾān 2 : 196. Pickthall's translation has been changed slightly; it reads: "Perform the pilgrimage and the Visit (to Mecca) for Allāh."

opponents restricted the meaning on the analogy of the remaining forms of worship when they are invalidated.

They agreed that an act invalidating *ḥajj* is either related to the commanded rites, like the dropping of the prescribed elements, which are a condition for its validity depending on their disagreement over what is an element and what is not, or it is related to one of the proscribed acts that are to be avoided, like sexual intercourse, even though they disagreed about the time at which sexual intercourse invalidates *ḥajj*. Their consensus about sexual intercourse as an invalidating factor for *ḥajj* is based upon the words of the Exalted, the Glorious, "And whoever is minded to perform the pilgrimage therein (let him remember that) there is (to be) no lewdness nor abuse nor angry conversation on the pilgrimage".[296] They agreed that the person who cohabits before the stationing at ʿArafa has invalidated his *ḥajj*. Likewise, one who has intercourse while undertaking the *ʿumra* before performing the circumambulation to be followed by the *saʿy*. They disagreed about the invalidation of *ḥajj* through sexual intercourse after the stationing at ʿArafa and prior to the throwing of pebbles at the *Jamrat al-ʿAqaba*, and also after throwing pebbles at it and before the *ṭawāf al-ifāḍa*, which is an obligation. Mālik said that the person who cohabits before throwing pebbles at the *Jamrat al-ʿAqaba* has invalidated his *ḥajj*, and he is liable for the offering as well as *qaḍāʾ*. This was also al-Shāfiʿī's opinion. Abū Ḥanīfa and al-Thawrī said that he is under an obligation to make an offering of a *badana* (she-camel), but his *ḥajj* is complete. An identical opinion is also related from Mālik. Mālik said that the pilgrim who cohabits after throwing pebbles at the *Jamrat al-ʿAqaba*, but before the *ṭawāf al-ifāḍa*, his *ḥajj* is complete. The majority maintain Mālik's view that cohabitation before the *ṭawāf al-ifāda* does not invalidate *ḥajj*, but the offering becomes binding upon him. One group of jurists said that the person who cohabits before the *ṭawāf al-ifāḍa* has invalidated his *ḥajj*. This is an opinion from Ibn ʿUmar.

The reason for disagreement is that there is for *ḥajj* a factor of completion that resembles the salutation in prayer (after which the pilgrim is free from the restrictions of the *iḥrām*). And this is of two types: full freedom (*taḥallul akbar*) which occurs after the *ṭawāf al-ifāḍa*; and partial freedom (*taḥallul aṣghar*) which occurs after the casting of pebbles at the *Jamrat al-ʿAqaba*. Is either form of freedom stipulated for the permissibility to engage in cohabitation or just one? There is no dispute among them that the minor *taḥallul*, which is due after the throwing of pebbles at the *Jamrat al-ʿAqaba* on the Day of Sacrifice,

[296] Qurʾān 2: 196.

disengages the pilgrim from all that was prohibited to him due to *ḥajj*, except sex activity, use of fragrance, and hunting game. The jurists differed, however, about what does become permissible. The well-known opinion from Mālik is that the pilgrim is free from all restraints except matters related to women, such as contracting marriage, intercourse, and the use of fragrance. It is said in a narration from him that the restraints are women, perfume, and hunting, because the apparent meaning of the words of the Exalted, "But when ye have been freed from the *iḥrām*, then go hunting (if ye will)",[297] refer to *taḥallul akbar*.

They also agreed that the person performing the *ʿumra* becomes free from the restrictions when he has made the circuits around the House and has performed the *saʿy* between al-Ṣafā and al-Marwa, even when he has not shaved his head or clipped his hair, because of the proof of this in the traditions, except for minor deviation (of opinion). It is related from Ibn ʿAbbās that this happens after the circumambulation. Abū Ḥanīfa said that the pilgrim is not free except after shaving his head, and if he cohabits before that his *ʿumra* is invalidated.

They disagreed about the nature of the cohabitation and the preliminaries that invalidate *ḥajj*. The majority of the jurists maintain that the union of the sexual organs invalidates *ḥajj*. It is likely that those who stipulate ejaculation along with the union of the sexual organs, as (factors) giving rise to the obligation for taking a bath, stipulate them also for *ḥajj* (as factors invalidating *ḥajj*). They disagreed about ejaculation outside of the vagina. Abū Ḥanīfa said that *ḥajj* is not invalidated except by ejaculation inside the vagina. Al-Shāfiʿī said that what results in the liability for *ḥadd* invalidates *ḥajj* (i.e., conditions associated with the act). Mālik said that ejaculation itself is sufficient for invalidating *ḥajj*, as are the preliminaries like fondling and kissing. Al-Shāfiʿī said that the person who performs the sexual act short of penetration should make an offering. They disagreed about the person who cohabits a number of times. Mālik said that he is liable for a single offering. Abū Ḥanīfa said that if cohabitation is repeated in a single session he is liable for a single offering, but if this occurs over several sessions he is liable for an offering for each act of cohabitation. Muḥammad ibn al-Ḥasan said that a single offering is sufficient even if the act is repeated a number of times, as long as he has not made the offering for the first act of cohabitation. All three opinions are related from al-Shāfiʿī; however, the well-known opinion from him is the same as that of Mālik's. They disagreed about the case of a person who cohabits out of forgetfulness. Mālik considered intention and forgetfulness to be the same in this case. Al-Shāfiʿī, in his last opinion, said that there is no expiation for

[297] Qurʾān 5 : 2.

him. They disagreed on whether a woman (in this case) is liable for making an offering. Mālik said that if he persuaded her she is liable for an offering, but if he forced her then he is liable for two offerings. Al-Shāfiʿī said that he is liable only for one offering, as was his opinion in the case of a person who cohabits during Ramaḍān.

The majority of the jurists maintain that if they (the cohabiting couple) perform *ḥajj* after this they have to do so separately, and it is also said that they are not to separate. The latter opinion is related from some of the Companions and the Tābiʿūn. This was also Abū Ḥanīfa's opinion. The opinions of Mālik and al-Shāfiʿī differed about the point at which they have to separate. Al-Shāfiʿī said that they have to separate from the time that their *ḥajj* has been invalidated, while Mālik said that they separate from the place where they commenced their *iḥrāms*, unless they did so before the *mīqāt*. Those who imposed separation upon them did so to eliminate the means (of corruption) and as a penalty, while those who did not impose this on them based their judgment on the principle that a *ḥukm* in this category cannot be issued unless it is based on a text.

They disagreed about the kind of offering that is obligatory on account of (proscribed) sexual intercourse. Mālik and Abū Ḥanīfa said that this should be a goat, while al-Shāfiʿī said that less than a *badana* (she-camel) is not enough, and if he cannot find one the value of the *badana* is to be converted into *dirhams* and the value of the *dirhams* into food, and he is then to fast one day for each *mudd* of food. He said that the offering and the food outside Mecca and Minā are not valid, but he may fast where he likes.

Mālik said that in the case of a deficiency that becomes associated with the *iḥrām*, whether it is due to cohabitation, or shaving of hair, or prevention, if the perpetrator of the act cannot find an offering he has to fast three days during *ḥajj* and seven when he goes back, and feeding of the needy does not enter into this. Mālik held the atonement by slaughtering an animal that is binding here should be similar to the atonement in the case of the *mutamattiʿ*, while al-Shāfiʿī held it to be similar to the atonement that is obligatory in *fidya* (ransom). Feeding of the needy in Mālik's view is only applicable in the expiation for killing game and the expiation for the elimination of an ailment. Al-Shāfiʿī maintains that fasting and feeding have been laid down as substitutes for the slaughtering of an animal in two places, while their substitute has not been mentioned on a single occasion, thus, the drawing of an analogy for the unexpressed cases from those that are expressed in the case of food is better. This then is what is specific to the invalidation occurring because of cohabitation.

With respect to invalidation occurring due to the lapse of time, which is the missing of the stationing at ʿArafa on the day of ʿArafa, the jurists agreed unanimously that the person who is in this situation is not released from his *iḥrām*, except by making the circumambulation of the House followed by *saʿy* between al-Ṣafā and al-Marwa, that is, he becomes free from the *iḥrām* after performing the *ʿumra*, and he is under an obligation to perform *ḥajj* in the next season. They disagreed over whether he is liable for the offering. Mālik, al-Shāfiʿī, Aḥmad, al-Thawrī, and Abū Thawr maintain that he is liable for the offering. Their reliance is upon their consensus that the person who has been delayed by illness until he missed the *ḥajj* is liable for the offering. Abū Ḥanīfa said that he is released from the *iḥrām* by undertaking the *ʿumra*. He is then to perform the *ḥajj* in the next season, and there is no liability (this time) for the offering. The evidence of the Kūfians is that the principle governing the offering is that it is a substitute for *qaḍāʾ*, thus, if he is liable for *qaḍāʾ* then there is no obligation for the offering, except in cases restricted by consensus.

Mālik, al-Shāfiʿī, and Abū Ḥanīfa disagreed about the case of a person who was *qārin* and has lost the *ḥajj*, whether he is to perform it (next time) as a *mufrid* (separately) or by combining it with *ʿumra* (as a *qārin*). Mālik and al-Shāfiʿī held that he is to perform it as a *qārin* as he is performing the *qaḍāʾ* of what he is liable for. Abū Ḥanīfa said that he is only under the obligation for the *ifrād* as he has already performed the circumambulation of his *ʿumra* and he is only to perform the *qaḍāʾ* of what he has missed.

The majority of the jurists maintain that the person who has missed his *ḥajj* is not to continue in the state of *iḥrām* till the next year, and this opinion was selected by Mālik, except that he permitted this so that the offering may be dropped from his liability, and he does not need to be released from the *iḥrām* by undertaking the *ʿumra*. The basis of this disagreement of theirs on this issue stems from their dispute about the person who forms the *niyya* of the *iḥrām* for *ḥajj* in days other than those of the *ḥajj* months. Those who did not consider such a person to be in a state of *iḥrām* did not permit the person who missed his *ḥajj* to remain in the state of *iḥrām* until the other year. Those who permitted the *iḥrām* in days other than the days of the *ḥajj* months permitted him to stay in the state of *iḥrām*.

The Qāḍī (Ibn Rushd) said: "We have discussed the expiations that are obligatory through the text in the case of *ḥajj*, the description of the *qaḍāʾ* for both the missed and the invalidated *ḥajj*, and the description of the acts of the person who has missed the *ḥajj*. We had discussed before this the expiations that are expressly laid down in the law and what the jurists had associated with them in the case of the person who invalidates his *ḥajj*. We are now left with the discussion of the expiations—over which they disagreed—pertaining to the omission of one of the rites of *ḥajj*, and these have not been expressly laid down".

9.3.5. Chapter 5 Discussion of Expiations not Expressly Laid Down

We say: The majority of the jurists agreed that the rites (of pilgrimage) are of two kinds: rites that are an emphatic *sunna* (*sunna mu'akkada*), and rites that are considered desirable. Those that are a *sunna* make the person who relinquishes them liable for atonement by slaughtering an animal, as his *ḥajj* becomes defective, the basis being the case of the *mutamatti*ʿ and that of the *qārin*. It is related from Ibn ʿAbbās that he said: "The person who misses a rite is liable for atonement by slaughtering an animal". The rites that are supererogatory were not considered by the jurists as giving rise to atonement by slaughtering an animal, but they disagreed extensively over each rite as to whether its relinquishment gives rise to atonement. This was based upon their dispute over the identification of a rite as a *sunna* or as supererogatory. They had no dispute about the principle that obligatory rites cannot be validated through atonement. They differed, however, over whether each of the acts itself was obligatory. The Ẓāhirites did not uphold the imposition of atonement unless it was laid down in the text, because of their rejection of (the validity of) *qiyās*, especially in cases of worship. Likewise, they agreed that if a pilgrim commits acts, avoidance of which is *sunna*, he is liable to the ransom for removing an ailment, but he is not liable for anything if he commits acts whose avoidance is considered desirable. The jurists disagreed about the consequences of the relinquishment of an act, because of their disagreement whether it was a *sunna*. And here again, the Ẓāhirites did not impose ransom except in cases that were laid down in the text. We shall mention the well-known disputes of the *fuqahā*ʾ over the relinquishment of each individual rite, that is, whether atonement by slaughtering an animal is obligatory. We shall take up these rites one by one, from the first rite to the last. So also we shall deal with the cases of the commission of prohibited acts.

The first rite that they disagreed about was the case of the person who passes the *mīqāt* without forming the intention of the *iḥrām* as to whether he is liable for atonement. A group of jurists said that he is not liable for atonement by slaughtering an animal (*dam*). Another group of jurists said that he is liable for atonement, even if he returns (to the *mīqāt* to form the *niyya* of the *iḥrām* there). This was the opinion of Mālik and Ibn al-Mubārak, and it is also related from al-Thawrī. A third group of jurists said that if he returns (to the *mīqāt*) he is not liable, but if he does not he is liable for atonement. This is the opinion of al-Shāfiʿī, Abū Yūsuf, Muḥammad, and the better known opinion of al-Thawrī. Abū Ḥanīfa said that if he returns pronouncing the *talbiya* he is not liable for atonement, but if he returns without pronouncing the *talbiya* he is liable. Yet another group of jurists said that returning to the *mīqāt* to form the *niyya* is an obligation and it cannot be rectified through atonement.

They disagreed about the pilgrim who washes his head with marsh mallow. Mālik and Abū Ḥanīfa said that he is liable for ransom. Al-Thawrī and some other jurists said that there is no liability upon him.

Mālik was of the view that entering a bath invokes the liability of ransom, while others permitted it. Entering the bath is attributed to Ibn ʿAbbās through authentic transmission.

The majority maintain that the person in the state of *iḥrām* is liable for ransom if he wears some of the things that he is prohibited from wearing. If he were to wear trousers in the absence of a loin-cloth is he is liable for ransom? They disagreed over this. Mālik and Abū Ḥanīfa said that he is liable for ransom, while al-Thawrī, Aḥmad, Abū Thawr, and Dāwūd said that there is no liability for one who does not have a loin-cloth. The reliance of those who disallowed this is the unqualified proscription about it, while the reliance of those who do not uphold ransom in this case is the tradition of ʿAmr ibn Dīnār from Jābir and Ibn ʿAbbās, who said, "I heard the Messenger of Allāh (God's peace and blessings be upon him) saying, 'Trousers are for the person who cannot find a loin-cloth and boots are for the person who cannot find sandals' ".

They disagreed about the case of a person who wears cut down boots when sandals exist. Mālik said that he is liable for ransom, while Abū Ḥanīfa held that he is not. Both opinions are related from al-Shāfiʿī. They disagreed about the case of a woman wearing gloves, whether she is liable to ransom. We have already discussed a large number of these *aḥkām* under the topic of *iḥrām*. They also disagreed about the case of a person who neglects the pronouncement of the *talbiya*, whether he is liable for atonement by slaughtering an animal. This too has preceded.

They agreed that the pilgrim who forgets to perform the circumambulation or who misses one of the circuits should perform it again as long as he is in Mecca, but they disagreed about what he should do when he has returned to his family. A group of jurists including Abū Ḥanīfa said that slaughtering an animal would atone for it. Another group of jurists said that he is to return and rectify what was defective, and slaughtering an animal will not compensate for it. Likewise, they disagreed about the case of a person who does not observe the *ramal* in the first three circuits. Its obligation was upheld by Ibn ʿAbbās, as did al-Shāfiʿī, Abū Ḥanīfa, Aḥmad, and Abū Thawr. The opinion of Mālik and his disciples differed over this.

The basis for the disagreement in all these issues is their dispute whether the act is a *sunna*. The discussion about all this has preceded.

If he misses kissing the Black Stone or kissing his hand after he has placed it on the Stone (in case he was not able to reach it), he is liable for atonement on the analogy of the *mutamattiʿ* in the view of those who do not consider it obligatory (i.e., consider it a *sunna*). Similarly, they disagree about the person who forgets to pray the two *rakʿas* of the circumambulation and returns to his homeland as to whether there is liability of atonement for him. Mālik said that he is liable for atonement, while al-Thawrī said that he may offer the two *rakʿas* as long as he is in the Ḥaram. Al-Shāfiʿī and Abū Ḥanīfa said that he may offer them wherever he pleases.

Those who upheld that the farewell circumambulation is not obligatory disagreed about the case of a person who neglects it and it is not possible for him to return to Mecca to perform it, whether he is liable for atonement. Mālik said that he is not liable for anything; however, he may return for it if he is near enough. Abū Ḥanīfa and al-Thawrī said that he is liable for atonement if he does not return. In their view he is to return as long as he has not reached the *mīqāt*. The argument of those who do not consider it a *sunna muʾakkada* (emphatic *sunna*) is that it is not obligatory upon the resident of Mecca or a menstruating woman.

In Abū Ḥanīfa's view if the person has not included the *ḥijr*[298] during the circumambulation he is to return to repeat the *ṭawāf*, as long as he has not left Mecca; if has left, he is liable for atonement by slaughtering an animal.

They disagreed about whether walking is a condition for the validity of the circumambulation for the pilgrim who is able to do so. Mālik said that it is a condition, like standing up in prayer. If he is unable to do so it is considered permissible like the prayer of the person observing it in a sitting posture. He is to return to repeat it (if he improves), unless he has returned to his homeland, in which case he is liable for atonement (*dam*). Al-Shāfiʿī said that riding during the circumambulation is permitted as the Prophet (God's peace and blessings be upon him) "performed the circumambulation of the House while riding, in the absence of an illness". He did so, however, in order to have a better view of the people.

Those who considered the *saʿy* to be obligatory imposed atonement for the person if he left for his homeland (without performing it), but those who considered it to be voluntary did not impose any liability. The discussion of their disagreement about the case of a person who performs the *saʿy* before the circumambulation has also preceded; it was then explained whether he is liable for atonement if he leaves Mecca (without repeating the rite).

They disagreed about the obligation of *dam* upon a person who left ʿArafa before sunset. Al-Shāfiʿī and Aḥmad said that if he returns and then leaves after sunset there is no atonement for him, but if he does not return by dawn (next morning) he is liable for atonement. Abū Ḥanīfa and al-Thawrī said that

[298] The open fenced area adjacent to the western wall of the Kaʿba is considered part of it and the pilgrim has to go around it during the *ṭawāf*.

he is liable for atonement whether he returns or he does not. This has already been discussed.

They disagreed about the person who stays at ʿUrana (and not at ʿArafa). Al-Shāfiʿī said that there is no *ḥajj* for him, while Mālik said that he is liable for *dam*. The reason for disagreement is whether the proscription of stopping there instead of at ʿArafa belongs to the category of prohibition or to that of disapproval. We have mentioned, in the section(s) on the performance of the acts of *ḥajj*, most of their disagreements about matters whose relinquishment prompts the imposition of *dam* and about those which do not, although the proper order requirs that they be mentioned here. But mentioning them on those occasions was easier.

The Qāḍī (Ibn Rushd) said: "We have discussed the obligation of this worship and the person on whom it is obligatory, as well as the conditions of its obligation and when it becomes obligatory. These are matters that form the preliminaries for the full knowledge of this worship. We discussed, thereafter, the time period of this worship, its location, and its prohibitions, and what acts are included in it with respect to each individual location out of the various locations, and also with respect to the individual segments of time among the various segments of time until the time for it is over. We then discussed the release from the restrictions of the *iḥrām* during this worship and also what is accepted by way of different forms of expiation for the rectification of defects as well as those acts that cannot be rectified and have to be repeated. We also discussed the *ḥukm* of repetition in accordance with the causes. In this topic was also included the case of a person who commences the worship, but is prevented from completing it by illness, or by the enemy, or by other things. What is left from the acts of this worship is the discussion of the offering (*hady*), because this is a kind of worship which is a part of the (larger) worship (of *ḥajj*) and which it is necessary to devote our attention to; so we now move to it".

9.3.6. Chapter 6 Discussion of the Offering (*Hady*)

We say: The study of the offering includes the identification of its obligation, the identification of its species, the identification of its age, the manner in which it is driven, from where it is to be driven and where it ends up after being driven, which is the place of sacrifice, and the *ḥukm* of its meat after slaughter.

We say: They agreed that the offering driven for this worship includes that which is obligatory and that which is voluntary. The obligatory offering is (either) obligatory through a vow, or it is obligatory in some forms of this worship, and it also includes that which is obligatory because it is an expiation.

The offering that is obligatory for some forms of this worship is the offering of the *mutamatti*ᶜ, by agreement, and the offering of the *qārin*, with accompanying disagreement. That which is (imposed as) an expiation is the offering for *qaḍā*ᵓ performance, in accordance with the opinion of those who stipulate an offering in it, the offering in the expiation for killing game, and the offering for removing ailments and dirt, and also the offerings resembling these offerings for which the jurists have drawn analogies for the case of each rite with cases that are explicitly mentioned in the texts.

With respect to the species of the offering, the jurists agreed that the offering should not be from things other than the eight categories explicitly laid down by Allāh, and that it is preferable that the offering should first be a camel then a cow then sheep then goats, but they differed about other slaughtered animals. With respect to the ages, they agreed that the *thanīy* (the age of one year for sheep, two years for cows, and five for camels) is valid, but a six-month old (*jadha*ᶜ) from among goats is not valid as an offering (*hady*) or as a blood sacrifice (*ḍaḥiya;* pl. *ḍaḥāyā*), because of the saying of the Prophet (God's peace and blessings be upon him) to Abū Burda, "It is valid for you but is not valid for anyone after you". They differed about the permissibility of offering a six-month old sheep. The majority of the jurists uphold its permissibility as an offering and as a blood sacrifice. Ibn ᶜUmar used to say that in offerings only a *thanīy* is valid from each species. There is no dispute that the more expensive the offering the better it is. Al-Zubayr used to say to his children, "O my children, none of you should make an offering to Allāh of that which he would be ashamed of offering to his benefactor, for Allāh is the Greatest of all benefactors, and deserves that the choicest thing be offered to Him". The Messenger of Allāh (God's peace and blessings be upon him) said in the case of slaves, when it was said to him which one of them has greater merit for emancipation, "The one that fetches the highest price and is the dearest to his masters".

There is no known limit for the number of offerings, and the offerings of the Messenger of Allāh (God's peace and blessings be upon him) were up to a hundred. The manner of driving them (to the place of offering) is by garlanding them and an indication (by incision) that it is an offering, "Because the Messenger of Allāh (God's peace and blessings be upon him) travelled in the year of al-Ḥudaybiya and on reaching Dhū al-Ḥulayfa he garlanded the offering, put distinguishing marks (by incision) on it, and then entered the *iḥrām*". When the offering is a camel or a cow, there is no dispute that it is made to wear one or two sandals around the neck, or whatever is similar for one who cannot find sandals. They disagreed about the garlanding of sheep.

Mālik and Abū Ḥanīfa said that sheep are not to be garlanded. Al-Shāfiʿī, Aḥmad, Abū Thawr, and Dāwūd said that they are to be garlanded on the basis of the tradition of al-Aʿmash from Ibrāhīm from al-Aswad from ʿĀʾisha "that the Prophet (God's peace and blessings be upon him) once took some sheep as an offering to the House and garlanded them". They considered it desirable to turn it toward the *qibla* while garlanding it. Mālik preferred the putting of distinguishing marks (by incision) on the left side, because of what he has related from Nāfiʿ from Ibn ʿUmar that when he made an offering, bringing them from Medina, he would garland them and place the distinguishing marks (by incision) on them at Dhū al-Ḥulayfa, and he garlanded them before placing the incisions. He would do this at one place when the offerings were turned toward the *qibla*. He would make them wear sandals (around the neck) and put the incisions on their left sides. He would then drive them down with them until he would stop with the people at ʿArafa, and then move with the people as they moved, and when they reached Minā in the early morning of the Day of Sacrifice he would sacrifice them before shaving his head or clipping his hair. He would sacrifice the offerings with his own hands, lining them up and making them face the *qibla*. He would then eat and feed others. Al-Shāfiʿī, Aḥmad, and Abū Thawr preferred the placing of incisions on the right side, because of the tradition of Ibn ʿAbbās "that the Messenger of Allāh (God's peace and blessings be upon him) observed *ẓuhr* at Dhū al-Ḥulayfa and then sent for his sacrificial animals. He made incisions on the right side of their humps (of the camels) after which he squeezed out the blood from them (the incisions). He garlanded them with two sandals. He then rode his mount and on reaching al-Baydāʾ pronounced the *talbiya* for *ḥajj*".

From where is the offering to be driven? Mālik said that the *sunna* for this is that it be driven from the outskirts of Mecca (*ḥill*), and because of this he maintained that the person who buys the offering from Mecca and did not bring it from the *ḥill* should take it with him for the stationing at ʿArafa, and if he does this he is liable for a substitute (*badal*). If he brought it along from the *ḥill* then it is desirable for him to take it along for the stationing at ʿArafa, which is the opinion of Ibn ʿUmar, and was upheld by al-Layth. Al-Shāfiʿī, al-Thawrī, and Abū Thawr said that the taking of the offering to ʿArafa is a *sunna*, but there is no penalty for the person who did not take it there, irrespective of his having driven it from the *ḥill*. Abū Ḥanīfa said that the taking of the offering to ʿArafa is not a *sunna*. The evidence of Mālik for the bringing of the offering from the *ḥill* into the Ḥaram is "that the Prophet (God's peace and blessings be upon him) did so and said, 'Acquire your rites from me'". Al-Shāfiʿī said that taking the offering to ʿArafa (*taʿrīf*) is a *sunna*, just like garlanding. Abū Ḥanīfa said it is not a *sunna*, and the

Messenger of Allāh (God's peace and blessings be upon him) did so as his residence was outside the Ḥaram. A choice in the matter of *taʿrīf* of the offering is related from ʿĀʾisha.

The destination of the offering is the Ancient House, as in the words of the Exalted, "And afterward they are brought to the Ancient House",[299] and His words, "As an offering to the Kaʿba".[300] The jurists agreed that no one is permitted to slaughter inside the Kaʿba, nor in al-Masjid al-Ḥarām, and that the meaning in the words of the Exalted, "As an offering to the Kaʿba",[301] is sacrifice in Mecca as a favor from Him for its needy and poor. Mālik used to say that the meaning of the words of the Exalted, "As an offering to the Kaʿba"[302] is Mecca, and he did not permit anyone who was slaughtering his offering in the Ḥaram to do it in a place other than Mecca. Al-Shāfiʿī and Abū Ḥanīfa said that slaughtering it in the Ḥaram outside Mecca is valid. Al-Ṭabrī said that the slaughter of the offering is permitted wherever the person making the offering desires, except for the offering of *qirān* and the killing of game, for they are not permitted in any place other than the Ḥaram. On the whole, the sacrificing at Minā is a point of consensus among the jurists, and at Mecca for the *ʿumra*, except for their dispute about the sacrifice made by the pilgrim who has been intercepted and prevented from completing *ḥajj*. In Mālik's view if the sacrifice is made for *ḥajj* at Mecca and for the *ʿumra* at Minā it is permitted. Mālik's evidence for stating that it is not permitted to sacrifice in the Ḥaram at a place other than Mecca is the saying of the Prophet (God's peace and blessings be upon him), "All the alleys of Mecca, and its streets are a place of sacrifice". Mālik exempted from this the offering due as ransom (*fidya*), and permitted it in a place other than Mecca.

With respect to the time of sacrifice, Mālik said that if the offering of *tamattuʿ* and of voluntary *ḥajj* are slaughtered before the Day of Sacrifice it is not valid, but Abū Ḥanīfa permitted it in the case of voluntary *ḥajj*. Al-Shāfiʿī said that it is permitted in both cases before the Day of Sacrifice.

There is no dispute among the jurists that the person who converts the offering into fasting may fast wherever he likes as there is no benefit in this to the residents of the Ḥaram nor to the residents of Mecca. They disagreed about the alms distributed in lieu of the offering. The majority of the jurists maintain that they are due to the needy of Mecca and the Ḥaram, as they are a substitute for the reparation of killing game, which is for them. Mālik said that feeding is like fasting and is valid outside Mecca.

[299] Qurʾān 22 : 29.
[300] Qurʾān 5 : 95.
[301] Qurʾān 5 : 95.
[302] Qurʾān 5 : 95.

The jurists agree unanimously about the description of the sacrifice that commencement with the name of Allāh is desirable in it as it is slaughter (*dhakāh*). Some of them preferred the pronouncement of *takbīr* along with the *tasmiya*. It is preferred for the person making the offering to undertake the sacrifice with his own hands, but if he delegates this it is permitted. This is what the Messenger of Allāh (God's peace and blessings be upon him) did in the case of his offerings. One of his *sunna*s is sacrificing while the animals are standing, because of the words of the Exalted, "So mention the name of Allāh over them when they are drawn up in lines".[303] The description of the sacrifice has preceded in the Book of Slaughtered Animals.[304]

There are a number of well-known issues about what is permitted to the owner of the offering with respect to utilizing it and consuming its flesh. The first is whether it is permitted to him to ride the obligatory or voluntary offering. The Ẓāhirites maintained that riding it is permitted in the case of necessity and even otherwise. Some of them made this obligatory. The majority of the jurists of the provinces considered riding it as abominable other than in cases of necessity. The evidence of the majority is what is recorded by Abū Dāwūd from Jābir when he was asked about riding the offering. He said, "I heard the Messenger of Allāh (God's peace and blessings be upon him) saying, 'Ride it with care if you are compelled to until you can find a mount' ". By way of reasoning, utilizing a thing through which the nearness to Allāh is sought is not allowed by the spirit of the *sharīʿa*. The evidence of the Ẓāhirites is what is related by Mālik from Abū al-Zinād from al-Aʿraj from Abū Hurayra "that the Messenger of Allāh (God's peace and blessings be upon him) saw a man leading his sacrificial animal, so he said, 'Ride it'. He said, 'O Messenger of Allāh it is an offering'. He said, on the second or third time, 'Ride it, woe unto you' ".

They agreed that the voluntary offering, after it has reached its intended destination (and killed), may be consumed (in part) by the owner like the rest of the people, but if it becomes sick before reaching its destination he is to leave it to the people and is not to eat from it. Dāwūd added to this that the person is not to feed any of his associates with it, because of what is established from the Messenger of Allāh (God's peace and blessings be upon him) that he sent an offering with Nājiyat al-Aslamī and said to him, "If some of it is fatigued, sacrifice it and dye the sandals in its blood, then leave it to the people". This tradition is related from Ibn ʿAbbās and he added to it the following words: "(Neither) you nor your associates are to eat from it". This addition was adopted by Dāwūd and Abū Thawr. They disagreed about the liability of the person who does eat of it. Mālik said that if he eats of it, its

303 Qurʾān 22 : 36.

304 The Book of *Hajj* was written last by the author. See the end of this section where this is mentioned.

substitute is due from him. Al-Shāfiʿī, Abū Ḥanīfa, al-Thawrī, Aḥmad, and Ibn Ḥabīb from the disciples of Mālik, said that he is liable for the value of what he has consumed or has ordered to be consumed in the shape of food that is to distributed as charity. This is related from ʿAlī, Ibn Masʿūd, Ibn ʿAbbās, and a group of the Tābiʿūn.

The offering that is hurt (injured) inside the Ḥaram before reaching Mecca, has it reached its destination? There is a disagreement about this based upon the preceding dispute as to whether the destination is Mecca alone or it is the Ḥaram. If, however, the obligatory offering is injured before reaching its destination, the owner has the right to consume it as he is liable for its substitute. Some of them permitted the sale of its meat in order to assist him in obtaining the substitute, but Mālik disallowed this.

They disagreed about eating (by the owner) from the obligatory offering if it reaches its destination. Al-Shāfiʿī said that he is not to eat anything from the obligatory offering, and all its meat is for the needy, so also its saddle, if there is any, for the needy as well as the shoes with which it was garlanded. Mālik said that he may eat from every obligatory offering, except the offering in expiation for killing game, that which is due to a vow for the needy, and that which is due to the elimination of ailment. Abū Ḥanīfa said that he is not eat from the obligatory offering, except from the offering of *tamattuʿ* and the offering of *qirān*. The reliance of al-Shāfiʿī is on the similarity between all kinds of offerings that are obligatory due to expiation. Those who made a distinction argued that there are two meanings which are apparent in the offering. The first is that it is a worship *ab initio*, and the other is that it is an expiation. One of these two meanings may be more obvious in some kinds. Those who gave predominance to its similarity with worship over its similarity with expiation, in each individual kind of offering, like the offering in *qirān* and the offering in *tamattuʿ*, especially those who said that *qirān* and *tamattuʿ* have greater merit, did not lay down the condition of non-consumption, because such an offering in their view is a merit and not an expiation repelling a punishment. Those who gave predominance to its similarity with expiation said that he is not to eat from it, because of their agreement that the person making the expiation is not to eat from the substance of the expiation. Insofar as the offering in the reparation for killing game and the ransom of eliminating ailment are apparently expiations these jurists did not disagree that he is not eat from them.

The Qāḍī (Ibn Rushd) said: "We have discussed the *ḥukm* of the offering, its species, its age, the manner of leading it, the conditions of its validity with reference to time and place, the description of its slaughter, and the *ḥukm* of utilizing it, and this is what we intended. Allāh is the Grantor of the truth. With the completion of this discussion, in accordance with our arrangement, the discussions of this Book have been completed, in conformity with our aim. All thanks and praise are due to Allāh, many times over, for He has granted success and guidance, and bestowed completion and perfection.

It was finalized on Wednesday, the ninth of Jumādī al-Ūlā, which is in the year five hundred and eighty-four. It is a part of *Kitāb al-Mujtahid*, which I have been compiling for more than twenty years or close to it. All praise is for Allāh, the Lord of the Worlds.

He, may Allāh be pleased with him, decided at first, when he was compiling the book, not to include the Book of *Ḥajj*, but he then started working on it and compiled it".[305]

[305] This is obviously the scribe's note.

X
THE BOOK OF *JIHĀD*

A comprehensive discussion of the principles of this subject is covered in two chapters. The first is about the identification of the elements of war. The second is about the *aḥkām* of the enemy's property when the Muslims come to own it.

10.1. Chapter 1 The Elements (*Arkān*) of War

There are seven sections in this chapter. The first is about the identification of the *ḥukm* of this activity and the persons for whom it is binding.. The second is about the identification of persons who are to be fought. The third is about the identification of each category of the enemy on whom harm may be inflicted, and those who are not to be hurt. The fourth is about the lawful conditions of war. The fifth is about the identification of the number (of opponents) from whom retreat is not permissible. The sixth relates to whether truce is permissible. The seventh deals with the question: why wage war?

10.1.1. *Section 1: Identification of the* ḥukm *of this activity*

With respect to the *ḥukm* of this activity, the jurists agreed unanimously that it is a collective and not a universal obligation, except for ʿAbd Allāh Ibn al-Ḥasan who said it is voluntary. The majority of the jurists adopted this view because of the words of the Exalted, "Warfare is ordained for you, though it is hateful unto you, but it may happen that ye hate a thing which is good for you, and it may happen that ye love a thing which is bad for you, Allāh knoweth, ye know not".[306] Its imposition as a communal obligation, that is, when some undertake it the rest are absolved of it, is based upon the words of the Exalted, "And the believers should not all go out to fight. Of every troop of them, a party only should go forth, that they (who are left behind) may gain sound knowledge in religion, and that they may warn their folk when they return, so

[306] Qurʾān 2 : 216.

that they may beware,[307] and on His words, "Unto each Allāh hath promised good, but he hath bestowed on those who strive a great reward above the sedentary".[308] Further, the Prophet (God's peace and blessings be upon him) never went out to battle unless he had left some of the people behind. Taken together all these (evidences) imply that this activity constitutes a collective obligation.

The activity is obligatory on men, who are free, have attained puberty, who find the means (at their disposal) for going to war, are of sound health, and are neither ill nor suffer from a chronic disease. There is no dispute about this because of the words of the Exalted, "There is no blame for the blind, nor is there blame for the lame, nor is there blame for the sick",[309] and His words, "Not unto the weak nor unto the sick nor those who can find naught to spend is any fault (to be imputed though they stay at home)".[310] With respect to the obligation being restricted to free men, I know of no disagreement. The jurists in general agreed that a condition for this obligation is the permission of parents, except when it becomes a universal obligation; for example, when there are not enough people to carry out the obligation unless all (present) undertake it. The basis for this is the established tradition which relates that "a person said to the Messenger of Allāh (God's peace and blessings be upon him), 'I wish to participate in the *jihād*'. He asked, 'Are your parents alive?' The man said, Yes'. He said, 'Then struggle in their cause'".

The jurists disagreed about the (need for the) consent of polytheist parents. Similarly, they disagreed about the consent of the creditor when a person is under debt because of the saying of the Prophet (God's peace and blessings be upon him), when a man asked him, "'Will Allāh pardon my sins if I die with forbearance sacrificing myself in the way of Allāh?' He replied, 'Yes, except for debts. That is what Jibrīl said to me lately'". The majority permit it, however, particularly when the person leaves something behind for the satisfaction of his debts.

10.1.2. *Section 2: Identification of the persons to be fought*

The jurists agreed, with respect to the people who are to be fought, that they are all of the polytheists (***mushrikūn***), because of the words of the Exalted, "And fight them until persecution is no more, and religion is all for Allāh",[311] except what is narrated from Mālik, who said it is not permitted to commence

[307] Qur'ān 9 : 122.
[308] Qur'ān 4 : 95.
[309] Qur'ān 48 : 17.
[310] Qur'ān 9 : 91.
[311] Qur'ān 8 : 39.

hostilities against the Ethiopians, nor against the Turks, because of the report from the Prophet (God's peace and blessings be upon him), "Leave the Ethiopians in peace as long as they leave you alone". Mālik was questioned about the authenticity of this tradition. He did not acknowledge it, but said, "People continue to avoid an attack on them".

10.1.3. *Section 3: Identification of the harm permitted to be inflicted upon the enemy*

Harm allowed to be inflicted upon the enemy can be to property, life, or personal liberty, that is enslavement and ownership. Harm that amounts to enslavement is permitted by way of consensus (*ijmāᶜ*) for all categories of the polytheists, I mean, their men and women, old and young, and the common people and the élite with the exception of monks. One group of jurists maintained that they (the monks) are to be left alone and not to be captured; in fact, they are to be left unharmed and not to be enslaved because of the saying of the Messenger of Allāh (God's peace and blessings be upon him), "Leave them and that to which they have devoted themselves", and also because of the practice of Abū Bakr.

The majority of the jurists maintained that the *imām* has different types of choices regarding the prisoners of war including their pardon, enslavement, execution, demand for ransom, and the imposition of *jizya* (poll tax) on them. A group of jurists maintained that it is not permitted to execute the prisoners. Al-Ḥasan ibn Muḥammad al-Tamīmī has related that there is a consensus (*ijmāᶜ*) of the Companions on this.

The reason for their disagreement stems from the conflict of the apparent meanings of the verses in this context, the conflict of the acts (of the Prophet), and the conflict of the apparent meaning of the Qurʾānic text with the acts of the Prophet Prophet (God's peace and blessings be upon him). This is because the apparent meaning of the words of the Exalted, " ow when ye meet in battle those who disbelieve, then it is smiting of the necks until, when ye have routed them",[312] is that after taking prisoners the *imām* can only pardon or take ransom. (This conflicts with) the words of the Exalted, "It is not for any Prophet to have captives until he hath made slaughter in the land",[313] and with the occasion of the revelation that indicates through the (case of the) prisoners of the battle of Badr that execution is better than enslavement. The Prophet (God's peace and blessings be upon him), however, executed the prisoners on some occasions, pardoned them (on others), and enslaved women.

[312] Qurʾān 47 : 4.
[313] Qurʾān 8 : 67.

Abū ʿUbayd has related that he never enslaved free male Arabs. The Companions, after him, agreed upon the permissibility of enslavement of the People of the Book, both male and female.

Those who maintained that the verse, which is specific about the matter of captives (prohibiting execution), has abrogated the acts of the Prophet, said that the captive is not to be executed. Those who maintained that the verse neither mentions captives nor is its purpose the final disposal of the question of what is to be done to the captives, and that the act of the Prophet (God's peace and blessings be upon him) is an addition to what is in the verse, when they take into account the censure of the failure to execute the captives said that the execution of the captives is permitted.

Execution is permitted in cases where the guaranty of safe conduct (*amān*) is not available. There is no disagreement among Muslims on this; however, they differ as to who can grant safe conduct and who cannot. They agreed on the permissibility of safe conduct granted by the *imām*. The majority of the jurists permitted safe conduct granted by free Muslim males, except that Ibn al-Mājishūn was of the view that it is contingent upon the consent of the *imām*. They disagreed about the safe conduct granted by a slave or a woman. The majority permitted this while Ibn al-Mājishūn and Saḥnūn used to say that safe conduct granted by a woman is contingent upon the consent of the *imām*. Abū Ḥanīfa said that safe conduct granted by a slave is not permitted, unless he participates in fighting.

The reason for their disagreement is the conflict of a general implication with that of analogical reasoning. The generality is in the saying of the Prophet (God's peace and blessings be upon him), "The blood of the Muslims has equal value among themselves (among themselves with respect to protection). Even the humblest endeavors for their (collective) protection, and against outsiders they form a single (protecting) hand". This implies, through its generality, that safe conduct granted by the slave is valid. The conflicting analogy arises due to the fact that safe conduct is contingent upon full legal capacity while the capacity of the slave is deficient due to his servility. Thus it is necessary that his servility should be effective in invalidating his *amān* on the analogy of its effectiveness in suspending many of the legal *aḥkām* in his case. The general implication must then be restricted by this analogy.

Their disagreement about the effectiveness of the safe conduct granted by a woman is based on their dispute about the meaning of the saying of the Prophet (God's peace and blessings be upon him), "We protect whom you have protected, O Umm Hānī", and on the analogy of women upon men (i.e. their equality). Those who understood from his saying, "We protect whom you have protected, O Umm Hānī", an endorsement of safe conduct granted by her and not its validity by itself, for had it not been for his endorsement, her guaranty of safe conduct would be ineffective, said that a woman cannot grant safe conduct unless it is endorsed by the *imām*. Those who understood from this that his endorsement of her (guaranty of *amān*) was with the view that *amān* had already been concluded and had taken effect, and not with a view that it was his endorsement that granted validity to its conclusion said that safe conduct guaranteed by a woman is permitted. Likewise, those who considered her equal to a man by way of analogy, and made no distinction between them, permitted safe conduct granted by her, while those who considered that she had a defective legal capacity as compared to a man did not permit such safe conduct.

Whatever the nature of the *amān* it is not effective (in affording protection) against enslavement, but only against execution. It is possible for us to relate this disagreement to their dispute about the words used for the masculine plural, whether they include women, that is,in accordance with legal usage.

The harm aimed at life is by killing, and there is no disagreement among the Muslim jurists that it is permitted in war to slay the male polytheists, who have attained puberty and are waging war. There is, however, disagreement about execution after captivity, as we have already discussed. Similarly, there is no dispute among them that it is not permitted to slay minors or women, as long as they are not waging war. If a woman fights the shedding of her blood becomes permissible. This was established as "the Prophet (God's peace and blessings be upon him) prohibited the killing of women and children, and said when he saw a slain woman, 'She was not one who would have engaged in fighting' ".

They disagreed about the case of hermits cut off from the world, the blind, the chronically ill, the old who cannot fight, the idiot, and the peasants and serfs. Mālik said neither the blind nor idiots nor hermits are to be slain, and enough of their wealth is to be left to them by which they may survive. Similarly, the old and decrepit are not to be slain, in his view, and this was also the view of Abū Ḥanīfa and his disciples. Al-Thawrī and al-Awzāʿī said that only the old are to be spared. Al-Awzāʿī added that the peasants are not to be slain either. According to al-Shāfiʿī's most authentic opinion, all of these categories (of people) are to be put to death. The basis for their disagreement stems from the conflict of the specificity in some traditions with the general implication of (some verses of) the Qurʾān, and also the generality of the authentic saying of the Prophet (God's peace and blessings be upon him), "I have been commanded to fight mankind until they say, 'There is no God but Allāh.' " The words of the Exalted, "Then, when the sacred months have passed, slay the idolaters wherever ye find them",[314] imply the slaying of

[314] Qurʾān 9 : 5.

every nonbeliever whether or not he is a monk, and so does the saying of the Prophet (God's peace and blessings be upon him), "I have been commanded to fight mankind until they say, 'There is no God but Allāh'".

The traditions laid down about the sparing of all these categories include the traditions related by Dāwūd Ibn al-Ḥuṣayn from ʿIkrimah from Ibn ʿAbbās "that the Prophet (God's peace and blessings be upon him) used to say while sending out his armies, 'Do not kill hermits'". There is also the tradition related from Anas Ibn Mālik from the Prophet (God's peace and blessings be upon him), "Do not slay the old and decrepit nor young children nor women, and do not purloin [the booty]". It is recorded by Abū Dāwūd. There is also among these the tradition related by Mālik from Abū Bakr that he said, "You will come across a people who will claim that they have devoted themselves to Allāh, so leave them and that to which they have devoted themselves", and it includes the words, "Never kill women, children, and the old weakened with age".

It appears that the chief source of disagreement in this issue springs from the apparent conflict between the words of the Exalted, "Fight in the way of Allāh against those who fight you, but begin not hostilities. Lo, Allāh loveth not aggressors",[315] and His words, "Then when the sacred months have passed, slay the idolaters wherever ye find them".[316] Those who held that the latter verse has abrogated the (meaning of the) words "Fight in the way of Allāh those who fight you",[317] as fighting is prescribed primarily against those who fight, said that the latter verse stands unrestricted upon its generality. On the other hand, those who maintained that the former verse is the governing verse, and that it includes all categories not involved in fighting, exempted it from the generality of the latter (in other words restricted the latter to those who do or can provide hostility, thus excluding children, old and decrepit etc). Al-Shāfiʿī argued on the basis of the tradition of Samura that the Prophet (God's peace and blessings be upon him) said, "Kill the old among the polytheists and keep alive their young". It appears that the effective underlying cause for slaying, in his view, is *kufr* (disbelief). It is necessary then that this cause be applied to all the non-believers.

Those who maintained that the peasants are not to be slain argued on the basis of what is related from Zayd Ibn Wahb, who said, "We received a letter from ʿUmar, may Allāh be pleased with him, saying, 'Do not misappropriate (the spoils), do not be perfidious, do not kill infants, and fear Allāh in the case of the peasants'". A prohibition has been laid down in the tradition of Rabāh

[315] Qurʾān 2 : 190.
[316] Qurʾān 9 : 5.
[317] Qurʾān 2 : 190.

Ibn Rabīʿ about the slaying of non-believing serfs, that "he went out with the Messenger of Allāh (God's peace and blessings be upon him) for a battle which he fought and he (Rabāh) and the Companions of the Messenger of Allāh passed by a slain woman. The Messenger of Allāh stopped near her and then said, 'She was not the one to be engaged in fighting'. He then turned to face the group and said to one of them: 'Hurry and go to Khālid Ibn al-Walīd (and convey to him) that he must not slay infants, serfs or women'".

The reason leading to their disagreement, on the whole, arises from their dispute about the effective underlying cause of slaying. Thus, those who maintained that the effective underlying cause for this is disbelief (*kufr*), did not exempt anyone out of the polytheists, while those who maintained that the underlying cause in it is the ability to fight, there being a prohibition about the killing of women though they be non-believers, exempted those who do not have the ability to wage war, or those who have not affiliated themselves with it, like the peasants and the serfs.

The proscription of mutilating the bodies (*muthla*) of the enemy is fully established. The Muslim jurists agreed on the permissibility of slaying them with weapons, but disagreed about burning them with fire. A group of jurists disallowed burning them with fire or even attacking them with it, and this is the opinion of ʿUmar and is also narrated from Mālik. Sufyān al-Thawrī permitted this, while some of them said: "If the enemy initiates this it is permitted, otherwise not".

The reason for their disagreement stems from the conflict of a general implication with a specific rule. The generality lies in the words of the Exalted, "Slay the idolaters wherever ye find them".[318] This does not make an exception for any kind of slaying. The specific implication was established when the the Prophet (God's peace and blessings be upon him), said about a man, "If you seize him, kill him, but do not burn him with fire for no one punishes (has the right to) with fire except the Lord of the Fire".

The majority of the jurists agreed about the permissibility of attacking fortresses by means of mangonels, irrespective of women or children being in them, because of the report that the Prophet (God's peace and blessings be upon him), positioned mangonels against the people of Ṭāʾif. If there are Muslim captives and Muslim children in the fortress then, according to a group, mangonels should not be used, and that is the opinion of al-Awzāʿī. Al-Layth permitted this. The reliance of those who do not permit this is on the words of the Exalted, "If they (the believers and the disbelievers) had been clearly separated We verily had punished those of them who disbelieved with

[318] Qurʾān 9 : 5.

painful punishment".[319] It appears that those who permitted this relied on jurisprudential interest (*maṣlaḥah*).

This, then, is the extent of harm that is allowed to be inflicted upon their life and liberty. The harm that is permissible in the case of their property, that is, buildings, animals, and crops, is a matter of controversy among them. Mālik permitted cutting of trees, picking of fruit, and destruction of inhabited buildings, but did not allow the slaughter of cattle and the burning of date-palms. Al-Awzāʿī disallowed the cutting of fruit-bearing trees and the demolishing of buildings – churches or other. Al-Shāfiʿī said that houses and trees may be set on fire if the enemy used them as fortresses, otherwise the destruction of houses and the cutting of trees is disapproved.

The reason for their disagreement springs from the conflict between the practice of Abū Bakr and that of the Prophet (God's peace and blessings be upon him). It is established that "the Prophet (God's peace and blessings be upon him) set fire to the date-palms of Banū al-Naḍīr", and it is also established that Abū Bakr ordered his troops: "Do not cut trees, do not destroy buildings". Those who maintained that the act of Abū Bakr was based on his knowledge about the abrogation of the act of the Prophet (God's peace and blessings be upon him)—as it cannot be conceived that Abū Bakr would act contrary to the practice of the Prophet when he was well aware of it—or that (the act of the Prophet) was restricted to the case of Banū al-Naḍīr due to their undue aggression against the Muslims, adopted the opinion of Abū Bakr. Those who relied on the act of the Prophet (God's peace and blessings be upon him), and did not consider the act of another as binding proof against it, adopted the view that trees are to be burnt. Mālik distinguished between animals and trees, as the killing of animals amounts to mutilation and the Prophet (God's peace and blessings be upon him) prohibited that. Further, it is not reported about the Prophet (God's peace and blessings be upon him) that he killed animals. This, then, is the identification of the harm that may be inflicted upon the disbelievers with respect to their life and property.

10.1.4. *Section 4: The condition for the declaration of war*

The condition for the declaration of war, by agreement, is the communication of the invitation to Islam, that is, it is not permitted to wage war on them unless the invitation has reached them. This is something upon which the Muslim jurists agreed because of the words of the Exalted, "We never punish until We have sent a messenger".[320] They disagreed on whether the repetition

[319] Qurʾān 40 : 25.
[320] Qurʾān 17 : 15.

of the invitation was required on the recurrence of war. Some of them made this obligatory, some considered it desirable, while some of them neither considered it obligatory nor desirable.

The reason for their disagreement arises from the (apparent) conflict of words (of the Prophet) with (his) acts. It has been established that the Prophet (God's peace and blessings be upon him) used to say to the commander upon sending a detachment, "When you come to face your enemy, the polytheists, invite them to opt for three choices or inclinations, and whichever of these they agree to, accept, and withhold the attack. Invite them to Islam, and if they agree refrain from attacking them. Call on them, then, to move from their territory to the territory of the Emigrants, and inform them that if they do this they shall have the rights granted to the Emigrants. If they refuse to do this, and choose their own abode, let them know that their status will be that of the Muslim Bedouin. The law of Allāh, which is applicable to the Believers, would be applicable to them, and they would have no share in the booty or in the spoils, unless they fight along with the Muslims. If they, then, refuse call on them to pay the *jizya* (poll tax). If they agree, accept it from them and refrain from (fighting) them, but if they refuse, seek support from Allāh and fight them".

It is, however, established from the Prophet (God's peace and blessings be upon him) that he used to ensnare the enemy and ambush them during the wars. Some of the jurists, and these are the majority, maintained that the acts of the Prophet (God's peace and blessings be upon him) abrogated his words, and that (the implication in his words) used to be valid in the early days of Islam before the Islamic movement had become widespread, on the evidence that there is an invitation to migrate. Some of the jurists preferred the words over the acts, by construing the acts to apply to specific cases. Those who preferred extending the invitation did so through an element of reconciliation (between evidences).

10.1.5. *Section 5: Identification of the number from whom retreat is not permissible*

With respect to the identification of a number from whom retreat is not permissible, it is double (the number of Muslims), and this by agreement, because of the words of the Exalted, "Now hath Allāh lightened your burden, for He knoweth that there is weakness in you. So, if there be of you steadfast hundred they shall overcome two hundred, and if there be of you a thousand (steadfast) they shall overcome two thousand by permission of Allāh".[321] Ibn

[321] Qur'ān 8 : 66.

al-Mājishūn held, and he also narrated from Mālik, that doubling here is to be related to strength and not to number, and that it is (therefore) permitted for one Muslim warrior to retreat from a single enemy if he has a better trained mount than his, has better weapons, or is superior to him in strength.

10.1.6. *Section 6: The permission for truce*

Is truce permissible? A group of jurists permitted this initially (without warfare) without necessity, if the *imām* considered it to be in the interest of the Muslims. Another group of jurists did not permit it, except on the basis of a compelling necessity, such as the avoidance of disturbances or for gaining from them some concessions for the Muslim community, which are not in the nature of *jizya* as the condition for *jizya* is that they be subject to the laws of the Muslims, or even without taking anything from them. Al-Awzāʿī permitted that the *imām* may negotiate a truce with the disbelievers on the basis of something that the Muslims would give to the disbelievers if that is required as a necessity for avoiding (greater) trials, or on the basis of any other necessity. Al-Shāfiʿī said that the Muslims are not to make any concession to the disbelievers, unless they fear that they would be overwhelmed by the sheer number of the enemy (in relation to) their own small numbers, or because of a severe ordeal that they are subjected to.

Those who upheld the permission of making a truce when the *imām* saw an interest (of the Muslims) in this are Mālik, al-Shāfiʿī, and Abū Ḥanīfa, except that al-Shāfiʿī stipulated that the duration of the truce should not be for a period greater than the one transacted by the Messenger of Allāh (God's peace and blessings be upon him) with the disbelievers in the year of al-Ḥudaybiya.

The reason for their disagreement over the permissibility of truce without a necessity stems from the conflict of the apparent meaning of the words of the Exalted, "Then, when the sacred months have passed, slay the idolaters wherever ye find them",[322] and His words, "Fight those who do not believe in Allāh nor the Last Day",[323] with His words, "And if they incline to peace, incline thou also to it, and trust in Allāh".[324] Those who maintained that the verse commanding fighting unless they believe or pay the *jizya* has abrogated the verse implying peace said that truce is not permitted, except in the case of necessity. Those who maintained that the verse implying peace has restricted

[322] Qurʾān 9 : 5.

[323] Qurʾān 9 : 29. Pickthall's translation has been changed here. His translation of this verse reads, "Fight against such of those who have been given the Scripture as believe not in Allāh nor the Last Day". This translation is correct, but only when the complete verse is taken into account. The translation of the complete verse appears a few paragraphs below.

[324] Qurʾān 8 : 61.

the other said that truce is permitted if the *imām* considers it proper. They supported this interpretation with the act of the Prophet (God's peace and blessings be upon him) in this case, because his (God's peace and blessings be upon him) truce in the year of al-Ḥudaybiya was not based upon necessity.

The principle for al-Shāfiʿī is the command to fight until they believe or pay *jizya*, and this, in his view, was restricted by the act of the Prophet (God's peace and blessings be upon him) in the year of al-Ḥudaybiya. He therefore did not approve that the period be in excess of what was negotiated by the Messenger of Allāh (God's peace and blessings be upon him). They disagreed about this period. It was said that it was for four years and it was said that it was for three years. It was also said that it was for ten years, and this was upheld by al-Shāfiʿī.

Those who permitted that the Muslims may conclude a truce with the polytheists on the terms that the Muslims would give them something, if this was required by necessity of avoiding tribulation or (the fulfilment of) some other pressing need, did so on the basis of the report that the Prophet (God's peace and blessings be upon him) was prepared to give part of the produce of Medina to some of the disbelievers who were among the forces mustered to attack Medina, but the Medinese did not agree, but Allāh granted him success (without his having made a concession to the unbelievers). Those who did not permit this unless the Muslims feared that they would be overwhelmed did so on the analogy drawn from their consensus on the permissibility of paying ransom for Muslim captives, the point being that Muslims in such a (weak) position are like prisoners.

10.1.7. *Section 7: Why wage war?*

Why wage war? The Muslim jurists agreed that the purpose of fighting the People of the Book, excluding the (Qurayshite) People of the Book and the Christian Arabs, is one of two things: it is either for their conversion to Islam or the payment of *jizya*. The payment of *jizya* is because of the words of the Exalted, "Fight against such of those who have been given the Scripture as believe not in Allāh or the Last Day, and forbid not that which Allāh and His Messenger hath forbidden, and follow not the religion of truth, until they pay the tribute readily being brought low".[325] The majority of the jurists also argued about the taking of *jizya* from the Magians, because of the saying of the Prophet (God's peace and blessings be upon him), "Establish with them the practice adopted for the People of the Book". They disagreed about the polytheists other than the People of the Book, whether *jizya* is to be accepted

[325] Qur'ān 9 : 29.

from them. A group of jurists said that *jizya* is to be charged from all polytheists. This is Mālik's opinion. Another group exempted from this the Arab polytheists. Al-Shāfiʿī, Abū Thawr, and a group of jurists said that *jizya* is only to be imposed upon the People of the Book and the Magians.

The reason for their disagreement stems from the conflict between the general and the specific implication. The general implication is in the words of the Exalted, "And fight them until persecution is no more, and religion is all for Allāh",[326] and in the saying of the Prophet (God's peace and blessings be upon him), "I have been commanded to fight mankind until they say, 'There is no God but Allāh'. If they say this their lives and wealth are protected from me, unless there is another claim on them, and their reckoning is with Allāh". The specific meaning is in the directive of the Prophet (God's peace and blessings be upon him) to the commanders of troops when he sent them to Arab polytheists who, it is known, were not the People of the Book, "When you come to face your enemy, the polytheists, invite them to opt for three choices", and he mentioned *jizya* as one of them. The tradition has already been mentioned.

Those who maintained that if a general command comes after the specific command it abrogates it, said that *jizya* is not to be accepted from polytheists other than the People of the Book. The reason is that the verses containing general commands for fighting them are later in time than this tradition, because the command to fight the polytheists is general and it occurs in *sūrat Barā'a*, which was (revealed in) the year of the conquest of Mecca, while the tradition is dated before the conquest on the evidence of the invitation to them to emigrate. Those who maintained that the general meaning is to be construed in terms of the specific, whether it is earlier or later or whether their being earlier or later with reference to each is not known, said that *jizya* is to be accepted from all the polytheists. With respect to the singling out of the People of the Book from all the polytheists, this exemption from the general meaning occurred, by agreement, in the the specific terms of the words of the Exalted, "Fight against such of those who have been given the Scripture as believe not in Allāh or the Last Day, and forbid not that which Allāh hath forbidden by His Messenger, and follow not the religion of truth, until they pay the tribute readily being brought low".[327] The discussion of the *jizya* and its *aḥkām* will be coming up in the next chapter of this Book.

These, then, are the elements of war. One of the well-known issues related to this chapter is the proscription of travelling to the land of the enemy with (a copy of) the Qur'ān. The majority of the jurists maintain that this is not

[326] Qur'ān 8 : 39.
[327] Qur'ān 9 : 29.

permitted because it was established from the Messenger of Allāh (God's peace and blessings be upon him). Abū Ḥanīfa said that it is permitted if it stays within the safety of military camps. The reason for their disagreement is whether the proscription is general having a general import or whether it is general with a specific implication.

10.2. Chapter 2 The *Aḥkām* of Enemy Property

A comprehensive discussion of the fundamentals of this chapter is also covered in seven sections. The first is about the *ḥukm* of the fifth. The second is about the *ḥukm* of the four-fifths. The third is about the *ḥukm* of *anfāl* (prize money, reward). The fourth is about the wealth of the Muslims found in the possession of the polytheists. The fifth is about the *ḥukm* of the two kinds of land. The sixth is about the *ḥukm* of *fay*ʾ (booty). The seventh is about the *aḥkām* of *jizya* and the wealth acquired from them through a truce.

10.2.1. *Section 1: The* ḥukm *of the fifth of spoils*

The Muslim jurists agreed that a fifth of the spoils, other than the lands acquired by force from the possession of the Byzantines belonged to the *imām* and (the rest) four-fifths of it were for those who seized it, because of the words of the Exalted, "And know that whatever ye take as spoils of war, lo! a fifth thereof is for Allāh, and for the messenger and for the kinsmen (of the Prophet) and orphans and the needy and the wayfarer, if ye believe in Allāh and that which We revealed unto Our slave on the Day of Discrimination, the day when the two armies met. And Allāh is able to do all things".[328] They disagreed about the fifth; there are four well-known opinions in this regard. The first is that the fifth is divided (further) into five parts in accordance with the explicitly mentioned shares in the verse. This is al-Shāfiʿī's opinion. The second is that it is to be divided into four parts, and that the words, "is for Allāh", are only an opening statement and do not imply a fifth share. The third opinion is that it is to be divided, today, into three shares, and that the share of the Prophet and the kinsman was eliminated with the death of the Prophet (God's peace and blessings be upon him). The fourth is that the fifth is of the same category as *fay*ʾ (booty) to which both the rich and the poor are entitled. This is Mālik's opinion and of the jurists generally.

Those who maintained that it is to be subdivided into four or five parts disagreed as to what is to be done with the share of the Messenger of Allāh

[328] Qurʾān 8 : 41. Pickthall's translation changed.

(God's peace and blessings be upon him) and that of the kinsmen after his death. One group of jurists said that it is to spread out proportionally among the remaining categories entitled to the fifth. Another group said that it is to be given to the rest of the army. A third group said that the share of the Messenger of Allāh (God's peace and blessings be upon him) belongs to the *imām*, and the share of the kinsmen is for the kinsmen of the *imām*. A fourth group said that it is to be used for arms and preparation. They disagreed as to who are the kinsmen? One group said that they are the Banū Hāshim alone, while another group said that they are Banū ʿAbd al-Muṭṭalib[329] and the Banū Hāshim.

The reason for disagreement over the question of whether the fifth is restricted to the stated categories or it can be extended to others besides them, stems from whether the purpose of mentioning these categories in the verse is the allocation of the fifth or the indication of their priority over others, in which case it would belong to a category of the specific with a general implication. Those who maintained that it is a category of the specific with a specific implication said that the fifth is not to be extended beyond these explicitly stated categories. This was adopted the majority of the jurists. Those who said that it is a category of the specific with a general implication said that it is permitted to the *imām* to spend it where he identifies the welfare of the Muslims.

Those who maintained that the share of the Prophet (God's peace and blessings be upon him) is for the *imām* after him argued on the basis of what is related from the Prophet (God's peace and blessings be upon him) that he said, "When Allāh provides the Prophet with a sustenance it goes to the successor after him". Those who would grant it to the remaining categories or to those who seized it do so on the basis of its similarity with the amount already earmarked for them.

Those who said that the next of kin are the Banū Hāshim and Banū al-Muṭṭalib argued on the basis of the tradition of Jubayr ibn Muṭʿim, who said, "The Messenger of Allāh (God's peace and blessings be upon him) divided the share of the kinsmen from the fifth among the Banū Hāshim and Banū al-Muṭṭalib". They said that the Banū Hāshim and the Banū al-Muṭṭalib are one category, while those who said that the banū Hāshim are a separate category did so on the grounds that *ṣadaqa* is not permitted to them.

The jurists disagreed about the share of the Prophet (God's peace and blessings be upon him) in the fifth. One group merely said that it is a fifth, and there is no dispute among them about the necessity (integrity) of his share irrespective of his being present or absent at the time of division. Another

[329] Banū (clan of) ʿAbd al-Muṭṭalib is a branch of the clan of Banū Hāshim.

group said that it is a fifth (if he is present) and the *ṣafīy* (the Prophet's choice).

Ṣafīy was a well-known share for the Prophet (God's peace and blessings be upon him), and it was something that he used to select from the undivided spoils, which could be a mare, a slave-girl, or a male slave. It is related that (the name) Ṣafiyya was from *ṣafīy*. They agreed that no one after the Messenger of Allāh (God's peace and blessings be upon him) is entitled to *ṣafīy*, except for Abū Thawr who held that it is to be treated in the same way as the share of the Prophet (God's peace and blessings be upon him).

10.2.2. *Section 2: The* ḥukm *of the four-fifths of the spoils*

The majority of the jurists agreed that four-fifths of the spoils are for those who seize them, if they acted with the permission of the *imām*. They disagreed about those who act without the permission of the *imām*, about the person entitled to a share in the spoils, about the time of the entitlement, how much, and also about the entitlement from the spoils before the division.

The majority of the jurists maintain that four-fifths of the spoils are for those who seize it whether they proceeded with the permission of the *imām* or without his permission, because of the general implication of the words of the Exalted, "And know that whatever ye take as spoils of war, lo! a fifth thereof is for Allāh, and for the messenger and for the kinsman (who hath need) and orphans and the needy and the wayfarer, if ye believe in Allāh and that which We revealed unto Our slave on the Day of Discrimination, the day when the two armies met. And Allāh is able to do all things".[330] A group of jurists said that if a detachment or an individual act without the permission of the *imām*, then, whatever either brings back is a reward (*nafl*) that is to be appropriated by the *imām*. Another group of jurists said that, in fact, all of it is to be taken by the person who seized it. The majority relied upon the apparent meaning of the verse, while the others relied upon the nature of the acts that occurred during the time of the Messenger of Allāh (God's peace and blessings be upon him). This is so as all troops used to proceed with the permission of the Prophet (God's peace and blessings be upon him), and it appears that they thought the permission of the *imām* was a requisite condition for it, but this is weak.

Who has a share in the spoils? They agreed that they are those who are males, free, and have attained puberty (among those who participated in the fighting). They disagreed about the case of the persons who have opposite characteristics, that is, women, slaves, and those who had not attained puberty

[330] Qur'ān 8 : 41.

but were nearing it. A group of jurists said that there is no share for women or slaves in the spoils, but some gifts are to be given to them. This was Mālik's opinion. Another group of jurists said that no presents are to be given to them nor is anything to be paid to them from the spoils. A third group said that they have the same share as the other sharers in the spoils. This was al-Awzāʿī's opinion. They also differed about the minor approaching the age of puberty (the adolescent). Some of the jurists said that a share is to be assigned to him. This was al-Shāfiʿī's opinion. Some of them stipulated that he should have the ability to fight. This was Mālik's opinion. Some said that he is to be given a gift.

The reason for their disagreement over slaves is whether the general communication of the law includes freemen and slaves together or only the freemen to the exclusion of the slaves. Further, the practice of the Companions is in conflict with the general implication of the verse. This is because it is was their general practice, may Allāh be pleased with them, that the slaves had no share. This is related from ʿUmar ibn al-Khaṭṭāb and Ibn ʿAbbās, and is related by Ibn Abī Shayba from them through various channels. Abū ʿUmar ibn ʿAbd al-Barr said that the most authentic report in this from ʿUmar is what is related by Sufyān ibn ʿUyayna from ʿAmr ibn Dīnār from Ibn Shihāb from Mālik ibn Aws ibn Ḥadthān, who said, "ʿUmar said, 'There is no one who does not have a right in this with the exception of those whom your right hands possess' ".

The majority of the jurists decided that a woman is not entitled to a share, but to a gift, on the basis of the authentic tradition of Umm ʿAṭiyya, who said, "We used to fight alongside the Messenger of Allāh (God's peace and blessings be upon him) tending the wounded and nursing the sick, and he used to give us gifts from the spoils". The reason for disagreement arises from their dispute over whether a woman is similar to a man in being effective in battle, if she participates in it. They agreed that it is permitted to women to participate in war; therefore, those who held them to be similar to men granted them a share in the spoils, while those who held them to be less effective in battle than men in this context either did not grant anything to them or granted them what was less than a share, and these were gifts. It is better here to follow the tradition. Al-Awzāʿī believed that "the Messenger of Allāh (God's peace and blessings be upon him) granted a share to women at Khaybar".

They disagreed about whether traders and mercenaries are to be given a share. Mālik said that they are not to be given a share, unless they have fought. A group of jurists said that they are to be given a share if they were present during the battle. The reason for their disagreement here stems from the restriction of the general implication of the words of the Exalted, "And know that whatever ye take as spoils of war, lo! a fifth thereof is for Allāh, and for the messenger",[331] by means of analogy that dictates a distinction between these people and the rest of the fighters entitled to the spoils. Those who maintained that the *ḥukm* of the traders and the mercenaries is different from the rest of the soldiers, because they did not intend to fight, but intended either to trade or to be hired for wages (for fighting), excluded them from the general implication of the verse. Those who maintained that the general implication is stronger than analogy let the general implication govern the issue. An evidence for those who excluded them is what is recorded by ʿAbd al-Razzāq that ʿAbd al-Raḥmān ibn ʿAwf asked one of the *muhājirūn*, who was a learned man, to go out to battle with him. He agreed to do so. When the time for departure came he called him, but he declined on the pretext of the needs of his children and wife. ʿAbd al-Raḥmān then gave him three *dīnārs* so as to make him accompany him. When they had routed the enemy the man asked ʿAbd al-Raḥmān for his share of the spoils. ʿAbd al-Raḥmān said to him, "I will mention your affair to the Messenger of Allāh (God's peace and blessings be upon him)". When he did mention it to him, the Messenger of Allāh (God's peace and blessings be upon him) said, "These three *dīnārs* are his share and portion from the battle with respect to this world as well as for the hereafter". Abū Dāwūd has recorded a similar tradition from Yaʿla ibn Munabbih.

Those who permitted them a share in the division held their case to be similar to the employment of hirelings, which is the assistance provided by some members of the *dīwān* to others, that is, like a person standing aside to support the warrior. The jurists disagreed about such hirelings, with Mālik permitting it and the others disallowing it. Some of the jurists permitted this if granted by the *sulṭān* alone, or when there was a necessity. This was the opinion of Abū Ḥanīfa and al-Shāfiʿī.

With respect to the condition which entitles a Muslim to a share of the spoils, most of the jurists said that it is his presence at the battle, even if he did not fight. If he arrives after the battle is over, he does not get a share of the spoils. This was upheld by the majority, while another group said that if he joins up with them before they move back into the *dār al-Islām* he is entitled to a share if he was employed somehow in its management. This is Abū Ḥanīfa's opinion.

There are two reasons for their disagreement: analogy and a tradition. The analogy is whether the role of the warrior in the preservation (and protection of the spoils) is similar to his role in its acquisition. This is so as the active participation of the person in the battle is effective in its acquisition, that is, in the acquisition of the spoils, because of which he is entitled to a share. The

[331] Qurʾān 8 : 41.

role of the person who arrives late, but before the Muslim army moves to the land of Islam, is effective in preserving (the spoils). Those who held his role in preservation to the role in acquisition said that he is entitled to a share even if he was not present at the battle. Those who said that such a role for purposes of preservation is weak (for analogy) did not consider him to be entitled to it.

There are two relevant traditions in this, but they conflict with each other. The first is related on the authority of Abū Hurayra, who said "that the Messenger of Allāh (God's peace and blessings be upon him) sent Abān ibn Saʿīd with a detachment from Medina towards Najd. Abān and his companions joined up with the Prophet (God's peace and blessings be upon him) at Khaybar after they [the Prophet and his Companions] had conquered it. Abān said, "O Messenger of Allāh, give us a share (of the spoils)". The Messenger of Allāh (God's peace and blessings be upon him) did not grant them a share". The second tradition is in the report "that the Messenger of Allāh (God's peace and blessings be upon him) said on the day of Badr, "ʿUthmān has departed on the business of Allāh and the business of his Messenger". The Messenger of Allāh (God's peace and blessings be upon him) then allotted a share for him, but he did not do so for anyone else who was absent from the battle". They said that he was entitled to a share as he was busy on behalf of the *imām*. Abū Bakr ibn al-Mundhir said: "It is established that ʿUmar ibn al-Khaṭṭāb, may Allāh be pleased with him, said, 'The spoils are for those who were present at the battle' ".

The troops that move out of the camps (for battle) are entitled to the spoils. The majority of the jurists maintain that the members of the camp participate with them in the spoils, even if they did not participate in the acquisition of the spoils or in the battle. This is because of the saying of the Prophet (God's peace and blessings be upon him), "The detachments (that went out to fight) should share (the spoils) with those (of them who are) stationed". It is recorded by Abū Dāwūd. Further, these people are also effective in the acquisition of the spoils. Al-Ḥasan al-Baṣrī said that if the detachment departs from the camp with the permission of the *imām* they divide the spoils into five parts, and what remains is for the members of the detachment, but if they went out without the permission of the *imām* they divide the spoils into five parts and what remains is for the rest of the troops. Al-Nakhaʿī said that the *imām* has a choice; if he likes he may divide into five parts what the detachment brought in or he may treat the whole as a reward (for the detachment). The reason for this disagreement also stems from the similarity of the effectiveness of the camp in the (acquisition of the) spoils by the detachment with the effectiveness of those who were present at the battle, and who are the members of the detachment.

A share in the spoils, then, in the view of the majority of the jurists, is given to the soldier on one of two conditions. He should either be one who had participated in the battle, or he should be one who had sheltered the fighting forces.

They disagreed about the share of the horse rider in the context of how much is due to the fighter. The majority said that the rider has three shares; one share for him and two for his horse. Abū Ḥanīfa said that only two shares are due to the rider, one for the horse and one for him. The reason for their disagreement arises from the conflict of the relevant traditions and the conflict of analogy with a tradition. Abū Dāwūd has recorded from Ibn ʿUmar "that the Prophet (God's peace and blessings be upon him) allotted three shares for a man and his horse, two shares for the horse and one for its rider". He also recorded a tradition from Mujammiʿ ibn Jāriyat al-Anṣārī that has the same import as the opinion of Abū Ḥanīfa. The analogy that conflicts with the apparent meaning of the tradition of Ibn ʿUmar is that the share of a horse should not be greater than that of a human being. This is why Abū Ḥanīfa preferred the tradition that conforms with this analogy over the tradition that opposes it. This analogy, however, does not hold, as it is the human being who is the rider of the horse and who is also entitled to the share of the horse, and it is not unlikely that the effectiveness of the rider riding a horse be thrice as much as the foot-soldier. This appears certain, along with the fact that the tradition of Ibn ʿUmar (maintaining this view) has greater authenticity.

The Muslim jurists, while considering how much a soldier is allowed to take from the spoils before division, agreed about the prohibition of purloining the spoils. This is based upon what is established from the Messenger of Allāh (God's peace and blessings be upon him) about this, like his saying, "Turn in the thread and the garment, for purloining is a shame and a disgrace, on the Day of Judgment, for those who practice it", along with other traditions that have been recorded on the subject.

They disagreed about the permissibility of consuming food seized by the fighters, while they are still on the battlefield. The majority of the jurists permitted this, while a group of jurists disallowed it, which is the opinion of Ibn Shihāb. The reason for their disagreement emanates from the conflict of traditions regarding the prohibition of purloining with those implying permissibility of eating food, like the traditions of Ibn ʿUmar, Ibn Mughaffal, and Ibn Abī Awfā. Those who restricted the traditions on the prohibition of purloining to these—which permitted the eating of food by warriors—held it to be permissible; those who preferred the traditions prohibiting purloining to these did not permit it. The tradition of Ibn Mughaffal is that he said, "I came upon a skin of fat on the day of Khaybar and whispered to myself, 'I will not give any of it (to anyone)'. I turned around and there was the Messenger of Allāh (God's peace and blessings be upon him) smiling at me". It is recorded by al-Bukhārī and Muslim. In the tradition of Ibn Abī Awfā, he said, "During our battles we came upon honey and grapes that we used to eat and did not turn them in". This is also recorded by al-Bukhārī.

They disagreed about the penalty of the person who purloins (the spoils). A group of jurists said that his baggage is to be set on fire, while others said that there is no penalty for him except reprimanding him. The reason for their disagreement arises from their dispute over the authenticity of the tradition of Ṣāliḥ ibn Muḥammad ibn Zā'ida from Sālim from Ibn ʿUmar that he said, "The Prophet (God's peace and blessings be upon him) said, 'Burn the baggage of the person who purloins'".

10.2.3. *Section 3: The* ḥukm *of* anfāl *(reward)*

The jurists agreed about the permissibility of the *imām*'s granting of a reward out of the spoils for whomsoever he likes, that is, to add to his share. They disagreed, however, about the items from which a reward is to be given, about its amount, and about whether it is permitted to promise it before the battle. Further, they disagreed whether a Muslim fighter is entitled to the possessions[332] of the disbeliever whom he has slain, or whether he is not entitled to it unless the *imām* grants it as a reward for him. These are four issues and they constitute the fundamentals of this section.

10.2.3.1. Issue 1

A group of jurists maintained that the *nafl* (reward) is to be paid from the *khumus* (fifth), which is due to the Muslim treasury. This was Mālik's opinion. Another group of jurists said that the reward is due from the fifth of the *khumus* alone, which is the exclusive share of the *imām*. This view was taken by al-Shāfiʿī. A third group of jurists said that such favours are to be granted from the spoils as a whole (before division). This was the opinion of Aḥmad and Abū ʿUbayda. Some of these jurists (in the third group) permitted (even) the giving away of the entire spoils as reward.

The reason for their disagreement stems from the question of whether there is a conflict between the two verses laid down about the spoils or whether they indicate a choice. I mean, between the words of the Exalted, "And know that whatever ye take as spoils of war, lo! a fifth thereof is for Allāh, and for the messenger and for the kinsman (who hath need) and orphans and the needy and the wayfarer, if ye believe in Allāh and that which We revealed unto Our slave on the Day of Discrimination, the day when the two armies met. And Allāh is able to do all things",[333] and His words, "They ask thee (O

[332] These would include his horse, sword, armour, clothes, and money.

[333] Qur'ān 8 : 41.

Muḥammad) of the spoils of war. Say: the spoils of war (*anfāl*) belong to Allāh and the messenger, so keep your duty to Allāh, and adjust the matter of your difference".[334] Those who maintain that the former verse, "And know that whatever ye take as spoils of war . . .", has abrogated the latter verse, "They ask thee (O Muḥammad) of the spoils of war . . .", said that the reward (*nafl*) is due from the fifth or the fifth of the fifth. Those who maintained that there is no conflict between the verses and that they indicate a choice, that is, the *imām* may grant a reward from the undivided spoils if he likes and he has choice of not granting any reward and of giving all four-fifths of the spoils to the persons acquiring them, said that he may grant the reward from the undivided spoils.

There are also two traditions on this issue. The first is related by Mālik from Ibn ʿUmar "that the Messenger of Allāh (God's peace and blessings be upon him) sent a detachment of troops toward Najd, and ʿAbd Allāh ibn ʿUmar was among them. They secured a large number of camels as spoils. Their two shares (of the spoils) came to twelve camels each, and they were also given a camel each as a reward". This indicates that the reward is given after the division from the fifth. The second is the tradition of Ḥabīb ibn Maslama "that the Messenger of Allāh (God's peace and blessings be upon him) used to grant an initial reward of a fourth [of the spoils] to the troops, upon their departure, after excluding the fifth, and thereafter he used to grant them a third as reward upon their return after excluding the fifth", that is, initially at the beginning of his battle and at the time of departure.

10.2.3.2. Issue 2

The second issue is about the amount that the *imām* may give away as reward. A group of those who permitted the giving of rewards from undivided spoils said that it is not permitted to grant more than a third or a fourth and this (prescription) is based on the tradition of Ḥabīb ibn Maslama. Another group of jurists said that the *imām* may grant a detachment all that it has acquired as spoils, and this is on the basis that the verse about *anfāl* is not abrogated and governs the issue, and that it is to be construed in its unrestricted general meaning. Those who maintained that it is restricted by this tradition said that it is not permitted to him to give as reward more than a fourth or a third.

10.2.3.3. Issue 3

Is the *imām* permitted to make a promise of reward before the battle? The jurists disagreed about this. Mālik disallowed this, while a group of jurists permitted it.

[334] Qur'ān 8 : 1. This is an example of the legal use of a term. The term *nafl* (pl. *anfāl*) is translated in the verse in its literal sense as spoils or booty, but the jurists focus on another literal meaning, namely "present" or "reward". They determine the latter to be the legal use of the term.

The reason for their disagreement stems from the conflict between the meaning of the purposes of the war and the apparent meaning of the tradition. The purpose of war is to seek the favour of Allāh, the Majestic, and that the word of Allāh should reign supreme. Thus, if the *imām* offers a reward before the battle there is an apprehension that the warriors will spill their blood for a cause other than seeking Allāh's favour. The tradition which implies through its apparent meaning the permissibility of declaring a reward before the battle, is the tradition of Ḥabīb ibn Maslama that the Prophet (God's peace and blessings be upon him) "used to announce a reward in battles for troops moving out of the camps at a fourth (of the spoils they would capture) and a third from what they captured on their return". It is obvious that the purpose in this was the active pursuit of the enemy.

10.2.3.4. Issue 4

The fourth issue is whether the slayer is entitled to appropriate (of his own accord) the spoils of the person slain, or whether he may do so only if the *imām* has determined it as a reward. They disagreed about this. Mālik said that the (believing) killer is not entitled to appropriate the spoils of the person killed, unless the *imām* considers it, by way of *ijtihād*, to be a reward for him, and this too after the battle. This was also the opinion of Abū Ḥanīfa and al-Thawrī. Al-Shāfiʿī, Aḥmad, Abū Thawr, Isḥāq, and a group of the predecessors said that the killer is entitled to it, irrespective of the the *imām*'s saying so. Some of these (latter) jurists deemed appropriation to be his right under all circumstances and they did not stipulate any condition for this. Some of them said that he has this right only if he slays the person face to face (in combat) and not treacherously or when the disbeliever is in retreat. This was al-Shāfiʿī's opinion. Some of them said that the killer is entitled to appropriate the property if he slays the enemy before the battle and not in the thick of it, or if he does so after the battle. If he kills him in the thick of battle he does not have the right to appropriate his property. This was al-Awzāʿī's opinion. One group of jurists said that if the declared reward (property of the enemy slain) is excessive, it is permitted to the *imām* to give a fifth of it.

The reason for their disagreement stems from the probability of meanings in the saying of the Prophet (God's peace and blessings be upon him) on the day of Ḥunayn when there was a setback in the battle, "Whoever slays a person shall have his spoils". It is probable that he meant this as a reward, but it can also be interpreted as a right of the slayer. For Mālik (God bless him) the stronger probability was that it was by way of reward on the grounds that it was not proved for him that the Prophet (God's peace and blessings be upon him) ever said this or decided it except on the day of Ḥunayn, and also because of its conflict with the verse of spoils if it is interpreted to convey a right of the slayer, I mean, the verse, "And know that whatever ye take as spoils of war, lo! a fifth thereof is for Allāh, and for the messenger".[335] The reason is that when it is explicitly laid down in the verse that a fifth is for Allāh it becomes obvious that the four-fifths are a right of those acquiring the spoils, just as when He laid down explicitly a third for the mother in inheritance it became obvious that the remaining two-thirds were the right of the father. Abū ʿUmar said that this saying was recorded from him (God's peace and blessings be upon him) on the Day of Ḥunayn as well as on the Day of Badr. It is related from ʿUmar ibn al-Khaṭṭāb that he said: "We did not divide the spoils of the slain into five parts during the period of the Messenger of Allāh (God's peace and blessings be upon him)". It is recorded by Abū Dāwūd from ʿAwf ibn Mālik al-Ashjaʿī and Khālid ibn al-Walīd "that the Messenger of Allāh (God's peace and blessings be upon him) gave a decision for appropriating the spoils of the slain". Ibn Abī Shayba has recorded from Anas ibn Mālik that al-Barrāʾ ibn Mālik made a charge toward al-Marzubān, on the day of al-Dāra, and struck his saddlebow with his lance killing him. His spoils (in monetary value) came to thirty thousand. When this report reached ʿUmar ibn al-Khaṭṭāb he said to Abū Ṭalḥa: "We did not divide the spoils of the slain into five parts, but the spoils for al-Barrāʾ have reached an exorbitant figure, and I have no choice but to add it to the spoils which have to be divided into five portions." Ibn Sīrīn said that Anas ibn Mālik related that this was the first *salab* from a slain person that were divided into five parts in Islam. This was relied upon by those who made a distinction between small and excessive possessions of the slain.

They disagreed about the spoils of the slain that are due (to the slayer). A group of jurists said that the slayer is entitled to all that he finds on the person of the slain. Another group of jurists excluded gold and silver from this (as these have to be added to general spoils).

10.2.4. *Section 4: The* ḥukm *of the property of muslims found in the possession of disbelievers*

They disagreed about the case of the property of Muslims that is recovered from the possession of the disbelievers. There are four well-known opinions on this subject. The first is that the wealth of the Muslims that is recovered by the Muslims from the possession of the disbelievers is for the owners of that wealth, and the warriors who recovered it are not entitled to any of it. Those who held this opinion include al-Shāfiʿī, his disciples, and Abū Thawr. The

[335] Qurʾān 8 : 41.

second opinion is that what is recovered by the Muslims is treated as spoils for the army and the owners are not entitled to any of it. This opinion was held by al-Zuhrī and ʿAmr ibn Dīnār, and it is also related from ʿAlī ibn Abī Ṭālib. The third opinion is that the owner of the property is entitled, without any payment, to what is discovered of the property of Muslims before division, but what is discovered after the division is to be given to the owner after he pays its value. Those who hold this opinion are divided into two groups. Some of them maintained that this rule applies to all (Muslim property) that is recovered by the Muslims from the possession of the disbelievers, whatever the manner in which it came into the possession of the disbelievers and at whatever location. Those who held this opinion include Mālik, al-Thawrī, and a group of jurists, and it is also related from ʿUmar ibn al-Khaṭṭāb. Some of them made a distinction between what came into the possession of the disbelievers by the use of force, and which they carried off until they transported it to the land of the polytheists, and between what was taken back from them before they were able to seize and carry off into polytheist territory. They said that this (the first kind of) property, if it is identified by the owner before its division, belongs to him, but if he comes across it after the division he has a right to it after paying its price. They maintained, on the other hand, that the property that was not gathered by the enemy so as to be transported to their land belongs to the owner before the division and after the division; and this is the fourth opinion.

Their disagreement arises from their dispute about whether the disbelievers can legally own the property of the Muslims taken by force. And the reason for their disagreement on this issue arises from the conflict of the relevant traditions, and also the conflict of analogy. This is so as the tradition of ʿImrān ibn Ḥuṣayn (the text of which is to follow) indicates that the disbelievers cannot own anything extorted from the Muslims. The tradition says: "The polytheists raided the freely grazing animals around Medina and snatched al-ʿAḍbāʾ, a camel belonging to the Messenger of Allāh (God's peace and blessings be upon him) along with a Muslim woman. One night, when they had gone to sleep, the woman arose, but any camel she touched would bray, until she came to al-ʿAḍbāʾ. It behaved in a docile manner, so she mounted it and headed for Medina, making a vow that if she was saved by Allāh, she would certainly sacrifice the camel. When she arrived in Medina the camel was recognized and she was brought to the Messenger of Allāh (God's peace and blessings be upon him). She informed him of her vow. He said, 'What an ungracious reward. A vow is not operable in what the child of Adam does not own, nor is there a vow for an evil deed'". Likewise, the apparent meaning of a tradition related by Ibn ʿUmar conveys the same meaning. Its content is that his horse ran away and was snatched by the enemy, but the

Muslims came upon it and it was returned to him during the lifetime of the Messenger of Allāh (God's peace and blessings be upon him). Both traditions are authentic. The tradition, on the other hand, that indicates the opposite, namely, that the disbelievers can own Muslim property stems from the saying of the Prophet (God's peace and blessings be upon him), "Has ʿAqīl left a house for us?" He (God's peace and blessings be upon him) had sold his house that he owned in Mecca after migrating from there to Medina.

The analogy is that those who considered wealth to be similar to the person (of an individual for ownership) said that just as the disbelievers cannot own our persons, as is the case of a rebel in comparison to a law-abiding person, that is, he cannot own any of the two things to the detriment of the rights of the law-abiding person. Those who said that the disbelievers can own (our wealth) argued that the person who does not own the wealth is liable for it if its substance is destroyed, and they agreed that the disbelievers do not compensate the property of the Muslims. From this it follows that the disbelievers can own captured Muslim property, for had they not been owners they would have been held liable for compensation.

Those who made a distinction between the *ḥukm* before the division of spoils and after it, and between what the polytheists acquire from the Muslims by force and what they get without violence, like a runaway slave going over to them of his own accord and a horse going back to them, have no legal basis. The reason is that there is no middle ground between saying that the disbelievers can own Muslim property and saying that they can not, unless this is proved through a transmitted evidence. The proponents of this opinion, however, made this distinction on the basis of the tradition of al-Ḥasan ibn ʿUmāra from ʿAbd al-Malik ibn Maysara from Ṭāwūs from Ibn ʿAbbās "that a man found his camel that had been taken away by the polytheists. The Messenger of Allāh (God's peace and blessings be upon him) said to him, 'If you came upon it before the division (of the spoils) it belongs to you, but if you came upon it after the division you have to pay its value'". Al-Ḥasan ibn ʿUmāra is by agreement a weak narrator and reliance is not placed upon his narration for argument by the traditionists. What Mālik had recourse to in this, as far as I know, is the decision of ʿUmar on the issue, but he did not rule that he should pay its price if he took it back after the division, judging on the basis of the apparent meaning of his tradition.

The exemption made by Abū Ḥanīfa in the case of an *umm al-walad*[336] and a *mudabbar*[337] out of all kinds of wealth is meaningless. This is so as he ruled that the disbelievers come to own all other kinds of wealth in the face of the

[336] A slave who bears a child of her master.

[337] A slave who becomes free upon the death of the master.

rights of the Muslims, except these two types. Likewise, Mālik's opinion requiring the *imām* to pay the ransom for the *umm al-walad* if her owner finds her after the division. If her master does not do so her master is to be compelled to pay the ransom, and if he does not have the money she is to be handed over to him and the person from whose share she has been taken out of is to pursue him (the owner) for her value, which is considered a loan until his condition improves. This too is an opinion for which there is no basis in analogy. If the disbelievers did not own her he has the right to take her back without paying the price, but if they did come to own her he has no claim upon her. Further, there is no difference between her and the remaining types of property unless a transmitted evidence were to establish this.

Under this principle, I mean, their dispute over whether the polytheist can come to own the property of Muslims, is the disagreement of the jurists about a disbeliever who converts to Islam and has in his possession the wealth of Muslims, whether his ownership is valid. Mālik and Abū Ḥanīfa said that it is validly owned by him, while al-Shāfiʿī, abiding by his principle, said it is not. Mālik and Abū Ḥanīfa disagree when a Muslim goes over to the side of the disbelievers by way of stealth and brings over property from their possession that belonged to Muslims. Abū Ḥanīfa said that he has a right to this property. If the original owner wants it back, he has to purchase it by paying the price. Mālik said that it belongs to the original owner, and here he did not maintain his principle.

Relevant to this topic is also their disagreement about a warring enemy who converts to Islam and migrates leaving behind in the *dār al-ḥarb* his children, his wife, and his wealth, whether there would be for what he left behind the same sanctity that is applied to the wealth of a Muslim, his wife and children, so that the Muslims cannot acquire them as spoils if they come to have dominion over them. Some of them said that all that he left behind has the protection of Islam, while others said that there is no sanctity whatsoever. Some of them made a distinction between his wealth, on the one hand, and his wife and children, on the other, saying that his wealth has no protection, but his children and wife stand protected. This runs contrary to analogy, and is the opinion of Mālik. The principle is that permissibility (absence of sanctity) of wealth arises because of disbelief, and the cause of sanctity is Islam. The Prophet (God's peace and blessings be upon him) said, "And when they pronounce it (the *shahāda*) their blood and wealth stand protected from me". This is an evidence against those who thought that there are factors other than Islam that make wealth permissible, like ownership by the enemy or other factors. Those making this claim need to adduce some evidence, and the fact is that there is no evidence on the basis of which they can oppose this principle, Allāh knows best.

10.2.5. *Section 5: The* ḥukm *of land conquered by the Muslims by the use of force* (ʿanwatan)

They disagreed about the land that is conquered by the Muslims by the use of force. Mālik said that the land is not to be divided and stays as a trust (*waqf*) with its *kharāj* (revenue) being spent for the interest of the Muslims, like the maintenance of those engaged in the defence of Islam, the construction of bridges and mosques, as well as other avenues of welfare. This is the case, unless the *imām* is at some time of the opinion that *maṣlaḥa* requires it to be divided, in which case he may do so. Al-Shāfiʿī said that conquered lands are to be divided like spoils, that is, into five parts. Abū Ḥanīfa said that the *imām* has a choice of dividing it or imposing *kharāj* on its disbelieving tenants leaving it in their possession.

The reason for their disagreement springs from what is thought to be a conflict between the verse of *sūrat al-Anfāl* and the verse of *sūrat al-Ḥashr.* This is so as the verse of *sūrat al-Anfāl* implies through its apparent meaning that anything acquired as spoils is to be divided, and these are the words of the Exalted, "And know that whatever ye take as spoils of war, lo! a fifth thereof is for Allāh, and for the messenger".[338] On the other hand, the words of the Exalted in the verse of *al-Ḥashr*, "And those who came after them say; Our Lord! Forgive us and our brethren who were before us in the faith, and place not any rancour toward those who believe",[339] when read in conjunction with the case of those to whom *fayʾ* (booty) was granted may indicate that all people, those present and the posterity, are partners in the *fayʾ*. It is related from ʿUmar (God be pleased with him) that he commented on the words of the Exalted, "And those who came after them say; Our Lord! Forgive us . . .", saying, "I do not think that this verse does anything but make it (the land) common for all the people, even for the shepherd at Kadāʾ", or words to that effect. He, therefore, did not divide up the lands of Irāq and Egypt that were conquered in his time by force of arms.

Those who maintained that both verses have been laid down in the same context and that the verse of *al-Ḥashr* restricts the verse of *al-Anfāl* exempted land from it. Those who maintained that the verses have not been laid down in the same context, but the verse of *al-Anfāl* is for spoils and the verse of *al-Ḥashr* is about *fayʾ* (booty) as is apparent from the context said that the land is to be divided up, and this is a must, especially when it has been established that the Prophet (God's peace and blessings be upon him) divided the land of Khaybar among the warriors. They asserted that it is necessary that the land be divided on the basis of the general implication of the words of the Book and

[338] Qurʾān 8 : 41.
[339] 59 : 10.

the acts of the Prophet (God's peace and blessings be upon him), which constitute, over and above the general implication, an elaboration of the unelaborated meanings.

Abū Ḥanīfa, on the other hand, upheld a choice between division and leaving the disbelievers in possession of it in lieu of *kharāj* that they would pay, because of his belief in the report "that the Messenger of Allāh (God's peace and blessings be upon him) gave out Khaybar for part of the produce, and later he sent Ibn Rawāḥa, who divided it up". They (the Ḥanafites) said that it appears from this that the Messenger of Allāh (God's peace and blessings be upon him) did not divide up all of the land, rather he divided up a segment of the land and left a segment undivided. It is therefore clear, they said, that the *imām* has a choice between dividing it up and leaving it in the hands of the disbelievers. This is what ʿUmar (God be pleased with him) did. If they convert to Islam after the conquest the *imām* has a choice of granting it to them or dividing it up as the Messenger of Allāh (God's peace and blessings be upon him) did in Mecca, that is, he granted it to them. This, however, can be used as an evidence in this context in accordance with the opinion of those who believe that Mecca was conquered by force. The authorities, however, disagree about this, though the correct view is that it was conquered by force, for that is what is related by Muslim.

It is necessary to know that the opinion of those who maintained that the verse of *fayʾ* and the verse of *ghanīma* are to be construed to convey a choice, and that the verse of *fayʾ* has abrogated the verse of *ghanīma*, or that it has restricted it, is a very weak opinion, unless the terms *fayʾ* and *ghanīma* carry the same meaning. If that is the case, then, the two verses conflict, as the verse of *al-Anfāl* imposes a division into five parts, while the verse of *al-Ḥashr* implies an unrestricted division, not limited to five parts. Thus, it becomes necessary that one of them is considered as abrogating the other, or that the *imām* be granted a choice between dividing into five parts or making a general distribution, and this would be for all the wealth acquired as spoils (land or other). Some of the learned have related that this is the opinion of some jurists, and I believe it is related from the School (Mālik's).

It is necessary for those who hold the opinion based upon a reconciliation between the two verses, deriving from it that land acquired as part of the spoils should be kept intact, undivided, but division should apply to whatever is besides land, to maintain that each of the two verses excludes part of what is in the other verse, or abrogates it. Thus, the verse of *al-Anfāl* excludes from the general implication of the verse of *al-Ḥashr* what is besides land imposing five-fold division in it, while the verse of *al-Ḥashr* excludes land from the verse of *al-Anfāl* so that the five-fold division is not carried out in it. This claim, however, is not valid in the absence of an evidence, along with the fact that the verse of *al-Ḥashr* apparently includes items of a kind that carry a different *ḥukm* from those that are included in the verse of *al-Anfāl.* This is so as the words of the Exalted, "And that which Allāh gave as spoil unto His messenger from them, ye urged not any horse or riding camel for the sake thereof, but Allāh giveth His messenger lordship over whom he please",[340] indicate the underlying cause for denying the army an exclusive entitlement to the exclusion of the people. Division (into five parts) is the opposite of this, as it applies to spoils acquired through "urging".

10.2.6. *Section 6: The division of* fayʾ *(booty)*

Fayʾ according to the majority of the jurists is all that moves from the possession of the disbelievers to that of the Muslims, because of intimidation and fear, without their having "urged any horse or soldier". The jurists disagreed about the avenues of its expenditure. A group of jurists said that *fayʾ* is for all Muslims, poor or rich, and the *imām* has the right to give from it to the fighters, to the administrators and governors, and to spend it on the places of frequent use by the Muslims like the construction of bridges and maintenance of mosques and other things, and there is to be no five-fold division in it. This was upheld by the majority, and it is established from Abū Bakr and ʿUmar. Al-Shāfiʿī said that there is *khumus* (one-fifth) in it, and this fifth is subdivided among the categories that have been mentioned in the verse of spoils. These are the same categories that have been mentioned for the division of the fifth of spoils (*ghanīma*). The remainder, he said, is to be spent in accordance with the *ijtihād* of the *imām*, and he may spend part of it upon himself and his family, and on whoever he deems rightly entitled. I think one group of jurists said that *fayʾ* is not subject to five-fold division and that it is to be divided among the five categories among whom the *khumus* is distributed. As far as I know, it is also one opinion of al-Shāfiʿī.

The reason for disagreement among those who maintained that all of it is to be divided among the five categories and those who said that it is to be spent according to the *ijtihād* of the *imām* arises from the same dispute as in the division of the *khumus* from the spoils, and this has already been discussed. I mean, those who considered the mentioning of the categories as an indication of some of those who have an entitlement to it said that it is for these categories as well as for others, while those who considered the mentioning of the categories as fixing the number of those who have an entitlement said that the expenditure is not to be extended beyond these categories, that is, they

[340] Qurʾān 59 : 6.

considered this to be a category of restriction (to these categories) and not an indication of their significance.

Taking a fifth out of *fayʾ* has not been maintained by anyone before al-Shāfiʿī, and he was led to this opinion because he held that in this verse it was *fayʾ* that was divided into the five categories among whom *khumus* is divided. He therefore believed that a fifth is to be taken from it, because he thought that this division is specific to the *khumus*, but this is not apparent. What is apparent is that this division is specific to the entire *fayʾ* not to a fifth of it, and that, as far as I know, was upheld by a group of jurists.

Muslim has recorded from ʿUmar that he said, "The wealth of Banū al-Naḍīr was bestowed by Allāh as *fayʾ* on his Messenger, and it was something for which the Muslims had not urged a horse or a riding camel. It was for the Prophet (God's peace and blessings be upon him) exclusively, and he spent from it on his family as maintenance for a year, and what was left he spent on horses and weapons in the way of Allāh". This supports Mālik's opinion.

10.2.7. *Section 7: Discussion of* jizya *(poll tax)*

A comprehensive discussion of the principles of this section is covered in six issues. The first is about the person from whom it is permissible to take *jizya*. The second is about the categories of people who are liable for *jizya*. The third is about the amount imposed. The fourth is about the time it is due and when it is waived. The fifth is about the types of *jizya*. The sixth is about the avenues of expenditure of *jizya*.

10.2.7.1. Issue 1

From who is it permissible to take *jizya*? The jurists agree unanimously that it is permissible to take it from the non-Arab People of the Book, and from the Magians, as has been mentioned. They disagreed about those who have no scripture, and about those who are the People of the Book but are Arabs, and this after they had agreed that it is not permissible to take it from a *Kitābī* who is from the tribe of Quraysh. The discussion of this issue has preceded.

10.2.7.2. Issue 2

This issue deals with the categories of people who are liable for it. They agreed that it is imposed on those who exhibit three characteristics: being a male, *bulūgh* [attainment of puberty], and being free. It is not imposed upon women or upon minors insofar as it is a substitute for being subject to slaughter, and slaying, by command, is directed at males who have attained puberty, and the slaying of women and minors is prohibited. Likewise, they agreed that it is not imposed upon slaves. They disagreed about some categories of such persons (i.e. those who are liable) including the insane and the crippled, the aged, and the monks, and the poor, whether they are to be considered as being liable for it when their condition improves. All these cases are a matter of *ijtihād* and there is no [specific] determination for them in the law. The reason for their disagreement arises their dispute about whether such a person can be lawfully slain (in war), that is, out of these types of persons.

10.2.7.3. Issue 3

What is the [annual] amount due? They disagreed over this. Mālik held that the amount due in this is what was imposed by ʿUmar (God be pleased with him), and this was four *dīnārs* for those who transact in gold and forty *dirhams* for those who transact in silver, along with provisions for Muslims and hosting them for three days, and is not to exceed this or to be less than this. Al-Shāfiʿī said that the minimum is fixed and it is one *dīnār* and the maximum is not fixed but depends on what they negotiate to pay. A group of jurists said that there is no determination in this and it is left to the *ijtihād* of the *imām*. This was maintained by al-Thawrī. Abū Ḥanīfa and his disciples said that *jizya* ranges between twelve *dirhams*, twenty-four *dirhams*, and forty-eight *dirhams*. The poor person is not to pay less than twelve *dirhams* and the rich person is not to pay more than forty-eight *dirhams*. The person of average means is to pay twenty-four *dirhams*. Aḥmad said that one *dīnār* or its equivalent in woven cloth (Yemeni), and it is neither to be increased nor decreased.

The reason for their disagreement springs from the variation in the traditions on the topic. It is related "that the Messenger of Allāh (God's peace and blessings be upon him) sent Muʿādh to Yemen and ordered him to take from every person over the age of puberty one *dīnār* or its equivalent in *muʿāfir*", which is cloth from Yemen. It is established from ʿUmar that he imposed *jizya* on those who transact in gold at (the rate of) four *dīnārs*, and on those who transact in silver at (the rate of) forty *dirhams* along with provisions for the Muslims and hosting them for three days. It is also related from him that he sent ʿUthmān ibn Ḥanīf and he imposed *jizya* on the residents of the *sawād* lands at the rates of forty-eight, twenty-four, and twelve (*dirhams*).

Those who interpreted all these traditions as granting a choice and adopted the general implication of the term *jizya*, as there is no tradition from the Prophet (God's peace and blessings be upon him) about its determination that is agreed upon for its authenticity, and the Book has mentioned it in general terms, said that there is no determination in this, and this appears to be the more obvious rule, Allāh knows best. Those who reconciled the tradition of Muʿādh and what is established from ʿUmar said that the minimum is fixed and there is no limit for the maximum. Those who preferred one of the traditions of ʿUmar either maintained that it is forty *dirhams* or four *dīnārs* or they held it to be forty-eight *dirhams*, twenty-four *dirhams*, and twelve *dirhams*, as has been mentioned. Those who preferred the tradition of Muʿādh, as it is *marfūʿ* (traced back to the Prophet) said that it is one *dīnār* or its equivalent in woven cloth (Yemeni) and is not to be increased beyond this nor is it to be decreased.

10.2.7.4. Issue 4

When is *jizya* due? They agreed that it does not become due except after the passage of one year, and it is to be waived for a person if he converts to Islam within the year. They disagreed over the case of one who converts after the passage of one year, whether he is to be charged *jizya* for the entire previous period of one year or for the portion that has passed. A group of jurists said that if he converts there is no *jizya* for him, whether the conversion was before the passage of the period or after it. This opinion was upheld by the majority of the jurists. One group of jurists said that if he converts after the passage of one year he is liable for *jizya*, but if he converts before the completion of the period of one year it is not imposed upon him.

They agreed that *jizya* does not become due before the passage of a year, as the *ḥawl* is a condition for its obligation, and if a cause for waiver is found, which is conversion to Islam, before the obligation is incurred, that is, before the existence of the condition of obligation, it is not to be imposed. They disagreed about the case after the passage of the *ḥawl*, for then it has become due. Those who maintained that Islam demolishes this obligation, just as it demolishes many other obligations, said that the liability against him is dropped even if his embracing of Islam occurs after the passage of the *ḥawl*. Those who said that embracing Islam does not demolish this obligation, just as it does not demolish many other claims like debts and other similar things, said that the liability is not dropped after the passage of the year. The reason for their disagreement stems from whether Islam eradicates the *jizya* that has become due.

10.2.7.5. Issue 5

What are the different types of *jizya*? *Jizya* in their view is of three types. The first is *jizya* resulting from conquest by force, and this is what we have discussed, that is, one that is imposed upon the warring enemy after they have been overpowered. The second type is *jizya* resulting from a negotiated settlement, and this is what they voluntary offer so that the Muslims may stay their hand against them. There is no fixing of amount in this type of *jizya*, neither in the obligation, nor with respect to the person on whom it is obligatory, nor in the time at which it becomes due. All these matters are dependent upon the agreement concluded between the Muslims and those opting for a peaceful settlement, unless someone were to say: "If the acceptance of the negotiated *jizya* is obligatory upon the Muslims it is necessary that there be for it some determined amount. When the disbelievers are paying it of their own accord and acceptance is binding upon the Muslims, there should be a fixed minimum and an undetermined maximum amount". The third type of *jizya* is related to *ʿushr*. The majority of the jurists maintain that there is no liability for *ʿushr* upon the *ahl al-dhimma* nor any liability for *zakāt* on their wealth, except what is related from one group among the jurists that the *ṣadaqa* required from the Christians of Banū Taghlab was doubled, that is, they were obliged to pay the double of what was imposed upon the Muslims, for each category of items on which *ṣadaqa* (*zakāt*) is charged from the Muslims. Those who held this opinion include al-Shāfiʿī, Abū Ḥanīfa, Aḥmad, and al-Thawrī, and it is also the decision of ʿUmar (God be pleased with him) in their case. There is no recorded statement from Mālik on this, in what they have related from him. All this has preceded in the Book of *Zakāt*.

They disagreed over whether *ʿushr* is to be imposed on them for the goods they trade in the land of the Muslims, and whether this becomes due automatically by the very act of trading—or through permission if they are warring enemies—or that this does not apply except through a stipulated condition. Mālik and many of the jurists held that in the case of traders from amongst the *ahl al-dhimma*, who enjoy peaceful stay in their own land on the payment of *jizya*, *ʿushr* must be charged to them on the goods freely traded all over the land, but only one-half of *ʿushr* on those goods that they send to a particular city. Abū Ḥanīfa agreed with him on the question of the imposition of the *ʿushr* by virtue of trade with permission or trade itself, but he differed with respect to the amount saying that their liability is for one-half of the *ʿushr*. Mālik did not stipulate for them the existence of a *niṣāb* nor the passage of a *ḥawl*, while Abū Ḥanīfa did stipulate for the obligation of one-half *ʿushr* the passage of a year and the same *niṣāb* that is laid down for the Muslims, and which is mentioned in the Book of *Zakāt*. Al-Shāfiʿī said that there is no obligation at all on them for *ʿushr*, nor for one-half *ʿushr*, because of trade, and there is nothing determined in this, except what is arrived at through a settlement or a condition. In this form the *jizya* based upon *ʿushr* becomes a type of negotiated *jizya*, and in conformity with the opinions of Mālik and Abū Ḥanīfa it becomes a third category of *jizya* that is not negotiated and is imposed upon individuals.

The reason for their disagreement is that there is no *sunna* on this from the Messenger of Allāh (God's peace and blessings be upon him) to which recourse can be had, but it is established that ʿUmar ibn al-Khaṭṭāb decided this for them. Those who maintained that this act of ʿUmar was based upon a precedent that he knew to be from the Messenger of Allāh (God's peace and blessings be upon him) held it to be their *sunna*, while those who maintained that this act of his was based upon a stipulation (between the parties), for had it been different from this he would have mentioned it, said that this is not binding on them, unless it is stipulated as a condition. Abū ʿUbayd has quoted in the *Kitāb al-Amwāl* one of the Companions of the Prophet (God's peace and blessings be upon him), whose name I do not remember at the moment, that it was said to him, "Why do you charge *ʿushr* from the polytheist Arabs?" He replied, "Because they used to charge *ʿushr* from us when we entered their territory". Al-Shāfiʿī said that the minimum that is to be stipulated in this is what was imposed by ʿUmar (God be pleased with him), and if they agree to more that is better. He said that the *ḥukm* of a *ḥarbī* if he enters upon *amān* is the *ḥukm* of the *dhimmī*.

10.2.7.6. Issue 6

On what is the *jizya* to be spent? They agreed that it is to be spent for the common interest of the Muslim without any limitations, as is the case with *fayʾ* according to the opinion of those who held that it is dependent upon the *ijtihād* of the *imām*, so much so that some of the jurists held that the term *fayʾ* is meant to apply to *jizya* in the verse of *fayʾ*. If that is the case, then, the revenue of the Muslims is of three types: *ṣadaqa*, *fayʾ*, and *ghanīma*.

This is sufficient for the discussion of the fundamentals of this book. Allāh is the Grantor of guidance against error.

XI

THE BOOK OF *AYMĀN* (OATHS)

This book is divided into two chapters. The first chapter is about the types of oaths and their *aḥkām*. The second is about the identification of things that remit binding oaths, and about their *aḥkām*.

11.1. Chapter 1 Types of Oaths (*Aymān*) and their *Aḥkām*

This chapter contains three sections. The first section is about permissible oaths and their distinction from those that are not permissible. The second is about the identification of ineffectual and effective oaths. The third is about oaths that are remitted by expiation and those that are not.

11.1.1. *Section 1: The identification of permissible oaths*

The majority of the jurists agreed that certain things can be objects of oaths in the law, while others cannot. They disagreed as to what things have these characteristics. One group of jurists said that swearing of an oath permissible in law is one sworn in the name of Allāh, and that the person swearing an oath by something other than Allāh is a sinner. Another group of jurists said that it is permitted to swear an oath naming anything that is venerated in the law (*sharʿ*). Those who maintained that permissible oaths are only those that are sworn in the name of Allāh, agreed about the permissibility of oaths sworn taking His (other) names, but they disagreed about oaths sworn naming His attributes and His acts.

The reason for their disagreement about an oath sworn taking a name beside Allāh's, but of a thing venerated in the law stems from the conflict between the apparent meaning of the (relevant words of the) Book and a tradition. This is so as Allāh has used oaths in the Book naming a number of things, as in His words, "By the heaven and the morning star"[341] and His words, "By the star

[341] Qurʾān 86 : 1.

when it setteth",[342] as well as other oaths occurring in the Qur'ān. It is established, however, that the Prophet (God's peace and blessings be upon him) said, "Allāh has prohibited you from swearing oaths in the names of your fathers, so he who has to take an oath should do so in the name of Allāh or remain silent". Those who reconciled the (meaning in the) Book and the tradition maintained that in the things mentioned in the Book the object of the oath is implied (though omitted in the text), and it is (the name of) Allāh, the Glorious and Exalted, therefore, the implied reading is, "the Lord of the star" or the "the Lord of the heaven". Thus, they said that permissible oaths are those that are sworn in the name of Allāh alone. Those who reconciled between them maintained that the purpose of the tradition is that the things not venerated by the law are not to be venerated, on the evidence of his (the Prophet's) saying, which includes the words, "Allāh has prohibited you from swearing oaths in the names of your fathers". They said that this is from the category of the specific by which a general meaning is implied. Thus, they permitted an oath in the name of anything venerated by the law. The reason for disagreement, then, springs from their dispute about the construction of the verse and the tradition.

The opinion of those who prohibited the swearing of oaths by taking the name of Allāh's attributes or by His acts is weak. The reason for the disagreement is whether to restrict the interpretation to the tradition by attaching the *ḥukm* with the name (of Allāh) alone or to extend it to apply to His attributes and acts as well. There is extreme rigidity in attaching the *ḥukm* to the name (of Allāh) alone, and it is similar to the attitude of the Ẓāhirites, though it was related from the School (Mālik's) as narrated by al-Lakhmī from Muḥammad ibn al-Mawwāz.

One group of jurists deviated (from all this) and prohibited an oath in the name of Allāh, the Majestic, but the tradition is explicit in opposition to this opinion.

11.1.2. *Section 2: Identification of ineffectual and effective oaths*

They agreed also that some of the oaths are ineffectual and some are effective, because of the words of the Exalted, "Allāh will not take you to task for that which is unintentional (*laghw*) in your oaths, but He will take you to task for the oaths that ye swear in earnest".[343] They disagreed about what is *laghw*. Mālik and Abū Ḥanīfa maintained that it is an oath that is sworn by naming a thing which the person swearing believes to be true, but it turns out to be the

[342] Qur'ān 53 : 1.
[343] Qur'ān 5 : 89.

opposite of what he swore the oath for. Al-Shāfiʿī said that a *laghw* oath is one in which the intention cannot be associated with the object, like the habit of a person saying in every day speech of saying, " o by Allāh, No by Allāh" which is something that is uttered by habit without believing it to be binding. This interpretation has been related by Mālik in *al-Muwaṭṭa*ʾ from ʿĀʾisha. The first interpretation is related from al-Ḥasan ibn Abī al-Ḥasan, Qatāda, Mujāhid, and Ibrāhīm al-Nakhaʿī. There is a third interpretation (of the *laghw*) oath, namely, that a person swears an oath when he is angry. This was maintained by Ismāʿīl al-Qāḍī, the disciple of Mālik. The fourth interpretation is that it is an oath sworn to undertake an unlawful act, and this is related from Ibn ʿAbbās. There is also a fifth interpretation that it is the case of a man swearing an oath not to eat a thing that is permitted to him by law.

The reason for their disagreement arises from the equivocality that is found in the term *laghw*. This is so as *laghw* sometimes means an invalid statement, as in the words of the Exalted, "Those who disbelieve say: Heed not this Qurʾān, and drown the hearing of it [i.e. deem it invalid]; haply ye may conquer",[344] and it sometimes means speech with which the intention of the speaker cannot be associated. The use of *laghw* in the verse indicates this meaning, which is the opposite of an oath that is effective, that is, confirmed, and it is necessary that the *ḥukm* of an opposite be an opposite (*ḥukm*). Those who maintained that *laghw* indicates the swearing of an oath to which the law does not attach any consequences, held, in accordance with this belief, that *laghw* here indicates a meaning that has technical usage in the law, and this relates to oaths about which the law has made clear, on a number of other occasions, that their *ḥukm* is to be dropped, as in the report "There is no divorce under duress", as well as in other cases. The more obvious meanings, however, are as in the first two opinions, that is, Mālik's and al-Shāfiʿī's.

11.1.3. *Section 3: Identification of oaths remitted by expiation*

In this section there are four issues.

11.1.3.1. Issue 1

They disagreed about effective oaths sworn in the name of Allāh whether they are remitted by expiation, irrespective of their being oaths sworn for a thing that was supposed to exist in the past, but actually did not, and this is known as the *yamīn ghamūs*, because the person lied intentionally, or for a thing that was to occur in the future on the initiative of the person swearing the oath or on the initiative of another under his influence and it does not happen. The

[344] Qurʾān 41 : 26.

majority of the jurists said that there is no expiation (*kaffāra*) for the *yamīn ghamūs*, and expiation operates for oaths pertaining to the future when the person swearing goes against the oath. Those who held this opinion include Mālik, Abū Ḥanīfa, and Aḥmad ibn Ḥanbal. Al-Shāfiʿī and a group of jurists maintained that expiation operates in it, that is, it remits the sin associated with it as it does for oaths other than the *ghamūs*.

The reason for their disagreement stems from the conflict between the general implication (of a verse) of the Book and a tradition. The words of the Exalted, "Allāh will not take you to task for that which is unintentional [*laghw*] in your oaths, but He will take you to task for the oaths that ye swear in earnest. The expiation thereof is the feeding of ten of the needy",[354] in the verse imply that there be an expiation in the case of the *yamīn ghamūs* as it is an effective oath. The words of the Prophet (God's peace and blessings be upon him), "Allāh has prohibited *janna* for the person who severed the right of a Muslim with his oath, and has made the Fire his due" imply that there is no expiation in the *yamīn ghamūs*. Al-Shāfiʿī, however, excludes the *yamīn ghamūs* from the oaths that do not destroy the right of another, and these are oaths mentioned in the text, or he says that the oaths destroying the rights of others combine the two factors of injustice and violation of the oath. Expiation, therefore, should not be able to obliterate both of them, or that it is not possible that is should to do away with violation without involving injustice, as remittance of violation through expiation is a kind of repentance, and repentance cannot be split up for the same single sin. If he repents, remedies the injustice, and makes the expiation then the entire sin is remitted.

11.1.3.2. Issue 2

The jurists disagreed about the (case of the person) who says, "I do not believe in Allāh," or "I associate others with Allāh", or "I am a Jew", or "I am a Christian, if I commit such and such act", whether there is expiation for him. Mālik and al-Shāfiʿī said that there is no expiation for him nor is this an oath. Abū Ḥanīfa said that this is an oath and he is liable for expiation if he acts contrary to the oath. This is also the opinion of Aḥmad ibn Ḥanbal.

The reason for their disagreement emanates from their dispute over whether an oath is valid in the name of anything that has sanctity or whether it is not valid without the use of the name of Allāh. Further, does it become effective if sworn? Those who maintained that effective oaths (with legal effects), that is, those pronounced employing the forms of an oath, are the ones sworn in the name of Allāh, the Glorious and Exalted, or by using His other names, said that there is no expiation in it (the oath in question) as it does not amount to

[345] Qurʾān 5 : 89.

an oath. Those who maintained that oaths become effective through all things whose sanctity is held in high esteem by the law said that there is expiation in this oath. The reason is that an oath for holding something in esteem is the same as an oath relinquishing the veneration, and because these things must be held in esteem it follows that their esteem is not to be negated. Thus, as the person who swears an oath about his owing a right of Allāh is bound by it, likewise, the person who swears to negate a due right is bound by it.

11.1.3.3. Issue 3

The jurists agreed about oaths that are not sworn by naming anything but are intended to be binding on the basis of a stipulated condition—like a person saying, "If I do such and such thing I am bound to walk up to the House of Allāh", or "If I do such and such thing my slave is free, or my wife stands divorced"—that they are binding in the case of an undertaking to worship, and also in what is binding by the law, like divorce and manumission. They disagreed over whether there is expiation for such oaths. Mālik held that there is no expiation in such oaths, and if he does not do what he undertook to do he has sinned without doubt. Al-Shāfiʿī, Aḥmad, Abū ʿUbayd, and others held that in this category of oaths there is expiation, except for divorce and manumission. Abū Thawr said that the person who took an oath of manumission must offer expiation. The opinion of al-Shāfiʿī is related from ʿĀʾisha.

The reason for their disagreement comes from whether this is an oath or a vow (***nadhr***). Those who said that it is an oath made expiation obligatory as it falls within the general implication of the words of the Exalted, "The expiation thereof is the feeding of ten of the needy".[346] Those who maintained that it is from the category of vows, that is, a category of things about which the law has stated that if a person imposes them on himself he becomes bound by them, said that there is no expiation in them. This, however, becomes difficult for the Mālikites for they designate these as oaths, but it is possible that they called them oaths in the figurative and wider sense. The truth, however, is that it is not necessary to call them oaths on the basis of the literal connotation, as oath in the usage of the Arabs has specific forms. Oaths are constituted by naming things that are venerated and the forms for stipulating conditions are not the forms for an oath. With respect to whether they have been designated oaths through legal usage and whether their ***ḥukm*** is the same as that for oaths, is a matter of investigation. This is so as it is established that the Prophet (God's peace and blessings be upon him) said, "The expiation of a vow is the expiation of an oath". The Exalted has said, "O Prophet! Why bannest thou

[346] Qurʾān 5 : 89.

that which Allāh hath made lawful for thee, seeking to please thy wives? And Allāh is Forgiving Merciful. Allāh hath made lawful for you (Muslims) absolution from your oaths (of such a kind), and Allāh is your Protector. He is the Knower, the Wise".[347] The apparent meaning of this is that in terms of the law a statement that was intended to be binding, without any stipulation or an oath, was called an oath. It is, therefore, necessary to construe all statement that run parallel to this as oaths, except those that have been specifically excluded by consensus from these, like divorce. The apparent meaning of the tradition conveys that a vow is not an oath, but its *ḥukm* is the same as that of an oath. Dāwūd and the Ẓāhirites held that such statements are not binding, that is, those expressed with a stipulation, except for those that have been deemed binding by consensus. The reason is that these are not vows so that they may be binding, nor are they oaths so that expiation may remit them. They, therefore, did not make it obligatory for the person who says "If I do such and such thing I am bound to walk up to the House of Allāh", either walk up to the House of Allāh or expiate. This is unlike the statement, "I am under an obligation to walk to the House of Allāh", for this is a vow by agreement. The Prophet (God's peace and blessings be upon him) has said, "One who vows to obey Allāh should obey Him, and one who vows to disobey Him should not disobey Him".

The reason for disagreement about statements that are expressed with a condition stems from whether these are considered oaths or vows, or whether they are considered neither oaths nor vows. Think over this so that it becomes evident, God willing.

11.1.3.4. Issue 4

They had three different opinions about the statement of a person who says, "I swear or I testify that if such and such happens . . ." as to whether it is an oath. It is said that it is not an oath. This is one of the two opinions of al-Shāfiʿī. It is said that it is an oath as opposed to the first opinion. This was held by Abū Ḥanīfa. It is said that if he intended to name Allāh it is an oath, but if he did not intend to name Allāh it is not an oath. This is Mālik's opinion.

The reason for the disagreement is what is to be taken into account: the form (style) of the words or the usual meaning or the intention. Those who gave consideration to the form of the words said that this is not an oath, as there is no mention of a name. Those who considered the form of words used in practice said that this is an oath, without doubt, with a word missing but implied, and that is the name of Allāh, the Exalted. Those who did not

[347] Qurʾān 66 : 1, 2.

consider these two factors and took intention into account, as the words could be valid for both cases, made a distinction in this as has been discussed.

11.2. Chapter 2 Remittance of Binding Oaths and their *Aḥkām*

This chapter is first divided into two parts. The first part is about exemptions. The second is about an examination of (the forms of) expiation.

11.2.1. Part 1: The Examination of Exemptions

There are two sections in this part. The first section is about the conditions that are effective in oaths. The second section is about the identification of oaths in which exemptions are operative and those in which they are not.

11.2.1.1. *Section 1: Conditions of exemptions effective in oaths*

They agreed that exemptions as a whole are effective in the absolution from oaths. They disagreed about the conditions of the exemptions for which such a *ḥukm* is operative, after they had agreed that there are three conditions for the effectiveness of the exemption: first, that it should accompany the oath; second, that it should be expressed; and third, that it should have the intention from the start that the oath will not be effective with the existence of the exemption. They disagreed on these three points, that is, if the exemption is separated from the oath, or when the person intends it but does not express it, or when he intends it to be an exemption later even when he pronounces it along with the oath.

11.2.1.1.1. Issue 1

This issue is about stipulating an exemption immediately after taking an oath. A group of jurists stipulated this condition, and it is the opinion of Mālik. Al-Shāfiʿī said that there is no harm in a brief silence between one and the other, like the silence of a man thinking or taking his breath or clearing his throat. A group of the Tābiʿūn (Successors to the Companions) said that it is permitted to the person swearing an oath to stipulate the exemption (at any time) as long as he has not moved away from the session (of the oath). Ibn ʿAbbās used to say that he has the right to introduce an exemption always, whenever he remembers. All of them agreed that the introduction of an exemption as the will of Allāh (saying if God wills) in the subject matter of the oath with reference to his act, if it is an act, or his relinquishment, if it is relinquishment, would absolve him from the oath, as an exemption does away with the binding nature of the oath. Abū Bakr ibn al-Mundhir said, "It is established that the Messenger of Allāh (God's peace and blessings be upon him) said, 'The person who swears an oath and says, "If God wills", has not violated the oath'".

They disagreed over whether the exemption is effective in an oath if it is not pronounced immediately following the oath; this is because of their dispute over whether an exemption does away with the effectiveness of the oath or whether it prevents the oath from taking effect. If we maintain that it prevents it from taking effect and does not eliminate it later, we would stipulate that it should immediately follow the oath, but if we maintain that it eliminates it, it would not be binding to make this stipulation. Those who agreed that it eliminates the oath disagreed over whether it absolves one from the oath if made shortly after it or even if it is (expressed) much later, as we have recounted. Those who maintained that it eliminates the oath if it follows shortly after, argued on the basis of what is related by Saʿd from Sammāk ibn Ḥarb from ʿIkrima, who said, "The Messenger of Allāh (God's peace and blessings be upon him) said, 'I swear by Allāh that I shall certainly fight the Quraysh'. He repeated this three times and then became silent. He then said, 'If Allāh wills'". This indicates that the exemption does away with the oath and does not prevent it from taking effect. They said that one of the evidences that it does away with the oath if it follows shortly after it is that if it was enough for absolution even if expressed much later, as has been maintained by Ibn ʿAbbās, the exemption would have done away with the need for making expiation (*kaffāra*). What they have said is evident.

11.2.1.1.2. Issue 2[348]

They disagreed about expressing the exemption in words. It is said that the exemption must be made in words, whatever words are used for (expressing) exemptions, and whether they are the words of exemption or those of restricting the generality of the oath or those qualifying an absolute oath. This is the well-known view. It is said that exemption is also valid through intention, only when it is not expressed using the word *illā*, that is, what is indicated by the word *illā*, but it is not valid in the case of other words. This distinction is weak. The reason for this disagreement stems from whether binding contracts become binding by virtue of intention alone to the exclusion

[348] The original text does not consider this as a separate issue and has listed only two issues under this section. The author's discussion at the beginning of the section, however, requires that there be three separate issues. An extra heading has therefore been introduced.

of expressions, or by expressions and intention together, as in the case of divorce, manumission, oaths, and others.

11.2.1.1.3. Issue 3

This issue relates to whether the intention of making the exemption is effective if it comes after the making of the oath. It is said in the School that it is valid if it occurs along with the exemption, and it is said that in fact it is valid if it occurs before the completion of the expression of the oath. It is also said that exemptions are of two kinds: exemption from a number, and exemption from the general implication by restriction or through the qualification of an unqualified meaning. The exemption from a number is not valid if the intention does not occur before the expression of the oath. The exemption from the general implication is valid even after the expression of the oath, if the exemption immediately follows the expression of the oath.

The reason for their disagreement springs from whether the exemption prevents the oath from taking effect or revokes it. If we say that it prevents it from taking effect, then, the stipulation of (the formation of) intention at the beginning of the oath is necessary, but if we say that it revokes it there is no need to stipulate this. ʿAbd al-Wahhāb denied that the (formation of) intention is to be stipulated at the beginning of the (expression) of oath so as to coincide, and he believed that the exemption acts in the same way as expiation for absolution from the oath.

11.2.1.2. *Section 2: Identification of oaths in which exemptions are effective*

They disagreed about oaths in which the stipulation of the will of Allāh as an exemption is effective, as distinguished from those in which it is not. Mālik and his disciples maintained that (the stipulation of) the will of Allāh (as an exemption) is only operative in those oaths that can be atoned through expiation, and these, in their view, are oaths sworn in the name of Allāh, as well as absolute vows that will be discussed in what follows. The exemption may be stipulated only in unconditional divorce and manumission, like saying, "She will be divorced, God willing", or "he will be free, God willing", for these are not oaths in their view. A stipulation of a condition, however, with divorce, like saying, "If such and such thing happens she is divorced, God willing" or "if this happens, he is manumitted, God willing" may also be made. There is no dispute in the school that in the first case the stipulation of the will of Allāh is not effective; but in the second case, which is an oath to divorce, there are two views in the school. The sounder view is that if he relates the exemption to the condition on which the divorce is contingent it is valid, but if he relates it to the divorce itself it is not valid. Abū Ḥanīfa and al-

Shāfiʿī said that the exemption is effective in all these cases, whether he has linked to statement made as a stipulation or to the statement that is expressed as a report.

The reason for disagreement, as we have stated, comes from whether the exemption revokes the oath or prevents it from taking effect. If we say it prevents it from taking effect, and the exemption is associated with the expression of an unconditional divorce, it has no affect on it, since the divorce is effective, I mean, in the case where the man says to his wife that she is divorced, God willing; this is so because the prevention, for a future happening, operates as long as the divorce does not take place. If we maintain that it revokes the oath, it is necessary that it be effective in the divorce even if it occurs. Think over this, for it is evident. The opinion of the Mālikites, that an exemption here is improbable as the divorce has occurred, is meaningless unless they believed that the exemption prevents the oath from taking effect and does not revoke it. Ponder over this, for God willing, it will be evident.

11.2.2. **Part 2: The Examination of *Kaffārāt* (Forms of Expiation)**

This part has three sections dealing with the fundamentals. The first section is about the cause of violation of the oath, its conditions and *aḥkām*. The second section is about atonement for the violation, and these are the various forms of expiation. The third section is about the time for atonement and the amount that achieves it.

11.2.2.1. *Section 1: The cause of violation, its conditions, and* aḥkām

They agreed that the cause of violation is opposition to the object of the oath. This is either an act that the person swearing the oath was to avoid or it is the failure to do what he swore to do, knowing that he has delayed the commission of the sworn act to a time in which it is not possible for him to perform it. This occurs in the oath of unqualified relinquishment, like his saying that he would certainly eat a particular loaf, which is then eaten by someone else, or he may postpone the act till a time that is not the time that he stipulated for its fulfilment. This occurs in an act for which a limited time has been stipulated, like his saying, "By Allāh, I will perform such and such act today", and if the day is over and he has not done so he has certainly violated the oath.

They disagreed over this subject on four points. The first is when he (the person swearing the oath) does the opposite of what he swore to do, out of forgetfulness or under duress. The second is whether the object of the oath is related to the minimum to which its name applies or to the whole. The third point is whether the oath relates to a synonym of the word expressed in the oath or to its specific connotation, and whether it extends beyond it. The fourth point is whether the oath is construed in accordance with the intention of the person swearing it or the intention of the person for whom it is sworn.

11.2.2.1.1. Issue 1

Mālik maintained that the person forgetting, and the person coerced, have the same status as the person acting intentionally, while al-Shāfiʿī maintained that there is no liability for violation for the person forgetting or for one coerced. The reason for their disagreement stems from the conflict of the general implication of the words of the Exalted, "But He will take you to task for the oaths that ye swear",[349] where no distinction has been made between a person acting intentionally or one forgetting, and between the general implication of the saying of the Prophet (God's peace and blessings be upon him), "Liability for forgetfulness and what they have been coerced to do has been lifted from my ***umma***". It is quite possible that these two general implications restrict each other.

11.2.2.1.2. Issue 2

This is the case of a person who swears that he would not perform a certain act, and then does part of it, or that he would perform an act but does not perform part of it. In Mālik's view if he said, "I will certainly eat this loaf", and then eats part of it he is not absolved unless he eats the whole of it, and if he said, "I will not eat this loaf", he violates the oath if he ate part of it. According to al-Shāfiʿī and Abū Ḥanīfa he does not violate the oath in either case, on the basis that the word is applicable to part of its meaning. Mālik's distinction between the commission and omission in this is not based upon a single principle, as he adopted for omission the minimum to which the name applies and adopted in the commission the application of the name to the whole. It appears that he was being cautious.

11.2.2.1.3. Issue 3

This is the case where a person swears to perform a specific act, but the implied intention is understood as meaning something wider than the specified act, or it is understood as implying a narrower meaning, or he swears to perform an act but forms an intention for a wider, or for a narrower, implication, or that the act specified is referred to by two different terms one of them being literal and the other technical, where one of them is more

[349] Qurʾān 5 : 89.

restricted than the other. Now, if he swore to perform a specific act he does not violate the oath, in the view of al-Shāfiʿī and Abū Ḥanīfa, except by doing the opposite with respect to this act, which is the subject-matter of the oath, even when the implied meaning is wider or narrower in terms of the technical meaning. Likewise, insofar as I know, they do not take into account an intention contrary to the specified act, and they take into account the expressed words alone.

The well-known opinion from Mālik is that the primary consideration, in his view, is for intention, for oaths in which no decision is to be rendered on their basis against the person swearing the oath. If that (the intention) is missing the context is to be taken into account, and in its absence the technical meaning of the expressed words is considered, and when that is absent the literal meaning is taken into account. It is, however, said that consideration is to be given to intention alone or to the apparent meaning of the words. It is also said that only the intention and the obvious circumstances are to be taken into account and no consideration is to be given to the technical meaning. In oaths, on the basis of which a decision may be rendered for the deponent, if the deponent comes seeking a verdict, the ***ḥukm*** for the oath is that of the oath in which a decision is not to be rendered against the deponent (that is) with respect to the consideration given to these things in that order. If the oaths are those on the basis of which a decision is to be rendered against him (when he is not the plaintiff) nothing but the apparent meaning is to be taken into account, unless there is corroborating evidence in the accompanying circumstances or in the technical meaning, for an intention contravening the apparent implication, which he claims to have formed.

11.2.2.1.4. Issue 4

They agreed that in claims (litigation) oaths are to be construed in conformity with the intention of the person seeking the oath (the opponent). They disagreed about other cases, like oaths in the case of promises, with a group of jurists saying that they are construed according to the intention of the deponent, and another group saying that they are construed in accordance with the intention of the person seeking the oath. It is established that the Messenger of Allāh (God's peace and blessings be upon him) said, "The oath is to conform to the intention of the person seeking the oath", and he (God's peace and blessings be upon him) also said, "Your oath is for what your companion will attest (as being the truth from you)". These two traditions have been recorded by Muslim. Those who maintained that the (construction of the) oath is dependent upon the intention of the deponent took into account the meaning assigned to the oath itself in the mind (of the deponent) and not the apparent meaning arising from the words.

In this topic there are a number of individual cases, but these four issues serve as the principles of the topic, as all the disagreement occurring in the topic can be referred back to them. For example, their disagreement about the case of the person who swears that he will not eat heads and then eats heads of whales, whether he has violated the oath. Those who took into account the technical meaning said that he has not, while those who took into account the connotations of the words said he has. Another example is that of the person who says that he will not eat meat and then eats fat. Those who considered the literal meaning of the word said that he has not violated the oath, while those who gave weight to the metaphorical meanings said that he has violated the oath.

Their disagreement, on the whole, in individual cases that fall under this heading refers to their disagreement over the four issues that we have mentioned, and also refers to their disagreement about the meanings of words used in the oath, as some of these are imprecise (*mujmal*), some apparent (for one out of several meanings), and some are unequivocal.

11.2.2.2. *Section 2: The remittance of violation*

They agreed that expiation for an oath has four forms that have been laid down by Allāh in His Book, in the words of the Exalted, "The expiation thereof is the feeding of ten of the needy with the average of that wherewith ye feed your own folk, or the clothing of them, or the liberation of a slave, and for him who findeth not (the wherewithal to do so) then a three days' fast".[350] The majority maintain that if the person swearing the oath violates it he has a choice between three of them, that is, feeding, clothing, and manumission, and that it is not permitted to him to fast unless he is unable to undertake (any of) these three, because of the words of the Exalted, "And for him who findeth not (the wherewithal to do so) then a three days' fast".[351] It is, however, related from Ibn ʿUmar that when the oath was for a solemn affair he used to set free a slave or provide clothing, and when it was not for something important he used to provide food.

They disagreed in this over seven well-known issues. The first issue is about the quantity of food to be given to each of the ten needy persons. The second is about the kind of clothing, when he chooses to provide it, and about the number (of garments). The third is about the stipulation of consecutive observance of the fasts of three days. The fourth is the stipulation of the number of the needy. The fifth is about the stipulation of being a Muslim and free as their qualifications. The sixth is about the stipulation of absence from

[350] Qurʾān 5 : 89.
[351] Qurʾān 5 : 89.

defects in the manumitted slave. The seventh is about the stipulation of belief (an Islam) for the slaves.

11.2.2.2.1. Issue 1

About the quantity of food, Mālik, al-Shāfiʿī, and the jurists of Medina said that each needy person is to be given one *mudd* of wheat in accordance with the *mudd* used by the Prophet (God's peace and blessings be upon him), except that Mālik said that the (restriction of one) *mudd* is specific to the people of Medina because of the restricted means of their livelihood, and all other cities are to base it upon the average quantity and quality of their food. Ibn al-Qāsim said that the *mudd* is to be used in each city, and this was the same as al-Shāfiʿī's opinion. Abū Ḥanīfa and his disciples maintained that they are to be given one-half *ṣāʿ* of wheat, or one *ṣāʿ* of barley or dried dates. They said that if he chooses to feed them lunch and dinner it is valid.

The reason for their disagreement over this stems from their dispute about the interpretation of the words of the Exalted, "The average of that wherewith ye feed your own folk",[352] whether it means one meal or the food of one day, which is lunch and dinner. Those who maintained that it is one meal said it is a *mudd* to satisfy the average appetite, while those who maintained that it is lunch as well as dinner said that it is one-half *ṣāʿ*. There is another reason for their dispute and that arises from the vacillation of this expiation between being the expiation of the intentional breaking of a fast during Ramaḍān and between the expiation for the elimination of an ailment (from the head during *ḥajj*). Those who held it to be similar to the expiation for breaking the fast said that it is one *mudd*, while those who held it to be similar to the expiation for removing an ailment said that it is one-half *ṣāʿ*.

They disagreed over whether there should be with bread something appetizing that is eaten with it (*idām*), and if it is to be there what is its quantity? It is said that plain bread is valid. Ibn Ḥabīb said that it is not valid. It is said that the average kind of *idām* is oil, while it is said that it is milk, butter, and dates.

Mālik's disciples differed about the people to whom average food has been attributed, in the words of the Exalted, "The average of that wherewith ye feed your own folk".[353] It is said that it is (the average for) the people of the person making the expiation, and on these grounds the average is to be worked out on the basis of the thing that forms his livelihood, if it is some sort of pulse, like peas, beans, or lentils, it is to be based upon it, and if it is wheat it is to be based upon wheat. It is also said that the average food is that of the

[352] Qurʾān 5 : 89.
[353] Qurʾān 5 : 89.

residents of the land in which he lives, and on this basis the consideration for what is due from him is given to the living standard of the land, generally, and not his own standard of living. On the basis of these two opinions the average quantity of food, that is "the average of that wherewith ye feed your own folk", is interpreted to be the average for his folk, or the average for the residents of the land of his folk, except in the specific case of Medina.

11.2.2.2.2. Issue 2

This issue is about the kind of clothing that is deemed sufficient. Mālik said that the obligation in this is to clothe them with garments in which prayer can be validly performed. Thus, if he gives men clothing comprising one garment and to women clothing comprising two garments covering their body and acting as a veil (it is valid). Al-Shāfiʿī and Abū Ḥanīfa said that the minimum to which the term is applied as being valid is a loincloth or shirt or trousers and a turban. Abū Yūsuf said that neither a turban nor trousers is valid. The reason for their disagreement stems from whether the obligation is to adopt the minimum literal implication or to adopt the technical meaning in the law.

11.2.2.2.3. Issue 3

This issue is about their disagreement over whether the observance of the fasts for three days is to be consecutive. Mālik and al-Shāfiʿī did not stipulate consecutive observance for this, though they considered it desirable, but Abū Ḥanīfa did stipulate it. There are two reasons for their disagreement over this. The first is whether it is permitted to act upon a variant reading that is not in the (popular and unanimously sound) *muṣḥaf*?[354] This is so as the reading of Ibn Masʿūd contains the words, "then three days of consecutive fasts". The second reason arises from their dispute over whether an unqualified command for fasting can be interpreted to mean consecutive fasting, as the principle in obligatory fasting prescribed by law is consecutive observance.

11.2.2.2.4. Issue 4

This is about the stipulation of the number of needy persons. Mālik and al-Shāfiʿī said that expiation is not valid for him unless he feeds ten (separate) needy persons. Abū Ḥanīfa said that it is valid if he feeds one needy person for ten days. The reason for their disagreement is whether there is in expiation a claim of the stated number of needy persons or whether it is a duty of the person making the expiation so that he may estimate the food for the number. If we say that it is a duty owed to a number like those in a bequest, then, it is necessary to stipulate the number, but if we say that it is the duty of the

[354] The written copy of the Qurʾān.

person making the expiation and if he estimated according to the number it is valid for him to feed one person with the amount required for the stated ten. The issue, however, is subject to interpretation.

11.2.2.2.5. Issue 5

The fourth issue is about the stipulation of being a Muslim and free (as qualifications) for the needy persons. Mālik and al-Shāfiʿī stipulated both conditions, but Abū Ḥanīfa did not. The reason for their disagreement arises from whether the entitlement to charity is on the basis of poverty alone, or because of Islam? The transmitted texts have indicated that there is reward for charity (not the *zakāt*) given to a poor person who is not a Muslim. Those who held expiation to be similar to *zakāt* and being obligatory for the Muslims stipulated that the alms of the expiation are to be given to a needy person who is a Muslim. Those who held it to be similar to voluntary alms permitted that it be given to non-Muslims.

The reason for their disagreement over the case of the slaves is whether need applies to them, as they are provided for by their masters in the usual cases, or whether they are to be counted amongst those who are to be provided for. Those who took into account poverty alone said that freemen and slaves are equal in this respect, for there could be slaves who are kept hungry by their masters. Those who upheld his obligatory right over others by law said that it is obligatory for the master to take care of his slaves, and this is to be enforced against him, and if he is hard up he is to be forced to sell his slave; therefore, the slaves are not in need of support from the alms of expiation and other similar alms.

11.2.2.2.6. Issue 6

Whether the slave (whose emancipation is an alternative form of expiation) is to be free from defects. The jurists of the provinces stipulated that freedom from defects is a condition as this influences the price. The Ẓāhirites said that this is not one of the conditions. The reason for their disagreement is whether it is necessary to adopt the minimum of what is implied by a noun or whether to apply it to the perfect form indicated by it.

11.2.2.2.7. Issue 7

This issue is about the stipulation of belief in Islam (as a qualification) for the slave. Mālik and al-Shāfiʿī stipulated this, while Abū Ḥanīfa permitted that the slave be a non-believer. The reason for their disagreement stems from whether an unqualified meaning is to be construed in the qualified sense for things that are similar with respect to the *aḥkām* although they have different causes, as in the case of this expiation in comparison with the expiation for imprecation (*ẓihār*). Those who maintained that the absolute is to be construed in its qualified meaning in this case stipulated belief in this by construing this through its stipulation in the case of the expiation of *ẓihār*, in the words of the Exalted, "Then (the penance) is to set free a believing slave".[355] Those who maintained that it is not to be qualified retained the implication of the word in its absolute meaning.[356]

11.2.2.3. *Section 3: The time for the remittance of the oath and its violation*

They disagreed about the time when the expiation remits the violation and erases its effect. Al-Shāfiʿī said that when he makes the expiation, whether he does so after the violation or before it, the sin is remitted. Abū Ḥanīfa said that the violation is not remitted except by the expiation that is made after the violation not before. Both opinions have been related from Mālik on the issue.

There are two reasons for their disagreement. The first is the variation in the narration of the saying of the Prophet (God's peace and blessings be upon him), "He who swears an oath [for doing something] and then sees something that is better than it he should do that which is better and make expiation for his oath". One group narrated it in this form, while another related it as, "He should make an expiation for his oath and do that which is better". The apparent meaning in the second narration is that expiation may be made before the violation, and the contrary meaning is found in the first version. The second reason arises from their dispute over whether the advancement of a duty before its due time is valid, as it is obvious that expiation becomes due after the violation, like (the payment of) *zakāt* becomes obligatory after the passage of a year. It may be said that expiation becomes due with the intention of violation and the determination to undertake it, as is the case in the expiation of *ẓihār*, therefore, no contradiction is found from this aspect.

The reason for disagreement by way of reasoning was whether expiation remits the sin after it occurs or it prevents it from taking effect. Those who said that it prevents it from taking effect permitted its advancement over the violation, while those who said that it remits it (after its occurrence) did not permit it, except after its occurrence.

[355] Qurʾān 4 : 92. This verse does not apply to *ẓihār*, but to homicide (*qatl*). The verse governing *ẓihār* is 58 : 3, which reads, "(The penalty) in that case (is) the freeing of a slave before they touch one another". What the author points out here is that despite the verse of *ẓihār* some jurists tried to extend the stipulation of the "belief" of the slave over to the issue of *ẓihār*. In other words, they attempted to qualify the unqualified meaning in the verse of *ẓihār*. What he appears to be saying is that a disagreement similar to the one existing over the faith of the slave in the case of imprecation is also to be found in this case. The source for the qualified meaning is found in the verse of homicide, which the author quotes. Please refer to the section on *ẓihār*.

[356] That is, in the Qurʾānic verse 5 : 89.

They agreed, as far as I know, about the number of expiations arising from swearing a number of oaths, that the person who swears to do different things through a single oath is to make expiation for a single oath. Likewise, as far as I think, there is no dispute amongst them that if he swears different oaths for doing the same thing the obligatory expiations for this correspond to the number of oaths, like the person swearing different oaths for different things. They disagreed, however, when he swears many times to do the very same thing. A group of jurists said that the expiation is that which applies to one single oath. Another group of jurists said that there is to be expiation for each of the oaths sworn, unless the intention was to emphasize the fact. This is Mālik's opinion. A third group of jurists said that there is a single expiation for it, unless he wanted to attach solemnity to the oath.

The reason for the disagreement derives from whether the cause for the multiplicity of expiations is the multiplicity of oaths by category or by count. Those who maintained that the distinction is based on count said that for each oath there is expiation if it is repeated. Those who maintained that the distinction is based upon category said that in this (disputed) issue there is a single expiation.

They disagreed over when he swears a single oath by using more than one attribute out of the attributes of Allāh as to whether the number of expiations should correspond to the number of attributes included in the oath or whether there is a single expiation for this. Mālik said that the expiations in this oath vary according to the number of attributes. Thus, the person who swears by "The Hearer", "The Knower", and the "The Wise", is liable for three expiations in his view. A group of jurists said that if he intends it to be a continuous expression and enumerates these as a single statement there is a single expiation for him if there was one oath.

The reason for their disagreement is the criterion for judging single or multiple oaths and this refers to the form of speech or to the number of things enumerated in the speech that is expressed as an oath. Those who took into account the form of speech said that there is one expiation, while those who considered the number of things included in the expression which can be sworn to individually, said that the expiations vary according to the number.

This is sufficient for stating the fundamentals of this book and for the reasons for disagreement in it. Allāh provides support through His mercy.

XII

THE BOOK OF *NUDHŪR* (VOWS)

There are three sections in this book. The first section is about the types of vows. The second section is about vows that are binding and those that are not, and about their *aḥkām* generally. The third section is about the identification of the duty that becomes binding through them and about its *aḥkām*.

12.1. *Section 1: The types of vows* (*nudhūr*)

Vows are divided into two categories. One category is (considered) from the aspect of expressions and the other from the aspect of things (objects) for which a vow is made. From the aspect of the form of the expression used it is of two types: absolute, and this is expressed in the form of a report, and qualified, which is expressed as a conditional statement. The absolute is of two sub-types: manifest in terms of the object of the vow and that which is not manifest. The first is like the statement of a person: "For Allāh, I vow to perform the *ḥajj*". The second is like the statement, "For Allāh, I am bound by a vow", in which the object of the vow is not stated. It is possible that in the first he may not mention the word "vow" or he may mention it, like his statement: "For Allāh, I am bound to perform *ḥajj*". When the object is qualified through a condition it is like the statement, "If such and such happens, I am bound by a such and such vow for Allāh, and I undertake to do such and such thing". In this he might make it contingent upon an act of Allāh, like saying that if Allāh cures his illness he would be bound by a certain vow, or he might make it contingent upon his own act, like saying that if he performed a certain act he would be bound by a certain vow. These are what the jurists term as oaths, and it was stated in our discussion that preceded that these are not (real) oaths. These are the vows with respect to the forms of expression used.

The types (of *nadhr*) from the aspect of things that constitute the category of objects of vows are of four sub-types: a vow for things that belong to the category of worship; a vow for things that belong to the category of disobedience; a vow for things that belong to the disapproved category; and a vow for things belonging to the permissible category. These four sub-types are divided into two kinds: vows for omission of the act and vows for the commission of the act.

12.2. *Section 2: Binding and non-binding vows*

With respect to what is binding and what is not binding out of these vows, they agreed upon the binding nature of the absolute vow for worship, except what is related from some disciples of al-Shāfiʿī that an absolute vow is not valid. They agreed about the binding form of the absolute vow when it is made willingly and not under pressure, and when the word *nadhr* is used explicitly in it, irrespective of whether the object of the vow is explicitly mentioned in it. Likewise, they agreed about the binding nature of the vow that is made contingent upon a condition, when it is a vow related to worship.

They agreed about the binding nature of vows on the basis of the general implication of the words of the Exalted, "O ye who believe! Fulfil your undertakings",[357] and also because Allāh has declared it commendable, as in His words, "(Because) they perform the vow and fear the day whereof the evil is wide-spreading".[358] Further, He has threatened to inflict punishment for its violation, saying, "And of them is he who made a covenant with Allāh (saying): If He give us of His bounty We will give alms and become of the righteous. Yet when He gave them of His bounty, they hoarded it and turned away, averse; So He hath made the consequence (to be) hypocrisy in their hearts until the day when they shall meet Him, because they broke their word to Allāh that they promised Him, and because they lied".[359]

The reason for their disagreement over the express use of the word *nadhr* in the absolute vow stems from their dispute whether a vow becomes operative because of intention as well as the expression taken together or by intention alone. Those who maintained that it becomes obligatory with both taken together (said that) if he says, "I am obliged to do such and such for Allāh", and he does not mention the words "as a *nadhr*", he is not bound by anything, as it is merely a report about the obligation of a thing that Allāh has not made obligatory for him, unless he expressly mentions it as an obligation. Those who maintained that the (express use of the) words is not a condition for it said that the vow is constituted even if he does not mention the words explicitly. This is Mālik's opinion, that is, if he does not use the word *nadhr* explicitly. He

[357] Qurʾān 5 : 1.
[358] Qurʾān 76 : 7.
[359] Qurʾān 9 : 75.

maintained that this vow is binding, although it is his opinion that a vow is not binding without words and intention, however, he held that the absence of the word *nadhr* in the statement is of no consequence, as the purpose of statements that are expressed as vows (is obvious) even though the word *nadhr* has not been used. This is the opinion of the majority of the jurists, while the first opinion is that of Saᶜīd ibn al-Musayyab.

It appears that those who did not uphold the binding nature of an absolute vow did so because they construed the command for compliance to imply a recommendation. The same is the case for those who stipulated consent in it, as they stipulated it because the desire to attain nearness to Allāh is fulfilled by way of choice and liberty, and not under pressure. This is al-Shāfiᶜī's opinion. In Mālik's view, on the other hand, a vow is binding in whatever way it is made.

This is what they disagreed about with respect to its binding nature from the aspect of the words used. The disagreement that they had with respect to its binding nature from the aspect of the things (acts) that are the object of the vow is covered in two fundamental issues.

12.2.1. Issue 1

They disagreed about the person who vows to undertake an act of disobedience. Mālik, al-Shāfiᶜī, and the majority of the jurists said that he is not bound by it in any way. Abū Ḥanīfa, Sufyān, and the Kūfīs said that it is binding, and the binding part in this for them is the expiation for an oath, not the commission of the act of disobedience.

The reason for their disagreement springs from the conflict of the apparent meaning of the traditions on the topic. Two traditions have been related in this subject. The first is the tradition of ᶜĀ'isha from the Prophet (God's peace and blessings be upon him), who said, "He who vows to obey Allāh should obey Him, but he who vows to disobey Him should not disobey Him". The apparent meaning of this tradition is that the vow of disobedience is not binding. The second is the authentic[360] tradition of ᶜImrān ibn Ḥuṣayn and the tradition of Abū Hurayra from the Prophet (God's peace and blessings be upon him), that he said, "There is no vow in disobeying Allāh and its expiation is the expiation for an oath". This is explicit in the sense of being binding. Those who reconciled the two for this meaning said that the first tradition contains the directive that disobedience is not binding, and this second tradition includes the obligation of expiation. Those who preferred the

[360] The author contradicts this himself a few lines down. It is apparently an error on the part of the scribe as this is the usual terminology used by the author for all authentic traditions unless the text reads as "attributed to" instead of "authentic", which appears more likely.

apparent meaning of ʿĀʾisha's tradition, as the traditions of ʿImrān ibn Ḥuṣayn and Abū Hurayra did not prove to be authentic for them, said that there is no obligation in a vow of disobedience. Those who adopted the method of reconciliation imposed in it the expiation for an oath. Abū ʿUmar ibn ʿAbd al-Barr said: The traditionists deemed this particular tradition related through both ʿImrān ibn Ḥuṣayn and Abū Hurayra to be weak, saying, "Because (the *isnād* of) the tradition of Abū Hurayra revolves around Sulaymān ibn Arqam and his traditions are rejected, while (the *isnād* of) the tradition of ʿImrān ibn Ḥuṣayn revolves around Zuhayr ibn Muḥammad from his father, and his father is unknown from whom none besides his son have related. Zuhayr himself relates *munkar* (denied) traditions. Muslim, however, has recorded this tradition from ʿUqba ibn ʿĀmir".

It was the practice of the Mālikites to argue on the basis of what he related "that the Messenger of Allāh (God's peace and blessings be upon him) saw a man standing in the sun and asked, 'What is his problem?' They said, 'He made a vow that he would not speak, nor seek the shade, nor sit, and he would continue to fast'. He said, 'Go and order him to speak and sit and complete his fast'. They said that he ordered him to perform what was in obedience to Allāh and to relinquish what was disobedience". It is, however, not apparent that giving up speech (as in this tradition) is an act of disobedience. Allāh has communicated (in the Qurʾān) that this was a vow made by Maryam. It also appears that standing in the sun is not an act of disobedience, except insofar as it is related to the infliction of pain on the self. If it is claimed that there is disobedience in this it can only be so by way of analogy and not on the basis of the text. It is originally a permissible act.

12.2.2. Issue 2

They disagreed about the person who prohibits for himself things that are permissible. Mālik said that this is not binding on him, except in the case of a wife. The Ẓāhirites said that there is no rule for this. Abū Ḥanīfa said that there is the obligation of the expiation of an oath in this case.

The reason for their disagreement arises from the conflict of juristic reasoning with the apparent meaning of the words of the Exalted, "O Prophet! Why bannest thou that which Allāh hath made lawful for thee, seeking to please they wives?"[361] This is so as a vow is not constituted in opposition to the *ḥukm sharʿī*, that is, as regards prohibiting what is permissible and permitting what is prohibited, because the jurisdiction over this belongs to the Lawgiver. It, therefore, follows from such an understanding that whoever prohibits for himself something that Allāh has permitted by law is not bound

[361] Qurʾān 66 : 1.

by it, just as he is not bound by a vow permitting something that has been prohibited by the law. The apparent meaning of the words of the Exalted, "Allāh hath made lawful for you (Muslims) absolution from your oaths (of such a kind), and Allāh is your Protector. He is the Knower, the Wise",[362] is that the affect of censure on prohibition gives rise to expiation for absolution from this declaration. If that is the case such a vow is not binding.

The first group interpreted the prohibition mentioned in the verse to mean that it was the swearing of an oath. They disagreed over the occasion for which this verse was revealed.[363] In the book by Muslim this was in the case of drinking honey, and there is a report from Ibn ʿAbbās, who said, "If a person prohibits his wife on himself it amounts to an oath that is remitted by expiation". He said, "There is for you in the example of the Messenger of Allāh an excellent model".

12.3. *Section 3: Things that become binding in vows and their* aḥkām

There is extensive disagreement among the jurists over what becomes binding in each individual vow, but we will only point out the well-known issues in this, and most of these are related to express provisions of the law, as has been our practice in this book. There are five issues here.

12.3.1. Issue 1

They disagreed about the obligation in an unqualified vow, in which the person making it does not identify any act except for saying, "I am bound by a vow for Allāh". Many of the jurists have held that there is expiation for an oath in this and nothing more. A group of jurists said that in fact there is for this the expiation of *ẓihar*. One group of jurists said that the minimum to which this name (*nadhr*) applies is the fast of one day or observance of two *rakʿas* of prayer.

The majority of the jurists decided in favour of the obligation of expiation in this because of the authentic tradition of ʿUqba ibn ʿĀmir that the Prophet (God's peace and blessings be upon him) said, "The expiation for a vow is the expiation for an oath". It has been recorded by Muslim. Those who maintained that the obligation is for a day's fast or prayer of two *rakʿas* did so

[362] Qurʾān 66 : 1.

[363] This appears to be the reason why the author did not use this verse in the previous issue concerning the obligation of expiation for vowing to commit an act of disobedience. The reasoning may be that if there is expiation for the remittance of a vow for prohibiting something that is permitted, then surely there must be expiation for vowing to commit an act of disobedience, an act which appears to be more grievous. The answer, as the author is indicating, is that this is the case of an oath, while that was the case of a vow.

by adopting the opinion that the valid performance is based upon the minimum implication of the term, and praying two *rakʿas* or fasting for one day is the minimum to which the term *nadhr* applies. Those who said that the obligation here is for the expiation of *ẓihār* has asserted something outside the ambit of analogy and the transmitted texts.

12.3.2. Issue 2

They agreed about the binding nature of a vow for walking to the House of Allāh, that is, if the person vows to go on foot. They disagreed over when he is unable to do so for part of the way. One group of jurists said that there is no obligation upon him, while another said that there is. The latter disagreed over his liability and had three opinions. The jurists of Medina said that he is to walk a second time from the place where he was unable to continue, and if he likes he may ride, which would be valid but he would be liable for atonement by sacrificing an animal (*dam*). This is related from ʿAlī. The jurists of Mecca said that he is liable for making an offering but not for making further attempts to walk. Mālik said that he is liable for both, that is, he is to return and walk from where it is obligatory and he is also to make an offering. The offering in his view is a she-camel or a cow, but if he does not find a cow or she-camel then a goat.

The reason for disagreement stems from the clash of principles and the conflict of traditions. This is so as those who held the person walking a second time to be similar to the *mutamattiʿ* or *qārin* (in *ḥajj*), because the *qārin* does in one journey what he was required to do in two and this person does in two journeys what he was obliged to do in one, said that he is liable for the offering made by the *mutamattiʿ* or the *qārin*. Those who held his case to be similar to all other acts of *ḥajj* that may be compensated by slaughtering an animal said that he is liable for *dam*. Those who adopted the traditions laid down on the subject said that if he is unable to do so there is no liability for him. Abū ʿUmar said that the authentic *sunan* laid down on this are an evidence for the avoidance of hardship, and one of these, as he said, is the tradition of ʿUqba ibn ʿĀmir al-Juhanī, who said, "My sister vowed to walk to the House of Allāh, the Lofty the Glorious, so she directed me to seek a ruling for her from the Messenger of Allāh (God's peace and blessings be upon him). I sought the ruling for her from the Prophet (God's peace and blessings be upon him), and he said, 'She may walk and she may ride'". It is recorded by Muslim. The tradition of Anas ibn Mālik is "that the Messenger of Allāh (God's peace and blessings be upon him) saw a man leaning on his two daughters. He asked about him and they said, 'He made a vow to walk'. The Prophet (God's peace and blessings be upon him) said, 'Allāh is not in need of this man's tormenting himself.' He then ordered him to ride". This too is an authentic tradition.

12.3.3. Issue 3

After agreeing about the obligation of walking during *ḥajj* and *ʿumra*, they disagreed over the case of the person who vows to walk to the Mosque of the Prophet (God's peace and blessings be upon him) or to the *Bayt al-Maqdis* (in Jerusalem) with the intention of praying there. Mālik and al-Shāfiʿī said that walking there is binding upon him. Abū Ḥanīfa said that it is not binding upon him and wherever he prays is counted as a valid substitute. In his view the same is the case about vowing to pray in the *Masjid al-Ḥarām*, but he upholds the obligation of walking to the *Masjid al-Ḥarām* for purposes of *ḥajj* or *ʿumra*. Abū Yūsuf, his disciple, said that the person who vows to pray in the *Bayt al-Maqdis* of in the Mosque of the Prophet (God's peace and blessings be upon him) is bound by his vow, but if he prays in *al-Bayt al-Ḥarām* it is to be considered sufficient (as a substitute). Most of the jurists maintain that vows for praying in mosques other than these three are not binding, because of the saying of the Prophet (God's peace and blessings be upon him), "A journey should not be undertaken except for three", and he mentioned *al-Masjid al-Ḥarām*, his own mosque, and the *Bayt al-Maqdis*. Some of the jurists maintain that a vow for visiting mosques in which greater merit is to sought is binding. They argued for this on the basis of the verdict issued by Ibn ʿAbbās for the son of a woman, who vowed to walk up to the mosque at Qubāʾ (close to Medina) but died, that he should do it on her behalf.

The reason for their disagreement over vows for mosques other than *al-Masjid al-Ḥarām* derives from their dispute over the meaning of undertaking a journey to these three mosques whether this is for observing obligatory prayers or supererogatory prayers in them. Those who maintained that this is for obligatory prayers and obligatory prayers in their view cannot be the object of a vow, as they are obligatory by law, said that a vow for walking up to these two mosques is not binding. Those for whom a vow can be made for an obligation or that the person can also vow to observe supererogatory prayers in these two mosques, because of the saying of the Prophet (God's peace and blessings be upon him), "A prayer in this mosque of mine is better than a thousand prayers in other mosques, except for *al-Masjid al-Ḥarām*", and because the term *ṣalāh* includes both obligatory and supererogatory prayers, said it is obligatory. Abū Ḥanīfa, however, interpreted this tradition to mean obligatory prayers, deciding on the basis of a reconciliation between this (tradition) and the saying of the Prophet (God's peace and blessings be upon him), "A prayer by one of you in his house is better than his prayer in this mosque of mine, except for the prescribed prayers", otherwise a contradiction would arise between these two traditions. This issue, though it is related to the second section, is better discussed here.

12.3.4. Issue 4

They disagreed about the case of a person who vows to sacrifice his son at the station of Abraham. Mālik said that he is to sacrifice a camel as reparation for him (his son). Abū Ḥanīfa said that he is to sacrifice a sheep, and this is also related from Ibn ʿAbbās. Some of the jurists said that he is to sacrifice a hundred camels, while others said that he is to make an offering of his blood-money (*diya*), and this is related from ʿAlī. Some of them said that he is to perform *ḥajj* together with his child. Abū Yūsuf and al-Shāfiʿī said that there is no liability for him, as it is an act of disobedience and there is no vow for disobedience.

The reason for their disagreement stems from the story of Ibrāhim (God's peace and blessings be upon him), that is, whether the way Ibrāhīm made his offering is binding upon all Muslims. Those who maintained that this is a law that was specific to Ibrāhīm said that the vow is not binding. Those who maintained that it is binding for us said that the vow is binding. The disagreement is the well-known dispute over whether the law for those before us is binding on us, but another disagreement impinges upon this. The apparent meaning of this act is that it was specific to Ibrāhīm and it was not a law for the people of his age, and on the basis of this it is not necessary that there be a dispute whether it is law for us. Those who maintained that it is law for us differed over the obligation arising from it with reference to the dispute whether the obligation in it is to be considered an obligation for Ibrāhīm or it is to be interpreted to mean one of the Islamic ways of attaining nearness (to Allāh). This would be (achieved) by making a charity of his blood-money, or by performing *ḥajj* with the child, or by an offering of a *badana*. Those who said that there are one hundred camels for it adopted the tradition of ʿAbd al-Muṭṭalib (when he vowed to offer his son ʿAbd Allāh, but was advised to offer one hundred camels instead).

12.3.5. Issue 5

They agreed that the person who vows to give his entire wealth in the way of Allāh or in a manner that denotes piety is bound by it, and there is no remittance for it through expiation. This is the case when the vow is in the form of a report and not a stipulation, which is what they call oath. They disagreed about the person who vows to do this contingent upon something, like his saying, "My wealth is for the needy if I do such and such thing", and then he does it. A group of jurists said that this is binding like a vow in the form of a report and there is no expiation for it. This is Mālik's opinion in the case of vows that are expressed in such forms, that is, there is no expiation in them (for remittance). Another group of jurists said that the obligation in this case is only for the expiation of an oath. This is al-Shāfiʿī's opinion for vows that are made contingent upon other acts, as he linked them to the *ḥukm* for oaths. Mālik, however, linked them to the *ḥukm* of vows, as has preceded in our discussion in the Book of Oaths.

Those who upheld the obligation of his spending his wealth in the manner that they adopted, disagreed about the extent of his liability. Mālik said that he is to give away only one-third of his wealth. A group of jurists said that in fact he is under an obligation to give away his entire wealth. This was maintained by Ibrāhīm al-Nakhaʿī and Zufar. Abū Ḥanīfa said that he is to give away all his wealth that is subject to *zakāt*. Some of them said that if he gives away an amount equal to the *zakāt* levied on his wealth it is sufficient. There is a fifth opinion on this, namely that if his wealth is abundant he is to pay a fifth, if it is average he is to give a seventh, and if it is a small amount he is to pay a tenth of it. The limit they fixed for abundant wealth was two thousand, for average wealth one thousand, and for a meagre sum it was five hundred. This is related from Qatāda.

The reason for their disagreement on this issue, that is, among those who said that all the wealth is to be given away in its entirety or one third of it, arises from the conflict of a principle of this topic with a tradition. It is related in the tradition of Abū Lubāba ibn ʿAbd al-Mundhir who sought the forgiveness of Allāh and decided to give in charity all his wealth. The Messenger of Allāh (God's peace and blessings be upon him) said, "A third of it is sufficient for you", and that is the governing opinion in Mālik's school. The principle requires that he is bound to give all his wealth in the light of the remaining vows, that is, it is obligatory for him to abide by it in the manner that he intended. It is necessary, however, to exempt this issue from this principle, as the text has exempted it, except that Mālik did not follow his principle in this issue. This is so as he said: If he swears an oath or vows to do a specific thing it is binding upon him, even if it is his entire wealth. Likewise, it is binding for him if he specified a part of his wealth that is more than a third. This is in conflict with the text related in the tradition of Abū Lubāba, and also with the saying of the Messenger of Allāh (God's peace and blessings be upon him) "to the person who came with gold equal to the weight of an egg. He said, 'I came across this in a mine, so take it, it is *ṣadaqa* and I do not own anything else'. The Messenger of Allāh (God's peace and blessings be upon him) looked away from him, but he came at him from his right, from his left, and from his back. The Messenger of Allāh (God's peace and blessings be upon him) took it from him and flung it at him, and had it hit him he would have been hurt. The Prophet (God's peace and blessings be upon him) said, 'One of you comes with all that he owns and says this is *ṣadaqa*. He then sits down begging from people. The best charity is that which leaves enough to fall back on'". This is explicit on the point that it is not binding to give determined wealth if it is offered as charity when it is the entire wealth of the person. Perhaps, these traditions did not prove to be authentic for Mālik.

The remaining opinions that have been advanced on the issue are weak, especially the opinions of those who fixed a limit other than a third. This is sufficient for explaining the principles of this book. Allāh guides to the truth.

XIII

THE BOOK OF *ḌAḤĀYĀ*[364] (SACRIFICES)

The principles of this book are covered in four chapters. The first chapter is about the *ḥukm* of sacrifices and the person to whom the command is addressed. The second chapter is about the kinds of sacrifices, their characteristics, ages (based on teeth), and their number. The third chapter is about the *aḥkām* of slaughtering them. The fourth chapter is about the *aḥkām* of the meat of the sacrificed animals.

13.1. **Chapter 1 The *Ḥukm* of the Sacrifices and the Person Addressed**

The jurists disagreed about sacrifices whether they are obligatory or are a *sunna*. Mālik and al-Shāfiʿī held that it is one of the *sunan muʾakkada* (emphatic *sunna*). Mālik made an exemption in the case of the pilgrims for relinquishing it at Minā.[365] Al-Shāfiʿī did not make a distinction between pilgrims and others. Abū Ḥanīfa said that sacrifice is obligatory for those residents of the cities who can afford it, and that it is not obligatory for travellers. He was opposed in this by his two disciples Abū Yūsuf and Muḥammad who maintained that it is not obligatory (but is a *sunna*). The same opinion as Abū Ḥanīfa's is also related from Mālik.

There are two reasons for their disagreement. The first is whether the act of the Prophet (God's peace and blessings be upon him) in this is to be construed as implying an obligation or a recommendation. This is so as the Messenger of Allāh (God's peace and blessings be upon him), in what is related from him, never gave up the offering of sacrifices even while travelling, as is laid down in the tradition of Thawbān, who said, "The Messenger of Allāh (God's peace

[364] The blood sacrifices offered on the Day of *ʿĪd al-Aḍḥā*.

[365] That is, when they are staying at Minā, busy with the concluding rites of the pilgrimage.

and blessings be upon him) slaughtered his sacrificial animal and said, 'O Thawbān carve out the meat of this sacrificed animal'. I continued to feed him [the Prophet] from its meat [to people] until he reached Medina". The second reason is their dispute about the traditions that lay down the *aḥkām* of sacrifices. It is established from the Prophet (God's peace and blessings be upon him) in the tradition of Umm Salama that he said, "When the first ten days (of Dhū al-Ḥijja) begin and one of you intends to make a sacrifice, he should not clip his hair or nails [until he makes the sacrifice]".[366] They said that his words, "one of you intends to make a sacrifice", contains an evidence that sacrifice is not obligatory. When the Prophet (God's peace and blessings be upon him) ordered Abū Burda to repeat his sacrifice for he had slaughtered it before the prayer, a group of jurists understood this to imply obligation. The opinion of Ibn ʿAbbās is that there is no obligation. ʿIkrima said that Ibn ʿAbbās sent him with two *dirhams* to buy meat, and said: Tell the person you meet that this is the sacrifice of Ibn ʿAbbās. It is related from Bilāl that he sacrificed a rooster. Arguing on the basis of a tradition that has not been laid down on the specific issue is weak.

They disagreed about whether it is binding upon a person, who intends to make a sacrifice, not to clip his hair and nails in the first ten days (of Dhū al-Ḥijja). The tradition about it is authentic.[367]

13.2. Chapter 2 The Categories of Sacrifices, Their Characteristics, Ages, and Number

In this chapter there are four well-known issues. The first is about the distinctive categories. The second is about the distinction of characteristics. The third is about the identification of age. The fourth is about their number.

13.2.1. Issue 1

The jurists agreed about the sacrifice of animals included in (the category of) cattle. They disagreed about what has greater merit out of these. Mālik maintained that there is greater merit in sacrificing rams followed by cows

[366] An implication of this tradition, though not directly related to the discussion here, is that the person who intends to make a sacrifice should not clip his nail or hair, even when he is not on the pilgrimage. The majority of the jurists do not consider this to be prohibited. Al-Shāfiʿī considers it disapproved, as does Mālik in one opinion. Abū Ḥanīfa deems it permissible.

[367] It might be possible to interpret the tradition in a different way by considering the third person pronoun in the tradition to apply to the sacrficial animal rather than the person making the sacrifice. Allāh knows best.

followed by camels, which is the opposite of his view in the case of offerings (during *ḥajj*). It is said, on his authority, that first come camels then cows and then rams. Al-Shāfiʿī maintained the opposite of what Mālik held, that is, first are camels then cows then rams. This was also the opinion of Ashhab and Shaʿbān.

The reason for their disagreement stems from the conflict of analogy with the evidence adduced from acts (of the prophet). This is so as it is not related from the Prophet (God's peace and blessings be upon him) that he made a sacrifice of anything other than a ram. This is an evidence of the fact that there is greater merit in sacrificing a ram, and it conforms with the narrations of some scholars. In al-Bukhārī there is a report from Ibn ʿUmar which indicates the opposite of this, and in which it is said, "The Messenger of Allāh (God's peace and blessings be upon him) used to slaughter and sacrifice (the animals)[368] at the place of prayer". The analogy is that as offerings (during *ḥajj*) are made in the same kind of animals, so it is necessary that those that have greater merit here should have greater merit there. Al-Shāfiʿī argued for his opinion on the basis of the general implication of the saying of the Prophet (God's peace and blessings be upon him), "He who goes out [for Friday prayer] in the early hour is like one who has made the offering of a camel, he who goes out in the next hour is like one making an offering of a cow, and he who goes out in the third hour is like one making an offering of a ram".[369] The obligation it appears is to construe this for all kinds of offerings in animals. Mālik, however, interpreted it to apply to offerings (during *ḥajj*) alone, so that the saying should not conflict with the acts (of the Prophet), and this is preferable.

It is possible that there be another reason for their disagreement, which is whether the great sacrifice (the tremendous victim) that was made by Ibrāhīm as ransom (for) his son Ismāʿīl persists as a *sunna* up to this day, and that was a sacrifice (of a ram), and whether this is the meaning of the words of the Exalted, "Then we ransomed him with a tremendous sacrifice. And We left for him among the later folk (salutation and the *sunna* of sacrifice)".[370] Those who adopted this meaning said that the sacrifice of a ram has greater merit, while those who maintained that this *sunna* does not prevail today did not consider it to be an evidence for assigning merit to the sacrifice of a ram. Further, it is

[368] It is difficult to convey the exact meaning of the tradition by using the words "slaughter and sacrifice". The words *dhabḥ* and *naḥr* have been used in the tradition. The word *naḥr* is used for slaughtering an animal by striking at the base of the neck. This method is used for animals with long necks, like the camel. The author provides the details in the next book. The tradition, therefore, goes against the first insofar as it indicates that both types of animals were sacrificed.

[369] The tradition has preceded in the Book of Prayer, in the section on the Friday prayer.

[370] Qurʾān 37 : 107, 108.

established "that the Messenger of Allāh (God's peace and blessings be upon him) made a sacrifice in both ways". If that is the case then it is necessary to rely upon al-Shāfiʿī's opinion.

All the jurists agreed unanimously that it is not permitted to make a sacrifice of an animal that is not in the category of cattle, except what is narrated from al-Ḥasan ibn Ṣāliḥ, who said that it is permitted to sacrifice a wild buffalo for seven participants, and a gazelle for one person.

13.2.2. Issue 2

As regards the condition of sacrificial animals, the jurists agreed about avoiding a lame animal with an obvious limp, the diseased animal that is obviously sick, and the emaciated animal that is not wholesome[371] on the basis of the tradition of al-Barrāʾ ibn ʿĀzib "that the Messenger of Allāh (God's peace and blessings be upon him) was asked about what should be left out in selecting sacrificial animals. He pointed with his hand and said, 'Four'. Al-Barrāʾ used to point with his hand saying, 'My arm is shorter than the arm of the Messenger of Allāh (God's peace and blessings be upon him). The lame animal with an obvious limp; the one-eyed animal with an obvious loss of one eye; the diseased animal with an obvious disease; and the emaciated animal that has no marrow in its bones'". Likewise, they agreed that a slight defect in these four types is not effective in denying their validity (for sacrifice).

They disagreed on two points. The first is about defects that are more acute than the four laid down in the text, like blindness and a broken leg. The second is about those that are equal in terms of the defect and disfigurement, that is, defects in the ears, eyes, tails, teeth, and in other limbs, (defects) that are not considered slight. On the first point, the majority of the jurists maintained that defects that are more grievous than the four mentioned in the text have a greater priority for avoidance in terms of their validity (for sacrifice). The Ẓāhirites maintained that these defects to not prevent such validity, and as a whole, nothing more than the four defects mentioned in the tradition should prevent sacrifice.

The reason for their disagreement derives from whether these words (in the text) are specific cases with a specific implication or that they are specific cases with a general implication. Those who maintained that they have a specific implication, and that was why a number was mentioned, said that only these four prevent their acceptance. Those who said that these are specific cases with a general application, and these are categories in which the minimum has been

[371] The editor of the original text gives a note that this is an animal having no marrow in its bones.

mentioned to indicate all that is more grievous, said that what is more grievous than the mentioned categories has a higher priority for rejection.

On the second point, that is, defects in the remaining limbs that are the equivalent of the defects mentioned in the text, they disagreed holding three different opinions. The first is that they are to be rejected like the cases mentioned. This is the prevalent opinion in Mālik's school as mentioned in the well-known books. The second opinion is that they do not prevent acceptance, even though it is desirable to avoid them. This was upheld by Ibn al-Qaṣṣār and Ibn al-Jallāb, and a group of the disciples of Mālik from Baghdād. The third opinion is that they are neither to be rejected nor is it desirable to avoid them. This is the opinion of the Ẓāhirites.

There are two reasons for their disagreement. The first is their dispute over the meaning of the preceding tradition. The second is the conflict of traditions on the subject. With respect to the preceding tradition, those who considered it to be a category of the specific applicable to the specific said that nothing is rejected except the four categories mentioned or what is similar to them or worse. Those who considered it to be a category of the specfic applicable generally, and these were the jurists, and considered such an application to be (intended) from a lower order meaning to a higher order meaning alone and not to equivalent meanings, said that those with more grievous defects are to be linked to these four cases, and the cases with equivalent defects are not to be linked to them, except by way of desirability. Those for whom it was an indication of both meanings, that is, what is more grievous than the categories mentioned and those that are equivalent said that the defects similar to those mentioned prevent acceptance, just as greater defects prevent its acceptance. This is one of the reasons of disagreement on the issue, and it belongs to the vacillation of (the meaning of a) word between being understood in a specific sense or in a general sense. Again, what kind of general implication is it, for those who understood it to be applicable in the general sense? Is it a general implication for more grievous defects or for those that are similar as well as the more grievous, as is the case (opinion) in Mālik's school.

The second reason is the existence of two conflicting traditions of the *ḥasan* category. Al-Nasāʾī has recorded from Abū Burda that he said, "O Messenger of Allāh, I detest the defect that is in the horns and ears [of the sacrificial animal]. The Prophet (God's peace and blessings be upon him) said, 'Leave what you detest, but do not forbid it for others'". ʿAlī ibn Abī Ṭālib said, "The Messenger of Allāh (God's peace and blessings be upon him) ordered us to be careful about the eyes and ears, and not to sacrifice the *sharqāʾ* or the *kharqāʾ* or the *mudābara* or the *batrāʾ*". The *sharqāʾ* is an animal with a cut up ear; the *kharqāʾ* is one with a hole in its ear; and the *mudābara* is one with its ears split from two sides from the back (and the *batrāʾ* is one with its tail cut). Those who preferred the tradition of Abū Burda said that only the four defects cause avoidance or what is more grievous than them. Those who reconciled the two traditions by construing the tradition of Abū Burda to apply to minor defects which are not obvious, and the tradition of ʿAlī to more grievous defects, which are obvious, linked with the cases mentioned what was similar to them. It was for this reason that the followers of this opinion decided to determine what kind of loss of limbs prevents acceptance (for sacrifice). Some of them took into account the loss of one-third of the ears and tail, while others took into account more than this. The same is the case with the loss of teeth and the skin of the udder. About the horns Mālik said that a partial loss is not a defect, unless they should bleed, in which case it is a disease in his view. There is no dispute that disease prevents acceptance for sacrifice. Abū Dāwūd has recorded "that the Prophet (God's peace and blessings be upon him) proscribed the [sacrifice of an] animal with split ears and a broken horn".

They disagreed about the *ṣakkāʾ*, which is an animal born without ears. Mālik and al-Shāfiʿī held that it is not permitted, while Abū Ḥanīfa maintained that if it is a birth defect it is permitted as in the case of one without horns. The majority of the jurists did not disagree that the cutting of the whole ear or part of it is a defect. All this disagreement refers to what we have already discussed. They disagreed about the animal with a cut off tail. a group of jurists permitted this on the basis of the tradition of Jābir al-Juʿfī from Muḥammad ibn Qaraẓa from Abū Saʿīd al-Khudrī, who said, "I bought a ram so as to sacrifice it, and a wolf ate up its tail. I asked the Messenger of Allāh (God's peace and blessings be upon him) about it and he said, 'Sacrifice it' ". This Jābir is not relied upon by most traditionists for argument. Another group rejected this because of the tradition of ʿAlī that has preceded.

13.2.3. Issue 3

This issue is about the identification of the ages stipulated for the sacrificial animals. They agreed that the *jadhaʿ* (six-month-old) is not sufficient, and it is the *thaniyy* (one-year-old) and whatever is older it is permitted, because of the tradition of the Prophet (God's peace and blessings be upon him) from Abū Burda when he ordered him to make the sacrifice again (saying), "A *jadhaʿ* is valid in your case, but for no one other than you". They disagreed about the *jadhaʿ* (six-month-old) in sheep. The majority of the jurists approved of this, but a group of jurists insisted that a sheep has to be the *thaniyya* (one-year-old).

The reason for disagreement arises from the conflict between the general with the specific implication. The specific meaning is found in the tradition of Jābir, who said, "The Messenger of Allāh (God's peace and blessings be upon him) said, 'Do not slaughter anything less than a *musinna* (a full grown animal), unless that is difficult for you, in which case you may slaughter a *jadhaʿ* from sheep'". It is recorded by Muslim. The general meaning is in the tradition of Abū Burda ibn Niyār regarding the saying of the Prophet (God's peace and blessings be upon him), "The *jadhaʿ* is not valid for anyone after you". Those who preferred this general implication over the specific (said that it is not permitted), and this is the opinion of Abū Muḥammad ibn Ḥazm on this issue for he claimed that Abū Zubayr[372] commits *tadlīs* (using subtle means of cheating) in the narration of traditions. And a tradition narrated by a *mudallis* using the term *ʿan* (on the authority of) rather than the terms *samiʿtu* (I heard) and *ḥaddathana* (he related to us) does not, in their view, have the same authority or recognition. There is, however, no objection against the tradition of Abū Burda. Those who construed the meaning of the general in terms of the specific, which is the well-known method of (the majority of) the experts on *uṣūl*, exempted the *jadhaʿ* in sheep mentioned in the text from this general implication, which is preferable. This tradition was deemed authentic by Abū Bakr ibn Ṣaffūr,[373] who held that Abū Muḥammad ibn Ḥazm made an error in what he had attributed to Abū Zubayr in his statement, according to my conviction, in which he sought to reply to Ibn Ḥazm on this issue.

13.2.4. Issue 4

This issue is about the number of sacrifices required from those making them. The jurists disagreed about this. Mālik said that it is permitted that a man slaughter a ram or a cow or a camel as sacrifice on his own behalf and on behalf of the members of his family whose maintenance is binding on him by law. The same applies to an offering, in his view. Al-Shāfiʿī, Abū Ḥanīfa, and a group of jurists permitted that a man sacrifice a camel or a cow on behalf of seven, as a sacrifice or as an offering. They agreed unanimously that a ram is sufficient only for one person (and his dependents), except what is related from Mālik that it is valid if the person slaughters it for himself and for the members of his family, not by way of participation but when he buys it alone. This is based upon the report from ʿĀʾisha that she said, "We were at Minā when meat of a cow was brought in to us. We said, 'What is this'. They said, 'It is the sacrifice of the Messenger of Allāh (God's peace and blessings be upon him) for his wives'". Abū Ḥanīfa and al-Thawrī opposed him in this, by way of disapproval not the lack of validity.

The reason for their disagreement stems from the conflict of a principle with analogy based upon a tradition laid down about offerings. The principle is that only one animal is valid for one person, because of which they prohibited

[372] It appears that his name occurs in the *isnād* of Jābir's tradition.

[373] The editor of the original text points out that this is how this name occurs in the manuscripts.

participation in sheep. We said that only one animal is valid for one person as the command for sacrifice cannot be split into parts as the person participating in the sacrifice is not covered by the designation "sacrificer", unless there is an evidence in law to this effect. The tradition on which the analogy, conflicting with this principle, has been constructed is what is related by Jābir, who said, "We slaughtered along with the Messenger of Allāh (God's peace and blessings be upon him) in the year of al-Ḥudaybiya a camel for seven persons". In some versions the words are: "The Messenger of Allāh (God's peace and blessings be upon him) established the *sunna* of [slaughtering] a camel for seven and a cow for seven". Al-Shāfiʿī and Abū Ḥanīfa constructed the analogy for sacrifices from offerings. Mālik preferred the principle over the analogy based upon this tradition, as he objected to the tradition on the grounds that this was when the polytheists prevented the Messenger of Allāh (God's peace and blessings be upon him) from reaching the House, and the offering of the person prevented (*muḥṣar*) was not yet obligatory in his view but was voluntary. Participation is possible in his opinion in a voluntary offering, but participation in an obligatory offering is not valid. On the basis of the opinion that sacrifices are not obligatory, however, it is possible to draw an analogy for them from these offerings. Ibn al-Qāsim related from him (Mālik) that participation is not permitted, either in voluntary offerings or in obligatory offerings. This appears to be the rejection of a tradition because of its opposition to a principle.

They agreed, however, that it is not permitted for more than seven persons to participate in sacrificial animals (in the *ḥajj nusuk*), even though it is related in the tradition of Rāfiʿ ibn Khadīj and through Ibn ʿAbbās and others that a camel may be shared by ten (persons). Al-Ṭaḥāwī said that the consensus on the point that more than seven persons cannot participate in sacrificial animals is an evidence that the traditions (implying the contrary) are not authentic. Mālik decided in favour of a man and his family participating in a sacrificial animal or an offering on the basis of what he related from Ibn Shihāb, who said, "The Messenger of Allāh (God's peace and blessings be upon him) did not sacrifice more than one camel or more than one cow for his family". Mālik was opposed in the case of sacrifices in this sense, that is, in participation, because of the consensus over the prohibition of participation in it with strangers, from which it follows that relatives in this case fall within the ambit of the analogy for strangers. Mālik, however, made a distinction in this between strangers and relatives on the basis of his analogy for sacrifices drawn from offerings in the tradition on which he relied, that is, the tradition of Ibn Shihāb. Their disagreement on the issue is based upon the conflict of analogies in the topic, I mean, either by linking relatives with strangers, or by drawing an analogy for sacrifices from offerings.

13.3. Chapter 3 The *Aḥkām* of Slaughter

The study of slaughter specific to sacrifices is related to the time and slaughter (itself). They disagreed over it on three points: its commencement, termination, and the intervening nights.

13.3.1. Issue 1[374]

With respect to the time of its commencement they agreed that slaughter before prayer is not permitted, because of the authentic saying of the Prophet (God's peace and blessings be upon him), "One who slaughters before prayer has [on his hands] a goat's worth of meat [not a sacrifice]". He ordered the person who had slaughtered before prayer to sacrifice again. Further, there is his saying, "The first thing we shall do on this day of ours (*ᶜĪd al-Aḍḥā*) is to pray, and then we shall make the sacrifice". Furthermore, there are other authentic traditions that convey the same meaning.

They disagreed about the case of a person who slaughters after the prayer, but before the *imām* has slaughtered (his animal). Mālik held that it is not permitted for any person to slaughter his sacrificial animal before the *imām* does. Abū Ḥanīfa and al-Thawrī said that it is permitted after prayer and before the *imām* has slaughtered his animal.

The reason for their disagreement derives from the conflict of the traditions in the topic. In some of these traditions it is related, "The Prophet (God's peace and blessings be upon him) ordered the person who slaughtered before prayer to make the sacrifice again", while in others (the words are), "He ordered the person who slaughtered before he [the Prophet] had to sacrifice again". The tradition is recorded in Muslim in the same meaning. Those who considered these (events) to be two separate incidents stipulated the prior slaughter by the *imām* as a condition for the validity of the slaughter (by the members of the congregation), while those who considered it to be a single incident took into account (the completion of) prayer alone for the validity of slaughter. The narration from Abū Burda ibn Niyār varies, as in some versions it reads, "he slaughtered before prayer so the Messenger of Allāh (God's peace and blessings be upon him) ordered him to make the sacrifice again", while in another versions "he slaughtered before the slaughter made by the Messenger of Allāh (God's peace and blessings be upon him), so he ordered him to make the sacrifice again". If this is the situation, then, it is preferable to interpret the versions about slaughter before prayer and slaughter before the slaughter undertaken by the Messenger of Allāh (God's peace and blessings be upon

[374] There are no headings for the first two issues in the original text, but there is one for the third issue. Headings are inserted here for the first two issues.

him) to be one incident, as the person who slaughtered before prayer did slaughter before the Messenger of Allāh (God's peace and blessings be upon him) had done so. It follows that the effective factor in the lack of validity is slaughter before prayer, as has been laid down in authentic traditions on the issue, like those of Anas and others "that he who slaughters before prayer has to make the sacrifice again". The reason is that the basis of the *ḥukm* from the Prophet (God's peace and blessings be upon him) conveys through the indirect implication of the text a strong evidence that slaughter after prayer is valid, for had there been an additional condition related to the validity of slaughter of the sacrificial animal the Messenger of Allāh (God's peace and blessings be upon him) would not have maintained silence when it was his duty to elaborate and explain. The text of this tradition of Anas is: "The Messenger of Allāh (God's peace and blessings be upon him) said on the Day of Sacrifice, 'He who slaughtered [his animal] before prayer should make the sacrifice again'".

They disagreed within this topic over a case that is not explicitly stated in the law, which is: when are the people in the remote countryside, who do not have an *imām* (in their locality), to slaughter their sacrificial animals. Mālik said that such people are to follow the *imāms* nearest their locality. Al-Shāfiʿī said that they are to wait for a length of time sufficient for the (*ʿĪd*) prayer and the sermon and are then to undertake the slaughter. Abū Ḥanīfa said that it is valid if anyone of these people should slaughter after the morning prayer, and he gave another opinion saying it is after sunrise.

Likewise, Mālik's disciples differed over another case, namely, when the *imām* does not slaughter his animal at the place of prayer. A group of jurists said that these people are to estimate the time for his slaughtering the animal after his departure, while another group said that this is not obligatory.

13.3.2. Issue 2

With respect to the end of the period determined for valid sacrificial slaughtering, Mālik maintained that the latest time is by sunset on the third day of the days of sacrifice. In his view slaughtering has to be undertaken on appointed days, which are the Day of Sacrifice and the following two days. This was also upheld by Abū Ḥanīfa, Aḥmad, and a group of jurists. Al-Shāfiʿī and al-Awzāʿī said that the time for sacrifice is four days, the Day of Sacrifice and the following three days. It is related from a group of jurists that they held the period of sacrifice to be a single day, which is the Day of Sacrifice specifically. It is also maintained by some that the period for slaughtering continues up to the last day of Dhū al-Ḥijja, but this is a deviant opinion and there is no evidence for it. All these opinions are related from the predecessors.

There are two reasons for their disagreement. The first comes from their dispute about the identification of the "appointed days" as to what are these in the words of the Exalted, "That they may witness things that are of benefit to them, and mention the name of Allāh on appointed days over the beast of cattle that He hath bestowed upon them. Then eat thereof and feed therewith the poor unfortunate".[375] It is said that these are the day of sacrifice and two days after it, and this is the well-known opinion. It is also said that it is the first ten days of Dhū al-Ḥijja. The second reason emanates from the conflict of the indirect indication of the text in this verse with the tradition of Jubayr ibn Mutᶜim, as in this tradition the Prophet (God's peace and blessings be upon him) said, "Each alley of Mecca is the place of sacrifice, and all the days of *tashrīq* are the period of slaughter". Those who maintained that the appointed days in this verse are the Day of Sacrifice and two days after it preferred the indirect indication of the text over this tradition and said that there is to be no sacrifice except on these (three) days. Those who reconciled the tradition with the verse maintaining that there is no conflict between them as the tradition implies a ***ḥukm*** in addition to the one in the verse and also maintaining that the purpose of the verse is not to fix the days of slaughter, while the purpose of the tradition is to do so, said that it is permitted to slaughter on the fourth day because, by agreement, the fourth day is one of the days of *tashrīq*.

There is no disagreement among them that the *ayyām maᶜdūdāt*[376] (the determined days) are the days of *tashrīq*, and they are the three days that follow the Day of Sacrifice, except what is related from Saᶜīd ibn Jubayr who said that the Day of Sacrifice is one of the days of *tashrīq*. They disagreed, however, about defining the *ayyām maᶜlūmāt* (appointed days) in accordance with the two preceding opinions. Those who said that it is the day of sacrifice alone did so on the basis that the "known days" are the first ten days (of the month of Dhū al-Ḥijja). They maintained that as a consensus has occurred that out of these (ten days) slaughter is not to be undertaken except on the tenth of that month, and this is the day of slaughter that is expressly stated, it follows that slaughter be undertaken on the day of sacrifice alone.

13.3.3. Issue 3

This relates to their disagreement about the nights intervening between the days of sacrifice. Mālik, in his well-known opinion, maintained that slaughter is not permitted during the nights between the days of *tashrīq*, nor is an offering. Al-Shāfiᶜī and a group of jurists maintained that it is permissible. The reason for their disagreement is the equivocality that exists in the term *yawm*. It is sometimes used by the Arabs to mean day as well as night, for

[375] Qur'ān 22 : 28.
[376] Qur'ān 2 : 203.

example, in the words of the Exalted, "Enjoy life in your dwelling-place for three days!"[377] and at other times it is applied to mean day and not the night, as in the words of the Exalted, "Which he imposed upon them for seven long nights and eight long days".[378] Those who determined that the word *yawm* includes both night and day in the words of the Exalted, "Remember Allāh through the appointed days",[379] said that slaughter is permitted during the day as well as the night in these days. Those who maintained that the term *yawm* in this verse does not include the nights said that neither slaughter for sacrifice nor for an offering is permitted during the nights.

Whether one meaning is more obvious than the other in the term *yawm* here is a matter of examination. It appears that it is more obvious in the meaning of day than it is for night, but even if we concede that the implication in the verse is for day alone this would not prevent slaughter during the night, except on the basis of a feeble evidence that rests on the indirect indication of the text, which is the assigning of the opposite *ḥukm* to the contrary implication of the term. This kind of implication of the text is the weakest, so much so that they (were led to) maintain what is held by al-Daqqāq from amongst the *Mutakallimūn*. Yet, someone may claim that the initial rule for slaughter is (general) prohibition and its permissibility (during the daytime) has been established (as an exemption) through an evidence, in which case those who permitted it during the night have to come up with an evidence.

With respect to the person who performs the slaughter, the jurists considered it desirable that the sacrificer should undertake the slaughter of his sacrifice with his own hands. They agreed that it is permitted to him to authorize someone else to perform the slaughter on his behalf. They disagreed over whether the sacrifice is valid if someone else should slaughter it without his permission. It is said that it is not permitted, while a distinction is also made between whether the person is a friend, a child, or a stranger, that is, it is not permitted if it is a friend or a child. There is no dispute (in this case) in the School that if it is done by a stranger it is not valid.

13.4. Chapter 4 The *Aḥkām* of the Meat of Sacrificed Animals

They agreed that the sacrificer is commanded to eat (some) of his sacrifice and to give (some of) it away as charity, because of the words of the Exalted, "Then eat thereof and feed therewith the poor unfortunate",[380] and His

[377] Qur'ān 11 : 65.
[378] Qur'ān 69 : 7.
[379] Qur'ān 2 : 203.
[380] Qur'ān 22 : 28.

words, "Eat thereof and feed the beggar and the suppliant".[381] There is also the saying of the Prophet (God's peace and blessings be upon him), "Eat, give it as charity, and store it". Mālik's school differed over whether the command is for eating and giving as charity together or whether the person has a choice to do one of the two things, that is, to eat all of it or to give it all away. Ibn al-Mawwāz maintained that he has the right to do either. A large number of jurists considered it desirable that he should divide it into three parts: a third for saving; a third for charity; and a third for eating. This is so because of the saying of the Prophet (God's peace and blessings be upon him), "Eat, give it as charity, and store it". ʿAbd al-Wahhāb maintained that eating from it is not obligatory in the School, as against a group of jurists who declared it obligatory. I believe the Ẓāhirites deem it obligatory to divide the meat into three parts that are included in the tradition.

The jurists agreed, as far as I know, that the sale of this sacrificial meat is not permitted. They disagreed about (the sale of) its skin and wool and other parts besides these that can be of benefit. The majority said that their sale is not permitted, while Abū Ḥanīfa permitted their barter for things other than *dirhams* and *dīnārs*, that is, in exchange for goods (barter). ʿAṭāʾ maintained that their sale is permitted in exchange for anything, *dirhams*, *dīnārs* and other things. Abū Ḥanīfa made a distinction between money and goods as he held an exchange for goods to be a kind of utilization, because of their consensus that it is permitted to benefit from them.

This is sufficient for the fundamentals of this book. All praise is for Allāh.

[381] Qurʾān 22 : 36.

XIV
THE BOOK OF *DHABĀ'IḤ* (SLAUGHTERED ANIMALS)

The comprehensive discussion of the fundamentals of this book are covered in five chapters. The first chapter is about the identification of the subject-matter of slaughter and sacrifice, and these are the slaughtered animal and the sacrificed animal. The second chapter is about the description of slaughter and sacrifice. The third chapter is about the identification of the instrument with which slaughter and sacrifice are undertaken. The fourth chapter is about the conditions of lawful slaughter (*dhakāh*).[382] The fifth chapter is about the persons who slaughter and sacrifice. The basic principles are (the first) four, and the conditions will possibly be covered in (all) four chapters, though it would have been easier to compile them in a separate chapter.

14.1. **Chapter 1** Identification of the Subject-matter of Slaughter and Sacrifice

Animals in terms of the stipulation of lawful slaughter (*dhakāh*) for their consumption are divided into two types: animals that are not lawful without lawful slaughter and animals that are permitted without slaughter. Included in these are some that the jurists agreed about and some over which they disagreed. They agreed that the animal whose meat becomes lawful for consumption is the warm-blooded land animal, which is neither prohibited by the law nor one with damaged vital organs nor that for which hope has been given up because of a fatal blow, goring, falling from a height, ravenous attack by a predator, or disease. And they agreed that the sea-animal[383] is not in need of *dhakāh*. They disagreed about animals (insects) that lack blood and whose consumption is permissible, like locust and similar creatures, whether

[382] *Dhakāh* includes two types of slaughter: *naḥr* and *dhabḥ*. *Naḥr* is the cutting of the jugular vein of the camel at the base of the neck. The details are explained by the author in what follows.

[383] This includes those in rivers, lakes, or any other reservoir or medium of water.

they are in need of *dhakāh*, as well as about (amphibious) animals that bleed, but live partly on land and partly in water, like the turtle. They disagreed about the effect of *dhakāh* on the categories of animals that have been prohibited for consumption in the Qur'ān (like the pig) with the object of making permissible the use and purification of their skins.

In this chapter then there are six fundamental issues. The first issue is about the effect of *dhakāh* on the five categories mentioned in the verse,[384] if they are caught alive. The second issue is about the effect of *dhakāh* on animals whose consumption is forever prohibited. The third issue is about the effect of *dhakāh* on a diseased animal. The fourth issue is whether the *dhakāh* of the fetus is achieved by the *dhakāh* of the mother. The fifth issue is whether there is *dhakāh* for locust. The sixth is whether there is *dhakāh* for (amphibious) animals that sometimes seek refuge on land and sometimes in water.

14.1.1. Issue 1

They agreed, as far as I know, about animals that have been choked, are struck by a blow, have fallen, are gored, or are attacked by a predator, that if the strangulation or fall (or any of the other threatening causes) has not left them in a state in which there is no hope (of survival) for them *dhakāh* will be effective (in making their consumption lawful), that is, if the animal seems most likely to survive, and this is when a vital organ has not been affected. They disagreed when there is a predominant probability that the animal will die, because of damage to a vital organ or some other reason. One group of jurists said that *dhakāh* is still effective in this case. This is the opinion of Abū Ḥanīfa and the well-known opinion of al-Shāfiʿī, and it is also the opinion of al-Zuhrī and Ibn ʿAbbās. Another group said that *dhakāh* is not effective in this case. Both opinions are related from Mālik, but the better-known opinion is that *dhakāh* is not effective in the case of an animal for which there is no hope of survival. Some of the jurists made an interpretation within the School that hopeless cases are of two types: desperate cases with some doubt, and hopeless cases whose death is certain, which is one with damaged vital organs, although there is a dispute about (the identification of the) vital organs. There are two well-known narrations in the School about the desperate case that is doubtful, but about the animal with damaged vital organs there is no transmitted dispute that *dhakāh* is not effective in it, even though a weak derivation can be made for its permissibility.

[384] See the following note.

The reason for their disagreement stems from their dispute about the meaning of the words of the Exalted, "Saving that which ye make lawful by *dhakāh*",[385] whether they form a linked exemption so that some of the animals in the categories are moved out, as is usual in the case of a linked exemption, from those included under each name. These are "the strangled, and the dead through beating, and the dead through falling from a height, and that which hath been killed by (the goring of) horns, and the devoured of wild beasts". In the alternative, it is a detached exemption that has no effect on the preceding statement, as that is usual with the detached exemption in the usage of the Arabs.

Those who maintained that it is a linked exemption said that *dhakāh* is effective in these five categories, while those who maintained that it is a detached exemption said that *dhakāh* is not effective in them. Those who maintained that it is a linked exemption argued on the basis of the consensus that *dhakāh* is effective in the hopeful cases and said that this indicates the effectiveness of the exemption, which is therefore of a linked category. Those who maintained that it is a detached exemption argued that the prohibition is not related to the corpus of these five categories when they are alive, but is related to them after their death, and if that is the case the exemption is not linked. This means that the words of the Exalted, "Forbidden unto you (for food) are carrion", would imply carrion-flesh, and likewise, it would mean the flesh of the beaten animal, or the animal that has fallen, or one gored, and of the rest, that is, carrion flesh resulting from these causes besides natural death, which is usually referred to as carrion in the usage of the Arabs or in its actual application. They said that since it has become clear that the prohibition is related to the corpus of these categories after their death and not when they are alive, because the flesh of a living animal is prohibited when it is alive on the evidence of the stipulation of *dhakāh*, and on the evidence of the saying of the Prophet (God's peace and blessings be upon him), "What is cut off from an animal when it is alive is carrion", it follows that the words of the Exalted, "Saving that which ye make lawful by *dhakāh*", are a detached exemption.

The truth, however, is that whatever the nature of the exemption it is necessary that *dhakāh* be effective in these five categories. The reason is that if we attach the prohibition to these five categories in the verse after their death it is necessary that they be subject to *dhakāh* as long as they are alive—these five categories and others besides them—because as long as they are alive they have the same status as other (living) animals for this purpose, that they accept being made lawful by way of *dhakāh*, as death caused through it is the cause of

[385] In the verse: "Forbidden unto you (for food) are carrion and blood and swine-flesh, and that which hath been dedicated unto any other than Allāh, and the strangled, and the dead through beating, and the dead through falling from a height, and that which hath been killed by (the goring of) horns, and the devoured of wild beasts, *saving that which ye make lawful*". Qur'ān 5 : 3 (emphasis added).

lawfulness. If, on the other hand, we say that the exemption is linked, then, there is no obscurity about it. It can probably be said that the generality of the prohibition may be understood as including the corpus of these five categories after their death as well as before it, as is the case of the swine for which *dhakāh* is not effective. In this case the exemption would remove the prohibition from their corpora as it expressly lays down the effectiveness of *dhakāh* on them. If that is the case, the objection of the objector who argues that the exemption is detached has no (persuasive) force.

Those who made a distinction between the animal with damaged vital organs and the doubtful case would probably maintain that the exemption is detached, and relying on the consensus about the effectiveness of *dhakāh* in the hopeful case they would construct from it an analogy for the doubtful case. It is also likely that they would say that the exemption is linked, but would then exempt the case of the animal beaten (gored etc.) on the basis of analogy. This is so as *dhakāh* is effective by necessity when it is certain that it is causing death, but when there is doubt that the cause of death was *dhakāh* or beating or goring or the remaining reasons it is not necessary that it be effective, and this is the case of the animal with damaged vital organs. They could rightfully say that the animal with damaged vital organs carries the *ḥukm* of carrion and that a condition for *dhakāh* is that it does away with confirmed life and not life that is departing.

14.1.2. Issue 2

They also disagreed over whether *dhakāh* is effective in purifying the hides of animals whose consumption is prohibited. Mālik said that *dhakāh* is effective in predatory animals, but not in swine. This was also Abū Ḥanīfa's opinion. The school, however, differed about the predatory animal being prohibited or abominable (*makrūh*), as will be coming up in the book of Foods and Beverages. Al-Shāfiʿī said that *dhakāh* is effective in (purifying the skin of) the animals prohibited as food,[386] so it is permitted to sell all its parts and to utilize them, except for their meat.

The reason for the disagreement is the dispute whether all the parts of the animal are dependent upon the rule governing the consumption of their meat. Those who maintained that they are dependent upon the *ḥukm* of the meat said that if *dhakāh* is not effective in their meat it is not effective in the other parts. Those who held that they are not dependent said that even if it is not effective in the case of meat it is effective in all the remaining parts of the animal. This is so as the basic rule is that it is (originally) effective in all parts, and if on the basis of an evidence of prohibition of meat its effectiveness for

[386] The editor in the original text says that this is not the well-known opinion from al-Shāfiʿī.

meat has been removed, its effectiveness for all the other parts remains, unless an evidence were to indicate its elimination.

14.1.3. Issue 3

They disagreed about the effectiveness of *dhakāh* on an animal that is in the throes of death due to the severity of the disease, and this after their agreement about its effectiveness in case of an animal that is about to die (but not from disease). The majority maintain that *dhakāh* is effective in its case too. This is the well-known opinion from Mālik, but it is also related from him that *dhakāh* is not effective in this case.

The reason for disagreement stems from the conflict of analogy with a tradition. The tradition is in the report "that a slave-girl of Kaʿb ibn Mālik was tending the sheep near Salaʿ when she found that one of the sheep was about to die. She took hold of it and killed it with a stone. The Messenger of Allāh (God's peace and blessings be upon him) was asked about it and he said, 'Eat it'". It has been recorded by al-Bukhārī and Muslim. The analogy is that as *dhakāh* is known to be effective in a living animal, and this animal is almost dead, therefore, all those who upheld its slaughter agreed that *dhakāh* is not effective in it unless it exhibits some evidence of life. They disagreed about the the valid signs (of life). Some of them took (a minor) movement in the slaughtered animal to be a sufficient indication of the existence of life, while others did not. The first is the view of Abū Hurayra and the second of Zayd ibn Thābit. Some of them insisted upon the existence of three types of movement in it: movement of the eyes, movement of the tail, and the movement of the legs. This is the opinion of Saʿīd ibn al-Musayyab and Zayd ibn Aslam, and this is what was preferred by Muḥammad ibn al-Mawwāz, while some of them stipulated breathing along with this, which is the opinion of Ibn Ḥabīb.

14.1.4. Issue 4

They disagreed over whether *dhakāh* of the mother is effective for the *janīn* (fetus) also, because it is dead when it comes out after the slaughtered mother. The majority of the jurists maintained that the *dhakāh* of the mother is the *dhakāh* of the *janīn*. This was the opinion of Mālik and al-Shāfiʿī. Abū Ḥanīfa said that if it emerges alive it is to be slaughtered and (may then be) eaten, but if it emerges dead it is carrion. Those who maintained that the *dhakāh* of the mother is the *dhakāh* of the foetus stipulated its full growth and the appearance of hair, and this was Mālik's opinion, while some did not stipulate this, and this was al-Shāfiʿī's opinion.

The reason for their disagreement arises from the authenticity of the tradition that is related on the issue from Abū Saʿīd al-Khudrī, along with its conflict with the principles. The tradition of Abū Saʿīd is that he said, "We asked the Messenger of Allāh (God's peace and blessings be upon him) about a cow, a camel, or a sheep when one of us sacrificed it and found a foetus in it, as to whether we were to eat it or throw it away? He said, 'Eat it if you like for its *dhakāh* is the *dhakāh* of its mother'". A similar tradition has been recorded by al-Tirmidhī and Abū Dāwūd from Jābir. They disagreed about the authenticity of this tradition with some of them declaring it as unauthentic and some declaring it authentic. One of those who considered it authentic was al-Tirmidhī. The conflict of the principle with the tradition on the subject is that if the foetus is alive and then dies due to the death of its mother, it dies because of suffocation, and it therefore becomes one of those that die due to choking, which the (Qurʾānic) text has prohibited. Abū Muḥammad ibn Ḥazm upheld its prohibition and he did not agree with the chain of the tradition.

With respect to the dispute of those who declare it permissible with the stipulation of the growth of its hair or without it, the reason stems from the conflict of the general meaning with analogy. The general content of the saying of the Prophet (God's peace and blessings be upon him), "its *dhakāh* is the *dhakāh* of its mother", implies that there be no separation between them, while its being an object of *dhakāh* requires that the existence of life be stipulated in it, on the analogy of animals for which *dhakāh* is required, and life cannot exist in it unless there is a growth of hair on the foetus, and the foetus itself must have been fully created (formed). This analogy is supported by the fact that stipulation of this condition is related from Ibn ʿUmar and from a group of the Companions. It is related from Maʿmar from al-Zuhrī from ʿAbd Allāh ibn Kaʿb ibn Mālik, who said, "The Companions of the Messenger of Allāh (God's peace and blessings be upon him) used to say, 'When the *janīn* grows hair its *dhakāh* is the *dhakāh* of its mother'". It is related by Ibn al-Mubārak from Ibn Abī Laylā, who said, "The Messenger of Allāh (God's peace and blessings be upon him) said, 'The *dhakāh* of the foetus is the *dhakāh* of its mother, whether it has hair or it does not'". Ibn Abī Laylā, however, is held to have suffered from an imperfect memory. Analogy implies that its *dhakāh* be included within the *dhakāh* of its mother as it is a part of it. If this is the case, then, there is no sense in stipulating the existence of life in it (when it emerges). It is, therefore, to be deemed weak that the general meaning in the tradition laid down on this be restricted by analogy as has been mentioned about the disciples of Mālik in what has preceded.

14.1.5. Issue 5

They disagreed about locust. Mālik said that it is not to be eaten without *dhakāh*, and their *dhakāh* in his view is that they are to be killed either by cutting off their head or some other part. The *fuqahāʾ* in general held that they may be eaten dead. This was the opinion of Muṭarrif. The *dhakāh* of any other thing (insect) that lacks blood, in Mālik's view, is the same as that of locust.

The reason for disagreement over dead locust comes from whether it is included in the term *mayta* (carrion) in the words of the Exalted, "Forbidden unto you (for food) are carrion . . ."[387] There is another reason for their disagreement, and that is whether they are sneezed out by the whales (and therefore they are a species of fish not needing *dhakāh*) or creatures of land.

14.1.6. Issue 6

They disagreed about creatures that have a habitat on land as well as in water as to whether they are in need of *dhakāh*. Some of the jurists gave predominance in this to the *ḥukm* of land, while others gave predominance to the *ḥukm* of water. Another group took into account the place where it has its habitat most of the time.

14.2. Chapter 2 Discussion of *Dhakāh* (Kinds of Lawful Slaughter)

There are two issues about the fundamentals of this topic. The first issue is about the types of *dhakāh* specific to each category of animals in cattle. The second is about the description of *dhakāh*.

14.2.1. Issue 1

They agreed that *dhakāh* for the animals included in cattle is either *naḥr* (slaughter of a camel by cutting the jugular vein at the base of the neck) and *dhabḥ* (slaughter by cutting the throat in other cases). They agreed that the *sunna* for sheep and birds is *dhabḥ*, the *sunna* for camels is *naḥr*, and that both *dhabḥ* and *naḥr* are permitted for cows. They disagreed whether *naḥr* is permitted for sheep and birds and *dhabḥ* for camels. Mālik held that *naḥr* is not permitted for sheep and birds nor is *dhabḥ* for camels, and this for cases other than those of necessity. A group of jurists said that all this is permitted without any abomination. This was the opinion of al-Shāfiʿī, Abū Ḥanīfa, al-Thawrī, and a group of jurists. Ashhab said that if *naḥr* is performed upon a thing for which *dhabḥ* is prescribed or *dhabḥ* is performed in place of *naḥr* the animal may be eaten but this is considered abominable. Ibn Bakīr made a distinction between sheep and camels alone saying that a camel may be eaten

[387] Qur'ān 5 : 3.

after *dhabḥ*, but a sheep is not to be eaten after *naḥr*. They did not disagree, however, about its permissibility in case of necessity.

The reason for their disagreement derives from the conflict between an act (of the Prophet) and the general implication. The general implication is in the tradition of the Prophet (God's peace and blessings be upon him), which reads: "(An animal) whose blood has been caused to flow by something and on which the name of Allāh has been pronounced may be eaten". The act is established "that the Messenger of Allāh (God's peace and blessings be upon him) performed *naḥr* on the camels and cows and *dhabḥ* upon sheep". They agreed about the permissibility of performing *dhabḥ* on cows because of (its application to cows in) the words of the Exalted, "And when Moses said unto his people: Lo! Allāh commandeth you to slaughter (*tadhbaḥū*) a cow",[388] and about *dhabḥ* in the case of sheep, because of the words of the Exalted about the ram, "Then We ransomed him with a tremendous slaughtered sacrifice (*dhibḥin ʿaẓīm*)".[389]

14.2.2. Issue 2

They agreed on the description of (valid) *dhakāh* that *dhabḥ* (slaughter) in which the two jugular veins, the gullet (esophagus), and the throat (pharynx) are cut is permitted for eating. They disagreed over this over several points. The disagreement is over whether it is obligatory to cut all four things or some of them, and whether it is obligatory to cut (each of) them completely or up to a greater part. Whether it is a condition for cutting that the *jawza* (prominent cartilage of the larynx; Adam's apple in humans) is to be on the side of the head and not the body (with respect to the blade), and whether it is permissible for eating if the cut is placed on the nape of the neck. Is it permitted (to eat it) if he extends the cut so that the spinal cord is severed? Is it a condition of *dhakāh* that the person should not lift his hand until the *dhakāh* is complete? These are six sub-issues about the number of the things to be severed, the extent of the cut, its location, the termination of the cutting, its direction, that is, whether it is to be from the front or the back, and about its description.

14.2.2.1 & 2 Sub-issues 1 and 2

The well-known narration from Mālik is about the severance of the jugular vein and the pharynx, and that less than this is not valid. It is also narrated from him that all four have to be cut, and it is narrated that only the jugular veins are to be cut. There was no dispute in the School about the condition

[388] Qurʾān 2 : 67. Picktall uses the term sacrifice, which has been changed to slaughter in this case.

[389] Qurʾān 37 : 107. Pickthall's translation has been changed again slightly to focus on the meaning intended by the author. He translates it as "a tremendous victim".

that the jugular veins be cut completely. They disagreed about the (extent of) cutting of the pharynx, in accordance with the opinion about its obligation. It is said that it is to be cut completely, while it is said that the major part is to be cut. Abū Ḥanīfa said that the obligation is to cut three undetermined things out of the four, either the pharynx and the two veins, or the gullet, pharynx, and one vein, or the gullet and the two veins. Al-Shāfiʿī said that the obligation is to cut only the gullet and the pharynx. Muḥammad ibn al-Ḥasan said that the obligation is to cut the larger part of each of the four things.

The reason for their disagreement stems from the fact that no transmitted condition is laid down in this, but there are two (conflicting) traditions. The first requires the flow of blood alone, while the second requires the cutting of the jugular veins along with the flow of blood. In the tradition of Rāfiʿ ibn Khadīj the Prophet (God's peace and blessings be upon him) said, "If (an animal's) blood has been caused to flow by something, and the name of Allāh has been pronounced on it, eat it". It is a tradition that is agreed upon for its authenticity by al-Bukhārī and Muslim. On the other hand, it is related from Abū Umāma from the Prophet (God's peace and blessings be upon him) that he said, "Whatever has cut the jugular veins eat it, as long as it was not snapped by a tooth or split with a claw". The apparent meaning of the first tradition implies that only a part of the jugular veins needs to be cut, as a cut is enough to cause the blood to flow. The second requires the complete severance of the jugular veins. The traditions, Allāh knows best, agree on the cutting of the jugular veins, either one of them, or part of both, or part of one. The basis for reconciling the two traditions is to understand the definite article in the word *alawdā*, "the jugular veins", in the saying of the Prophet (God's peace and blessings be upon him), as implying a part and not the whole, as the definite article in Arabic sometimes indicates a part of the defined word.

Those who stipulated the cutting of the pharynx and the gullet do not have an argument based upon transmitted evidence, and more than this is the view of those who stipulate the cutting of the gullet and the pharynx to the exclusion of the jugular veins. It was for this reason that a group of jurists held that the obligation is to cut that which has been accepted unanimously. As *dhakāh* is a condition (they maintained) for making things lawful, and there is no text on what is to be done, it follows that the obligation in this is what has unanimously been agreed upon, unless an evidence were to indicate an exemption from it. This, however, is weak, because the point on which consensus has occurred is not necessarily a condition of validity.[390]

[390] What he means is that even if something is agreed upon through the consensus of the jurists, it may not constitute a condition for the validity of an act. It does not mean that the consensus is being rejected. In other words, the act agreed upon may simply be a recommendation and not binding.

14.2.2.3. Sub-issue 3

This issue is about the location of the cut. The jurists in the school differed about when the *jawza* falls towards the body. Mālik and Ibn al-Qāsim said that the carcass is not to be eaten. Ashhab, Ibn ᶜAbd al-Ḥakam, and Ibn Wahb said that it may be eaten. The reason for the disagreement is whether the cutting of the pharynx is a condition of *dhakāh*. Those who maintained that it is a condition said that it is necessary to cut the *jawza*, because cutting above the *jawza* would mean that the pharynx has remained in one piece. Those who maintained that it is not a condition said that if the cut is placed above the *jawza* it is permitted.

14.2.2.4. Sub-issue 4

This issue is about the cutting of the organs of *dhakāh* from the nape of the neck. There is no disagreement in the School that this is not permitted. This is the opinion of Saᶜīd ibn al-Musayyab and Ibn Shihāb as well as others. Al-Shāfiᶜī, Abū Ḥanīfa, Isḥāq, Abū Thawr permitted this. This is related from Ibn ᶜUmar, ᶜAlī, and ᶜImrān ibn Ḥuṣayn.

The reason for their disagreement is whether *dhakāh* is effective in the case of an animal with ruptured vital organs, because the person cutting the organs of *dhakāh* from the nape of the neck cannot reach the organ of *dhakāh* except after cutting the spinal cord, which is one of the vital organs. *Dhakāh* in this case would be performed on an animal whose vital organ is damaged. The basis for disagreement on this has preceded.

14.2.2.5. Sub-issue 5

This is about the instance where a person who continues cutting until the spinal cord is cut. Mālik considered it abominable when the cutting is extended without initially intending to cut the spinal cord, because if he intended this form of slaughter from the start he would be making a resolve to perform *dhakāh* in an unlawful manner. Muṭarrif and Ibn al-Mājishūn maintained that the animal is not to be eaten if the person did this intentionally and without a lack of knowledge, but if he made a the cut by mistake or in ignorance it may be eaten.

14.2.2.6. Sub-issue 6

The sixth issue relates to whether it is a condition of *dhakāh* that it be performed in a single uninterrupted movement. The School did not disagree that this is a condition of *dhakāh*, and if the person raises his hand before the completion of the slaughter and then resumes cutting after an interval the *dhakāh* is not valid.

They disagreed over the instance of when he brings his hand back immediately and within a very short space. Ibn Ḥabīb said that if he brings his hand back immediately it is permitted, while Saḥnūn said that it is not to be eaten. It is said that if the person raises his hand to check whether *dhakāh* has been completed and brings it back immediately when he realises that it is not completed it may be eaten. This is one interpretation of Saḥnūn's, and his opinion is also construed to imply abomination. Abū al-Ḥasan al-Lakhmī has said that if the opposite of this was maintained it would have been better, I mean, (the opposite of the statement that) if the person lifts his hand thinking that he had completed the *dhakāh*, but it becomes obvious to him that he has not, and he brings it back, the animal may be eaten. The first action was on the basis of doubt and this (moving it back) is on the basis of his conviction. This is based upon the consideration that cutting of all the organs is a condition of *dhakāh*. When he lifts his hand before completing the *dhakāh* the animal becomes one whose vital organs have been cut, and moving his hand back is no longer effective, as it (now) amounts to the *dhakāh* of an animal with ruptured vital organs.

14.3. **Chapter 3 With what instrument is *Dhakāh* Performed?**

The jurists agreed that anything (instrument) causing the blood to flow and the jugular veins to bleed is valid, whether it is made from iron, rock, or wood, or a reed. They differed about three things: teeth, claws, and bones. Some of the jurists permitted *dhakāh* with bones, but prohibited it with teeth and claws. Some of those who prohibited it with teeth and claws made a distinction between their being detached or being attached, and they permitted *dhakāh* with them if they were detached, but they did not when they were attached. Some of them said that *dhakāh* with teeth and bones is abominable but not prohibited. There is no dispute in the School that *dhakāh* is permitted with bones if they cause blood to flow. They disagreed about teeth and bones holding three different opinions, I mean, about their absolute prohibition, about the distinction between their being detached or attached, and about (the *ḥukm* whether it entails) abomination and not prohibition.

The reason for their disagreement arises from their dispute about the meaning of the proscription laid down in the saying of the Prophet (God's peace and blessings be upon him) in the tradition of Rāfiʿ ibn Khadīj, who said, "O Messenger of Allāh, we shall be meeting the enemy tomorrow and we do not have knives, may we then slaughter (animals) with a (sharpened) cane?" The Prophet (God's peace and blessings be upon him) said, "Whatever causes the blood to flow, with the name of Allāh pronounced on it (the animal), as long as it is not a tooth or claw, and let me tell you about them. The tooth is a bone and the claw is the knife of the Abyssinians". Some of the jurists understood this to mean that it is not in the normal nature of these things to cause blood to flow, while some of them understood from this that this law has no underlying reason. Some of those who understood from it that the law has no underlying reason believed that the proscription indicates the invalidity of the thing proscribed, some believed that it does not indicate the invalidity of the thing proscribed, while some believed that the proscription is laid down by way of disapproval not as a prohibition. Those who understood the meaning to be that blood is not usually spilled with these things said that if one of these is able to cause blood to flow it is permitted. It is for this reason that some of them maintained that they be detached as the flow of blood can be caused when they are in this form. This is Abū Ḥanīfa's opinion.

Those who maintained that their proscription is a law without an underlying cause and that it indicates the invalidity of the thing proscribed said that if slaughter is performed with them *dhakāh* is not valid, even when blood has been made to flow. Those who maintained that the proscription does not indicate the invalidity of the thing proscribed said that if the person does it and causes the blood to flow he has sinned, but the slaughtered animal is permitted. Those who maintained that the proscription is laid down by way of disapproval considered it abominable but not prohibited. There is no substance to the opinion of those who made a distinction between bones and teeth, as the Prophet (God's peace and blessings be upon him) declared the underlying cause of the prohibition of teeth to be the fact that it is a bone.

There is no dispute in the School about the disapproval of using any sharp thing other than that made from iron with the availability of the iron instrument, because of the saying of the Prophet (God's peace and blessings be upon him), "Allāh has prescribed the doing of good deeds to everyone, therefore, when you kill do it in a decent manner, and when you slaughter do it in the best way, and let him who does it sharpen his knife and lay the animal on its side". It has been recorded by Muslim.

14.4. Chapter 4 Conditions of *Dhakāh*

There are three issues in this chapter. The first issue is about the stipulation of the *tasmiya* (saying "I begin with the name of Allāh"). The second is about turning the slaughtered animal toward the *qibla*.[391] The third is about the stipulation of intention.

[391] There is an error in the original manuscript where the first issue is repeated for the second also. The discussion in the issue is about pointing the animal toward the *qibla*.

14.4.1. Issue 1

They disagreed about the *ḥukm* of *tasmiya* over the slaughtered animal and expressed three different opinions. It is said that it is an absolute obligation. It is said that it is an obligation when remembered, but is dropped in the case of forgetfulness. It is said that it is an emphatic *sunna* (*sunna mu'akkada*). The first opinion was held by the Ẓāhirites, Ibn ʿUmar, al-Shaʿbī, and Ibn Sīrīn. The second opinion was held by Mālik, Abū Ḥanīfa, and al-Thawrī. The third opinion was held by al-Shāfiʿī and his disciples, and is also related from Ibn ʿAbbās and Abū Hurayra.

The reason for their disagreement arises from the conflict between the apparent meaning of the Book on this and a tradition. In the Book it is the words of the Exalted, "And eat not of that whereon Allāh's name hath not been mentioned, for lo! it is an abomination".[392] The *sunna* opposing this verse is what has been related by Mālik from Hishām from his father, who said, "When the Messenger of Allāh (God's peace and blessings be upon him) was asked, 'O Messenger of Allāh, people from the desert bring us meat, and we do not know whether they have mentioned Allāh's name over it'. The Messenger of Allāh (God's peace and blessings be upon him) said, 'Mention the name of Allāh over it (the meat) and then eat it'". Mālik held that the verse abrogates the tradition and he interpreted the tradition as belonging to the first period of Islam. Al-Shāfiʿī did not uphold this, as the apparent implication of the tradition is that the incident occurred in Medina, while the verse about mentioning the name of Allāh is from the Meccan period. Al-Shāfiʿī adopted the method of reconciliation, because of this, by construing the (Qur'ānic) command for *tasmiya* to imply recommendation. Those who stipulated remembrance for the obligation did so on the basis of the saying of the Prophet (God's peace and blessings be upon him), "Liability has been lifted from my *umma* for (what they do by) mistake or forgetfulness and for what they are compelled to do".

14.4.2. Issue 2

A group of jurists considered it desirable to turn the animal brought to slaughter in the direction of the *qibla*. Another group of jurists permitted this. A third group considered it obligatory. A fourth group deemed it abominable when the animal was not made to point toward the *qibla*. The opinion about abomination as well as that about prohibition are found in the School, and it is an issue that is not expressly stated in the texts. The original rule in this is of permissibility, unless an evidence indicates this stipulation (of turning toward the *qibla*). There is no suitable case in the law from which an analogy can be

[392] Qur'ān 6 : 121.

drawn for this issue, unless *qiyās mursal* is adopted, which is analogy that does not rely on a specific rule, according to those who permit it, or a remote *qiyās al-shabah* may be adopted, and this indicates that *qibla* is a venerated direction and the act is a worship, therefore, it is necessary that this direction be adopted. This, however, is weak, because it is not every worship for which the assumption of this direction is stipulated, except for *ṣalāh*, and the analogy for *dhakāh* drawn from *ṣalāh* is weak, as well as that drawn from the taking of the direction of *qibla* for the dead.

14.4.3. Issue 3

The stipulation of intention (*niyya*) is deemed obligatory in the School, and I do not recall at the moment the dispute over it outside of the School. It appears, however, that there are two opinions about this. An opinion upholding its obligation, and an opinion dropping the obligation. Those who upheld its obligation said that it is a worship in which attributes and number are stipulated, therefore, it follows that intention be a condition. Those who did not deem it obligatory said that it is a rational act that leads to the taking of life, which is its purpose; therefore, intention should not be stipulated for it as a necessity, and it is just like the washing of impurities that leads to the removal of their substance (without the stipulation of intention).

14.5. Chapter 5 The Person who Can Validly Perform *Dhakāh*

There are three categories mentioned in the law: a category about the performance of whose *dhakāh* they agreed, a category about the invalidity of whose performance they agreed, and a category over which they disagreed. The category about the performance of whose *dhakāh* they agreed is one that gathers in it five qualifications: Being a Muslim, being a male, the age of puberty, sanity, and regular observance of prayer. The category whose performance of *dhakāh* is prohibited are the polytheists who worship the idols, because of the words of the Exalted, "And that which hath been immolated unto idols",[393] and His words, "And that which hath been dedicated unto any other than Allāh".[394] The category about which they disagreed comprises many sub-categories, but the well-known are ten: the People of the Book, the Magians, the Sabians, a woman, a minor, and insane person, an intoxicated person, one who neglects prayer, a thief, and one who misappropriates the property of others.

[393] Qur'ān 5 : 3.
[394] Qur'ān 5 : 3.

The jurists are agreed unanimously about the permissibility of the slaughtered animals of the People of the Book, because of the words of the Exalted, "The food of those who have received the Scripture is lawful for you, and your food is lawful for them",[395] but they disagree about the details. They agreed that if they were not from the Christians of (the Arab tribe of) Banū Taghlab nor from the apostates and they slaughtered the animals for themselves when it was known that they mentioned the name of Allāh over them and the slaughtered animal was one that was not prohibited for them in the Torah, nor did they prohibit it for themselves, it is permitted, except for fat. They disagreed about the opposites of these characteristics, that is, when they slaughter for a Muslim, who has authorized them, or when they are the Christians of Banū Taghlab or the apostates, and when it is not known that they have mentioned the name of Allāh, or when the purpose of the slaughter by them is unknown, or when it is known that they have mentioned the name of other than Allāh in what they slaughter for their synagogues or churches and for their feasts, or the slaughtered animal is one that is prohibited for them by the Torah, as in the words of the Exalted, "Unto those who are Jews We forbade every animal with claws",[396] or it is one that they have prohibited for themselves, like the slaughtered animals that are not permitted to the Jews because of a shortcoming with which the animal is created.[397] They also disagreed about fat.

14.5.1. Issue 1[398]

In the case where they slaughter under authorization from a Muslim, the narration in the School from Mālik is that it is permitted, and it is also said that it is not permitted. The reason for disagreement stems from whether the belief in the permissibility of the slaughtered animal, in accordance with the Islamic conditions, is a prerequisite for the slaughter performed by a Muslim. Those who held that intention is a condition for this said that the slaughter undertaken by *Kitābī* for a Muslim is not valid, as Islam is a condition for the validity of intention. Those who maintained that it is not a condition, and who gave predominance to the general implication in the Book, that is, the words of the Exalted, "The food of those who have received the Scripture is lawful for you",[399] said that it is permitted. The same is the case for those who believe that the intention of the person authorizing (Muslim) is enough. This is the basis for Ibn Wahb's opinion.

[395] Qurʾān 5 : 5.
[396] Qurʾān 6 : 146.
[397] See Leviticus 29—41.
[398] The heading for the first issue does not appear in the manuscript.
[399] Qurʾān 5 : 5.

14.5.2. Issue 2

This issue relates to the animals slaughtered by the Christians of Banū Taghlab and the apostates. The majority of the jurists maintain that the *ḥukm* of the slaughtered animals of the Christian Arabs is the same as that for the People of the Book. This is the opinion of Ibn ʿAbbās. Some of them did not permit their slaughtered animals. This is one of the two opinions of al-Shāfiʿī, and is also related from ʿAlī (God be pleased with him). The reason for disagreement is whether the Arab Christians and Jews are both included in the meaning of the term *ahl al-Kitāb* meaning "those who have been given the Book", just as it primarily includes those nations specifically attributed with the possession of the Book, and these are the Banū Isrāʾīl, the Romans, and the Byzantines.

With respect to the apostates, the majority maintain that animals slaughtered by them are not to be eaten. Isḥāq said that animals slaughtered by them are lawful, while al-Thawrī said that they are disapproved (*makrūh*). The reason for disagreement is whether the apostate is included within the meaning of the People of the Book. Thus, he may or may not have the sanctity provided to the People of the Book.

14.5.3. Issue 3

In the case where it is not known that the People of the Book have mentioned the name of Allāh over the slaughtered animal, Mālik said that it may be eaten, which is also related from ʿAlī, and I do not remember a disagreement about it at the moment. It can probably be said that the principle is that their slaughtered animals are not to be consumed except those which conform to the conditions of Islam, and if it is agreed that *tasmiya* is a condition for *dhakāh* it follows that they should not be eaten because of doubt.

Some jurists considered it abominable to eat the animals that they slaughter for their feasts and places of worship, and this is Mālik's opinion. Some of them declared it permissible, which is the opinion of Ashhab. Some prohibited it, and that is al-Shāfiʿī's opinion. The reason for their disagreement arises from the conflict of two general implications in the Book on this subject. The words of the Exalted, "The food of those who have received the Scripture is lawful for you",[400] may be interpreted to have restricted His words, "And (forbidden is) that which hath been dedicated unto any other than Allāh",[401] as each of these can validly make an exemption from the other. Those who considered the words "dedicated unto any other than Allāh" to have restricted

[400] Qurʾān 5 : 5.
[401] Qurʾān 5 : 3.

the words "The food of those who have received the Scripture is lawful for you" said that what has been dedicated to their houses of worship and feasts is not permitted. Those who deemed it to be the other way around said that it is permitted.

When an animal that is prohibited for them is slaughtered by them, it is said that it is permitted, and it is also said that it is not permitted. A distinction is also made between what is prohibited to them by the Torah and that which they prohibited for themselves, that is, by permitting what they prohibited for themselves and prohibiting what is prohibited for them by Allāh. It is also said that it is considered abominable and not prohibited. All four opinions are found in the School. The prohibition is related from Ibn al-Qāsim, permissibility from Ibn Wahb and Ibn ʿAbd al-Ḥakam, and the distinction from Ashhab. The basis for the disagreement stems from the conflict between the general implication of the (relevant) verse and the meaning of the stipulation of intention, that is, the belief in the permissibility of the slaughtered animal because of *dhakāh*. Those who maintained that it is a condition for *dhakāh* said that these slaughtered animals are not permitted, as they believed that they would become permissible with *dhakāh*. Those who maintained that it is not a condition for it relied upon the permitting general implication of the verse and said that these slaughtered animals are permitted.

This (reason for disagreement) is the very basis for the disagreement they have about eating fat (tallow) from their slaughtered animals, and no one disagreed over it except Mālik and his disciples. Some of them said that this fat is prohibited, and it is the opinion of Ashhab. Some said that it is abominable. Both opinions are related from Mālik himself. Some said that it is permissible. In the case of fat another reason, from among others, intervenes, besides the conflict between the general implication and the stipulation of the belief that the slaughtered animal becomes permissible through *dhakāh*. That reason is whether *dhakāh* can be viewed in separate segments. Those who maintained that it can be viewed in parts said that (this) fat is not to be eaten, while those who maintained that it is not to be split up said that the fat may be eaten. The permissibility of fat from their slaughtered animals is indicated by the tradition of ʿAbd Allāh ibn Mughaffal when he came upon a skin (leather bag) of fat on the day of Khaybar. It has been mentioned in the Book of *Jihād*.[402] Those who made a distinction between what was prohibited to them out of these by their original law and what was prohibited by them of their own accord said that what was prohibited for them was the truth and *dhakāh*

[402] The tradition of Ibn Mughaffal is: "I came upon a skin (leather bag) of fat on the day of Khaybar and said to myself, 'I will not give any of it [to anyone]'. I turned around and there was the Messenger of Allāh (God's peace and blessings be upon him) smiling at me".

cannot be effective in it, but what they prohibited for themselves is based on falsehood and *dhakāh* is effective in it.

The Qāḍī (Ibn Rushd) said: The truth is that what was prohibited for them and what they prohibited for themselves became, at the time of the *sharīʿa* of Islam, a nullity, as it (the *sharīʿa* of Islam) abrogates all preceding laws. It is, therefore, necessary not to take into account their belief about it, nor should it be stipulated that their belief about the permissibility of slaughtered animals be the same as the belief of the Muslims or that of their (own) laws, because if this is stipulated the eating of their slaughtered animals would not be valid from any aspect, for their belief in their *sharīʿa* in this respect stands abrogated, and their belief based upon our *sharīʿa* is not valid. This is a *ḥukm* that Allāh, the Exalted, has laid down specifically for them. Thus, their slaughtered animals are permitted to us, Allāh knows best, without qualification, otherwise the *ḥukm* of the verse permitting this would stand lifted completely. Think over this, for it is evident, Allāh knows best.

The majority of the jurists maintain that the slaughtered animals of the Magians are not permitted, for they are polytheists. A group of jurists permitted them and relied for their permissibility upon the saying of the Prophet (God's peace and blessings be upon him), "Establish with them the practice adopted for the People of the Book". With respect to the Sabians, the disagreement is based upon the dispute whether they are from the People of the Book.

In the case of a (Muslim) woman and a (Muslim) minor, the majority of the jurists maintain that animals slaughtered by them are permitted and are not disapproved. This is Mālik's opinion. Ibn al-Muṣʿab considered them disapproved. The reason for their disagreement is the deficient legal capacity of the woman and a minor. The majority did not disagree in the case of a woman because of the tradition of Muʿādh ibn Saʿīd "that a slave-girl of Kaʿb ibn Mālik was tending the sheep near Salaʿ when she found that one of the sheep was about to die. She took hold of it and slaughtered it with a stone. The Messenger of Allāh (God's peace and blessings be upon him) was asked about it and he said, 'There is no harm, so eat it'". This is regarded as an authentic tradition.

Mālik did not permit the animal slaughtered by the insane and the intoxicated person, but al-Shāfiʿī did. The reason for disagreement derives from the stipulation of intention in *dhakāh*. Those who stipulated intention for this disallowed it, as it (intention) is not valid when formed by the mentally ill or the intoxicated person, especially the mentally ill.

The majority of the jurists permit the *dhakāh* performed by the thief and the usurper, but some of them disallow this and hold it to be similar to carrion, and this was upheld by Dāwūd and Isḥāq ibn Rāhwayh. The reason for their disagreement stems from whether the proscription indicates the invalidity of the thing proscribed (i.e., the object of the act proscribed, which is the stolen property). Those who maintained that it does indicate this said that the thief and the usurper are prohibited from slaughtering it, consuming it, or owning it; thus, if they subject it to ***dhakāh*** the ***dhakāh*** becomes invalid. Those who maintained that it does not indicate this, unless the forbidden act is a condition for (the validity of) such an act, said that their ***dhakāh*** is valid as the validity of ownership is not one of the conditions for ***dhakāh***. In the *Muwaṭṭa'* of Ibn Wahb (his narration) it is related that "The Messenger of Allāh (God's peace and blessings be upon him) was asked about it, and he did not raise any objection against it". Its permissibility, along with abomination, is laid down in what is related from the Prophet (God's peace and blessings be upon him) about the sheep slaughtered without the permission of the owner. The Messenger of Allāh (God's peace and blessings be upon him) said, "Feed it to the prisoners (of war)".

This is sufficient for the fundamentals of this book, Allāh knows best.

XV

THE BOOK OF *ṢAYD* (HUNTING)

In this book too the fundamentals are covered in four chapters. The first chapter is about the *ḥukm* of hunting, and about its object. The second is about tools with which hunting is undertaken. The third is about the description of the *dhakāh* of game and the conditions stipulated for undertaking *dhakāh* in game. The fourth is about the person who can hunt lawfully.

15.1. Chapter 1 The *Ḥukm* of Hunting and its Object

The majority of the jurists maintain that hunting is permissible, because of the words of the Exalted, "To hunt and to eat the fish of the sea is made lawful for you, a provision for you and for the seafarers; but to hunt on land is forbidden you so long as ye are on the pilgrimage. Be mindful of your duty to Allāh, unto Whom ye will be gathered;"[403] after this He said, "But when ye have left the sacred territory, then go hunting (if ye will)".[404] The jurists agreed that the command for hunting in this verse after the proscription indicates permissibility, in the same way that they agreed it does in the words of the Exalted, "And when the prayer is ended, then disperse in the land and seek of Allāh's bounty", that is, the purpose of the issuance of the command after the proscription is to indicate permissibility, although they did differ as to whether a command after a proscription implies permissibility or whether it indicates an obligation in accordance with its original application.

Mālik considered wasteful hunting to be abominable. The later jurists in his School go into its details and the summary of their views is that some of its types are obligatory for some people, prohibited for some, recommended for some, and disapproved for others. This kind or reasoning in law delves deep into analogy and is far removed from the principles expressly stated in the law, and it does not suit this book of ours, as our purpose is to mention those

[403] Qur'ān 5 : 96.
[404] Qur'ān 5 : 2.

(issues) that are expressly stated in the law or are closely related to those so stated.

With respect to the object of hunting, the jurists agreed that its object is the different types of fish among the creatures of the sea (water) and the permissible non-domesticated animals from among the animals on land. They disagreed about the domesticated animals that have turned wild so that it is not possible to catch them nor to subject them to *naḥr* or *dhabḥ*.[405] Mālik said that they are not to be eaten unless those that are subject to *naḥr* are killed by *naḥr* and those subject to *dhabḥ* are slaughtered, or unless they are subject to either method, if they belong to a category that is subject to both. Abū Ḥanīfa and al-Shāfiʿī said that if a runaway camel cannot be subject to *dhakāh* it is to be killed like game.

The reason for their disagreement stems from the conflict of the principle in this matter with a report in this regard. The principle in this topic is that a domesticated animal is not to be eaten except after *dhabḥ* or *naḥr* and that the wild animal is eaten after shooting it down. The report opposing these principles is the tradition of Rāfiʿ ibn Khadīj, in which he said, "One of the camels bolted and there were few horses with the group. They chased it but it exhausted them, so a man shot an arrow at it and Allāh prevented it from running away. The Prophet (God's peace and blessings be upon him) said, 'In some of these animals are untamed ones like the untamed wild animals, so if any of them bolts this is what you do to it'". It is preferable to base the opinion on this tradition because of its authenticity, for it does not necessarily amount to an exemption from the principle. It could, however, be said that it is in conformity with the relevant principle, because the underlying cause for wounding (*ʿaqr*) being the *dhakāh* in some of the animals is nothing more than not being able to catch it. Analogy and transmission (of a tradition), therefore, conform with each other.

15.2. Chapter 2 The Things with which Hunting is Undertaken

The sources of this chapter are two verses and two traditions. The first verse contains the words of the Exalted, "O ye who believe! Allāh will surely try you somewhat (in the matter) of the game which ye take with your hands and your spears".[406] The second contains the words of the Exalted, "Say (all) good

[405] The distinction between *naḥr* and *dhabḥ* has already been explained by the author in the previous book.

[406] Qurʾān 5 : 94.

things are made lawful for you. And those beasts and birds of prey which ye have trained as hounds are trained, teaching them what Allāh taught you; so eat of that which they catch for you and mention Allāh's name upon it, and observe your duty to Allāh, Lo! Allāh is swift to take account".[407] Among the two traditions, the first is the tradition of ʿAdiyy ibn Ḥātim, in which the Messenger of Allāh (God's peace and blessings be upon him) said to him, "If you dispatch your trained dogs after mentioning the name of Allāh over them, then, eat what they catch for you. If the dog eats (part of) what it catches do not eat it, for I am afraid that it has then caught for itself. If other dogs mix up with them do not eat it, as you have taken the name of Allāh over your dog and not on dogs besides it". He (also) asked him about *miʿrāḍ* (a featherless arrow)[408] and he replied, "If it hits it with the broad side, do not eat it, for it has died with a blow". This tradition is the fundamental source for most of what is in this book. The second tradition is that of Abū Thaʿlaba al-Khushanī, and in this the words of the Prophet (God's peace and blessings be upon him) are, "Eat what you hunt with your bow when you take the name of Allāh over it. Eat what you catch with your trained dog after taking the name of Allāh over it, but eat what you catch with your untrained dog after you have been able to slaughter it". These traditions are recorded by the compilers of the *ṣaḥīḥ* traditions.

The instruments (weapons) used for hunting include those over which they agreed as a whole, and also those over which, and about whose description they disagreed, and these are three: predatory animals, sharp instruments, and blunt weapons. They agreed about instruments sharpened to kill, like spears, swords, and arrows, because they are mentioned explicitly in the Book and the *sunna*. Likewise, they agreed about things similar to those used for wounding, except for the things whose effectiveness they disagreed about in the case of the *dhakāh* of domesticated animals, like teeth, claws, and bones. The discussion of these has preceded and there is no sense in repeating it.

With respect to the blunt weapon, they disagreed about hunting with it, like hunting with *miʿrāḍ* and stones. Some of the jurists did not permit this, except for those animals that were caught alive and slaughtered. Some of them permitted it without qualification. Some made a distinction about animals killed by *miʿrāḍ* or with the sharp or blunt part of a stone when these tore the body of the prey. They permitted it when the body of the animal was torn, and they did not permit it when it was not. This opinion was held by the famous jurists of the provinces, al-Shāfiʿī, Mālik, Abū Ḥanīfa, Aḥmad, al-Thawrī,

[407] Qurʾān 5 : 4.

[408] Causing death by the shock of a blow, like hitting with the broad side of a spear or arrow, and not by causing a wound that bleeds.

and others besides them, and it refers to the principle that there is no *dhakāh* without a sharpened instrument.

The reason for the disagreement is based on the conflict of some principles of this topic with others, and on the conflict between a tradition and the principles. It is a principle of this topic that an animal killed with a blow is prohibited by the Book and by consensus. Another principle is that *ʿaqr* (wounding with a cut) is the *dhakāh* for game. Those who held that what is killed by the blunt edge of a weapon is killed by a blow prohibited it absolutely. Those who held it to be *ʿaqr* of a kind permitted it absolutely. Those who made a distinction between what causes a rupture and what does not decided on the basis of the tradition of ʿAdiyy ibn Ḥātim that has preceded, and this is correct.

With respect to (using) predatory animals, the agreement and disagreement about them relates to the species and the condition, and in the case of some only to the condition. The species over which they agreed is that of dogs with the exception of a black dog; a group of jurists, including al-Ḥasan al-Baṣrī, Ibrāhīm al-Nakhaʿī, and Qatāda disapproved of black dogs. Aḥmad said that he knew of no one who made an exemption in the case of a jet-black dog. This was also the opinion of Isḥāq. The majority of the jurists permitted the game hunted by it, if it was a trained to do so.

The reason for the disagreement arises from the conflict of analogy with a general implication. This is so as the words of the Exalted, "And those beasts and birds of prey which ye have trained as hounds are trained, teaching them what Allāh taught you",[409] implies the inclusion of all kinds of dogs in it, while "the command of the Prophet (God's peace and blessings be upon him) to kill the jet-black dog" implies by way of analogy (for this case) that game hunted by it is not permitted in accordance with the opinion of those who believe that a proscription indicates the unsuitability of the thing related to the proscribed act.

The other kinds of predatory animals over which they disagreed, include the birds of prey and other predatory animals. Some of them permitted hunting with all of them if they were trained, even a cat as is held by Ibn Shaʿbān, and this is the opinion of Mālik and his disciples, as well as that of the jurists of the provinces. It is also related from Ibn ʿAbbās, that is, any predatory animal or bird of prey that is receptive to training becomes a lawful instrument of *dhakāh* for game. A group of jurists said that there is no (lawful) hunting with predatory animals besides the dog, neither with the falcon nor the hawk nor with the others, unless *dhakāh* is performed on the game if caught alive. This is the opinion of Mujāhid. Some of them made an exception for the falcon

[409] Qurʾān 5 : 4.

alone from among the birds of prey, and said that only the game hunted by it is permitted.

The reason for disagreement in this topic is based upon two factors. The first is the analogy for all the predatory animals and birds of prey from the case of the dog, because it is believed that the text has permitted it for dogs, that is, in the words of the Exalted, "And those *jawāriḥ* (beasts and birds of prey) which ye have trained as hounds are trained, teaching them what Allāh taught you",[410] unless it is interpreted to mean that the word *mukallibīn* (in the verse) is derived from the pouncing[411] of the predatory animals, and not from the meaning of the word dog. This is indicated by the generality of the word *al-jawāriḥ* used for predatory animals and birds of prey in the verse. On the basis of this the reason for disagreement is the equivocality of the word *mukallibīn*.

The second reason is about the stipulation of catching that it (the animal) should catch for its master. If this is a condition, then, does it apply to animals other than the dog? Those who maintained that an analogy for the remaining animals is not to be drawn from the dog, and that the word *mukallibīn* is derived from the word meaning "dog" and not from any other term, or that catching can only be achieved by the dog, that is, for its master (and on his bidding), and that this is a condition, said that hunting is not to be undertaken with any predatory animal except the dog. Those who made an analogy for all predatory animals drawn from the dog, and did not stipulate in the act of catching the condition that it be on the bidding of the master, said that hunting with all other predatory animals and birds of prey is permitted as long as they are amenable to training. Those who made an exemption only for the falcon alone decided on the basis of the tradition of ʿAdiyy ibn Ḥātim, who said, "I asked the Messenger of Allāh (God's peace and blessings be upon him) about the game caught by a falcon and he said, 'Eat what it catches for you'". It is recorded by al-Tirmidhī.

These, then, are the reasons for their agreement and disagreement about the different kinds of predatory animals and birds of prey.

The conditions stipulated for the predatory animals and birds of prey over which they disagreed include those that they agreed to as a whole, and this is training, because of the words of the Exalted, "And those beasts and birds of prey which ye have trained as hounds are trained, teaching them what Allāh taught you,"[412] and also the words of the Prophet (God's peace and blessings be upon him), "If you dispatch your trained dogs". They disagreed about the

[410] Qurʾān 5 : 4.

[411] The meaning here could also be "rabid predatory animals"; however, training a rabid animal for hunting would be out of the question insofar as it conveys the meaning of a diseased animal.

[412] Qurʾān 5 : 4.

description of the stipulated training and its conditions. A group of jurists said that training is of three types. The first is that you call the predatory animal or bird of prey and it comes to you (responds). The second is that you set it off to pursue game and it does. The third is that you deter it from doing something and it stops. There is no disagreement among them about these three conditions in the case of the dog. They disagreed about deterrence in the case of all other animals (used for hunting). They also disagreed over whether it is a condition that the animal should not eat (from) what it has caught. Some of them stipulated this without qualifications, while others stipulated it for the dog alone. Mālik's opinion is that these three conditions are to be stipulated for dogs as well as other animals. Ibn Ḥabīb, one of his disciples, said that deterrence is not to be stipulated for those animals that are not amenable to it, like falcons and hawks. In Mālik's view it is not a condition, either for dogs or for other animals, not to eat (what they catch), while others stipulated it for the dog, but not for the birds of prey. Some of them stipulated it, as we have said, for all. The majority of the jurists permit the eating of game caught by the falcon and the hawk even if they eat of it, because it is prompted to catch for eating.

The disagreement, then, in this topic refers to two points. The first is whether it is a condition for training that it should be deterred, if that is in its nature. The second is whether it is a condition that it should not eat (of what it catches). The reason for disagreement over the stipulation of not eating is based upon two factors. The first is the conflict of traditions over this, and the second is whether it is still effective as trained catcher if it eats part of the catch. The traditions include that of ʿAdiyy ibn Ḥātim, which has preceded, and in it are the words, "If the dog eats (part of) what it catches do not eat it, for I am afraid that it has then caught for itself". The tradition that conflicts with this is the tradition of Abū Thaʿlaba al-Khushanī, who said, "The Messenger of Allāh (God's peace and blessings be upon him) said, 'If you let go your trained dog after mentioning the name of Allāh over it, then eat (what it catches)'. I said, 'Even if it eats from it, O Messenger of Allāh?' He said, 'Even if it eats of it'". Those who reconciled the two traditions by construing the tradition of ʿAdiyy ibn Ḥātim to imply recommendation, and this for permissibility, said that it is not a condition that jthe animal should not eat (of the prey). Those who preferred the tradition of ʿAdiyy ibn Ḥātim—as it is a tradition agreed upon by al-Bukhārī and Muslim, while the tradition of Abū Thaʿlaba is disputed, for which reason the two Shaykhs, al-Bukhārī and Muslim have not recorded it—and (in addition) maintained that it is a condition for catching that it should not eat from it on the basis of the mentioned tradition, said that if it eats of the caught game it is not to be eaten. This was upheld by al-Shāfiʿī, Abū Ḥanīfa, Aḥmad, Isḥāq, and al-Thawrī, and it is also the opinion of Ibn ʿAbbās. An exemption was made, as we have said, in the eating of what it (the trained animal) has (partly) eaten, by Mālik, Saʿīd ibn Mālik, Ibn ʿUmar, and Sulaymān.

The later Mālikites maintained that eating (by the dog) is no indication that it did not catch for its master nor is catching for its master a condition for *dhakāh*, as the intention of the dog is not known, as it may catch for its master at first and it may then suit it to have it all for itself. This statement of theirs, however, is in conflict with the text of the tradition and is contrary to the apparent meaning of the Book, that is, the words of the Exalted, "So eat of that which they catch for you".[413] There is a method for identifying what is caught for the master of the dog, and that is practice; therefore, the Prophet (God's peace and blessings be upon him) said, "If the dog eats (part of) what it catches do not eat it, for I am afraid that it has then caught for itself".

With respect to their disagreement over deterrence, there is no reason for it besides analogy drawn for the remaining animals and birds from the case of the dog, as the dog that is not deterred cannot, by agreement, be called trained. Can animals and birds be called trained if they are not deterred? Their is a vacillation in this and that is the basis for the disagreement.

15.3. Chapter 3 *Dhakāh* Specific to Game and its Conditions

They agreed that *dhakāh* specific to game is *ʿaqr* (shooting to kill). They disagreed extensively over its conditions. If its principles, which are the basis of disagreement, are taken into account, besides the conditions stipulated for the instrument and the hunter, you will find them to be eight conditions. Two are common to the two kinds of *dhakāh*, I mean, the *dhakāh* of game and the *dhakāh* of animals other than game. These are intention and the *tasmiya*. Six of them are specific to this kind of *dhakāh* of game. The first is that if a (hunting) weapon or a predatory animal has not struck the game by damaging one of its vital organs, then, it is necessary that it be subjected to the form of *dhakāh* meant for a domesticated animal, before it dies from whatever has struck it whether it was a predatory animal or a blow. If, however, one of its vital organs has been damaged this is not necessary, even though it is desirable. The second condition is that the act of hunting the game must be initiated by the hunter and not occurring by chance as in the case of a snare (net), or spontaneously by a predatory animal as is the case of a dog that springs of its own accord. The third condition is that a thing not valid for lawful hunting should not be

[413] Qurʾān 5 : 4.

coupled with his action. Fourth, the hunter should not be in doubt about the identification of the particular game that he has struck, and this may happen when it disappears from his sight. Fifth, the game should not be in a position of being (easily) caught at the time of dispatch (when it could have been caught and slaughtered like a domesticated animal). Sixth, its death should not be caused by its terror of the predatory animal or by a collision with it.

These are the fundamental conditions the stipulation of which, or the lack of it, led the jurists to disagree. Sometimes they agreed about the necessity of some of these conditions, and disagreed about their existence in each particular incident. This is like the agreement of the Mālikites that the act causing death should be initiated by the hunter, and their disagreement over the case where the predatory animal or bird of prey springs from his hand or takes off on its own and the hunter urges it on afterwards. They disagreed as to whether this catch would be permissible, because of the vacillation whether this condition has been fulfilled in this situation. Again, it is like the agreement of Abū Ḥanīfa and Mālik that when he (the hunter) comes upon a prey that does not have a wounded vital organ the condition is that he should subject it to *dhakāh* before it dies, but they disagreed when he retrieves it alive and it dies in his hand before he is able to slaughter it. Abū Ḥanīfa forbids its consumption like that of carrion. Mālik permitted it and considered it to be similar to the first case, I mean, when he is not able to retrieve it from the predatory animal until it dies. This is so, because of the vacillation of this situation between saying that he appears negligent, as he caught it without its vital organs having been damaged when it was not in the clutches of the predatory animal, and saying that he does not appear to be negligent.

As these conditions are the foundation for the conditions stipulated for game, along with all the remaining conditions that have been mentioned about the instrument and the hunter himself, as will be coming up, it is necessary that we mention what they agreed upon from among these and what they differed over, as well as the reasons for disagreement in these and the cases that arise from the well-known issues.

We say: The discussion about the disagreement over *tasmiya* and intention has preceded, along with the reasons for it, in the Book of Slaughtered Animals. With reference to intention in *dhakāh* according to those who stipulate it, it is not permitted (to eat the game) when the hunter sets his predatory animal after the game and another (predatory animal owned by him) executes the *dhakāh* for this game. This is Mālik's opinion. Al-Shāfiʿī, Abū Ḥanīfa, Aḥmad, and Abū Thawr said that this is permitted and may be eaten. Of the same nature is the disagreement among Mālik's disciples about setting a predatory animal after unseen game, like setting it after possible game in a swamp covered with trees or after newborn game or something behind a hillock, when he does not know whether there is something over there, as the intention here is based on ignorance.

The first condition specific to the *dhakāh* of game, out of the six that we have mentioned, is that the wound inflicted by the predatory animal, when it is not (inflicted) on a vital organ, amounts to *dhakāh* if the hunter is not able to catch the game alive. The majority of the jurists upheld this stipulation, because of what is related in the tradition of ᶜAdiyy ibn Ḥātim, where in some of its versions the Prophet (God's peace and blessings be upon him) said, "If you catch it alive, slaughter it". Al-Nakhaᶜī said: "If you catch it alive and you do not have a sharp instrument, set the dogs after it until they kill it". This was also maintained by al-Ḥasan al-Baṣrī deciding on the basis of the general implication of the words of the Exalted, "So eat of that which they catch for you".[414] On the basis of this condition, Mālik said that the hunter dispatching his predatory animal is not to be sluggish in finding the game, and if he is lazy and finds the game dead, then, if it died from damage to a vital organ with an arrow eating it is permitted otherwise it is not permitted, for had he not been lazy about it he would have been able to catch it alive without its vital organs being damaged.

The second condition is that the act should be initiated by the trapper and should be continuous until the prey is caught. With reference to their dispute over this they disagreed about what is caught in the snare or net, if a vital organ is struck by a sharp instrument inside these. Mālik, al-Shāfiᶜī, and the majority of the jurists prohibited this, while al-Ḥasan al-Baṣrī made an exemption for it. Under this rule Mālik did not permit the *dhakāh* the game when the predatory animal, having been dispatched, becomes occupied with something else and later comes to it (the prey) of its own accord.

The third condition is that nothing else should participate with it in wounding the prey when the wounding by such other thing is not valid as *dhakāh*. This is a condition that is unanimously agreed upon, as far as I can recall, as it is not known what killed it (the prey).

The fourth condition is that there should be no doubt about the corpus of the prey or about the predatory animal having killed it. With reference to this they disagreed about eating the game when the target has disappeared from the hunter's sight. Mālik said, once: "There is no harm in eating game when the target dropped has disappeared from your sight, if you find the marks of your dog upon it or if you find your arrow in it, as long as it has not been there overnight, for if it has been there overnight I consider it abominable". Al-Thawrī also considered it abominable. ᶜAbd al-Wahhāb said that if the prey has taken shelter overnight (after being struck) it is not to be eaten (when

[414] Qurᵓān 5 : 4.

found). There is a disagreement about the arrow. Ibn al-Mājishūn said that it is to be eaten in both cases, if it is found to have a damaged vital organ. Mālik maintained, according to *al-Mudawwana*, that it is not to be eaten in either case, if it stays out overnight and has a ruptured vital organ. Al-Shāfiʿī said that on the basis of analogy it is not to be eaten if its track has disappeared. Abū Ḥanīfa said that if the game conceals itself and the dog continues to search for it, if the hunter finds it dead it is permissible for eating as long as the dog has not given up the hunt, but if it gives up the search eating the game is disapproved.

The reason for their disagreement is based upon two things. The first is the doubt occurring about the corpus of the game or about its *dhakāh.* The second is the conflict of traditions on the issue. Muslim, al-Nasāʾī, Al-Tirmidhī, and Abū Dāwūd have recorded from Abū Thaʿlaba from the Prophet (God's peace and blessings be upon him) about the person who finds his game after three days. He (the Prophet) said, "Eat it as long as there is no stench". Muslim has recorded, also from Abū Thaʿlaba from the Prophet (God's peace and blessings be upon him), that he said, "If you shoot your arrow and the target drops, but disappears from your sight, eat it as long as it does not elude you overnight". In the tradition of ʿAdiyy ibn Ḥātim the Prophet (God's peace and blessings be upon him) said, "If you find your arrow in it and you do not find marks from beasts of prey on it, and you know that it is your arrow that killed it, then, eat it".

Within this topic is their disagreement about game that is shot by an arrow or has been struck by the hunting animal but falls into water or falls from a height. Mālik said that it is not to be eaten as it is not known from which of the two causes it has died, unless the arrow has penetrated a vital organ and there is no doubt that it has died from it. This was upheld by the majority of the jurists. Abū Ḥanīfa said that a prey with a damaged vital organ is not to be eaten if it falls in the water, but it may be eaten if it falls from a height. ʿAṭāʾ said that it is not to be eaten at all if it falls into water or from a height, after it was struck in a vital organ, because of the possibility that it died because of the fall or the water before it was affected by the damage to its vital organ.

With respect to its death due to a collision with the hunting animal, Ibn al-Qāsim prohibited (eating it) on the analogy of death by a blunt weapon. Ashhab permitted it because of the generality of the words of the Exalted, "So eat of that which they catch for you".[415] The School did not disagree that what dies of terror of the hunting animal has not been subjected to valid *dhakāh.* With respect to the condition that the prey be out of reach at the time of dispatching the hunting animal, it is agreed upon as far as I know, and this

[415] Qurʾān 5 : 4.

condition prevails when the game is within reach without any apprehension or risk (of its fleeing). This happens in situations when it is entangled in something or something is clinging to it or has a broken wing or leg due to a shot. There are a number of cases in which the game vacillates between its being within reach or out of it, like the dogs pursuing it until it falls into a ditch. It is maintained in the School that in this case it may be eaten, and it is also said that it is not to be eaten.

They disagreed about the description of striking the game (*ʿaqr*) when one of its limbs is severed by the hit. It is said that the game may be eaten and not what is severed, while a group of jurists said that all of it may be eaten. Another group of jurists made a distinction between whether the severed limb was a vital part or some other part, and they said that if it was a vital limb the whole may be eaten but if it was not a vital limb the game may be eaten and not this limb. This is the meaning of Mālik's opinion. It is the background to their disagreement when the game is cut into two equal parts or when one is larger than the other.

The reason for their disagreement stems from the conflict between the saying of the Prophet (God's peace and blessings be upon him), "What is cut off from the animal when it is alive is carrion", and the general implication of the words of the Exalted, "So eat of that which they catch for you",[416] and His words, "The game which ye take with your hands and your spears".[417] Those who gave predominance to the *ḥukm* of game, which is the effectiveness of the *ʿaqr*, without qualifications, and interpreted the tradition to apply to domesticated animals, said that the game and the severed limb of the game may be eaten. Those who interpreted the tradition to be applicable to both domesticated as well as wild animals, and who excluded from the general implication, through this tradition, the severed limb said that the game may be eaten and not the severed limb. Those who took into account the term *ḥayāh* (life) in the Prophet's saying, "while it is alive", to mean the normal unthreatened life, made a distinction based on whether the severed part was vital.

15.4. Chapter 4 Conditions for the Hunter

The conditions for the hunter are the same as those for the person slaughtering, and these have preceded in the Book of the Slaughtered Animals, whether they were agreed upon or disputed. There is an additional condition

[416] Qurʾān 5 : 4.
[417] Qurʾān 5 : 94.

specific to hunting land, which is that he should not be in the ritual state of *iḥrām*. There is no dispute about this because of the words of the Exalted, "But to hunt on land is forbidden you so long as ye are on the pilgrimage".[418] If he does hunt, is this game to be considered as permitted for those not in the state of *iḥrām* or is it to be considered carrion not permitted for anyone at all? The jurists disagreed about it. Mālik maintained that it is carrion, while al-Shāfiʿī, Abū Ḥanīfa, and Abū Thawr held that it is permitted to the person not in a state of *iḥrām* to eat it.

The reason for their disagreement derives from the well-known principle whether the proscription renders the object of the act proscribed as invalid. This is similar to the *ḥukm* of slaughter (of the stolen or misappropriated animal) by a thief or by a person who misappropriates.

Within this topic they disagreed about hunting with a dog belonging to the Magians. Mālik said that it is permitted to hunt with it, as the consideration is to be given to the hunter not the instrument he employs. This was also the opinion of al-Shāfiʿī, Abū Ḥanīfa, and others. Jābir ibn ʿAbd Allāh, al-Ḥasan, ʿAṭāʾ, Mujāhid, and al-Thawrī disapproved this, because the communication in the words of the Exalted, "And those beasts and birds of prey which ye have trained as hounds are trained",[419] is directed at the believers.

This is sufficient in accordance with our aim in this book. Allāh is the Grantor of the truth.

[418] Qurʾān 5 : 96.
[419] Qurʾān 5 : 4.

XVI

THE BOOK OF *ʿAQĪQA* (SACRIFICE FOR NEWBORN INFANTS)

The comprehensive discussion of the fundamentals of this book is covered under six topics. The first is about the identification of its *ḥukm*. The second is about the identification of its subject-matter. The third is about the person for whom *ʿaqīqa* is to be made and the number (of animals sacrificed). the fourth is about the identification of the time of this rite. The fifth is about the age of the sacrificial animal for this rite and description. The sixth is about the *ḥukm* of its flesh and its other parts.

With respect to its *ḥukm*, a group of jurists, including the Ẓāhirites, maintained that it is obligatory. The majority of the jurists held that it is a *sunna*. Abū Ḥanīfa held that it is neither an obligation nor a *sunna*, and it is said that in the final analysis it is, in his view, voluntary.

The reason for their disagreement stems from the conflict of traditions on the subject. This is so as the apparent meaning of the tradition of Samura implies obligation, and this is the saying of the Prophet (God's peace and blessings be upon him), "Each boy is held in pledge for his *ʿaqīqa*, which is slaughtered on his behalf on the seventh day, and the harm is removed (by shaving his hair)". The apparent meaning of the saying of the Prophet (God's peace and blessings be upon him), when he was questioned and said, "I do not like the breaking of ties (*ʿuqūq*), and he to whom a child is born, if he wishes to perform the rite for it, he may do so", implies recommendation or permissibility. Those who understood it to imply a recommendation said that *ʿaqīqa* is a *sunna*, while those who understood it to mean permissibility said that it is neither a *sunna* nor an obligation. Both traditions have been recorded by Abū Dāwūd. Those who relied upon the tradition of Samura deemed it obligatory.

The majority of the jurists agreed about its subject-matter that nothing is valid in it except what is valid in making sacrifice from the eight pairs. Mālik, however, preferred sheep in accordance with his views in the case of sacrifice. His opinion differed over whether a camel or cow is valid. The remaining jurists abide by their principle that a camel has greater merit than a cow and a cow has greater merit than sheep.

The reason for their disagreement arises from the conflict between traditions on the subject and analogy. The tradition is that of Ibn ʿAbbās, "that the Messenger of Allāh (God's peace and blessings be upon him) performed the *ʿaqīqa* for al-Ḥasan and al-Ḥusayn with a ram each", as well as his saying, "For a girl is one sheep and for a boy two". These are recorded by Abū Dāwūd. The analogy is that it is a religious rite, therefore, it is necessary that first priority should be for the one having greater merit on the basis of analogy drawn from offerings.

About the person for whom *ʿaqīqa* is to be offered, the majority of the jurists maintain that it is only for the newborn infants, male and female. Al-Ḥasan deviated and said that *ʿaqīqa* is not to be performed for a girl, while some permitted it for grown-up persons. The evidence of the majority for its restriction to infants is the saying of the Prophet (God's peace and blessings be upon him), "On the seventh day", and the evidence for its relevance for the girl is the saying of the Prophet (God's peace and blessings be upon him), "For a girl is one sheep and for a boy two". The evidence of those who confined it to the male is the saying of the Prophet (God's peace and blessings be upon him), "Each boy (*ghulām*) is held in pledge for his *ʿaqīqa*".

The jurists also disagreed about the number of animals sacrificed. Mālik said that one sheep each is to be sacrificed for the male and the female. Al-Shāfiʿī, Abū Thawr, Abū Dāwūd, and Aḥmad said that one sheep is to be sacrificed for a girl and two for a boy. The reason for their disagreement springs from the conflict of traditions on the subject. These include the tradition of Umm Kurz al-Kaʿbiyya, who said, "I heard the Messenger of Allāh (God's peace and blessings be upon him) saying about *ʿaqīqa*, 'For the boy are two similar sheep, and for the girl one sheep'". Similarity here implies equivalence (for exchange). This implies a distinction between a male and a female, while the tradition related about his performing *ʿaqīqa* for al-Ḥasan and al-Ḥusayn with one ram each implies an equality between them (male and female).

With respect to the time of this rite, the majority of the jurists maintain that it is the seventh day after birth, but Mālik does not count the day on which the child is born, if it is born during the day, while ʿAbd al-Malik ibn al-Mājishūn counts it. Ibn al-Qāsim has stated in *al-ʿUtbiya* that if the sacrifice is made during the night it is not valid. Mālik's disciples disagreed about the commencement of the time of validity. It is said that it is the time for sacrifices, that is, after sunrise, while it is said that it is after dawn on the analogy of Mālik's opinion about offerings. There is no doubt that those who permitted sacrifices during the night permitted this too, during the night. It is said that it is permitted on the second and the third seventh (the fourteenth and the twenty-first).

The ages and the description (of the sacrificial animals) for this rite are the ages of sacrifices and their valid attributes, that is, the defects avoided for the sacrifices must be avoided in the case of *ʿawīq* too. I do not know of a disagreement over this within the School, nor outside it.

The *ḥukm* of its meat, skin, and the remaining parts of the animal is the *ḥukm* of the meat of the sacrifices with respect to eating, giving as alms, and (prohibition of) sale.

All of the jurists maintain that the pre-Islamic custom of smearing the head of the child with blood of the sacrifice stands abrogated in Islam. This is because of the tradition of Burayda al-Aslamī, who said, "In the days of *jāhiliyya*, when a son was born to one of us, a sheep was slaughtered for him and his head was smeared with its blood. When Islam came, we (stopped that practice and instead) slaughtered (a sheep) and shaved his head and smeared it with saffron". Al-Ḥasan and Qatāda deviated and said that the head of the child is to be touched with cotton that has been dipped in blood. It is considered desirable to break the animal's bones in order to be at variance with the custom of *jāhiliyya*, when the people used to sever them from the joints.

They disagreed about the shaving of the head of the child on the seventh day, and over giving alms worth the value of the weight of his hair in silver. It is said that this is desirable, while it is said that it is not desirable. Both views are narrated from Mālik. Desirability is preferable, and this is the opinion of Ibn Ḥabīb, because of what has been related by Mālik in *al-Muwaṭṭa'* "that Fāṭima, the daughter of the Messenger of Allāh (God's peace and blessings be upon him), shaved the hair of al-Ḥasan, al-Ḥusayn, Zaynab, and Umm Kulthūm, and gave alms in silver equal to the weight of the hair".

XVII

THE BOOK OF FOODS AND BEVERAGES

The discussion of the fundamentals of this book is covered in two chapters. In the first chapter we shall mention the things prohibited in a state of choice. In the second chapter we shall mention the situations arising under duress.

17.1. **Chapter 1 The Prohibited Foods and Beverages**

Human foods are vegetation and animals. The animals that are consumed for nutrition include those that are permissible by law and those that are prohibited. Of these some exist on land and some on water. The things prohibited include those that are prohibited in themselves and those that are prohibited for a cause that is imposed externally. In all of these there are some that are agreed upon by the jurists and some that are disputed. The things prohibited because of an external reason are nine (in number) as a whole: carrion, strangulated animals, those dead from a blow, those dead after a fall, those dead after being gored, those (partly) devoured by a predatory animal, those for the consumption of which *dhakāh* is stipulated but they lack one of its conditions, animals that consume filth, and food smeared with filth.

With respect to *mayta* (carrion), the jurists agreed about the carrion on land. They disagreed about carrion found in the sea into three opinions. One group of jurists said that it is permitted absolutely, while another group said that it is prohibited absolutely. One group said that what floats on the sea is prohibited and what is left (on the coast) by the tide is permitted.

The reason for their disagreement arises from the conflict of traditions on the subject, and the conflict of the general implication with some of them, at the level of the principle, while conforming with them some and conflicting with some at the level of cases. The general implication is found in the words of the Exalted, "Forbidden unto you (for food) are carrion . . ."[420] The traditions conflicting with this generality on the level of the principle are two.

[420] Qur'ān 5 : 3.

The first is agreed upon by al-Bukhārī and Muslim, while the other is disputed. The tradition agreed upon is that of Jābir, in which it is said, "The companions of the Messenger of Allāh (God's peace and blessings be upon him) found a whale known as *ʿanbar*, or some animal, that had been brought in by the tide. They ate from it for about twenty days or a month, and then came up to the Messenger of Allāh (God's peace and blessings be upon him) and informed him about it and he said, 'Do you have some of its meat with you?' They sent him some meat and he ate of it". This conflicts with the Book on principle through its implication not its words. The second tradition is disputed, and it is what has been related by Mālik from Abū Hurayra "that he (the Prophet) was asked about the water of the sea and he said, 'Its water is pure and its carrion is permissible'".[421] The tradition that partially conforms with the general implication (of the verse) is what is related by Ismāʿīl ibn Umayya from ʿAbū al-Zubayr from Jābir from the Prophet (God's peace and blessings be upon him), who said, "Eat what is thrown out by the sea or is left by the tide, but do not eat what floats on it". It is, in their view, weaker than the tradition related by Mālik (above). The reason for the weakness of Mālik's tradition is that there is a narrator in the chain who is unknown, and that it has been transmitted through a single *isnād*. Abū ʿUmar, however, maintains that its narrators are known and it has been transmitted through various channels. The reason for the weakness of Jābir's tradition is that though the narrators in its *isnād* are reliable, the name of Jābir's disciple who is supposed to have narrated from him is dropped, and the tradition is attributed to Jābir directly be the disciple's disciple (*mawqūf* at Jābir).[422]

Those who preferred this tradition of Jābir over Abū Hurayra's tradition, because of the support of the general implication of the Book for it, did not exempt anything from it (the general rule), except what is brought in by the tide, as no conflict arises from it. Those who preferred Abū Hurayra's tradition upheld absolute permissibility (of the carrion from the sea). Those who upheld its absolute prohibition decided on the basis of preference for the general implication of the Book. Absolute permissibility is upheld by Mālik and al-Shāfiʿī, while absolute prohibition is maintained by Abū Ḥanīfa. A group, other than these jurists, upheld the distinction (between what floats and what comes in with the tide).

[421] This tradition is in conflict with the Qurʾānic verse, but apparently it restricts its meaning to the carrion of the land.

[422] When the name of the Companion, who is supposed to be the immediate narrator of a tradition, is missing from the *isnād* and the text of the tradition is attributed to the Prophet directly by a disciple from the second Muslim generation, the tradition is known as *mursal*. If the name of the second narrator, the Companion's disciple, is dropped, the tradition is known as *mawqūf*.

There is no disagreement among the jurists that the five other categories laid down by Allāh along with carrion also carry the *ḥukm* of carrion. They disagreed with respect to the eating of *jallāla*, which is an animal that consumes filth. The reason for their disagreement stems from the conflict of analogy with a tradition. The tradition is in the report "that the Messenger of Allāh (God's peace and blessings be upon him) proscribed the meat of the *jallāla* as well as its milk". It is recorded by Abū Dāwūd from Ibn ʿUmar. The analogy conflicting with this is that what enters the mouth of the animal is converted into its flesh and other elements. Thus, if we say that the flesh of an animal is permitted, though it is converted and developed from food consumed by the animal which became filthy in the animal's stomach, then, the *ḥukm* of all converted material must be the same, and this includes flesh, and also when that is converted to dust, or when blood is converted into flesh.[423] Al-Shāfiʿī prohibits *jallāla*, while Mālik considers it disapproved.

With respect to filth being mixed up with permissible food, the source is the well-known tradition from Abū Hurayra and Maymūna "that the Prophet (God's peace and blessings be upon him) was asked about a mouse falling into butter, and he said, 'If it was in a solid state, throw it (the mouse) out and what was around it, but eat the rest, but if it was melted, spill it or do not touch it' ". The jurists have two opinions on filth mixing up with eatables. The first is the opinion of those who took into account mixing alone for purposes of prohibition, even if the food has not changed in colour or smell or in taste because of the filth that is mixed up with it. This is the well-known opinion and is maintained by the majority of the jurists. The second opinion is held by those who take change into account. This is the opinion of the Ẓāhirites and is a narration from Mālik.

The reason for their disagreement arises from the dispute over the meaning of the tradition. This is so as some of them considered it to be a specific application intended to apply to a specific case, and these are the Ẓāhirites. They maintained that this tradition is to be considered in its apparent meaning and all other things are to be considered with respect to the change caused in them by the filth. Some of them considered it to be a specific case intended to apply generally, and these are the majority. They maintained that the meaning of the tradition is that it is the mixing up of the filth itself that makes a permissible thing filthy, otherwise he (the Prophet) would not have elaborated upon the distinction for them as to whether the filth mixed up with it was in a solid or melted state, as things mix more readily when they are in a liquid state. It follows from this that it is necessary to distinguish between small and

[423] The author appears to be saying here that according to analogy the *hukm* of permissibility cannot be based upon chemical conversions. For example, if blood changes into flesh and other constituents of the body, then the consumption of blood is prohibited and meat is not.

large amounts of filth. As they did not distinguish between them, it appears that they confined some of the implications to its apparent meaning and constructed analogies from some. It was for this reason that the Ẓāhirites construed the entire tradition in its apparent meaning.

The jurists also agreed about some of the things that are prohibited in themselves and they differed about others. The Muslim jurists agreed about two of these things: swine-flesh and blood. With respect to the swine, they agreed about its fat, meat, and skin. They disagreed about the utilizing of its bristles and the purification of its skin, whether tanned or untanned. This has preceded in the Book of Purification. With respect to blood, they agreed about the prohibition of blood that flows out from an animal subjected to *dhakāh*, but they disagreed about blood that does not flow out. Likewise, they disagreed about the blood of a whale. Some of them held it to be filthy, while others did not. The disagreement about all this is found within Mālik's school and outside it. The reason for disagreement about blood that does not flow out derives from the conflict of the unqualified implication with the qualified. This is so as the words of the Exalted, "Forbidden unto you (for food) are carrion and blood . . .",[424] imply a prohibition of flowing as well as non-flowing blood, while the words of the Exalted, "Say: I find not in that which is revealed to me aught prohibited to an eater that he eat thereof, except it be carrion, or blood poured fourth . . .",[425] implies through the indirect indication of the text the prohibition of the flowing blood alone. Those who preferred the unqualified implication to the qualified stipulated the prohibition of flowing blood. Those who maintained that the unqualified meaning implies an additional *ḥukm* over the qualified, and that the conflict between the unqualified and qualified meanings is a category of the indirect implication of the text whereas the unqualified meaning has a general implication, the general implication being stronger than the indirect indication of the text, decided to give predominance to the unqualified meaning over the determined and said that small as well as large quantities of blood are prohibited.

The condition of "flowing" stipulated in the proscription of blood relates to blood flowing from the animal subjected to *dhakāh*, that is, the blood flowing out at the time of *dhakāh* from an animal that is permissible for eating. The blood flowing out from an animal, while that animal is alive, is prohibited in small or large quantities, similarly, the blood that flows from an animal which is prohibited for eating, even when this animal is subjected to *dhakāh*. Small as well as large quantities of it are prohibited, and there is no dispute about this.

[424] Qur'ān 5 : 3.
[425] Qur'ān 6 : 146.

With respect to their disagreement about the blood of a whale, the reason for disagreement is the conflict of a general implication with analogy. The general implication is in the words of the Exalted, "and blood . . ."[426] The analogy is based on the assumption that the *hukm* of blood follows the *hukm* of the dead animal, that is the blood of that whose carrion is prohibited is also prohibited, and if the animal is permissible its blood should also be permissible. It was for this reason that Mālik held that animal with no blood is not carrion.

The Qāḍī (Ibn Rushd) said: We have discussed this issue in the Book of Purification. The jurists quote a tradition in this context that restricts the general implication of the prohibition of blood. This is the saying of the Prophet (God's peace and blessings be upon him), "Two kinds of carrion are permitted for us as are two kinds of blood".[427] The authenticity of this tradition is probable (*ẓannī*), as it is does not exist in the well-known compilations of *ḥadīth*.

The things prohibited (perpetually and) in themselves, and which are disputed, are four in number. The first is the flesh of birds of prey and four-footed predatory animals. The second are domesticated animals with hoofs. The third is the flesh of animals the killing of which is prescribed in the Ḥaram. The fourth is the flesh of animals for which there is a natural aversion and which appear repulsive by nature. Abū Ḥāmid has related from al-Shāfiʿī that he prohibited the flesh of animals whose killing[428] is prohibited, like the *khuttāf* (a type of swallow) and the bee. This makes it the fifth of the disputed species.

17.1.1. Issue 1

This deals with predatory quadrupeds. Ibn al-Qāsim has related from Mālik that they are disapproved (*makrūh*). This is the opinion on which his disciples have relied and it is the prominent opinion in their view. Mālik has mentioned something in *al-Muwaṭṭa*, which indicates that they are prohibited. This is so as he said immediately after the tradition of Abū Hurayra from the Prophet (God's peace and blessings be upon him), "Eating of all predators with fangs is prohibited. That is the position taken by us". Al-Shāfiʿī, Ashhab, the disciples of Mālik, and Abū Ḥanīfa upheld their prohibition, except that they disagreed about the species of the predators with Abū Ḥanīfa saying that anything that eats meat is a predator, so that even the elephant, the hyena, and the gerbil are also included under predators, as are cats. Al-Shāfiʿī said that the hyena and the fox may be eaten, and the predators are those that attack humans, like the lion, leopard, and the wolf. Both views are to be found in the

[426] Qur'ān 5 : 3.

[427] The remaining text of the tradition is: "the fish and locust, and the liver and the spleen."

[428] The text in the original mentions the word "eating", that is, animals whose eating is prohibited; however, a comparison with the text two pages later reveals that this should be "killing".

School. The majority of the jurists maintain that the monkey is not to be eaten and not to be benefited from, and in al-Shāfiʿī's view even the dog is prohibited and is not to be benefited from, as he concluded its filthiness in itself from the filthiness of its saliva.

The reason for their disagreement about the prohibition of the flesh of quadruped predators stems from the conflict of the Book with traditions. This is so as the apparent meaning of the words of the Exalted, "Say: I find not in that which is revealed to me aught prohibited to an eater that he eat thereof, except it be carrion, or blood poured fourth . . .",[429] implies that whatever is besides what is mentioned in the verse is permitted. The apparent meaning of the tradition of Abū Thaʿlaba al-Khushanī, who said, "The Messenger of Allāh (God's peace and blessings be upon him) proscribed the eating of all predators with fangs", implies that the predators are prohibited. This is how it has been recorded by al-Bukhārī and Muslim. The version related by Mālik in the same context on the authority of Abū Hurayra conflicts more obviously, and it states that the Messenger of Allāh (God's peace and blessings be upon him) said, "The eating of any predator with fangs is prohibited". This is so as a reconciliation is possible between the first tradition and the verse by construing the proscription laid down in it to imply abomination. A reconciliation between the tradition of Abū Hurayra and the verse is not possible, unless it is assumed that it abrogates the verse, in accordance with the view of those who maintain that an addition amounts to abrogation and that the Qurʾān may be abrogated by the *sunna* that is *mutawātir*. Those who reconciled the tradition of Abū Thaʿlaba and the verse construed the tradition about the flesh of predators to imply abomination. Those who maintained that the tradition of Abū Hurayra includes an addition over what is in the verse prohibited the flesh of predators. Those who maintained that the hyena and the fox are prohibited did so through the general implication of the term "predators". Those who exempted from this the hostile decided on the basis of what is related by ʿAbd al-Raḥmān ibn ʿAmmār, who said, "I asked Jābir ibn ʿAbd Allāh about the hyena whether it is to be eaten. He said, 'Yes'. I said, 'Is it to be hunted?' He said, 'Yes'. I said, 'And you have heard this from the Messenger of Allāh (God's peace and blessings be upon him)?' He said, 'Yes'". Though this tradition is related by ʿAbd al-Raḥmān alone he is a trustworthy narrator according to the leading traditionists. Further, they relied upon the tacit approval of the Prophet (God's peace and blessings be upon him) when the hyena was eaten before him.

With respect to the birds of prey, the majority of the jurists maintain that they are permitted because of the verse mentioned, but a group of jurists

[429] Qurʾān 6 : 146.

prohibited them, because of what is related in the tradition of Ibn ʿAbbās, who said, "The Messenger of Allāh (God's peace and blessings be upon him) proscribed the eating of all predatory animals with fangs and all birds of prey with claws". This tradition, however, has not been recorded by the two Shaykhs (al-Bukhārī and Muslim), but it has been recorded by Abū Dāwūd.

17.1.2. Issue 2

This issue is about the domesticated animals with hoofs, I mean, horses, mules, and donkeys. The majority of the jurists agreed about the prohibition of eating the meat of the domesticated donkey, except what is related from Ibn ʿAbbās and ʿĀʾisha, who used to consider it permissible. It is related from Mālik that he used to consider it abominable, while a second narration from him is the same as that of the majority. Mālik, Abū Ḥanīfa, and a group of jurists maintained that eating horses is prohibited, while al-Shāfiʿī, Abū Yūsuf, Muḥammad, and a group of jurists upheld its permissibility. The reason for their disagreement over the domesticated ass is the conflict of the mentioned verse with authentic traditions on the topic from Jābir and others. He said, "The Messenger of Allāh (God's peace and blessings be upon him) proscribed on the Day of Khaybar the meat of the domesticated ass and permitted the meat of horses". Those who reconciled the verse and this tradition construed it to imply abomination. Those who maintained that it is a case of abrogation upheld the prohibition of the donkey, or they maintained that it is an additional *ḥukm* without invoking abrogation. Those who did not uphold the prohibition argued on the basis of what is related from Abū Isḥāq al-Shaybānī from Ibn Abī Awfā, who said, "We came across an ass when we were with the Messenger of Allāh (God's peace and blessings be upon him) on the day of Khaybar and cooked it. The crier sent by the Messenger of Allāh (God's peace and blessings be upon him) announced that the pots should be turned over with what is in them". Ibn Isḥāq has said, "I mentioned this to Saʿīd ibn Jubayr and he said that this proscription was laid down as it eats filth".

Their disagreement about mules is based upon the conflict of the indirect implication in the words of the Exalted, "And horses and mules and asses (hath He created) that ye may ride them, and for ornament",[430] (read) along with the words of the Exalted in the case of cattle, "Allāh it is Who hath appointed for you cattle, that ye may ride on some, and eat of some",[431] with the verse comprehensively detailing the prohibited things, because the indirect meaning of the communication indicates that the permissibility in the case of mules is for riding, as well as the analogy for mules drawn from donkeys. The

[430] Qurʾān 16 : 8.

reason for their disagreement about horses arises from the conflict of the indirect implication of this verse with the tradition of Jābir, and the conflict of the analogy for the horse drawn from the mule as well as the donkey with it; however, the permissibility of horseflesh is explicit in Jābir's tradition, and it is not imperative to oppose it with analogy or the indirect implication of the communication.

17.1.3. Issue 3

This issue is about their disagreement over animals whose killing is prescribed within the Ḥaram, and these are five that have been expressly mentioned (in the texts): the raven, the kite, the scorpion, the mouse, and the ferocious dog. A group of jurists understood from the command to kill them, along with the proscription of killing animals that are permitted for eating, that the underlying cause (*ʿilla*) for this is that these five creatures are prohibited for eating. This is al-Shāfiʿī's opinion. Another group of jurists understood from this the reason to be the of hostility (found in these creatures) and not prohibition. This is the opinion of Mālik and Abū Ḥanīfa and of the majority of their disciples.

With respect to the fourth species that is repulsive for humans, like insects, frogs, lobsters, turtles, and other similar creatures, al-Shāfiʿī considered them prohibited while others permitted them. Some of them merely considered them abominable. The reason for their disagreement is their dispute over the term *khabāʾith* (foul, gross) in the words of the Exalted, "He will make lawful for them all good things and prohibit for them only the foul".[432] Those who maintained that these are the things prohibited by the text of the law did not prohibit those that are repulsive for humans, as long as there was no explicit text forbidding them. Those who maintained the foul things are those that are found repulsive by humans said that these are prohibited.

What Abū Ḥāmid has related from al-Shāfiʿī about his prohibiting the flesh of animals whose killing is proscribed is conjecture, for I do not know where the traditions about this occur. Perhaps, they are in books other than those that are well-known to us.

The jurists agreed unanimously about the permissibility of eating animals of the sea, as long as their names do not coincide with the names of land animals that are prohibited. Mālik said that there is no harm in eating all the animals of the sea, except that he considered the porpoise (*khinzīr al-māʾ*)[433] abominable, and said: you call it *khinzīr*. This was also the opinion of Ibn Abī

[432] Qurʾān 7 : 157.

[433] This is the name given to the porpoise which, according to the dictionary, is a name for a number of gregarious toothed whales. *Porcus* in Latin is pig, while *piscis* is fish. Together they form porpoise, which is *khinzīr al-māʾ*.

Laylā, al-Awzāʿī, Mujāhid, and the majority of the jurists, except that they stipulated *dhakāh* in things other than fish, and this has already been mentioned. Al-Layth ibn Saʿd said that the *insān al-māʾ* (manatee)[434] and the porpoise are not to be eaten under any circumstances.

The reason for their disagreement is whether the terms "human beings" and "swine" include these things in the literal meaning or whether this is the technical application in the law. On the basis of this, the discussion must turn to every animal of the sea that has a counterpart in name in the language or in the technical application among the animals prohibited upon land, like the dog, according to those who consider it prohibited. The examination of this issue refers to two factors. The first is whether these names are literal. The second is whether an equivocal term has a general application. For example, *insān al-māʾ* and the swine of the water (porpoise) are referred to in the terms "swine on land" and "*insān*". Those who accepted that these terms are literal, and who held that the equivocal terms have a general application, were bound to uphold their prohibition. Mālik, therefore, reserved his view and said: you call it *khinzīr*.

This is the position about animals prohibited for eating and those permitted.

All vegetation that provides nutrition is permitted, except for *khamr* (wine) and all other intoxicating beverages derived from juices that ferment and from honey itself.

With respect to *khamr*, they agreed about its prohibition in small or large quantities, I mean, that which is derived from grape juice. In the case of the other intoxicating beverages, they disagreed about a small quantity that does not intoxicate. They agreed that the amount which intoxicates is prohibited. The majority of the jurists of Ḥijāz, as well the majority of the traditionists, maintained that small and large quantities of intoxicating liquor are prohibited. The Irāqīs, Ibrāhīm al-Nakhaʿī from the Tābiʿūn, Sufyān al-Thawrī, Ibn Abī Laylā, Shurayk, Ibn Shubrama, Abū Ḥanīfa, and all the remaining jurists of Kūfa, as well as the majority of the jurists of Baṣra maintained that what is prohibited in all the remaining beverages (that is, besides wine derived from grape juice) is intoxication itself and not the substance (of the beverages).

The reason for their disagreement springs from the conflict of traditions and analogies on the issue. The jurists of Ḥijāz have two methods for establishing their opinion. The first is through the traditions laid down on the issue. The second is by designating all the intoxicating beverages, in their totality, by the name *khamr*. One of the best known traditions that the jurists of Ḥijāz used as evidence is what is related by Mālik from Ibn Shihāb from Abū Salama ibn

[434] Manatee is probably what is intended here. The dictionary defines *insān al māʾ* as a sea-animal with a tail. The description fits manatee, which is also known as a sea-cow.

ʿAbd al-Raḥmān from ʿĀʾisha that she said, "The Messenger of Allāh (God's peace and blessings be upon him) was asked about *bitaʿ* (wine from honey and dates) and *nabīdh* from honey (mead) and he said, 'Any drink that intoxicates is prohibited' ". It is recorded by al-Bukhārī. Yaḥyā ibn Maʿīn said that this is the most authentic tradition related from the Prophet (God's peace and blessings be upon him) about an intoxicant. There is also the tradition recorded by Muslim from Ibn ʿUmar that the Prophet (God's peace and blessings be upon him) said, "Each intoxicant is *khamr*, and each *khamr* is prohibited". These two are authentic (*ṣaḥīḥ*). The first one is agreed upon by all, while the second is declared authentic by Muslim alone. Al-Tirmidhī, Abū Dāwūd, and al-Nasāʾī have recorded from Jābir ibn ʿAbd Allāh from the Messenger of Allāh (God's peace and blessings be upon him) that he said, "(If) something intoxicates in a large quantity its small quantity is prohibited". This is explicit on the point at issue.

The second argument is that all (intoxicating) beverages are called *khamr*. For this they have two methods. The first is from the aspect of establishing names by way of derivation. The second is by way of transmission. They said, from the aspect of derivation, that it is known to the experts of language that *khamr* has been called *khamr* because it clouds (veils) the intellect, therefore, it follows that the term *khamr* be applied to everything that befuddles the intellect. There is a disagreement among the experts on *uṣūl al-fiqh* over this method of establishing names, and it is not acceptable to the Khurāsānians. The second method is by way of transmission. They maintained that even if it is not conceded to us that intoxicating beverages are designated in the language by the term *khamr*, yet they are called *khamr* in the legal sense. They argued for this on the basis of the tradition of Ibn ʿUmar that has preceded and by what is related by Abū Hurayra that the Messenger of Allāh (God's peace and blessings be upon him) said, "*Khamr* is from these two trees: the date-palm and the grapevine". Further, on what is related from Ibn ʿUmar that the Messenger of Allāh (God's peace and blessings be upon him) said, "*Khamr* is from grapes. *khamr* is from honey, *khamr* is from raisins, *khamr* is from wheat, and I forbid you from using all intoxicants". These are the arguments of the jurists of Ḥijāz for the prohibition of all intoxicating beverages.

The Kūfians relied for their opinion upon the apparent meaning of the words of the Exalted, "And of the fruits of the date-palm, and grapes, whence ye derive strong drink, *sakar*, and good nourishment",[435] and on traditions that they related on the issue, as well as upon *qiyās maʿnawī* (primary form of analogy).

[435] Qurʾān 16 : 67.

With respect to their arguments on the basis of the verse, they said that *sakar* is an intoxicant and if it had been prohibited in its substance Allāh would not have designated it as "good nourishment." Among traditions that they relied upon in this topic, the best known, in their view, is the tradition of Abū ʿAwn al-Thaqafī from ʿAbd Allāh ibn Shaddād from Ibn ʿAbbās from the Prophet (God's peace and blessings be upon him), who said, "*Khamr* is prohibited for its substance", and intoxication in things besides it. They said that this is explicit and is not susceptible to interpretation. The jurists of Ḥijāz considered it weak as some of its narrators related the words: "intoxicant from other things". Further, there is the tradition of Shurayk from Sammāk ibn Ḥarb with its *isnād* from Abū Burdā ibn Niyār, who said, "I used to forbid you from drinking beverages in certain containers, so drink what you like but do not get intoxicated". It is recorded by Al-Ṭaḥāwī. It is related from Ibn Masʿūd that he said: "I witnessed the prohibition of *nabīdh* (mead) as you witnessed it, thereafter, I witnessed its permissibility. I remembered and you forgot". They related from Abū Mūsā that he said, "The Messenger of Allāh (God's peace and blessings be upon him) sent me as well as Muʿādh to Yemen. We said, 'O Messenger of Allāh, there are two beverages there that they make from wheat and barley. One of them is called *mizr* and the other is called *bitaʿ*.[436] Which one should we drink'. He said, 'Drink (both) but do not get intoxicated' ". This is also recorded by al-Ṭaḥāwī. There are other traditions also that they narrated on the subject.

In their argument by way of reasoning they said that the Qurʾān has explicitly laid down that the *ʿilla* (underlying cause) of prohibition of *khamr* is that it prevents the remembrance of Allāh and breeds enmity and hatred, as the Exalted has said, "Satan seeketh only to cast among you enmity and hatred by means of strong drink (*khamr*) and games of chance, and to turn you from remembrance of Allāh and from (His) worship". This *ʿilla* (they said) is found in a certain quantity of the intoxicating liquor not in what is less than that; it follows therefore that this quantity be prohibited, except on what a consensus has taken place regarding small as well as large quantities of *khamr*. They said that this kind of analogy is linked with the text, and it is one in which the underlying cause is indicated by the law.

The later analysts said that the argument of the jurists of Ḥijāz is stronger with respect to transmission, while the arguments of the Irāqīs by way of analogy are better. If this is as they say, then, their disagreement refers back to their dispute about giving predominance to traditions over analogy, or to analogy over tradition, when they conflict. It is an issue that is disputed, but the truth is that if the tradition is explicit and authentic, then, it must be

[436] *Mizr* is Abyssinian beer made of millet, barley, or grain. *Bitaʿ* is an intoxicating drink made from honey and dates.

granted predominance over analogy; however, if the apparent meaning is subject to interpretation, the analysis vacillates between reconciling the two through the interpretation of the text and between granting predominance to the apparent meaning over the implications of analogy. This varies with the strength of the words used in the apparent text as well as on the strength of the analogy that confronts it, and the distinction between them cannot be grasped except through mental skill (taste), just as (the distinction between) balanced and unbalanced speech (or poetry) is grasped. Perhaps, both kinds of skills are equal and because of that there is extensive disagreement over this category, so much so that some have said: each *mujtahid* is correct.

The Qāḍī (Ibn Rushd) said: As it appears to me, Allāh knows best, although the saying of the Prophet (God's peace and blessings be upon him), "Each intoxicant is prohibited", can probably be interpreted as meaning the *ḥukm* of a certain quantity of the intoxicant and not its category, it is more likely to mean the prohibition of the category rather than the quantity, because of the conflict of analogy with this as has been construed by the Kūfians. It is not unlikely that the Lawgiver prohibit a small amount of the intoxicant for the purpose of plugging of the channels (to an agreed unlawful end) and by way of emphasis, even though the harm appears to occur when excessive amounts (of the intoxicant) are taken. Moreover, it is established from the state of the law, by consensus, that the Lawgiver has considered the category in the prohibition of *khamr* and not the requisite quantity. It follows that whenever the underlying cause of *khamr* is found it (the intoxicant) should be linked with *khamr*. And those who believe in the existence of a distinction should come up with an evidence for this. This is the case when they do not concede to us the authenticity of the saying of the Prophet (God's peace and blessings be upon him), "(If) something intoxicates in a large quantity its small quantity is prohibited." If they concede it, they will not find any way of avoiding our conclusion, as it is explicit on the point of dispute, and (besides this) it is not proper to oppose explicit texts with analogies. Further, the law has communicated that in *khamr* there is harm as well as benefit. The Exalted has said, "They question thee regarding strong drink (*khamr*) and games of chance. Say: In both there is great sin, and (some) utility for men".[437] If the aim of analogy is to reconcile the negation of the harm and the existence of the benefit, it would prohibit larger quantities and permit smaller quantities, but when the law has given predominance to the *ḥukm* of the harmful in the case of *khamr* and has prohibited small as well as large quantities of it, it is necessary that it be the same for everything in which the underlying cause of prohibition is found, unless there is established in it a legal distinction.

[427] Qur'ān 2 : 219.

They agreed that the making of beverages is permitted, as long as the intensity of fermentation related to ***khamr*** does not exist in them, because of the saying of the Prophet (God's peace and blessings be upon him), "Make (fermented) beverages, but each intoxicant is prohibited", and also because of what is established from the Prophet (God's peace and blessings be upon him) "that he used to make ***nabīdh*** (fermented beverage), but he used to spill it on the second or third day". They disagreed about this on two issues. The first is about utensils in which fermentation is undertaken. The second is about fermentation of two things together like fresh and ripe dates, and dried dates and raisins.

17.1.4. Issue 1: Fermented beverages

They agreed unanimously about the fermentation of drinks in water-skins, but they differed about fermentation in other containers besides this. Ibn al-Qāsim has related from Mālik that he used to disapprove fermentation in gourds and vessels smeared with pitch, but he did not disapprove of it in things besides these. Al-Thawrī disapproved fermentation in gourds, green jars, hollow stumps, and vessels smeared with pitch. Abū Ḥanīfa and his disciples said that there is no harm in fermenting drinks in all (kinds of) vessels and utensils.

The reason for their disagreement derives from the conflict of traditions in the topic. This is so as a proscription is related on the authority of Ibn ʿAbbās in four things that were disapproved by al-Thawrī. It is an authentic tradition. It is related by Mālik from Ibn ʿUmar in *al-Muwaṭṭaʾ* "that the Prophet (God's peace and blessings be upon him) proscribed the fermentation of drinks in a gourd or a vessel smeared with pitch". It is laid down in the tradition of Jābir from the Prophet (God's peace and blessings be upon him) on the authority of Shurayk from Sammāk that he said, "I used to forbid you from fermenting drinks in a gourd, green jars, hollow stumps, and a jug smeared with pitch. Ferment the drinks, but an intoxicant is not permitted". The tradition of Abū Saʿīd al-Khudrī, which is related by Mālik in *al-Muwaṭṭaʾ*, is that the Prophet (God's peace and blessings be upon him) said, "I used to forbid you from fermenting drinks. Ferment them and each intoxicant is prohibited".

Those who maintained that the earlier proscription, which was abrogated, was a proscription about fermentation in these utensils, as another proscription besides this is not known, said that fermentation is permitted in all utensils. Those who maintained that the earlier proscription, which was abrogated, was an absolute proscription of fermentation said that the proscription of fermenting in these utensils persists. Those who relied on the tradition of Ibn ʿUmar upheld the proscription for the two utensils mentioned in it. Those who relied upon the tradition of Ibn ʿAbbās upheld the proscription for four utensils, as it includes an additional *ḥukm*, and because the conflict between this tradition and the tradition of Ibn ʿUmar belongs to the category of the indirect indication of the text. In the book of Muslim the proscription is about fermentation in a green jar, and it says that he made an exemption for them in using it if it was not smeared with pitch.

17.1.5. Issue 2: Fermented beverages

This issue is about the fermentation of two mixed constituents. The majority of the jurists maintained the prohibition of mixed constituents of things that are amenable to fermentation. A group of jurists said that (such) fermentation is abominable. Another group of jurists said that it is permitted. One group said, as far as I know at the moment, that a mixture of two constituents is prohibited even if they are not those that are amenable to fermentation.

The reason for their disagreement stems from their ambivalence as to whether the proscription laid down in this indicates disapproval or prohibition. If we maintain that it indicates prohibition, then, does it indicate the invalidity of the object of the act proscribed? This is so as it is established from the Prophet (God's peace and blessings be upon him) "that he proscribed the mixing of dried dates and raisins, of blossoms and ripe dates, and of unripe dates and raisins." In some versions the Prophet (God's peace and blessings be upon him) said, "Do not ferment blossoms and raisins together, or dates and raisins together, and ferment each separately". On the basis of this, three opinions are derived: an opinion prohibiting it, an opinion upholding permissibility along with the accompanying sin (inherent) in fermenting, and an opinion upholding abomination.

Those who maintained that it is permissible probably relied upon the general implication of the tradition about fermentation in the tradition of Abū Saʿīd al-Khudrī. Those who prohibited all mixing of constituents either adopted the prohibiting underlying cause, which is mixing itself and not what results from the intensity of the fermented drink, or they adopted the general implication of the tradition in which he proscribed the mixing of constituents.

The jurists agreed that if the *khamr* turns into vinegar (of itself) its consumption is permitted. But they had three opinions about what would be the case when its conversion into vinegar is initiated by human intervention: prohibition, abomination, permissibility. The reason for their disagreement stems from the conflict of analogy with a tradition, as well as their dispute over the meaning of the tradition. This is so as Abū Dāwūd has recorded a tradition from Anas ibn Mālik "that Abū Talḥa asked the Prophet (God's peace and blessings be upon him) about orphans who had inherited wine. He said, 'Spill it'. He asked, 'Should I not turn it into vinegar?' He replied, 'No'". Those who understood the prohibition to be a plugging of the channels (to an unlawful end) construed it to mean abomination. Those who interpreted the proscription as having no underlying cause upheld prohibition. From this it can be derived that there is no prohibition even according to the opinion of those who believe that a proscription renders unlawful the object of the proscribed act. With respect to the conflicting analogy in the case of the prohibition of turning it into vinegar, it is known from the law by necessity that the different *aḥkām* are for different substances, and the substance of *khamr* is different from the substance of vinegar, and vinegar, by consensus, is permitted. Thus, when the substance of *khamr* is converted into the substance vinegar it is necessary that it be permitted, whatever the manner in which it was converted.

17.2. Chapter 2 The Use of Prohibited Things under Duress

The source for this topic are the words of the Exalted, "He hath explained unto you that which is forbidden unto you, unless you are compelled thereto".[438] The study of the topic relates to the legalizing cause, about the category of a thing made lawful, and its quantity.

The cause is the necessity of eating, that is, when nothing permissible is found that may be eaten, and there is no dispute about this. The second is the seeking of a cure, and this is disputed. Those who permitted it argued on the basis of the permission granted by the Prophet (God's peace and blessings be upon him) to ʿAbd al-Raḥmān ibn ʿAwf to wear silk because of a (skin) rash that he had. Those who prohibited it did so on the basis of the saying of the Prophet (God's peace and blessings be upon him), "Allāh has not placed the cure for my *umma* in things that he has prohibited for it".

The category of things made lawful (due to necessity) includes every thing prohibited, like carrion and others. The disagreement is about *khamr* when it is used for medicinal purposes but not about its use as food (under duress); therefore, they permitted a thirsty person (dying of thirst) to drink it if that can quench his thirst, and the person who is burned by the sun to do away with the burns.

With respect to the quantity that may be eaten under duress from carrion and other things, Mālik said that the limit for this is to stay hunger and to make provisions until other food is found. Al-Shāfiʿī and Abū Ḥanīfa said that he is not eat more than what is enough to sustain life, and this was also upheld by some of Mālik's disciples. The reason for disagreement is whether the thing permitted to a person in a state of duress is the whole quantity

[438] Qurʾān 6 : 120.

(available) or what will sustain life. It is apparently the whole of it because of the words of the Exalted, "But he who is driven by necessity, neither craving nor transgressing".[439]

Mālik and al-Shāfiʿī agreed that it is not permitted for a person under duress to eat carrion if he has undertaken his journey in disobedience, because of the words of the Exalted, "Neither rebellious nor transgressing".[440] Other jurists upheld its permissibility.

[439] Qurʾān 2 : 173.

[440] Qurʾān 2 : 173. Pickthall's translation changed slightly to convey the literal meaning intended in the discussion.

Glossary

ʿadāʾ: Payment of a debt. The term is also applied to the timely performance of an act of worship, as distinguished from *qaḍāʾ*, which is delayed performance.

ʿadāla: The attribute of justice, moral uprightness. The qualification of being a legally acceptable witness in the court of a *qāḍī*. See also *ʿādil.*

aḍḥā: Animals sacrificed during *ʿīd al-aḍḥā*. The term *yawm al-aḍḥā* is applied to mean the *ʿīd* day.

adhān: Call for prayer.

ʿādil: A just person, that is, one who avoids major sins (*kabāʾir*) and does not persist in minor sins. A witness whose testimony is admissible under Islamic law. A just ruler (*imām ʿādil*) is one who governs in accordance with the dictates of the *sharīʿa*.

adilla: The plural of *dalīl*, which means guide. In the technical sense, the term *dalīl* is applied to mean an evidence leading to the discovery of a rule of law or *ḥukm*. The term *adilla tafṣīliyya* is used for specific evidences within the general evidences, like the individual verses of the Qurʾān, and is distinguished from the term *adilla ijmāliyya* insofar as the latter term applies to general evidences that contain the specific evidences; namely, the Qurʾān, *sunna*, *ijmāʿ*, and *qiyās*.

ʿadl: Justice. See *ʿadāla* and *ʿādil.*

āḥād: Derivative of *wāḥid* (single). *Ḥadīth al-āḥād* means a tradition that has not reached the level of a continuous narration. To be specific, it is an individual narration, that is, it was narrated by a single individual in the first generation after the Prophet, as compared to a continuous narration (*mutawātir*), which has multiple chains.

aḥkām: (Plural of *ḥukm*). See *ḥukm*.

ahl al-Kitāb: The People of the Book, that is, Jews and Christians.

ahl al-dhimma: Free non-Muslims who are citizens of a Muslim state or country.

ʿamal: Act; practice. The term includes internal acts like intention. In the technical sense, it means the juristic principle adopted by Mālik, and in that sense it is applied to mean the rule of law maintained by the jurists of Medina. It is also understood generally to mean the practice of the people of Medina, but there is a need to be careful in the use of this term, because usually Ibn Rushd uses this term to mean the jurists of Medina, though the wider application is not excluded.

amān: The assurance of safe-custody given by a free Muslim to a foreigner, especially from an enemy state, planning to visit the grantor's country. A kind of a visa.

āmīn: Amen.

ʿāmm: A general word that includes all the categories to which it is applied. If an injunction is expressed in general terms, it is considered to apply to all its categories, that is, the *ḥukm* contained within the general word is applicable to each category without restriction or qualification. The implication of such a command is considered to be definitive (*qaṭʿī*) by the Ḥanafīs, who maintain that such a command will apply to all its categories unless another equally strong and definitive evidence singles out one of its categories and assigns it a different *ḥukm*. The Shāfiʿīs do not consider a general word to be definitive, thus, they permit its restriction by a probable evidence.

amn: The period of peace between two wars.

amr: A command that is the bearer of a *ḥukm.*

ʿanāq: The *jafra* and *ʿanāq* are goats, with the difference that the *jafra* is a young goat that has started eating and is past the age of weaning, while the *ʿanāq* is said to be older than the *jafra*. It is also claimed that it is younger than the *jafra*.

ʿanbar: The name of a whale that had been brought in by the tide during the period of the Prophet. It is referred to while deciding the question whether seafood brought in by the tide can be consumed lawfully.

anfāl: Plural of *naḟl* (reward). It is the reward promised by the commander to combating forces out of the spoils to be won by them.

ʿanwatan: Land conquered by the force of arms as compared to land that is surrendered through negotiation. The former is treated as spoils and is to be distributed, while the latter becomes *kharāj* land.

ʿanz: A goat that has given birth to offspring, or a goat of the same age. It is offered as compensation for a gazelle hunted unlawfully.

ʿāqila: A group of persons responsible for paying the blood-money (*diyah*) on behalf of an offender. Usually they are agnates or all the relations on the paternal side, but the term was also applied to the *dīvān* of a soldier.

ʿaqīqa: An offering made for newborn infants.

aqiṭ: Cheese.

ʿaqr: A cut on the legs of an animal during hunting to make it fall. It is also applied to mean any wound inflicted on a hunted animal that would amount to legally valid slaughter of such animal.

ʿArafa: The Arafat mountain near Mecca where the pilgrims gather on the ninth day of the *ḥajj* rites.

ʿarḍ: Chattel or goods of trade (*ʿurūḍ*).

ʿariyya: Plural *ʿarāyā*. The fruit left on the trees by the owner of an orchard for the consumption of the poor. The sale of *ʿariyya*, on the other hand, involves the exchange of dry dates with fresh dates still on the trees.

arkān: Plural of *rukn* (element). The essential ingredient of an act of worship, other act, or contract, the absence of which renders such act or transaction invalid.

ʿĀshūrāʾ: The tenth day of Muḥarram.

ʿaṣr: The time after the declining of the sun, that is, afternoon. The word is also applied to mean the prayer for which the legally appointed time is *aṣr*. This prayer is also referred to as the middle prayer.

athar: Plural *āthār*. Acts and sayings attributed to the Companions of the Prophet. The term is also applied to mean the legal effects of a contract or transaction.

ʿawra: Private parts that need to be covered.

al-awdā: The jugular veins.

awqiya: Unit of weight that varies for certain commodities. It is generally equal to 127 grams, but for gold and silver it is 119 grams.

awsuq: It is the plural of *wasq*, which is a unit of measure that is equal to one camel-load.

aymān: Plural of *yamīn*. See *yamīn*.

ayyām maʿdūdāt: The three determined days that follow the Day of Sacrifice, also known as the days of *tashrīq*. See *tashrīq*.

badal: Substitute.

badana: A term applied to both camels and cows that are sacrificed, but it has been restricted to a she-camel in this book.

balāgh: A term used by the Mālikites for wages of a person who offers his services for the performance of *ḥajj*. The amount must be sufficient for covering provisions and the cost of a riding animal. If the wages actually paid fall short of the *balāgh*, the person hired is to be paid what would be enough, and if an excess is left he is to return it.

barāʾa aṣlīya: Freedom from liability. This is the original rule of permissibility for an act that is asserted in the absence of a rule or *ḥukm* for such an act.

barīd: A measure of distance that is roughly equal to twelve miles.

basmala: Reciting the formula: "In the name of Allāh, the Beneficent, the Merciful." See also *tasmiya*.

batrā': An animal whose tail has been cut off or is missing.
bayān: Elaboration; explanation. In Islamic jurisprudence, the term is applied generally to mean interpretation. In a restricted sense it means the explanation or elaboration required for an obscure term in the texts called *mujmal*. The explanation in such a case is usually sought from the *sunna*.
bayāt: It means "during the night".
al-Bayt al-Ḥarām: The Kaʿba in Mecca. This name was given to it because of the prohibition of hunting inside it or around it.
binā': A method of interpretation in which the interpreter resolves the apparent conflict between traditions by adding up or structuring their meanings instead of preferring one tradition over the other.
bint labūn: A she-camel that has entered the third year of its age.
bint makhāḍ: A camel that has entered the second year of its age.
Bi'r Jamal: The name of a well in Medina.
bitaʿ: An intoxicating drink made from honey and dates. Also called *bitʿ*.
bulūgh: The literal meaning is "attaining" or "reaching." In the technical sense it means reaching the age of marriage. The apparent sign for such age is the attainment of puberty. In the absence of such signs the age is eighteen for a male and seventeen for a female in the opinion of Abū Ḥanīfa. The age for the presumption of puberty is fifteen for females according to the majority of the jurists.
ḍabʿ: Hyena.
ḍaḥiya: Plural *ḍaḥāyā;* Offering; blood-sacrifice.
dalālat al-lafẓ: Implication of the text.
dalīl al-khiṭāb: The indirect or opposite implication of the text. The author uses this term in the sense of *mafhūm al-mukhālafa*. An example is the statement: "In the pasturing animals there is *zakāt*". The indirect or opposite implication would be that there is no *zakāt* in non-pasturing animals.
dalīl: See *adilla*.
dam: Blood. The word is used by the jurists for atonement by sacrificing an animal, usually in the case of violation of the rites of *ḥajj*.
dār al-ḥarb: Enemy territory.
dār al-Islām: The area within the jurisdiction of the Islamic state as distinguished from the *dār al-ḥarb*, which is enemy territory.
dayn: Debt. It is distinguished from *ʿayn*, which is a commodity or property that is present, because a debt is not tangible and present, it is associated with the *dhimma* as a liability.
dhabḥ: Plural *dhabā'iḥ*. Slaughter; slaughtered animal.
dhakāh: Slaughter. See also *naḥr*.
dhikr: Remembrance of Allāh.
dhimmī: A non-Muslim citizen of an Islamic state.

dhirāʿ: A unit of length; an arm-length.

dhū maḥram: A relative of the prohibited degree for marriage.

diya: Blood-money; reparation.

duʿāʾ: Supplication.

fajr: Dawn.

faqīr: A poor person as distinguished from the needy person (*miskīn*). According to the distinction, a poor person (*faqīr*) is better off than the needy (*miskīn*).

faraq: A unit of measure equivalent to fifteen *ṣāʿs*. See also *ṣāʿ*.

farḍ: An obligation established by a definitive evidence. The Ḥanafīs make distinction between *farḍ* and *wājib*, but the other schools do not.

farḍ kifāya: A communal obligation. If some members of the community performs the obligation, liability for its performance is removed from the other members.

farīḍa: An obligation imposed by the Lawgiver.

fāsiq: A disobedient person.

Fātiḥat al-Kitāb: The Opening of the Book. The first chapter of the Qurʾān.

fayʾ: The booty acquired during war without fighting.

fī al-riqāb: According to Mālik, the term is used for slaves who are to be set free by the *imām* after ensuring that they are loyal to the Muslims. Al-Shāfiʿī and Abū Ḥanīfah maintained that these are the *mukātab* slaves, that is, those who have entered into a contract of freedom with their masters.

fidya: Ransom.

al-fiqh: Islamic jurisprudence. *Fiqh* is knowledge of the law as distinguished from *sharīʿah*, which is the law itself.

fisq: Disobedience in the observance of religious duties.

fitna: Trial; sedition.

al-fiṭr: Alms given at the end of Ramaḍān.

fiṭr: The cutting off of fasting. *ʿĪd al-fiṭr* is the first day of Shawwāl following Ramaḍān.

fiṭra: Alms given on *ʿīd al-fiṭr*.

fuqahā: Jurists; experts in *fiqh*. The term is distinguished from *mujtahid* insofar as the *mujtahid* is a jurist who is qualified to derive the law independently, while the *faqīh* may not be qualified to derive the law independently though he is trained in the law.

furūḍ: Plural of *farḍ*; obligations.

ghamūs: See *yamīn ghamūs*.

ghanīma: Spoils.

gharīb: Strange; stranger.

ghulām: Male slave.

ghurar: The thirteenth, fourteenth, and fifteenth days of each month.

ghusl: bath; bathing.

ḥabs: To arrest, confine. The term is used for *waqf* as well, because it amounts to setting aside of property for a charitable purpose.

ḥadath: Impurity. Impurity (*najāsa*) is divided by the jurists into two kinds: actual (*haqīqīya*) and technical or legal (*ḥukmīya*). The term *ḥadath* is applied to legal or technical impurity, while *khabath* is used for actual impurity. *Ḥadath* may be minor, which is removed through ablution, or it may be major (sexual defilement and menstruation) and is removed through bathing (*ghusl*).

ḥadd: A fixed penalty prescribed in the texts as a right of Allāh, like the penalties for unlawful sexual intercourse and theft. In general terms the word is used for all duties determined to be the rights of Allāh.

ḥadīth: Saying. In the technical sense, the term is used for the written record of the *sunna*, thus a *ḥadīth* may contain more than one *sunan*.

hady: Gift, offering.

al-ḥajar al-aswad: The Black Stone affixed in the eastern corner of the Kaʿba.

ḥajj: Annual pilgrimage to Mecca.

ḥalāl: Permitted. In a technical sense, the Lawgiver is indifferent to the performance of the act. In another sense, each permitted category may be obligatory or prohibited as a whole. Thus, the Lawgiver is indifferent to how much a person eats, but total abstention from eating is prohibited insofar as it leads to the loss of life. In such a case it is obligatory for the person to eat for the preservation of his life, which is an acknowledged purpose of the *sharīʿah*.

al-ḥamd: Praise of Allāh.

ḥāqin: A person suppressing the call of nature during worship.

haqīqiya: Actual as compared to *ḥukmiya* (legal).

ḥarām: Prohibited.

ḥarbī: Enemy.

ḥasan: A tradition that has within it all the conditions laid down for a *ṣaḥīḥ* (sound) tradition, but one of it narrators is considered weak, because he may not have a sound memory.

ḥawl: One year. The period is relevant for purposes of *zakāt*.

ḥayāh: Life.

ḥayḍ: Menstruation.

ḥijr: The northern wall of the Kaʿba.

ḥill: The area beyond the boundary of the Ḥaram; outskirts of Mecca.

ḥiqqa: A she-camel that has entered the fourth year of its life.

ḥukm: A rule of law; judgement; decision. The word is also used for the effects of a contract.

ḥukm sharʿī: A primary rule that creates an obligation or duty by declaring an act to be obligatory, prohibited, recommended, disapproved, or permissible.

ḥukm waḍʿī: A secondary rule of law that does not create an obligation by itself, but determines the relationship between obligation creating laws, their causes, conditions, and obstacles.

ḥukmiya: Legal.

ḥukūma: The estimation of damages in injury or loss, when it is not possible to refer to a fixed prescribed amount.

iʿāda: Repetition. The term is used for repetition within the prescribed time of a ritual performed irregularly.

ʿibāda: Worship.

ʿibādāt: Plural of *ʿibāda* (worship).

ʿibādī: a ritual (non-rational) meaning underlying a rule of law.

ibn labūn: A camel that has entered the third year of its age.

ʿīd: Celebration.

ʿĪd al-Aḍḥā: The celebration, accompanying sacrifice, at the end of the *ḥajj* pilgrimage.

ʿĪd al-Fiṭr: The celebration following Ramaḍān, which is accompanied by the giving of alms (*fiṭr*).

idām: An appetizer eaten with bread, usually oil.

ifrād: A method of performing the pilgrimage where the worshipper starts with the *ḥajj* alone, and *ʿumra* is performed later on.

iḥrām: Intention; the dress required for performing *ʿumra* and *ḥajj*.

ijmāʿ: Consensus. In the technical sense it is the consensus of the jurists within a period of time after the death of the Prophet on a *ḥukm sharʿī* (point or rule of law).

ijtihād: Striving. In Islamic law it is the effort that the jurist exerts to discover the law from the sources. *Ijtihād* is not a source of law, as is assumed by some, it is merely the effort invested in interpretation according to a prescribed methodology.

ijtihādiya: An issue that admits of discussion and interpretation; a moot point.

ikhāla: A method followed by the Shāfiʿī jurists in which they derive an underlying cause for a rule to be extended to other cases through their reasoned conviction. The other schools consider this to be based on conjecture rather than on the texts. The cause so derived is called *mukhīl.*

ikhtilāf: Disagreement. The term is applied to mean the differences of opinion among jurists whether they belong to the same school or to different schools. According to al-Ghazālī the science of *khilāf* is a discipline in itself as distinct from *uṣūl al-fiqh. Uṣūl al-fiqh* may be called theoretical *uṣūl* where the assumptions of each school of interpretation are described with respect to the sources of Islamic law. The science of *khilāf* may be referred to as applied *uṣūl* where the assumptions and principles of each school are put to the test to see how the law is actually derived.

īlāʾ: An oath by the husband that he will refrain from sexual intercourse with his wife.

ʿilla: Underlying cause for a rule; *ratio decidendi.*

imām: The Muslim ruler or leader. The term is also applied to mean the person leading congregational prayers.

imāma: The office of the *imām*. The office is not to be construed as a juristic or fictitious person, in the sense of the English common law or of Western law in general.

īmān: Faith.

ʿishāʾ: The last of the five daily prayers.

iʿtidāl: Moderation. In the context of the praying postures, it means keeping a straight back while bowing.

iʿtikāf: Seclusion in a mosque for the remembrance of Allāh.

insān al-māʾ: A sea-animal with a tail. The description fits manatee, which is also known as a sea-cow.

insān: Human.

iqʿāʾ: Sitting on the buttocks and folding up the knees, a posture disallowed during prayer.

iqāma: The commencement of congregational prayer.

iqrār: Admission; acknowledgement; confession.

ishtirāk: Equivocality.

isnād: The chain of transmission of a tradition.

istiḥāda: Unhealthy bleeding associated with menstruation.

istiḥsān: A principle used by the Ḥanafīs and Mālikīs in which the rule pointed to by strict analogy or syllogism is ignored and another rule based on other factors, like a general principle or necessity, is preferred. An example is the contract of hire. Strict syllogism (*qiyās*) maintains that a contract cannot be concluded for benefits that are not in actual existence. In the contract of hire for wages, for example, the services of the worker will emerge when he commences work, but they do not exist at the time of the contract. The Ḥanafīs would say that the contract is permissible on the basis of necessity, because there is no way that the benefits to be derived from the worker can be brought into existence before the contract. The same situation prevails in the hiring of property and many other cases. The juristic preference here is called *istiḥsān*.

istinjāʾ: Washing of the private parts during ablution or otherwise after answering the call of nature.

istinshāq: The snuffing up of water into the nostrils during ablution.

istisqāʾ: Prayer for rain.

jabr: Rectification of excesses or shortfalls by means of prostrations for forgetfulness in prayer.

jadhaʿ: A two year old goat.

jafra: A four month old goat.

jāhiliyya: The period of ignorance before the dawn of Islam.

Jamrat al-ʿAqaba: The location at which pebbles are to be cast during the pilgrimage, especially on the tenth day of Ḥajj. The term *jamra* in its original meaning is applied to pebbles; it later came to be used for the location at which the pebbles are cast. There are three such locations in Mina at which pebbles are thrown during the pilgrimage.

jallāla: An animal that consumes filth.

jamʿ: Combining prayers.

jamāʿa: Congregation.

jamra: Plural *jamarāt*; one of the three locations in Minā at which pebbles are thrown during the last days of Ḥajj.

janāba: Major form of ritual impurity arising from sexual activity.

janāza: Plural *janāʾiz*; body of a deceased person; also used to mean the funeral.

janīn: Foetus.

janna: Heaven.

al-jawāriḥ: Beasts or birds of prey.

jawrabayn: Socks.

jawza: The prominent cartilage of the larynx; Adam's apple in humans.

jihād: War prescribed for Muslims for the defence of their faith and lands.

jimār: Plural of *jamra*.

jinn: Genie.

jizya: Poll-tax levied on the non-Muslim citizens of a Muslim state.

jumuʿa: Friday; the Friday congregational prayer.

junub: A person who has acquired a major ritual impurity.

kaʿb: Ankle.

kabāʾir: Major sins.

kabsh: Ram.

kaffāra: Plural *kaffārāt*. Expiation; atonement.

karāha: Disapproval; abomination; one of the categories of the *aḥkām*.

kawmāʾ: A camel with a mounting hump.

khāṣṣ: Particular; specific. A term applied to the particular word as distinguished from the general word (*ʿāmm*).

khabāʾith: Foul; gross.

khabath: Plural *khabāʾith*; foul; gross. Actual impurity as distinguished from legal impurity.

khamr: Wine from grapes, as distinguished from other forms of liquor.

kharāj: Tax levied on land that has come into the control of Muslims without fighting.

kharqāʾ: An animal with a hole in its ear.
khawf: Fear; fear arising from threat of attack by enemy.
khiṭāb: Address; communication.
khinzīr al-māʾ: Porpoise.
khinzīr: Swine.
khuṭba: Sermon.
khumus: One-fifth.
Kitābī: A person from among the People of the Book.
kubrā: Major.
kufr: Infidelity.
kusūf: Eclipse. *Ṣalāt al-kusūf* is the prayer during eclipse.
laghw: Meaningless; futile oath.
madhy: Prostatic secretion prior to cohabitation.
maḍmaḍa: Rinsing of the mouth.
maʿḍūb: The name assigned to a legal issue where a relative or other person is willing to perform the pilgrimage on behalf of another person with his own wealth.
maghrib: Evening; sunset; the evening prayer.
maḥram: Husband or relative of the prohibited degree for marriage.
makrūh: Disapproved, reprehensible.
maʿlūl: Defective.
mandūb: Recommended.
maniyy: Sperm.
marīḍ: Sick person.
marfūʿ: A tradition whose chain of narration reaches the Prophet.
masāʾil: Legal issues.
masḥ: Wiping; rubbing.
mashaqqa: Hardship, especially in the performance of a religious duty.
masīl: Bottom of the valley; bed of the stream.
maṣlaḥa: Plural *maṣāliḥ*. Interest; benefit. A principle of interpretation that seeks to protect and preserve the interests identified by the *sharāʿah* as the purposes of law. It is different from the principle of utility advocated by Jeremy Bentham.
maṣlaḥī: A rule that is based on the principle of *maṣlaḥa*.
mass: Touching.
mawāqīt: Plural of *mīqāt*.
mawlā: Master of a slave.
mawqūf: Suspended; see also *mursal*.
mayta: Carrion.
mīqāt: Limits; limits of time as well as locations.
miʿrāḍ: A featherless and blunt arrow used for shocking the hunted bird or animal.

miskīn: A needy person.
mithl: Similar, equivalent.
mithqāl: A unit of measure.
mizr: An Abyssinian beer made of millet, barley, or grain.
muʿāfir: A kind of cloth made in Yemen.
muʾakkada: Emphatic. The term is used for *sunna* of the Prophet, and it is an act that he performed persistently.
muʿawwidhatān: The two short chapters of the Qurʾān beginning with: "Say, I seek refuge with the Lord of the daybreak . . .,' and 'Say, I seek refuge with the Lord of mankind. . . ."
mubāḥ: Permissible. One of the five categories of the *aḥkām.*
mubāshara: Performing or committing an act directly. The word is also used in the sense of touching or coming into physical contact with a woman other than sexual intercourse.
mudābara: An animal with its ears split from two sides.
mudabbar: A slave who becomes free upon the death of the master, in accordance with a declaration made by the master during his lifetime.
mudallis: A person who uses subtle means of cheating or deception. See also *tadlīs.*
mudd: A unit of measure for grains. It is equivalent to two rotls according to the Ḥanafīs.
mudīr: Manager; administrator. The word has been used in the context of *zakāt* for the active trader, who does not have time to record each and every transaction that he concludes, like the busy shopkeeper.
mufassar: An elaborated statement or word.
mufrid: A person who is undertaking the *ifrād* form of *ḥajj.*
mughallaza: Heavy; enhanced.
al-muḥṣar: Surrounded; besieged by the enemy.
muḥkam: A governing rule or verse of the Qurʾān.
muḥrim: A person in the ritual state of *iḥrām.*
muḥtamal: A probable meaning.
mujmal: An obscure term that needs explanation from the *sunna* or other sources, like the term *ribā* used in the Qurʾān for usury. The meaning of the term *ribā* is not explained in the Qurʾān. It is, therefore, necessary for the jurist to look for its *bayān* (explanation) in the *sunna* before trying to discover its meaning through literary or other sources.
mujtahid: A fully qualified and independent jurist, who not only derives the law independently but also lays down the rules of interpretation for himself and for his school or for those who follow him. It is prohibited for such a jurist to follow the opinion of another jurist; it is obligatory on him to derive the law himself.

mukātab: A slave who enters into a contract with his master through which he buys his freedom.

mukallaf: A person who fulfils the conditions for the acquisition of obligations and the performance of duties; a subject who is a major having attained puberty.

mukallibīn: A term used in the Qur'ān for the pouncing of predatory animals.

mukhīl: Reasoned; convincing; conjectural; an underlying cause determined by a jurist through his personal conviction rather than through explicit or implicit meanings in the text.

mukhaffafa: Light; reduced.

mu'min: Believer.

munāsib: Suitable; compatible. The term is used for the underlying cause of a rule of law when such cause is compatible with the general propositions and purposes of the law.

munkar: Denied; rejected; inconsistent.

munqaṭiʿ: A tradition whose chain of narration is broken and is not complete.

mursal: When the name of the Companion, who is supposed to be the immediate narrator of a tradition, is missing from the *isnād* and the text of the tradition is attributed to the Prophet directly by a disciple from the second Muslim generation, the tradition is known as *mursal.* If the name of the second narrator, the Companion's disciple, is dropped, the tradition is known as *mawqūf.*

muṣḥaf: Copy of the Qur'ān within two covers.

muʿtakif: The person who secludes himself in a mosque for worship and remembrance of Allāh.

mushrikūn: Polytheists.

musinna: A grown animal; a two year old cow.

musnad: A tradition whose chain can be traced to the Prophet; a compilation of traditions arranged according to the names of the Companions narrating from the Prophet.

mustaḥāda: A woman suffering from unhealthy or irregular menstrual bleeding.

mustaḥabb: Approved; recommended.

mutʿa: A temporary form of marriage; the conversion of a declared intention of *ḥajj* into one for *ʿumra.*

mutābaʿa: The conformity in traditions when one narrator narrates from the *shaykh* of another narrator or from one above the *shaykh.*

mutamattiʿ: A person undertaking the *tamattuʿ* form of *ḥajj.*

mutawātir: A continuous narration. A tradition or report that has been narrated by so many persons in the first generation after the Prophet that any agreement or conspiracy on their part to propagate a falsehood is ruled out.

muthāl: Mutilation of bodies during war; torture. Also *muthla*.
muṭlaq: Absolute; unqualified.
muzābana: The sale of fruit on trees in exchange for other measured fruit.
Muzdalifa: Place near Mecca where the pilgrims spend the night on their return from the station at Arafat.
nabīdh: A beverage made from dates, which is considered by some to be prohibited like other intoxicants.
nadb: Recommendation.
nadhr: Vow.
nāfila: Supererogatory worship.
nafl: Supererogatory worship.
nafs: Life.
naḥr: A method of slaughtering camels or animals with long necks, as distinguished from *dhabḥ*, which is used for other animals.
nahw: Grammar.
nahy: Proscription; prohibition.
najāsa: Impurity, actual or legal.
naʿlayn: Pair of slippers or shoes.
naqḍ al-witr: Making the prayer odd by adding another *rakʿa*.
naskh: Abrogation of one text by another.
naṣṣ: Text; explicit word that does not admit of more than one meaning.
niṣāb: Scale; minimum prescribed number or value. The term *niṣāb* has relevance for *zakāt*, theft, and testimony. For *zakāt* it is the minimum value on which the duty can be levied. In the case of theft, it is the minimum amount that the thief must steal in order to invoke the penalty prescribed in the Qurʾān. For testimony it is the ratio of two women for one man.
niyya: Intention.
qaḍāʾ: Judgement; the office of the *qāḍī*; delayed performance of a worship.
qādhif: A person who falsely accuses women or men of having committed unlawful sexual intercourse.
qāḍī: Judge.
qalb: Heart.
qārin: A person who undertakes the *qirān* form of *ḥajj*.
qassīy: A silk striped garment.
qaṭʿī: Definitive.
qatl: Homicide.
qirān: One of the three forms for the performance of *ḥajj*.
qīrāṭ: A measure of small lengths.
qiyās: Syllogism; analogy. A method of extending the *ḥukm* for one case to another case through equivalent meanings of a specific (*khāṣṣ*) word carrying the *ḥukm*. If the meaning is being extended to a higher-order or lower-order

meaning, like extending the meaning of the word "fie," occurring in a verse of the Qur᾿ān, to more grievous acts of beating and abusing, the analogy is considered to be very strong and is called *qiyās al-maᶜnā*. This, in fact, is not *qiyās*, but the extension of the meaning through a literal implication of the word. In equivalent meanings, an underlying cause is determined for the *ḥukm* provided and the rule is extended through this cause. If the cause discovered does not meet all the conditions, but appears to be an apparent attribute in both cases, the analogy is referred to as *qiyās al-shabah*.

qiyās al-ᶜilla: See *qiyās*.

qiyās maᶜnawī: See *qiyās*.

qiyās al-shabah: See *qiyās*.

qiyās mursal: A name given to the principle of *maṣlaḥa*, which is a refined form of analogy based on the combination of two or more general principles.

qulla: A measure of water.

qunūt: Supplication; prayer.

qur᾿: Period; period of ritual purity followed by menstruation or the duration of menstruation itself.

raghā᾿ib: Desirable acts that are of a lesser status than the *sunan*.

rājiᶜ: For purposes of *ḥajj*, it is the person who has completed his return journey or one who is in the middle of such a journey.

rakᶜa: A unit of the Muslim prayer.

ramal: Rhythmic trot while shrugging the shoulders. It is adopted for the first three circuits of the circumambulation of the Kaᶜba.

ramḍā᾿: Scorching heat.

raqabah: Slave; literally neck.

raṭl: Rotl.

ra᾿y: A term applied to the interpretations of the law on the basis of one's personal opinion. The method is associated with the Ḥanafīs, however, it really means a method in which the literal meaning of the text is evaded, and importance is given to the general principle or the spirit of the law.

ribā: Interest; usury.

rikāz: Treasure which may include minerals.

riqa: A term for both gold and silver.

rukhṣa: Exemption.

rukn: Element; ingredient. The performance or bringing about of a *rukn* is essential for the validity of a transaction or worship.

al rukn al-aswad: The corner of the Kaᶜba with the Black Stone.

al rukn al-yamānī: The corner of the Kaᶜba pointing in the direction of Yemen.

rukūᶜ: Bowing, especially in prayer.

ṣāᶜ: A measure of volume.

ṣabī: Minor; a boy who has not attained puberty.

ṣadāq: Dower.

ṣadaqa: (Plural *ṣadaqāt*) charity; also applied to mean *zakāt*.

sadd al-dharāʾiʿ: A principle of interpretation for the derivation of laws that permits the plugging of lawful means to unlawful ends.

ṣafīy: An item of property that was chosen by the Prophet from the spoils of war before they were distributed into prescribed shares.

ṣaḥīḥ: One of the six compilations of sound (*ṣaḥīḥ*) traditions. The term *ṣaḥīḥayn* refers to the two leading compilations by al-Bukhārī and Muslim.

ṣaʿīd: Clean soil that may be used for *tayammum*, which is a substitute for ablution with water when water is lacking.

sāʾima: Pasturing animal.

sakar: A nourishing drink prepared from the date-palm. The term is mentioned in the Qurʾān.

ṣakkāʾ: An animal born without ears.

ṣalāh: Prayer.

salab: Spoils acquired from a slain person.

salām: An advance payment made for the delivery of goods at an agreed later date. The contract of *salam* is permitted as an exemption from the principles of *ribā*.

ṣalāt al-khawf: Prayers offered in a congregation on the front under threat of attack.

ṣalāt al-marīḍ: The prayer offered by a sick person.

sanad: Authority; basis. The *sanad* of a tradition is the chain of authorities reporting the tradition. The *sanad* of consensus (*ijmāʿ*) is the evidence on which the agreed upon rule or principle is based.

satr al-ʿawra: Covering of the private parts.

sawād: The fertile lands of Irāq.

saʿy: The circuits between al-Ṣafā and al-Marwah.

shafaq: Twilight.

shahāda: Testimony; evidence.

shāhid: Witness.

shahīd: Martyr.

sharʿ: The law.

sharʿī: Legal.

sharīʿa: The law of Islam.

sharqāʾ: An animal with a cut off ear.

shibr: A measure of length that is equal to the size of the spread out hand.

sidr: Lotus.

ṣiyām: (Plural of *ṣawm*) fasts; fasting.

ṣubḥ: Morning.

ṣughrā: Minor.
sūra: Chapter of the Qurʾān.
sujūd: (Plural of *sajda*) prostrations.
sulṭān: The ruler.
sunna: (Plural *sunan*) practice of the Prophet, that is, a precedent laid down by him either in the form of a saying, or an act, or an approval.
sunna muʾakkada: (Plural *sunan muʾakkada*) emphatic practice of the Prophet. An act that was persistently performed by the Prophet when the act was not declared as obligatory.
sutra: A curtain placed before a person when he is praying.
tabīʿ: A one year old cow.
Tābiʿūn: Followers of the Companions of the Prophet.
tadlīs: Cheating; deception; misrepresentation. See also *mudallis.*
tafath: Dirt.
taḥallul: Freedom from the restrictions of the *iḥrām*. It is of two types: full freedom (*taḥallul akbar*), which occurs after the *ṭawāf al-ifāḍa*; and partial freedom (*taḥallul aṣghar*), which occurs after the casting of pebbles at the *Jamrat al-ʿAqaba*.
ṭahāra: Ritual purification.
taḥrīm: Prohibition.
takbīr: Saying *Allāhu akbar.*
takhlīl: Combing the beard with wet fingers during ablution.
taklīf: Obligation; liability.
talbiya: The words pronounced on various occasions during *ḥajj* and *ʿumra*. The words of the *talbiya* are: *labbayk Allāhumma labbayk, labbayka lā sharīka laka labbayk, inna ʾl-ḥamda wa ʾn-niʿmata laka wa ʾl-mulk, lā sharīka lak* (At Your command, O Allāh, at Your command; at Your command, You have no partner, at Your command; all praise and grace are Yours, and Yours the dominion; You have no partner).
tamattuʿ: One of the three forms for the performance of the annual pilgrimage to Mecca.
tamr: Dates.
tarabbus: A sitting posture during prayer.
tarāwīḥ: Prayers performed in the night during Ramaḍān.
taʿrīf: Definition; identification; delineation.
tarjīʿ: The dual pronouncement of the *shahāda* in a lower tone followed by its dual pronouncement in a louder voice.
tarjīḥ: Preference of one legal evidence over another.
tarwiya: The eighth day of Dhū al-Ḥijja.
taqlīd: Following the opinion or ruling of another without enquiring into the *dalīl* or evidence for such ruling in the texts. In Islamic law, it is a name

given to a judicial method for following precedents, that is, a junior jurist or *qāḍī* following the rulings given by senior jurists or the *imāms* of the schools. It is similar to the system of precedents that judges follow in the English common law. In general terms, it would mean following the opinion of a specialist: a doctor, lawyer, or any other specialist. Modern life, it can be easily seen, is based upon *taqlīd*. The principle of *taqlīd* is condemned by many in modern times as the cause for the stagnation of Muslims, especially in the area of law. This allegation needs to be reconsidered, because the real cause of stagnation could be the subjugation of Muslims and the colonization of their lands. It cannot be denied, however, that blind following of an opinion even in the law, when the jurists lock up their own faculty of reasoning, is to be condemned.

tasbīḥ: Saying *subḥāna Allāh*, that is, words glorifying Allāh.

taṣfīq: A method for women to alert a person who forgets while leading prayer. It consists in stroking the back of the left hand with the palm of the right hand.

tashahhud: Words recited within the regular prayer while in the sitting posture.

taṣḥīf: An error made by the scribe.

tashrīq: Days following the day of sacrifice.

tasmiya: Basmala, the words meaning, "In the name of Allāh, the Beneficent, the Merciful".

ṭawāf: Circumambulation of the Kaʿba.

ṭawāf al-ifāḍa: The obligatory circumambulation of the Kaʿba during *ḥajj* after throwing pebbles at the *jamarāt*. It is also known as *ṭawāf al-ziyāra*. As distinguished from this a final farewell *ṭawāf* is called *ṭawāf al-widāʿ*, which is performed before departure for home.

ṭawāf al-qudūm: The first circumambulation of the Kaʿba made by the worshipper coming from outside Mecca.

tawātur: Continuous narration of a report by a number whose agreement on propagating a falsehood is ruled out.

tawjīḥ: According to al-Shāfiʿī it is a statement after *takbīr* in prayer, "I (have) turned my face to One Who created the heavens and the earth". According to Abū Ḥanīfa it is the glorification of Allāh. According to Abū Yūsuf, the disciple of Abū Ḥanīfa, it is a combination of both.

tayammum: Ablution with clean soil. It is provided as a substitute for ablution with water in the absence or lack of water.

thaniyy: The term is used for one or two year old cows and five year old camels.

thawāb: Reward in the hereafter.

ṭuhr: Purification; period following menstruation.

umm al-walad: Slave mother of the master's child.
ʿumma: The Muslim nation.
ʿumra: A visit to the House of Allāh in a state of *iḥrām*. It consists of *ṭawāf* and *saʿy*.
ʿumrat al-qaḍāʾ: *ʿUmra* with delayed performance. The Prophet performed an *ʿumra* in the year after the year of al-Ḥudaybiya as *qaḍāʾ* for the *ʿumra* he had missed in the previous year. It is, therefore, called the *ʿumrat al-qaḍāʾ*.
umūm al-balwā: The need for a thing being so widespread that it would be impossible for a prohibition of the thing by the Lawgiver to have remained unknown.
ʿuqūq: Ties.
ʿurūd: Chattel; goods of trade.
ʿushr: A ten per cent levy on the produce of the earth that is to be paid as a religious duty.
uṣūl: Sources; principles; foundation; roots; principal amounts.
uṣūl al-fiqh: Islamic jurisprudence; Islamic legal theory. The discipline that describes the methodology for the derivation of law from its sources.
wady: Fluid preceding or following urination.
wājib: Obligation.
wājib mukhayyar: An obligation for the performance of which an option is provided to the worshipper.
wālī: Ruler.
walī: Guardian.
waqf: Trust; endowment.
waqṣ: A case where the payment of *zakāt* involves fractions, like payment of one and one-half cows.
wars: A dye for cloth.
waṣiyya: Bequest; testament.
wilāya: Guardianship; jurisdiction; domain.
witr: Odd; the odd prayer.
wuḍūʾ: Ablution with water.
wujūb: Obligation.
wuqūf: Suspension.
yadd: Hand; forearm; arm.
yamīn: Oath.
yamīn ghamūs: False oath.
ẓāhir: Apparent; the apparent meaning in two or more probable meanings of a word.
zakāt: The poor-due that has been made obligatory on wealth as a religious duty.
zakāt al-fiṭr: The obligatory amount to be paid on *ʿīd* day following Ramaḍān.

ẓannī: Probable; conjectural.

ẓihār: The oath by a person that his wife is like the back of his mother for him, that is, declaration of abstention from sexual intercourse; injurious assimilation.

ẓuhr: Afternoon; the afternoon prayer.

Index for Volume One

www.ingramcontent.com/pod-product-compliance
Lightning Source LLC
Chambersburg PA
CBHW061351240926
51846CB00007B/1375
9788119005765